WRITING
WORTH READING

A Practical Guide with Handbook

SECOND EDITION

WRITING

WORTH READING

A Practical Guide with Handbook

Nancy Huddleston Packer
STANFORD UNIVERSITY

John Timpane
LAFAYETTE COLLEGE

A Bedford Book
ST. MARTIN'S PRESS • NEW YORK

For Bedford Books:
Publisher: Charles H. Christensen
Associate Publisher: Joan E. Feinberg
Managing Editor: Elizabeth M. Schaaf
Developmental Editor: Ellen Darion
Production Editor: Chris Rutigliano
Copyeditor: Susan M. S. Brown
Text Design: Anna Post
Cover Design: Richard Hannus

For information, write: St. Martin's Press, Inc.
175 Fifth Avenue, New York, NY 10010

Editorial Offices: Bedford Books of St. Martin's Press
29 Winchester Street, Boston, MA 02116

ISBN: 0-312-01257-8

ACKNOWLEDGMENTS

W. H. Auden, "Law Like Love." Copyright 1940 and renewed 1968 by W. H. Auden.
    Reprinted from *W. H. Auden: Collected Poems*, edited by Edward Mendelson, by per-
    mission of Random House, Inc. and Faber and Faber Ltd.
Isaac Babel, "My First Goose." Reprinted by permission of S. G. Phillips, Inc. from *The
    Collected Stories of Isaac Babel*. Copyright © 1955 by S. G. Phillips, Inc.
Emily Dickinson, "A word is dead . . ." Copyright 1951, © 1955, 1979, 1983 by The
    President and Fellows of Harvard College. Reprinted by permission of the publishers
    and the Trustees of Amherst College from *The Poems of Emily Dickinson*, edited by
    Thomas H. Johnson, Cambridge, Mass.: The Belknap Press of Harvard University
    Press.
Richard E. Emery, from "Creating Crime" and Thomas Reppetto, from "Sound Prac-
    tice." Copyright © 1988 by The New York Times Company. Reprinted by permission.
Robert Frost, "Bravado." Copyright 1947 by Holt, Rinehart and Winston, Inc. and re-
    newed 1975 by Lesley Frost Ballantine. Reprinted from *The Poetry of Robert Frost*
    edited by Edward Connery Lathem, by permission of Henry Holt and Company, Inc.
Joel W. Hollenberg and James Gleick. From "Secret of the Knuckleball's Dance." Copy-
    right © 1988 by The New York Times Company. Reprinted by permission.

*Acknowledgments and copyrights are continued at the back of the book on page 573 which
constitutes an extension of the copyright page.*

PREFACE FOR INSTRUCTORS

This book is based on the belief that writing does not exist in a vacuum but is part of a continuum of thinking-reading-writing. To write effectively, students must learn to think critically about significant matters. A giant step toward critical thinking is critical reading. When students learn to engage and challenge difficult texts their thinking and their writing will improve. And, mysterious though it may sound to those who have never taught composition, good writing—including such things as the appropriate use of the semicolon—gives rise to better thinking and better reading. The best way to improve one part of the process is to work on all parts.

So goes the credo on which we based the first edition of *Writing Worth Reading*. This second edition reflects this belief even more strongly. We hope that you will feel this emphasis throughout the book whether the subject is persuasion or word choice or documentation of sources.

Much is old here and much new. As before, we focus on the five most important moments in the college writer's career: the selection of a subject; the process of revision, the encounter with reading, the transfer of reading into writing, and the twin processes of doing research and writing it up. As before, we aim to address the elements and habits crucial for any writer of expository prose: the skeptical attitude, the constant focus on one's own thinking, critical distance from one's writing, recognition and understanding of rhetoric and argument, an analytical approach to reading, an informed and organized approach to research, an appropriate and imaginative personal style, and a firm knowledge of the rules and conventions of English prose.

The first part of the book, entitled "Overture: The Writing Process," is indeed an overture, an introduction to the main theme: the process of inventing, organizing, drafting, and revising. New material on the thesis appears in the second chapter, and there is also a case study that follows a student through the entire process. For this student, revision included large-scale rethinking, not just line editing and moving blocks of text here and there.

By far the most significant change from the first edition comes in our new Part Two, Steps to Good Thinking: The Critical Process. Here we devote five chapters to critical thinking, beginning with suggestions on how to open one's mind and prepare to think. How and where does one start? What are the good habits to cultivate and the bad habits to avoid? How does one distinguish between acceptable and unacceptable rhetoric, correct and faulty logic, cogent and sloppy argumentation? Beyond this new beginning, our chapter on logic is much expanded. It includes the proper and improper uses of induction and deduction, a new section on the enthymeme, and some of the more familiar logical fallacies.

We have also expanded our already extensive coverage of critical reading. The steps to good reading are again here, as are the practical questions a reader can ask to get the most from reading. How does one bring one's reading and thinking into prose? How does one construct an argument from one's notes? We follow the case study of a student's response to a text. We read along with the student, watch him take notes, make an outline, and draft and revise.

Persuasion comes next. We provide some thinking tools for constructing a strong argument. Like all writers, students think more clearly and argue more effectively when they understand the importance of evidence. Therefore, Part Two concludes with a chapter on the use and evaluation of evidence.

Part Three, The Heart of the Matter: The Paragraph, treats the paragraph both as a concrete unit and as the product of strategies of development, such as illustration or definition. Unity, development, and coherence are here, as they should be, and our treatment of topic sentences and thesis statements is much augmented. We have expanded our discussion of the strategies both here and throughout *Writing Worth Reading*. After all, they are ways of thinking that the writer can use at any stage in the writing process. We have added a section on selecting the right strategy and using strategies to govern groups of paragraphs. Part Three concludes with a chapter on three often misunderstood elements of writing: the beginning, the ending, and the title of an essay.

Part Four, The Art of the Writer: Sentences, Diction, Style, investigates the elements of stylistic choice—sentence structure, word choice, and tone. A stylistic choice is a moment, a crucial moment, of critical thinking. It involves the writer's understanding of self, purpose, and audience. We describe a style appropriate for college writing and suggest how students can achieve it.

The fifth part of the book, entitled "Putting It All Together: College Writing," treats four of the most common college writing tasks: the research project, the report, the essay on literature, and the in-class essay examination. Our account of the research process now spans two chapters. Chapter 14, Doing Research, carries the student from interpreting the assignment and choosing a subject through compiling a bibliography and writing a first draft. Much new material is here on how to avoid plagiarism; how and when to summarize, paraphrase, and quote; and how to integrate sources into one's own text. Chapter 15, Writing Research, carries the story from documenting sources to revising and presenting the final draft. Our treatment of the MLA parenthetical references and list of works cited format is greatly expanded from the first edition. The chapter concludes with a thoroughly annotated case study.

Chapter 16, The Report: Writing in All Disciplines, is new. We added this chapter because we recognized that the nonargumentative project is perhaps the most common form of writing assigned outside the humanities. We discuss ways of organizing material and writing the report. Especially prominent here is the organizational thesis, used when the primary purpose of the project is not to argue a thesis but to present information. Common organizational strategies, including the ready-made format for scientific reports, appear here as well.

We turn then to other important kinds of college writing. Chapter 17, Reading, Interpreting, and Writing about Literature, covers topics important to all literature as well as topics specific to fiction and poetry. Here we offer more on methods and levels of interpretation. Why, after all, discuss the objects of literary analysis without discussing the methods? To demonstrate ways of thinking about literature, we describe how a student might prepare to write a literary paper. Chapter 18, The In-Class Essay Examination, offers advice on preparing for the examination as well as on actually taking it. For a case study, we include one of the best in-class essays we have ever read.

Any essay that neglects or ignores the conventions that readers need will fail, no matter how brilliant it may be. What was once an appendix—the "Handbook" in the last edition—has thus become Part Six, The Nuts and Bolts: A Handbook of Grammar, Punctuation, Mechanics, and Usage. We have "promoted" this material to emphasize that these conventions are not imposed on students to curb spontaneity but rather are essential parts of the writing enterprise. This part includes rules and advice governing all those little problems—from dangling modifiers through incorrect use of the semicolon to misused words—that we composition teachers find all too common, all too exasperating. Because most of our students will travel and write far from the discipline of English, we have included as appendixes discussions of the APA reference format and the old MLA footnotes and bibliography system as well as a list of style manuals and handbooks students may find useful in other disciplines and in their careers.

Precept and example are perhaps the two oldest tools for teaching. We have both in this book, as we did in the first edition. We offer general advice on specifics of writing and careful analysis of examples. The general advice is summarized as "Tips" at the end of each chapter or section. We would not want these tips misunderstood. We see no quick and easy—and certainly no mechanical—way to write well. The tips only represent pieces of advice students can use as a checklist. We analyze writing by students and professional writers, writing with problems and writing that works. Understanding why a passage succeeds can be informative and encouraging. When a passage has a problem, we analyze the problem and suggest possible solutions. Such comparison may furnish a model for the kind of close reading we advocate.

The Resources for Teaching contain sample syllabuses, overviews of each chapter (including lists of "demonstration points"—places in the text that deserve classroom discussion), analyses of exercises, and suggestions for teaching strategies in each section. We have tried to make these notes thorough and detailed.

Acknowledgments

We have learned from many other composition teachers and writers. We have also learned from our students. We wish particularly to thank those at Stanford University, Rutgers University, and Lafayette College who were, perhaps without knowing it, the guinea pigs on whom we tried out many of our ideas and exercises. Most of all we would like to acknowledge the help of Larry Boyd, Cornelia Condry, Kimberly Corsaro, Christina Gerke, Stephanie Klein, Jeri Shikuma, and Jeff Sloan. We thank them for letting us use their work and for being such good writers.

We also want to thank the following people, who helped us with the first edition: David Bartholomae, Helen Brooks, Mary Butler, Robert DiYanni, Howard Dobin, Kevin Dungey, Irv Hashimoto, Maria-Christina Keller, Barbara King, George Lee, Robert Levine, Dagmar Logie, Dennis Matthies, John McClure, Tom Miller, Geoffrey Moore, Shirley Morahan, Joseph O'Mealy, Mike Rose, Martin Schwartz, Haskell Springer, and Ann Swidler.

We owe a debt of thanks to the many teachers who used the book and commented on it, especially those who so carefully and helpfully responded to our inquiries about the first edition: Randall Bass, Jenny Franchot, Richard McLellan, Marian Price, Sister Susan Rieke, Lolly Ockerstam Snyder, Sharon Thomas, and Lee Upton. Pat Donahue, Michael Robertson, Ralph Slaght, and James Woolley made important and helpful suggestions for this edition. Marci Lingo, Linda K. Robertson, and Patricia Skarda commented not only on the first edition but also on an early draft of the second, and we are in their debt. We also thank Michael Meyer, who commented on early drafts of both editions. To John Ruskiewicz we owe a special thanks for his thorough review of the first edition and his critique of a draft of the second. We would also like to thank Pilar and Conor Timpane for various forms of inspiration.

The staff of Bedford Books has been wonderful. Every contact with the Bedford people has increased our admiration. They have saved us from horrendous gaffes, solved problems that caused us to throw up our hands, and accepted with good grace our occasional churlishness. Sometimes the good suggestions have been so deft that we have not known from whom they came. And so we thank everyone at Bedford, particularly Charles Christensen and Joan Feinberg for guidance and general help, and Ellen Darion, Chris Rutigliano, Elizabeth M. Schaaf, Susan M. S. Brown, Julie Shevach, and Matthew Carnicelli for their special care for our manuscript.

The book, finally, is ours, and we take full responsibility for it. We hope you find it writing worth reading.

BRIEF CONTENTS

CONTENTS

PART FOUR   THE ART OF THE WRITER: SENTENCES, DICTION, STYLE   *241*

11. *The Sentence from Many Angles*   *243*

PART FIVE   PUTTING IT ALL TOGETHER: COLLEGE WRITING ***319***

WRITING WORTH READING

A Practical Guide with Handbook

INTRODUCTION FOR STUDENTS

He wins every hand who mingles profit with pleasure, by delighting and instructing the reader at the same time.

HORACE (65–8 B.C.)
ROMAN POET

The only thing we have to fear is fear itself.

FRANKLIN D. ROOSEVELT (1882–1945)
PRESIDENT OF THE UNITED STATES

No one is born knowing how to write. Unlike breathing, walking, even talking, writing has to be consciously learned. It doesn't come naturally. Most of us don't think in nice, well-rounded sentences and neat paragraphs. In conversation, we don't start out with our main point firmly in mind and immediately back it with proof—often we don't even recognize our main point until halfway through the conversation.

Writing well takes effort. As the Renaissance poet Ben Jonson said, "Who casts to write a living line must sweat." Improving your writing is hard work. So, too, is learning to program a computer, to play tennis or chess, to clone a cell or set a bone. Like all these activities, writing can be very rewarding. You can communicate with your readers, inform them, change their minds, maybe, show them how the world looks to you. Getting it right is worth the sweat. And all the best writers—novelists, journalists, letter writers, people in almost every walk of life—work and work to get it right. Their writing may seem effortless, but then so does Michelangelo's *David,* and that was once just a hunk of rock.

At this point, you may be asking yourself why, in an age of instant communication by satellite or terminal or telephone, you should struggle to write better. We think there are two very good answers to that question, one professional, one personal.

1

First, the professional. Perhaps computer scientists can envision a world without paper, with everything on a silicon chip. But a world without a written record would be chaos. We would not know where we had been, what we had promised, where we hoped to go. All through our working life, most of us are called on to put our ideas into orderly and more or less permanent form. Police officers take evidence and describe crimes and accidents. Engineers write abstracts of projects they hope to undertake. Executives write reports to the boss and directives to the staff. Lawyers present briefs for judges to study, and judges hand down written opinions. And with every rung of the ladder, people rely more and more on writing.

Second, the personal. We think the second reason is even more important. Writing is a road to knowledge, to knowledge both of the subject of the writing and of the self who writes. We write and we remember better. We write and we understand. Above all, we write and we find out what we really think. And the better we write, the better we think.

Many people are afraid of writing. That blank piece of paper can look as resistant as any rock. Many times as we approached a new chapter of this book, we were a good deal less than eager. But because both of us have done a fair amount of writing, we believed we could do it, and we went ahead. You may not yet possess that confidence. Perhaps when you were in the second grade, you overheard your mother or your teacher say something like "That child will never learn to write!" and you have believed it ever since. Or perhaps writing just did not interest you because your imagination whirled with colors, numbers, animals, plants, music—not with words and sentences. Or perhaps you always assumed you wrote well until that first assignment in Western Civ, when you began to fear you would never understand the hard reading and would never be able to write anything worth reading.

Our experience as teachers and writers tell us that fear is the most pervasive reason people cannot write well. It paralyzes, it stultifies. If you suffer from fear of writing, your first task is to get over it. You can write, if you will. It will require work, yes, but armed with knowledge, seasoned by practice, you can get beyond the fear to the confidence.

For writing is not a mystery. It is, as the English novelist Laurence Sterne observed over two hundred years ago, "when properly managed . . . but a different name for conversation." When you write, you must of course be a little more careful than when you speak, but with the proper management your meaning can be just as powerful.

This book is about proper management. It is about finding something to say that is worth saying. It is about reading more productively and thinking more forcefully in order to write more persuasively. It is about identifying your audience and shaping your language, though not your opinion, accordingly. If you want to improve your organizational skills, you should find some helpful tips here. If you want to make certain once and for all that you know the proper use of the colon and the semicolon, that is here, too. Our aim in writing this book was to provide help with whatever you write, be it an essay, a business letter, a report, a law brief, or an exam.

We don't expect you to come up with a *David*: Michelangelo, Mozart, Shakespeare had a brilliance no one can teach or learn. We do, however, expect you to learn to write what you mean—and with a touch of style.

PART ONE

Overture:
The Writing Process

1
GETTING READY TO WRITE

What we need to learn to do
we learn by doing.
ARISTOTLE (384–322 B.C.)
GREEK PHILOSOPHER

Writing is both a thing we read and an action we perform, a product and a process. As readers, we look at the product. We want to know what is being said and how well. As writers, however, we must look at the process. We want to be sure that we are getting across what we want to say and that what we want to say is worth reading.

The writing process is a continuing development, a growing through time, one stage shaped by the preceding stage and shaping the following. No two writers go through the process in exactly the same manner. One person may have a rich fund of ideas but may need to make several drafts and revisions. Another may find that ideas come slowly but once they arrive the rest is easy. And the process may vary according to subject and occasion. If, for instance, an instructor assigns an explicit topic, you will not need to find your own. If you are required to hand in a first draft, you will not revise.

But in most cases the writing process occurs in four stages:

generating ideas

settling on a subject and thesis

getting the ideas written

getting the writing right

Writers do not always follow this order: sometimes in drafting an essay the writer discovers a better subject; sometimes the most effective ideas are generated during revision. But almost all writing goes through these stages in one way or another.

Before discussing the four stages, we want to discuss two concerns all writers must bear in mind: purpose and audience. No matter what kind of writing we do, we write with a purpose and for an audience. These concerns provide the context for the whole process and govern what we say and how we say it.

Lord, let me shake with purpose.

JAMES DICKEY (B. 1923)
AMERICAN POET AND NOVELIST

PURPOSE: THE AIMS OF WRITING

Behind all good writing is a writer with a purpose. The purpose is like the destination of a journey. Where do we want to end up? with what effect?

Sometimes our true purpose will emerge in the process of writing. We may need a few paragraphs or even a full draft before we know our destination, as when on a journey we take a wrong turn or even go down a long wrong road. But when we hold our destination in mind, we find the whole process easier.

Our overall purpose in all kinds of writing is to learn what we think and to communicate it. This means we have to get the facts clear, distinguish the important from the trivial, recognize relationships and hierarchies, and write correct and interesting prose. We also intend to convey a particular kind of information. What Aristotle said about speech making holds for writing: our purpose will usually be to report, to explain, or to persuade.

Almost all the writing you will do in school—and most of your writing after you graduate—will have one of these purposes. You may be asked to *report* on the contents of a book or on the performance and results of an experiment. You may be asked to *explain* the causes of war or rust or inflation. You may want to *persuade* someone that the sound of the clarinet is more beautiful than the sound of the oboe or that careerism is destroying education.

Often you will have several purposes within a single piece of writing. In an essay on inflation, for instance, you may need one section to *report* a particular example of inflation—say, the last twenty years in Israel—one section to *explain* how inflation generally works, and one section to persuade your reader to undertake a specific course of action to stop inflation. Whatever your purpose or purposes, bear it or them in mind as you go through the writing process.

To Report

Good reporting is a faithful, detailed account of something. By *faithful*, we mean presenting the facts as truthfully as we can. Just as though we were witnesses in a court of law, we swear to tell the truth, the whole truth, and nothing but the truth. We do not repress the unpleasant or the contradictory. We do not distort in order to support a point of view.

By *detailed*, we mean presenting specific and concrete facts. When statistics are relevant, we cite them. When the story is at issue, we narrate. When how something looked is important, we describe it as exactly and vividly as we can. We try to bring the reader close to the subject.

Sometimes we will base a report on firsthand information, as we might if we were documenting a psychological experiment, describing a sporting event, or narrating an episode from our lives. Sometimes we will base a report on information gleaned from books or articles, as we would if we were narrating a marriage ceremony in Ghana or describing how Social Security works. However we obtain our information, we must bear our purpose in mind: to tell the facts. And we must remember to be accurate and organized throughout our presentation. (For more on reporting, see Chapter 16, The Report.)

To Explain

Explaining goes beyond presenting simple facts to interpreting, accounting for, and making sense of a subject. If we were only reporting on the Black Death, which historians say killed 20 million people beginning in 1347, we might write,

> Sufferers from the plague exhibited swellings the size of an orange in their groin or armpit. Sometimes victims lasted five days; sometimes they were dead within twenty-four hours.

Something concrete and physical, like the appearance of the victims, can be reported, that is, described and narrated in a straightforward manner. But if something is obscure or complex, the reader will probably need more information, placing the event or idea in a larger context or showing how it functions and why it happened. In discussing the Black Death, for instance, we might want to explain where it came from and how it affected victims, and so we might write,

> The disease was brought to Italy by infected rats from Eastern ports. Fleas carried by these rats infected other rats and people. The plague affected three areas of the body: the lymph glands, the lungs, and the blood.

Now we show what caused the plague and what it caused. We indicate the process and the principles by which it worked. We show the relation of the parts to the whole and to each other. Within the word *explain* lies the idea of making obscure or complex things *plain.*

Explanation is a large part of most college papers. In a chemistry class, you might explain how the nonmetallic element bromine works on metals and on skin or what other elements it combines with to do what. In an American history class you might explain Lyndon Johnson's decision to withdraw from the presidential campaign in 1968. In a communications class, you could explain how Capitol Records' marketing strategies changed in the 1970s. Virtually every paper requires some form of explanation.

To Persuade

Persuasion builds on both accurate reporting and clear explanation. In addition, it requires the ability to identify the crucial issues, muster the supporting evidence, and present the whole so that it appeals to both reason and emotion. Only then will we achieve our purpose: to convince the reader that our view of a controversial issue is a reasonable one.

Many college papers will require you to take a position on a debatable subject and defend it. Suppose you were to write about Argentinian politics and to identify responsibility for the troubles of that nation. You would first report the facts and then explain the country's political history, the legacy of the dictator Juan Perón, the role of the military, the effect of U.S. policy, as well as that of other nations. Then you would reason carefully to show how the facts lead to your assessment of the responsibility.

You would also need to discuss these controversial issues in the right tone, using the words appropriate to your own feeling and conviction. Part of the purpose of a persuasive essay is to get the reader to feel the emotion the writer feels—joy, anger, indignation. Emotion can be a helpful tool in constructing an essay. It can also be dangerous. It cannot be ignored. (We have more to say on this issue in Chapter 3, The Critical Sense, and Chapter 6, Writing to Persuade.)

TIPS FOR PURPOSE

- As you write, keep your purpose in mind.
- When reporting, concentrate on accuracy.
- When explaining, concentrate on clarity.

- Pay careful attention to how the parts of your subject are connected to one another and to the whole.
- When persuading, remember that you must appeal to both reason and emotion.

Exercises for Purpose

1. Think of an intense experience you had last year, and report it as factually as possible. Who was there? Exactly what happened? In your last paragraph, evaluate your ability to be objective in recounting the experience. Would an observer have reported it differently?

2. Write one paragraph explaining why you decided to attend your present school. Write a second paragraph reporting on your first week of classes. Now write a third paragraph claiming that your decision was correct.

3. Read the following four opening paragraphs and identify the purpose of each—whether to report, to explain, or to persuade. What elements point especially clearly to each passage's purpose? Identify the specific sentences and words that express emotion. Write a paragraph in which you justify your assessment of one of the paragraphs.

    The environmental crisis tells us that there is something seriously wrong with the way in which human beings have occupied their habitat, the earth. The fault must lie not with nature, but with man. For no one has argued, to my knowledge, that the recent advent of pollutants on the earth is the result of some natural change independent of man. Indeed, the few remaining areas of the world that are relatively untouched by the powerful hand of man are, to that degree, free of smog, foul water, and deteriorating soil. Environmental deterioration must be due to some fault in the human activities on the earth. (Barry Commoner, *The Closing Circle: Nature, Man, and Technology*)

    Niagara Falls is a city of unmatched natural beauty; it is also a tired industrial workhorse, beaten often and with a hard hand. A magnificent river—a strait, really—connecting Lake Erie to Lake Ontario flows hurriedly north, at a pace of a half-million tons a minute, widening into a smooth expanse near the city before breaking into whitecaps and taking its famous 186-foot plunge. Then it cascades through the gorge of overhung shale and limestone to rapids higher and swifter than anywhere else on the continent. (Michael Brown, *Laying Waste: The Poisoning of America by Toxic Chemicals*)

    Everyone lives on the assumption that a great deal of knowledge is not worth bothering about; though we all know that what looks trivial in one man's hands may turn out to be earth-shaking in another's, we simply cannot know very much, compared with what might be known, and we must therefore choose. What is shocking is not the act of choice which we all commit openly but the claim that some choices are wrong. Especially shocking is the claim implied by my title: There is some knowledge that a man *must* have. (Wayne Booth, "Is There Any Knowledge That a Man *Must* Have?")

Sagebrush and lizards rattle and whisper behind me. I stand in the moonlight, the hot desert at my back. It's tomato harvest time, 3 A.M. The moon is almost full and near to setting. Before me stretches the first lush tomato field to be taken this morning. The field is farmed by a company called Tejo Agricultural Partners, and lies three hours northeast of Los Angeles in the middle of the bleak, silver drylands of California's San Joaquin Valley. Seven hundred sixty-six acres, more than a mile square of tomatoes—a shaggy vegetable-green rug dappled with murky red dots, 105,708,000 ripe tomatoes lurking in the night. The field is large and absolutely level. It would take an hour and a half to walk around it. Yet, when I raise my eyes past the field to the much vaster valley floor, and to the mountains that loom farther out, the enormous crop is lost in a big flat world. (Mark Kramer, *Making Milk, Meat, and Money*)

I shot an arrow into the air,

It fell to earth, I knew not where.

HENRY WADSWORTH LONGFELLOW
(1807–1882)
AMERICAN POET

AUDIENCE:
IS ANYONE OUT THERE LISTENING?

Although writing and talking are similar, there is one enormous difference: when we talk, we have that other person sitting there asking questions, interrupting, responding with body language as well as with words. We probably know something about that person, including prejudices and cherished values. As we speak, we naturally adjust what we say to fit the listener.

Similarly, when writing we adjust to the audience. In writing a personal letter, we have an image of the recipient and gauge the most effective way to reach him or her. A student visiting in Italy might want to express the glories of the trip. To her close friend, she might send a postcard of the Tuscany countryside, describing a bicycle ride down the mountain in the rain. The student might send her mother a postcard of Giotto's *Madonna and Child*, saying she had been to the Uffizi Gallery twice and this was her favorite painting. Both true, both wonderful examples, but different—because the audience is different.

Most people find writing an essay more perilous than talking or sending postcards. We may not have a clear idea of the purpose or know what the reader needs to be told. We may not even know who the reader is. Too often, we don't think of our writing as communicating with a reader. When we have to write, we just start in. No wonder writing frequently seems scattered, unfocused—it's not aimed anywhere. "I shot an arrow into the air,/It fell to earth, I knew not where." Chances are it got stuck in the trees, far from any target.

Sometimes an instructor will set up the target. One instructor we know tells students, "Think of the reader as an intelligent person, familiar with the subject but not expert, and eager to know what you think most important or misunderstood about it." Another says, "I want you to prove to me you understand the basic concepts." A third says, "Write for your classmates. Give them what they need in order to understand your position." More likely, however, the instructor will say something like "Write a five- to seven-page paper on some aspect of the subject that catches your fancy." And you start shooting arrows.

Stop. Lay down your quiver and bow until you have set up your target. Make that target as specific as possible. Think about your potential reader: a TA, the instructor, a student? Imagine the reader's values, biases, and knowledge or lack thereof. When you aim your essay—or any writing—you have a much better chance of hitting the bull's-eye.

With your target in mind, think about these questions:

What does my audience know, and what does it need to know?

What ideas and information do my reader and I share?

Will I need to argue about values?

What level of detail will be necessary?

What response do I want, and what can I expect from this audience? respect? amusement? agreement? action? feeling?

What kind of language will elicit the response I desire?

Are technical items appropriate?

What illustrations and examples will achieve the desired effect?

These questions boil down to two very important ones: How much and what kind of information must I supply to this audience? And what kind of writing will be most appealing?

Suppose you were writing a persuasive essay calling for more nuclear power plants. If you were writing for a professor of physics, you could assume a good deal of scientific knowledge, no doubt more than your own, and a familiarity with the technical terms as well as the background of the debate. You would not, for instance, need to define the difference between fusion and fission unless showing your knowledge was a purpose of the assignment, but you would need to treat the economics of the various forms of energy, a subject in which your professor may not have expertise. And because you were writing for a scientific audience, you probably would attempt to sound objective and judicious.

If, however, you were writing the same essay for a wider, less specialized audience, you would take a different tack. You would probably define in simple terms the difference between the two kinds of nuclear energy. Furthermore, you would make a major effort to examine the safety of nuclear power plants. And you might mention how savings from nuclear energy could be used for other programs, such as highway construction, child care, and so on. You would probably make an effort to write with more emotion than usual.

We are not suggesting that you shape your opinions and values to please your audience. Your writing would be worthless if it only reinforced someone else's ideas. It becomes worthwhile when it carries your conviction about a significant subject. What is important to you is exactly what your reader wants to know. The goal is to persuade your audience to *your* way of looking at something or *your* plan for doing something. To reach that goal, you must bear your audience in mind throughout the writing process.

TIPS FOR AUDIENCE

- Visualize your reader before you start writing.
- Ask yourself how much background your reader needs.
- Decide what details will appeal to that particular audience.
- As you write, stop occasionally to think about your reader.

Exercises for Audience

1. Select one of the topics below. Decide whether you will argue for or against it. Now consider Audience 1. Compile a list of the points that would best make your case with Audience 1, and then write a paragraph arguing that case for that audience. Now repeat the process for Audience 2 and Audience 3, maintaining your pro or con stance.
   a. Topic: a more stringent grading policy for college papers
      Audience 1: president of your institution
      Audience 2: an instructor you now have
      Audience 3: your fellow students
   b. Topic: a proposal to allow oil drilling in Yellowstone National Park
      Audience 1: President of the United States
      Audience 2: head of the Union of Oil Workers
      Audience 3: a meeting of the Friends of the Earth conservation group
   c. Topic: a proposal to allow marijuana to be used as pain relief for terminally ill cancer patients
      Audience 1: president of the American Medical Association
      Audience 2: director of the FBI
      Audience 3: a local pastor

2. Write a short essay in which you discuss how the change in audience affected your argument in Exercise 1. Did you need special appeals for the audiences? What appeals did you think would or would not work for which audience?

3. Imagine that last night while kidding around, your friend balanced your typewriter or word processor on the windowsill and it fell two floors to a cement driveway. Write letters explaining this event to your mother or father, the dean of the school, and your best friend at another institution. To each, tell the truth, the whole truth, and nothing but the truth. Write up a brief analysis of the differences.

"Fool!" said my muse to me,
"look in thy heart, and write."
SIR PHILIP SIDNEY (1554–1586)
ENGLISH POET AND STATESMAN

INVENTION: GENERATING IDEAS

I don't know what to write. I don't have anything to say. I don't know what the instructor wants.

As soon as we are required to write on a particular topic, many of us find writing the last thing in the world we want to do and our topic the least interesting. And, of course, the more we resent or fear the task, the more difficult going on impossible it is to get started.

A first step to getting started is to find a way to care about the subject. If the writer does not care, the reader will not care either. And caring is almost impossible to fake. Yes, we can be sure all the commas are screwed into place and the topic sentences all present and accounted for. But mechanical or surface correctness, though necessary, is not sufficient for good writing. Unless we write about something that engages our imagination and intelligence, our writing will be sluggish, doughlike, dull.

No matter what the subject, there is apt to be something to engage us. "Nothing in mankind is foreign to me," said the Roman dramatist Terence. And nothing need be inaccessible to any of us. Some would probably groan audibly if asked to write on the Spanish-American War, the fight against malaria, or *Moby-Dick*. But we could probably find in the recesses of our imagination a way in which each of those subjects could interest us: the dissolution of the Spanish Empire or the beginnings of American imperialism; the selfless desire to eradicate disease or the economic costs of poor health; the destructive power of obsession or the courage of seamanship.

Almost every subject is multifaceted. When we enter the writing task with sincerity and an open mind, we can discover something that will stimulate our imagination and generate energy. Our ideas find roots in the real world. We begin to see enriching connections. We enjoy writing much more.

In the following pages, we describe five invention techniques that may help you discover your way into a subject:

brainstorming

free writing

clustering

designing a topic tree

directed questioning

You can use these techniques at almost any point in the writing process. They can help you get ideas, see connections, discover evidence, even organize an essay. Not every one will work for all writers or under all circumstances. One technique may be right for one assignment, another for a different assignment. Tried seriously, one of them may help you break up a mental logjam.

Brainstorming

Brainstorming usually refers to the way a group of people—movie writers, advertising agents, political advisers—throw ideas and questions at one another, banging out the shape of a project or generating ideas to solve a problem. Writers, too, can brainstorm, alone or with friends. Brainstorming requires an open mind, a fearless attack on a subject, and a tolerance for some temporarily disordered searching.

Although brainstorming follows no set pattern, you might try this four-step process. First, think about the general subject, to the best of your ability ridding your mind of extraneous ideas. Second, jot down as many questions about the subject as you can think of, whether you know the answers or not. Third, narrow in on the questions that spark your imagination, and make brief notes on the answers, if any. Don't bother with full sentences or attempt perfect mechanics. Just try to generate a mass of questions and ideas, however outrageous and remote. Fourth, now that you have narrowed your focus, go through the process again in the area you find most interesting. This process may lead you to an idea you want to pursue in an essay.

The following is an example of brainstorming on the subject of secondary education:

Four years in high school. Yikes. But teachers
forever. Didn't they once teach lots of things like
in grammar school? Did they always have special
subjects like trig over and over again year after
year? Trig was awful why did they make me study
it? Why did I have to study 50% of the stuff I
did? Useful? But boring. Why was I so bored?
Waiting for after school? outside activities more
fun? Yeah but why do they allow so much outside?
Doesn't it compete for our attention? Athletics?
Why that production of <u>A Midsummer Night's Dream</u>?

After a rather desultory start, the brainstormer warmed to the process and began to get closer to something interesting. He wrote down answers to some of the questions he had asked.

They made me study trigonometry as a way to get me
to think in abstract ways.
I was bored because I didn't understand half of what
they were telling me——and because I didn't realize
how important some of it really was.
They allowed so much outside stuff because maybe
they felt sorry for us, or maybe because they wanted
us to be well rounded.
Athletics exercised my body like trig was supposed
to exercise my brain.
I learned a lot being Puck in that play.

With the questions at least partly answered, the writer looked over his notes. He decided that "outside activities" and the way they competed for "our attention" needed more thought. And so he brainstormed again.

Were the outside activities just fun? or something
else?
What about the play?
What do people get out of the debate team or choir?
Would some guys drop out without sports?

Unsystematic as this questioning was, it brought out unexpected ideas or points and perspectives the brainstormer might otherwise have missed. Once he brainstormed "other activities competing with studies," the point he found most interesting, he was only a short jump from beginning to write the paper.

Free Writing

If brainstorming leaves you with a messy lump of questions but no clear direction, try free writing. It is similar to brainstorming, but it can offer a steadier vision of your subject.

Free writing, as developed by Peter Elbow, is based on the notion that writing is a process and that you may need to be in the process, writing and rewriting, to find out what you think and know. This notion has much in common with the saying "How do I know what I think until I hear what I've said?"

The method is called free writing because you write for a designated period completely free of censorship or editing. You do not stop writing for any reason. You do not think about what you are writing; you just write. Evaluating your ideas or your sentences before or during the writing may abruptly halt the flow of words. Just let yourself go—no one else will read or judge what you write. Try to get as much out as you can, regardless of form. Editing will come later, after you recognize what you really want to say.

You can free-write as long as you like, but of course you should make sure you stick to the designated task and the time you establish. Here is a free-writing procedure that we think works very well:

With the overall subject firmly in mind, write for ten consecutive minutes without lifting your pen. Put down anything that pops into your head, relevant or irrelevant, sense or nonsense. In fact, don't even think about relevance and sense at this stage. Don't judge; keep writing. If your mind goes blank, write "My mind is a blank on subject X, my mind is a blank on subject X . . ." and keep on writing it until your mind begins to function. Don't let your hand stop writing.

If instead of brainstorming on the subject of secondary education our student had tried free writing, he might have come up with something like this during the first ten-minute period:

```
The last thing I want to write about is education
it's so general and I can't think of anything except
chalkboards that awful scratching sound with the
fingernail lots of math equations trigonometry I
```

```
hated worst except the lit class we read Crime and
Punishment was it?  it was punishment all right that
man murdered the old lady who needs it?  I liked Pip
though he was okay but not trig I hated my mind's a
blank on education just like that fourth question on
the final I couldn't even begin I'd rather have been
outside the sun was shining but funny old man Puntz
really liked that trig stuff his big grin when I
finally worked out that problem Puntz was an okay
guy and he really liked math but maybe lots of
teachers don't like the subject I bet they're bored
what would it be like if they switched around and
Puntz taught lit and Demoully taught math?  Imagine
Puntz talking about butchering old ladies.
```

Time's up.

We recommend a five-minute break after the first ten-minute effort: Get some water or do a math problem. Then read what you have written. Most of it will probably sound like gibberish. But you will very often find something worth thinking about. Throw away the results of the first step and repeat the exercise, again writing freely without stopping or editing. For a second effort our student might have written this:

```
The teachers are interested because that's all
they know maybe.  Mrs. O'Reilly knew about butter-
flies but became a history teacher.  Hard remember-
ing all that stuff they have to remember.  And they
don't get paid much either.  My mind's a blank on
education my mind's a blank on education And half
the kids are asleep even though when you have to
tell them to be quiet just when we were having a
good time laughing in trig he had to say everything
at least five times and he really must have been
bored but wouldn't want us to know he was bored.
But that grin when I was right.  I was pretty
pleased myself.  I wonder what he really thought. He
probably didn't know what I thought either. Maybe if
```

```
students and teachers saw the other side it wouldn't
be so difficult.  Bull sessions with teachers!
```

After the second writing, again do something else for five minutes. Then read what you have written, think about it, and repeat the ten-minute exercise.

By the end of the third step, you will probably be honing in on a subject. In our example, the student might be ready to concentrate on the difference between the way a student perceives education and the way a teacher does. After going through the process yet again, he might be ready to state a thesis, the specific point his essay will make:

```
To reduce the almost inevitable antagonism between
high-school students and teachers, I propose a
weekly bull session of an hour, complete with soft
drinks and fudge brownies.
```

Keep repeating the exercise until your ideas have crystallized and you have developed a line of thought or at least recognized what material you need. You may need to go through the process four or five times. At the end, flesh out your ideas with the necessary support, arrange them appropriately, revise, and polish.

Free writing doesn't work equally well for all writers. It seems most helpful to those who cannot decide on a thesis and who find themselves blocked when faced with a blank page.

Clustering

Clustering is somewhere between free writing and the more systematic forms of invention. It works best when you have a topic—perhaps one assigned by an instructor—but no clear ideas about it. Suppose you are asked to write about your family, a popular first assignment in a variety of courses, from composition to sociology. If the ideas are not exactly flowing, take a sheet of paper and somewhere near the middle write "My family." Circle the words. Now think about your family. As other ideas emerge—topics, memories, images, names—jot them down anywhere on the paper (see Figure 1.1).

After you have a number of ideas, circle the ones you find most intriguing and begin to make clusters around them. Around "Girls and boys treated differently" you might write "Mother easier on boys" and "Father easier on girls," and you might use "Father easier on girls" to form another cluster, which might include "Changed when Maggie went

Figure 1.1 Clustering

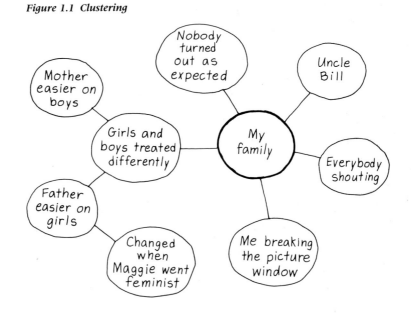

feminist." Make clusters around each of your subordinate ideas. Now you can do one of two things: note which ideas are connected and cluster around the connection, or choose a phrase, image, or idea that appeals to you, write it on another sheet of paper, and do the clustering process all over again. If the clustering around "Father changed when Maggie went feminist" interests you, you could start a new sheet of paper with that as the central idea.

As you cluster and connect, you will find your ideas getting more and more specific and insightful. In our example of "Father changed when Maggie went feminist," you might begin a new cluster that would develop into the idea that family relationships necessarily change, especially when children take contrary positions. You might analyze the consequences. By this time you would be fairly close to starting your essay.

Designing a Topic Tree

The topic tree combines elements of brainstorming, clustering, and directed questioning (see the next section). To make a topic tree, draw a diagram of your topic that resembles a tree. First, draw the "trunk," which is your general subject. Now draw the tree's main "branches"—that is, general aspects of your topic. You'll have to brainstorm these. Keep the

Figure 1.2 Topic Tree

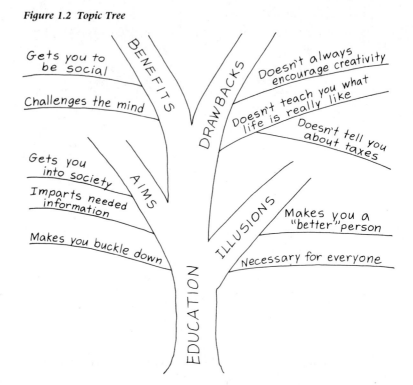

number of main branches small, or your tree will turn into a tangled mess. In the case of education, four main branches might be the aims, benefits, drawbacks, and illusions of education. From these main branches, draw examples of the main divisions. The only rule is that a branch must be directly related to the subject from which it branches. At any time, you can "break off a branch" and use it as a slip from which to start a new tree. Figure 1.2 shows what a topic tree for education might look like. Topic trees help you see your topic grow before your eyes. They can be useful ways to elaborate on a subject.

Directed Questioning

When you already know what interests you about the general subject but aren't sure how to approach it, try directed questioning. Instead of encouraging your mind to go where it will, with this method you close in on the major points. For when you have your basic ideas in mind, you want to limit and focus, not search and expand. Two directed questioning techniques are the journalistic method and the classical method.

THE JOURNALISTIC METHOD. The journalistic method simply answers six questions: who? what? when? where? why? how? Asking these questions may help to narrow your focus and order your thoughts. The questions will prove particularly useful when you narrate or describe human events. (We discuss this important method fully in Chapter 16, The Report.)

THE CLASSICAL METHOD. Many teachers suggest that rhetorical devices used by the ancient Greeks and Romans can help today's writers. The ancients analyzed a topic by using definition, comparison, relationship, and testimony. You will get to know some of these devices later as "strategies" you can use to construct a paragraph. Using them to analyze a subject can help you develop ideas about it. If the student who wrote on secondary education had used the classical method, his questions and answers might have followed this pattern:

Definition—What is it? What isn't it? What are its characteristics? What are its parts? Are there concealed implications or values? Are all the terms sufficiently clear?

He might have started with the dictionary definition: "The process of being trained or gaining knowledge through a formal or informal course of instruction." Then he might have gone on to think about that definition:

> Suppose I learned how to shoplift—is that education? How can you tell the difference between a good education and a bad one? I think it's what you know. How well adjusted you are to society. Whether or not you have skills so you can support yourself afterward. Some people would not agree. Definitions vary from person to person.

Comparison—How does your subject resemble something else and how does it differ? Are the differences trivial or significant? Is the comparison compelling enough for an entire essay?

> Education is like other ways of socializing people to participate in society, like joining the army or becoming a member of a club. Going to school is not the only way to get an education. You could listen to informed people, read books and magazines, get some on-the-job training. But school is different. Maybe because so much of what goes on is brain training, which you may get occasionally in these other activities but only incidentally.

Relationship—What preceded and what followed the subject? What were its causes and what were its consequences? What events happened at the same time, and how did they relate to the subject?

> What precedes education is not being educated. What happens at the same time? Well: life. While learning one kind of thing in school you learn other things outside. Everything from how to play the xylophone

to how to fly a plane. But inside and outside often connect. What follows education is what the debate is all about: happiness? maturity? success? or being a cog in the economic machine?

Testimony—What has previously been said and written on this issue? Have opinions changed over time? How does your view differ from "received" or conventional opinion? Why?

> Plenty has been said and written, including "A little learning is a dangerous thing." Ideas about education are always changing. Once teachers would try anything in class, but they are getting conservative. Seems to be a pendulum, from conservative to liberal and back. And that is good. When new ideas are being tried, even when they are really old ideas, students get more interested.

The student would have covered vast territory. Depending on his interests and impulses, he could select any of his answers as a starting point. He could compare the structured learning in school with the unstructured learning out of school, or he could trace the various changes in schoolroom tactics. The advantage of the classical method is that it puts ideas into categories and directs that all-important fund of ideas, daydreaming.

TIPS FOR INVENTION

- There is nothing about which you have nothing to say; you only need to find a way to care about a subject.
- Keep an open mind about all the techniques of invention: brainstorming, free writing, clustering, designing a topic tree, and directed questioning.
- Remember that one technique may be effective for one kind of task, another for another kind.

Exercises for Invention

1. From the following topics, choose one that interests you and free-write on it for ten minutes. Read what you have written, and select the idea you find most interesting. Using it as your starting point, free-write on it for another ten minutes. Stop again and select the most appealing sentence. Free-write on it for a final ten minutes.

   heroes
   temptations to lie or steal
   being a foreigner

parents
why biology, or any academic subject, is fascinating

2. Write a paragraph in which you describe doing Exercise 1. Was it easier or harder to free-write the second and third times? Did you develop unexpected ideas? Look at your first free writing. What ideas might you have pursued instead of the one you did? Why did you choose the one you did?

3. This exercise takes a partner. Agree on one of the following topics, and then brainstorm separately for ten minutes. Compare your notes. List the ideas and images that appear on both sheets. Which seem most promising as writing topics? Choose one of these items and repeat the process. Now each of you write an essay on an item from the second brainstorming list. Compare the two essays and account for the differences. What choices did each of you make? Why?

entering a party full of strangers
the hazards of exercising
taking responsibility for your actions
the value of intramural sports
the difficulties of choosing a career

4. Cluster ideas around one of these large topics. From this first cluster, pick an idea and cluster another set of ideas around it. Choose one of the ideas in this second cluster and cluster ideas around it. Write an essay on an idea in your third cluster. Explain your choice.

foreign policy
intercollegiate athletics
imports from Asia
studying philosophy
college education for everyone

5. Use a topic tree to generate ideas on one of the following topics. (If you do not have information about the topic, consult the reference section of your library.) Compare your ideas with those of classmates who chose the same topic. After seeing your classmates' work, would you go about the task in a different way? Explain why or why not in a paragraph.

Harry Truman's election as president
special awards at high-school graduation
the Donner Party
the law of gravity
a specific athletic event

6. The classical method was originally used to generate ideas from general topics. Try it on one of the following: civil disobedience, faithfulness in marriage, racial diversity, the Third World, social welfare programs. Now write an essay on one of these topics. At the end of the essay, discuss which strategy—definition, comparison, and so on—was most fruitful. Which led you to your topic? Why?

2

PUTTING WORDS
ON PAPER

There is nothing to write about, you say. Well,
then, write and let me know just this—that
there is nothing to write about.

PLINY THE YOUNGER (C. 61–C. 112)
ROMAN ORATOR AND STATESMAN

SUBJECT AND THESIS: SAYING SOMETHING

Generating ideas is a first step toward writing, but once you have a fund of possibilities, you need to decide which idea or ideas are worth writing about.

In the Introduction, we mentioned some of the things we hope you will get from this book, and we started the list with "finding something to say that is worth saying." We started there because, of course, that is the most important part of writing. If there is nothing to say, there is no point writing. All of us know people—and some of us have dear friends—who chatter on about nearly nothing. We put up with it because we love the person or the voice is soothing or the sound serves as a cover for our thoughts. But imagine finding that same chatter in print. We would not read it.

Writing worth reading must have both a worthwhile subject and a thesis, or interesting approach to the subject. The invention methods we discussed in Chapter 1 may help a writer settle on a subject and an approach before actually beginning to write. Frequently, however, something worth saying does not precede the writing. In the act of writing, you may come upon the subject just meant for you. Putting sentences or paragraphs onto the paper may continue the invention process.

The Subject

The subject of an essay is often the "given" of a writing assignment. It may be as broad as the title of a course: "Soviet-American Relations after World War II," "Abnormal Psychology," "Classical Greece." More often than not, the instructor will narrow down the subject: "Soviet-American Relations and the Third World," "Anorexia Nervosa," "Socrates." Even so, you won't be expected to cover the whole subject.

Think of the possible ramifications of "Soviet-American Relations and the Third World." Most of the world is the Third World—you could not write about every country. Nor could you discuss all aspects of superpower and Third World relations: military, political, social, economic, and so on. You would have to narrow the subject to a size commensurate with your knowledge, your interests, the time you can allot, and the number of pages the instructor has requested.

Sometimes instructors provide a narrow subject with built-in limits that tell you where you can and cannot go. These limits, implicit and explicit, help you focus in on the subject. Even then, you have to do some narrowing of your own. Suppose you receive this assignment in a course called "Classical Greece":

> Compare the preoccupations and methods of Socrates with those of the pre-Socratic philosophers. Six to eight pages.

This is a huge topic. Books have been written on it and barely scratched the surface. A whole army of important Greek philosophers lived before Socrates, and, of course, Socrates alone is an immense subject. Your instructor would expect you to *select* one or perhaps two pre-Socratics for consideration. You might decide that Pythagoras is representative and interesting (besides, you have known his name ever since high-school geometry).

You would now have set up the two sides of the comparison: Socrates and Pythagoras. But you would still need to narrow the focus: "preoccupations and methods" covers just about everything. You would limit the number of headings under which to compare Pythagoras and Socrates. You might brainstorm a list of the preoccupations the two philosophers had in common:

> the irrational
>
> problems in perception
>
> the physical universe

and many more. Which of these topics do you want to analyze? The same constraints operate: your knowledge, your interests, and the time and space allotted.

You may be drawn to "the irrational," just as Pythagoras was. You may "feel" a distinct difference between Pythagoras and Socrates on this subject, but you may not know exactly what that difference is.

At this stage, let the problem percolate. Review all you have read by and about the two philosophers. Compare representative passages from their writings. Review your class notes ("Socrates distrustful of irrational beliefs"). When something strikes you, jot it down. But also let your mind wander (Hey, didn't Pythagoras believe in reincarnation?). Follow your thoughts wherever they lead. Take the brakes off your imagination. Speculate.

When a central concern begins to firm up in your mind, concentrate on it. Write it down so you will be sure not to forget: "What the two philosophers thought about the limits of reason." Having narrowed your subject and thereby set up a manageable comparison, you are well on your way to developing your thesis.

The Thesis

The basic idea around which your essay is organized and to which all the parts contribute is called a thesis. It is the point of the essay. In the following sections we discuss two kinds of thesis: the argumentative thesis, which argues a point, and the organizational thesis, which organizes information.

THE ARGUMENTATIVE THESIS.   When assigning an essay, most instructors call for an *expository* essay, that is, an interpretation of a topic. They expect students to develop an idea about a subject and then argue to prove it. This process demonstrates how students think, how they handle concepts, and how much they understand.

The argumentative thesis represents your opinion on the subject, your conviction, your evaluation, your discovery, your approach, your point of view. Note the word *your*. The subject belongs to the world; the thesis is your stamp on it.

You must, of course, get to the narrowed subject before you arrive at your thesis idea. The following examples show the narrowing process:

Assignment: A three-page essay on a difficult social issue

Broad subject: Smoking in public places

Narrowed subject: The rights of nonsmokers

Thesis: Because of the danger to the health of nonsmokers, smoking should be restricted to designated areas.

Assignment: A six-page essay on a novel read in this course

Broad subject: Charles Dickens's *Great Expectations*

Narrowed subject: The protagonist Pip (still too broad)

More narrowed subject: Important places in Pip's life

Thesis: Three important places—the forge, Satis House, and the grave-yard—shape Pip's possibilities in life.

Notice that the subjects are sentence fragments, but the theses are complete sentences. They make a completed thought about each subject.

You may not know what your thesis is when you start writing—it may result from putting ideas and impressions down on paper. But when you set about writing your final draft, you will certainly need to know your thesis. An essay without a thesis is like a ship without a rudder. It moves in circles or in zigzags. It spins with the wave and sinks with the trough. It will probably swamp.

Although a thesis need not necessarily be stated in a sentence or two, such an explicit statement can help you and your reader. Like a lodestar, it can help you stay on course and enable your reader to determine whether you are actually traveling where you said you would. Usually this explicit statement will occur in the first or second paragraph. From then on, you and your reader can check whether the essay is on course.

More often than not, the thesis will be encapsulated in a single sentence. There may be times, however, when your idea would burst out of a single sentence because it requires immediate explanation or qualification. You may then need two or more sentences. But remember that the longer the thesis, the more difficult for the reader to grasp. Try to make your thesis statement hard, tight, unmistakable.

A thesis is not a litany of cold facts. Facts say nothing about themselves. They simply are. When we write, we must show how facts connect and what they mean. In short, we must interpret. In a class on twentieth-century European history, the assignment was "In a four- to six-page paper, discuss the Aisne-Marne offensive." One student wrote this as his thesis:

On July 18, 1918, a quarter of a million American troops began the month-long Aisne-Marne offensive. This offensive forced the Germans to retreat to the Vesle River. It was followed by the Meuse-Argonne drive. The armistice was signed on November 11, 1918.

This paragraph is all facts you could find in any encyclopedia. The writer did not say why the facts are important. The rest of the essay was a simple chronology. This happened and then this and then this. The facts are cold indeed.

The writer warmed the facts up in his revision:

> On July 18, 1918, a quarter of a million American troops began the month-long Aisne-Marne offensive. This offensive halted what had seemed to be an irresistible German attack, fortified the sagging Allied defenses, served notice of the American presence, and—perhaps most significant—caused widespread dissatisfaction and political unrest in Germany. It was the turning point of the war.

He now had the start of a very meaty six-page essay.

A thesis is not a gusher of feeling. We are not against feeling. On the contrary, we are all for expressing it in essays. But feeling alone will not help the cause. Readers will not be stampeded—they can be persuaded. "Computers are fantastic and fun" is not very arguable or scintillating. Neither is "Jeanette MacDonald and Nelson Eddy had the most beautiful voices ever," or "Abortion is a horrible sin." These explosions of feeling hardly promise an essay worth reading, one that is reasoned and supported.

In a second effort, the computer fancier tried to modulate her tone:

> Computers are the most fantastic innovation ever to revolutionize human life.

Imagine trying to prove that a piece of hardware is "the most fantastic innovation." What about the internal combustion machine, the lever, and the wheel? This thesis is still too large and too emotional for an essay. The writer made a final try:

> Computers have revolutionized human life by drastically shortening the time it takes to perform previously difficult and lengthy intellectual operations.

The writer still has her work cut out for her, but now it is doable.

The thesis is not a grandiose generality. It is an assertion you can support in the time and space allotted. In a six- to eight-page paper, you can neither prove nor disprove the superiority of capitalism over socialism or vice versa. You can neither prove nor disprove that the novel is dead. These assertions are too far-reaching for an essay. Don't claim more than you can support. Be modest. If the economies of Burma and Thailand can be considered typical, Communism has not provided as high a standard of living in Asia as has capitalism.

The thesis is not a recitation of the obvious. No one wants to read that "senators are subject to pressure from special-interest groups." We know that already. We know that slavery is evil, that defense costs money, that science is challenging. Conventional opinions do not a lively essay make.

If something is not worth arguing about, it is unlikely to be worth writing about. A good thesis is controversial. Although it should not be wild or crazy, it ought to have a sharp edge.

Sometimes you can turn blank statements of received wisdom—like those in the previous paragraph—into sharp statements with an argumentative edge:

> Because special-interest groups—such as blacks, unions, and corporations—have become so powerful, balancing their demands is at the heart of the American political system.

> Slavery helped to bring about the development of democracy in Greece by providing philosophers leisure from onerous work.

> If it causes us to stop building intercontinental ballistic missiles, Star Wars may save money in the long run.

> An obsessive desire for scientific knowledge can be dangerous, because, as the Frankenstein story suggests, the results can be unpredictable.

We do not necessarily agree with these assertions, but they do have an argumentative edge, and we want to read what the writers have to say about them.

A thesis is not just the assertion of an opinion. The best theses do not make bald statements of opinion, however reasonable. A reader wants to know right away whether the issue is worth discussing and whether the writer will pursue an interesting idea. The following flat-footed assertions offer little for a reader to anticipate:

> Live theater is a declining entertainment.

> We should turn the churches into grain bins or art museums.

> I prefer men who know they are chauvinists but don't care to men who are chauvinists but don't know it.

Why? why? and why again? Answering *why?* would limit the thesis, direct the discussion, sharpen the argumentative edge, and promise a more interesting essay. Look at the difference between

> We should not allow the president to wage covert wars

and

> We should not allow the president to wage covert wars because such a right would upset the balance of powers mandated by the Constitution.

Another writer on waging covert wars might frame the thesis this way:

> If we let the executive branch wage covert wars, we sacrifice the very basis of our constitution.

Many theses will answer not *why?* but *how?* This question becomes particularly important when we make a proposal. Here is a proposal that could use a dose of *how?* to lift it above the platitudinous:

High-school students can become more sensitive to the needs of the elderly.

Sure, but ho hum. Add the *how?* and the idea becomes more interesting:

If the school hired retired people as teachers' aides, high-school students would become more sensitive to the needs of the elderly.

Suppose we keep the *how?* and add a *why?*

From such contact, students would learn how the elderly view the world and why they see it that way.

Now the writer promises a thoughtful essay.

Sometimes answering the question *under what circumstances?* can make a drab thesis more compelling:

Experimentation on animals should not be allowed.

can become

Unless laboratory scientists place the highest priority on not causing pain to the animals, experimentation on animals should not be allowed.

Although and *when* clauses can suggest the circumstances under which the thesis assertion is true:

When voters suffer economically, they blame the party in control of the White House rather than Congress.

Although some individuals still manage to climb the social ladder, social class is largely predetermined on the basis of inherited wealth and privilege.

A thesis that answers a question predicts the shape and even the content of the essay. It tells the writer what kind of support is needed, and it tells the reader that the journey won't be shrouded in fog but will be sharp and clear.

The most effective theses are succinct and their terms clear. The following thesis may well contain an idea worth pursuing, but the language in which it is expressed is so vague and scattered that we don't know what it really means:

The U.S. government has concealed the whole question of the MIAs in its own conception of what the American people really want and believe, and the Vietnamese haven't bothered to be straight about what is really going on, and I think that explains what some of the problems are in the exchange.

What conception? What does *straight* mean? What problems? This thesis is so wordy and imprecise that the reader can have little idea what is coming. The student redesigned the thesis this way:

> Because of partisan politics in the United States and deviousness in Vietnam, the MIAs will probably never be accounted for.

The vague references to our government's policy and Vietnamese behavior have been focused in the forthright phrase *partisan politics in the United States and deviousness in Vietnam.* The explanation for "some of the problems" is the subject of a straightforward assertion: "the MIAs will probably never be accounted for."

In the revision, the student dropped the *I think.* Because the reader will assume the ideas belong to the writer, phrases such as *I think* or *I feel* are unnecessary. When you clutter up your prose with them, you sound unsure of yourself. The thesis is your special twist on the subject; *you* are the expert on what you think.

THE ORGANIZATIONAL THESIS.   Thus far we have been discussing the expository essay, in which the writer makes an arguable assertion and then sets out to prove it. You may often be asked, in school and out, to do other kinds of writing—book reports, personal essays, explications, surveys of writings about a subject. You may be asked to narrate or describe, summarize or analyze. For these kinds of assignments, you will need to determine the most effective way to present the information. Accumulating and throwing facts at the reader higgledy-piggledy would lead to chaos. You need an *organizational thesis.*

Unlike the argumentative thesis, the organizational thesis does not primarily represent a point of view or an opinion. Rather, it prepares the reader for the information to come. It suggests the form and the focus of that information. It is as essential to the report and summary as the argumentative thesis is to the expository essay. Even a straight newspaper article has an organizational thesis, as in this opening paragraph:

> As stock markets soared this year, a chorus of pessimists warned that 1987 looked more like 1929, when a stock market crash ushered in the Great Depression. Yesterday, after a plunge reminiscent of the worst days of 1929, the most pressing question was whether the aftershocks would be as devastating to individuals and the nation at large. (Eric Gelman, "Does 1987 Equal 1929?")

Now we know what kind of information to expect: a comparison of the two periods in regard to potential for economic disaster.

(For a full discussion of various kinds of organizational theses, see Chapter 16, The Report.)

TIPS FOR SUBJECT AND THESIS

- Narrow your subject to a manageable size.
- In papers that support an opinion, devise a sharp and clear argumentative thesis.
- Ask yourself, Is my thesis too factual? too emotional? grandiose? trite?
- Have you made your thesis interesting by answering how? or why? or under what circumstances?
- Are the terms of your thesis succinct and clear?
- In your thesis, avoid phrases such as *I think* or *I feel.*
- For reports or summaries, be sure you have a good organizational thesis.

Exercises for Subject and Thesis

1. The following subjects are too broad for an essay of 750–1,000 words. Reduce four of them to an appropriate size. You need not construct a thesis: this is an exercise in narrowing the subject. Be prepared to explain how and why you narrowed as you did.

newspapers	American children	DNA
violence	women in literature	missionaries
Brazil	building bridges	rodents

2. Sometimes it is a good idea to narrow step by step. Choose two of your subjects from Exercise 1 and narrow them a step at a time four times.

3. With a partner, select three of the following overly broad assertions and separately write thesis statements appropriate for an essay of 750–1,000 words. Assert the negative if you prefer. Test the statements by the standards discussed in this chapter. Compare your thesis statements with your partner's. What kinds of differences do you find?

   James Joyce was the greatest writer of this century.
   The quality of life ought to be improved.
   Affirmative action is essential.
   Taxes should be reduced.
   Genetic engineering is dangerous.
   Movies are more entertaining than television.

4. Rewrite the following statements to give them an argumentative edge.
   a. Beethoven was a musician.
   b. Waterskiing is exciting.
   c. In time of war, traitors should be punished.
   d. Police should be nice.

5. Evaluate the effectiveness of the following statements as theses for essays of 750–1,000 words. Rewrite the ineffective ones to make them workable. Bear in mind why? how? and under what circumstances? Note: you may not know what the writer had in mind—a major flaw in some thesis statements. If this is the case, construct a sound thesis for the indicated subject.
   a. Fraternity initiations are like animal aggression.
   b. The feminist movement threatens the institution of marriage.
   c. Wood stoves obviate the internal redistribution of thermal energies.
   d. Violence on television is a complex topic, but in this paper I will attempt to deal with it.
   e. Private ownership of handguns poses a serious problem.
   f. City planners may be eliminating the private dwelling.

6. Scan this week's issues of *Time, Newsweek,* and *U.S. News and World Report* and select a major story that all three magazines covered. The coverage, emphasis, and depth of the stories will differ. Now write an organizational thesis for a report on that story. Repeat the process for two other major stories. In each case, consider the following questions: How did you choose your thesis? What elements did you decide to include and discard and why? Do you think you chose the proper point of view in each case?

A man may write at any time, if he will set himself doggedly to it.

SAMUEL JOHNSON (1709–1784)
ENGLISH WRITER AND CRITIC

DEVELOPING, ORGANIZING, DRAFTING: GETTING THE IDEAS WRITTEN

To get a workable and interesting thesis may take several tries, and you may even change your thesis after you finish your first draft. But when you feel you have a pretty good idea of what you are going to write, it is time to begin to get those thoughts clear and to put them on paper.

Writing involves our psychological state and our physical state, so much so that the ease of it depends on how good we feel, how much we expect to enjoy the process, what response we hope for or fear, even our regard for the audience. No wonder it can sometimes not be "free-form fun." As Samuel Johnson suggests, we must sometimes just be dogged about it.

Getting Ready

Before you start, plan your attack on the project. Think through your best way of getting down your thoughts. This part of the process will vary from person to person. Some will want to be tightly organized; others will just start writing. Save time and energy by proceeding in the way best for you.

The following advice should help with any writing task. It contains no big secrets or surefire tricks, only some points that will make your writing more enjoyable during the process and more effective with your audience.

First of all, make it easy on yourself. Start early. Some writers begin halfway between the assignment of the project and the deadline. If they have two weeks, for instance, they start writing one week before the due date. They don't wait until the last minute. Starting early provides a margin for error as well as ample time to perform the task.

Schedule a block of time to write, and do nothing else during that time. When you write in tidbits, you are constantly starting up. This is as hard on writing as stop-and-go traffic is on cars.

Put yourself out of temptation's way. Find a quiet, well-lighted nonsocial place where you won't be disturbed. Take the phone off the hook. Have a snack or soda nearby.

Keep supplies handy. When you have a head of steam, going off to the store for a new pencil or eraser will undoubtedly dissipate it.

Be sure your references and source materials are easily accessible. Your dictionary should always be nearby. Keep *Writing Worth Reading* around for questions about writing. If you are using research, check to see that your major sources are with you. Be sure your notes are together, legible, and in order.

Developing

Once you have settled on a subject and formulated a thesis, however tentative, start jotting down major supporting ideas. A good source of supporting ideas is what you generated from brainstorming, directed questioning, or one of the other invention techniques. Identify the ideas that relate directly to the thesis you are working on. Perhaps you should try the invention technique again, this time with your thesis in mind.

Your major supporting ideas will probably be somewhat general or abstract, and you will need to develop evidence for them. *Evidence* is whatever the reader will accept without further explanation. It includes numbers, quotations, examples, the word of someone you and your reader both trust, the values you know you share. It is the common ground you and your reader can stand on. Be sure your evidence connects directly with a major point.

Evidence lies also in your sources. If you are, for instance, writing an essay on a novel, refer to notes you took while reading, and page through the book itself for apt quotations or examples. If you are writing about history, look in your textbook and other readings for facts you can use. If you are discussing a problem in sociology, develop your ideas by working up a chart or graph based on some statistics you have collected. Always, always take careful notes.

You might find the *reasons chain* helpful in developing support. This is a chain of *becauses*. Write down your thesis, and then write down *because*. Fill in the answer, and again write *because*. Keep going along that chain until the answer is self-evident. Then go back to the beginning and see if you can develop another chain of *becauses*.

Here is the reasons chain in action:

Thesis: The college should retain its two-semester "Western Civilization" requirement.

Because: It is the best way to ensure a knowledge of our history and our cultural values.

Because: Only with the knowledge of history can we fully understand contemporary society.

Because: Only when we fully understand our society will we know how to protect our democracy.

Because: History teaches us that forces hostile to democracy lurk just below the surface of society and can break out at any time.

Because: The frequent reorganization of the Ku Klux Klan is an example.

We have probably hit the self-evident wall here, and so we try another chain based on the same thesis:

Because: Without a requirement, many students would not take the Western Civ course.

Because: The drive toward professionalism is so great in our schools.

That may or may not be self-evident. If not, the *because* might require some statistical evidence.

Now we should look back at all the *becauses* to be sure we have followed them. We can see, for instance, that the first *because* mentions cultural values, but we did not build a chain on that. Now is the time to forge that chain of reasons. By means of the reasons chain, you can extend your understanding of your thesis and be far along the way to organizing.

Organizing

When you organize, you systematically arrange the ideas and evidence that you intend to use in your essay. If you're not certain about your thesis, you may need to draft first, organize later. But if you have a good idea of what your thesis is, then organizing before you write provides a sense of direction through the morass of facts and helps you find connections between important points.

As a first step, identify your major supporting ideas, making sure they are neither repetitious nor irrelevant. Under each, place the supporting evidence. If a piece of evidence won't fit, don't force it. If you have not generated enough evidence, try one of the invention techniques—they can work for small as well as for large points. Invention techniques can also help you get started organizing because they can help you see connections and group similar ideas.

SUMMARY PARAGRAPH.   At this stage you might try writing a paragraph that begins with your thesis and continues with each major point expressed in a complete sentence. Such a summary paragraph could help you determine your general direction and focus. Here is a paragraph encompassing the thesis and all the major ideas for an essay on the Electoral College:

> Because the Electoral College is unnecessary and potentially dangerous, we should support efforts to change the system. It once worked. The "winner-take-all" principle for each state's delegates is unfair to minority political groups. It violates the "one-person, one-vote" principle. It threatens the federalist system. There is also the problem of small states having inordinate influence. The victory could go to a candidate the majority of people don't want. Many have suggested changes. The best would be direct election.

Although it will not appear in the final essay, this paragraph—the whole essay boiled down—will help the writer see forward.

OUTLINING.   Whether you are writing a personal essay or a lengthy research paper, outlining can help you organize and develop your material. When you outline, you first divide your thesis into major components or headings, and then arrange your ideas under those headings. This process can help you in several ways:

It forces you to get that thesis down on paper.

It identifies the main points.

It indicates at least a tentative organizational plan.

Outlines come in both informal and formal varieties.

Informal outlines or scratch lists: Making an informal outline, or scratch list, sometime during the writing process can help you figure out where you're going and how to get there. To write an informal outline, divide your thesis into its major parts and use each part as a heading under which you place your supporting ideas.

Suppose your thesis is "The affluence of American society has changed the values of all but the lowest economic class." Within that sentence lie several major ideas, which you can jot down in a word or short phrase:

> affluence
>
> American society
>
> values
>
> lowest economic class

You can then place your supporting ideas under the relevant headings. Under *affluence,* for instance, you might jot down a reminder to "compare standard of living in 1930s and now" and "compare consumption patterns in the United States and the Third World." Under *values,* you might list "attitudes toward family," "religion," "education," or "sense of community responsibility." After following this pattern, you would know pretty well the shape of your essay. Of course, the more detailed your outline, the closer you are to the completed essay.

Formal outlines: If you undertake a large project, you may want to devise a formal outline. Formal outlines break down, group, and arrange your ideas more thoroughly than informal outlines, or scratch lists. We call this type of outline *formal* because it is a detailed, methodical effort to set forth the ultimate shape and even the content of your paper.

As with the informal outline, you start by dividing your thesis into major elements. Now, just as you carefully divided your thesis, you divide your major elements into their component ideas, and, where feasible, continue to subdivide until you have all your evidence clearly identified. In this way, you preserve your major divisions and establish the relative importance of your minor ideas.

In devising a formal outline, follow the conventional system of numbered or lettered headings. In the following example, we outline an essay on the gun control controversy:

> Thesis: The two sides of the gun control controversy line up over the issue of individual rights versus society's needs.
>
>   I. Background
>
>   A. Description of issue
>
>   B. Evidence of controversy
>
>   1. News media

   2. Legislative action
    a. Federal action
    b. State and local laws and ordinances
  II. Individual rights
   A. Constitutional rights
    1. Right to bear arms
     a. Legislative history
     b. Supreme Court interpretations
    2. Right to self-defense
   B. Tradition of vigilantism or citizen policing
   C. Need to exercise rights
    1. Increase in crime
    2. Inadequacy of police
 III. Society's need
   A. Access to firearms
    1. Easy to purchase
    2. Hard to control
   B. Relation of legal gun ownership to use of firearms
    1. Crimes
     a. Comparison of United States and Great Britain
     b. Domestic violence and violence against strangers
    2. Accidents
     a. Children
     b. Adults
   C. Changes in society since Constitution
    1. Intention of Founders
    2. Growth of police forces

This outline is called a *topic outline* because it sets forth the paper's main topics in words and phrases. If you want more detail, try a *sentence outline*. Write a complete sentence for each item. Number III.A.2. above might read

> States that try to control traffic in firearms fail because different states have different laws and purchasers can simply go into an adjacent state.

You can add more detail if you wish. You could, for instance, subdivide III.A.1. into a. and b. and write:

> a. Sporting goods stores often provide handguns without identification.
> b. Many people order handguns from mail-order businesses, as did Lee Harvey Oswald, who killed John F. Kennedy.

How much you subdivide depends on how near the completed essay you want to get by means of an outline. A complete formal outline appears on pages 394–397.

  Three general rules apply to making outlines. First, items on the same level should be of the same general importance, that is, I. should be of equal importance to II., A. to B., and so on. After all, the point of the outline is to understand the relative importance of topics.

Second, whenever you divide a level, you need at least two parts beneath it: you can't cut a cake into one piece. Under I., if you have A., you need B., and so on. Each level in the preceding outline follows this rule.

Third, items at each level should be grammatically parallel. If A. is a complete sentence, B. should be also. If (1) is a phrase, (2) should be a phrase. Otherwise, you may find it difficult to grasp which ideas belong together and in what way.

Even if your outline is less formal than our example, be sure you

connect all points in intelligible order

distinguish major points from minor ones and emphasize them accordingly

gather evidence adequate to support each point.

ORGANIC PROGRESSION. Organization is not only form, but order. How do we decide what order our ideas should follow? The very best organization is, not surprisingly, organic: one idea grows out of another, and the essay proceeds according to inherent connections. To see these connections, do as much reading as you think you should—in fact, do more. Be as comfortable with the subject as possible. And then, after reviewing your notes, free-write, brainstorm, talk it out with a friend, or just think about it. The more familiar you are with the subject, the more likely you are to see connections that appear natural, even inevitable. Here is the summary of one essay that grew organically:

Because of the inevitable depletion of fossil fuel sources, we must immediately seek new sources of energy.

Coal is becoming scarce and more hazardous.

People have therefore turned to nuclear energy.

Fission has great problems, including safety.

Fusion is safer but costly.

Wind and waves produce energy but can't be major sources.

A major source has been hydroelectric power, but its capacity is limited.

Although expensive, unlimited solar energy promises to be our best source of energy.

This "organic" progression is actually quite logical. The first idea (depletion of resources) leads to an example (coal) and a cause-and-effect argument (because coal is scarce, people have turned to nuclear energy) and so on: the seed idea of depletion grows into the final thought.

The least interesting essays are those in which one idea is placed next to another without thought to connection, like stacking logs. "First, second, third, and so on." To test whether your essay is a stack of logs, reverse the order of its ideas. If it still makes sense, you have a stack of logs.

Drafting

However you organize your material, a time comes when you must start drafting. Drafting should be the least pressured stage of writing. You should let your ideas flow—no one is going to read your first efforts. Drafting can be free-form fun, a snap compared with the other stages.

Well, that is a bit of an exaggeration. It does not work that way every time. Sometimes getting that first draft on paper is painfully slow. Perhaps the subject is genuinely difficult, and it takes time to cobble together all the bits of information or fill out each step in a closely reasoned argument. You may spend hours at a midparagraph sentence. Sometimes those very first inkblots are paralyzing. Even James Joyce, a great writer, would stare out the window for hours on end seeking the right word.

Although no method is right for everyone, here are some suggestions for the drafting stage:

1. Keep three basic elements of your paper always in view: your purpose, your audience, and the big picture. Think about your goal. Can you get there from here? Have new ideas opened up new routes? Consider whether you should revise your plan. Think about your audience. Imagine how the essay will sound, how it will look, and how it will be received.

2. Don't try to write and edit at the same time. Writing a sentence, crossing it out, rewriting it, and worrying over the grammar or the wording can slow you down and endanger your mental health. When you hit on a new twist, you don't need to go back right away to adjust the beginning—you can do that on the next draft. If a start-and-go-back method is the best way for you, however, then follow it. But most of us find it easier and more effective to write now, edit later.

By all means, when those blinding flashes of insight tell you, "Hold on! That sentence on page 3 should have read . . ." or "Use that juicy Smith quotation on page 5," obey them. Fix up the suddenly offending passage, or at least make a note of it. And if you have an idea you know will work beautifully at the end of the essay, be sure to make a note of that. But what writers usually need most at this stage is a natural rhythm in writing, not an agonizing halt-and-about-face process. Try to press on.

3. Do not, however, force sections that just will not come. Many writers cannot begin with the introduction: they think it demands too much formality and precision all at once. Yet some cannot get started until that first paragraph is right.

Don't fret: if you feel happiest writing middle paragraphs, go straight to one. Start with a section you think may be easy to write. Use any invention technique at any point in drafting. The satisfaction you derive from the easier writing will often speed the harder writing.

4. Read aloud to yourself. When you come to a natural pause—the end of a paragraph or a section—give voice to your silent words. Reading aloud is a good way to stay in close touch with your writing. It will tell you if you are moving at an appropriate pace and if the writing flows smoothly. Of course, you will revise later, but reading aloud can help you to anticipate your next moves. It may give you some new ideas, reveal rough spots, or encourage you.

5. Recognize signs of tension. This may sound more like therapy than writing advice, but it concerns every writer. Frustration tends to grow slowly for a while and then hit a point where it sends you through the roof. If you feel frustration building, stop before you explode. Take a break. Take a walk. Take a nap.

Like frustration, fatigue is an enemy of good writing. If you begin to get very tired, rest your eyes and your mind. Stop writing. If your paper is due in two hours, not writing may be hard to do—a good reason to make sure you are never in that position.

6. Regard the first draft as provisional. Few if any writers ever get it right the first time. A first draft is almost bound to be changed, and improved. Be ready—perhaps even eager—to revise.

TIPS FOR DEVELOPING, ORGANIZING, DRAFTING

- Look in your background material and your invention notes for evidence and ideas that need developing.
- Identify your main ideas and place supporting ideas under them.
- Select a congenial method of organization: a summary paragraph, an informal outline, or a formal outline.
- Think about the organic progression of your major ideas; avoid stacking ideas.
- While drafting, bear in mind your purpose, your audience, and the big picture.
- Use the invention techniques to develop points.
- Remember that few writers can write and edit at the same time.
- Treat your first draft as temporary, subject to drastic change.

Exercises for Developing, Organizing, Drafting

1. Choose two ideas from a recent invention exercise you've done—brainstorming, free writing, clustering, designing a topic tree—and develop each one with three pieces of evidence. Draft a paragraph for each.

2. Imagine that you have been asked to write your autobiography, including your life-to-be. Free-write or brainstorm your life, and then plan how you would go about writing it. Divide the subject into major periods, themes, events, people, or however you want to organize it. Turn in your organizational plan.

3. With a partner, determine the major supporting ideas for or against one of the following theses. Now each of you choose a form of organization from this list: summary paragraph, informal outline, formal outline. Compare what you have done. What differences do you find? Which organization seems better and why?

   Because of hazards to health, smoking should be prohibited in all buildings on the campus.

   Contracts between childless parents and surrogate mothers should be outlawed because such contracts infringe on the constitutional rights of the surrogate mothers.

   To control the spread of drug abuse, federal employees should be subject to random testing.

4. From the following list, choose the topic that most appeals to you. Construct a thesis, develop support, organize your ideas, and draft an essay—in that order.

   anything that makes you particularly angry
   the virtues and foibles of your mother's family
   allergies you have known
   the value of wearing, or not wearing, a wristwatch
   the pitfalls of borrowing and lending

I'm goin' to change my way of livin'
  and if that ain't enough,
Then I'll change the way I strut my stuff. . . .
BILLY HIGGINS AND W. BENTON OVERSTREET
AMERICAN POPULAR-SONG WRITERS

REVISING: GETTING THE WRITING RIGHT

Novelist Vladimir Nabokov once said, "I have rewritten—often several times—every word I have ever published. My pencils outlast their erasures." Professional writers like Nabokov do not treat a first draft as sacred, engraved in stone. They know that words rarely march onto the page in perfect order, thoughts clear, sentences elegant, phrases vigorous, punctuation accurate. They know that to be a good writer is to be a good rewriter.

Although with most people revision is about as popular as house-breaking puppies, it is the most important stage of writing. We need the spontaneity of the first draft, yes, but the first draft is only *a first draft*. First, not last. If we are honest with ourselves, we know we will need a second go, and probably a third.

Revising brings into play everything this book covers, from thinking large thoughts to selecting the proper dot or dash. Like writing, revising is a process. When we revise, we make a series of decisions and we try out alternative ideas and words. We reorganize, perhaps even find a better thesis. We experiment with sentence shapes and with emphasis. We keep on changing things until we are satisfied—or have run out of time.

Some people write a first draft and then in the name of revision gussy it up with a few minor changes before presenting it to their bosses or instructors. Here it is, folks: the first-and-a-half draft. That is not revision. Revision follows a slow and objective reexamination of that first draft. It allows us to react to our first thoughts and to refine and expand them.

The Critical Distance

A brand-new piece of writing is like a brand-new baby: it looks perfect. We can no more read our recent writing objectively than we could list the baby's flaws. We need critical distance. We need to separate ourselves from our creation. Before trying to revise, you should put your essay away for a while. The Roman poet Horace recommended nine years. If you don't have that sort of time, try a few hours. Take a walk, see a movie, practice the flügelhorn—anything that will give your objectivity a chance to grow.

If you would like to know what critical distance feels like, find a letter or essay you wrote two years ago, or five. If you have the sensation of reading someone else's writing, you are feeling critical distance. The perfect writer would treat his or her first draft like another person's writing—that would guarantee that the distance would be critical. Because most of us are not virtuous enough to attain such a state, we take a long break between drafts.

Once you have achieved some critical distance, return to your first draft. Read it. Read it aloud. Have a friend read it to you. Hearing your written words is almost always surprising. You may even want to interrupt with an occasional "Well, that isn't exactly what I meant." Feel the critical distance grow.

Blowing the Essay to Pieces

If you start revising line by line straight through, you risk seeing the essay the way you first saw it. Good revisers try to break the pattern in order to get a clearer look. They have various ways of blowing the essay to pieces.

Some writers start at the end and work backward. They check the conclusion against their purpose. They compare the ending and the opening to see if they can get to one from the other. Going backward, they note the transitions between paragraphs. They read sentences out of context— and perhaps wonder what they meant.

A few actually take scissors to their first effort. They cut it up into sections and arrange them in different combinations. Wrenched from their context, passages lose that "finished" look.

Anything that disrupts the way you are used to seeing or thinking about your writing helps you lose the pride of ownership that makes objectivity so difficult. It allows you to read with fresh eyes.

Once you have established the distance needed for a rigorous examination, you are ready to revise. You will probably want to cross out repetitions, underline good points, write questions to yourself, circle ideas, draw boxes and arrows. Gather some pens or sharp pencils and erasers. If you cut and paste, you will need scissors and tape or staples. And you will need plenty of time. This process cannot be rushed.

When the actual rewriting begins, most good revisers start at the beginning and work through methodically.

Revising with Word Processors

Word processors make revision both easier and riskier. It's easier because nothing is final: on a word processor, you can change anything at any point. More important, your word processor can save drafts at each stage for the purpose of comparison. We suggest that you print out your hard copy, do large-scale revision by hand, then enter the changes. Some of our students print out two or three drafts and lay them next to one another on a table or floor. That way they can see how their essays evolve. If they work on revision with a partner, they can now easily compare different drafts and discuss what they changed and why.

Many fine programs are now available to make revision easier. We especially like those displaying split screens so that you can see text and revision side by side. Other programs can save both original and changes, highlighting the latter so that you can decide which changes you want to keep. Search programs that count how many times words are used can help you avoid repetition. Other programs—much less useful, we think—can assist you with grammar and punctuation.

Word processors make revision riskier for three main reasons:

You can be tempted to change too much too often.

You can usually see only a paragraph or two at a time, making large-scale revision difficult.

Because of the ease and speed of word processing, you can be tempted to start too late and not do any real revision at all.

And let us take up arms against the great myth of word processing: that it makes revision quicker or unnecessary. Give yourself just as much time to draft, revise, and complete an essay as you ever did. You can use every minute.

The Levels of Revision

Revision takes place on two levels, with a number of discrete tasks on each. As you revise, you'll find that you naturally move between levels. Changing a single word will sometimes mean changing your whole organization—just as changing a single note changes the whole tune. And huge changes in thought compel changes in commas and periods. Our advice is work first on the biggest elements (we call this *macrorevision*) and then the smaller *(microrevision)*, but don't be rigid: let yourself move freely between levels.

MACROREVISION.   The most important level of revision is what could be called macrorevision. On this level you rethink your big ideas. You must be ruthless with yourself, perhaps eliminate what cost you anguish to create.

First, think about your thesis. Are the terms clear and succinct enough for your reader? Perhaps you should try to sharpen the wording for the next draft. If any of the terms seem vague or too abstract, define them—and then be sure you include that definition in the next draft. Is the thesis strong enough? A weighty essay cannot stand on a weak thesis. Having gone through all the writing, do you think that thesis is what you now want to say? And is it worth writing about? If not, find another.

Look separately at each major supporting idea. Does it support the thesis, or have you let a digression slip in? If you find a digression, get rid of it. Are any of the ideas, though expressed differently, really the same? Combine them. If forgotten good ideas come back to you now, try to work them in if they fit. If you feel your essay is skimpy, look back at your earlier notes or try an invention technique to generate more material.

Check your evidence. Do you provide the common ground for you and your reader to stand on? Is there enough support for your major ideas? If a weak thesis provides a poor foundation for your thought, scanty evidence makes for a shaky scaffolding. If you need more evidence, do the necessary research or go through another invention process. Be sure to adjust your thesis and your major ideas accordingly. Don't try to prop up a rickety argument.

Step back a bit and look at your organization. Try a paragraph-by-paragraph outline of the first draft. Just jot down in a sentence the topic discussed in each paragraph. This technique will help even if you used an outline initially. The sentences ought to read like a tightly focused (although general) paragraph.

Having such an outline allows you to see how your essay developed. If there are no missing links, then you know you have not omitted a major idea in the chain of argument. If one of the sentences seems to stand out, examine it closely to be sure it isn't a digression. Ask yourself if the ideas flow smoothly toward the conclusion or if they are just logs stacked one on another. It isn't too late to write new paragraphs.

MICROREVISION.   On the second level of revision, microrevision, you look at your writing phrase by phrase, sentence by sentence, paragraph by paragraph. And you ask hard questions. Is the topic of each paragraph clear, whether stated or implicit? Do all the points relate to the topic? Are the sentences in the right order? Is the meaning of each sentence clear? Is there ample variety in the writing? And what about word choice: is the writing concise, concrete, and vivid?

Reading an essay aloud is particularly helpful for microrevision. Be sure you have a pencil handy to mark those places where you question the shape or sound of your prose. If your first draft is too simple or too complicated, you can change it in the second draft.

The last task at this level is pencil editing, correcting grammar, punctuation, spelling, and mechanics. For specific information, check Part Six, The Nuts and Bolts: A Handbook of Grammar, Punctuation, Mechanics, and Usage.

Often, microrevising for style turns into rethinking. If, for instance, you find your illustrations inadequate or uninteresting, you may try to think up additional ones, and that could lead you to conclude that a point you made really was not justified. You would then go back and rethink the point and its relation to your whole argument. If excess verbosity or pomposity has made your prose fat, the slimming process may make your point more visible. Searching for a better word may lead to a better idea.

(For appropriate manuscript form, see pp. 389–391.)

CASE STUDY:
THE TRUE CONFESSIONS OF AN ESSAY

Here is the story of how a writer made her way from a first draft that embarrassed her to a final draft that was much better. Her task, set by the instructor, was to define one of a list of terms: *creativity, prejudice, mental health,* or *mental illness*.

Inventing

The student, Kimberly Corsaro, first spent a few minutes thinking about the terms. *Prejudice* did not appeal to her, and she knew she would not do a good job if she did not like the subject. Although *mental illness* was interesting, she knew so little about it that she would have to do research, and that was not the point of the assignment. The point was to think. *Mental health* seemed to her a very broad term—too broad for a short paper. In the end, nothing attracted her as much as *creativity*.

She had always enjoyed free writing, and so she chose that as the way to get deeper into the subject.

```
Creativity.  Poets, dancers, painters, musicians.
But don't all of us have some somewhere?  My pic-
tures look like baby scrawls.  Can't carry a tune.
But funny--Mother's friend laughed when I sang that
song.  Still, I tried.  Nobody quite like you in the
whole human race or something.  No two pictures
alike.  Twins even but each has thoughts nobody else
has.  I can't do it but I can think it.  Where do I
fit?  Creative?  Not just artists.  Would anyone
agree with that?  My ideas may be different.
```

Developing, Organizing, Drafting

When Corsaro read over her free writing, she identified three major ideas:

My definition differs from most people's
everybody distinctive in some way
creativity is not limited to artists

The second idea seemed vague, and she decided that the best way to sharpen it was to use artists themselves as the model for distinctiveness. That would help tie the paper together. She still believed in the third idea, but she had to admit that too often she felt quite uncreative. At the bottom of her page of free writing, she wrote, "More creative if less time in groups? Do I lose my indiv. or not?" After a moment, she added, "Not."

She thought she was probably interpreting the assignment in a way her instructor had not intended, but that was all right because the instructor—her audience—liked students to take chances with their writing.

Here is her first draft:

Most people think of something physical or tan-   1
gible when they think of creativity. However, the
most creative thing that I am capable of doing is
neither visible nor concrete. It is my ability to
think as an individual.

There are many people who may be artificially   2
talented, but it is through their imagination that
we see their creativity. Without thought and imagination from individuals, creativity would be nonexistent and consequently this would be a rather dull
and boring place to live.

This is not to say that I or other people do   3
everything differently from others, because that
would be an exaggeration. It is very common for
people to do things in large groups because they
enjoy company and I am no exception. However, you
can be yourself and part of a group at the same time.
Nobody is you, and you are nobody else. You can see
this most clearly if you think about artists.
If a group of artists were asked to draw a picture
of a house, all the pictures would be different.
The theme of the pictures is all the same, but yet
all the houses vary. This is because each artist has
his or her own ideas; each perceives a house differently. This is where uniqueness and originality
enter into a person.

Everyone has the potential to be creative. It ₄
is dependent upon the person to develop his or her
own talents. In the cases of some people, such as
artists or musicians, the creativeness is somewhat
obvious, whereas others' talents are less apparent.

Creativeness is the ability to be inventive or ₅
to transform original thoughts into something others
can enjoy. To most people a creative work is a
painting or great music. While these are good examples of creativity, it can also be expressed in various other ways, such as a poet or a writer.

But as I said above, I cannot paint or sing. ₆
When I draw it looks terrible, and when I sing everybody asks me to stop. But I do think for myself,
and that is creative. If it was not, I would be
thinking everyone else's thoughts. It can be very
difficult to think for yourself, because there are
many pressures to conform to other people's ways of
thinking. I try not to do that, though I catch myself doing or thinking somebody else's way. Sometimes I am glad I have other role models. If we did
not have other people telling us how to think when
we were younger, how would we know how to think at
all? But I still think I put my thoughts together
in my own way. That is my creativity.

Corsaro put the essay in a drawer.

Revising

When Corsaro returned five hours later to take a fresh look, she blew
the essay to pieces. She looked first at the conclusion. It seemed jumbled.
She didn't know how she had arrived there. She checked it against the
opening. That opening, she saw, was thin. She began to read the essay
aloud. *She* wrote *that*? The essay started and stopped. Some paragraphs
seemed to lack a topic. She wasn't sure what she meant by certain phrases,
and the writing was awkward. The critical distance became so great she
almost ran out of the room. She was ready to revise.

MACROREVISING.   Corsaro was concerned about her thesis. She didn't want her own creativity to be the central idea. She tried again: imagination, not works of art, is the important part of creativity. Although it needed work, the idea was worth arguing.

She turned to the evidence. Her first evidence had been "Most people think of something physical or tangible when they think of creativity." To make that less vague, she needed an example, and she found one in the fifth paragraph: "To most people a creative work is a painting or great music." She thought it ought to be even more specific, and so she added, "like the Sistine Chapel or Beethoven's Fifth Symphony."

She realized she had not fully established the difference between her definition and the conventional one, which was a main idea. After a trip to the dictionary, she wrote: "Dictionaries often define the word as the ability to be inventive, or to transform one's original thought into a form others can enjoy." Then she saw that both the dictionary and "most people" defined the word according to the *results* of creativity—what it creates. In contrast, she was concerned with imagination itself, a quality possessed by all people, not just artists.

Now she stated her thesis more clearly: "Creativity exists in each person's particular thoughts and imagination." She wrote a new second paragraph to focus this idea and then systematically checked the thinking in all the paragraphs.

In the old second paragraph, the phrase *artificially talented* no longer made sense. She looked up *artificial* in the dictionary: "of a human, as opposed to natural, agency." So what was human? Hard work, training, performance. People like Lewis Thomas, Leontyne Price, Fred Astaire. And what was *natural*? Imagination was natural because we all have it. Eureka: she had clarified her own half-articulated distinction. She was ready to write a new third paragraph, one related to her thesis and illustrated concretely.

The central idea of the old third paragraph seemed to be that "you can be yourself and part of a group." Or was it that "each artist has his or her own ideas"? Whichever, she couldn't see how it related to her thesis. She put it aside. That decision was extremely important: Corsaro had resisted the temptation to preserve at all costs her original organization.

Her main point was that everyone has imagination and so is potentially creative. Her original fourth paragraph—three diffident and unsuccessful sentences—had pawed at that idea. How to improve it? Give an example of "everybody." Well, although her own creativity was not *the* central issue, it could serve as an example. By thinking for herself, she demonstrated her own imaginativeness. She had said this in the old sixth paragraph. Polished and refined, that paragraph could become the new fourth.

And then she saw that the old third paragraph had a place after all. In her new third paragraph she could combine the material about the distinctiveness of artists with the idea of how hard artists work. She could put the material about everybody's distinctiveness in a strong new fourth paragraph.

She looked at the old fourth and fifth paragraphs and realized they were floating loose. The fourth was simply a summary of the whole essay she was better off without. As for the old fifth paragraph, she had already transplanted its heart—the example about painting and music—to the new first paragraph. All she needed was a strong concluding paragraph. She decided to finish with creativity and society.

Now she made an outline of her essay:

Paragraph 1—Most people think of great works of art when they think of creativity.

Paragraph 2—All people share imagination, the most important and least understood part of creativity.

Paragraph 3—Artists differ from other people in their dedication to work and training, not in possessing imagination.

Paragraph 4—Having one's own distinctive thought is a creative act.

Paragraph 5—We can be ourselves and part of a group.

She felt good about the rethinking.

MICROREVISING.   Now it was time to examine the details and how the different parts fit. Her second paragraph was a problem:

> I fit the first part of the definition (I have original thoughts) but not the second (I can't transform them into creations other people can enjoy). A person's unique thoughts and imagination are the most important part of creativeness, and that is the part most people know the least about.

The connection between the two sentences was not clear—hadn't she heard someplace that two-sentence paragraphs are dangerous because often the connecting link is missing? She put in the link:

> I fit the first part of the definition (I have original thoughts) but not the second (I can't transform them into creations other people can enjoy). I and people like me nonetheless qualify as creative. That is because a person's unique thoughts and imagination are the most important part of creativity, and that is the part most people know the least about.

The last sentence looked limp. "That is because" was wordy and imprecise, and the word *unique* was overused. Worse yet, the elongated ending dragged down the thought. She revised: "A person's thoughts and imagination are the most important, though least understood, part of creativity." By reducing eleven words to three, and incorporating them in the middle, she had improved her clarity.

Corsaro went through the same kind of analysis for all the other paragraphs. She put in connecting links, cut back verbiage, added examples, moved always toward the clearer support of her thesis. She was shocked by how often she had used *creative* and *creativity, because* and *people.* These repetitions were nothing compared with the many clumps of the lazy verb *to be.*

As she deleted *to be's* and *people's,* she discovered that her language became more vivid. She noticed that she had concluded the third paragraph with "Without thought and imagination from individuals, creativity would be nonexistent and consequently the world would be a rather dull and boring place to live"—a dull and boring sentence. She now had a second chance at that statement, and she wrote, "Creativity begins when individuals think and imagine. Their actions light up the world." Then she extended the metaphor: "but their imaginations provide the current."

This image created a transition problem. She was no doubt delighted when she came up with "Like most of the human race, I have the current but not the light," as a new first sentence of the next paragraph. She went back over the manuscript to sharpen all her transitions. She did not find another quite as brilliant as that, but she locked her paragraphs tightly together.

As a last task in revising, she went to work on her grammar, punctuation, spelling, and mechanics. She used her handbook and her dictionary.

Was this essay perfect? No. There is no such thing as a perfect draft. Professional writers revise twelve, twenty, thirty times. One of the authors of this book revised a short story over twenty times—the story was published and won a prize. It could have been better. Corsaro's essay still has awkward moments and almost-but-not-quites. She knew her last sentence was not strong—perhaps she would revise it again. But with revision her essay had become fuller and more interesting. For us, the essay provides the most exciting reward of reading: the sense of a mind moving.

New Meaning for an Old Word

When most people think of creativity, they   1
think of something tangible--Michelangelo's Sistine
Chapel or Beethoven's Fifth Symphony. Dictionaries
often define the word as the ability to be inventive, or to transform one's original thoughts into a
form others can enjoy. Since dictionary definitions
often reflect widespread attitudes, it is not surprising that even <u>Webster's</u> stresses the results of
creativity rather than the thing itself.

I have a problem with such definitions--namely 2
that I fit the first half (I have original thoughts)
but not the second (I cannot transform them so other
people can enjoy them). I and people like me nonetheless qualify as creative. A person's thoughts
and imagination are the most important, though least
understood, part of creativity.

We share this gift of imagination with stars 3
and geniuses--Lewis Thomas, Leontyne Price, Fred
Astaire--whose creativity shines through in performance, the product of many hours of training and
hard work. What sets them apart is not their natural talent, for many people have an aptitude for
science, a fine voice, or a sense of melody or
rhythm. The true difference began even before they
held a test tube, sang a note, or danced a step. It
was their outlook, their approach to what they do,
and their personal sense of style. Creativity
begins when individuals think and imagine. Their
actions light up the world, but their imaginations
provide the current.

Like most of the human race, I have the current 4
but not the light. When I draw, my pictures resemble nothing in the real world, and when I sing, everybody asks me to stop. I do think for myself,
though. My thoughts are my own and no one else's--
quite an achievement, just as difficult as many
other creative acts. Just think of all the pressures to conform to other ways of thinking, to
accept what others believe. Parents, teachers, and
friends all have their own influences to exert. Just
having a thought of my own is a creative act.

I do not mean to say I am totally original. 5
Nobody is. If we did not like to do things in
groups, we would hardly be human. We also owe a

great deal to the parents, teachers, and friends who teach us how to think in the first place. But what we learn from them is a sort of creative conformity: we learn to be ourselves and part of a group at the same time.

TIPS FOR REVISING

- Unless you are an extremely talented writer, be sure to revise your first drafts.
- Develop critical distance: separate yourself from your work.
- Read your first draft aloud or ask someone else to read it to you.
- Don't edit in a straight line; blow your essay to pieces.
- Start by revising large elements; move to small elements later.
- Stay flexible: be ready to change anything at any time for any good reason.

Exercises for Revising

1. Rewrite your most recent essay. Reorganize the sentences in at least two paragraphs; rewrite your opening paragraph; change the last sentence of the essay; reword at least eight sentences. Write one paragraph describing the changes in detail, and write another paragraph comparing the old essay with the new one.

2. With a partner, select a topic from the following list and separately write a first draft of an essay on that topic.

   an actor you think is bad
   your preference for either dogs or cats
   a crowd activity you did or did not participate in
   student politics on campus
   respecting other cultures
   a book you've both read

   Make an extra copy. Exchange drafts, and revise each other's essay. Be respectful but pitiless.

3. Compare your first draft for Exercise 2 with your partner's revision of it. Evaluate the changes. Write a paragraph on your comparison and evaluation. Give the paragraph to your partner. Be honest but kind.

PART TWO

Steps to
Good Thinking:
The Critical Process

3

THE CRITICAL SENSE

The critical sense is so far from frequent that it is absolutely rare, and the possession of the cluster of qualities that minister to it is one of the highest distinctions.

HENRY JAMES (1843–1916)
AMERICAN NOVELIST AND ESSAYIST

Just as we try to sell our ideas when we write or speak, so other people try to sell us theirs. But good consumers of persuasion refuse to buy whatever happens to be on the market. They are as skeptical about ideas as they would be about a used car. They know that some ideas wouldn't make it off the lot before breaking down. They always carefully examine the product, read the warranty, kick the tires. Only when satisfied with the overall quality will they buy.

Good consumers of ideas are always critical. By *critical* we don't mean having disrespect for others, faultfinding, or carping over details. We mean a healthy skepticism, an unwillingness to accept something at someone else's evaluation, a willingness to postpone agreement or disagreement until after thorough analysis.

We are all skeptical in some areas of life. As soon as an elected official opens his or her mouth, "Oh yeah?" "Who says?" and "So what?" ready themselves for the asking. Each time we see an automobile commercial featuring a sleek cheetah, a brilliant desert landscape, a beautiful woman clad in flowing chiffon, and a virile-looking, handsome man, we feel a scoff coming on.

And we should. We know that politics and commercials are notorious for humbug. Perhaps less obviously, humbug and sleights of hand exist throughout the world of ideas. A healthy skepticism uncovers less obvious humbug.

In this chapter, we offer some observations and suggestions we hope will help you become a better consumer of ideas.

OPENING THE MIND: CLEARING OUT THE UNDERBRUSH

The thinker about whom few of us are skeptical enough is our very own self. When we believe something, we assume we have it right. If we weren't right, we would believe something different that *was* right, wouldn't we? We certainly don't need to listen to conflicting views. We lock the doors of our mind.

Yet all of us have been wrong and have had to change our minds. A person we disliked on what we thought were good grounds becomes a dear friend. A candidate we vehemently supported turns out to be morally flawed. A policy or rule we opposed suddenly makes good sense. We have either learned more or listened to someone else who persuaded us otherwise. When we open our minds to new ideas and fresh insights, we gain a better understanding of the world.

In this section we suggest ways of opening the mind and clearing out bad thinking habits and attitudes that stunt intellectual growth.

Shedding Stereotypes

To stereotype means to judge another person according to some preconceived ideas about a group that person belongs to—a race, religion, gender, nationality, physical type, occupation, and so on. Stereotyping assumes that all members of the group share the same set of fairly simple characteristics, frequently unpleasant and sometimes immoral. Too often, the more ignorant we are, the more certain. We don't have to think: our judgments come to us precast.

Germans are authoritarian.

Fraternity men drink.

Mack wouldn't mind being called Fatty (all fat people are good-natured).

Surely you aren't consulting a woman lawyer (women lack reasoning power).

Kinnard was elected only because he's black (blacks aren't really qualified).

To bring the injustice of this kind of judgment close to home, think of a stereotype an outsider might have of a large group to which you belong. Are you Italian? left-handed? a midwesterner? a woman? a "rich kid" or a "poor kid"? How do you feel about that stereotype? Compare yourself with the other people like you. When we've seen one, have we seen 'em all? Are the differences trivial or significant? Would you be willing to be judged solely on the basis of your membership in this group?

To stereotype others hurts us as well as those who are prejudged. It encourages us to shut ourselves off from enlarging experiences and limits the range of our understanding. And so we misinterpret signals and act inappropriately. If, for instance, we assumed that all politicians were corrupt and we heard a politician make an important proposal, we might ignore it—and thereby close ourselves off from the debate.

Questioning Authority

No one can study every subject, and all of us rely on authorities for information and ideas. (See the first section of Chapter 7 for a discussion of using expert testimony as evidence.) What were the causes of the Second World War? Read what historians have to say. Is cholesterol bad for me? Just ask nutritionists. How can I collect the money my ex-brother-in-law owes me? Get a lawyer.

But we need to remember two things about authorities. First, most issues worth discussing usually have at least two sides, and authorities can be found on both. One economist wants to raise taxes to decrease the deficit; another wants to lower taxes to increase the gross national product. Their debate helps us to clarify the issues. As nonexperts, we listen carefully, analyze the evidence and the reasoning, challenge with further questions—and then take responsibility for our own thinking.

Second, expertise in one field rarely extends into another. As a coach or a television commentator, John Madden speaks as an authority on football and could give an expert analysis on the choice for most valuable player. But his background and experience do not qualify him as an authority on beer, cameras, or even philanthropic organizations. Scientists and artists often express their opinions on political matters, and they certainly have that right. But their opinions are no more authoritative than any citizen's and should never be accepted without a thorough analysis. (When we appeal to unqualified "experts," we commit the logical fallacy called *ipse dixit*, a Latin phrase meaning "He himself has spoken.")

In your everyday life, you confront important decisions: career choices, how to invest, what to believe about U.S. policy in Central America. Listen to the experts in their own fields, but remember that no human being has cornered the market on truth. Learn what others think—and then do your own thinking.

Slowing Down Judgment

We are constantly making generalizations. Indeed, we couldn't do without them. When we look both ways as we cross the street, we are generalizing about automobiles: all cars are big and powerful, and if one hits me it will probably hurt. We generalize almost daily about the weather: when we see dark clouds, we decide to wear a raincoat. We base our generalizations on past experience and use them to anticipate the future.

A problem emerges, however, when we make what logicians call a *hasty generalization*, that is, when we rush to an unwarranted conclusion from insufficient evidence:

> That banana I bought was soft inside. The fruit in that grocery store is rotten.
>
> I can't do calculus. I'd better quit school.
>
> Abraham Lincoln did not start pushing the Emancipation Proclamation until 1863. He did not really care about the problem of slavery.

One tiny fact—a soft banana, difficulty with a subject—is hardly a sound basis for rushing to a conclusion. And weren't there other reasons for Lincoln's delay? Doesn't other evidence suggest that he cared deeply about the enslaved? The writer has generalized too hastily.

> Neither Senator X nor Senator Y went back home after leaving the Senate. Senators would rather live in Washington.

But Senator X and Senator Y may not be typical. We need a broader base of evidence, and even then, unless we know what happened to every single senator, the claim cannot be absolute—we must qualify it accordingly:

> If the experience of twenty-five senators is typical, then many senators remain in Washington after they leave the Senate.

Qualifying a generalization to fit the evidence is an important thinking skill. (We discuss qualification in "Considering the Opposition" in Chapter 6.)

Acknowledging Complexities

Almost any idea worth thinking about is complicated. If it weren't, we wouldn't have to think about it. Unfortunately, most of us try to fly over the complications. We seek a simple explanation, we ignore contrary evidence, we settle for the obvious conclusion. In short, we indulge in the logical fallacy *oversimplification*.

Oversimplification takes many forms. Sometimes we claim that a problem has only one solution:

> If we want to improve education, we have no choice but to eliminate electives from the curriculum.

Slow down. This issue is too important to treat it superficially. Mightn't reducing extracurricular activities or raising teacher salaries have some good effect?

Similarly, we often justify a belief or a course of action on the basis of one single reason:

> We would never have had a drug problem had it not been for rock and roll music.

Even if rock and roll is *one* reason for the drug problem (and that itself is a very debatable claim), it is certainly not the only reason, and may not even be a main reason.

Occasionally we consider only the positive side of a proposition, ignoring the negative or harmful effects:

> Let's disband the CIA in order to improve the reputation of the United States.

For all its problems, the CIA helps the United States in many ways, and if we disbanded it, we could lose those benefits. Few proposals have only good effects.

When a certain goal is desirable, we may believe that it does not matter how we achieve it. We say the end justifies the means.

> We should remove restraints on police behavior because they interfere with apprehending criminals.

It's not that simple. Apprehending criminals is certainly desirable, but removing restraints could lead to excessive force and lack of accountability by the police. We have to examine the means of attaining a proposed end at least as closely as we examine the end itself.

Putting issues into their simplest form is natural. It saves time and allows us to get on with something else. It makes us feel good about ourselves and confident that we have a grasp of the world. But it doesn't lead to good thinking. When we oversimplify, we distort reality and kid ourselves into thinking we have accurately pictured the world, when in fact we have only drawn a cartoon.

TIPS FOR OPENING THE MIND

- Unlock your mind and let in new ideas.
- Don't let stereotypes shut you off from real people.
- Listen to the experts but decide for yourself.
- Don't base generalizations on insufficient evidence.
- Avoid oversimplified analyses and solutions.

Exercise for Opening the Mind

Read the following statements and identify the "underbrush" that needs clearing out (there may be several specimens in each):

   a. No point in even discussing the issue: I know what I think.

   b. I don't like broccoli or spinach. I won't like asparagus.

   c. Vietnamese are gifted in math. Three of them got A's in our calculus class.

   d. I won't go to Calcutta. The poverty there would ruin the visit.

   e. What a glorious tenor—he could only be Italian.

   f. Only believe people who have firm, incontrovertible evidence for their opinions.

   g. A well-organized and secret left-wing group opposes this nomination. Patriots support it.

   h. Those who oppose a "Western Civilization" requirement must not believe that ideas are important.

   i. Did Grandpa remember you when you visited him last week?

   j. I saw Pavarotti put one of these lozenges in his mouth—they must be best for keeping the throat moist.

   k. Everybody knows children should be seen and not heard.

   l. Don't argue with him about health-care systems: he's a chemist.

   m. I don't know anything about art, but I know what I like.

   n. Right after Carl started using Odoroff Deodorant, Wanda agreed to go dancing with him. Odoroff does it again!

   o. The president should have the right to make national security decisions without media criticism.

   p. The threat of inflation caused the stock market crash.

   q. Drug abusers are mentally ill. My mother is a lawyer and has defended a lot of them, and she says so.

   r. A man who would do something like that should never be allowed to run for public office.

   s. Priests make lousy marriage counselors.

   t. Instead of revising your paper on a word processor, print out the original and make changes in the old way.

u. Democrats tend to be incompetent and Republicans corrupt.

v. Thanks but no thanks—these new dances are for young people.

w. The way to fix our problems in the U.S. Postal Service is to sell the whole operation to some private vendor.

RECOGNIZING RHETORIC: SEEING BEHIND THE WORDS

At the beginning of the chapter, we mentioned that people are always trying to get us to think or behave in a particular way. To persuade us, they use *rhetorical* skills. Aristotle defined rhetoric as "the art of discovering the available means of persuasion in a given case." Some people use the word only to mean "lacking in truth or substance" or "artificial and overly elaborate language." But the the term *rhetoric* also refers to expressing ideas in a manner that persuades other people to think or feel in a certain way. It includes the appeal to reason as well as the appeal to emotion: rhetoricians employ valid ideas as well as forceful language.

"Sticks and stones may break my bones but words can never hurt me" is a patently untrue saying. Rhetoric can be quite as powerful as sticks and stones. The rhetoric of poetry can bring great joy and help us articulate our experience: the rhetoric of politics can make a population docile or even cruel or can inspire people to a great cause. Rhetoric can fog an issue or it can lead us to greater understanding.

In this section we analyze some of the most important problems with evaluating rhetoric. In Chapter 4, The Logic of Argument, we discuss in greater detail the part of rhetoric called *argument*.

Weighing Emotional Appeals

Sincere and honest emotion has a legitimate and significant place in our thought. Used with care and scruple, it can be an effective ally of reason. In many situations, it would be foolish to pretend that reason performed alone and that we didn't *care* one way or the other. To discuss without emotion a famine in Ethiopia or a hostage crisis in Lebanon would be perverse. In virtually everything we read or hear, the appeal to emotion is part of the message. Even the new superconductors can hardly be described by scientists without expressions of joy and pride. As the philosopher Ludwig Wittgenstein pointed out, being convinced is an emotional condition, even if reason leads us to it.

Writers and speakers often arouse our emotions by appealing to our *values*. When an American scientist speaks to Americans of superconductors, he or she appeals to our hope for progress and the betterment of humanity. Values, of course, vary from culture to culture. An Iraqi writing to Iraqis would perhaps appeal to the audience's reverence for Islam. A Japanese writer might appeal to tradition or respect for elders. Appealing to the values the audience shares is an important technique of the rhetorician.

What values do contemporary Americans share? Two communications experts examined this question and came up with the following list:

value of the individual

achievement and success

change and progress

ethical equality

equality of opportunity

effort and optimism

efficiency, practicality, and pragmatism

rejection of authority

science and secular rationality

sociality

material comfort

quantification

external conformity

humor

generosity and "considerateness"

patriotism

(E. D. Steele and W. Charles Redding, "The American Value System: Premises for Persuasion")

Not all Americans share all these values, and some of the values even seem contradictory, for example, "external conformity" and "value of the individual." But speakers and writers appeal to one or many of them—often with conscious intent. Here is a speech writer's proposal for a successful acceptance speech by the Democratic presidential nominee:

In 1988, the nominee might begin by saying: "We are a party of diversity and we are strong because of our diversity, but there are common beliefs that unite us." The writer would then invoke the defeated candidates, one by one, to emphasize the ties that unify the party. "Senator Sam Nunn," at which point people would applaud, "a great chairman of the Armed Services Committee who would make a great Secretary of Defense," at which point everybody would again applaud, "is right when he says that the Democratic Party must stand for an end to the arms race before it ends the human race." (Robert Shrum, "Word Perfect")

Shrum thus ticks off several shared political values. Some you can find in the preceding list, including "value of the individual," "generosity and considerateness," and change and progress." Others, such as a strong defense and an end to the arms race, are more relevant to the moment. We can almost hear the convention stomping.

Effective use of emotion need not be as direct as a political speech. In her coolly rational and factual dissection of the rise of Nazism, Hannah Arendt writes,

> Many Germans and many Nazis, probably an overwhelming majority of them, must have been tempted *not* to murder, *not* to rob, *not* to let their neighbors go off to their doom (for that the Jews were transported to their doom they knew, of course, even though many of them may not have known the gruesome details), and not to become accomplices in all these crimes by benefiting from them. But, God knows, they had learned how to resist temptation. (*Eichmann in Jerusalem*)

The emotion is carried by the italicized *not*s, by heavily freighted words such as *doom* and *temptation*, and by potent words such as *murder* and *neighbors* and that final cry from the heart, "God knows." Take away those words and the facts may remain but the significance, and maybe the reader, is lost.

We need to bear in mind that emotion is a potent ingredient, volatile and sometimes overwhelming. With clever manipulation of language, the unscrupulous can mask their real message by arousing our emotions. Too often appeals arouse not our best emotions, such as sympathy and generosity, but the morally debilitating and destructive:

> Rock music is turning our youth into enervated zombies, sapping the strength of the American character from within and exposing us to our enemies without.

> Unless we want our children to grow up to work for the Japanese, we should not allow foreign cars into this country.

> Gun control would undermine the very fiber of this nation and destroy what makes us great.

> Try some of this stuff—everybody is doing it.

> If the administration did away with student aid, it could lower tuition, and we would all have more money.

> Any intelligent person would agree that we need a proctoring system at this school because only a small fraction of the student body has the inner strength to resist cheating.

Each of these appeals goes right to the heart of a basic human emotion: fear, prejudice, pride, conformism, greed, vanity. We could find examples of appeals to sloth, lust, and all the rest of the sins, deadly and venial.

Awareness of language can protect us against unwanted or dishonest appeals to emotion. We can become more sensitive to vocabulary. Certain words come ready-made to excite our emotions: *brutal, vicious, stealthy, innocent, baby, soft, gentle,* and *honorable* are a few that spring to mind. Notice the difference between these two sentences:

The dog attacked the man.

The vicious dog brutally attacked the man.

The first is a fact; the second is an outrage. But how about

The dog attacked the stealthy intruder.

Pin a medal on that dog.

A second way to become more sensitive is to be aware of the emotive impact of images. Notice the difference between these two sentences:

Yeats spent seven hours a day carefully crafting his poems.

Yeats was a slave to the grinding process of creating poems.

In the first we have an image of a serious artist; in the second he's a drudge. (We have more to say on the power of words, especially on connotation and imagery, in Chapter 12, Working with Words.)

Appeals to our values and our emotions are legitimate—and inevitable. To think clearly, however, we need to recognize the appeals and stay out of their grasp, at least until we have evaluated them.

Separating Fact from Opinion

Some statements are facts, some are opinions. Nothing is more essential to good thinking than being able to tell the difference. A fact is a certainty, a statement agreed on by all those in a position to investigate the matter. Some facts are obvious or known to everyone:

The sun moves from east to west.

Other facts are known to experts:

Pellagra is caused by an inadequate amount of niacin in the diet.

When experts agree that something is a fact, the rest of us generally accept it. (See "Expert Testimony" in Chapter 7 for more on this point.)

An opinion is a belief not based on certainty or agreement by those who investigate. It is a personal statement that something is true or false, good or bad.

Once soccer catches on, people will prefer it to baseball.

An opinion may turn out to be a fact: in twenty years we may find that soccer *is* more popular than baseball. That the earth revolves around the sun was once an opinion but is now a fact.

Some opinions cannot become facts because they express personal preference:

Chocolate ice cream tastes better than strawberry.

Ballet is more enjoyable than opera.

If we recognize the unstated "in my opinion," we don't bother to argue.

A problem arises, however, when the line separating fact and opinion is blurred. This can happen when we read or listen carelessly. Someone may say,

Baseball is called the favorite national pastime

and we disagree. Disagree with what? The statement does not say that baseball *is* the favorite national pastime (an opinion in the absence of evidence), only that it is *called* so (a fact). We need to pay close attention to what is actually being said.

More frequently, an opinion claims to be a fact:

Left-handed people are smarter than right-handed people.

This is not a matter of personal preference but of opinion pretending to be fact. There is no evidence for it. The sound of certainty is no substitute for the real thing.

Sometimes an opinion subtly assumes the status of fact:

Because the Filipinos hate their present government, we should support the New People's Army.

We all recognize that the last part of the sentence is opinion, but the writer apparently wants us to assume that the first part is an established fact, when it isn't.

Often received opinion masquerades as incontrovertible wisdom:

Male children are better at math than female children but not as good at language.

Maybe, maybe not. The jury is still out.

We all have opinions. We eat, buy, vote, marry, all on the basis of our opinions. It is our right to express them. We need to recognize, however, that not all opinions are equally valuable or equally useful to others. An opinion is only as good as the facts and reasoning on which it is based.

Don't study German: it's the most difficult language to learn could be based on knowledge of only one other language, in which case the listener should not act on this advise. We might be impressed by the statement

> Plato's *Republic* is irrelevant to our society

until we discover the speaker has never read any Plato. It is idle chatter for me to say

> Candidate J is the most qualified of all the candidates

if I know nothing about the other candidates.

Our opinions aren't sacrosanct. Learning is the process of gathering information, rethinking, and then reformulating our opinion. Even a personal preference can be more or less valuable. Our liking for chocolate ice cream becomes more interesting when we've sampled other flavors.

Uncovering Assumptions

An assumption is a belief that we take for granted as a basis for an assertion. All kinds of statements rely on assumptions—questions, commands, promises, assertions. The simple command *Pass the salt* is based on several assumptions, including that the salt can be passed, that you can pass it, and that I have the right to ask you to pass it. Some assumptions are unexpressed. We would be the joke of the neighborhood if we went around articulating our assumptions every time we asked someone to pass the salt.

We get into thinking trouble, however, when we fail to recognize important assumptions that subtly guide our thoughts. Sophocles said,

> Reason is God's crowning gift to man.

A statement like this seems innocent enough. When we think about it, we easily recognize that he was basing his idea on two major assumptions: (1) that man has a mind, and (2) that God exists. So far we may agree.

Hidden in the statement, however, are some subtle assumptions, not all of which we support. Here are some of the more obvious: (1) God is a personal force capable of making a gift; (2) reason is a more important gift than heart, soul, or body; and maybe (3) woman's mind is not a gift of God. Once we articulate these assumptions, we might disagree.

Or suppose we read the following statement:

> To alleviate overcrowding in prisons, we should convert prison sentences to community service. The inmates then could expiate their sins through retribution to society and at the same time discover that doing something useful can be quite satisfying.

Sounds pretty good, but concealed in all the high-minded words are some dubious assumptions:

1. Converting a prison sentence to community service is not itself against the law.
2. Retribution and rehabilitation, rather than keeping criminals off the streets, are the main purposes of prison sentences.
3. Community service would serve more or less the same purpose as a prison term.
4. Requiring prisoners to perform community service will not have a destructive effect on the community.
5. Experience can change character.
6. "We" have the right to change matters.

There are other assumptions, but this list should be enough to warn us against jumping on that bandwagon before thoroughly examining the assumptions underlying it.

Hidden assumptions are not necessarily dishonest: the salt can be passed and the prisons are overcrowded. Nevertheless, we can avoid many thinking problems by becoming more sensitive to the assumptions of others and more critical of our own.

Finding the Argument

When we use the word *argument* in the following pages, we don't mean a violent disagreement often leading to anger and perhaps a confrontation out in the alley. We mean a statement supported by reasons. Arguments answer questions all of us have: Why should I believe this? Why is it true? Why should I do this? Why is it worthwhile?

Not all statements are arguments. Notice the difference between these two (possibly familiar) sentences:

Pick up your room

and

Pick up your room or no television tonight.

The first is an *assertion*, for which no reasons are provided. The speaker gives us nothing to think about. That's not an argument. The second makes the same statement but also provides a reason. This *is* an argument. Now we have to think about whether or not the reason is persuasive. Is watching television worth picking up the room?

When an assertion lacks reasons, all we can do is vote it up or down:

When volatized, bromine is irritating to mucous membranes.

Deforestation will affect world peace more than terrorism will.

These statements offer no justification for our agreeing with them. When we ask Why? they are silent. When people make assertions like these, they may have reasons in mind, but we can't evaluate them because they aren't stated.

Of course, not every statement needs its supporting reasons to be articulated right out loud. We do share certain values and beliefs.

> The rule of law is essential to a democracy.

This may be a platitude and not worth saying, but for most of us it needs no support.

> Drive carefully

is a command we are always making, but we seldom provide reasons for it. Some statements based on common knowledge need no justification:

> Paul was converted on the road to Damascus.

Statements like this are often the accepted basis for what will be an argument:

> When Paul was converted on the road to Damascus, Western civilization was changed.

Because we accept the first part of the assertion, the writer can spend his or her time and energy arguing the second part. If we had to provide reasons for everything, we would never get to the crux of the matter.

Some statements that are phrased as simple assertions contain hidden arguments:

> The great biologist Camille Fox believes vitamin K can cure insomnia. (If a great scientist believes it, it must be true.)

> Don't put that greasy stuff on your pretty hair. (Your hair won't be as pretty if you do.)

Television advertisers use this kind of hidden argument all the time. A beer company shows young men cavorting at a bar, and the voice-over says, "Drink Brand X." The hidden argument is

> If you drink Brand X, you will be one of a happy gang of attractive, fun-loving friends.

Ha!

If we aren't aware of the hidden arguments, they can have a very insidious effect: we may find ourselves wide awake with a carload of vitamin K, no hairdressing, and a colossal hangover.

TIPS FOR RECOGNIZING RHETORIC

- Think about the values that underlie what you read and what you write.
- In everything you read or write, be aware of the important role of rhetoric.
- Avoid being trapped by an emotional appeal you don't share.
- Distinguish between fact and opinion.
- Articulate the clear assumptions and uncover the hidden ones, your own or someone else's.
- Remember that an opinion is only a valuable as the knowledge and experience on which it is based.
- Differentiate between flat assertions and arguments, that is, assertions backed up by reasons.
- Be aware of hidden arguments, particularly in advertisements and politics.

Exercises for Recognizing Rhetoric

1. Automobile bumper stickers are public appeals to (presumably) shared values. To which values do the following bumper stickers appeal?
   a. Touch dis truck and I'll rip yer face off!
   b. Overworked Mother on Board
   c. Easy Does It
   d. Teachers Do It with More Class
   e. If You Can Read This Sign You're Following Too Closely

2. Referring to the list of values on page 66, read the following passages and determine what appeals to value each contains. In each one, the writer is attempting to establish common ground with the reader. What is that common ground?
   a. I believe the American people expect sex-ed courses to teach their children the relevant physiology, what used to be called "the facts of life," but they also expect that those facts will be placed in a moral context. In a recent national poll, 77 percent of the adults surveyed said they thought sex-education programs should teach moral values, and about the same percentage believe the programs should urge students not to have sexual intercourse. And believe it or not, teens agree. According to a recent survey, seventh- and eighth-graders who have chosen not to engage in intercourse say that the greatest influence on their decision is the fact that "It is against my values for me

to have sex while I am a teenager." (William J. Bennett, "Why Johnny Can't Abstain")

b. The proper question, I believe, is not, How good a document is or was the Constitution but, What effect does it have on the quality of our lives? And the answer to that, it seems to me, is, Very little. The Constitution makes promises it cannot by itself keep, and therefore deludes us into complacency about the rights we have. It is conspicuously silent on certain other rights that all human beings deserve. And it pretends to set limits on governmental powers, when in fact those limits are easily ignored. (Howard Zinn, "Some Truths Are Not Self-Evident")

c. Nothing in the world can take the place of persistence.
Talent will not; nothing is more common than unsuccessful men with talent.
Genius will not; unrewarded genius is almost a proverb.
Education will not; the world is full of educated derelicts.
Persistence and determination alone are omnipotent.
("Press On," motto of McDonald's Corporation)

3. The following sentences are problematic in their rhetorical appeal. Identify the problem in each.
   a. You are either part of the solution or part of the problem. ([Leroy] Eldridge Cleaver)
   b. Prisons teach inmates to be better criminals.
   c. Because thin people tend to be neurotic, we should insist that our children eat five full meals a day.
   d. You should wear the same uniform as the rest of the cadets.
   e. Because the English have government drug clinics, they have fewer addicts than we do.
   f. Although our standard of living depends on increased military spending, we should consider cutting back in the interest of our foreign policy.
   g. People are no damn good.
   h. If you're nice to him, he'll give you a ride in his Jaguar.
   i. Get an engineering degree if you want to get a good job.
   j. Be aware of hidden arguments in advertisements.
   k. In my opinion, the whole discussion of cholesterol is silly.
   l. Wheaties—the breakfast of champions.
   m. You wouldn't want anyone to see you crying, would you?

4. Every writer has an aim and manipulates words, thoughts, and feelings to achieve that aim. Read each of the following passages. What is the writer trying to achieve? What aspects of the writing are meant to achieve that aim? What is meant to be persuasive in each one?
   a. Hundreds of white women swarmed along Hill Street—our route and the university's fraternity row. They huddled in packs, hugging and squealing and sometimes singing, defiantly stopping traffic. The crowd reeked of money: pearl necklaces and the effects of orthodon-

tia were everywhere in evidence. (M. G. Lord, "Frats and Fraterni-
ties: The Greek Rites of Exclusion")

b. The majority of homeless single individuals have not spent time in
mental institutions. Even among the 22 percent of men in emergency
centers who once were institutionalized, almost half had been dis-
charged at least five years before they become homeless. And two-
thirds of the homeless in families are children who have no history
of institutionalization. (Peter Marcuse, "Why Are They Homeless?")

c. Therefore to our best mercy give yourselves,
Or like to men proud of destruction,
Defy us to our worst; for as I am a soldier,
A name that in my thoughts becomes me best,
If I begin the battery once again,
I will not leave the half-achieved Harflew
Till in her ashes she lies buried.
The gates of mercy shall be all shut up,
And the fleshed soldier, rough and hard of heart,
In liberty of bloody hand, shall range
With conscience wide as hell, mowing like grass
Your fresh fair virgins and your flowering infants.
(King Henry V to the surrounded town of Harflew, in
William Shakespeare, *Henry V*)

d. What is the key to [Barbara] Walters's success? On your TV screen,
you behold a large but sleek common-looking woman, with a brash-
ness that has been cosmeticized into proto-polish, who might be the
wife of a Seventh-Avenue clothing magnate or, as it happens, the
daughter of a man who owned a large, vulgar night club. She wears
her bought respectability with a certain bravura, although her over-
eagerness to be gracious collapses when, for instance, [Barbra] Streis-
and's phone rings in mid-interview and Walters shrills in mingled
panic and outrage, "Don't answer that phone!," the Park Avenue
gloss on her voice cracking to reveal the Bronx. (John Simon, "Verbal Barbarisms")

5. Each of the following passages contains an argument. Determine what
that argument is and whether it is reasonable.

a. I don't know where Hoboken is. Pull into this gas station and let's
ask the attendant.

b. Well, if he's rich and has a nice car, he'll probably be fun on a date.
Call him back.

c. I called you Friday, and you said you were sick. I called you Saturday, and you said you had homework. I called you Sunday, and you
said you had church all day long. Don't you like me or something?

d. Scientists are calling AIDS fatal because no AIDS patient has been
known to live longer than six years after diagnosis of the disease.

e. Let's go to Asbury Park. That's the place Bruce Springsteen is always
singing about.

f. So I looked again at all the acts of oppression which were being done under the sun. And behold, I saw the tears of the oppressed and that they had no one to comfort them; and on the side of their oppressors was power, but still the oppressed had no one to comfort them. So I congratulated the dead who are already dead more than the living who are still living. (Ecclesiastes 4:1–2)

g. The moon causes the ebb and flow of the tide. The human body consists of about 70% water. Therefore, the moon influences our bodies. (*Aries 1971 Horoscope*)

h. Overheard at a discotheque: "You can see why it's easy to hate Stevie Wonder. He's talented, he's black, and he's got money."

i. If God hadn't wanted there to be poor people, He would have made us rich people more generous. (Caption of a *New Yorker* drawing by Dana Fradon)

j. She's cool. She's bright. She's alive. She uses Glam-Glop.

k. If you haven't driven a Tapir, you haven't driven a real automobile.

l. Dear Miss Lonelyheart: Between you and me, the people who write to your column are either scoundrels or idiots.

4
THE LOGIC
OF ARGUMENT

But there must be some use for reason. There
is a real world of people, things, and events.
F. G. BAILEY (b. 1924)
ENGLISH ANTHROPOLOGIST

Thus far, we have focused on some of the difficulties we face in analyzing ideas. We've discussed various impediments to clear thinking, of
our own creation or buried in what we hear and read. Now we turn to a
discussion of logic. Logic is our intellectual tool for understanding a reasoning process, our own and others'. By means of logic we evaluate the
relation between evidence and the conclusion we draw from it. We answer
the question, Am I justified in thinking this is true?

PREMISES AND INFERENCES:
THE PATH TO CONCLUSIONS

The terms *premise* and *inference* are not as difficult as they may sound.
All they refer to is the point where an argument begins and the process of
arriving at the conclusion.

Premises

When we reason, we have to start somewhere, with some idea or
fact or belief. That starting point is called a premise. A premise is the idea
we don't try to prove. We assume it is true. A premise is our reason for
concluding something.

PREMISE	My dog ate arsenic.
CONCLUSION	He may die.
PREMISE	All living things require water.
CONCLUSION	A cactus requires water.

When we reason, we combine two or more premises and draw a conclusion based on their connection:

PREMISE 1	Any thirty-five-year-old or older nonfelon born in the United States is eligible for the presidency.
PREMISE 2	James is a thirty-eight-year-old nonfelon born in the United States.
CONCLUSION	James is eligible for the presidency.

Not all premises are stated. Some may be implicit or hidden. In the preceding reasoning about arsenic, the unstated premise is "Arsenic kills." In the reasoning about the cactus, the unstated premise is "A cactus is a living thing." (For a discussion of hidden assumptions, see "Uncovering Assumptions" in Chapter 3 and "What's Behind All This?" in Chapter 5.)

The premises must be true to justify the conclusion. If, for instance, James is a felon, we are not justified in concluding that he is eligible for the presidency. Basing an argument on an untrue premise makes for faulty reasoning.

Even true premises may not justify a conclusion. Good reasoning requires that the premises include *all* relevant considerations. If James had relinquished his U.S. citizenship or served in a foreign army, he would not be eligible for the presidency. Had the premises included these relevant facts, we would surely have drawn a different conclusion. Premises must be true *and* adequate.

In reasoning, especially about values, we may disagree vociferously about what constitutes an acceptable premise. And if you disagree with the premises, you won't think the conclusion is justified. Here is a familiar argument:

> Controlling crime and criminals is the most important problem in our society. If the police violate due process once in a while, well, that's too bad.

If you don't accept the premise that controlling crime is the most important problem in our society, you might conclude that it is worse than "too bad" to violate due process.

Inferences

The process of moving from the premises, or reasons, to the conclusion is called inference. Based on what we know or believe, we infer ideas about what we don't know:

We know we see smoke. Where there's smoke, there's fire. We infer a fire.

When we analyze inferences, we are evaluating not the truth or adequacy of the premises but whether the reasoning from them to the conclusion is justified. When we make an inference, we consider the premises and then derive a conclusion that follows from them.

We know people are standing in line in front of a movie theater. We infer they will attend the movie.

The strength or weakness of an inference depends on the extent to which the premises compel us to the conclusion. In any argument, we need to evaluate how compelling those premises are.

Each of the following statements contains a premise and an inference. How compelling are the premises and how strong are the inferences?

I wrote her twelve letters but she never answered. She does not want to correspond with me.

Although we have been in two classes together, David has never invited me to go mountain climbing. David hates me.

Transcendental meditation gives a person self-knowledge, and self-knowledge is desirable. TM should be required in high schools.

In the first statement, the premise is so compelling that no one would quarrel with the inference, although we might be amused that a person bothered to draw such an obvious conclusion.

In the second, David's failure to extend an invitation to climb a mountain hardly justifies the conclusion "David hates me." The inference is weak to ridiculous.

The third statement is trickier. Even granting the truth of the explicit premises—that TM does give self-knowledge and that self-knowledge is good—is the inference strong or weak? Can we confidently take the step to the conclusion?

Three steps can help us evaluate inferences. First, we should articulate both the stated and the unstated premises to make sure we understand what is being claimed. For the first example, an unstated premise is

If she had wanted to correspond with me, she would have answered at least one of my letters.

Reasonable enough, but it hardly needed saying. But for the transcendental meditation argument, we have some fairly important and subtle unstated premises to analyze. In laying out the argument, we might come up with something like this:

Transcendental meditation gives a person self-knowledge. Self-knowledge is desirable. We should require in the curriculum whatever is desirable. Being required will not undermine the benefits derived from TM.

We have identified just two of the many unstated premises here, but they give us a better idea of whether the inference is strong or weak.

Second, we should state the argument in its baldest terms by adding a *therefore* before the conclusion.

> Transcendental meditation gives a person self-knowledge, and self-knowledge is desirable. Therefore, TM should be required in high schools.

Put like that, the conclusion receives its full weight of absoluteness, and you might decide you don't agree. Often poor reasoning is concealed because it is worded in moderate terms. When put baldly, you can decide if the conclusion is justified, as, for instance, it is in the cactus argument:

> Therefore, a cactus requires water.

Finally, we should reframe the conclusion to test its limits. First, reframe to make the inference less of a jump:

> Transcendental meditation gives a person self-knowledge. Self-knowledge is desirable. Therefore, we might offer TM as an elective course in high school.

How does that strike you? Now make the inference more of a jump:

> Transcendental meditation gives a person self-knowledge. Self-knowledge is desirable. Therefore, TM should be required for all citizens.

Given this range, you can better determine what inference is justified, and you may want to disagree with the original conclusion. Even with these helps, you are really on your own when it comes to evaluating inferences. It is often a matter of *feeling*, of gauging how strongly the premises compel you to the conclusion.

INDUCTION AND DEDUCTION: HOW WE REASON

Through induction and deduction we reason from what we do know, or believe, to draw conclusions about what we don't know. Although they follow more or less the same form—from premise by means of inference to conclusion—they differ in the kinds of premises we start with and in the degree of certainty we end with.

Induction

Induction is the process of reasoning from premises that constitute good, but not absolutely certain, reasons to a conclusion that is *probably* correct. We do this kind of reasoning all the time—choosing a college, making a career choice, even buying sneakers:

> It's time to buy new sneakers. I've had five pairs of Nikes and never had any foot problems. Adidas caused me blisters, and Pumas made my ankles ache. Therefore, I probably ought to buy Nikes.

The conclusion to buy Nikes is based on experience with Nikes, Adidas, and Pumas, good premises from which to reason. We cannot be absolutely certain, however, that this conclusion is the correct one. Perhaps the problem was with only a particular pair of Pumas, and all the others are fine, or perhaps the machinery on which the Nikes were made has been replaced, and the sneakers will never be the same. Or perhaps . . . the possibilities are endless. It could have been a phase of the moon that made the Adidas cause blisters. Nonetheless, the inference is strong, the conclusion justifiable. Go with the Nikes.

Scientists often use the inductive process for making new discoveries. They start with particular facts, analyze their connections, and reason to conclusions. A doctor sees many patients who are suffering from swollen tongues, loose teeth, and watery eyes. By asking questions, the doctor discovers that all these patients have the same kind of diet. Reasoning from these two premises—the symptoms and the diet—the doctor tentatively concludes that the problem is dietary, a deficiency in a particular vitamin. This hypothesis is tested by depriving laboratory rats of the vitamin. When rat after rat develops the symptoms, the doctor firms up the conclusion.

Judges and juries also reason inductively. They bring together all the pieces of evidence (the premises) presented by the lawyers and come up with a verdict (the conclusion). Here is the summary of the evidence a lawyer makes in a custody case before a judge:

> Mrs. Wiggs sometimes left the seven-year-old to look after the two younger children. Therefore, Your Honor, custody should be denied Mrs. Wiggs and given to my client, Mr. Wiggs.

Hardly an adequate premise for inferring such a momentous conclusion. Did Mrs. Wiggs just go next door, or was she out all night? The lawyer provides other premises:

> The neighbors have testified that Mrs. Wiggs drinks and leaves the children alone at night. Because she did not pay her bill, her electricity was shut off for a week during the winter. Therefore, Your Honor, custody should be denied Mrs. Wiggs and given to my client, Mr. Wiggs.

The judge is beginning to find this lawyer's reasons compelling and the inference strong.

Mrs. Wiggs's lawyer likewise offers a compelling reason:

> Mr. Wiggs watches pornographic movies on his VCR.

The judge decides to investigate on his own.

Even months of investigating, however, could not uncover every relevant fact: Will one or both parents cease their vices? Which is worse for these particular children, the booze or the movies? Would one parent be better for the seven-year-old and the other for the younger children? With less than complete knowledge, the judge must decide what is *probably* in the best interest of the children.

The best inductive arguments are only "highly probable," probable enough to justify the movement from the premises through the inference to the conclusion.

Deduction

When we reason deductively, we move from general statements we accept as true to an inevitable conclusion. When the general statements are indeed true and the reasoning valid, then the conclusion is *certainly* true. (Remember that in inductive reasoning, the conclusion is never more than highly probable.) The most famous example of deduction is

> All men are mortal.
>
> Socrates is a man.
>
> Therefore, Socrates is mortal.

Logicians refer to this form of argument as a *syllogism*. It contains two statements and a conclusion. The first statement makes a general assertion, called the *major premise*. This assertion is the foundation of the argument. For the argument to proceed, we have to accept that all men are mortal. The second statement, called a *minor premise*, provides a specific instance of the major premise. Without the minor premise, we would have

> All men are mortal.
>
> Therefore Socrates is mortal.

But we don't know about this thing called Socrates. Is it a city?

> Socrates is a man.

The minor premise links the major premise to the conclusion. It indicates the way in which the conclusion fits into the major premise. Reasoning from the two premises, the conclusion is inevitable. If all men are mortal and Socrates is a man, then he is mortal.

Scientists and physicians sometimes think deductively:

> White blood cells multiply to combat infection. This blood sample indicates a rapid rise in the white blood cell count. There must be an infection.

So do plumbers, electricians, secretaries, and automobile mechanics:

> The car's electrical system is not operating. The battery is the source of electricity. I'll check the battery.

We frequently use this form of reasoning in everyday life too, as in this statement:

> All movies starring Kevin Costner are enjoyable. He's in a new movie. This new movie will be enjoyable.

Usually our deductive reasoning is more casually formulated and takes place so fast we hardly know we're doing it:

> I like Russian novels and haven't read this one by Dostoevsky. I think I'll buy it.

As with inductive reasoning, in deductive reasoning, to agree with the conclusion, we must agree with the premises. Both premises. Here is an argument based on a dubious major premise:

> All my friends are brilliant.
>
> Conrad is my friend.
>
> Therefore, Conrad is brilliant.

We have to wonder about the truth of these premises. Surely everyone has at least one friend who isn't brilliant.

Even when we accept the major premise, we need to look carefully at the minor premise. Here are the bases for two deductive arguments regarding test-tube fertilization. They are based on the same major premise but arrive at opposite conclusions.

> Major premise: Any practice that detracts from the dignity of human life should be illegal.

The minor premise of one side of the argument is

> Test-tube fertilization detracts from the dignity of human life.

The minor premise of the other side is

> Anything that denies infertile couples the right to have children detracts from the dignity of human life.

Never the twain shall meet. We need to analyze the minor premise as closely as we do the major.

We often think in syllogisms when we try to anticipate the consequences of a course of action. We set up a hypothesis and see how things work out. The major premise projects a condition that *if* something is the case, *then* something else will be or will happen:

> *If* I see someone cheating, *then* I am honor bound to report it.

The minor premise states that the condition of the *if* clause does exist in a particular case:

> I saw that student cheating.

The conclusion states that the *then* clause obtains in the particular case:

> *Then* I am honor bound to report him.

> We use forms of hypothetical reasoning every day in subtle ways:

> If a highway patrolman observes me speeding, he will give me a ticket. A highway patrolman is hiding behind that billboard. I will slow down.

> If I eat any more pizza, I will gain weight. I love pizza, but I won't have any more.

Very few arguments in real life are completely deductive. Most are based on some prior induction. In the argument about white blood cells, for example, the major premise—that white cells multiply to combat infection—is the product of an inductive process. And of course we wouldn't know that all men are mortal if we hadn't known about particular people who had died. When you come across a deductive argument, look closely at the inductive argument on which it probably rests. That is the best way to test it.

Enthymemes

We turn now to a discussion of arguments in which one part—either of the premises or of the conclusion—is missing. This is a common form of argument and is called an *enthymeme*.

> The leaves of my camellias are yellowing. I should put on some nitrogen.

Missing is a second premise necessary to justify the conclusion:

> Yellow leaves usually indicate that a plant needs nitrogen.

A nongardener would probably have needed that second premise to understand the conclusion. Often, however, the missing premise is just too obvious to require stating:

> He just committed a murder. Arrest him.

No one would bother to say,

> Anyone who commits a murder should be arrested.

Or the conclusion may not need stating:

If you don't mail your taxes in by April 15, you're going to get hit with a huge penalty. Tomorrow is April 15.

It would actually be less effective to state the conclusion outright:

So you should send in your taxes by tomorrow.

While enthymemes can be quite innocent, as these examples suggest, sometimes they create problems in reasoning, because they can be used to deceive:

Koop is a South African. Therefore, he accepts apartheid.

Missing from this deductive argument is the major premise:

All South Africans accept apartheid.

We know this statement to be false, and if it were stated we would challenge it. When it is unstated, however, we may be misled into accepting the argument.

Asserting two premises and leaving the conclusion unstated can be even more insidious:

All South Africans accept apartheid. Koop is a South African.

We're supposed to fill in the blank:

Koop must accept apartheid.

Stated, this could be grounds for a libel suit. We should insist that people who make sly insinuations draw their own conclusions.

Sometimes unintentional enthymemes confuse the reader, as did this one from a student essay:

Ernest Hemingway loved big-game hunting and contests of strength and skill. He often had fights with friends and competitors, and he especially loved boxing and bullfighting. His stories are often about men trying to prove their masculinity. It seems as though he was very much afraid that he wasn't much of a man.

The missing part of the argument is

Any writer so concerned with masculinity must be insecure about his own manliness.

We would want to examine that premise before we agreed with the conclusion.

Sometimes a good argument seems absurd because an important part is missing:

You should exercise daily because blood lactates are responsible for mental dullness and lethargy.

Huh? Missing premise, please:

Exercise lowers the quantity of blood lactates.

Oh.

Although enthymemes can be dangerous, they can also enrich prose. They can have a strength and elegance that every writer should try to master. Enthymemes involve the audience in the argument by inviting them to supply the missing part of the syllogism—as the enthymeme about April 15 did. They work best when the part to be supplied is reasonably apparent and is something the reader will either agree with or find interesting. Supplying that missing part can be a great source of reader satisfaction.

We see this use of enthymemes every day. Here is the same movie review put into three different enthymemes. Can you supply the missing part?

> *Dark Passions* does not have good acting, brisk direction, or especially good cinematography. That's why it won't be getting many Academy Award nominations.

> A movie needs good acting, brisk direction, and especially good cinematography to earn Academy Award nominations. That's why you won't be seeing *Dark Passions* among the nominees this year.

> A movie needs good acting, brisk direction, and especially good cinematography to earn an Academy Award nomination. *Dark Passions* has none of these.

Write out the complete syllogism, and you'll be able to see why each enthymeme has an unmistakable—and completely different—impact.

As a reader, be aware of enthymemes. Supply missing elements in reasoning. Say them aloud to yourself, or just make a mental note. By doing so you will learn more about both the writer's intention and your own reasoning process. As a writer, experiment with enthymemes. They invite the reader to join you in the process of reasoning.

FACTS OR VALUES: TELLING *IS* FROM *OUGHT*

In deciding whether a reasoning process is valid and we agree with its conclusion, we need to recognize exactly what kind of argument is being made, whether of fact or of value.

In an argument of fact, the conclusion establishes what was, is, or will be:

John von Neumann was largely responsible for inventing the computer.

If we let people use water indiscriminately, we will deplete our water supplies.

Lower taxes will lead to greater federal revenues.

These conclusions rest on factual premises shared by anyone in a position to investigate. The premises behind "John von Neumann was largely responsible for inventing the computer" might be various expert studies on the history of the computer, testimony of contemporary witnesses, and the influence of von Neumann's ideas on contemporary computer design—all facts. Environmentalists arguing that indiscriminate use of water will deplete the water supply would base their argument on, among other facts, documented examples of such occurrences elsewhere and an examination of current water tables. Because the conclusion "Lower taxes will lead to greater federal revenues" anticipates future events, economists so concluding would base their argument on mathematical models.

Sometimes arguments of fact are not valid, as we suggested earlier in this section. Perhaps the facts are not true or not adequate, or the inference is weak. Nonetheless, the argument rests on fact.

In an argument of value, the conclusion establishes whether an idea or an object is or is not worthwhile, whether a person should or should not do something, whether an action is good or bad. Conclusions of value rest not on established facts but on norms, a sense of what is right or wrong, good or bad. The writer seeks to persuade us not of what is, was, or will be but of what ought to be. No investigation, no experimentation, no mathematical model could prove these conclusions of value:

Capital punishment should be outlawed.

Star Wars is the greatest movie ever made.

The state should prohibit surrogate motherhood.

Sometimes arguments of value are premised on a fact. In arguing against capital punishment, for instance, a writer might claim as one premise the fact that innocent people have been executed. But the importance or weight of that fact rests upon an unstated premise of value: nothing justifies executing innocent people.

Arguments of value cannot be directly proven, for finally they rest on personal interests and considerations and emotionally charged beliefs. This does not mean that we should dismiss such arguments—they involve the most important issues of our lives. But it does mean that we should be clear about what kind of argument is being made. For an argument of fact, when we muster sufficient evidence, we will probably persuade our audience. But it is extremely difficult to persuade another person that our values are superior to his or hers. No amount of haranguing will help. The best we can do is express our own values clearly and hope that in some way we touch the reader.

PROBLEMS IN LOGIC:
IDENTIFYING LOGICAL FALLACIES

The validity of an argument, whether inductive or deductive, depends on both the premises and the reasoning to the conclusion. Errors in either premises or inferences can lead to logical fallacies. Logical fallacies are patterns of reasoning that are at worst completely invalid and at best weaker than they appear to the unwary. Human beings have invented so many logical fallacies that we could never name, let alone discuss, all of them. In Chapter 3, The Critical Sense, we discussed several, including hasty generalization and oversimplification. Here we discuss other fallacies you will often encounter.

The Undistributed Middle

Logicians point out that a syllogism won't work unless the assertion found in the major premise is true of all members of the group. In the Socrates syllogism, "mortality" is true of "all men." But look at this syllogism:

Most little children fib.

Timmy is a little child.

Therefore, Timmy fibs.

The major premise does not claim that fibbing is true of "all" children: although Timmy is a child, he may not be one of the fibbers. The syllogism is faulty because what is true of "most" may not be true of a specific individual. Logicians call this the fallacy of the undistributed middle, meaning that the middle term (fib) is not necessarily true of, or "distributed to," all members of the group (children). Carefully check the wording to be sure you know exactly what is being asserted.

Affirming the Consequent

Although its name may be a bit daunting, the fallacy called "affirming the consequent" is important and frequent enough to merit study.

The state punishes embezzlers.

The state punished Lester.

Therefore, Lester is an embezzler.

The facts here may be correct, but the reasoning is faulty because the major premise does not specifically exclude punishing criminals other than embezzlers. The state may be punishing people for other crimes. Lester may have robbed a bank for all the two premises tell us. If the major premise had stated

> The state punishes only embezzlers,

the reasoning would have been valid, and we would know Lester to be an embezzler. Make certain the major premise specifically includes the minor premise.

Circular Reasoning

Occasionally people will argue in a circle, using as a premise what in fact they are setting out to prove.

> Freud's investigations were truly scientific because they were based on Freud's own clinical research.

In this argument we end up where we started out. Some logicians call this *begging the question* because the careful thinker would ask something like, Why are Freud's clinical studies scientific?

Another form of circular reasoning is the *tautology,* that is, an argument that only repeats the same idea in different words:

> This car doesn't work because something is wrong with it.

And slightly more subtly:

> We must preserve the American way of life because without it, we won't be able to live the way Americans should.

This is a tautology because it is a tautology.

Non sequitur

The Latin phrase *non sequitur* means "it does not follow." It applies to any argument whose conclusion simply has nothing to do with its premises:

> Warfield will make an excellent governor because he was a fine captain of his football team.

Football experience has little relevance to political skill and tells us nothing about political goals. The premise may be correct, but the conclusion does not follow.

As we suggested in the discussion of assumptions in Chapter 3, television commercials specialize in non sequiturs. Just because we see a sleek cheetah, a handsome man, a beautiful woman, a desert landscape, and a car, it does not follow that we should buy that car.

As we suggested earlier, sometimes what seems to be a non sequitur is really an enthymeme.

Although human beings did not eat barley in the sixteenth century, barley was necessary for war.

This apparent non sequitur is really an enthymeme lacking a part:

War making depended on horses, and horses ate barley.

Be sure you fill in all the necessary parts of an argument.

Post hoc, ergo propter hoc

Also from the Latin, *post hoc, ergo proper hoc* means "after this, therefore because of this." We commit this fallacy when we argue, without other reasons, that because X occurred before Y, X caused Y.

Herbert Hoover was inaugurated as president in the spring of 1929, and that autumn the stock market crashed. Hoover must have caused the crash.

The causes of the stock market crash go much further back than the spring of 1929 and involve much more than the actions of a single individual.

A variant of the post hoc fallacy is the argument that because A was one of the conditions for bringing B about, we can eliminate B by eliminating A.

Neville Chamberlain's negotiation with Adolf Hitler allowed Germany time to rearm and increased its ability to wage war. To avoid war, we should never negotiate.

It may not have been wise to negotiate with Hitler, but this does not mean that negotiation is always unwise. Be sure to examine the connection between things that are claimed as causes and their effects.

Ad hominem

Still another Latin phrase, *ad hominem* means an argument "to the man," that is, to the person making the statement. Someone guilty of this fallacy argues by making irrelevant assertions—usually character slurs—about the opponent, rather than attacking the opponent's reasoning.

Ralph Nader's attacks on environmental laws don't amount to a hill of beans. He is conceited and self-righteous.

Maybe he is, but his *opinion* is the point, not his character; he may still have important claims to make about environmental laws.

Ridicule is a particularly insidious ad hominem technique because it is based on humor. Once when he saw Stafford Cripps, an old opponent with a reputation for arrogance, Winston Churchill said, "There but for the grace of God goes God." Nevertheless, Churchill had finally to debate the merits of Cripps's arguments.

TIPS FOR THE LOGIC OF ARGUMENT

- Check all premises to be sure you agree with them. Remember premises must be true and adequate for an argument based on them to be true.
- Articulate stated and unstated premises to be sure you understand the argument.
- To evaluate an inference, state the argument in its baldest terms.
- Test an inference by reframing the conclusion less drastically and then more drastically.
- Remember that even in the best case, a conclusion from induction is only highly probable.
- Check both premises and reasoning to evaluate a deductive argument.
- Remember that most deductive arguments rest on prior induction.
- Check enthymemes to be sure the missing part—whether premise or conclusion—doesn't change the argument.
- Carefully distinguish between arguments of fact and arguments of value.
- Be aware of logical fallacies: for instance, the undistributed middle, affirming the consequent, circular reasoning, non sequitur, *post hoc, ergo propter hoc,* and ad hominem.

Exercises for the Logic of Argument

1. In the following passages, identify the premises, stated and implied:
   a. It is outrageous for GoodHealth Insurance Company to cancel insurance for 8,000 people on the ground that the policies did not pay for themselves. What further proof do we need that the health-care industry cares only about money? The state should provide coverage for all people at a cost proportionate to their income.

   b. When a tourist brochure suggested that Robin Hood was just a greedy outlaw, the Nottingham city fathers feared tourism would be hurt. The present sheriff said, "I would like to see the authors of this brochure locked up in the dungeons of Nottingham Castle."
   c. Let's not argue. I've made up my mind.
   d. Laugh and the world laughs with you;
      weep, and you weep alone. (Ella Wheeler Wilcox)
   e. At this college, freshmen are required to take a full year of a foreign language. Since you are just beginning your college career, sign up for a foreign language.
   f. The air in this city is full of pollen that makes me sneeze. I feel rotten. I think I'll move.
   g. The reason Robert Bork was not confirmed as a Supreme Court justice was that dishonest self-seekers and special-interest groups mounted a personal attack.

2. What inferences are you expected to make in the following examples? Are the inferences strong or weak?
   a. At a grocery store checkout counter: "She's eighty-five and she has six shopping bags to carry to her car."
   b. What America needs is someone who can lead the country. My opponent has never run a business, never been a lawyer, and never served in Congress.
   c. If the Olympic Committee barred every athlete who ever used drugs, Andorra would win all the gold medals.
   d. Only drink when you're alone or with somebody else. (Meredith Wilson, "Belly up to the Bar, Boys")
   e. There are old pilots and there are bold pilots—but there are no old, bold pilots. (Air Force slogan)
   f. Persons attempting to find a motive in this narrative will be prosecuted; persons attempting to find a moral in it will be banished; persons attempting to find a plot in it will be shot. (Samuel Clemens, *The Adventures of Huckleberry Finn*)

3. Determine whether each of these arguments is inductive or deductive, and then evaluate the reasoning.
   a. There has never been a female president. There has never been a female vice president. There has never been a female secretary of state, treasury, or defense. Women have no chance in politics in this country.
   b. The pound picks up all stray dogs. The pound picked up Rover. Therefore, Rover must be a stray dog.
   c. Cats are vicious creatures. They disturb the dogs in the neighborhood and sometimes kill birds. If their owners let them out of the house, the neighbors ought to have a right to shoot them.
   d. You live next door, don't you? You must drive a Buick or a Chevy. Most of the people around here drive GM cars.
   e. The law says that you are liable for taxes on your share of the taxable income of any partnership in which you are a partner. Your share of

the income of our partnership was $500. Therefore, you must pay taxes on $500.

4. Rewrite the arguments in Exercise 3 to make them more acceptable. Change the premises or the conclusion as necessary.

5. Here are a series of enthymemes. Which part of each argument is missing? Restore the missing part, and then determine if the argument is valid.

   a. Used-car salesman: "So you're a student. Well, here's a 1963 Lemon. It's sort of beat up, but, heck, it runs, and it's cheap."

   b. Overheard at a bar: "What do you mean, is my wife temperamental? She's a woman, isn't she?"

   c. On a sports talk show: "What you need to win the Super Bowl is great passing, superb defense, and good special teams. That's why Denver is a lock on the Bowl this year."

   d. Tennessee Williams's plays are all tragic and decadent; the people in them are all sick, wasted, or confused. If my kid sees his plays, he's going to shoot himself.

   e. You know as much about embroidery as a pig does about rocket science.

   f. A truly desirable home is hard to find. So are the homes at Hidden Hollow Estates.

   g. A bill before the Maine legislature in 1969: "Every person residing in Maine who earns less than $4,000 annually shall be furnished a hearing aid free of charge by the Department of Health and Welfare."

   h. Mother to daughter: "You're going to have to take off your ice skates if you want me to believe you are too sick to go to school."

   i. It is the policy of this college not to bail any of its students out of jail. That's something better left to parents.

   j. If I'm smart enough to be in college, I'm smart enough to choose my own courses.

   k. Here's a surefire way to make sure the East Germans don't win the next Winter Olympics: don't invite them.

   l. Homosexual acts between consenting adults are victimless acts and therefore should not be considered criminal.

   m. Water pollution is everybody's fault. That means it is your duty to help clean it up.

6. Which of the following conclusions would be based on fact and which on value? Explain your identifications.

   a. If you see a situation in which something is wrong and you could rectify it yet do nothing, then you are also responsible for that situation.

   b. Meat eaters have a much higher chance of developing cancer of the digestive system than do vegetarians.

   c. Watching television makes a child less sensitive to violence and an adult more indifferent to actual violence in the world.

   d. I prefer Kobe's peach ice cream because it contains real fruit.

   e. Writing well is the sign of an educated person.

7. Identify all the logical fallacies in this letter written to the editor of a newspaper.

Dear Editor:

For the very reason the minimum wage should be lowered for teenagers, it should be abolished for everyone. Just as shoppers at my grocery store will buy more blueberries if the price is lower, employers will hire more laborers at a lower rate. That, of course, would mean less unemployment, and less unemployment would mean less welfare, and that would mean lower taxes. If people did not have to pay so much money in taxes, they would have increased purchasing power. And that in turn would make for more workers being employed. We would be far along in solving our economic problems. If we don't get rid of the minimum wage, we might as well give up pretending we have a free-enterprise system.

8. Try your hand at some illogical writing. Write a paragraph about one of the following subjects, making sure you have at least one thinking problem in each sentence.

No one over eighty should serve in the U.S. Senate.

Zoos should be outlawed.

Any person driving a car above the speed limit should spend the night in jail.

Anyone convicted of a drug-related crime in which someone was murdered should automatically receive the death penalty whether or not he or she committed the murder.

5
CRITICAL READING

Reading is to the mind what exercise is to the body.

SIR RICHARD STEELE (1672–1729)
ENGLISH ESSAYIST AND PLAYWRIGHT

Understanding a text is not an automatic consequence of running our eyes over the print. To read well takes more than vision: it takes full engagement of the mind. Some writing is, of course, not difficult—just look at the sports page or popular novels. We can usually understand this easy-access reading on the first try and without effort. But college reading is by its very nature different. Its purpose is not to divert but to inform and stimulate thought. It almost always requires a second and often a third try, for the meaning accumulates from page to page. College reading requires, then, that we put our minds in gear and feel the traction as our thought moves over the writer's thought.

We call this process *critical reading.* By *critical,* we do not mean fault-finding or carping over details. We mean a healthy skepticism—respectful but inquisitive—and a willingness to analyze a text step by step. Critical reading helps us to remember. When we read casually, uncritically, we don't nail the text into our memory. When we read critically, however, the ideas and facts stay in place. Being more engaged, we pay closer attention. We relate one idea to another and notice similarities. As we read, our knowledge accumulates and our understanding grows.

We do not naturally adopt a critical stance when we read. We tend to accept what we see in print, forgetting that no matter how well qualified writers may be, they are nonetheless fallible. We cannot assume that mistakes, deceptions, and illogicalities just won't appear in what we read. They will.

A CRITICAL ATTITUDE: ENGAGING THE TEXT

This chapter covers certain habits of mind appropriate to reading. Some of its terms will be familiar from previous chapters. Here we discuss ways of sifting out the good in what you read and throwing away the bad.

Critical readers perform three main activities:

They participate. They do not sit back and read passively. Before starting to read, they map the whole terrain they will cover. They look ahead and know what to expect. They make notes, put concepts into their own words, group important topics, relate main ideas. They summarize or paraphrase, the better to capture the essence of a thought or a text.

They analyze. Developing analytical skills is a—perhaps *the*—major purpose of a college education. To analyze is to break large items or ideas into smaller units or complex items into simpler components. Critical readers look at each major idea separately and examine its subordinate parts. They study how major ideas connect to make up the whole.

They interrogate the text. Critical readers know that almost all writers—whether of textbooks, essays, editorials, or advertisements—are trying to impose their opinions and thoughts on their readers. Critical readers are always on the lookout for sloppy reasoning, missed steps, "fast ones," or hidden assumptions. They assume neither the best nor the worst. They judge for themselves.

AN OVERVIEW: MAPPING THE TEXT

You have a piece of writing before you. It could be a textbook, a newspaper editorial, a magazine article, or a roommate's essay that you have just been asked to look at. In each case, you have a good reason to read critically: you want to learn, you want to understand, or you want to help. The following four tactics will give you an effective way to map the text:

1. When you write, you think about your purpose for writing; when you read, think about your purpose for reading. Do you need to accumulate facts or to understand the development of an idea? Are you studying the text to prepare for an examination, or will you be writing a paper on it?
2. Take a quick tour of the ground to be covered. First, note the title and the author's name and read any information about the author.

Next, scan the table of contents. Page through and note any head-notes, subdivisions, or illustrations. Note repeated terms and names. Finally, scan the questions, if any, at the end of the chapter or article to determine what the author thinks is important. At this point, although you have not started your actual reading, you are already familiar with the whole piece.

3. Check the length of the piece and estimate how long it will take to read. Don't always try to finish in one sitting. Your brain likes to store information gradually rather than to have everything rammed in at once. We recommend that when reading textbooks, you read in a fifteen- to twenty-minute chunk, take a short break, and start again.

4. Respond. This may be the most important phase of critical reading. You cannot expect to understand and retain important material if you just turn pages. Some people underline or use marking pens to highlight significant passages. This process has drawbacks, however: it allows the reader to register passively that a word or phrase is important but not *how* it is important. We once saw a copy of *Othello* that was almost entirely highlighted, because almost every line has something good. You could sit there highlighting all day.

   We strongly urge you to take notes, putting what you have read in your own words. Taking notes forces you to discriminate constantly, reducing and reorganizing the ideas as your understanding grows. Some people prefer to write their notes in the margins of the text, but then the notes remain scattered and are difficult to use. We recommend jotting your notes in a notebook or on notecards. This method forces you to organize the notes apart from the text—a good way to get a handle on the material—and provides quick access for review. And if you are writing a paper on the reading, your notes will put you one step closer to the finished product.

The following are suggestions for note taking:

1. Summarize the text, writing down the primary ideas and most significant evidence. You can go back to fill in details.
2. Note page numbers or paragraph numbers so that you can easily find specific material.
3. Include in your notes your agreement or disagreement and any reservations you have—but be sure to keep these comments separate from the summary.
4. After completing your reading, make an outline of the main points and supporting ideas so that you can see how the text was organized, how the parts were related, and how the argument developed. (For a discussion of outlining, see "Organizing" in Chapter 2.)

Yes, all this is trouble, and yes, it is worth it. Reading critically will vastly enhance both your retention and your understanding.

EIGHT QUESTIONS: EVALUATING READING

In the following section, we discuss eight questions a critical reader can use to interrogate difficult texts as an aid to understanding and retention. Thinking through—or even better, writing down—the answers to these questions can help you know what is really in the text and develop an informed opinion about it.

1. What are they talking about? The Subject

You cannot enjoy a game unless you know who is playing, and you cannot start understanding your reading until you know what it is about. Your first task is to articulate the subject.

The title will sometimes, but not always, indicate it. "Politics and the English Language" does—"Boring from Within" does not. When a title does not communicate the subject, try the first two or three paragraphs and then the last two or three. Page through to see if subheadings disclose the subject. Don't go any further with your reading until you know what the subject is. Don't assume you know it. Say it aloud or write it out just to be sure. Or put the subject in the form of a question the whole text will answer: for example, "What is the function of the mitochondrion within the cell?" At the head of your notes, write down your idea of the subject. Now you have made it yours.

2. Why are they talking about it? The Purpose

Writers have different purposes for writing. Usually, as we saw in Chapter 1, these break down into three motives: to report, to explain, or to persuade. Sometimes the purpose is concealed and sometimes it is right out front. Some writers—journalists, for instance—have a clear purpose: to report an event or describe a situation or scene. Remember, though, that some writing that purports to be pure reportage has a concealed motive. Here is an interesting headline from a newspaper:

Fed Official Chides Bad-Mouth Economists

Even allowing for the distortions of brevity, such "reportage" is hard to accept. One *chides* a child; *bad-mouth* suggests an unfair criticism. The headline implies that critical economists behave like little children. Consciously or unconsciously, the writer of that headline meant not merely to report but to persuade. Bias has a way of slipping in, and a good reader will be on the lookout for it. When you find evidence of bias in a piece that pretends only to report, be wary.

Much of what you read in college will be not reporting but explaining: *The Rise of the Novel,* "Letter to a Young Surgeon," "Magic and Ritual—The Art of Prehistoric Man," "Kant and Hegel: The Emergence of History," *Science and the Modern World.* As these titles suggest, the writers of these works are explaining how something came about, how it works, what it is, what its consequences are, how to do something. What the writing will explain is usually made explicit fairly early. In "Letter to a Young Surgeon," Richard Selzer's first sentence is "At this, the start of your surgical internship, it is well that you be told how to behave in an operating room." The purpose is clear.

Frequently you will read works whose purpose is to persuade the reader that a particular view or course of action is the right one. We can usually discern that persuasive purpose in an early sentence. In his "Letter from Birmingham Jail," Martin Luther King, Jr., begins,

> While confined here in the Birmingham city jail, I came across your recent statement calling my present activities "unwise and untimely." Seldom do I pause to answer criticism of my work and ideas. If I sought to answer all the criticisms that cross my desk, my secretaries would have little time for anything other than such correspondence in the course of the day, and I would have no time for constructive work. But since I feel that you are men of genuine good will and that your criticisms are sincerely set forth, I want to try to answer your statement in what I hope will be patient and reasonable terms.

His purpose—to persuade "men of genuine good will" to join his crusade for justice—is clear.

3. What's the big idea? The Thesis

THE EXPLICIT THESIS.   As we have said, the single most important sentence in most essays is the thesis statement, that is, the articulation of the author's main idea. Recognizing the thesis is important for understanding the rest of the essay. The first paragraphs may not contain the thesis. There may be anecdotes, accounts of recent controversies, disclaimers, all manner of greetings and promises before the writer hones in on the thesis. Even so, as you read you will probably feel the subject area narrowing, narrowing, until the author's point becomes clear.

Most frequently, however, an introductory paragraph establishes the subject, narrows it, and then presents the thesis:

> Only in the nineteen-sixties did the textbooks finally end their rearguard action on behalf of a Northern European America. The civil-rights movement had shattered the image of a homogeneous American society

and, for the first time in the twentieth century, raised profound questions about the national identity. The answer given by that movement and accepted as orthodoxy by most state and big-city schoolboards was that the United States is a multiracial, multicultural society. This formula, however, raised as many questions as it answered. Was the United States really like Yugoslavia—a country held together only by a delicate balance among ethnic and cultural groups? Or was there some integration of these groups? Was there a dominant culture—and was that a good thing? Was there some principle of unity that Americans ought to support apart from that of the state? The current texts show signs of struggle with these questions. The struggle has had no clear outcome, for the social portrait drawn by the texts remains divided and confused. (Frances FitzGerald, *America Revised: History Schoolbooks in the Twentieth Century*)

FitzGerald gives the background for the debate and ends this introductory paragraph with her thesis statement.

Occasionally a writer comes right out and identifies the essay's point or argument with words and phrases that advertise it: "My thesis in this section will be . . . " "It is, however, more likely that . . . " or "The answer is . . . " Watch for words that indicate either the assertion of a differing opinion *(on the contrary, nevertheless, although)* or a conclusion *(therefore, because, for)*—frequently words like these introduce the thesis statement.

THE IMPLICIT THESIS.   When the thesis is not directly stated, the author will usually try to make the main point as obvious as possible without actually expressing it. Identifying implicit theses can be a tricky business, because we could always be wrong about what the author means us to infer. Still, at times the thesis will shine as clear as day:

> It is still the rainy season in Haiti, and with the sporadic but vengeful rains, and then the mud, and then the dust that hides everything, it has been difficult to get around, and even harder than usual to find out what is happening across town, much less outside the capital. "It's the rain," officials tell you when telephone communications are cut the minute unrest breaks out. "It's the rain," when the electricity goes off just as night falls and the army starts shooting. But rain cannot explain away the recent massacre of hundreds of peasants nor the beatings and arrests of people in the parish of Haiti's most outspoken bishop, nor the ham-handed attempt to silence the country's best-known and best-loved progressive priest. (Amy Wilentz, "Letter from Haiti: The Priest Who Fights the Regime")

This writer relies on her manipulation of language to make her thesis clear. Note "vengeful rains," "the dust that hides everything," "ham-handed," "best-loved." From such hints, we identify the thesis: the Haitian government tries but fails to hide its responsibility for the violence. Wilentz's careful writing makes the thesis as clear as any explicit thesis statement.

When you have identified the thesis, check for vague or ambiguous terms, and then be sure they are defined later and used consistently. If not, be wary. And look for qualifying words or phrases, such as *sometimes, may, perhaps, to some extent.* Careful writers use words like these to limit exactly what they intend to argue, and readers have to evaluate the argument accordingly.

THE ORGANIZATIONAL THESIS.   Many of the texts you read will simply report or explain, and thus have an organizational, not an argumentative, thesis. A political science textbook, for example, could purport to "discuss various forms of contemporary political organization." All the information in the book would be viewed from that perspective and fulfill that purpose. For a book describing the approaches to literary criticism, the author might indicate in a thesis statement that the material is organized around a few important themes. Two social scientists undertook to preserve the history of Amoskeag, an old mill in New Hampshire. Their organizational thesis informed the reader that they would base their work on systematic interviews with former workers and their families. The organizing idea of a manual for assembling an amplifier would no doubt be chronology. Identifying the organizational thesis can help organize the way we read a text. (See Chapter 16, The Report, for a full discussion of the organizational thesis.)

4. How do you figure? Main Supporting Points

Now the real analysis starts. Pay attention to the main supporting points under the thesis. You can often spot these ideas in the topic sentence or main statement of each paragraph. Write out the main supporting points, especially if the reading is difficult, and note how they tie into the thesis.

In his essay "Were Dinosaurs Dumb?" Stephen Jay Gould puts forth the thesis that dinosaurs were as smart as one ought to expect. He provides three main supporting points that could be summarized this way:

1. Dinosaurs had the right size brain for reptiles of their body size.
2. Dinosaurs exhibited intelligence in their behavior.
3. As a species, dinosaurs survived for a relatively long period of time.

Arranging the main points in clear relation to the thesis or purpose lets us see the argument develop and opens a clear path into real critical analysis.

Once you've done your analysis, ask the following questions:

1. Do the main points directly support the thesis? If not, what is their purpose?
2. Are they logical and relevant divisions of the thesis? Were you con-

fused or surprised by any of them? If so, was your reaction the result of careless reading or careless writing?

3. How much space is devoted to each point? The greater the emphasis, probably the more important the point.

4. Does the author seem equally confident of all the points? If one point is significantly more hedged with *maybe*'s and *possibly*'s, perhaps it is the weak link.

5. Are there any big jumps from one main point to another? If so, how badly does the jump damage the argument?

5. What's behind all this? Assumptions

An assumption is anything taken for granted. (In Chapter 3, The Critical Sense, we discussed assumptions, particularly in our own thinking.) Some wonderful jokes depend on a fairly obvious but unspoken assumption. Will Rogers said, for instance,

> I don't belong to any organized political party. I'm a Democrat.

Sometimes assumptions, however, are not merely unspoken but hidden:

> Rock stars became folk heroes to young men precisely because of the strings that were obviously not attached. Lead singers could attract as many women as they wanted and jettison them in full view of the public. They flitted from flower to flower, virile, cheerful, and irresponsible—and they got away with it.

The hidden assumption here is "And that's what men want—right?" You as critical reader are the one to say "right" or "wrong." When you become aware of hidden assumptions you don't agree with, your attitude toward the argument will change. If you think men can be sensitive people, you won't like the crude stereotype of male desire behind this passage.

Hidden assumptions may be all right for humor or fairly harmless in topical journalism, but they can be dangerous in serious written argument. Important assumptions should be explicit and detailed, for then the reader can judge their validity. If we do not agree with a writer's assumptions, we will never agree with his or her arguments.

In the following four examples, we present the same assertion supported by four different bits of evidence. In each case, there is a hidden assumption. Before reading the analysis, try to put the assumption into your own words. Determine whether the assumption is valid, and whether the writer should make it explicit.

> Soviet behavior around the world is hostile to the United States. Russian troops just blew up the Washington Monument.

The hidden assumption is that any foreign power that blows up the Washington Monument is hostile to the United States. This assumption is obvious and acceptable, and the author need not make it explicit.

> Soviet behavior around the world is hostile to the United States. Russian-made missiles have been sighted in Cuba.

The hidden assumptions are that these missiles are threatening to the United States and that anything Cuba does Russia instigates. Most, though not all, readers would find such assumptions acceptable. Cuba is 90 miles from the United States, and sighting Russian missiles there is cause for thinking Russia is involved. Many people would agree without further explication.

> Soviet behavior around the world is hostile to the United States. The Russians invaded Afghanistan.

The hidden assumptions are that America has important interests in or near Afghanistan and that this invasion intentionally threatens those interests. Their validity is shaky. The Washington Monument is right at home and Cuba only 90 miles from our shores, but Afghanistan is half the world away. Perhaps the author thinks that the USSR plans to cut the United States off from the oil fields of the Middle East and that the invasion is one more step toward this goal. If so, these are exactly the kinds of assumptions that the author must write out.

> Soviet behavior around the world is hostile to the United States. The Soviets persecute those who practice their religion.

The hidden assumption is that because the United States allows freedom of religion, religious persecution in Russia is a strike at our values. This assumption is unacceptable. The Communist system has always inhibited religious practice, even in times of friendship between the two countries. Once we make this assumption explicit, we reveal a hole in the argument. Now the author must either find evidence to provide the connection between Soviet policy on religion and hostility toward the United States or give up this line of argument.

Most evidence is neither as self-evident as the first example nor as invalid as the last. The middle two examples represent the middle ground where you must evaluate the assumptions.

Very often, honest and careful writers will take pains to make sure their important assumptions are out on the page, in full view for the reader to inspect. They will lay out the ideas behind their ideas. Writers who do this gain our trust. Writers who don't make us suspicious: are they lazy? sloppy? shifty?

Where are we likely to find assumptions we ought to analyze? At almost any point, but particularly in

introductory paragraphs

definitions

pivotal or impassioned moments.

INTRODUCTORY PARAGRAPHS. Writers often feel the need to justify or defend what they are about to do at the very beginning of their essays. They cart out their assumptions for all to see. To establish the common ground with the reader, they state the facts and values they believe in. In beginning an argument to limit immigration into the United States, the sociologist Garrett Hardin identifies several assumptions:

> Though insisting on their commitment to democracy, most Americans conveniently close their eyes to two facts. First, ours is not a democracy in the original Greek sense but a representative government in which the many vote for a few and then the few make the laws that govern all. The consequences of this arrangement have never been fully worked out in political theory. Particularly—and this brings us to the second aspect of our willful blindness—it should be noted that very frequently the will of the majority can be thwarted for a long time by the normal working of the machinery of representation. The fact deserves the closest study by those who want the will of the majority to prevail. ("Smoke-screens and Evasions;" our underlining)

Are these stated assumptions self-evidently true, or are there some hidden assumptions behind them that need stating and support?

DEFINITIONS. When writers define their central terms, they can't help bringing important assumptions to light. In his famous essay "The Art of Moving Pictures," Bruno Bettelheim, a Freudian scholar and interpreter of modern culture, selects some movies he finds especially valuable for modern viewers. He tells us that he has picked these particular movies because they offer "an affirmation of man." Immediately he attempts to clarify what he means and reveals some assumptions that we have underlined:

> When I speak of an affirmation of man, I do not mean the presentation of fake images of life as wonderfully pleasant. Life is best celebrated in the form of a battle against its inequities, of struggles, of dignity in defeat, of the greatness of discovering oneself and the other.

Not only has Bettelheim defined the kind of "affirmation" he is looking for in pictures but he has also given us a very important assumption about how life is "best celebrated." This assumption runs forward and backward throughout his essay.

PIVOTAL OR IMPASSIONED MOMENTS. When an argument heats up at controversial or emotional moments, writers often reveal important beliefs and opinions—again bringing assumptions to light. In the following example, Richard C. Cowan argues that the government itself has been one of the main causes of the current drug crisis—a controversial point indeed. Note all the important assumptions that come to light at this heated moment in his argument:

> The American criminal-justice system, meanwhile, is on the verge of collapse because of drug prohibition. Even if expensive drug habits did not create criminals—and there is no doubt that they sometimes do—the cost of illegal drugs certainly increases the number of crimes that criminal addicts must commit. Drugs are without a doubt the most powerful corrupters of the police and the court system. For those who have not been corrupted, the failure of the drug laws to have a positive impact on the drug problem has caused great frustration. This has led to calls for more power to be given to the police, and even for calls for suspending the Constitution. There is no prospect of this happening on a wholesale basis, but our liberties are being incrementally eroded at a rapid pace. The existing and proposed laws constitute the basic elements of a socialist police state. There are already controls on cash and capital transfers, calls for the canceling of hundred dollar bills, violations of the long-standing principle of lawyer-client confidentiality, and the authority to seize the accused's property *before* trial or even *after* acquittal. ("How the Narcs Created Crack;" our underlining)

Note that the author italicized certain words. When writers raise their voices like this, they direct us to important assumptions. Here, Cowan wants us to see the terrible breach of constitutional rights when authorities seize people's property in this way.

Anywhere a writer has something at stake, he or she may well bring assumptions to light. Look carefully at concluding paragraphs—where writers make a last effort to convince readers—and at all moments when the heat rises.

Here are some pieces of advice for dealing with assumptions, the trickiest part of reading:

1. Subject all arguments to intense scrutiny at the beginning to determine whether you share a starting point with the author. Think about a writer's stated assumptions. Do you find them biased? naïve? unreasonable? Or are they what you would assume in the same instance? If you disagree with the assumptions on which the argument is clearly based, you will probably not accept the rest of the argument. If, for instance, you believe desirable social change can come about peacefully, you no doubt will disagree with an essay based on the assumption that change will come only with revolution. But you need to be clear about that assumption.

2. Find and articulate the hidden assumptions. When the tone or an-

gle of a piece strikes you as unusual or unexpected, look carefully to determine what is behind it. When you suddenly find yourself confused about where an idea came from or why it appears where it does, trace the confusions to their source. Are there missing steps or strange twists? Once you isolate the hidden assumptions, ask yourself whether you share them. You may have spotted a dark corner where an unacceptable assumption lurks.

6. Did they prove it? Evidence

Without some hard evidence, an argument is just talk. (Throughout this book, we have much to say about evidence, and we refer you to Chapter 7 for a detailed discussion.) When you have ascertained the thesis and main supporting point and articulated all the assumptions of a work, you must delve even further and evaluate the evidence that backs up every step in the argument. Be especially tough on the evidence provided for crucial points. Ask each bit of proof the following six questions:

1. Is it relevant? Does it directly and unambiguously support the point?

2. Is it accurate? Three things can produce inaccurate evidence. The first is simple human error. The *Manchester Guardian* once quoted the U.S. secretary of the treasury as saying, "We will make certain that there will be calamities in the banking system." One tiny missing *not* invalidated the evidence. If you find errors in quotations or statistics, begin to wonder about the writer. The second cause of inaccuracy is ignorance. Some writers present obsolete research or peddle pop wisdom as fact. The third cause is plain human guile. Writers may disguise or distort the meaning or context of a piece of evidence, the better to fit it into their argument. You must test each piece of evidence to make sure it is accurate.

3. Is it specific and detailed? Vague allusions to "the thinking of Freud" or "the well-known development of South American dictatorships" will never be enough to prove a point. The closer the evidence is to facts, numbers, actual quotations from the text, the better. Demand a thorough analysis of such references as "Freud's notion of the Oedipal complex" or "the strife between the press and the dictatorship of Chile in 1983."

When an author paraphrases rather than quotes another author, be alert. A paraphrase poses tricky questions, since you must trust that it fairly represents the original. Don't just accept it; analyze it. Does the paraphrase sound accurate? Is it enough to make the point believable?

4. Are the sources for the evidence clear? You have the right to know the source of all evidence, and the writer has the responsibility to provide it. We are not suggesting that you look up every reference or follow every footnote. When you hit a surprising or unclear bit of proof, however, pursue it further. If the source is suppressed or vaguely presented, you may begin to doubt the author.

5. Is there enough support? Only you can decide whether the author has presented enough proof to persuade you. Withhold your assent until you feel ready to give it. Sheer quantity is not the criterion, however. Sometimes you will find that good arguments are based on quite scanty evidence; sometimes a flood of facts will not suffice. Look for the intelligent commentary that makes the evidence relevant.

6. Is the evidence clearly linked to the main point? Or do you have to make a great leap to determine how the evidence actually supports the point? When the leap is too great, perhaps the evidence doesn't really fit.

7. So what? The Conclusion

The conclusion is the payoff to the argument. Locate it—it is usually in the last few paragraphs or the last chapter of a book, but some writers offer it in a next-to-last section and then discuss its implications in the final section. And some studies in the social and natural sciences offer conclusions in the beginning and then show how the authors reached those conclusions. Track the conclusion down, and compare it with the thesis. How has the thesis changed in the conclusion? Does the conclusion surprise you? Can you think of alternative conclusions that would follow from the same discussion?

Notice we said "Compare the conclusion with the thesis." Often they are similar; just as often, however, the author has argued the thesis in order to point out a larger significance for his or her piece of writing. The last sentence of Gould's essay on the dinosaur makes an unexpected point:

> Do you know anyone who would wager a substantial sum, even at favorable odds, on the proposition that *Homo sapiens* will last longer than Brontosaurus?

Hardly a person would read that ending without feeling the sudden chill of nuclear anxiety.

Frequently an argument develops from the thesis to the conclusion. Comparing the two is a useful way to keep track of where an argument has led. Here is a very simplified version of the thesis and conclusion of Sigmund Freud's *Civilization and Its Discontents:*

> Thesis: The individual's instincts of aggression and self-destruction inevitably conflict with the prescriptions of civilized life.

> Conclusion: Whether instinct will finally triumph over culture is the fateful question facing the human species.

The thesis and the conclusion are similar, but they harbor a crucial difference. The conclusion suggests that unless controlled, the conflict could lead to great problems. It makes no sense to accept the conclusion unless you understand the thesis and believe that the argument has adequately supported it. Follow that argument.

If you think creatively, you can sometimes come up with a different conclusion from the one the author has drawn. Here is a familiar argument:

> For five years, five rats were forced to breathe in the smoke of x number of cigarettes. Of the five rats, four died of lung cancer. For experimental purposes the physiology of rats is close to that of human beings.
>   Therefore:

Before reading further, imagine some possible conclusions. The results can be enlightening. Here are just a few:

> You shouldn't do things like that to rats.
>
> Any human being who smokes x number of cigarettes a day for five years has a 20 percent chance of survival.
>
> One out of every five rats has a constitution stronger than that of human beings.
>
> Eighty percent of the rat population will not last five years.
>
> Cigarette smoking may cause cancer in human beings.

All these conclusions follow, more or less validly, from some or all of the evidence. The point of imagining alternatives is that *no conclusions are inevitable: all depend on the author's analysis of the evidence.*

8. *Was it all worth it? The Whole Work*

When you have finished reading, sit back and take stock of the book or essay and decide what you think of it. Page back through and pause at important points. Carefully examine the evidence. Think about the definitions. Think about the overall argument: was it closely and persuasively reasoned, or were you forced to make some pretty strenuous leaps across the gaps? Was the conclusion justified? When you read critically and actively, you will be in a good position to evaluate even the most illustrious authors, for you will have a deeper understanding and a more secure memory of what they wrote.

CASE STUDY:
GETTING WRITING FROM READING

Going from reading to writing includes nine steps:

mapping the text

reading and taking notes

rereading and taking more notes

asking the eight questions

forming a thesis

planning the essay

selecting evidence

drafting

revising

In this section we tell the story of how one student, Larry Boyd, read a difficult essay and, by reading critically, was able to turn his reading into a serious and satisfying piece of work. He more or less covered the nine steps, though he raced down a few.

Mapping the Text

In a class on twentieth-century American society, the instructor assigned a paper on Robert Nisbet's essay "Victimology." She said she expected not a paraphrase but a critical evaluation.

In his initial overview, Boyd learned that the essay came from Nisbet's *Prejudices: A Philosophical Dictionary*, a collection of short essays under topics such as "Alienation," "Permissiveness," and "War." According to the blurb, Nisbet has written several books on similar subjects. Boyd learned that Nisbet is Albert Schweitzer Professor of Humanities, Emeritus, at Columbia University in New York. He looked up *emeritus* and discovered it means "retired."

Boyd noticed that the essay was a little over three pages long. It had no headings or questions at the end. As he quickly turned the pages, he picked up important information for mapping ahead: the word *victim* appeared frequently, as did *liberal*. He checked the word *liberal* in the dictionary: "having, expressing, or following political views or policies that favor civil liberties, democratic reforms, and the use of governmental power to promote social progress; having, expressing, or following views or policies that favor the freedom of individuals to act and express themselves as they choose."

Boyd thought he could do a first reading and take notes in about thirty minutes. He gathered three pens—no point having to search around if one went dry—a dictionary, and notecards. He was ready to read and take notes.

Victimology

This word will not be found as yet in most dictionaries and doubtless ₁ will strike the sensitive ear harshly. But so far as meanings go, this word has as much prima facie right to existence as *criminology*, the study of criminals and what they have in common. It only later occurred to students of crime that victims in the aggregate might also be shown to have a good deal in common.

There are those who victimize—dominating parents, older brothers   2
and sisters, employers, police, asylum tenders, and physicians as well as
common ordinary felons. Victimizing comes more easily and naturally
to some than to others in the population. But so does victimhood come
more easily to some than to others. Clinical psychologists assert that
some people need and subconsciously enjoy being victimized, being ex-
ploited, browbeaten, tightly ruled. It is as natural for them to be victims
as for others, of different temperament, to be victimizers.

Although interest in the class characteristics of victims of crimes goes   3
back to the founders of criminology in the nineteenth century, it was
not until the middle of the twentieth century that victimology became a
specialty within sociology and social psychology. The scientific research
conducted so far leaves no doubt that the study of victims of thefts, robberies, rapes, assaults, murders, and other crimes is almost as rewarding
and illuminating as is the study of criminals. The inescapable fact is that
just as there are murderers, so there are murderees. Without victims
there can be no victimizers, and temperaments of certain individuals
have been shown to lead to ways of behavior which come close to inviting victimization, such as theft, rape, or assault. This does not mean
that people conspicuously lacking in the stigmata of victimhood do not
also suffer victimization of every kind. It is simply a matter of statistical
probability. The majority of those who are mugged on the city streets
have in common certain attributes which are less likely to be found
among those never or rarely mugged. In sum, precisely as one cannot
learn all there is to be learned about leadership without attending also
to followership, so with peccadilloes, cruelties, sins of man against man,
and crimes: the victim is as important to a knowledge of crime as is the
perpetrator.

But there is very different and wholly political meaning today to the   4
words *victim* and thereby *victimology*. This meaning is inseparable from
the welfare Leviathans that have been built up in the West during the
last century or two. The source of this meaning is the do-gooder and
uplifter that became widespread in the nineteenth century. Those who
were poor, unemployed, chronically drunk, and even criminal in tendency were, by some sociological legerdemain, decreed to be victims—
of society. This form of thinking allows two victims for any given crime
and no victimizer or criminal. The individual robbed, raped, or slain is
certainly a victim, but so is the robber, rapist, and murderer a victim—
of circumstances, of poverty, of broken family, in sum, of society. Few
things please the liberal heart more than a victim, especially that of society, and when a choice has to be made between the rights of the victim
who was robbed and the victim of society who did the robbing, the
right-thinking humanitarian almost tropistically sides with the latter.

In this special, very modern social sense of victimhood, there can be   5
no end to the process of creating victims. At this moment, at least 75
percent of the American people are victims. From the point of view of
the ardent women's liberationist, all women, or some 51 percent of the
population, are victims. Add the blacks, Hispanics, Indians, farmers ex-

posed to drought, unemployed, mentally disturbed, pupils in the public schools, and many other groups in the population, and even an estimate of 85 percent might seem absurdly low. Wealth and high status are no protectors. A new species of victimhood has just been publicized with excellent market results: children of celebrities. They too must be seen as victims. In wife beating there is manifestly a female victim, but the subtlety of the victimological mind should never be underestimated. The husband administering the beating is also a victim—of childhood, say, in a wife-beating home atmosphere—and cannot properly be held accountable.

Accountable! Human society is ultimately possible only when people are accountable for their actions, that is, responsible. The moron who murders, the poverty-stricken who steals, the clinical sadist who tortures and mutilates, the psychologically disturbed who rapes, the insane who slaughters boys by the dozen after sodomizing them, assassins and would-be assassins of Presidents and other high officials of state—all of these are manifestly the causal agents of their various crimes and are recognized as such. Once they would also have been declared responsible and accountable for their crimes. They would have been duly punished by execution, sometimes in a manner as painful or nearly as painful as that inflicted upon their victims. Punishment would have been swift and public, for punishment can exert its cathartic effect upon a community that has been grievously violated only if the punishment is observable by all. 6

Correctly did Maistre maintain after the Revolution in France that the executioner is the necessary symbol of the social order. If everyone is a victim of some sort, even a Gacy in Chicago who sodomized, strangled, and buried under his house some three dozen boys and men, then there are no criminals. If there are no criminals, there cannot logically be any punishment. Nor can rehabilitation be the goal, since most students of the rehabilitation process, even at its most expert and humane, pronounce it a failure. 7

There is no substitute for punishment in a social order, and that means holding human beings accountable, treating them as human and therefore responsible. Concern for human rights is rampant these days, but a right is possible in the strict sense only for beings who can be rationally regarded as responsible. The celebrated dignity of man oozes away in an atmosphere where man is so little prized for his unique mental and moral qualities as to be classified from the start a victim. Rights, duties, responsibilities, restraints, consciences, moral codes, all of these are visibly softening and decaying under the influence of victimology—no longer a specialty of criminology but a gigantic malaise of Western society. 8

More victims, of a different order, have appeared during the last year or two on the American scene: college students, writers, artists, and musicians. They are all victims, it is said, of the federal government's effort to reach a balanced budget without placing punitive taxes on other citizens. For many years government loans were available to nearly all stu- 9

dents who requested them; often these loans were not paid back, with
government agencies reluctant to prosecute lest they seem to make victims of the delinquent. Now when something of a cut is made in the
funds for loan use, or at least a slight deceleration in the rate of increase
of these funds, thousands of new victims, the middle-class students, suddenly appear.

Similarly, although the budgets of the National Endowments of the   10
Arts and Humanities rose in the fifteen years between 1965 and 1980
from 10 million to around 170 million each, the result has been only to
create more victims, among artists, writers, and musicians. Testimony
before Congress by a best-selling novelist, himself acquainted with grants
by taxpayers, tells the story: "The truth is, if you are going to take away
the lunches of school children, payment to miners with black lung, store
front legal assistance, you might as well cut the budget of poets, artists,
and musicians. You cannot rip up the texture of our national life and
expect it to survive. . . . What does it matter if our theaters go dark or
if the libraries close their doors. . . . I recognize a simple undeniable
eviction procedure in which most of us are the widows and or-
phans. . . . As a writer of fiction, I could not relate or tell of this. I
could not get away with a portrayal of such sanctimonious cruelties."
The entire reason for this bleat was simply that a few million dollars
were to be lopped from the proposed increases in the budgets of the two
endowments. One wonders how Dreiser, Cather, Hemingway, Faulkner,
and Cozzens were able to do their writing in an era when there was no
endowment, or how the scholarship of McIlwain, Kittredge, and their
many peers across the country came about without such endowment.
The truth is that they were victims, and egregious ones for they did not
even know they were victims.

But Americans do now. By the year 2000, the whole of American   11
society will be composed of victims, or so perceived by the prophets of
liberal cant, and perceived no doubt the same way by those aggressive
enemies abroad who in their own Soviet-communist garrison states do
not recognize victims.

Reading and Taking Notes

Boyd's first set of notes read like this:

Paragraph 1—Victims have something in common.

Paragraph 2—Victimizing comes easy to some, victimhood easy to
others.

Paragraph 3—V-ology in mid-20th c.: understanding vic as important as
understanding criminal.

Paragraph 4—"Do-gooder" and "uplifter" consider criminal victim of
society. Libs side vs. society, behave "tropistically" (dictionary says
"reflex action" = dig at libs.)

Paragraph 5—As defined, maybe 85% vics. (Lumping rich kids, women, and minorities = unfair emotional appeal?)

Paragraph 6—says human society possible only when "accountable" = his main idea. Punishment used to be "swift" and "public" and was catharsis for society.

Paragraph 7—Executioner symbol of social order. (Wow!) Rehabilitation a failure (authority for this?)

Paragraph 8—Concern for human rights "rampant," but rights possible only if person responsible (dictionary: a right is "a power or privilege to which one is justly entitled.") Otherwise: "a gigantic malaise of Western society."

Paragraph 9—Even middle-class students and artists called victims of balanced budget.

Paragraph 10—How did writers manage before, when not "victims"? (More irony, or is this sarcasm?)

Paragraph 11—By 2000 even "aggressive enemies" will see us as victims. Scary.

Rereading and Taking More Notes

Boyd read the essay several times, adding to and revising his notes and including some useful dictionary definitions of words such as *stigmata* and *Leviathan*. He jotted down more impressions of the author's attitude, noting that *do-gooder* and *uplifter* make a questionable emotional appeal and that the last paragraph suggests a closed mind. But he thought Nisbet had made some very strong points and was right about holding people responsible.

Eventually, Boyd was ready to answer the eight questions. Being a conscientious student, he wrote out the answers; as a reader, you at the very least should "talk out the answers" to yourself.

Asking the Eight Questions

1. Subject: Thinking people are "victims" of society
2. Purpose: To persuade reader that identifying people this way is dangerous
3. Thesis: Mostly implicit, but the strongest statement of it is:

Rights, duties, responsibilities, restraints, consciences, moral codes, all of these are visibly softening and decaying under the influence of victimology.

4. Main supporting points:

We are almost as interested in victims as in criminals.

Liberals refer to many people as victims of society, including criminals, and so not accountable.

All sorts of political groups see themselves as victims.

Accountability is what makes society possible.

By holding criminals accountable, punishment makes society possible.

As a result of liberal influence, morality is decaying.

5. Asumptions: Nisbet assumes liberals don't distinguish between a poor person and a murderer, and that "do-gooders" only do harm. Does he assume minorities and women aren't victims at all? Ignores bad effects punishment may have on society, like encouraging cruelty.

6. Evidence: Nisbet calls on history, recent events, quotations, a congressional report. Sometimes doesn't document his ideas. Could quote some liberal hearts. Who thinks rehabilitation is a failure? (Does he mean scholars?) He probably knows, but he should name them.

Still, he does bring most of his assumptions to light when he starts talking about accountability. I guess his main assumption that account-ability is about the most important thing in society.

7. Conclusion: If they listen to the liberals, soon all people will con-sider themselves victims. Then Nisbet has this image of the Soviets seeing us as weak in the year 2000.

8. The whole work: I see what he means, and I agree with most of it, though not all. What he says about punishment bothers me. Public executions? But the essay isn't about victims and criminals, but about the bad effect liberals have on society. Provocative. Made me think. Worth reading.

Forming a Thesis

After this analysis, Boyd was ready not to paraphrase but to respond to Nisbet's essay. While reading he had been particularly struck by the fact that the essay was not really about what the title indicated. He didn't have to brainstorm or free write; he had his thesis:

Nisbet's essay is not really about victimology but about liberal ideas and institutions that Nisbet thinks produce such thinking.

Planning the Essay

Boyd turned to his notes. Although extremely useful when we turn reading into writing, raw notes, that is, those taken while reading, are not a good basis for organizing an essay. They follow the shape of the reading, and adhering closely to them usually makes for a poorly constructed essay. Successful essays seize on a significant point and organize the writer's thinking around that. An argument's shape must take priority over the shape of the text.

An outline can help at this point. It allows the writer to devise a general structure and then to place the ideas where they belong. It provides a plan to work by. Here is Boyd's first try at an informal outline:

I. "Victimology" really an ironic attack on "the liberal heart" and the consequences of liberal social views
"welfare Leviathans" (para 4)
victimology appeals to "liberal heart" (para 4)
rehabilitation "a failure" (para 7)
concern for human rights "rampant" these days (para 8)
liberals "bleat" (para 10)

II. Argues for a social order of accountability, punishment for misdeeds, and responsibility
A. Accountability
society "possible only when people are accountable for their actions, that is, responsible" (para 6)
even "moron who murders" should be accountable (para 6)
B. Punishment (enforces responsibility)
"cathartic effect" of punishment (para 6)
used to have punishment "as painful . . . as that inflicted upon their victims" (para 6)
C. Responsibility
without it dignity of man "oozes away" (para 8)
"Rights, duties," etc. (para 8)

III. Much truth in Nisbet's argument
A. Problems with welfare state
B. Inconsistency in society's views of criminals

IV. Some not true
A. Overstates his criticism
B. Executioner a bad symbol: executioner as "necessary symbol of the social order" (para 7)

V. Things not as bad as he says: "garrison states" (para 11)

Selecting Evidence

Notes are the relay station between reading and writing. From our notes we identify our major support, select examples, distill what we need from the text, and remind ourselves of our thoughts. After establishing his outline, Boyd went over his notes and decided what to put where. When our notes are organized according to the plan for the essay, the writing is simpler, almost a matter of filling in the blanks.

Drafting and Revising

After he had reorganized his notes, Boyd went back over his outline. Because he was writing an analytical essay about a difficult work, he knew his writing had to be especially clear and precise. He had to do justice both to Nisbet's thinking and his own thinking. He decided that his thesis statement could be clearer and more precise if he answered the question Why? He began to write. Several drafts later, he had this version.

Victims of Victimology

Robert Nisbet tells us that the recently coined word <u>victimology</u> will probably "strike the sensitive ear harshly." After reading his essay, the reader has little doubt that both the word and the idea strike Nisbet very harshly indeed. He argues that too many Americans consider themselves victims, and as a result society is becoming weaker and weaker. His central target is not victimology as such, but rather the "prophets of liberal cant" who are responsible for such thinking. The liberal viewpoint endangers society, he says, by allowing criminals to escape accountability for their crimes, and this detracts from the rights and dignity of the rest of society.

Nisbet attacks the "welfare Leviathans that have been built up in the West during the last century or two." He also criticizes other liberal causes, including women's liberation, minority rights, and prisoner rehabilitation. He says, for example, that the last is simply a failure.

Nisbet's worst sarcasm is at the expense of the "liberal heart." He never defines what that heart is, but he clearly thinks liberals are too ready to forgive criminals, and this endangers the rest of society. He traces the "sociological legerdemain" of the nineteenth century which first made victimology popular. This way of thinking allowed early liberals to get things backward:

> Few things please the liberal heart more than a victim,. especially that of society, and when a choice has to be made between the rights of the victim who was robbed and the victim of society who did the robbing, the right-thinking humanitarian almost tropistically sides with the latter.

Nisbet would agree with John F. Kennedy's famous "Ask not what your country can do for you—ask what you can do for your country." However, he believes the liberal heart assumes the opposite. This is why, in Nisbet's words, "concern for human rights is rampant these days." For the liberal heart, a right is what society owes the individual, no matter what; for Nisbet, a right is something that places the individual at some obligation to society. Thus, Nisbet has little patience with the liberals who "bleat" about society's victims.

The central passage in the essay concerns Nisbet's idea that "human society is ultimately possible only when people are accountable for their actions, that is, responsible." A society is a group of people bound together by mutual rights; these rights have no meaning if some are allowed to trample upon them and escape responsibility. Thus, everyone must be held accountable, including "the moron who murders, the poverty-stricken who steals." Instead of making excuses for everyone, society should uphold the dignity of its members by punish-

ing criminals, no matter what the explanation behind
their crimes. We can infer that for Nisbet, the opposite is happening today: no one is accountable,
and society is threatened.

Perhaps that is why punishment is the American
institution Nisbet discusses most. Punishment
defends and upholds the dignity of human beings.
Also, it has a "cathartic effect" that helps people
get rid of their outrage and sorrow caused by crime.
He looks back to the days when punishment was "swift
and public" and sometimes "as painful as that inflicted upon [the] victims." Nisbet probably does
not think much of the Constitution's forbidding
cruel and unusual punishment or of the lengthy
trials and long delays that characterize the legal
system today. Above all, he probably thinks that
American society does not punish criminals with a
force equal to their crimes.

Through punishing criminals, society enforces
responsibility. But that is not what is happening
now. With contemporary society's obsession with
victims and deemphasis of responsibility, the actual
rights of the people are diminished. When everyone
is a victim, "the celebrated dignity of man oozes
away":

> Rights, duties, responsibilities, re-
> straints, consciences, moral codes, all of
> these are visibly softening and decaying
> under the influence of victimology--no
> longer a specialty of criminology but a
> gigantic malaise of Western society.

This is the climax of his essay, the place where
Nisbet not only defines victimology but also reveals
that he is really talking about the decline of our
way of life.

Much of what Nisbet says about America is defi-

nitely true. There have been problems with the so-
called welfare state since World War II. Many programs, like Social Security, have grown too large
and cost too much, leading people to question the
ideas that created the programs in the first place.
American society has also shown inconsistency and
unfairness in the way it views criminals and victims, sometimes showing more sympathy for the
criminals.

Nisbet overstates his case, however. The trend
of victimization may just be temporary. Lately, it
seems as if things are swinging back in a direction
Nisbet likes. And I would not accept all the examples he cites of victimology. Many students could
not go to college without financial aid, and needing
financial aid does not mean they think they are victims. Although Nisbet is right when he says that
some people have portrayed women and minority groups
as victims of society, he takes the idea too far.
Most women and minorities do not want to be thought
victims. They only want to get the very rights Nisbet is talking about.

Although I agree that accountability is important to society, he takes the idea too far when he
says "the executioner is the necessary symbol of social order." Few people would want to identify with
such a symbol. Perhaps some other symbol, like the
builder or the teacher, would be better for an accountable society.

If things were really as bad as Nisbet thinks,
we would, he says, be in danger from "those aggressive enemies abroad who in their Soviet-communist
garrison states do not recognize victims." Things
are not that bad. Nisbet ignores the millions of
people who just lead their lives the best way they
can and would never think of themselves as victims.

TIPS FOR CRITICAL READING

- Read critically; that is, participate, analyze, interrogate the text.
- Before starting to read, leaf through the text to get some clues about its most important ideas.
- To help both understanding and retention, take notes on what you read.
- Summarize the main ideas and the most important supporting ideas.
- Use the eight questions to analyze the text.
- Consider the entire argument when you have finished reading.
- Follow the nine steps when writing about reading: map, read and take notes, reread and take more notes, ask the eight questions, form a thesis, plan your essay, select evidence from the text, draft, and revise.
- Let the organization of your argument take priority over that of the text.
- When writing an analytical essay, take special care to write clearly and precisely.

Exercises for Critical Reading

1. In a large general encyclopedia, follow all the steps under "Mapping the Text" for one of these entries: Rabindranath Tagore, Omar Khayyám, Lao-tzu. What is the writer's purpose? What is the article's thesis or organizing principle? Are there hidden assumptions that should have been explicit? What is your overall evaluation of the article? Write a short essay on your reading of this text.

2. In the library you will probably find copies of *Dissent, Policy Review, New Criterion, The Nation,* or *National Review.* Using the eight questions, analyze an article from one of these periodicals. Was the article persuasive? Should the author have added anything or made the assumptions more explicit? Write an essay evaluating the article.

3. Using the *Readers' Guide to Periodical Literature,* the *Humanities Index,* the *Social Sciences Index,* or the index to a major newspaper, locate one article or column for and one against one of the following controversies of the not-too-distant past:

   establishment of a new court just below the Supreme Court to cut down on the Supreme Court's work load
   a constitutional amendment to ensure a balanced budget

the quality of large cultural awards such as the Pulitzer Prize or the Nobel Prize in literature

legalization of cocaine

Analyze the two articles. Would you have preferred a clearer thesis in either? Was the support adequate? Do you think either should have made its underlying assumptions more explicit? Your answers to these questions could take the form of either a short essay or an in-class report.

4. Here are some definitions. What assumptions underlie them? Do you agree or disagree with any of the definitions? Where you disagree, can you come up with your own definition?

Graft: The main element in any smoothly running government
Immorality: What you do that I wish I could do but cannot
Free enterprise: The same thing as greed
Liberalism: The guilty conscience of people who are well off
Conservatism: Defending old ideas in the absence of new ones

5. *Time, Newsweek, U.S. News and World Report,* and the *New York Times* "Week in Review" cover some of the same topics. Choose a topic prominent in last week's news and analyze how it was treated in these four publications. Write an essay on the different treatments.

6

WRITING TO PERSUADE

His gentle reason so persuasive stole
That the charmed hearer thought
it was his own.
JAMES THOMSON (1700–1748)
SCOTTISH POET

In much of your college writing, you will try to persuade your reader to see things your way. In a political science class you may want to persuade your instructor that voting patterns changed in 1980 because of growing affluence. In an American literature class, you may want to argue that the three major characters in Melville's *Billy Budd* represent the three main American national character types. In a history class, you may want to claim that America's participation in the Korean War of 1950–1953 was, or was not, imperialistic.

And after you graduate, you will constantly exercise your skill in persuasion. Lawyers try to persuade juries that their clients are innocent. Engineers and executives try to persuade boards of directors to support their projects. Parents try to persuade school boards, traffic violators try to persuade traffic officers, husbands try to persuade wives and vice versa. The stronger the skill, the more likely the desired outcome.

In *The Uses of Argument*, the philosopher Stephen Toulmin describes how to build a strong argument. Although he uses different terms from those you learned in Chapter 4, he is talking about the same ideas: premises, inferences, enthymemes, and the like. In this chapter we will use Toulmin's terms, but we will indicate when one of his terms has the same meaning as a term we've used previously.

THE BASIC MOVES:
CLAIM, EVIDENCE, WARRANT

Toulmin calls the three basic components of argument *claim, evidence,* and *warrant.* We can illustrate these ideas with an example found in Chapter 4.

James is eligible for the presidency. He was born in Cincinnati, is thirty-eight, and has never been arrested, and any thirty-five-year-old or older nonfelon born in the United States is eligible for the presidency.

This is an argument with a claim (James is eligible for the presidency), a piece of evidence (He was born in Cincinnati, is thirty-eight years old, and has never been arrested), and a warrant (any thirty-five-year-old or older nonfelon born in the United States is eligible for the presidency). The claim makes an assertion; the evidence supports it; the warrant explains how the evidence supports the claim. This a sturdy three-legged stool on which you can rest an argument.

Claim

The claim is the assertion the argument will back up. It is the *conclusion* of the argument. Here are some claims:

Aerosol spray cans should be outlawed.

Cytochrome is important in cell respiration.

All students should take computer science.

Arthur killed Daphne in self-defense.

Claims have two parts: the topic and what is asserted about the topic:

TOPIC	ASSERTION
Aerosol spray cans	should be outlawed
Cytochrome	is important in cell respiration
All students	should take computer science
Arthur killed Daphne	in self-defense

An expository essay contains a large claim—the thesis—that the essay as a whole supports. In the process of supporting the thesis, the writer makes smaller claims, generally supported in a paragraph. There may be several claims within a paragraph, all needing support. Sometimes a single sentence contains a claim and its support:

You better slow down because a policeman is tailing us.

Because a policeman is tailing us is evidence to support the claim *you better slow down.* A good claim tells the audience exactly what is being argued. Only when the claim is clear and unambiguous can the evidence be properly weighed.

Evidence

Evidence is any support for your claim that your audience accepts without further proof: the specific example, the statistic, the fact, the next logical step, the quotation, the shared belief about what is right or good. It is a *premise* for the argument. If the premises are adequate, you can logically infer the claim. Consider the lawyer's argument in Arthur's murder trial.

> Arthur does not deny that he killed Daphne. In fact, several witnesses say they saw the two of them struggling, saw Daphne fall, and saw the gun in Arthur's hand. But it was clearly self-defense. Daphne was out to kill Arthur, and he had to protect himself. Daphne's friend Louella testified that Daphne admitted hating Arthur and said he ought to be done away with. Louella quoted Daphne as saying, "If no one else will do it, I will." And the deed was done with Daphne's gun.

A pretty good case. Each piece of evidence supports the claim: the struggle, the killing, Daphne's statement of her motive, the ownership of the gun. The jury would probably begin to think that, yes, the claim of self-defense is upheld by the evidence.

Arthur's lawyer knows, however, that the prosecutor may question whether the gun was actually Daphne's, and that might undermine the defense argument. So the lawyer constructs a subargument to support the subclaim that the gun was Daphne's.

> The gun, as I say, belonged to Daphne. It had been purchased by her two days before her death. The police found in her handbag a receipt indicating she had charged the gun on her American Express card.

If the prosecutor challenged the signature on the charge receipt, the defense lawyer would have to construct another subargument regarding the signature. Could this go on forever? It could, until the evidence had become so detailed that no further proof was necessary to convince the jurors.

Writing a college paper bears a close resemblance to arguing in a court of law, for it also requires a claim supported with evidence. Suppose we were writing an essay on the poet Robert Frost, and we devised this thesis:

> Although his poems are direct and accessible, Robert Frost himself was a many-sided person, ambitious and competitive, yet kind and generous.

To set out to prove this large claim, we would divide it into subclaims, to be treated separately in a paragraph or two each.

1. Frost's poems are direct and accessible.
2. Frost was extremely ambitious for fame and admiration.
3. He was highly competitive with other poets of his time.
4. But he responded to kindness with kindness.
5. He was generous to students and loving to old friends.

We would now need to develop evidence for each subclaim, just as Arthur's lawyer developed evidence for each subclaim in Arthur's defense. We might, for instance, support the third point this way:

> He was highly competitive with other poets of his time. Edwin Arlington Robinson seemed to give him the most trouble. Even the poet Archibald MacLeish came in for attack. Frost did not hesitate to show disdain for Ezra Pound and Wallace Stevens. He seemed unable to accept the success of his peers.

After providing this series of what could be called subsubclaims, we ask ourselves if in doing so we have reached the common ground or need still more detailed evidence. We examine each subclaim. Standing alone, the sentence

> Edwin Arlington Robinson seemed to give him the most trouble

is too vague. What kind of trouble? Maybe Robinson beat Frost at poker or squash. We add some more evidence:

> for time and again Frost expressed a deep-seated jealousy of him.

But is it clear what kind of jealousy this was? Did they fight over a woman? We need to demonstrate what we mean by *jealousy:*

> Perhaps he thought Robinson's fame was greater than his.

When we provide similar evidence for the other points, we get this:

> He was highly competitive with other poets of his time. Edwin Arlington Robinson seemed to give him the most trouble, for time and again Frost expressed a deep-seated jealousy of him. Perhaps he thought Robinson's fame was greater than his. Even the poet Archibald MacLeish, seldom considered as good as either Frost or Robinson, came in for attack. At a testimonial dinner, Frost so upstaged MacLeish that the audience became hostile. Frost did not hesitate to show disdain even for those whom some consider the most important poets of the era, Ezra Pound and Wallace Stevens. Frost made open fun of Pound and had several heated arguments with Stevens. He seemed unable to accept the success of his peers.

Now we have reached the common ground.

Warrant

A warrant is the glue that holds an argument together. It links the evidence to the claim. It says something like "This evidence supports this claim because . . . "

CLAIM	I think you should join my t'ai chi class.
EVIDENCE	T'ai chi clears the mind and brings peace to the soul.
WARRANT	As an airline pilot, you need a clear mind and a peaceful soul.

Although an argument can be presented in any order, most start with the claim, move straight to the evidence, and wrap things up with the warrant. You can see this pattern in many essays and even in paragraphs.

Because people sometimes have trouble with the word *warrant,* we want to clarify it right off. Its oldest meaning is a "protector" or "defender." It also means "justification or reasonable grounds for an act or belief" as well as "an authorization or assurance or guarantee." In signing a warrant for someone's arrest, the judge authorizes that arrest. In sentencing a criminal, the judge indicates that the crime warranted the punishment. When Ford provides a warrant for a truck, it guarantees that the truck will operate properly.

These meanings are included in Toulmin's use of the term. A warrant in an argument authorizes or provides the justification for linking the evidence to the claim. It guarantees that the claim is supported by the evidence.

CLAIM	Forks were not used in France in the fifteenth century.
EVIDENCE	Paintings of banquets from that period show no forks on the tables or people eating with them.
WARRANT	Contemporary paintings are very good indications of the customs of an age.

Without a warrant to explain why the evidence or premises support the claim adequately, your audience may not understand your argument. The argument in the following example is impossible to follow:

> The most popular soap opera on American television is *Wild Wet Winds of Love.* We know that because fully 76 percent of the viewing public in Wadkins, Florida, watches this program.

What does that prove? the reader wants to know. Who cares about some little town in Florida? Warrant needed:

> And the viewing public in Wadkins, Florida, is a cross section of viewers much like those in the rest of the United States. Thus, a show's popularity there indicates its popularity throughout the land.

Now we have the missing link in the chain of argument. We may or may not accept the warrant, but at least we know why the writer thought the evidence supported the claim.

Sometimes the connection between the claim and the evidence is so obvious that the writer does not need to state it in a warrant:

Someone has been eating my porridge. It's eaten all up.

Perhaps you recognized that this argument is an enthymeme (Chapter 4). The missing warrant is

When my porridge is gone and I didn't eat it, I can safely assume that someone else did.

Not even the bears needed to spell it.

Let's go back to the murder trial, where Arthur's lawyer is constructing a subargument about Daphne's ownership of the gun.

The police found in her handbag a receipt indicating she had charged the gun on her American Express card. The police verified that it was her signature on the receipt.

The lawyer pauses. Is the connection clear? Does he need a warrant? If stated, the warrant would be

Charge receipts are reliable proof of purchase when the signatures on them have been verified.

Deciding not to risk insulting the juror's intelligence, the lawyer moves on to the next point. If you make every single warrant explicit, your audience may find you condescending.

More frequent than overdoing warrants, however, is underdoing them. People often leave out warrants essential to understanding the argument, as in this pair of conflicting arguments:

First Baseball Fan.

| CLAIM | Ty Cobb is the best hitter in baseball history. |
| EVIDENCE | He had a lifetime batting average of .367, the highest of any player. |

Second Baseball Fan:

| CLAIM | Hank Aaron is the best hitter in baseball history. |
| EVIDENCE | He had more total homers, runs batted in, and extra base hits than any other player. |

Both arguments are based on valid evidence, but the claims conflict. How can that be? What is wrong? To get at the problem, we need those warrants:

| FIRST FAN'S WARRANT: | Lifetime average is the best measure of a hitter. |

SECOND FAN'S
WARRANT: Power statistics are the best measure of a hitter.

If these two fans are to resolve their dispute, they will have to argue the validity of their warrants. The warrants would become subclaims, and the two fans would have to provide evidence for each of them. If the fans cannot resolve their differing criteria for the best hitter, they will have to agree to disagree. In the meantime, by presenting their warrants they at least identify the real argument.

When should warrants be stated, and when can they be implicit? When the evidence obviously illustrates the claim, you do not need a warrant. When, however, the connection is at all unclear or complicated, write out the warrant. This decision is, of course, a matter of judgment. In this as in all aspects of expository writing, err on the side of overclarification.

PUTTING THE COMPONENTS TOGETHER: BINDING THE ARGUMENT

So far we have looked at claim, evidence, and warrant as separate building blocks. In an argument, however, they form a unit of continuous thought. The following is a passage from an essay whose thesis is "Computer-aided instruction can be extremely valuable in teaching writing":

> Computers have many advantages over human teachers when it comes to giving the repetitive drills needed to teach writing. Computers are more patient and can run the same drill over and over until the student masters it, something few teachers can endure. Computers can provide instant feedback, which busy teachers often cannot do. Where large classes make it difficult for teachers to gear their instruction to the needs of individual students, computer programs are entirely adaptable to each student's pace. Best of all, they cost almost nothing to operate. 1
>
> A computer really is a video textbook. It presents information on screens rather than on sheets of paper. Students press buttons instead of turning pages or writing down answers. Quizzes appear every few screens to ensure that students are getting the point. If they pass these quizzes, students can go on; otherwise, they must go back, review the material, and take the quiz over. Video textbooks can do anything regular textbooks can do, from drills to the actual teaching of writing. 2
>
> In sum, the computer can engage students' attention and guide their progress without involving a teacher. Thus, it is preferable to today's expensive and often ineffective methods of teaching writing. 3

The first paragraph consists of a claim, evidence, and warrants. The claim appears in the first sentence. The rest of the paragraph is composed of pieces of evidence and warrants connecting the evidence to the claim. Diagramed, the first paragraph would appear like this:

Claim: "Computers have many advantages over human teachers when it comes to giving the repetitive drills needed to teach writing."

First piece of evidence: "Computers are more patient and can run the same drill over and over until the student masters it,"

Warrant: "something few teachers can endure."

Second piece of evidence: "Computers can provide instant feedback,"

Warrant: "which busy teachers often cannot do."

Third piece of evidence: "Computer programs are entirely adaptable to each student's pace."

Warrant: "Large classes make it difficult for teachers to gear their instruction to the needs of individual students."

Fourth piece of evidence: "Best of all, they cost almost nothing to operate."

Warrant: not needed because the connection is obvious. It would insult the intelligence of the reader to say "and human teachers must be paid."

The same ingredients appear in the second paragraph, but in a different form:

Claim: "A computer really is a video textbook."

First piece of evidence: "It presents information on screens."

Second piece of evidence: "Students press buttons instead of turning pages."

Third piece of evidence: "Quizzes appear every few screens."

Fourth piece of evidence: "If they pass these quizzes, students can go on;"

Fifth piece of evidence: "otherwise, they must go back, review the material, and take the quiz over."

Warrant: "Video textbooks can do anything regular textbooks can do, from drills to the actual teaching of writing."

Notice that instead of having a warrant for each piece of evidence, in this paragraph the final sentence is an overall warrant that connects all the evidence to the claim. In writing, then, we need not have one warrant for each piece of evidence, but we do need to be sure the evidence is securely attached to the claim.

The third paragraph might be called a *reinforcing warrant*. It treats as a unit all the evidence and warrants in the first two paragraphs and connects that unit to the thesis of the essay. Stopping to combine paragraphs into summary units like this and then tying each unit to the thesis helps maintain clarity for both reader and writer. (We have more to say about this in "Linking Paragraphs: Using Overarching Strategies" in Chapter 9.)

The process doesn't have to be this mechanical. In most essays, you naturally give warrants as you explain or interpret your evidence. Some evidence, like the bears' missing porridge, is self-explanatory; other evidence calls for *you* to make sense of it, and when you do that, you provide the warrant.

CONSIDERING THE OPPOSITION: BACKING, REBUTTAL, CONCESSION/QUALIFICATION

The claim-evidence-warrant model is fine if you think your audience is open to your line of argument. Careful writers, however, assume skeptical readers, who wait to be convinced. Skeptical readers ask hard questions, demand more evidence if they are not satisfied, and attack weak places in the argument. Writing for a skeptical reader demands three further tools: backing, rebuttal, and concession/qualification.

Backing

Backing shores up a warrant. When you cannot assume your audience will accept that your warrant is true, you need to prove it. To do this, you treat the warrant as a claim that needs evidence.

Suppose you were sick of living in a sloppy dormitory, so you made the following argument in a meeting with college administrators:

> The college should provide janitorial service for the dorms. The dorms are falling apart, and it is costing the college a great deal of money to maintain them. *This high cost of maintenance justifies hiring janitors.*

Skeptical administrators might ask, What have maintenance costs to do with the janitors?

You would need to respond by building an argument around the warrant, italicized in the following paragraph:

> *The high cost of maintenance justifies hiring janitors.* Because of yearlong neglect, dorm rooms are in such serious disrepair that they must be painted and refurbished at the end of the spring term, and this costs nearly $1 million per year. If the college had routine janitorial service, we would not need annual painting and refurbishing.

The administrators might also question the warrant of the argument found in the last sentence here: Why would routine janitorial service make annual painting and refurbishing unnecessary?

You would answer with still more backing:

> *Routine janitorial service would make annual painting and refurbishing unnecessary.* If walls were washed regularly, they would not need painting every year. If floors were swept and carpets vacuumed regularly, they would last much longer.

Backing clarifies and supports weak or unclear connections.

When you use backing, you are not assuming that your audience disagrees with you, only that they hold an understandable skepticism. Rebuttal and concession/qualification, however, presume a doubting or even antagonistic audience. Anyone who wants to convince such an audience— a very common kind—must address their contrary beliefs or opinions.

Rebuttal

Rebuttal is the process of refuting the opposing view. In essence, it says, "People who say *X* are wrong because . . ." Rebuttal demands a great deal of tact because it is aggressive. You want to confront the differing opinion without alienating readers so that they refuse to hear what you say. If you imply that a reader is a fool or a knave, as in these openings, you will fail to persuade:

> Ignorant people would perhaps think . . .
>
> People with bad judgment or ulterior motives would claim . . .

Writers sometimes begin their rebuttals by attributing the erroneous view to some hypothetical group.

> Some people may think . . .
>
> There is a widely held but false view that . . .

More diplomatic writers might go even further.

> Many reasonable people do hold this opinion, even though it has turned out to be mistaken.

Once you have found the right tactful entry into your rebuttal, you face the real work. You must fairly present the opposing claim and then show why it is invalid.

Suppose that in the argument about janitors, the administration has asked you to put your proposal in writing for the board of trustees. In writing the report, you anticipate that the trustees will say something like

> College kids can clean up after themselves. They never had janitors at home—why should they have them in college?

You rebut this point by fairly paraphrasing the opposing claim and acknowledging the evidence on which it rests. If you distort the claim or ignore the evidence, your audience will lose confidence in you.

> Many people may think that students can be made to care properly for their rooms themselves. Certainly, these people argue, the students never had a janitor at home.

Now it is time to erect your counterclaim.

> Our experience, however, indicates that students will not take care of their dorm rooms, no matter how they behaved at home. Three years ago, the college instituted a program of weekly inspections. After one semester, the administration abandoned the program as a failure. There was no good effect, and in fact students, their parents, and faculty complained. Last year the college tried again, providing housekeeping equipment and supplies to each wing of every dormitory. The students agreed to keep their particular wings clean. In one wing the original bottle of cleanser was three-quarters full at year's end. In another, students used the broom to prop open a window. Apparently, whatever action the college takes, the problem persists.

Because the evidence is sufficient, the argument effectively refutes the opposition.

Concession/Qualification

At times all of us have to make concessions. When you cannot find a way to refute the opposition, there is nothing to do but admit it: "You have a good point—I'll give you that one." It would be counterproductive to deny a solid claim just because the opposition has made it. It would be equally useless to hold tenaciously to an untenable position. Just concede the good point and qualify your own claim accordingly: that is, redefine it so that it no longer conflicts with the valid claim the opposition made.

In response to your report about the need for janitors in the dorms, suppose the trustees say,

> Students are, after all, adults and should be fully capable of taking care of their living accommodations. They should be trained to do so.

Now that is a good point. Who would want to argue that students are not adults or are not capable of taking care of their rooms? You'll have to concede these opposing claims and then find a way around them.

> Of course, students ought to be more responsible than they have shown themselves in this matter, but that is a problem for society, not for the school. The issue here is whether janitorial service makes good economic sense.

Figure 6.1 The Full Toulmin Model. This model for a persuasive argument says, in effect, "I have evidence that warrants a claim. Because I anticipate skepticism from my audience, I will provide additional backing for warrants, rebut any conflicting arguments that I can, concede opposing arguments I cannot rebut, and qualify my original claim to account for the concession." Mastering this form can help you conduct a persuasive argument.

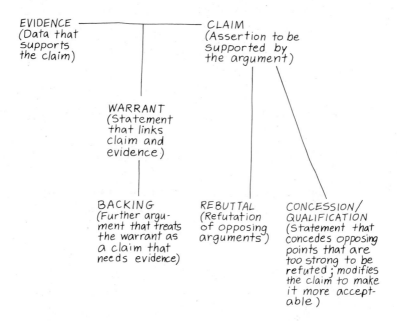

You acknowledge that students should be responsible enough to take care of their rooms and then qualify your claim by limiting it to a point the trustees will accept: dollars and cents. See Figure 6.1 for a full Toulmin model.

CASE STUDY: ARGUMENT IN ACTION

In the following essay, Stephanie Klein bravely argues in defense of the harp seal hunt. Such a controversial and emotionally charged issue required the utmost in reasoning and tact. In order to prepare her backing, rebuttal, and concession/qualification, the writer brainstormed the concerns, objections, and contrary opinions of the opposing side. She came up with this list on her word processor:

```
danger of extinction
immoral or unethical
ecological damage
```

She wrote this essay:

In Defense of the Harp Seal Hunt

The yearly hunt for the baby harp seal has   1
aroused the American public's indignation for over
twenty years. The controversy began after film-
makers distributed across the United States some
powerful film clips of the kill. Seeing the killing
of the seal pups triggered an immediate public out-
cry against the hunters. Supported by celebrities
like Brigitte Bardot, opponents organized a nation-
wide campaign to ban the hunt. Although no doubt
well-intentioned, the opponents of the seal hunt
have been influenced more by emotion than by facts.
If we look at the evidence, we see a different, and
much more complex, picture.

The seal hunt is not a sport but a necessity.   2
The hunters do not kill for pleasure, as perhaps do
hunters of fox and deer and doves. The seal hunt
provides the livelihood of a large population that
has for many generations survived by hunting. "It
is," explained one hunter, "both a cherished tradition and a livelihood" (Lavigne 139). These hunters
are hardly growing rich from hunting. The average
sealer earns from all sources less than $8,000 a
year. To deprive the sealer of hunting income
would reduce this paltry sum by as much as 30
percent. It would remove millions of dollars a
year from an "already depressed Atlantic economy"
(Bryden 69).

Sealing provides not only employment but also   3
essential goods. Contrary to the propaganda, the
hunters do not leave the carcasses to rot on the
ice. Although most of the income to the sealer
comes from selling the fur, much more than the pelt

is salvaged. Both the meat and the oil are pro-
cessed. The hides can be used for boats. As with
the livestock industry, the by-products are almost
as important as the main product.

The fishing industry indirectly benefits from   4
the seal hunt. The seals are a carnivorous species
that consumes schools of fish. Without the hunt,
the fishing industry in this poor area of the world
would be damaged (Lavigne 139).

Despite the economic necessity of the seal   5
hunt, many people argue that it must be stopped, and
they offer several reasons. They argue that the
hunt threatens the harp seals with extinction. If
true, this is a powerful argument. As a nation, we
are determined to protect other species from extinction. The efforts made to save the condor are a
good example. The fact is, however, that the harp
seal is not an endangered species. According to
studies made by the North Pacific Fur Seal Commission and Convention, the seal population has actually increased during the past seventy years and
continues to grow at the rate of 2 percent a year.
In 1911, only 200,000 harp seals had survived the
uncontrolled commercial slaughter at sea. In 1975,
there were over 1.3 million harp seals ("Seals and
Seal Fisheries" 483).

The increase resulted from hunting regulations   6
imposed by the Canadian government. Beginning in
1965, the government established quotas limiting the
number of seals that can be taken each year. In his
book An American Crusade for Wildlife, James Trefethen points out that the Front population of
seals—the herd that winters in Labrador—is now
fully protected against all hunting (326). In the
Gulf of St. Lawrence, sealing is closed to aircraft

and ships over 65 feet in length. Other restric-
tions also apply. Although sealing continues, the
Canadian government closely monitors it (Bryden 69).

Even environmental organizations, quick to pro-   7
tect nature, acknowledge that the seal is not on the
verge of extinction and that the population will
remain stable through regulation of hunting. According to Lewis Regenstein in The Politics of Extinction, many conservation groups "have implicitly con-
doned this and other seal 'harvests' as long as they
are done . . . as part of a sound, rational management program" (87). The harp seal "has not been
classified as an endangered species" (88).

Whether the seals are endangered or not, the   8
question of the cruelty of the hunt remains. Opponents have asserted that the pups suffer unduly, and
indeed are even skinned alive. Anyone who has seen
pictures of these little pups can hardly be unaf-
fected by that argument. But what is the evidence?

The means and the manner of death are also reg-   9
ulated by the Canadian government. The pups are
struck with clubs, and death is almost invariably
instantaneous. The tales of skinning them alive are
untrue. Government agents have inspected hundreds
of baby seal carcasses and found almost all the pups
to be dead before skinning began ("Seal Hunt" 62).
As for the clubbing, it does seem cruel, but Victor
Scheffer, author of A Voice for Wildlife, compares
it to the slaughterhouse and says it is "no worse
than the killing of lambs in an abbatoir" (67).

We can't view the hunting of the seal in isola-   10
tion as a special case. It is part of the larger
issue of the protection of nature and our duty to
other species. We are naturally moved by film clips
depicting cute little seal pups, as we would be by

pictures of lambs and calves. We should never allow
any harmless species to suffer or die simply because
we have technology and intelligence on our side.
Yet surely our compassion must extend in both directions: to the seal that is hunted and to the human
being whose livelihood depends on hunting. Only
when we examine these complex issues coolly——taking
into account all the economic, ethical, and cultural
ramifications——can we expect to arrive at an intelligent understanding.

Works Cited

Bryden, Ronald. "They Impale Bleeding Hearts, Don't
    They?" Maclean's 20 Mar. 1978: 69.

Lavigne, David. "Life or Death for the Harp Seal."
    National Geographic Jan. 1976: 129–142.

Regenstein, Lewis. The Politics of Extinction. New
    York: Macmillan, 1975.

Scheffer, Victor. A Voice for Wildlife. New York:
    Scribner's, 1974.

"Seal Hunt." Life 21 Mar. 1969: 61–63.

"Seals and Seal Fisheries." Encyclopedia Americana.
    1985 ed.

Trefethen, James. An American Crusade for Wildlife.
    New York: Winchester, 1975.

(In her notes and bibliography, Klein used the MLA parenthetical references and list of works cited format. For detailed information on this system, see Chapter 15.)

The first paragraph provides the background and sets up the argument. Notice the subtlety of the thesis in the last sentence of that paragraph. Before making her argument, Klein did not want to arouse the
hostility of the audience by baldly stating the thesis: the seal hunt should
not be banned. Rather, she allows for the good intentions of the opposition
and suggests the need for more evidence. The thesis promises that the
essay will provide that evidence.

In the second, third, and fourth paragraphs, Klein makes her case for
the seal hunt, a case based largely on economic necessity. She provides

hard data regarding employment and the use of the seal remains. In each paragraph she makes a claim, develops evidence, and ties the two with a warrant. In the third paragraph, for instance, the claim is that the seal provides essential goods. The evidence is that the fur is sold, and the by-products—flesh, oil, and hides—can be used. The value of the fur needs no warrant, for we understand that. But Klein warrants the other evidence with "the by-products are almost as important as the main product." Notice, too, the mention of the livestock industry; it will reappear later.

In the next four paragraphs, Klein backs, rebuts, concedes, and qualifies. In paragraphs 5 through 7, she challenges, with data, the idea that the seals are threatened with extinction. She makes a concession: yes, the seals were once threatened, but no more, because the Canadian government now monitors the industry. And she backs up her assertion by referring to evidence from environmental organizations.

In paragraphs 8 and 9, she turns to what is really the heart of the argument: the cruelty of the hunt. She first qualifies her largely economic argument by suggesting that cruelty is an important issue. She then rebuts that argument by providing evidence about the manner of the killing and compares it with slaughtering a lamb.

In the conclusion she suggests, without actually stating it and thus running the risk of alienating her reader, that the opponents of the seal hunt are either hypocritical or intellectually narrow in not placing the issue in its context. Her final, and rather large, concession is that though we must fulfill our obligation to our own species, we must not become cruel, willful tyrants of the earth.

In "Recognizing Rhetoric" in Chapter 3, we suggested that virtually every argument that uses words has an emotional component. Klein certainly recognizes both the rhetoric of her opponents and the need for rhetoric of her own. Her reference to "the killing of lambs in an abbatoir" is an example. The comparison of the seal hunters with sportsman hunters of other animals (in paragraph 2) is another. Even the phrase *the protection of nature and our duty to other species* carries an emotional charge. Klein has argued with reason and with feeling.

TIPS FOR WRITING TO PERSUADE

- Make your claims clear and unambiguous.
- Be sure you have sufficient evidence to support all parts of the claim.
- When the connection between the claim and the evidence is unclear or complicated, provide the warrant.

- If a connection seems weak, supplement it with backing.
- Anticipate the opposing arguments and provide rebuttal.
- When an opposing idea is too strong to be denied, concede the point and qualify your argument accordingly.
- After completing a draft, check to be sure you have used claim, evidence, warrant, backing, rebuttal, and concession or qualification as appropriate.

Exercises for Writing to Persuade

1. Choose either the affirmative or the negative of one of the following claims:

   Creationism should be taught in high school along with evolution.
   Pay television should be censored.
   The government should decriminalize possession of marijuana.
   The state should help finance parochial schools.

   List points of evidence to support your position and all the opposing points you can think of. Now try to rebut each point on both lists. Write a paragraph accounting for any discrepancies or failure to rebut. With the opposing points in mind, qualify your claim.

2. Here is a list of claims, each of which is paired with a piece of evidence:
   a. Dolphins should be considered equal to human beings. They have their own language.
   b. Shakespeare must not have been interested in women. His female characters are not drawn in detail.
   c. The Beatles were better musicians than Elvis Presley. They sold more records than Elvis did.
   d. We must all start learning Chinese. Otherwise we cannot hope to understand China.
   e. Women should not wear the same clothes as men. If both sexes dress alike, we won't be able to tell them apart.

   What is the implied warrant for each argument? Is it persuasive? If the warrant needs backing, provide it.

3. Here is a claim followed by supporting statements. Which statements would a reader accept as evidence, and which require more proof? Explain. *Claim:* This institution should discontinue participation in intercollegiate football.

   Evidence:

   a. Played through out the United States, football is a brutal sport.
   b. Our school should not give even tacit approval to anything brutal.
   c. Players often are injured during games.

d. Few if any people like to see players injured.

e. Only players benefit from whatever character building football provides.

f. Studying history also can build character for all students.

g. Basketball has become a dangerous contact sport.

h. Playing in or watching football games may distract students from important intellectual pursuits.

i. The school may be liable for injuries incurred during practice or games.

4. From the following list of topics, choose one that you and a partner disagree about.

All students should be required to take computer science.
All students should be required to take a foreign language.
Playing radios and stereos should be forbidden every evening between seven and ten o'clock and after midnight.
Automobiles should be excluded from campus.

Write an essay stating your belief and providing an argument. Try to anticipate what your partner will say. Exchange essays. Now revise your essay, backing, rebutting, and conceding or qualifying on the basis of what your partner wrote.

5. Write an essay in which you argue for one side of one of the following controversies:

A terminally ill patient should/should not be allowed to end his or her life.
Taxpayers should/should not be able to withhold part of their taxes when they are dissatisfied with government actions.
Female reporters should/should not be allowed access to male locker rooms following sports events.

Provide three reasons why you think the way you do; give an example for each. These reasons will now become the main supporting points for your chosen thesis. Provide at least one claim of fact and one claim of value to support each reason. (See "Facts or Values" in Chapter 4.) Accompany these claims with one sentence each of further explanation.

6. Here is a passage of argumentative writing. Read it closely and analyze the structure of the argument.

Photographing is essentially an act of nonintervention. Part of the horror of such memorable coups of contemporary photojournalism as the pictures of a Vietnamese bonze reaching for the gasoline can, of a Bengali guerrilla in the act of bayoneting a trussed-up collaborator, comes from the awareness of how plausible it has become, in situations where the photographer has the choice between a photograph and a life, to choose the photograph. The person who intervenes cannot record; the person who is recording cannot intervene. Dziga Vertov's great film, *Man with a Movie Camera* (1929), gives the ideal image of the photographer as someone in perpetual movement, someone moving through a panorama of disparate events with such agility and speed that any intervention is out of the question. Hitchcock's *Rear Window* (1954) gives the complementary image: the photographer played by James Stewart has an intensified relation to one event, through his camera, precisely because he has a broken leg and is confined to a wheelchair; being temporarily immobilized prevents him from acting on what he sees, and makes it even more important to take pictures. Even if incompatible with intervention in a physical sense, using a camera is still a form of participation. Although the camera is an observation station, the act of photographing is more than passive observing. Like sexual voyeurism, it is a way of at least tacitly, often explicitly, encouraging whatever is going on to keep on happening. To take a picture is to have an interest in things as they are, in the status quo remaining unchanged (at least for as long as it takes to get a "good" picture), to be in complicity with whatever makes a subject interesting, worth photographing—including, when that is the interest, another person's pain or misfortune. (Susan Sontag, *On Photography*)

Write an essay in which you identify the passage's main claim, evaluate the evidence it puts forward, and discuss the warrants that tie the claim to the evidence—remember, some of the warrants may be implicit, and you will need to put them in your own words. In your conclusion, evaluate the argument as a whole. Do you agree or disagree? Which pieces of evidence are especially convincing or especially weak? Which warrants are especially strong or especially questionable?

7. Here are opposing arguments from interviews in the *New York Times* on the issue of police decoys, that is, disguising police officers in order to trap suspects in criminal acts. Analyze both arguments for effective persuasion, claim, evidence, warrant, backing, rebuttal, concession and qualification. Also, evaluate the use of emotion in the arguments. Write an essay taking the same general position as the side you support, but include a rebuttal of all the points the opposition made and, if necessary, conceding points you cannot rebut.

I think decoy squads, even well trained and well supervised, eventually self-destruct. This is a result, in most cases, of the inevitable pressure to produce when there is this much investment in personnel and resources in what usually turns out to be not an extremely productive squad. You have four or five officers on a detail, spending one set of tours at least and probably more, five days a week, conducting operations which result in sometimes several but other times not so many arrests. And there is an inevitable, inexorable pressure to justify that expenditure.

Regrettably, the only way the police have traditionally attempted to justify that enormous expenditure is through arrests. Consequently decoy squads are under pressure, at the end of a week when there have been few arrests, to move toward entrapment, toward framing somebody, toward "flaking" [that is, planting evidence on] somebody.

They usually think they can get away with it and they usually can get away with it, because it's four or five officers' words against one suspect, who's usually picked because he or she is vulnerable. But sooner or later that sort of scam catches up with the decoy squads, just as it did in the mid-1970's when the "dollar collars" scandal ended the last transit decoy squad. That's when kids were lured by dollars hanging out of decoys' pockets.

There's concern at this point over evidence of alleged flakes of suspects, where valuables are planted on arrestees by decoy officers, and robberies are staged between decoys to rope in an innocent bystander who's the target and has the goods dumped on him by one of the decoys posing as the mugger.

The tragedy of the decoy squad is that if improper arrests are made, it is extremely difficult to defend against them. Any defendant caught up in a decoy scam stands almost no chance at all. There's this large number of cops, and their testimony will be tailored, given their extensive training and understanding of the entrapment laws, to obtain a conviction. and the target will often be a person with a criminal record, even though he or she did not commit this particular offense.

There is also something just fundamentally offensive about cops creating crime. Obviously, targeting people who are predisposed to criminal conduct is a desirable law enforcement technique. It's efficient, and it protects the public. But creating temptations that are often questions of instantaneous judgment for the target, where it's extremely ambiguous as to what the target's intent really was at the time he or she was arrested, is a very, very troubling side of police work, and really walks on the precipice of a violation of due process.

(Richard D. Emery, former staff counsel to the New York Civil Liberties Union)

It's better that the crime victim be a trained officer with a backup team than an innocent citizen walking the streets or the platforms of the subways. That's why the decoys were put in there. They're put in where there have been a lot of reports of crime. I would expect that on a referendum it would get 99 percent of the vote.

It's also very strong from a legal standpoint. You've got a police officer who's trained. You've got an ironclad case, as opposed to a citizen who may not have seen the person, who may be afraid to follow through and make a complaint. So, with the police officer, it's the same as with a drug sale. If you sell to an undercover officer, you've got an ironclad legal case.

It's also a theory called proactive policing, as opposed to reactive policing. All progressive police administrators today try to be proactive. Instead of waiting around for things to happen, they go out where the numbers say there is a lot of crime. If the numbers say a lot of businesswomen are getting mugged, you might put a female officer out there with a briefcase.

It is dangerous, even with a backup team. The perpetrator can get in some pretty good licks. But you're doing something about preventing crime, rather than waiting and writing a report on it. My basic quarrel with the extreme civil liberties point of view is that most everything they've been criticizing is good, solid, sound police work. If it's done in the wrong way, the answer is not to say, ''Let's abolish it.''

The basic principle is that these things are not some weird idea that somebody thought up. They're based on standard police practices. And if you posit the idea that there are crime problems in the subways, and I think everyone would agree that there are, then the way you deal with it is with standard police practices.

A police force is created to maintain order and protect people against crime, and it isn't always going to come out neat and sweet. Most cases are not 100 percent clear-cut either way. A lot of them are judgment calls. Certainly there are ethical difficulties. The rule has always been that you're not supposed to flash money. The standard on entrapment is you're not supposed to persuade people to commit a crime who would not have committed a crime otherwise.

(Thomas Reppetto, president of New York City's Citizens' Crime Commission)

7

USING EVIDENCE

Some circumstantial evidence is very strong,
as when you find a trout in the milk.
HENRY DAVID THOREAU **(1817–1862)**
AMERICAN WRITER AND NATURALIST

Although we discussed evidence as part of an argument in Chapter 6, we are now going to examine evidence more closely in its own chapter. We have three reasons for this special treatment. First, evidence will take up the bulk of your argument essays. For a single claim, you may need to present two, three, or perhaps four pieces of evidence. Second, handling evidence well is essential. The processes of gathering, evaluating, interpreting, and defending evidence are major parts of any college work. Third, evidence is extremely varied and therefore complicated. In an essay on the effect of pollution on southern California's ecology, for instance, you would certainly call on expert testimony to analyze the situation, statistics to indicate the rate of increase in pollution, examples of damage, and perhaps other kinds of evidence as well. What evidence you use will depend on what you are trying to prove and to whom.

In the following pages, we discuss seven kinds of evidence available and how to use them.

EXPERT TESTIMONY: LEARNING FROM THOSE WHO KNOW

Learning to evaluate experts and what they have to say is one of the most important goals of education. All our lives, our opinions and even our values and actions are shaped by experts—the doctor, the lawyer, the engineer, the secretaries of the treasury, state, defense. These experts will not always agree with one another. One lawyer may advise suing, another negotiating. One foreign policy expert says we should send financial aid to Country *Y*, another says absolutely not. Most of us have not had legal training, and few will know much about Country *Y*. We have to rely on experts.

What is an expert? An expert is someone who has special skill and knowledge based on careful study and wide experience in a certain area. More than that, an expert has tested his or her skill and knowledge in a public forum—through books, articles, performances, lectures, debates— where other experts can challenge any idea or opinion. Expertise must be able to survive public scrutiny. Clearly, the testimony of self-styled experts carries little weight. Albert Einstein did not achieve the status of authority until other scientists found evidence for his theory of relativity in their own calculations and experiments. Gregory Bateson became an expert in anthropology by first doing fieldwork and then publishing his findings so that other anthropologists could examine them.

Many assignments in college will test your ability to use expert testimony. An economics instructor could ask you to write an essay on monetary theorists. An Asian history instructor could assign a study of the various interpretations of the 1899–1900 Boxer Rebellion in China. They will want you not merely to condense and repeat what the experts say but to evaluate it and then use it to help you form your own opinion. Once your opinion is firm, you can use expert testimony to support it. To use expert testimony wisely, be both respectful and critical.

You will need to differentiate among three kinds of evidence that experts provide: facts, informed opinions, and speculations. First are *facts*. Facts are incontrovertible: anyone investigating a subject would come up with the same facts, the same numbers, the same report.

The United States has experienced inflation almost steadily since 1776.

Until recently, bacteria were a genuine household threat.

If you use only recognized experts, you can rely on the validity of the factual evidence they supply.

Experts become experts not only by knowing facts but also by developing *informed opinions* about them; this is the second kind of evidence they provide. Facts need the play of the human intellect to give them significance. Careful experts constantly bring facts together and interpret them. When a scholar or professional concludes that the facts justify a particular generalization, you can use that generalization as support for your claim. It is not quite a matter of "If Professor *X* thinks so, it must be so"—Professor *Z*, also an expert, may disagree. But if Professor *X* thinks so, then that does carry some weight. For instance, the historian A. J. P.

Taylor's opinion that the major factor leading to the end of World War I was a revolution in Germany lends considerable, if controversial, strength to any argument advancing the same point.

The third kind of evidence experts offer can be dangerous for the unwary to use. It is *speculation,* neither contradicted nor adequately supported by the facts. As do the rest of us, experts like to project their ideas beyond provable limits. Often this imagining opens up new areas for research and study and may give rise to new facts. But speculation is only what one person, albeit an expert, thinks is plausible. It should be treated as merely a suggestion, a hypothesis, something that *could* be true.

When experts speculate, they qualify their hypotheses with words and phrases such as *perhaps, seems, may be, conceivable, possibly.* It is up to the reader to notice those qualifiers and to use the statement accordingly, that is, not as a claim or as an interpretation but as a conjecture.

Check the credentials of any authority you cite. Find out the background and the source of his or her expertise. Assess the range and breadth of any bibliographies provided at the end of articles or books. Check for possible bias—a scientist employed in industry may be slow to find harm in his or her company's products, and a scholar holding a government post may have lost some objectivity. Be aware, too, that their opponents could be equally biased. Be particularly careful with eyewitness accounts in which the observer has a stake in what happened. For example, you should check the official account of the 1966–1976 Cultural Revolution in China against the descriptions by experts with other political and cultural viewpoints. The same goes for the CIA account of its activities in foreign countries.

STATISTICS AND SAMPLES: THE MAGIC OF NUMBERS

Whether they are raw data or translated into charts and figures, numbers are powerful evidence. Properly used, they can prove a claim rapidly and conclusively. Understanding numbers has become essential to a college education. It is basic to the sciences and the social sciences and is increasingly important to disciplines such as history.

Statistics are numerical data gathered and tabulated to yield significant information. Statistical data can be used in many ways. An investigator who had collected a mass of data on grades in a chemistry class, for instance, could construct from it a graph in the form of a curve. At one end of the curve would be the highest grade and at the other end the lowest. If the curve is a bell curve, a gradual increase of numbers would appear from the lowest grade to the middle grade and then a gradual decrease to the highest. Most students, that is, would fall in the middle, where the curve bulges. Or the investigator could compare each individual's performance with that of the rest of the class by placing him or her at the appropriate place on the curve.

An investigator could also determine the performance of the statistically average student. There are three ways to do this. To compute the *mean,* you add all the grades and divide the total by the number of students. To compute the *median,* you find the grade in the exact middle of the range from highest to lowest. Half the grades would be above the median, half would be below. To compute the *mode,* you determine what grade the greatest number of students achieved. When dealing with averages, pay close attention to which of these methods is used, for computing the mean, median, and mode will render different results.

Scientists often use the technique called *sampling* to discover the typical acts, beliefs, characteristics, or qualities of a very large population. Rather than trying to interview or test each individual, the investigator studies a representative number in a group. This is the technique used by Gallup polls. To discover what the American public thinks about an issue, Gallup poll-takers interview a small representative group of Americans.

The problem arises in selecting the individuals to be studied because they must truly represent the group as a whole. The findings of a study on what Americans think about pornography on cable television, for example, would be distorted if the proportion of pornography watchers in the group studied was higher than in the general population. The result would almost certainly indicate a higher percentage of approval than is the case. Be sure any sampling data you use comes from a representative group.

Numbers can mislead the unwary. Say you are going to write an essay on unemployment. In your research you find a graph in a reputable journal indicating that *X* million Americans are presently employed, the largest number of workers in America's history. You would perhaps conclude from this that unemployment is not a problem. But then you read in another reputable journal that *Y* percent of Americans are presently out of work, the largest percentage since 1940. Based on this evidence, you would perhaps conclude that unemployment is in fact a serious problem. Both journals are correct. The problem is that different ways of calculating the numbers tell different stories.

Deep down most of us still believe in the magic of numbers. We trust them. But alas, nothing obscures the truth more effectively than numbers misused. Fifty million Frenchmen can't be wrong, says the song. If polls say Senator Smith will be defeated, why bother to vote? Cite numbers, yes, but handle with care.

EXAMPLES: BEING SPECIFIC

Every day of your life you use examples as evidence for your claims. You might say, "*King Kong* has some marvelous scenes. In one scene, Kong is on top of the Empire State Building and the whole thing is swaying." Or you might write to your parents, "Sorry I haven't written much but I've been very busy. I spent last week in the library, bent over the books studying for two midterms." In each case, you establish your claim ("*King Kong* has some marvelous scenes," "I've been very busy") and you back it up with a specific example.

Examples serve three purposes. First, they clarify meaning. Your parents may not know exactly what you mean by *busy* until you show them. Second, examples demonstrate why, at least in one instance, you are justified in making your claim. Studying for two midterms does sound like being busy. Third, examples make for entertaining reading. Abstractions are dry. Claiming that you are busy isn't very interesting. But the image of you bent intently over a book probably pleases your parents, who may now forgive you for not writing.

We wish we could offer a rule about how many examples you need to prove what, but of course the number varies. The best we can say is, err on the side of abundance, but don't exhaust your reader.

PERSONAL EXPERIENCE: WHAT YOU KNOW ON YOUR OWN

If we actually experience something directly, we don't need experts or statistics to back us up. We saw the robber running from the scene of the crime. We know people lose contact with high-school friends. Although we know that our experience is not totally reliable—the robber turned out to be a cocker spaniel—until proven wrong, we trust our senses and our ability to understand our personal experience.

In complex matters, however, beware of jumping to conclusions based on limited personal experience. One occurrence does not make an immutable law. Your experience may help to explain, but it cannot prove a more general thesis. Knowing someone who cheats on her income tax does not prove that the problem with income tax cheaters is pervasive. Even if you know five or ten or twenty cheaters, all that proves is that you are unlucky in your acquaintances. For such a complex subject, you need more than personal experience. You need statistics and expert interpretation.

Personal observation can be useful, nonetheless. In an essay opening it may sharply focus your argument. In a conclusion it may sum up points more emphatically than further exposition. Throughout an essay it may powerfully illuminate facts and figures. Personal experience may not prove much, but it makes for lively reading.

ANALOGY: SHOWING HOW THINGS ARE SIMILAR

An analogy is a comparison of apparently dissimilar things, and its purpose is to illuminate one thing by showing how it is like and not like the other. To the extent that analogies make a point easy to see, they are evidence. But they don't prove the point—they can never be sufficient evidence for a complex idea. A student wrote an essay on World War II in which she wanted to suggest that General Eisenhower functioned as coordinator of the armies in the European theater rather than as strategist, tactician, or field commander. She constructed this analogy:

> Eisenhower served as the conductor of the invasion of Europe. He did not write the music or play an instrument, but he selected the music and the musicians, determined the interpretation, kept the beat, and then evaluated the whole performance.

Although this analogy does not prove that Eisenhower was only the co-ordinator, it clarifies what the student wanted to say. Because she had other powerful evidence, the analogy drove the point home.

Problems may arise, however, when writers either ignore or suppress differences that invalidate the analogy. Analogies can be weak, unclear, or false depending on how damaging the differences are.

> We can view the African practice of sister trading to be exactly analogous to conversation, the trading of words.

This analogy is false: conversation is portable and repeatable in a way a sister is not, and it has no inherent right to be treated with dignity and consideration.

Sometimes a writer uses an analogy indirectly to argue a point the reader would not otherwise agree with, as here:

> Human beings in society are like the bees in a hive. Each person's identity is determined by his or her function and place in the overall system. Like drones, no one has any identity apart from the work he or she does. If people do not work or refuse to conform to the role the system has assigned them, they, like weak or unfit bees, should be thrown out of the system to live or die on their own.

Hey, wait a minute. Analogies are valid only when the two things compared are clearly similar, which beehives and human society are not. The difference between bees and human beings is too great. Think of dissimilarities, and keep your eye on where an analogy will lead you.

KNOWN FACTS AND SHARED BELIEFS: WHAT WE ALL HAVE IN COMMON

When writing, you can safely assume that you and your reader share a vast body of facts and beliefs. You do not need to provide evidence for things your reader already knows or believes. You do not need to point out that Columbus arrived in America in 1492, that Theodore Roosevelt was once president, that fascism is evil. No one wants to waste time and eyesight reading that sort of thing.

But generally known facts can be effective when used in a surprising context.

> Columbus presumably brought civilization to the Western Hemisphere in 1492, but the Mayans knew mathematics and astronomy and practiced urban planning long before that.

Juxtaposing this generally known fact with less familiar information about the Mayans can underscore our cultural bias. Or you might write,

> We all believe fascism is evil, but what do we believe about social programs that incarcerate unwilling bag ladies in overnight shelters?

Here, reference to the truism about fascism aggressively questions some elements of our liberal, democratic tradition. When we appeal to known facts and shared beliefs, we strengthen our point.

REASONING AND LOGIC: THINKING IT THROUGH

Sometimes the only evidence you bring to bear is your ability to reason and employ logic. If, say, your instructor asked you to respond to Plato's *Apology* or John Stuart Mill's *On Liberty,* he or she would want to know about these works. The only relevant evidence would be your reasoning. In Chapter 4, we discussed the basic ways of reasoning. Here, we just want to point out that in your arsenal of evidence, thinking itself is a very powerful weapon.

CRITERIA FOR GOOD EVIDENCE: MAKING SURE

Solid evidence of every variety exhibits the following five qualities: relevance, representativeness, accuracy, detail, and adequacy.

Relevance

Good evidence speaks directly and unequivocally to the point. You should select a particular piece of evidence because it supports the point, not because it is novel or comic or elegant. In discussing similarities between the foreign policies of Presidents Nixon and Carter, for instance, describe their attitudes toward Israel, for they are relevant. Don't present evidence that the two men are sixth cousins—even though a genealogist claims they are. Their possible kinship is irrelevant. Be sure your evidence speaks to the topic.

Representativeness

Evidence should fairly represent its source or the situation it describes. Sometimes writers ignore large segments of relevant information in order to make a point, as this one did:

> The people of California enjoy an incredibly high standard of living. Malibu has one of the highest concentrations of wealth in the world.

The writer misrepresents the situation by ignoring much poorer cities such as East Palo Alto, San Jose, and Fresno. Be sure you let your reader know the full context of any material you use.

Accuracy

The writer is responsible for the accuracy of all evidence. Even if evidence appears to be from a bias-free source, cross-check it with other sources. In writing a paper about America's economic condition, don't rely only on *Time* or the *New Republic* or *National Review* or *Partisan Review* or even the *New York Times* or the *Los Angeles Times*. Verify the facts.

Detail

The closer your evidence is to the concrete—facts, numbers, quotations from a text—the more believable and acceptable it is. If you were describing the ill effects of working around asbestos, you might write,

Of hundreds of asbestos workers studied in the 1970s, more than a third were dying of cancer.

But how much more potent to do what Paul Brodeur did in "The Asbestos Industry on Trial":

Dr. Selikoff and his colleagues at Mount Sinai had continued to observe the cause of death among an original group of six hundred and thirty-two asbestos insulators they were studying, and by 1976 a broad picture of the asbestos-disease toll among them had become tragically clear. Nineteen percent of them were dying of lung-cancer; nine percent were dying of gastro-intestinal cancer; eight percent were succumbing to mesothelioma; and nine percent were being killed by asbestosis and other noninfectious lung diseases.

This level of detail is more effective than paraphrase or summary. Except where space dictates otherwise, provide the poet's own words, the pollster's charts, the Health Department's statistics. Then interpret them.

Adequacy

No one can state a general rule for the appropriate quantity of evidence. We think lavishness is preferable to stinginess. But choose your places to be lavish. Your supporting points that most importantly support your thesis deserve the most detailed and concrete substantiation. Your second-level points need evidence, too, but don't let them overshadow more important ideas. Your third-level points are lucky to be there at all. And don't be sentimental: if you can't make the evidence fit the idea, let the idea go. In the end, the best way to determine whether or not you have enough evidence is to ask a familiar question: Would a reasonable member of my intended audience be convinced? Once again, put yourself in the reader's place.

TIPS FOR USING EVIDENCE

- When examining what experts say, distinguish facts from informed opinions and speculation.
- Be careful when using statistics: they can be dangerous.
- Use examples to clarify meaning, demonstrate why, or entertain your reader.
- Use personal experience sparingly.
- Remember that although they can clarify a point, analogies cannot prove anything by themselves.
- Use known facts and shared beliefs to highlight a point.

- Remember that reasoning can provide powerful evidence.
- Be sure your evidence exhibits relevance, representativeness, accuracy, detail, and adequacy.

Exercises for Using Evidence

1. Read the following paragraph:

   I suspect that any new religions that appear in the '80s and '90s will have the computer figuring prominently in them, just as some of the religions of the '60s and '70s have been built around the image of the flying saucer. In some it will play a Satanic role, and it is conceivable that any anti-computer movements of the future will have a mystical—and therefore particularly dangerous—thread running through them. Once again there are straws in the wind. The "down with Western technology" and "back to the fundamental religion" movements which are at this time of writing wracking Iran, Turkey, and Pakistan seem to be manifestations of a more general disquiet but perhaps, unconsciously, *all* human beings deeply resent the advance of science and the inhospitable view of the universe that it is painting, and yearn for a more primitive view of things. These feelings of resentment are only surfacing at the moment in countries where technology is a recent import, but they may in due course surface in the heavily mechanized West, in which case the '90s would turn out to be unexpectedly turbulent. But there also remains the real chance that computers will be seen as deities, and if they evolve into Ultra-Intelligent machines, there may even be an element of truth in the belief. (Christopher Evans, *The Micro Millennium*)

   How much credence would you give each kind of evidence the author brings forward? Which elements are fact? informed opinion? speculation? Write a paragraph about the passage in which you evaluate the persuasiveness of its evidence.

2. Write an essay in which you interpret the following examples and statistics concerning the crime rate in Bodie, California, a frontier town that boomed in the late 1870s and early 1880s.

   Fistfights and gunfights were regular events.
   Stagecoach holdups were not unusual.
   The old, the young, the weak, and the female were generally not harmed.
   In modern American cities, the old, the young, the weak, and the female are often the objects of crime.
   There were 11 stagecoach robberies in Bodie between 1878 and 1882, and in 2 instances passengers were robbed. Highway robbers usually took only the cashbox carried on the coach.
   There were only 10 robberies and 3 attempted robberies of individuals in Bodie from 1878 to 1882.
   Bodie's total of 21 robberies over a five-year period converts to the rate of 84 robberies per 100,000 inhabitants per year.
   New York City's robbery rate in 1980 was 1,140 per 100,000 people; Miami's was 995; and Los Angeles's was 628.
   The rate for the United States as a whole in 1980 was 243 per 100,000 people.

Between 1878 and 1882 there were 32 burglaries in Bodie; 17 were of homes and 15 were of businesses.

At least 6 of these burglaries were thwarted by the presence of armed citizens.

Bodie's burglary rate for those five years was 128 per 100,000 inhabitants.

Miami's burglary rate in 1980 was 3,282 per 100,000 people; New York's was 2,661; Los Angeles's was 2,602.

The crime rate for the United States as a whole in 1980 was 1,668 per 100,000 people.

In the relevant period in Bodie, only one woman, a prostitute, was robbed; there were no rapes.

Thirty-one people in Bodie were shot, stabbed, or beaten to death from 1878 to 1882.

The homicide rate was 116 per 100,000 inhabitants per year.

In 1980, Miami led the nation with a homicide rate of 32.7 per 100,000 people; Las Vegas was second with 23.4.

The homicide rate for the United States in 1980 was 10.2 per 100,000 people.

The majority of Bodie's residents were young, single males.

Courage was the most admired characteristic.

Alcohol was heavily imbibed.

Most of the young men carried guns.

Most of the shootings in Bodie between 1878 and 1882 involved willing combatants. (Based on Roger D. McGrath, ''The Heritage of the Frontier'')

3. What kinds of evidence are represented by the following?

If the efficiency of the car had improved at the same rate as that of the computer over the last two decades, a Rolls-Royce would cost about three dollars, would get 3 million miles per gallon of gas, and would deliver enough power to propel an ocean liner.

The notion that the best way to avoid war is to destroy nuclear weapons goes against common sense.

A baby chimpanzee far outstrips a human infant in the rate of development of its motor ability, reflexes, and physical coordination.

We once lived next door to some Somalis. Their house, was of course, always dirty.

Evaluate the quality of the evidence. Write a statement that each item could be used to illustrate. Now decide if you would need another illustration to make the point. If so, provide it (make it up if you must). Make the whole into a paragraph.

4. Find the answers to three of these questions:

What is the dollar-and-cents value of the human body?

What were the numbers and national origins of immigrants to America between 1900 and 1910?

In which countries is French the official language, and how was it established in each?

What area in the United States had the highest cost of living in 1980, and what area had the lowest? (Be sure to explain how the term *cost of living* is defined.)

What professional basketball team's players received the highest average salaries in 1988, and how did their salaries compare with the average salaries of players on the best-paying teams in football and baseball?

Describe how the statistics or facts in your answers were arrived at. Explain and define any statistical concepts you came across in your research.

5. Write an essay in which you use personal experience to support or attack one of the following statements:

Americans allow their children's adolescence to continue too long.
Memory is a crucial social asset.
Most people pay more attention to their bodies than to their brains.
A high-school education has no practical value and is only a way of keeping young people off the street and out of the job market.

Be sure you tie your experience directly to your thesis statement. In a separate paragraph, indicate how much credence you believe the experience deserves. If the statement needs further evidence, what kind should it be and where would you find it?

6. Using as many different kinds of evidence as you can, write an essay about your family. If you have the information, go back three generations. Include date and place of birth, age, sex, national origin, and occupation for each family member mentioned. In your last two paragraphs, speculate on the future you see for the family as a whole. Base your speculation on the evidence presented in the essay.

PART THREE

The Heart
of the Matter:
The Paragraph

8

THE STRUCTURE OF THE PARAGRAPH

Sentences are not emotional but paragraphs are. . . . I found this out first in listening to Basket my dog drinking.

GERTRUDE STEIN (1874–1946)
AMERICAN WRITER

Writers use paragraphs to help their readers. The paragraph break allows a pause for the eye and for the mind. During that pause, however brief, the reader can absorb what the previous paragraph said and take a breath in readiness for the next. The paragraph also serves to package the writer's ideas. It indicates units of thought. It marks the completion of one idea and the promise of another. Knowing how to shape a paragraph is essential to good writing.

Many people, however, write paragraphs by charging ahead in a straight line, one sentence after another, not one look back until they run out of words or their fingers get tired. Then they draw a deep breath, indent five spaces, and start up again. This may be fine for a first draft, when we are still sifting ideas and discovering what we want to say, but it won't do for a finished essay. No reader would be able to follow the thoughts, and few would be willing to try.

No matter how wonderful our ideas are, we still need to organize and package them carefully. Suppose you took a sackful of coins to the bank and demanded a twenty-dollar bill. Before any bank teller would give you the money, you would have to sort the coins into those thick paper wrappers, perhaps all the pennies in red wrappers, all the nickels in blue, and so on. That is what paragraphing is all about: sorting, combining, packaging ideas so that the reader can figure out how much each packet is worth and whether you get the twenty-dollar bill.

Successful paragraphs share three main qualities. They have *unity,* or a sense of togetherness; *development,* or a sense that the paragraph's topic has been discussed adequately; and *coherence,* or a sense of hanging together.

UNITY: A SENSE OF TOGETHERNESS

As the bank teller needs packets organized around only one kind of coin, so the reader needs paragraphs organized around one idea, or main point. This main point is what the paragraph as a whole supports or proves. What does not support or prove the main point doesn't belong in the paragraph. In the following passage, Malcolm Cowley states the main point in the first sentence and supports it in the following sentences:

> The vanity of older people is an easier weakness to explain, and to condone. With less to look forward to, they yearn for recognition of what they have been: the reigning beauty, the athlete, the soldier, the scholar. It is the beauties who have the hardest time. A portrait of themselves at twenty hangs on the wall, and they try to resemble it by making an extravagant use of creams, powders, and dyes. Being young at heart, they think they are merely revealing their essential persons. The athletes find shelves for their silver trophies, which are polished once a year. Perhaps a letter sweater lies wrapped in a bureau drawer. I remember one evening when a no-longer athlete had guests for dinner and tried to find his sweater. "Oh, that old thing," his wife said. "The moths got into it and I threw it away." The athlete sulked and his guests went home early. ("The View from 80")

The first sentence identifies the main point. It is a statement of the idea that governs the paragraph. Cowley first turns to the ex-beauties and then to the ex-athletes. He demonstrates why it is "easier . . . to explain, and to condone" the vanity of old people.

Sometimes no single sentence announces the main point, but all the sentences work so closely together that just to read them is to understand what main point they are making. The following paragraph contains one main point, but no single sentence conveys it:

> I don't find evidence, as some radical feminists do, for the claim that all men are rapists and murderers. If all men are, potentially, rapists and murderers, then they are so only as women, too, have a potential for destructive behavior. Women, however, have been traditionally trained away from such behavior (how else would the two-year-olds of the world survive?), except as we can turn it on ourselves in madness and self-destruction. Why else would Sylvia Plath's suicide inspire myths rather than simple pity? Men are trained to kill in circumstances of war. Because for most men such behavior is abhorrent, it must continually be

glorified to persuade them against their own moral sense to destroy rather than protect other members of their own species. (Jane Rule, "Pornography Is a Social Disease")

Every sentence contributes to make the main point, that both men and women are conditioned to behave in certain ways. That is the point that unifies the whole paragraph.

Staying with the Main Point

Every idea, every fact, every opinion in the paragraph must be part of the main point. No extraneous ideas should be dropped in, no matter how witty or arresting—no nickels among the pennies. A paragraph may, more than likely will, have more than one sentence. It may include statistics, quotations, facts, observations, assertions of value. But they must all unite to form the main point.

The following paragraph comes from a student essay whose thesis was "Most country and western performers are mockeries of real cowboys."

> The clothes that country and western performers wear bear little resemblance to those of the authentic cowboy. The cowboy's hat was made of rough leather to protect him against the relentless, corrosive western sun. Bandanas also protected the cowboy from the sun and served as swabs to mop up the inevitable sweat: they were made of plain cotton cloth. Chaps and boots, rough leather like the hats, were not ornaments: they helped ease chafing of the legs and thighs during the rough riding the cowboy did each day. From these homely and practical garments, country and western singers have somehow derived a costume of black velvet hats, alligator boots, satin pants, and phosphorescent bandanas. Perhaps they figured that cowboys wore fancy clothes in their spare time, to go to the local square dance. Whatever their reasoning, the result is a travesty of history. And of common sense. I can't picture any self-respecting horse allowing a hot-pink, rhinestone-studded dude to get within ten feet, let alone to ride him out on the range.

The writer fully develops one way—clothes—in which country and western singers are mockeries of real cowboys. The first sentence sets out the main point, and all the other sentences work to support that point. The writer has resisted the temptation to talk about hairdos, accents and voices, or music (she takes up those subjects in other paragraphs). After all, there is a good and ample point to be made—and much fun to be had—just with clothes. Such a sharp, consistent focus illustrates the virtues of unity. United the paragraph stands; divided it probably would have fallen.

We must resist beguiling, even fascinating, associations that will lead us away from our main idea and probably right out of our paragraph. Imagine a paragraph with consecutive sentences on these subjects: paint, color, green, blue, blues, jazz, rock, stone, stoned. We have rarely seen paragraphs that aimless, but we have seen some in which the writer similarly drifts down the stream of consciousness. Here is a fairly tame example:

> When we think about animal experimentation, we should look at the animals used. Because so many are required, only abundant species are chosen. Scientists may test a drug on anything from a small mouse to a monkey. Testing is helpful to scientists because it enables them to study the effects of new chemicals. Limiting tests to cell and tissue cultures only is inadequate. Scientists can find out a good deal from tissue analysis, but drugs do not act the same way when other kinds of tissue are absent. Not even with the capabilities of computers can scientists discover enough about the effects of drugs. Tests on experimental animals are still our best means, short of human trials, of learning how drugs work in human bodies.

The paragraph's first sentence seems to promise a discussion of the lab animals, and for the next two sentences that is what we get. But the word *testing* in the fourth sentence diverts the writer from her point, and she drops the animals. If the student had checked each sentence against that initial promise, she would have seen right away that at her fourth sentence she had begun to go astray. In the fifth and sixth sentences, she discusses another kind of test, and in the seventh, quite far afield, she points out the inadequacy of computers. The closing sentence brings us back to animals but makes an extraneous point.

In the revision, the writer refuses to be diverted and concentrates on supporting her main point.

> When we think about animal experimentation, we should look at the animals used. Because so many are required, only abundant species are chosen. Scientists may test a drug on anything from a small mouse to a monkey. They choose animals that share certain biological functions with human beings. By observing the effect of drugs on these animals, they can learn something about the effects of the drugs on human beings. This kind of testing is still our best means, short of human trials, of learning how drugs work in human bodies.

Getting Help from the Topic Sentence

Often the main point of a paragraph is indicated in a single sentence, called the *topic sentence*. Usually it either expresses the main point outright or makes that point unmistakably clear. Because it must hold all the sentences together in a unity, the topic sentence will be the paragraph's most general and inclusive sentence. It says, "This is what this whole paragraph is all about."

Having such an explicit statement can help both the writer and the reader. It is a constant reminder of what kinds of evidence can be included. Bearing this statement in mind while revising, the writer can check the other sentences to gauge the unity of the whole paragraph. The reader can more easily pick up the main point and evaluate the evidence accordingly. It is like "$2 in nickels" written across the blue wrapper.

"The vanity of older people is an easier weakness to explain, and to condone" (p. 158) is a topic sentence that informs the reader that the paragraph will be about the vanity of older people. "The clothes that country and western performers wear bear little resemblance to those of the authentic cowboy" (p. 159) is a topic sentence that indicates the paragraph will be about clothes. These two sentences are general enough to include all the evidence the writers provide, and they thus hold the paragraph together.

Although a topic sentence can come anywhere in a paragraph—first sentence, second, middle, last—the first is the most common position. Placing it at the top alerts the reader to what will be coming up. Look at these initial topic sentences, and think about the expectations they create:

> In astronomy, although the sun, moon, and stars continue to exist year after year, yet in other respects the world we have to deal with is very different from that of everyday life. (Bertrand Russell, "Touch and Sight: The Earth and the Heavens")
>
> The intellectual interest of a child in the riddle of sexual life, his desire for knowledge, finds expression at an earlier period of life than is usually suspected. (Sigmund Freud, "The Sexual Enlightenment of Children")
>
> The modern business organization, or that part which has to do with guidance and direction, consists in numerous individuals who are engaged, at any given time, in obtaining, digesting or exchanging and testing information. (John Kenneth Galbraith, "The Technostructure")

Each of these sentences makes a promise to the reader: this is what the following evidence will support. What exact form that evidence takes—example, comparison, analysis, definition—is often suggested by the topic sentence as well. We might expect, for instance, that Galbraith will describe how exchange and testing go on, that Freud will give some examples of the child's desire for knowledge, that Russell will analyze some of the differences between astronomy and everyday life. However the writer presents the evidence, the topic sentence tells us what the evidence means. We would be startled and confused if the subject were dropped, if, for instance, Freud went on to provide examples not of a child's interest in sex but of an adult's.

Frequently a first sentence does not state the main point but only provides a transition from the previous paragraph. The topic sentence may then appear later in the paragraph. Arguing that the Soviet Union is less likely to trigger World War III than the United States, Jan Morris follows a transitional sentence with the topic sentence:

> Of course, you [the United States and the USSR] are both paranoiac—two ideologically stunted giants, neither of whom really wants to conquer the world by force but whose preposterous dinosauran posturings menace the survival of everyone. But the Russians have cause to be paranoiac! Their history has been one long misery, one long failure perhaps, distorted always from afar by psychotic fear of the outside world—time and again, after all, the outside world has brutally attacked them. They are not as we are—of course they aren't. They have different values—of course they do. But they are a grand and tragic nation, struggling always, if often in ways we do not like, to find some fulfillment of their own. ("Down, Down on America")

Notice that after the transitional sentence, the United States is not part of the discussion. The rest of the paragraph is about Russian paranoia.

Paragraphs sometimes conclude with a topic sentence. So placed, it seems to sum up the earlier sentences. In the following example, the writer—novelist and naturalist Wendell Berry—could have begun the paragraph with the last sentence, but note the impact of placing it at the end:

> In the early spring of 1965 I had planted a small orchard; the next spring we planted our first garden. Within the following six or seven years we reclaimed pastures, converted the garage into a henhouse, rebuilt the barn, greatly improved the garden soil, planted berry bushes, acquired a milk cow—and were producing, except for hay and grain for our animals, nearly everything that we ate: fruit, vegetables, eggs, meat, milk, cream, and butter. We built an outbuilding with a meat room and a food-storage cellar. Because we did not want to pollute our land and water with sewage, and in the process waste nutrients that should be returned to the soil, we built a compacting privy. And so we began to attempt a life that, in addition to whatever else it was, would be responsibly agricultural. We used no chemical fertilizers. Except for a little rotenone, we used no insecticides. As our land and our food became healthier, so did we. And our food was of better quality than any that we could have bought. (*Recollected Essays: 1965–1980*)

Berry has carefully guided the reader through a narrative of his life on the farm. That last sentence is like putting the sum at the bottom of a column of figures. The reader says, Ah, now I know what all these ideas mean.

In the hands of a superb writer like Berry, the topic sentence can be very effective in the last position. But unless carefully tended, this arrangement has dangers. The reader, abruptly arriving at the final sum, may have to retrace the steps to be sure they were tallied correctly. Write paragraphs with topic sentences at the end, of course, but double-check them.

Sometimes a writer places the topic sentence deep in the paragraph, as in this passage describing the plight of some college students:

> The unhappiness and discontent of young people is nothing new, and problems of adolescence are always painfully intense. But while traveling around the country, speaking at colleges, and interviewing students at all kinds of schools—large and small, public and private—I was overwhelmed by the prevailing sadness. It was as visible on campuses in California as in Nebraska and Massachusetts. <u>Too many young people are in college reluctantly, because everyone told them they ought to go, and there didn't seem to be anything better to do.</u> Their elders sell them college because it's good for them. Some never learn to like it, and talk about their time in school as if it were a sentence to be served. (Caroline Bird, "Where College Fails Us")

The main idea, underlined in the fourth sentence, summarizes the description in the first three sentences and anticipates the explanations of the last two. It encompasses the whole paragraph.

Sometimes a paragraph reaches back to a previous paragraph to find its main idea. In "The View from 80," Cowley ends one paragraph with

> We start by growing old in other people's eyes, then slowly we come to share their judgment.

In the next paragraph, he provides the evidence for that main point.

> I remember a morning many years ago when I was backing out of the parking lot near the railroad station in Brewster, New York. There was a near collision. The driver of the other car jumped out and started to abuse me; he had his fists ready. Then he looked at me and said, "Why, you're an old man." He got back in the car, slammed the door, and drove away, while I stood there fuming. "I'm only 65," I thought. "He wasn't driving carefully. I can still take care of myself in a car, or in a fight, for that matter."

Likewise, writers will often continue a topic in a second or even a third paragraph without any additional topic sentence. In an essay comparing our fears with those of the Eskimo, Loren Eiseley begins one paragraph this way:

> For what is it that we do? We fear. We do not fear ghosts but we fear the ghost of ourselves. We have come now, in this time, to fear the water we drink. . . .

He finishes that paragraph with a series of things we fear and then goes to a new paragraph and continues listing our fears:

> We fear the awesome powers we have lifted out of nature and cannot return to her. We fear the weapons we have made, the hatreds we have engendered. We fear the crush of fanatic people to whom we readily sell these weapons. We fear for the value of the money in our pockets that

stands symbolically for food and shelter. We fear the growing power of the state to take all these things from us. We fear to walk in our streets at evening. We have come to fear even our scientists and their gifts. ("The Winter of Man")

The topic sentence controls the development of both paragraphs.

Paragraphs containing only a topic sentence also occur occasionally; their main idea is so obvious that it needs no further support. Frequently these one-sentence paragraphs are rhetorical questions, as in this example from Eiseley's essay:

Has the wintry bleakness in the troubled heart of humanity at least equally retreated?—that aspect of man referred to when the Eskimo, adorned with amulets to ward off evil, reiterated: "Most of all we fear the secret misdoings of the heedless ones among ourselves."

Almost always, however, you will need to flesh out the topic sentence with a series of supporting sentences.

Our examples of topic sentences so far have laid out the main point in fairly explicit terms. Some topic sentences are more subtly phrased yet express the main point. In an essay on criminal justice, the writer summarizes what he found wrong with indeterminate sentencing and then asks,

Then should we get rid of indeterminate sentencing?

He follows this question with reasons why we shouldn't. The question provides the context for the reasons. Another writer presents the opposition's view of animal experimentation in one paragraph and begins the next paragraph with

But that is all wrong . . .

and proceeds to explain why. In neither instance, does the topic sentence indicate exactly what opinion the paragraph will support. It nonetheless guides the reader into the subject.

The best writers use a variety of paragraph constructions, none of which is ever mechanical. Their topic sentence may be first, middle, or last, or only implied. They are guided by the flow of ideas between and within paragraphs.

Inexperienced or uncertain writers, however, will find topic sentences very helpful, particularly when they come at the beginning of the paragraph. Starting a paragraph with the main point clearly stated can help to keep the writer on track and serve as an ever-present reminder of the paragraph's point.

One further suggestion: a bold and intriguing topic sentence up front can entice readers into the paragraph. Make your topic sentence interesting so that the reader will want to read on.

A Special Word about the Thesis and the Topic Sentence

Topic sentences not only tie all the sentences of a paragraph together but also tie the whole paragraph to the essay's thesis. The topic sentence says, This is what this paragraph has to do with the argument developing through the whole essay. When the topic sentences are clearly related to the thesis, they help keep the whole essay together.

Remember Stephanie Klein's essay on the harp seal hunt in Chapter 6? By analyzing it, we can see how the topic sentences relate to the thesis and promote the argument:

Thesis: If we look at the evidence, we see a different, and much more complex, picture [rather than supporting the notion that the harp seal hunt should be banned].

Topic sentence 1: The seal hunt is not a sport but a necessity.

Topic sentence 2: Sealing provides not only employment but also essential goods.

Topic sentence 3: The fishing industry benefits from the seal hunt.

Topic sentence 4: Despite [assertions to the contrary] the harp seal is not an endangered species.

Topic sentence 5: Although sealing continues, the Canadian government closely monitors it.

Topic sentence 6: Even environmental organizations . . . acknowledge . . . that the [seal] population will remain stable through regulation of hunting.

Topic sentence 7: The question of the cruelty of the hunt remains.

Topic sentence 8: The means and the manner of death are also regulated by the Canadian government [and the cruelty has been exaggerated].

Concluding topic sentence: Only when we examine these complex issues coolly—taking into account all the economic, ethical, and cultural ramifications—can we expect to arrive at an intelligent understanding.

Each topic sentence is both a logical development from and a support for the thesis. If you read them as though they formed a single paragraph, you will see how tight and clear the argument is. We suggest you do this sort of postwriting outline of your topic sentences to see how well your argument has turned out.

TIPS FOR UNITY

- Be sure each of your paragraphs has a single main point.
- Remember that all ideas must relate to that main point.
- Delete any sentences not related to the main point, no matter how clever or intriguing.
- Think about using a topic sentence to express the main point.
- Putting the topic sentence at the beginning of the paragraph can help you stay on course.
- When you place the topic sentence in the middle, be sure it combines both ends of the paragraph into a single idea.
- When you place the topic sentence at the end, be sure all sentences lead to it.
- Remember that every main point, whether expressed in a topic sentence or implied, should relate to the essay's thesis.

Exercises for Unity

1. Revise the following paragraph for unity, cutting out extraneous material and correcting any digressions. To revise effectively, first identify the topic sentence and then analyze whether the other sentences are clearly moving in the direction it lays out.

   The apparent advantage of dialogue over lecture as a way of teaching critical thinking is that it can involve students in more than one viewpoint and help them develop their own ideas. But even Plato, usually acknowledged as a master of the dialogue form, sometimes fails to bring off this advantage. In *Republic*, for example, he has Socrates question Glaucon about the nature of life, but Plato makes Glaucon such a yea-sayer that the reader never gets a proper interplay of ideas. It is like a class in which the teacher asks leading questions but will only accept one answer—one that agrees with his. Students sense that they are being unfairly manipulated and are not being taken seriously, and soon most will lapse into indifference. The teacher then complains to other teachers that the Socratic method is a waste of time. Some of his more open-minded colleagues may protest that the method must be properly used, but the old guard nod sagely to one another as if to say, "Another one of us has come of age." Life is full of such rites of passage, and in some circles they pass for wisdom. But education of this sort never got anyone out of the cave.

2. The following two paragraphs lack unity because their authors have gone off on tangents:

   Popular fiction focuses on a few basic fantasies, continually readapting them to the latest fashions in the culture. In the 1950s, for example, the private eye was the basic adventure hero, in the 1960s it was the spy, and in the 1970s the ex-Vietnam veteran against organized crime. But each hero faces essentially the same challenges—rich and powerful supervillains—and has the same resources—hand-to-hand combat skills, inventive intelligence, and that most crucial of all ingredients, sex appeal. Indeed, whatever the decade of their flourishing, these heroes always succeed in seducing women. And this is what their readers want to experience vicariously. In airports, on trains, at bus stops, you see mild-mannered and well-groomed men, briefcases in hand, reading the latest stories. Who would suspect the brutal and lascivious fantasies exploding within their brains? As Gilbert and Sullivan once observed, "Things are seldom what they seem."

There is great power not only in the denotative meanings of words but in their connotations as well. Consider, for example, this familiar phrase: "We hold these truths to be self-evident." Ask yourself, How is this different from "We hold these truths to be sacred and undeniable"? Thomas Jefferson himself actually wrote the second phrase. The Continental Congress, however, delegated the task of writing the Declaration of Independence to five men, including John Adams and Benjamin Franklin. Adams had suggested that Jefferson write the document by himself, in part because Jefferson was known to be a good writer, in part because he was a Virginian and Adams wanted to secure Virginia's support for the rebellion. Who actually changed the wording, though, we do not know.

In each case, identify the point at which the paragraph gets off track and then compose a new ending starting at that point.

3. Here are four pairs of sentences, one a topic sentence for a paragraph and the other a piece of support. Identify the topic sentence in each pair.
   a. Blessed are the children who always eat the same flavor of ice cream or always know beforehand what kind they want. It's a sad thing to observe a beautiful young child who has always been perfectly happy with a plain vanilla cone being subverted by a young schoolmate who has been invited along for the weekend—a pleasant and polite visitor, perhaps, but spoiled by permissive parents and scarred by an overactive imagination. (L. Rust Hills, "How to Eat an Ice Cream Cone")
   b. Perhaps the finest painting in the church is Lorenzo Lotto's *St. Anthony Giving Alms* in which the warm colour scheme seems to have been derived from the soft Turkish carpets which play a prominent part in the composition. Although the church is not as rich in paintings as in sculpture, it contains several of note. (Hugh Honour, *The Companion Guide to Venice*)
   c. The Beatles could afford not to grow up because a certain childlike magic had always been central to their appeal. They were bound up with the decade in more ways than one, for the sixties were a period that believed in magic and innocence, that had a touching faith in the omnipotence of individual desire. (Morris Dickstein, *Gates of Eden: American Culture in the Sixties*)
   d. Early one morning the sub-inspector at a police station the other end of the town rang me up on the phone and said that an elephant was ravaging the bazaar. It was a tiny incident in itself, but it gave me a

better glimpse than I had had before of the real nature of imperialism—the real motives for which despotic governments act. (George Orwell, "Shooting an Elephant")

4. Identify the topic sentence in each of the following paragraphs.

I used to cut vegetables in the kitchen. String beans had to be cut in one-inch pieces. The way you were supposed to do it was: You hold two beans in one hand, the knife in the other, and you press the knife against the beans and your thumb, almost cutting yourself. It was a slow process. So I put my mind to it, and I got a pretty good idea. I sat down at the wooden table outside the kitchen, put a bowl in my lap, and stuck a very sharp knife into the table at a forty-five-degree angle away from me. Then I put a pile of the string beans on each side, and I'd pick out a bean, one in each hand, and bring it towards me with enough speed that it would slice, and the pieces would slide into the bowl that was in my lap. (Richard P. Feynman, *"Surely You're Joking, Mr. Feynman!"*)

The Hebrews craved to settle for good in the fertile plains. But characteristically they dreamed of lands overflowing with milk and honey, not lands of super-abundant crops like those the Egyptians imagined for their hereafter. It seems that the desert as a metaphysical experience loomed very large for the Hebrews and coloured all their valuations. It is, perhaps, the tension between two valuations—between a desire and a contempt for what is desired—that may explain some of the paradoxes of ancient Hebrew beliefs. (H. and H. A. Frankfort, *Before Philosophy*)

They fished, trolling hooks with strips of canvas greased with fat. Bonitos would grab them and be hauled like silvery-finned melons, shuddering and tail-tapping, into the scuppers; they were eagerly eaten, as were the sharks, the ominous "sea-lawyers" that followed patiently at the vessel's stern. These "were pronounced excellent; the most trifling change of circumstance in so long and wearisome a voyage being greedily grasped at and joyfully entertained." Now and then sailors would catch albatrosses with baited hook and a sounding-line, drag them screaming on board, slaughter them, and skin them, there being a market for their stuffed carcasses. (Robert Hughes, *The Fatal Shore*)

5. Each of the following statements could serve as a thesis for an essay:
   a. Attempting suicide should/should not be a crime.
   b. The government should/should not provide funds for abortions for women on welfare.
   c. Freshmen at this institution should/should not be required to take a sequence of courses on Western civilization.
   d. This institution should/should not participate in intercollegiate athletics.

For each, write four topic sentences suitable for supporting paragraphs. Exchange your sentences with a partner and discuss the differences.

6. Examine a recent essay of yours paragraph by paragraph. Identify the topic sentences. Do all clearly relate to the thesis? Do any paragraphs fail to adhere to their topic sentence? Do any end far away from where they began? If you find examples of disunity, revise them.

DEVELOPMENT: EXPANDING ON THE MAIN IDEA

In the first section of this chapter, we discussed the need for unity in a paragraph, for having only a single main point. Now we turn to developing that main point through the paragraph.

Completing the Thought

At the end of a well-designed paragraph, we have the feeling of coming to a natural stop. But at the end of some paragraphs (particularly in the second half of an essay), we have only a feeling of hunger for more. For some writers offer only such skimpy and fleshless fare as this paragraph, written to answer the assignment "Describe the God of the Old Testament":

> The God of the Old Testament is uncompromising in the demands He makes on humanity. Commanding Abraham to sacrifice Isaac is a case in point. The fate of Job is another. There is no reasoning with the All-Powerful.

That's it. Good-bye. Hope you enjoyed it. Thinking the task completed, the cook turns off the burners, leaving us with little to chew on. Unified, yes, and with a lead-off topic sentence, but not very nourishing. Remind us of Abraham, we want to say. How is his story a "case in point"? What had Job done, and what happened to him? As for that fine last sentence (like many of us, this writer writes better beginnings and endings than middles), how did we get there? We may have other unanswered questions, too. In the Book of Hosea, for instance, didn't God compromise a little? How did He compromise?

Whether such writing results from impatience, stinginess, or timidity, we of course don't know. But we do know that no writer should expect the reader to fill in the blanks. When we provide an illustration, we should indicate exactly what is being illustrated and exactly how it supports the main point. When we use a term in a special way—for example, "no reasoning" in the preceding example—we should define the term. Writers ought to cook up a healthy diet of explanation, not a thin gruel.

Here is another paragraph that leaves the reader begging for more:

> Among the misconceptions regarding nutrition is the belief that athletes need extra protein. This misconception is common among weight-lifters and football players. But there is no evidence that a high-protein diet constructs more muscle.

This paragraph has a strong topic sentence, and every sentence relates to it. It is unified, certainly, but we would like to know much more about proteins and muscle development.

Why did this student serve us such meager fare? We think it was because the whole issue of diet and strength is complex and controversial, and he probably didn't want to take the trouble of going into it. But it is impossible to avoid trouble when discussing a proposal or arguing for a new idea. There is no point in dodging complexity. The audience expects not avoidance but explanation.

In the revision, the student provided some important evidence:

> Among the misconceptions regarding nutrition is the belief that athletes need extra protein. Many athletes believe that protein improves athletic performance by increasing muscle mass. The belief is especially common among weight-lifters, prompting them to consume large quantities of high-protein foods and dietary supplements. Like weight-lifters, football players consume too much protein, expecting it to produce additional muscle and energy. Although it is true that muscles contain more protein than do other tissues, there is no evidence that a high-protein diet actually constructs more muscle tissue than a normal diet. Nutritionists point out that muscle cells grow not from excess protein but from exercise: when a muscle is used, it pulls in protein for its consumption. This is how the muscle grows and strengthens.

Now the student has laid out specific details of both the misconception and the truth. The last sentence responds to the eternal So what? and provides *closure*—that is, the feel of completion as well as the fact of it.

That feeling of closure is important. Readers often take away from the paragraph the thought expressed in the last sentence. Although no degree of eloquence in the wrap-up will make a thin broth into a robust soup, a strong last sentence can contribute to the reader's sense of satisfaction.

How do you know when enough is enough and not too much? Readers will think a paragraph is too much when one or both of these things happen: they find it difficult to retain the overall shape of the argument, or their eyes and mind begin to tire. Try to anticipate both of these problems. If you find one of your paragraphs requires more than ten sentences or spreads over a whole page, double-check it to be sure you aren't repeating yourself or haven't buried a second main point somewhere in the middle—you may need another paragraph.

No hard and fast rules can govern how well-developed a paragraph should be, but our experience tells us that writing is one area in which fat is generally better than skinny. Where do you find the details, the explanations, and the examples that develop your thoughts? In your own mind, of course. Chapter 9 suggests strategies that can help you locate them.

Accentuating the Important

Good writers distinguish between important ideas and lesser ones. They decide who are the stars of the show, bring them front and center, and direct the spotlight accordingly. They give them the best lines and the most lines. The minor players stay back in the shadows. These decisions usually boil down to choices about the extent of the discussion and placement of the major points.

EXTENDING THE DISCUSSION. Some writers seem to know intuitively which points to play up and which to play down. But for most of us, this is a tricky business. We worry that if we don't hammer a point home the reader may miss it altogether. But at the same time we worry about over-emphasizing a minor point and knocking our argument out of shape.

Some decisions about emphasis are, of course, easy. We don't need to emphasize what everybody knows and agrees to. We need not slave to prove that Apple Computers is innovative: everybody already believes that. We can just say, "Always innovative, Apple Computers . . ." and everyone will go on reading. If we start citing examples of Apple's innovation ("Apple Computers, which developed Apple I, Apple II, the Mac, the mouse and . . ."), readers will see that we are wasting their time. We have to be wary of saying too much.

We must be wary, however, of saying too little. Controversial ideas dropped in a paragraph without elucidation can distort the balance of an argument. And the more controversial the point, the more we need to say. If we want to argue that Apple really has not been innovative but has merely built on the ideas of other companies, we will need much more than a paragraph, maybe more than an essay (if we seriously try to argue that point at all).

Sometimes writers lose sight of important points because they become enamored of minor points and spend too much time on them. In the following paragraph, the writer argues that our sense of time depends on how involved we are in what we are doing. The notion of "psychological time" is interesting, but the writer loses sight of the important points and offers too much evidence for tangential ideas.

> Our sense of how fast time passes indicates our involvement in what we are doing. In any activity—like studying at the library—we experience periods of absorption punctuated by periods of disengagement. Then we usually glance around, or perhaps actually get up for a drink of water, take a walk, or go to the bathroom. These breaks may hark back to the survival instinct, readily witnessed in films of animals in the wild pausing in the midst of feeding or drinking to take a look around and sniff the air. Even while dashing across the plains, the whole herd

may stop as though to take its bearings. When we do look around, we check the time. We compare the reading with what time we expect it to be. Intense involvement can distort our expectation. We can be so absorbed in an activity that we are not aware of time passing, and we expect that a normal interval has passed when it has been longer. We get the idea that time passed swiftly. But who ever heard of a clock going faster at one time and then slower at another?

Unity is not the problem here. Every sentence is about interrupted time. Nor is completeness the problem. The information is adequate and not excessive. The problem is emphasis. The paragraph bulges out of shape. So much time is spent describing the lessons of the wildlife documentaries that a reader may begin to think the subject is the sense of time of animals. The writer jams discussion of the real subject—the disparity between clock time and perceived time—into a few short sentences. At the end, she seems to be on a mad dash out of the paragraph.

The revision retains the virtues of the original but improves on its wandering ways:

> Our sense of how fast time passes indicates our involvement in what we are doing. In any activity—like studying at the library—we experience periods of absorption punctuated by periods of disengagement, in which our minds pull back from the immediate situation. We glance around at our surroundings, and we usually manage to check the time. When we do, we compare the reading with what we expect it to be, based on our normal span of involvement. For some this may be twenty minutes, for others forty; but however long, it tends to remain fairly constant. Intense involvement, however, can extend this time markedly: when we are intensely absorbed we have little sense of time passing. When we check the clock, we discover that it is much later than we expected. Thus, we get the idea, patently illogical, that time itself has passed swiftly.

In revising, the writer sorted out her main idea (that our perception of time depends on how involved we are) and added to the two major supports (the normal expectation of time passing and the effect of absorption). She de-emphasized everything else. Removing her reference to the animals was painful: this was the writer's favorite material. Nevertheless, out it went, and with it the improper emphasis.

PLACING THE ACCENT. Placement creates emphasis. Your major points—the ones you want the reader to carry out of the paragraph—should come at the beginning and the end. In writing, as in life, those are the most emphatic places to make a statement.

Sometimes you can present your material so that the paragraph rises to a peak. If, for instance, you have three points, you can arrange them so that the paragraph moves from interesting point to more interesting point to most interesting point. Speech writers, novelists, movie-makers, and musical composers are well aware of the advantages of this order. They build toward a climax of increasing interest and tension.

You should go to almost any length, short of distortion, to avoid a sudden drop in tension, or anticlimax. Anticlimax creates confusion and a sense of disorder. The following paragraph brims with marvelous details, but it suffers from anticlimax:

> Living in England for two years convinced me that the Who was rock's most representative group. Their music was challenging, violent, as repetitive and insistent as the throb of a broken jaw. That music, at times the closest thing to pain I had ever heard, seemed to be me and say me. Their lyrics spoke of the undeniable facts of life at eighteen: you are caught in the middle, not a schoolboy and not ready to be a working man, old enough to want power and young enough never to have it. The Who looked like skinny, awkward kids: defiant pairs of deep, hungry eyes, a chipped tooth here, a huge nose there.

In revising, the writer evaluated the impact of each sentence, and then arranged them in order of climax:

> Living in England for two years convinced me that the Who was rock's most representative group. They looked like skinny, awkward kids: a huge nose here, a chipped tooth there, defiant pairs of deep, hungry eyes. Their lyrics spoke of the undeniable facts of life at eighteen: you are caught in the middle, not a schoolboy and not ready to be a working man, old enough to want power and young enough never to have it. Their music was challenging, violent, as repetitive and insistent as the throb of a broken jaw. That music, at times the closest thing to pain that I had ever heard, seemed to be me and say me.

Now the writer has a much more dramatic and entertaining paragraph.

Because the beginning and ending are the most important positions in a paragraph, writers work hard to make them right. With a strong beginning, they can entice the reader to read on. The reader will probably scoop up an emphatic opening and carry it all the way through the paragraph. The interest it arouses provides the energy for reading the rest. If, however, the opening sentence fizzles, the reader may have to struggle on to the end. The art of the opener—the grabber, the hook—is one to be mastered.

The following paragraph opens with a dull, unemphatic, and imprecise sentence:

> <u>Many of us spend hours every week listening to television.</u> After the networks have finished trying our patience, the local stations demand equal time. We are shown products guaranteed to automate and begadget the most mundane household tasks. We are subjected to "Amazing!" shaves and "Miraculous!" washes. If we tried all the beers we are

invited to taste, we would float down the avenue—and get run over by all those fast cars our neighbors have been seduced into buying. To close the evening, Cutprice Records presents its Infinite Original Hits: Do you remember this? and that? It is not the commercials that interrupt the programs, but the programs that interrupt the commercials, ever more briefly.

The paragraph itself is not bad, but who would get to it after that dull start? And what is the paragraph going to be about? What major idea does the writer want us to carry forward? All this writer needed was a snappier and more informative opening:

The barrage of commercials never ends.

The word *barrage* alerts us; the word *commercials* tells us exactly where we are going. An emphatic opening sentence acts like a magnet, drawing the other sentences toward it.

The other traditional place for emphasis is the end of a paragraph. In some ways this position is even more important. Leave 'em laughing, says the comedian. Just as the first sentence can provide momentum into the paragraph, the last sentence can provide momentum into the *next* paragraph. If the last sentence is a bore, the reader may be reluctant to push on.

The following paragraph comes from an essay on children not raised in human communities, that is, wild children:

The wild children that horrify anthropologists are made into heroes by fiction writers. For anthropologists, the wild children were animalistic and repulsive and did not demonstrate many human values and characteristics. The scientists describe, for example, children eating live chickens and garbage. But fiction writers idealized wild children. Both Tarzan of the Apes and Mowgli are noble and represent the very best of the human species. The anthropologists didn't find that at all.

This paragraph has a point, but it is not pointed. It fizzles. No thought, no energy, concentrates at the end to carry the reader onward. In revising this interesting material, the student replaced the last uninspired sentence with an emphatic one:

But the anthropologists looking for a noble savage looked in vain.

Just as the "barrage" sentence exerted an upward surge, this new ending exerts a strong forward pull. It properly focuses the reader's attention on the significance of the difference between the fiction writers and the anthropologists. Now the reader wants to know what resulted from this difference.

TIPS FOR DEVELOPMENT

- Check to be sure you have provided enough information in your paragraphs, particularly in the last half of your essay.
- Don't expect your reader to fill in information.
- Prefer well-developed paragraphs to skinny paragraphs.
- Differentiate important points from unimportant details.
- Ask yourself if you need to add emphasis to the important points.
- Limit discussion of unimportant points, no matter how fascinating.
- Sentences you want to emphasize should come at the beginning or the end of the paragraph.
- Try to build to a climax.
- On your first draft underline the most important point in each of your paragraphs, and if any points are improperly placed, move them.

Exercises for Development

1. Here are three skinny paragraphs.

   America's many foods take their characters from their countries of origin. Spaghetti is a good example, as are tacos and burritos, which are both spicy and hot. And we must not forget the hamburger, one of America's most popular foods.

   Children learn language by imitating their parents. At first, all a newborn can do is cry, but then it can see better. It starts imitating its parents, and soon it can make sentences by itself. Now it is a member of society.

   Roads are becoming a real problem for modern cities. Many cities have grown too fast. They build new roads. As those fill up, soon they have no place to put more roads. Public transportation is the only solution.

   Study each one, determine where the gaps are, and fill them in, providing missing material and connections. Feel free to rewrite any of the sentences if that will help. After you finish revising, be prepared to discuss what you added and why.

2. Find a recent essay of yours and look for skinny paragraphs. Revise it, adding what is needed. What did you add and why? (You can do this with a partner, too: exchange recent papers and look for skinny paragraphs. Then take your own paper back and revise it. Or revise a skinny paragraph in your partner's essay.)

3. The following paragraphs have improper emphasis. This may show up

as either too much discussion on a particular subject or misplaced discussion.

> Pulling a person out of quicksand is a delicate process. You must lie on the
> nearest solid piece of ground. The ground can be wet or even a little sandy, but
> you must test it to make sure it will hold when you start pulling. Wind your rope
> around one shoulder. Two-thousand-pound nylon test is the best, though con-
> ventional silk-wound or hempen rope will do. Some rescuers have used their
> own belts, but these must be of leather rather than the weaker synthetic materi-
> als. The whole question of exactly what material to use is sorely debated. Then
> throw the rope and pull the victim out.

> A good diplomat must possess three essential qualities: discretion, social grace,
> and political savvy. Without discretion or political savvy, the diplomat will be a
> liability in times of international tension. Without social grace (a knowledge of
> local habits and customs, easy affability), the diplomat will be a bore at parties
> and will fail to build that system of informal contacts so crucial for keeping
> abreast of local developments. For this reason, the diplomat should purchase full
> sets of silverware and tablecloths and practice eye contact and conversational
> skills. Spare no expense: stingy diplomats make poor impressions.

Revise each paragraph to correct its problem, deleting unnecessary elaboration or adding what is missing. Be prepared to answer the question
What did you change and why?

4. Here are three theses, each followed by a list of points.
    a. Rich countries must sacrifice to help poor countries. Time is running
       out.

    > The richer countries can afford it.
    > It is hard for any sensitive person to go on watching the famine and suffering
    >   without doing something about them.
    > Poor countries cannot help themselves.
    > The individual sacrifice would not be very large.

    b. Space exploration has had many benefits.

    > It has expanded the human imagination.
    > It has helped humanity develop new technologies that would have been im-
    >   possible to develop on earth.
    > It has allowed women, minorities, and people from many other countries to
    >   join in a great project.

    c. Most popular music is based on a strong rhythmic beat and not much
       else.

    > Writers design their songs that way to capture the dance market.
    > If you actually listen, many of the melodies are undistinguished and
    >   indistinguishable.
    > The words are usually vapid as well.

Choose one thesis and determine which of the points you would emphasize most in a paper on that topic and which ones you would emphasize less. Arrange the points according to your analysis, with the
most important point last; then write a paragraph using your rearranged
as an outline. Devote two additional sentences to the point you feel is
most important. Give less important points one additional sentence. If

you wish to leave a point unemphasized, do not add to it. Be ready to explain which points you emphasized most and why.

5. For ten minutes, use one of the invention techniques in Chapter 1 on one of the following topics, jotting down as many different ideas as you can.

the Statue of Liberty
sibling rivalry
the Grand Canyon
babies' lack of knowledge
traffic signs
the Mississippi River
alcohol as a dangerous drug
the Liberty Bell

Go over your ideas to see which are important. Now write a paragraph or two on the subject, using as many ideas as you can from the invention but bearing in mind an appropriate emphasis.

COHERENCE: HANGING IDEAS TOGETHER

A good paragraph hangs together. One thought logically and naturally follows from the preceding thought and gives rise to the next. The sentences are locked one to the other like the cars of a train. Few aspects of writing are as important as how you lock your ideas together.

In this paragraph from "Letter from Birmingham Jail," Martin Luther King, Jr., maintains coherence in a passage of rich detail, subtle thought, and moving argument:

> In your statement you assert that our actions, even though peaceful, must be condemned because they precipitate violence. But is this a logical assertion? Isn't this like condemning a robbed man because his possession of money precipitated the evil act of robbery? Isn't this like condemning Socrates because his unswerving commitment to truth and his philosophical inquiries precipitated the act by the misguided populace in which they made him drink hemlock? Isn't this like condemning Jesus because his unique God-consciousness and never-ceasing devotion to God's will precipitated the evil act of crucifixion? We must come to see that, as the federal courts have consistently affirmed, it is wrong to urge an individual to cease his efforts to gain his basic constitutional rights because the quest may precipitate violence. Society must protect the robbed and punish the robber.

This statement of conscience gains power with each sentence. Each idea builds upon the one before it and increases the intensity of the argument. All the questions point to that completely persuasive reference to the crucifixion in the fifth sentence. At the end King wraps up his thought by referring back to the robbed and the robber. Every sentence illuminates the main idea. In addition, each sentence seems to rise from the one before it and to reach out for the one after it. The ideas grow as if organic, and with each sentence the impact builds.

When a paragraph is coherent, thoughts and ideas develop continuously, and the relationships are clear. The current of thought flows. There are no jerks, no backing and filling, no long leaps from the period of one sentence to the capital letter of the next.

Paragraphs can fall apart for many reasons. Thoughts may appear out of logical order. A subject may give way to another and then be picked up later. Connections between ideas may be fuzzy. All these disorienting problems appear in this paragraph from an essay arguing for changes in the rules of professional football:

> The technique of tackling known as "spearing"—charging helmet first into the opposing player's body—ought to be outlawed. Getting speared is very much like getting hit with a cannonball. Yet ballcarriers are likely to be in the forefront of those resisting this rule change. Why do we allow spearing to continue? And if the tackler hits at the wrong angle, he can break his back. Playing with pain has become a sign of manliness. A tackler could give himself a concussion—padding can only absorb so much shock. There are, in short, things in this world of more value than demonstrating manliness through enduring pain—things like maintaining the health of one's body for an active life, not just for a few "playing years." The modern helmet is as hard as iron, and with 250 pounds of charging linebacker behind it, the impact is awesome. At best the ballcarrier will come out with a bruise, but it is all too likely that the blow will break a rib or even puncture a lung. Football has been plagued from the outset by a macho image.

It is all in there—the ballcarrier, the tackler, the need for rules changes—but what a confusion. The writer didn't finish one thought before he was off to another. He did not, for instance, fully describe the damage to the runner, and so he had to return to the subject. The topic sentence does not promise discussion of the tackler. And there are some fairly body-shocking leaps. The whole paragraph zigzags back and forth among the various ideas.

Dizzying shifts and turns like these called for revision:

> The technique of tackling known as "spearing"—charging helmet first into the opposing player's body—ought to be outlawed. It jeopardizes the health of both the ballcarrier and the tackler. For the ballcarrier, getting speared is very much like getting hit with a cannonball. The modern helmet is as hard as iron, and with 250 pounds of charging linebacker behind it, the impact is awesome. At best the ballcarrier will come out with a bruise, but the blow could break a rib or even puncture

a lung. Nor does this practice leave the tackler unscathed. If he hits at the wrong angle, he can break his back, or, because padding can only absorb so much shock, he may give himself a concussion. Yet players themselves resist rule changes in their interest. Football and individual football players have been plagued from the outset by a macho image. Playing with pain has become a sign of manliness, and perhaps it is. But there are things of more value than such manliness, for instance, the health of one's body over a whole lifetime.

Because the writer started the revision with a more inclusive topic sentence, we know that the paragraph will treat both ballcarriers and tacklers. The writer grouped all the sentences referring to the ballcarrier and all those referring to the tackler. In the last sentences he explained the problem for both the ballcarrier and the tackler and tightly fastened all the other sentences together.

In the pages that follow we will discuss ways to make paragraphs hang together.

Grouping Related Ideas

Sometimes when we write, we stop one thought, go to the next, realize we have more to say on the first, and return to it. It is natural to write this way on a first draft, because ideas take awhile to develop. But we must group all related ideas together by the final draft. If we don't, the reader's mind will be shifting back and forth, forth and back. It can be like watching a Ping-Pong match.

In an essay arguing that first-year college students should be required to live on campus, a student wrote this paragraph:

> Living in a dormitory can facilitate the difficult transition from dependence on parents to independence. For students who live near their parents, the change is not so dramatic. But for most students college is the first experience of living far from their parents. Without recognizing why, they may feel lonely and deserted. Students living near home can visit or call when they feel the need. Those who live far away may fear rejection. Discussing the problem with others similarly situated can ease the transition. For some students, the transition is not so difficult. There are those who have gone off to boarding schools and so have probably made something of an adjustment. Students who have never lived away before and who don't live near their parents now will find understanding and sympathy from others in the same situation. Other freshmen may not offer quite the acceptance of parents, but living with them beats living in a lonely apartment in town.

By the end of this paragraph, the reader's mental eyeballs are weary.

In the revision the student grouped similar ideas (the exceptions and the typical), finished each thought before going to the next, and thus did not need to return. Notice, too, that the grouping removes the awkward phrasing "Students who have never lived away before and who don't live near their parents now" and substitutes a pronoun. Reading this paragraph is no longer like watching the little white ball bouncing back and forth.

> Living in a dormitory can facilitate the transition from dependence on parents to independence. The transition is easier for some than for others. Students who go to college near their parents won't find the change so difficult. They can visit or call when they feel the need. And students who have attended boarding schools have probably made some adjustment already. But for most students college is the first experience of living away from their parents. Without recognizing why, they may feel lonely and deserted. In a dormitory, they can find sympathy from others in the same situation. Other freshmen may not offer quite the acceptance of parents, but living with them beats living in a lonely apartment in town.

Thoughts Descending a Staircase

Movement between ideas should be gradual enough for the reader to step from one idea to the next without feeling jolted. But some paragraphs—usually underdeveloped, "skinny" paragraphs (see "Development: Expanding on the Main Idea")—suffer from a dangerously steep staircase. The steps may all be there, but they are too far apart. Readers may feel as though they are dropping into space. Such is the case in reading this paragraph, in which a student discusses Carl Sagan's essay "The Abstractions of Beasts":

> Research indicates that certain kinds of monkeys have considerable language skills. Carl Sagan deals primarily with three chimpanzees— Lucy, Lana, and Washoe—who were taught Ameslan (American Sign Language) and developed vocabularies ranging from 100 to 200 words and eventually were capable of constructing phrases. James Dewson and colleagues found that chimpanzees have a language center in the neocortex of the left hemisphere of the brain, just as human beings do. Apes are thought to transmit extragenetic or cultural information. Differences in group behavior have been documented among chimpanzees and other related species.

Although all the sentences relate to the topic, something seems to be missing. How does the reader get from the three chimps to James Dewson? What is the connection between cultural information and differences in group behavior? The last four sentences are piled one on top of the other without relation to the first or to each other—like pancakes tossed on a plate. And one thing a paragraph should not be is a pile of sentences tossed anywhere.

Recognizing the gaps between the ideas and the apparent discontinuity of his thoughts, the writer went back to work. He provided elaboration of some ideas and even additional sentences. These changes help us to descend through the paragraph.

> Research indicates that certain kinds of monkeys have considerable language skills. Carl Sagan deals primarily with three chimpanzees—Lucy, Lana, and Washoe—who showed considerable linguistic talent. When they were taught Ameslan (American Sign Language), they were able to develop vocabularies that ranged from 100 to 200 words and eventually to form phrases. Medical research provides further support for the idea that chimpanzees are capable of linguistic tasks. James Dewson and colleagues found, for example, that monkeys have a language center in the neocortex of the left hemisphere of the brain, just as human beings do. This center may explain why their language capacity is far beyond that of other lower mammals. In addition, investigators think apes transmit extragenetic, or cultural, information that differs from tribe to tribe depending on the environment and what is needed to survive. Differences in group behavior among chimpanzees and related species have been documented. Such differences could come about, some investigators claim, only through language skills.

In the revision the writer does more than merely list pieces of evidence about the monkeys and the neocortex. Recognizing that the steps between the main idea and some of the concrete evidence are too steep, he builds intermediate steps. The addition to the second sentence allows us to move gracefully from the main idea to the Sagan research. The intermediate step in the fourth sentence eases us from the Sagan research to the evidence on the neocortex. These two steps help us descend through the paragraph. The last sentence is not so much a new step as an elevator: it carries all the freight back up to the topic sentence. Without it, and without those intermediate steps, all that evidence would lie inert in the basement of the paragraph.

We can think of the paragraph as a staircase the reader can smoothly descend, one foot safely on a step before the other foot moves. If the steps are too steep, the reader must jump and may fall. We must build in the intermediate steps—those statements somewhat less general than the topic sentence, somewhat more general than the evidence, that make for continuity of thought.

Something Old, Something New

Even when our ideas are properly grouped and the staircase well constructed, we still must provide clear transitions between sentences. As it introduces a new thought, each sentence almost always refers to something in the previous sentence. This reference backward indicates the connection between one thought and another. It helps the reader feel secure and oriented.

To see how something old, something new works, look at the paragraph by Martin Luther King, Jr., on page 177. The second sentence asks a question about the first. The third repeats the question, in a more concrete form. The fourth and fifth continue the questioning in the same form. Each sentence seems to reach back for an idea from the previous sentence and then to modify it. The thought is continuous, the connections firm.

Here is a paragraph of seemingly unconnected ideas:

> Housing prisoners one to a room is a controversial proposition. Some citizens say our society is already too permissive with criminals. Army recruits live in barracks. Some people see real advantages. Hardened criminals would have less opportunity to corrupt first offenders. Violence would decrease. Prisoners would have a chance to reflect on their past actions. Everybody agrees that taxpaying citizens are in no mood to underwrite experimentation in any area of government service. It might have ended up saving money, not to mention lives.

All the ideas are there, but we didn't have any pleasure reading them. Every sentence contains something new but hardly anything old. The writer might as well have made a list headed by "Pro" and "Con."

A writer can provide something old, something new in three ways:

1. by repeating words or phrases
2. by carefully using pronouns and demonstrative adjectives
3. by repeating a grammatical construction.

In revising, this writer used all three. Note the underlined words.

> Housing prisoners one to a room is a controversial proposition. Some citizens oppose such housing as unwarranted luxury. They say our society is already too permissive with criminals. They say that army recruits live in barracks. Other citizens claim that there are real and practical advantages to the plan. They say it would offer less opportunity for prison violence. It would offer less opportunity for hardened criminals to corrupt first offenders. At the same time it would offer more opportunity for prisoners to reflect on their past actions. These citizens also recognize that, despite the advantages, taxpayers are in no mood to underwrite experimentation in any area of government service. But they contend that it might end up saving money, not to mention lives.

REPETITIONS AND SYNONYMS.   When a writer repeats a word or uses its synonym from sentence to sentence, the reader recognizes that the same subject is being discussed. That recognition ties the two sentences together. The revised paragraph on housing prisoners contains many examples of this kind of reinforcement. The synonym *criminal* takes the place of, and makes more emphatic, the word *prisoner*. Notice how *they say* is repeated, as are *opportunity, advantages,* and *citizens*. These words are like Velcro, binding the sentences together.

Sometimes repeating a word throughout a paragraph tightens the connections:

> Experience, intelligence, and personality would not be enough to elect a person president. There must be money. Money influences delegates. Money buys airtime. Money pays for television advertisements. Money pays for hairstylists and speech coaches. Money pays for the campaign directors, whose main job is to find more money.

PRONOUNS AND DEMONSTRATIVE ADJECTIVES. The revised passage on housing prisoners uses both pronouns (*they, it*) and demonstrative adjectives (*such, that*) to connect ideas. When readers see a pronoun, they expect that the writer will say more on the same subject and that the ideas will accumulate, as in this example:

> Your basic president is a man who combines the common and the uncommon. He is white, and he stands somewhere around six feet tall. He is always religious, or at least a member of a religious organization. He is almost always a millionaire.

What holds true for pronouns also applies to demonstrative adjectives such as *this, that, these, those,* and *such*. The paragraph on presidents goes on to say:

> These qualities do not prevent his being an astute politician with many supporters. Those supporters get him to the White House, and, if he is at all competent and lucky, keep him there.

Read these sentences substituting *the* for *these* and *those*. Although you can figure it out, your reaction time is just a little slower. Your eye climbs back through the sentences, seeking connections that the demonstrative adjectives make plain.

PARALLEL CONSTRUCTION. Later we will discuss parallel construction in regard to both diction (see Chapter 12, Working with Words) and grammar (see Chapter 20, Problems in Sentences). Here we want to point out that repeating a grammatical form links sentences and helps to make a more coherent paragraph. Responding to the repeated pattern and the repeated rhythm, the reader makes connections more easily.

This passage from John F. Kennedy's inaugural address is an excellent example of the power of parallel construction:

> To those old allies whose cultural and spiritual origins we share, we pledge the loyalty of faithful friends. United, there is little we cannot do

in a host of cooperative ventures. Divided, there is little we can do, for we dare not meet a powerful challenge at odds and split asunder.

To those new states whom we welcome to the ranks of the free . . .

And on he went, holding firmly both his sentences and his audience.

Transitional Words

No matter how hard we try, we sometimes cannot write a paragraph that holds together without outside help. Frequently we need to insert transitional words, such as *furthermore, however,* and *for instance.* These linchpins help us keep our ideas logically connected. They explain whether the previous idea is being modified, qualified, amplified, or contradicted.

Before we discuss transitional words in depth, we want to make two important points. First, you will not need to insert such a word in absolutely every sentence. Whole paragraphs, in fact, can flow along without a single *however, thus,* or *furthermore,* just on the strength of a strong topic sentence and implicit relationships among ideas. In fact, overused, explicit transitions make writing wooden and mechanical. But carefully and sparingly employed, they make writing tight, emphatic, and clear. Second, transitional words carry a meaning and function of their own. They help determine the meaning of a sentence. Thus, you must be sure to choose a word that does exactly what you intend. Don't, for instance, use *therefore* when you mean *furthermore.*

Here are eight relations that transitional words can signal, with examples of each:

NUMBER. *First, second, third, finally.* If you have a series of complex ideas, you can give your reader a sense of order by treating the ideas as a list and numbering them. To show that you are closing the list—or to show that you are ending a narrative—you can use the word *finally.*

> In becoming a successful owner of securities, follow these four basic steps. First, learn to read Standard & Poor's monthly stock guide, which shows price/earnings ratio, long- and short-term debt, and so on, of many companies. Second . . . Third . . . Finally, be prepared to tolerate some wrong judgments.

ADDITION. *And, furthermore, moreover, in addition, besides.* When you attach another idea to a point already made, use one of these words or phrases.

> And everything will be crystal clear. Moreover, your writing will be smoother.

COMPARISON. *Similarly, likewise, in the same way.* One of these words or phrases will tell the reader to notice that two ideas are alike.

> Western explorers have always misunderstood the foreign cultures they "discover." In the same way, most American and European listeners fail to comprehend Indian music and think of it as a mixture of nasal caterwauling and groaning strings.

CONTRAST. *Even so, still, nonetheless, but, yet, notwithstanding, nevertheless, however, on the other hand.* To signal the reader that a new idea differs from the previous idea, insert one of these words or phrases.

> Babe Ruth was overweight, bandy-legged, often drunk, and always slow. He became, nevertheless, one of baseball's greatest hitters.

EXAMPLE. *For instance, for example, to illustrate, in particular.* When you use an example to support a statement, flag the example.

> Earning a college degree in the sciences is only one of many ways to a promising future. You could inherit your father's oil well, for instance, or score 100 points a game for your high-school basketball team.

CONCESSION. *Of course, to be sure, granted, given that, no doubt.* Concessions are an important part of any argument. They demonstrate that you are aware of other ways of looking at questions.

> More wars have been fought in the name of money than in the name of religion. Granted, millions have suffered and died for their religious beliefs. But behind every religious purge we can usually find an economic motive.

SUMMARY. *Briefly, in short, in conclusion, in sum, to sum up.* These signals warn your reader that you have ended your argument and want to make it a bit plainer by summing it up.

> Templeton's writing style is full of dense sonorities, a polished perfection that serves to avoid the untidy, irrational moment. In short, it stinks.

CONSEQUENCE OR CONCLUSION. *Thus, and so, as a result, consequently, therefore, hence, accordingly.* These words and phrases provide a sense of finality. We want to caution you, however, against using such words inaccurately. Be sure you don't claim a conclusion you haven't earned. For example, we could not in all conscience now write.

> Thus have we exhausted the subject of transitions, and you therefore know all you ever need to know.

With this brief survey, we have not earned either the *thus* or the *therefore*.

As their name indicates, transitions assist the flow of your thought from one sentence or phrase or clause to the next. They are the bridges over which your thought moves. Rather than asking your reader to jump the gap between thoughts, you provide a bridge.

Coherent writing conveys the reader smoothly and considerately from thought to thought. Much of your writing will do this naturally, but when rereading and revising your writing, watch for the gaps or missed connections that could cause your reader to stumble. Working for coherence will help your reader understand and will also help you chart the progress of your thought.

TIPS FOR COHERENCE

- Remember that few considerations are as important as how you get from one idea to the next.
- Finish one idea before you take up another so that you won't have to double back.
- Be sure your reader doesn't have to jump too far between steps in the paragraph.
- Check your sentences for something old, something new.
- Be both sparing and accurate with transitional words; make sure you earn your *therefore*s and *moreover*s.

Exercises for Coherence

1. Underline everything in these two passages that aids coherence, particularly all transitional words.

Sport may be the toy department of life, but one of its abiding compensations is that, at least on the field, it is the real thing. Much has been done in recent years in the attempt to ruin sport—the ruthlessness of owners, the greed of players, the general exploitation of fans. But even all this cannot destroy it. On the court, down on the field, sport is fraud-free and fakeproof. With a full count, two men on, his team down by one run in the last of the eighth, a batter (as well as a pitcher) is beyond the aid of public relations. At match point at Forest Hills a player's press clippings are of no help. Last year's earnings will not sink a twelve-foot putt on the eighteenth at Augusta. Alan Page, galloping up along the quarterback's blind side, figures to be neglectful of that quarterback's image as a swinger. In all these situations, and hundreds of others, a man either comes through or he doesn't. He is alone out there, naked but for his ability, which counts for everything. Something there is that is elemental about this, and something greatly satisfying. (Joseph Epstein, "Obsessed with Sport")

In Mexico, orphaned when he was eight, my father left school to work as an "apprentice" to an uncle. Twelve years later, he left Mexico in frustration and arrived in America. He had great expectations then of becoming an engineer. ("Work for my hands and my head.") He knew a Catholic priest who promised to get him money enough to study full time for a high school diploma. But the promises came to nothing. Instead there was a dark succession of warehouse, cannery, and factory jobs. After work he went to night school along with my mother. A year, two passed. Nothing much changed, except that fatigue worked its way into the bone; then everything changed. He didn't talk anymore of becoming an engineer. He stayed outside of the school while my mother went inside to learn typing and shorthand. (Richard Rodriguez, "The Achievement of Desire")

2. Go through a recent essay of yours and locate a passage near the middle. If you can, find a passage you recall writing with special ease. Now read that passage closely. How did you get from sentence to sentence? What is it about your sentences that made transitions possible? Look carefully for passages *without* either repeated words or transitional words.

3. Revise the following pairs of sentences so that something old and something new are in the second sentence of each pair.
   a. In the nineteenth century, being well padded with flesh was a sign of beauty. My friends like the slender look.
   b. Football games are not called on account of weather. Rain fell and they postponed the third game of the World Series.
   c. Pug dogs are fawn colored. Siamese cats are fawn colored.
   d. Genes are the elements that determine human inheritance. Some people believe we may eventually abuse our ability to change things that were not defects in the first place.

4. Revise the following passages to improve coherence.
   a. One writer suggests that solar power is the answer to our energy needs. Nuclear power should be our source of energy is what the other writer argues. Solar power is too expensive for many homes. No commercially viable power source has been devised on a scale large enough for private use. Nuclear power is used on a national scale.
   b. Antivivisectionists are opposed to any scientific experimentation on animals. The desire for new and safe cosmetics does not justify the pain and death necessary to test various products. Scientists want to learn the effects of chemicals and drugs on human beings.

9

STRATEGIES FOR DEVELOPING YOUR THOUGHTS

I hate definitions.

BENJAMIN DISRAELI (1804–1881)
BRITISH PRIME MINISTER AND AUTHOR

When you want to share your thought with someone else, you can't merely assert it in its bare form. You need to explain what it means and how it works. You take your main ideas, and you amplify, modify, qualify, exemplify them. In this chapter we examine eight strategies for developing your thought:

describing

telling stories

illustrating

analyzing a process

tracing cause and effect

classifying and dividing

comparing and contrasting

defining

These strategies help you to develop your ideas. You can use them at any stage in the writing process. As invention strategies (see Chapter 1, Getting Ready to Write), they can help you discover ideas. They can also, of course, help develop those ideas once discovered. They can help organize your thoughts. And—as we discuss in this chapter—they can help you draft and revise for complete and effective paragraphs. They are natural ways of thinking. As we write or speak, we use them without thinking.

Government is invading our lives. Take taxes, for example.

We've just used illustration, one of the most basic strategies.

I'm not getting a permanent. If I did, all my friends would laugh at me.

This sentence is developed by cause and effect.

All you have to do is take hold of the handle and turn.

Process analysis.

Sometimes a paragraph will be developed according to a single strategy. You will see examples of such paragraphs throughout this chapter, paragraphs of description, process analysis, classification, and so on. More often, a paragraph will intermingle several strategies. In discussing the idea of a "career," the sociologist Erving Goffman uses comparison and contrast, illustration, and cause and effect, with a bit of definition thrown in.

> One value of the concept of career is its two-sidedness. One side is linked to internal matters held dearly and closely, such as image of self and felt identity; the other side concerns official position, jural relations, and style of life, and is part of a publicly accessible institutional complex. The concept of career, then, allows one to move back and forth between the personal and the public, between the self and its significant society, without having to rely overly for data upon what the person says he thinks he imagines himself to be. (*Asylums*)

Writers often build whole essays around a central strategy. Other strategies will also be used in the process. Few essays go by without a paragraph or two of definition, illustration, and cause and effect, and almost certainly description or narration.

Look at the following passage, in which Richard Rodriguez argues against bilingual education:

> I hear of something called "bilingual education"—a scheme proposed in the late 1960s by Hispanic-American social activists, later endorsed by a congressional vote. It is a program that seeks to permit non-English-speaking children (many from lower class homes) to use their "family language" as the language of school. Such, at least, is the aim its supporters announce. I hear them, and am forced to say no: It is not possible for a child, any child, ever to use his family's language in school. Not to understand this is to misunderstand the public uses of schooling and to trivialize the nature of intimate life.
>
> Memory teaches me what I know of these matters. The boy reminds the adult. I was a bilingual child, but of a certain kind: "socially disadvantaged," the son of working-class parents, both Mexican immigrants.
>
> In the early years of my boyhood . . . (*Hunger of Memory*)

After defining two terms (*bilingual education* and *socially disadvantaged*), Rodriguez offers himself as an illustration of his point, and then begins to narrate, the major strategy of his essay. Within the narration will be description and more illustration.

The strategy you use at any particular point will depend on your purpose. You wouldn't use the same strategy to convey the impression of a Zulu war dance that you use for placing surrealism in its historic context. The dance requires description, narration, and perhaps process analysis. Surrealism must be defined and illustrated and then analyzed for its historic causes and effects. With each task, you will have to decide what strategy or strategies to employ. And after the decision comes the performance. In the following pages, we suggest ways of effectively using each of the eight strategies.

DESCRIPTION: SHOWING IT

When we put into words what our senses tell us, we are describing. "Meet me by the broken copper fountain under the gnarled old tree that gives off a pungent, almost acrid smell." We frequently use description in our college work as well. In a film class, the instructor might assign the description of a scene from a movie; in a history class, a battle or a political event; in a law class, a court trial or an accident.

Description is one of the most basic strategies. We can use it by itself or to support other strategies. A narration almost always includes description. A definition frequently relies on describing.

What Description Is

In the following passage, James Agee describes the great movie comedian Buster Keaton:

> No other comedian could do as much with the dead pan. He used this great, sad, motionless face to suggest various related things: a one-track mind near the track's end of pure insanity; mulish imperturbability under the wildest of circumstances; how dead a human being can get and still be alive; an awe-inspiring sort of patience and power to endure, proper to granite but uncanny in flesh and blood. Everything that he was and did bore out this rigid face and played laughs against it. When he moved his eyes, it was like seeing them move in a statue. His short-legged body was all sudden, machinelike angles, governed by a daft aplomb. When he swept a semaphorelike arm to point, you could almost hear the electrical impulse in the signal block. When he ran from a cop his transitions from accelerating walk to easy jogtrot to brisk canter to

headlong gallop to flogged-piston sprint—always floating, above this frenzy, the untroubled, untouchable face—were as distinct and as soberly in order as an automatic gearshift. ("Comedy's Greatest Era")

Agee re-creates in our mind's eye the brilliant comedian. First he sets up the angle from which we will view Keaton's deadpan face. Then, like a camera zooming in on a scene, he moves us closer and closer to the details of Keaton's face, body, and performance. We see the eyes moving in the immobile face. We see the movements of the short-legged body and arms. In the seventh sentence, he brings the whole description—face and body— brilliantly alive in a specific, and typical, scene: Keaton running from the cops. And always the deadpan face, the organizing principle of the passage.

Agee avoids the vague and the abstract. Notice the words *statue, frenzy, soberly, gearshift*. Each calls up a distinct image. He uses the word *mulish* before *imperturbability*, so we think of the dumb, unyielding mule. When we read "easy jogtrot to brisk canter to headlong gallop to flogged-piston sprint," we conjure up images associated with these words.

At every step of the way, Agee had choices to make. He might, for instance, have written "a donkeylike imperturbability"—a donkey is about as stubborn as a mule. But *donkey* would call up the unwanted association of almost frivolous stupidity. A mule is mulish, but it is not a jackass. Agee did not write "a large, jutting, rough-edged hunk of gray granite." The single word *granite* sufficed. He knew that a few well-chosen details would suffice to suggest a complete picture and that unimportant details would only confuse.

Agee made a point with this description: the source of Buster Keaton's power and appeal is that face. By the end of the passage, we can understand why he found Keaton so wonderful. This is exactly what good description does: it conveys an idea and the images it is based on from the mind of the writer to the mind of the reader. When the description is good, the idea lives in the reader's mind.

Writing Description

The writer's task is, as Joseph Conrad said, "by the power of the written word, to make you hear, to make you feel—it is, before all, to make you *see*." The details we choose for a description must be vivid enough to call up images from the reader's store of remembered impressions. Good description demands the exact, the concrete, and the familiar. Abstract or imprecise words make for slower understanding and are generally less effective. Using an invention technique can help make ideas more specific and vivid.

Details must add up to something, however: an impression, an effect, such as Agee's idea about the source of Keaton's appeal. Only when we select details with our idea in mind will the reader *see*.

The following passage describes a great painting:

> The *Mona Lisa* is a portrait by Leonardo da Vinci of an Italian woman about whom we know little. Her hands are folded in her lap. She is looking out of the painting, wearing her famous smile. She has on dark clothes and is poised at a window. Her hair is mostly straight. The surface of the painting has deteriorated so that closer examination is difficult.

This description is too vague. It doesn't tell us, for instance, whether the folded hands are tensely gripping each other or are loose and relaxed. The phrase *her famous smile* could mean a death's-head grin for all we know. The condition of the painting's surface appears as an isolated fact. The details are too disorganized to make a point. Indeed, there was apparently no point.

The revision is considerably better:

> Everything in the *Mona Lisa* communicates serene repose. Her hands, folded loosely, and her gaze, neither avoiding nor confronting the viewer, indicate a woman at peace with herself and the world. Her smile bespeaks inner contentment, not an effort to entertain or impress the world. Da Vinci reinforces this mood of quiet by using muted hues— dark hair, dark clothing, the distant, obscure valley. Yet even here there are bits of brightness, in both the wisp of curl framing the subject's face and the river behind her. Time itself has supported da Vinci's theme, for the deteriorating surface of the painting thwarts the microscopic examination that would set mood aside to analyze structure. One must instead absorb the *Mona Lisa* whole, and in this way, perhaps, come away a bit more serene oneself.

Now we can see the kind of smile it is, the hands as part of the whole, the window as framing the river. All the details are relevant. We understand that the hues reinforce the meaning of the smile.

TIPS FOR DESCRIPTION

- Use details vivid enough to call up an image in the reader's mind.
- Emphasize important details; eliminate unimportant ones.
- Make sure there is a point to the description; have it contribute to a larger idea.

Exercises for Description

1. Think about a movie you have seen recently and conjure up a particular scene. Focus in on just one moment in that scene, as if you were selecting one frame of film for a publicity still. Describe that frame in vivid, concrete detail and suggest the overall impression it makes. Now change one major detail—the general appearance of a character, the number of characters present, the setting, the dominant color. How would the change affect the overall impression?

2. Think back over your childhood and recall an object you especially cherished. Describe it as objectively as you can from your present perspective. Now describe it as you think you saw it when you were a child. What is the difference?

3. Choose an object that has become something of a symbol of the American way of life; for example, a McDonald's or a football. Using either free writing or clustering, develop ideas about the object. Now describe it. Emphasize details that strike you as important, and explain their significance in relation to your interpretation of American culture.

4. Go to the library and find a photograph of one of the following people:

Billie Holiday	Robert E. Lee
Jim Thorpe	Shirley Chisholm
Calvin Coolidge	Golda Meir
Jean Harlow	Indira Gandhi
Marie Curie	Charles Darwin

   Photocopy it and describe it in a paragraph. All the paragraphs will be reproduced and distributed in class, and the photocopied photographs will be passed around. Members of the class will try to match the descriptions to the photocopies.

NARRATION: TELLING IT

"Where did you go?"
"Out."
"What did you do?"
"Nothing."

When we tell what happened, even if it was "nothing," we narrate. A narration is an account of what happened. Short stories and novels are narrations, but so is a joke, an anecdote, or an autobiography. We narrate when we summarize the plot of a novel, tell what happened during a rebellion, or trace the course of a disease. We also narrate a lab report or a summary of a research project.

After description, narration is the most basic writing strategy. Frequently, we use it in conjunction with other strategies. When we write a descriptive piece, we almost always narrate part of it. Often our examples are narrations. And we may use narration in process analysis, cause and effect, and definition.

What Narration Is

In the following passage, George Orwell skillfully narrates a poignant but challenging event to support his argument against capital punishment:

> We set out for the gallows. Two warders marched on either side of the prisoner, with their rifles at the slope; two others marched close against him, gripping him by the arm and shoulder as though at once pushing and supporting him. The rest of us, magistrates and the like, followed behind. Suddenly, when we had gone ten yards, the procession stopped short without any order or warning. A dreadful thing had happened—a dog, come goodness knows whence, had appeared in the yard. It came bounding among us with a loud volley of barks, and leapt round us wagging its whole body, wild with glee at finding so many human beings together. It was a large woolly dog, half Airedale, half pariah. For a moment it pranced round us, and then, before anyone could stop it, it had made a dash for the prisoner and, jumping up, tried to lick his face. Everyone stood aghast, too taken aback even to grab at the dog.
>
> "Who let that bloody brute in here?" said the superintendent angrily. "Catch it, someone!" ("A Hanging")

This powerful narrative helps Orwell drive his points home. The scene is deftly set. The action is continuous, from "set out" to "'Catch it, someone!'" Something is always happening, and every happening contributes to the point. The passive prisoner is never the grammatical subject of a sentence, yet we cannot forget him for a moment. When the dog gives the prisoner the canine kiss of love, one "pariah" accepts another. The dog offers a sympathy that we and perhaps the officials in the narrative like to associate with human beings.

As this passage unfolds, we become uneasy. By its end, we may find ourselves pondering a serious moral question: what love should we offer criminals, outcasts, pariahs? This question takes on life not in a sermonette but in a narrative.

Writing Narration

The building blocks of good narration are the same as those of good description: a point to be made and concrete, relevant details. To help the reader get the point, concentrate on the most illuminating events. Let the story unfold scene by scene. Using vivid detail—concrete nouns, active verbs, exact adjectives and adverbs—try to re-create the narrative in the reader's imagination. *Show* rather than *tell* the story, as though the reader were actually watching and listening. Arrange the scenes so that they rise to a climax, a dramatic high point.

The following passage attempts to narrate an important event in the life of the writer:

> When we came back from the store that Christmas Eve, I realized I had been given too much change from my final purchase. I showed the money to my brother and then to my father. My father didn't like it and he made me give back the money. My brothers and sisters all laughed at me. I should have returned the money myself, without father's having to tell me.

This narrative is an abstract and general summary of happenings, without dialogue, contrasts, or drama. The writer tells everything and shows lit-tle—and yet many important questions are ignored: we don't really know why the father took the narrator back to the store or why the siblings laughed. As for the point, at the end the writer tries to incorporate a neat—far too neat—little moral. But does the story only want to tell us to be honest? Do we really need to be reminded of that?

In the revision the writer thought through what point she wanted to make. Then she made an effort to visualize the happenings and present them as vividly as she could.

> When the salesclerk gave me back my change, I thought she had given me too much. At age six, I didn't count money very well, and so when we got home, I showed the coins to my brother. "I gave her fifty cents," I said, "and she gave me this."
>
> "That's sixty cents," he said in an admiring voice I seldom heard from him. "You're smarter than I thought." Beaming with pride, chortling over my new fortune, I went sailing in to my father to receive his praise.
>
> "The salesclerk gave me too much change," I said.
>
> With deliberation, he went over all my purchases with me. He ex-amined my dog-eared Christmas list and the sales slips. "Get your coat," he said.
>
> The news flashed through the house, and, as my father and I pre-pared to leave, my brothers and sisters hid behind the banisters and si-lently mocked me.
>
> "Honor," my father said as he closed the front door. "Honesty," he said as we walked to the car. "Fairness," he said as he started the car. "These are virtues without which civilization cannot endure. Money," he went on as we backed away from the curb, "may threaten virtue but must never be allowed to defeat it. Let this be a lesson to you." And in truth it was, though I could not have said in what.

In her revision, the writer lets us watch the people act and hear them talk. The scenes now build to the climax. Perhaps the greatest improvement, however, is in the point of the story. Now it is left ambiguous, as it should be. Sibling rivalry, parental instruction, honesty, the joys of praise and of money—all are inextricably mixed in the young narrator's mind. The whole narrative supports that point.

TIPS FOR NARRATION

- Before writing, decide what point your narrative should have.
- Choose events, details, and language to support your point.
- Show, don't tell; develop your narrative scene by scene.
- Build to a climax.

Exercises for Narration

1. Report an incident, at home or at work, as if you were giving information to a specific person; for instance, a police officer or supervisor. Think about what kind of detail the audience needs. Think about the purpose.

2. Narrate a story having to do with one of the following feelings: pain, fear, hunger, affection, hope. Do not name the feeling. Let your choice of events and the words you use communicate it.

3. Make up an encounter in which you and a stranger have a disagreement. Be sure it has a climax and a point, but don't state the point. In a follow-up paragraph, describe how you selected the key events to make the episode climactic. Now state the point and evaluate your skill in conveying it.

4. After developing ideas through the journalistic or classical method (see "Directed Questioning" in Chapter 1), write a page narrating one of the following events:

   high-school commencement
   your arrival at college
   registration for classes
   the first meeting of this class
   the first social occasion at school

   Now exchange your essay with a partner, each analyzing the other's essay. Based on your partner's critique and your own increased focus on narration, rewrite your essay.

ILLUSTRATION: MAKING IT SPECIFIC

When we see a questioning look on our listener's face, we instinctively provide an illustration, an example of what we mean. "Ingmar Bergman is excellent at portraying intricate family relationships—in *Autumn Sonata,* for example, he captured mother-daughter rivalry." In much of your college writing, you will need to provide illustrations. When you make a point about a work of literature, you must go to the text to find illustrations for it. When you generalize about a historic event, illustrations clarify your meaning. They support your assertion about a work of art, a social phenomenon, a laboratory procedure.

Illustrations serve three purposes. First, they clarify your thought by bringing the general idea to a more easily understood specific level. Second, they help prove your idea by showing that, at least in this particular instance, your assertion is reasonable. Third, they make reading more entertaining. Nothing brings the reader and the writer together quite so quickly and effectively as the well-chosen illustration.

What Illustration Is

The writer of the following passage states a point and then makes it more specific by providing illustrations.

> Little girls learn early in life that the boy's role is one to be envied and emulated. Child psychologists have pointed out that experimenting with the role of the opposite sex is much more acceptable for little girls than it is for little boys. For example, girls are free to dress in boys' clothes, but certainly not the other way around. Most parents are amused if they have a daughter who is a *tomboy,* but they are genuinely distressed if they have a son who is a *sissy.* The names we give to young children reflect the same attitude. It is all right for girls to have boys' names, but pity the boy who has a girl's name! Because parents keep giving boys' names to girls, the number of acceptable boys' names keeps shrinking. Currently popular names for girls include *Jo, Kelly, Teri, Chris, Pat, Shawn, Toni,* and *Sam* (short for *Samantha*). *Evelyn, Carroll, Gayle, Hazel, Lynn, Beverley, Marion, Francis,* and *Shirley* once were acceptable names for males. But as they were given to females, they became less and less acceptable. Today, men who are stuck with them self-consciously go by their initials or by abbreviated forms such as *Haze, Shirl, Frank,* or *Ev.* And they seldom pass these names on to their sons. (Alleen Pace Nilsen, "Sexism and Language")

The assertion in the first sentence of this paragraph is abstract, but the illustrations are specific. They become more and more so as the paragraph continues, until we encounter that cascade of names toward the end. Nilsen's deft use of illustration accomplishes two things: it makes her point very clear indeed, and it makes that point persuasive.

Writing with Illustration

As with all strategies, writers must plan and arrange illustration carefully. Each illustration must be relevant to the subject and accessible to the reader.

In this paragraph, from an essay analyzing the distinctive qualities of various movie stars, the writer uses illustrations in his discussion of Humphrey Bogart:

> Humphrey Bogart occupies a unique and permanent place in the imagination of the American moviegoer. The key to his success lies in his ability to portray a complex character, at once a ruthless, utterly self-seeking loner, and a tender, even sentimental, defender of the weak. In *The African Queen,* Bogart is a buffoon and Katharine Hepburn is the tough one. In *The Desperate Hours,* Bogart displays love for his brother but cruelly jeopardizes the family he holds hostage. When he dies, we feel both relief and a touch of sorrow. Fredric March plays the father, who is loving and selfless. In *To Have and Have Not,* Bogart is again both hard and sensitive. Lauren Bacall is as usual honest and humorous. Moviegoers still value the qualities Bogart represented and look for them in today's actors. But we can no more imagine a new tender-tough Bogart than we can a new Garibaldi riding through the Italian countryside, unifying his country.

Did you feel this paragraph going awry? The writer has a great many details, but he has not selected them wisely or arranged them well. Notice that he reverses the description of Bogart from tough-tender to tender-tough and then back to tough-tender. Once we establish an order, we ought to stick to it. Otherwise the reader's eyes will be flying up and down the page, looking for home base.

Many of the details are irrelevant. The references to Katharine Hepburn and Fredric March distract the reader. The writer has an interesting point about Bogart as a buffoon; however, he introduces this idea far too early—before he has developed his main idea—and muddles the discussion. The comparison in the last line is farfetched. Few readers would easily connect Garibaldi, the nineteenth-century Italian revolutionary leader, with Bogart, the twentieth-century actor. And *The Desperate Hours* is an obscure film. The writer should have told the reader more about this important but unfamiliar illustration.

Still a Bogart fan, the writer went back to the writing desk.

Humphrey Bogart occupies a unique and permanent place in the imagination of the American moviegoer. The key to his success lies in his ability to portray a complex character, at once a ruthless, utterly self-seeking loner and a tender, even sentimental, defender of the weak. A good example of this character can be seen in *The Desperate Hours*. In this movie, Bogart's willingness to destroy his fellow convict, to pistol-whip the innocent father of the family he holds hostage, and to jeopardize the lives of the family exists side by side with his love for his brother and, finally, his unwillingness to harm the little boy in the family.

In *To Have and Have Not,* Bogart again plays the tough-tender guy, but his toughness is softened by Lauren Bacall's irony and his sentimentality undercut by her honesty. Bogart did not always play the same role, of course—in *The African Queen* he is a weakling and a buffoon until near the end—but he was always most appealing in his tough-tender guise. Moviegoers still value the qualities Bogart represented and look for them in today's actors. But we can no more imagine another tough-tender Bogart than we can another ironic-honest Bacall.

Here the writer maintains the tough-tender order all the way. He sticks to his subjects, and where needed he elaborates with more detailed illustrations. At the end, he illustrates his point by a comparison with the well-known Lauren Bacall.

TIPS FOR ILLUSTRATION

- When providing illustrations, follow the same pattern as the idea the illustrations support.
- Be sure your illustrations are clearly related to the point.
- Use illustrations that your reader will find easily understandable.
- If necessary, offer more detailed illustrations.

Exercises for Illustration

1. Find a passage in one of your textbooks in which the author illustrates a point. Be ready to present the passage to the class and answer these questions:

   Why did the author use the illustration or illustrations?
   Would fewer or more illustrations have improved the passage?
   How could you make this passage more effective?

2. Think up two illustrations for each of the following statements:

   Money is the root of all evil.
   Shyness can be an asset.
   Buying stocks can be hazardous to your financial health.
   Politics is the art of the possible.

   Exchange your illustrations with a partner. Choose one of the statements and write a paragraph analyzing the difference between your illustrations and those of your partner. Which are more accessible? Which need to be more specific? How would you make your partner's illustrations better?

3. Take your most recent essay and find places where you need more illustrations of your point. Rewrite the essay accordingly.

PROCESS ANALYSIS: EXPLAINING HOW IT WORKS

Process analysis is a special kind of narrative, one that shows *how* something happens. We often use process analyses to *instruct*. If we want to teach someone how to use a computer, how to dissect a frog, how to get there from here, we focus on the process.

We use process analysis also to *explain*. Scientists use process analysis to explain how a strand of DNA, deoxyribonucleic acid, replicates. Economists use it to explain how bank clearinghouses work. If psychologists wish to explain the development of human personality in the infant, they will probably call on this strategy. It is important in virtually every academic discipline and outside of school too.

What Process Analysis Is

The following passage instructs novices in how to save work when using WordStar, a word processing program:

Every half hour or so, while editing a file in WordStar, type ↑-K ↑-S. This will save everything you have typed so far on the disk and return you to the top of the file. After the computer has finished saving the file, type ↑-Q ↑-P to return to where you were before.

When you have finished an editing session and are ready to turn off the computer or remove a text diskette, save the file by using ↑-K ↑-X, which will write your file on the disk and return you to the operating system. The computer will display a "B↑" prompt (because you changed the logged drive to B: after you entered WordStar—see step 4.c above). *Do not remove any diskettes* until you have returned to the operating system and the red lights on both disk drives are off. If you wish to do other things on the computer (i.e., not using WordStar), type A:<RET> to log in Drive A. (Tiro Project, "Instructions for Start-Up, Disk Handling, and File Maintenance")

This analysis of how to operate WordStar is unusually good. Bearing in mind the purpose—to save edited material—the writer breaks the process into major elements and deals with each as an entity, a miniprocess: analyzing first how to save what you have typed during an editing session and then how to save work when you are finished. Within each major element, the writer narrates the process step by step and shows how each step is related to the previous one.

Rather than saying "Do this, do that," the author explains consequences. He interrupts the analysis to fix the process in the reader's mind by summing up the process so far. He indicates exactly when to take the next step. These signals increase the user's understanding and retention, the goals of any instruction.

The writer avoids unnecessary detail. He does not spend words telling the user to press the control key with the index finger or to sit up straight. He sticks to the essential, makes the language simple and direct, and keeps technical terms to a minimum. The most nervous, inexperienced user would soon master the system by following his instructions.

When we use process analysis to explain, the goals are similar: to set forth the process in all its richness, to make clear the sequence of states or steps, and to present the analysis so that the reader can easily understand and remember it.

In the following passage the authors analyze one of baseball's most mysterious pitches, the knuckleball:

> A deliberately awkward grip makes it possible to throw a baseball with almost no spin. While the standard curveball uses rapid spin to create a sideways force, the knuckleball gets its curve from the effect of its protruding stitches. The stitches interfere with the smooth flow of air around the ball. When they are positioned asymmetrically, they deflect the low-pressure wake that forms behind the ball, and that, in turn, makes the pitch curve sideways. A typical knuckleball may start by curving to the left. But then the slow rotation changes the stitches' orientation. A midcourse correction results. Suddenly the new sideways force pushes the ball to the right—and increased drag from the stitches may also cause it to plunge. (based on Joel W. Hollenberg and James Gleick, "Secret of the Knuckleball's Dance")

Hollenberg and Gleick start by dividing the process into its major components—the awkward grip, the effect of the protruding stitches, and the aerodynamics of the pitched ball. Each of these components is shown in action, and the significance of each is explained for us. Finally, we are shown the result of all three acting together: the unpredictable, maddening flutter of the knuckleball. Thanks to such writing, something we may have considered a mystery is now not so mysterious.

Writing Process Analysis

Process analysis may seem easy because it is, like most writing, a written version of a natural way of thinking. We often wonder how things happen or work, and if we can figure them out, we think we should be able to explain them. As with most writing, however, a gap exists between understanding a process and effectively conveying it in writing. And sometimes in our headlong rush to get it down, we fall into that gap.

The first step in writing process analysis is to articulate its purpose or its ultimate goal and identify the audience. If you are telling someone how to put together a bicycle, say so right off. The purpose determines both the order of the presentation and the emphasis each part receives. And knowing the audience will determine how much background you need and how specific you should be.

The second step is to divide the process into major and minor elements. In explaining the assembly of a bicycle, you would divide the process into assembling the frame, fitting the gears, and attaching the wheels, and then discuss the minor elements as subdivisions. If you tried to deal with one operation after another without grouping—bolt 1, bolt 2, bolt 3, and so on to bolt 25—the reader would have a difficult time understanding and remembering.

You will need to decide which details are essential to your analysis. You don't want your reader to get bogged down in excess, but you do want to provide an adequately concrete analysis. Because a process is a sequence of steps or operations, you need to show how one step is related to the previous and the following steps. Clear transitions help to keep the order in focus. It is also important to stop every once in a while and recapitulate briefly where you are in the process.

The final step is to suit your language to your audience and purpose. You would not discuss circumference/velocity ratios on a bicycle with someone who merely wanted to get the thing on the road. But do not hesitate to use special terms when they are the best way to convey your meaning; just be sure to define them clearly the first time they come up.

When process analysis goes wrong, the writer usually has not articulated the overall purpose, emphasized major steps, or shown how the parts connect, as this passage demonstrates:

> To buy a house will probably take about three months. Look the place over to be sure it meets your family's needs. If you have young children, you may want a play yard; if the children are older, perhaps a family room. You will want to show the house to family members. Next

draw up a contract. Then come the title search and the house inspection. This house inspection should include termite infestation, structural integrity including the roof and beams, and quality of water, sewer, gas, and electrical systems. Almost everyone needs a mortgage. And a lawyer. Once the bank makes the commitment, you can close and move in.

Too much important information is missing and too much irrelevant information is emphasized for this paragraph to work as a process analysis. What is the writer's overall purpose? What are the main elements of the process? How are the steps in the process related? What is a title search, and how can I inspect the house for termites? Why a lawyer? And why three months—will it take that long for all those family members to troop through?

In the revision, the writer addressed these problems.

Buying a house is seldom either smooth or easy, but anticipating what lies ahead—from signing the contract through buying to taking actual possession—may lessen the difficulties. First, you and the seller draw up a contract establishing the purchase price and the date on which the sale will be completed. Before signing and making the down payment, you should get a lawyer's advice about the legality and adequacy of the contract. Your lawyer can also perform a title search, that is, make sure that no one other than the seller has a claim on the house. Your next step is to hire experts to inspect the house for problems that might not be visible to the naked eye, like insect infestation or the quality of the electrical system. If anything is amiss, you may have to renegotiate the contract. Unless you are a millionaire, your next step is to apply for a mortgage, the most trying aspect of the whole process. The lending institution will want to know everything about your financial condition, including your tax returns. No matter how quickly you comply, the bank can take up to three months to decide. When your mortgage is approved, you can "close"—that is, make the agreed-upon payment to the seller and get the house and the keys in return.

The writer starts with a clear statement of purpose, indicates the broad outlines of the process, and discusses the major steps in chronological order. She defines terms and relates each step to the whole. She does not dwell on unimportant details. And she left that extended family back home.

TIPS FOR PROCESS ANALYSIS

- Identify your audience and their level of knowledge on your subject.
- Tell your reader the purpose of your analysis.

- Group elements into major components.
- Include only essential details.
- Occasionally point out where you are in the process.
- Be sure your language is appropriate to your audience; where necessary, define terms.

Exercises for Process Analysis

1. Choose something you do well—playing a musical instrument, operating a machine, waterskiing, playing tennis—and write an essay in which you explain to a novice the skills necessary for this activity. At the end, describe the perfect practitioner of your activity and identify all the qualities that make for that perfection.

2. Outline a plan for a major enterprise, such as converting the campus food service to a student-run operation, setting up a summer camp for blind children, or developing a transportation system for the campus. Your purpose is to persuade the authorities, who know nothing of this plan, that they should institute it as soon as possible.

3. Write a paragraph in which you explain first to a ten-year-old and then to a contemporary one of the following:

   achieving a checkmate in chess
   betting in a poker game
   performing a suicide squeeze in baseball
   assuming a body position that signals defensiveness
   performing an *entrechat*

   Specify the functions of each part in relation to the overall strategy, attack, or defense involved.

4. Choose one of the following topics and, after you have done the necessary research, write a process analysis of it:

   how an Individual Retirement Account works
   the courting rituals of the praying mantis
   how one becomes a Methodist minister
   how continental drift works
   how a "rite of passage" functions

CAUSE AND EFFECT: EXPLAINING WHY IT HAPPENED

Cause and effect analysis answers the question *why*? Why did you ruin the peas? I left the burner on too long. Why is Joe in the hospital? He had a car accident. Why did he have the accident? He was driving too fast, the roads were wet, and there was a sharp curve. Breaking down a train of events into causes and effects can be a powerful analytical tool. It can help us to understand not only small, simple events, such as burning the peas, but also large, complicated ones. When California passed New York as the nation's most populous state, experts argued over the causes and the effects of the demographic redistribution. Futurologists attempt to analyze what life will be like when people shop and pay bills and even entertain via television and computers.

Cause and effect analysis helps answer two fundamental questions about an event. The first is, Why did something happen? To answer that, we look for causes. What factors, for example, allowed California to surpass New York in population? Did people move to California because of the weather? because of the decay of cities in the East? because the international economic focus was shifting from Europe to Asia? The second question is, What happened because of it? To answer this question, we look for effects. What changes resulted from the migration to California? Has the California style of living become more attractive than other styles of living? Has the quality of life in California declined because of overcrowding?

Because this form of analysis is so important to understanding our world, instructors often assign cause and effect essays. A psychology instructor may assign a paper on the causes of neurosis. A history instructor may assign one on why the Weimar republic collapsed. A physics instructor may ask for an analysis of the effects of ultraviolet radiation on the skin. Most research projects and most argumentative essays include cause and effect passages to support their theses because almost always we want to know why.

What Cause and Effect Is

In the following passage, the sociologist William Helmreich speculates about the causes behind the stereotype of the warm Hispanic:

> The anthropologist Oscar Lewis often observed that Hispanic families he studied had warm, emotional ties, especially between mother and child. Psychiatrists have pointed out that Hispanic mothers kiss and cuddle infants more than Anglo mothers, and remain intensely involved with their children throughout their lives.
>
> Researchers have attributed such behavior to the extended family structure common among Hispanics. As a result, the child learns to regard a greater number of people with warmth and affection. Others note that historically Hispanics have come from societies where the individual was born into a social and economic system that remained fixed throughout his life. They therefore tended to place more importance on personal qualities to make distinctions among those with whom they lived. ("Stereotype Truth")

Helmreich examines each of the causes—warm emotional ties, extended family, importance of personal qualities—and explains the importance of each in the causal chain. Each cause is defined and explained, and its significance evaluated. Each cause is placed in context and thus also becomes an effect in its own right, a part of the causal chain.

Writing Cause and Effect

In constructing a cause and effect argument, you start with a situation and work your way forward to the effects or backward to the causes. This process can be an intellectual adventure and may include both research and speculation. A good way to begin is to brainstorm and then organize the individual possibilities into large groups. This way you can distinguish essential elements from incidental ones. Organizing your ideas can help clarify relationships, establish a hierarchy of importance, and ensure that your analysis is comprehensive.

Beware of oversimplification. Sometimes we think we have discovered *the* cause or *the* effect when in fact we have only come upon one of several. Complex phenomena have more than one cause or result in more than one effect. Even a simple effect, such as "I ruined the peas," cannot be explained simply by saying "I left the burner on too long." Of course, if the focus was only on the agent—or *precipitating* cause—of the ruin, "I left the burner on" would be enough. In most cases, however, we would need to explain why the burner was left on: the telephone rang and I answered it and it distracted me because it was long distance, there had been an accident, Joe was injured . . .

In constructing a cause and effect essay, you must also distinguish between *remote* causes and close or *proximate* causes. Proximate causes contribute directly and forcefully to the effect: "The telephone rang" is a proximate cause and must be included in any explanation of burning the peas. To say "The peas were ruined because Joe was in the hospital" would not make much sense: what has Joe's being in the hospital to do with burning the peas? You must include the proximate cause of each effect: "The telephone call informing me that Joe was in the hospital distracted me, and I left the burner on too long, ruining the peas."

Remember the old saying "For want of a nail the shoe was lost, for want of a shoe the horse was lost, for want of a horse the rider was lost"? Causes happen in chains, and every cause has causes. Yet there is a limit to how far we want to extend our search for causes. In explaining the peas, we might trace the causal chain to Joe's reckless driving, and then we might conclude, "Joe's mother didn't discipline him when he was a child." Joe's recklessness may indeed go back to being overindulged by his mother, but mentioning his upbringing as a cause of ruining the peas only confuses the issue.

How far back to go is a matter of judgment. Purpose is the key to making that judgment. If the purpose is to explain the ruined peas, we do not need to state that Joe's mother did not discipline him. If, however, the purpose is to explain Joe's recklessness, we probably do need to talk about his mother's overindulgence.

We cannot include everything that may have contributed—we may have burned those poor old peas in part because the range light was dim, we were tired, and we have always loathed peas. Even though these facts contributed marginally, we clutter up our argument by trying to be all-inclusive. We should mention only causes that contribute significantly.

Sometimes we mistake coincidence for cause. We think that because something happened either before or at the same time as the effect, then that something caused the effect. (This fallacy is called *post hoc, ergo propter hoc* and is discussed in Chapter 4.) "Joe never had an accident until he got that convertible. Obviously, convertibles aren't safe." This is patently illogical. The convertible did not cause either the accident or Joe's recklessness. You must limit your discussion to causes that have real agency.

When cause and effect analysis fails, it is usually because the writer has not sorted out the essential elements from the nonessential, or has not thought through his or her purpose. Such is the case in the following paragraph from an essay on the changing status of women in American society:

> The main reason that women improved their position is that the media focused so much attention on the women's liberationists at the beginning of the 1970s. Sexual emancipation also contributed, as did fairer hiring policies in business and government. A liberal political climate and a succession of Democratic presidents and Congresses in the 1960s cleared the way for the climb, as did the invention of the Pill. Women in high places—like Golda Meir, Indira Gandhi, Margaret Thatcher, senators and representatives, business executives, university presidents—became role models. Rising divorce rates also contributed. Of course, many minorities of other sorts were seeking their rights at the same time. Many women were not interested any longer in the traditional roles of housekeeper, wife, and mother. Women had been a large part of the war effort during the Second World War, and afterward more women started going to school and earning higher degrees.

It is all in there somewhere—yet something is missing. The writer does not evaluate his findings. Which causes does he think are important, and why? All receive the same treatment. Nor does he differentiate between causes and effects. In the first sentence, media attention is called the main reason, but media attention was probably an effect of the change, not a cause. It was without doubt not the main cause.

The writer establishes no chain of causation and does not show how the elements he lists are related. Is there, for instance, a connection between women participating in the war effort and women not being inter-

ested in traditional roles? between the contraceptive pill and sexual emancipation? The writer does not say. By slapping the causes on the page
without grouping them or analyzing the chain in which they figure, the
writer fails to provide a clear explanation of how this enormous social
change came about.

For the revision, he decided that the two most important causes were
women's experience in industry and contraception. He clustered his other
causes around these and showed how they were connected.

> The improvement of the position of women in American society re-
> sulted from many events occurring in the last half of the twentieth cen-
> tury. During World War II, the country and women themselves learned
> that women could perform well in an industrial society. This success led
> to a demand for greater opportunities in education and employment.
> With the advent of effective contraceptive devices, especially the Pill,
> women began to feel that they were not bound to motherhood. This
> sexual emancipation became a symbol for other kinds of freedom: free-
> dom to pursue education and a career, and freedom to reject the tradi-
> tional roles of housekeeper, wife, and mother. When the civil rights
> movement focused national attention on the rights of minorities, people
> began to see more clearly that women, too, had been denied rights. The
> liberal political climate of the 1960s and 1970s led to fairer hiring poli-
> cies in business and government. And, as though they had been waiting
> in the wings, there emerged a group of prominent public women—
> Golda Meir, Indira Gandhi, Margaret Thatcher, senators and repre-
> sentatives, business executives, university presidents—ready to show
> younger women the path to the halls of power.

Improvement begins early with a very firm topic sentence that brings previously scattered points into order, sets forth a hierarchy of causes, and
controls the rest of the paragraph. Notice that the writer maintains clarity
by dealing first with the more remote cause—the experience during World
War II—before turning to the recent chain of events. And he completes the
analysis of causes before going on to the effect. By careful use of transitional
devices—"This success," "this sexual emancipation," "women, too, had
been denied rights"—he indicates relations between the various ideas.

TIPS FOR CAUSE AND EFFECT

- List all possible causes and then narrow down to the important ones.
- Distinguish between significant causes and incidental ones.
- Resist the temptation to look for an only cause or single
  effect.

- Differentiate between the remote causes and the proximate causes.
- Let purpose determine how far back to go in the causal chain.
- Separate real causation from coincidence.

Exercises for Cause and Effect

1. Here is a list of words often used in causal arguments: antecedent, component, condition, consequence, constituent, determinant, element, factor, influence, ingredient, issue, occasion, prerequisite, result. Look each one up in your dictionary and determine the distinctions among them. Which identify the most important causes? Arrange the words in ascending order of importance.

2. For each of these effects, determine a remote cause and a proximate cause. You might find the topic tree helpful here.

   your being in this writing class
   your living in this state
   the fact that you speak English
   your choice of the clothes you are wearing
   what you did last Saturday night

3. Here is a list of possible causes for the increased suicide rate among Americans aged fifteen to twenty-four from 1960 to 1977:

   political and social decline of America since 1960
   trauma of the Vietnam War
   alienation from society
   economic policies of the government
   unemployment
   racial tensions
   sexual and love-related matters
   parents too permissive
   parents too strict
   migration to big cities
   lack of clear and consistent values

   Which do you think are proximate causes? Which are remote? Which do you reject? Put them in ascending order of significance.

4. Find three causes of one of the following effects:

   the rise in the number of American bison since 1911
   the upward trend in sports salaries
   the constant appeal, whatever the economic situation, of diamond rings
   the disappearance of the California condor
   the overthrow of the Somoza regime in Nicaragua

   Determine the importance of each cause, and argue for your interpretation.

DIVISION AND CLASSIFICATION: PUTTING IT IN ITS PLACE

When we divide, we start with a single entity and break it into its parts. To say something useful about the practice of medicine, we might first divide it into its functional components: diagnosing, treating, curing, and preventing disease. We may need to subdivide: diagnosing includes use of sight to observe the patient, touch to determine abnormalities, hearing to examine functioning of lungs and heart, and microscopic, chemical, and bacteriological examination of blood and urine. And we could divide further.

Dividing is often the first step in the other strategies. When we write process analysis, cause and effect, or definition, we almost always begin by dividing the whole subject—the whole picture, the whole event, the whole world—into parts. Even when we compare and contrast, we divide items into their attributes. And division is at the heart of the strategy we call classification.

When we classify, we sort individual items into categories based on shared attributes or qualities. First we define the categories. For example, if we are classifying dogs, we might set up categories based on size: small, medium, large. Once we have set up the category, we can make general observations about all the individual items within it; describing the shared attributes or qualities. We can say small dogs eat less, bark more, learn quickly, or whatever we find to be true of small dogs. Now when we meet up with a small dog, we can say that it will probably eat less, bark more, and learn quickly—because those are attributes of individuals in the small dog category.

By putting any phenomenon into a classification, we often understand it better. A new government takes over a country, and we immediately want to place it: is it in the Soviet sphere of influence, the American sphere of influence, or neutral? We hear music on the radio, and without even thinking we shuffle it into a known category: rock, country and western, classical, soul.

Fields of knowledge are often defined by what they classify and how they classify it. In biology, animals are classified according to family, genus, and species. In geology, rocks are classified as igneous, sedimentary, and metamorphic. In geological time, eras are classified as Cenozoic, Mesozoic, Paleozoic, and Precambrian. Often instructors ask students to apply what they have learned by classifying individual items into the proper categories. Is this poem lyric or narrative? Is that note A sharp or E flat? Is a rabbit really a rodent like a rat? These categories are all given, ready-made. Often, however, you must invent your own classification.

What Division and Classification Are

In this passage Eric Berne suggests that human personality is based at least in part on which layer of the body—inward organs, muscles, or nervous system—is most developed in the individual:

> We can thus say that while the average human being is a mixture [of brains, muscles, and inward organs], some people are mainly "digestion-minded," some "muscle-minded," and some "brain-minded," and correspondingly digestion-bodied, muscle-bodied, or brain-bodied. The digestion-bodied people look thick; the muscle-bodied people look wide; and the brain-bodied people look long. This does not mean the taller a man is the brainier he will be. It means that if a man, even a short man, looks long rather than wide or thick, he will often be more concerned about what goes on in his mind than about what he does or what he eats; but the key factor is slenderness and not height. On the other hand, a man who gives the impression of being thick rather than long or wide will usually be more interested in a good steak than in a good idea or a good long walk. (*Mind in Action*)

This classification conveys the sense of a creative mind making meaning of the world he experiences. Like all good classification, it is based on significant aspects of the subject: body type and personal interests. To categorize according to a trivial or irrelevant quality—for example, surnames or color of hair—would provide little useful information. Whether a person is named Jones or Domjanovich says nothing about the influence of body type on personality, which is Berne's topic. Preference for steak over walks says a good deal.

Whenever we classify, our categories should all contain the same kind of information. Otherwise, an individual item might fit in more than one category. If Berne's categories had been, for instance, "redheads," "people named Jones," and "North Dakotans," he might well have found that some redheads named Jones live in North Dakota. Berne's categories are mutually exclusive; that is, each individual can be placed in only one category.

Berne also made sure that his classification was comprehensive enough to include all individuals in his subject. Notice that at the beginning of the passage he limits his subject: "while the average human being is a mixture, some people are mainly 'digestion-minded,' some 'muscle-minded,' and some 'brain-minded,' and correspondingly digestion-bodied, muscle-bodied, or brain-bodied. He then goes on to classify the "some people." We are left with the impression that his three categories pretty much cover the limited subject without trivializing the differences they identify. From his classification, we gain insight into the relation of body type and personality.

Writing with Division and Classification

Classifying people, places, ideas, and acts is natural, but doing it well requires care. First of all, articulate the point so that you will have it clearly in mind. Second, settle on a principle of classification. For Berne, the principle was the relation between body type and personality. The principle should divide the whole subject in categories into which all the individual items can fit. Then define the categories so that they will not overlap: an item should fit into only one category.

When writing, be sure you describe the categories in the same terms. Decide which characteristics differentiate the categories, and then describe all the categories according to the differentiating characteristics. And, of course, these characteristics should be significant to the subject and relevant to the point you are making.

When a writer ignores these guidelines, a first draft may look like this:

> The men at this college fall into categories. First are the hackers, who are round-shouldered and bleary-eyed from all-night sessions with the computer. Next are the fraternity boys, many of whom come from well-off families. Next are the athletes, who are shaped like V's and call women *babes* and *chicks*. Next are the men who wear jeans and sneakers. Next are the hard-working types, who will probably go to law or medical school. Then there are the men who spend most of their waking hours drinking beer or smoking dope. And finally there are the ones who wear their shirts open down to their navels and have a little gold chain nestling in their chest hair.

This classification is not a success. Its problems are twofold: lack of a clear purpose or unifying point and failure to hit upon a consistent principle for grouping the men on campus. Individuals are not confined to a single category. Some hackers may have money, some athletes may wear jeans and sneakers. Furthermore, the categories do not exhaust the subject: where are the foreign students, the married students, the commuters?

The writer went back for a second go. First, she came up with a point: from their clothing, an observer can tell a good deal about male students, how they view themselves, and what their aspirations are. Next, she *divided* the whole topic into categories that were mutually exclusive. Luckily, a natural division stood waiting: preppy, jock, grind. When she asked herself if the categories exhausted the whole, she decided she had to add one more: others.

With her point clear and categories established, she was ready to write.

> We can learn a good deal about college men from their clothes. The preppy's uniform—a boat-neck sweater over a blue cotton button-down

shirt above a pair of wrinkled chinos above Top Siders—says he comes from the best suburbs and the good prep schools. For him, college is a rehearsal for the good life. The giant V-shaped jock wears a shiny shirt so tight you can see his tattoo and pants so form-fitting you can see the freckles on his knees. His shoes say Nike, Adidas, or Puma. He, too, is rehearsing: for pro scouts, big bucks, adoring fans. Those who want to advertise that they are grinds also do it through the choice, or lack of choice, of their clothes. Notice the row of pens or the calculator hooked to the pockets of white, probably polyester, shirts, wash-and-wear pants, hard-soled shoes and maybe mismatched socks. These men take their studies very seriously.

As extremes of fashion, these three stereotypes make clear what is also true for the others, whose nameless sneakers and nondescript jeans make them harder, but not impossible, to read. The way a college man dresses indicates an attitude—toward performance in school, toward social acceptance, toward the future beyond school.

In this draft each category is treated in the same manner: description, then interpretation of clothes. The last sentence makes the categories significant, for now we see that they have helped to convey a meaningful point about students and clothing.

TIPS FOR DIVISION AND CLASSIFICATION

- Remember that to use the other strategies, you almost always must first divide the subject.
- Decide first on the point or purpose of the classification.
- Choose a significant principle of classification and stick to it.
- Make sure your categories are mutually exclusive.
- Describe all the categories in the same fashion.
- Make sure all the individual items fit in your categories.

Exercises for Division and Classification

1. Create three categories under each of the topics below. Choose one of the topics and provide two examples for each category you created.

fast foods	religions
middle-class people	airliners
forms of government	sports played with a ball

2. Write an essay about living arrangements for students in your school. Free-write or brainstorm until you have a thesis. Divide the subject, and

then develop a system of classification that allows you to support your thesis.

3. Choose one of the following abstract terms:

language   wars
classification   beauty
goodness   immorality

Find a way to divide it and classify its components.

4. Divide your class on the basis of three different principles. Although you need not place individuals in categories, be sure each system of classifying is comprehensive and each category exclusive. Be prepared to share your systems with the class.

COMPARISON AND CONTRAST: SHOWING LIKENESS, SHOWING DIFFERENCE

We should not make an important decision without deliberately and carefully comparing and contrasting one possibility with another. In deciding which college to attend, or whether to attend at all, most people consider as many possibilities as they can think of—cost, social life, sports, and, of course, academic challenge. They then compare and contrast them. Once they have evaluated differences and similarities, they can make a more informed, intelligent choice.

In college essays and examinations, students are often asked to compare or contrast two or more ideas or things: investment in equities, bonds, or real estate; reproduction in amoebas and paramecia; the treatment of Hell in Milton's *Paradise Lost* and Marlowe's *Doctor Faustus*; the views and actions of Presidents Kennedy, Johnson, and Nixon in the Vietnam War. Sometimes the point will be to show the depth of our knowledge, at other times to make a choice and back it up. Comparison and contrast can make almost anything clearer.

What Comparison and Contrast Are

Here is a complex but carefully controlled comparison:

An orange grown in Florida usually has a thin and tightly fitting skin, and it is also heavy with juice. Californians say that if you want to eat a Florida orange you have to get into a bathtub first. California oranges are light in weight and have thick skins that break easily and come off in hunks. The flesh inside is marvelously sweet, and the segments almost separate themselves. In Florida, it is said that you can run over a California orange with a ten-ton truck and not even wet the pavement. The differences from which these hyperboles arise will prevail in the two states even if the type of orange is the same. In arid climates, like California's, oranges develop a thick albedo, which is the white part of the skin. Florida is one of the two or three most rained-upon states in the United States. California uses the Colorado River and similarly impressive sources to irrigate its oranges, but of course irrigation can only do so much. The annual difference in rainfall between the Florida and California orange-growing areas is one million one hundred and forty thousand gallons per acre. For years, California was the leading orange growing state, but Florida surpassed California in 1942, and grows three times as many oranges now. California oranges, for their part, can safely be called three times as beautiful. (John McPhee, *Oranges*)

In this passage—from an essay describing the history, sociology, and delights of the orange—McPhee compares orange growing in Florida with orange growing in California in terms of a range of aspects. He describes a specific aspect of Florida's orange-growing industry and then compares it with the same aspect of California's orange-growing industry or vice versa. He develops the paragraph attribute by attribute: skin and juice of the fruit, rainfall, production rates, beauty of the fruit. When he discusses an attribute of the Florida orange, he will discuss the same attribute in regard to the California orange.

Writing Comparison and Contrast

Although comparison and contrast support and clarify your ideas, you still need a thesis. When, for instance, you compare and contrast the three presidents' involvement in Vietnam, you might say something like, "A comparison of the three presidents indicates that though Kennedy seldom receives blame for the war, his actions were at least as misguided as those of Johnson and Nixon."

Maintaining a consistent pattern or focus is also extremely important. There are two ways to organize a comparison and contrast. Attribute by attribute is one way. Whatever attribute you identify in one item you must also identify in the other, and in the same order. The second way is to present one item, describe all its relevant attributes, and then do the same for the item with which you are comparing and contrasting it. If McPhee had used this method, he would probably have written a paragraph about Florida oranges, describing skin, juice, weather conditions, quantity, and appearance, and only then turned to California oranges, and dealt with skin, juice, weather conditions, quantity, and appearance. He would have made sure that both items received the same treatment in the same order.

Unfortunately, unless the writer stays alert, he or she may intermix the pattern and confuse the reader, as happened in the following paragraph:

> It is funny to think that both the *New York Times* and the *New York Daily News* are published in New York City. The *Times* doesn't have a long sports and entertainment section as does the *Daily News*. The *Daily News* will usually have a long section on deejays and soap operas. It runs huge headlines that scream out raw, sometimes profane headlines. The *Times* is written in an objective, balanced way. It may have a long article on Mozambique's political situation. Many of its foreign correspondents, like Joseph Lelyveld and David K. Shipler, have written books about their assignments. The *Daily News* has huge photographs, often of partially clad young women. There's not much room for print. The *Times* has introduced a new section on the legal profession to go along with its section on science. The *Daily News* has a lot about celebrities, though. The two papers are obviously imagining different audiences.

Though vigorously written, this comparison and contrast is rather a mess. First the writer has not identified his thesis well enough. He presents a lot of little facts without any context. The item-by-item pattern at the beginning gives way to attribute by attribute. Nor has he made clear the terms of comparison or grouped the facts so that they more directly make the comparisons. He also violated the rule of parallelism: there is nothing to balance the mention of the foreign correspondents of the *Times*. The reader's head spins.

With a little rethinking, the writer made it work. He decided to establish the overall point, to stick to the attribute-by-attribute pattern, to group the facts, and to omit any extraneous references.

> The *New York Times* and the *Daily News* are like night and day in the news business. Even a quick glance indicates a major difference. The *Times* is famous for running long articles accompanied by very few pictures, while the *Daily News* runs huge photographs—often of a partially clad young woman—with only a little explanation. A closer look suggests an even more important difference: what is covered. The *Times* concentrates on presenting national and world affairs, spending whole columns, for instance, on the political situation in Mozambique; sports and entertainment have their own sections, but they are usually much shorter than the news sections. The *Daily News*, by contrast, obviously has other priorities: the entertainment and sports sections take up more than half the newsprint. The rest of the paper focuses on such things as deejays, soap operas, and celebrities. Even the tone in which all this is presented is different. The *Times* is written in an objective, balanced way, whereas the *Daily News* screams out raw, sometimes profane headlines and concentrates on the sensational aspects of the news. The two papers are obviously imagining different audiences. The *Times* assumes its readers want to know what is happening in the world and why; the *Daily News* assumes its readers have short attention spans and little interest in the outside world.

This revision is effective because it is consistent, clear, and parallel. The items are compared under three clearly defined attributes: balance between print and pictures, coverage, and tone. Best of all, the writer concludes with an observation that ties the comparison and contrast together.

TIPS FOR COMPARISON AND CONTRAST

- Be sure you have an overall point, and make it clear, preferably at the beginning.
- Follow a consistent pattern throughout, either attribute by attribute or item by item.
- Provide the same kind of information in the same order for all items.

Exercises for Comparison and Contrast

1. Write a brief consumer report comparing and contrasting two brands of a product you would like to buy, perhaps a car, a computer, a stereo, or even blue jeans, pizza, detergent, or shampoo. Justify buying one brand over the other.

2. Select a news story and compare and contrast the way two newspapers or magazines presented it. Draw conclusions as appropriate.

3. Using illustrations, compare and contrast two abstract words that are often taken to be synonymous—happiness and joy, sorrow and despair, solitude and loneliness, boredom and apathy, and so on. Don't forget to establish an overall purpose.

4. Write an essay on the kinds of social encounters you prefer. To illustrate your preference, think about two families that you visited recently. Think about free writing to get your ideas flowing. Narrate the two visits to provide comparison and contrast.

DEFINITION: ESTABLISHING WHAT A WORD MEANS

Whether you write about art or science, world affairs or personal affairs, you will probably need to define some term. What is it? What is it not? What are its uses? What are its characteristics? Can I recognize it on the street if I see it? Can I recognize it in this essay?

In college writing, you will often use complex terms—meiosis, abstract expressionism—and you must define them so that your readers will have the same idea you have. Most often you can define in a single sentence ("Crime is conduct forbidden and punishable by law"), but when the term is especially complicated, it can take a paragraph or even a whole essay. Chapter 5 contains an entire essay devoted to the word *victimology*. The context as well as the word will determine the lengths to which you must go in defining it.

What Definition Is

A formal definition—like those found in dictionaries—has three parts: the name of the thing to be defined, the class to which it belongs, and the quality that distinguishes it from other members of its class. Formal definitions are useful for fairly straightforward words. A cheetah, for instance, "is a large cat native to Asia and Africa, possessing tawny fur with black spots and long back legs that make it unusually swift." For the most part, you will not need to define concrete words such as *chair* or *painting*. An informative adjective, however, can often more exactly locate an idea in a proper context: wing chair, cubist painting.

Simple definitions like these, however, are not adequate for complex terms or terms used in special ways. The formal definition of *modernism*, for instance, would be "a movement supporting modern practices, trends, ideas, and so forth, or showing sympathy with any of these." With that definition, we would not get a very deep understanding of the great cultural movement called modernism. To define that term would probably require paragraphs.

Sometimes, though, we can define a rather complicated or mysterious term briefly right in the text and then go on with what we are saying. In the following sentence a writer parenthetically defines the technical term *stagflation*:

> Worries about stagflation—that is, economic stagnation at a time of inflation—depressed private investors and the U.S. stock market in general during the late 1970s.

Now the writer can use *stagflation* with confidence through the essay.

Even a summary of complex ideas can serve as a definition. In the following sentence, nineteenth-century German philosopher Arthur Schopenhauer's belief is summarized:

> At one time Nietzsche was deeply influenced by Schopenhauer's belief that reality is blind force expressed in human beings as the will to live.

The reader now has some idea of what Schopenhauer's philosophy is. Of course, this summary hardly does justice to Schopenhauer. If his philosophy were important to the whole discussion, the writer would have to devote much more time to defining it.

Figures of speech—metaphors, similes, analogies, and the like—often sharpen our definitions and can make them unmistakable.

> To succeed in business in the 1950s and 1960s, some women felt they had to suppress their womanliness, as had the Amazons, who sliced off their right breasts to improve their aim with the bow and arrow.

We may not agree with the writer, but we certainly know what she means by "suppress their womanliness." (For a discussion of figures of speech, see "Writing with Flair" in Chapter 12.)

Greater difficulty comes with words that have several meanings or meanings that are confusing or controversial. The writer must define these terms precisely. Suppose, for instance, that a writer says, "Nude sunbathing is normal." *Normal* has many meanings. It could mean "conforming, adhering to, or constituting a usual or typical pattern, level, or type" or "functioning or occurring in a natural way" or "average in intelligence, ability, and emotional traits or personality"—other definitions from mathematics and chemistry are also possible. We see a world of difference between "average," "natural," and "conforming to the usual." Which does this writer mean? Einstein was natural, and he conformed to a type, albeit the type called "genius," but he was far from average. Was he "normal" or not?

We can resolve any confusion in several ways. We can substitute a more specific phrase: "Nude sunbathing is accepted at certain beaches in Greece." We can provide a context that makes the use clear: "Nude sunbathing is normal among indigenous populations on some South Sea islands." Or we can stipulate—that is, simply assign—the meaning: "By normal, I mean typical behavior at that time and place."

When we *stipulate,* we say in effect, "Exactly *this* is what I will mean when I use this word." We specify a condition of our argument, and the reader must recognize that condition or miss the argument. Stipulating is particularly useful for limiting the range of a discussion. When, for instance, we say, "Crime is conduct forbidden by law and resulting in punishment," we exclude behavior that is not forbidden by law and does not result in punishment.

Terms such as *normal, average, natural,* even *crime* are tough enough, but some words are dynamite and a lighted match. Words such as *fascism, patriot,* and *Christian* can arouse great passions. To use them well, you must define them with care. Even with these loaded words, you can stipulate a definition: "By Christian, I mean any person who is actively engaged in a Christian community of believers" or "By Christian, I mean any person who has been baptized." You cannot now say, "Anyone who accepts abortion is not a good Christian" or "Anyone who fails in generosity to the poor is not a good Christian," because you did not allow for those exclusions in your definition. When you shift your meaning or leave it vague, your reader won't be able to follow your argument. You have to stay within your stipulation.

Writing Definition

Few things are more challenging than establishing meaning. To communicate meaning you must define all terms that your reader may not know or that you may use differently. As a first step, check the dictionary, but then go beyond it. You can seldom get a truly complicated or subtle understanding without thinking about all the meanings of a word. You may even need to trace the history of its usage and examine how it is used in a particular context.

Definition often involves the other strategies. To get at its essential meaning, you may need to compare and contrast a term with similar words. Except for the most obvious definitions, you will almost certainly need to provide illustrations. Remember that in definition, as in all strategies, you are trying to bring your reader to the common ground, to establish a meaning that the reader will accept. Thus, even with abstract terms you need to be as specific and concrete as possible.

To deal with attitudes toward war of the World War II and Vietnam generations, a student defined *patriotism.*

> In evaluating the two generations, we should think about whether or not they were patriots. *Patriotism* is love of country and a willingness to sacrifice for it. During the Vietnam War, many young Americans refused to take up arms to fight for their country, some going so far as moving to another country, others serving time in jail. The generation of 1941 was more patriotic and willing to fight for the country.

Did you feel disappointed, as though you had been promised steak and been given white bread? What are "love of country" and "willingness to sacrifice"? This simple, and abstract, definition is inadequate for such a highly charged issue.

Once he had achieved some critical distance, the writer recognized that what he had written was platitudinous. He spent a few hours doing research and discovered that the meaning of *patriotism* has varied from place to place and time to time. During the American Revolution, the idea of *patriot* was purely affirmative. Writing about the Boston Tea Party, John Adams said, "There is a dignity, a majesty, a sublimity, in this last effort of the patriots that I greatly admire." Across the water, however, the word had a different meaning. In eighteenth-century England, it meant "a factious disturber of the government," and the contemporary writer Samuel Johnson said, "Patriotism is the last refuge of a scoundrel." Were Johnson and Adams talking about the same thing? What *were* they talking about?

The writer then looked up material on attitudes toward World War II and the Vietnam War. He discovered that veterans of World War II had accused the anti-Vietnam demonstrators of not being "patriotic" because they did not support all the decisions of the president and the Congress. But many of the men who refused to fight in Vietnam claimed that a true patriot would not support a cause that destroys the values the country cherishes. They felt that they were the "true" patriots.

The writer decided to brainstorm on the subject. Why should we let other people in government determine our lives? What would happen if we had no obligations except to our own ideas? Could a country continue if every citizen could, in the name of the higher "patriotism," decide what laws to obey? What would happen to society if we all refused to pay taxes when we didn't like the way the money was spent?

After absorbing all these ideas, the student tried again to define the word *patriotism*:

> In 1941, for most people patriotism meant an immediate response to the war effort; such a definition was understandable and reasonable in light of the clear threat posed to the nation by the belligerent forces of Japan and Germany. In 1965, the threat in Vietnam was neither as clear nor as present. Patriotism for many meant upholding certain values like questioning authority and refusing to serve in what they considered an unjust war. For our time, perhaps we should put these two experiences together and define the word anew. In a society like ours, patriotism cannot be blind, or we chance losing the very values that have established our country. At the same time, we cannot expect to enjoy the privilege of those values without being willing to sacrifice to maintain them. Patriots, then, will be critical of their country for the country's own good, and yet be ready to sacrifice for it when reason, combined with the force of events, tells them they must.

This paragraph shows that the writer went far beyond the dictionary to gain his understanding of the word. When it came to writing, he was explicit about the different definitions, stating exactly how the experience of the two generations differed. Notice the careful comparison and contrast. The writer divided the concept into its two parts: the willingness to sacrifice and the necessity to uphold values. Thus he made a fairly complex definition clear to the reader.

TIPS FOR DEFINITION

- Use the dictionary, but go beyond it to subtle meanings.
- Be as specific and concrete as you can.
- Use other strategies—such as narration or illustration—to help you define.

Exercises for Definition

1. Research and define one of the following words or phrases: *anima, balance of power, karma, law of supply and demand, Occam's razor, Planck's constant, surrealism, transubstantiation.* In a short essay, describe the process you went through in formulating your definition.

2. Define from your own experience one of the following words: apathy, discipline, egotism, fantasy, insecurity, negotiation, nostalgia, power, success, wealth. Try one of the invention methods to help you sharpen your ideas. Narrate an experience of yours that illustrates your definition. If you think your definition may be unusual, account for the difference.

3. Trace the different definitions of the word *law* in this section of the poem "Law Like Love," by W. H. Auden.

   Law, say the gardeners, is the sun,
   Law is the one
   All gardeners obey
   To-morrow, yesterday, to-day.

   Law is the wisdom of the old,
   The impotent grandfathers shrilly scold;
   The grandchildren put out a treble tongue,
   Law is the senses of the young.

   Law, says the priest with a priestly look,
   Expounding to an unpriestly people,
   Law is the words in my priestly book,
   Law is my pulpit and my steeple.

   Law, says the judge as he looks down his nose,
   Speaking clearly and most severely,
   Law is as I've told you before,
   Law is as you know I suppose,
   Law is but let me explain it once more,
   Law is The Law.

   Yet law-abiding scholars write:
   Law is neither wrong nor right,
   Law is only crimes
   Punished by places and by times,
   Law is the clothes men wear
   Anytime, anywhere,
   Law is Good morning and Good night.

   Others say, Law is our Fate;
   Others say, Law is our State;
   Others say, others say
   Law is no more
   Law has gone away.

   And always the loud angry crowd

> Very angry and very loud
> Law is We,
> And always the soft idiot softly Me.

4. For a classtime game: All students in the class will be asked to write a definition of each of the following words: omphaloskepsis, ngwee, constringe, doss house, deodand, oxytocic, primipara. The instructor will secretly give one student the correct definition. All the students will read out their definitions, and the class will try to decide which is the correct one.

CHOOSING STRATEGIES: QUESTIONING YOUR MAIN POINT

Good tennis players don't rely on just one shot. Instead, they use the shot appropriate to the specific situation—crosscourt, drop shot, volley, lob—and combine them in a game for the greatest effect. The same with good writers. They select the right strategy for the particular idea they want to get across, and then combine it with other strategies.

As you think of an idea you want to write about, a particular strategy may occur to you. Don't fight it—give it a try. See if it gives rise to other ideas or ties into another main point you've already made or intend to make. When your ideas are rolling, roll with them. Don't stop and judge them.

If you don't know what strategy to use, try questioning the main points you want to make. Write them down on a page, and ask these questions (in any order):

Will the reader know what I mean by the significant or special words I use? Try a definition or an illustration.

Will the reader find a point vague? (See pp. 280–282 for a discussion of "The Specific and the General.") Clarify with an example or describe concretely.

Is the subject markedly like or unlike another subject? Compare and contrast them.

Would separating a particular point into its components make it clearer? Try dividing it. If it is part of a sequence of actions, perhaps a process analysis would support it best.

Will it help the reader to know how the subject came into existence or what resulted from it? A cause and effect analysis or a straight narrative might effectively place the idea.

Don't try to cram everything into one paragraph. Allow your answers to the questions to expand. You may find that a whole series of paragraphs can be combined under one strategy.

LINKING PARAGRAPHS:
USING OVERARCHING STRATEGIES

You have probably noticed how in some essays paragraphs come in groups within the sweep of an argument. An overarching sense of purpose seems to create a "throughline," that is, an idea running through several paragraphs and organizing them into a subunit of the essay.

These throughlines have in common a strong controlling statement at the beginning of the series of paragraphs—somewhere between a thesis statement and a topic sentence. This statement identifies the overall strategy that will be used in this group of paragraphs. An essay may have several throughlines. The white space frequently found in professional essays usually indicates the end of one throughline and the beginning of another. You can choose throughlines the same way you choose individual strategies, that is, by questioning your main point.

In the pages that follow, we discuss some natural throughlines.

Extended Definition

An extended definition can serve as a throughline. The writer often will establish an overall definition as the thesis and then elucidate, using different strategies, over the next few paragraphs. An example is the definition of patriotism on page 221.

> Patriots . . . will be critical of their country for the country's own good, and yet be ready to sacrifice for it when reason, combined with the force of events, tells them they must.

Can you predict how the rest of this section of the essay went? The writer used the definition as a throughline. He identified the various elements of the definition and wrote one or two paragraphs on each.

Critical of the country for the country's own good
    Defined *critical*
    Compared and contrasted being critical and not being critical
    Gave illustrations of "critical for country's own good"
Ready to sacrifice for it
    Defined *sacrifice*
    Illustrated with sacrifices
    Narrated a story of a particularly poignant sacrifice
When reason, combined with the force of events, tells them they must
    Stipulated meaning of *reason*
    Used cause and effect to show force of events

Each of the main ideas served as a throughline for a part of the essay, employing different strategies to give substance and content along the way. Note that at several points, the extended definition required definitions of other terms.

When writing an extended definition, be sure you

Establish clear boundaries for the extended definition, and then stay within them. Don't be distracted even by fascinating sub-topics.

Finish one part of the definition before starting the next. If you let ideas stray back and forth, you will lose coherence.

Provide clear transitions between paragraphs. Repetition of the word being defined is one way of providing a transition. For the patriotism essay, the writer introduced the second part of the definition ("Ready to sacrifice for it") with "But patriotism is not only an attitude but also an action: sacrifice." With such a clear transition, the reader knows that the throughline is continuing.

Write with concrete details. This is a truism of writing, of course, but never more necessary than with an extended definition. Too often writers move toward the abstract, wrongly thinking that way lies precision of thought. On the contrary: generally speaking, that way lies dullness and vagueness.

Extended Narrative

Because readers have listened to stories since childhood, time sequence is an excellent and natural throughline. Sometimes whole essays, and often several paragraphs, are organized chronologically. The reader easily follows the events. Consider how the following paragraph's strong topic sentence establishes chronology as the throughline in this section of an essay arguing against gun control laws.

> Gun control is not a new idea. The first government restrictions on handgun ownership in the United States were implemented in the post–Civil War South as part of the Black Codes—a body of laws designed to keep the blacks in legally mandated serfdom. (Bruce Powell Majors, "Gun Control: Historically Ineffective, Imprudent, and Coercive")

In the next paragraph, he takes the narrative through the late 1800s and early 1900s, in the next paragraph down to the 1920s, and so on to the present day. Once he has finished his historical survey, he will move on to another aspect of the subject.

Chronology provides excellent organizing throughlines when we write about history, narrate a story, explain a process, or examine a cause and effect relation. When using this method, remember two things:

Divide the time sequence into major periods, according to what is important. Don't get bogged down in too many small subdivisions about which you have little to say. Group shorter or less important periods under the major ones.

Let your reader know when you have moved to the next period in the sequence. We do not suggest that you begin the discussion of each new period with the date, but we do think your reader has a right to know when you enter a new part of the sequence.

The term *chronological development* suggests that time brings significant changes. Thus, narrative throughlines often take the shape of a comparison and contrast between what was and what is. In such cases, follow the general procedures discussed under "Comparison and Contrast" earlier in this chapter.

Assertion and Illustrations

When we argue a highly controversial main point, we probably will need to support the point with many examples, and if those examples are fairly complex, we will need to enlarge on each of them, with more illustrations, definitions, narratives. The main point can serve as the throughline on which we string all the examples.

In the following passage, watch how the strong assertion in the lead paragraph binds the subsequent paragraphs.

> President [of Costa Rica] Oscar Arias Sánchez's efforts to find a peaceful solution to the conflicts of Central America and his refusal to allow the Nicaraguan *contras* to operate out of his country have provoked strong economic and political retaliatory measures by the Reagan Administration.
>
> "The [U.S.] Administration is very angry with Oscar, and Reagan will continue to be very tough," said one of Arias' top advisers. He and others interviewed conceded that the United States wields enormous political and economic power in Costa Rica, and Arias "has very few cards to play" in return.
>
> No U.S.-appropriated funds have been disbursed to Costa Rica during the past six months. An embassy official puts the amount withheld at $85 million, while Costa Rican and U.S. Congressional officials say the total is $140 million.
>
> During the previous administration, that of Luis Alberto Monge, who quietly collaborated with the United States and the *contras,* U.S. aid soared to more than $200 million annually. "Costa Rica has not received a penny [of U.S. aid] since almost the beginning of the peace plan effort. That, of course, is purely coincidental," one Arias insider remarked sarcastically.

[The next paragraph discusses U.S. bans on flowers, clothing, and other Costa Rican exports.] (Martha Honey and Tony Avirgan, "Leaning on Arias")

Note that the authors start the third paragraph right out with an interesting fact rather than something like "Another example of this point is . . ." When the throughline is strong, we can do without those clumsy crutches.

A variation of this technique occurs when the throughline is classification and the topic sentence in the lead paragraph establishes the class of objects or ideas to be discussed. In an essay arguing that propaganda is everywhere in commercials and advertisements, one writer uses this technique:

What kind of propaganda techniques do advertisers use? There are seven basic types. (Ann McClintock, "Propaganda Techniques in Today's Advertising")

In subsequent paragraphs she identifies and discusses each type.

TIPS FOR CHOOSING STRATEGIES AND LINKING PARAGRAPHS

- If a particular strategy occurs to you, go with it.
- Question your main points to decide on the appropriate strategy or strategies for developing those points.
- Develop the body of your essay by means of throughlines that bind groups of paragraphs.
- Find throughlines the same way you find strategies.

Exercises for Choosing Strategies and Linking Paragraphs

1. Here is a controversial thesis supported by four main points.

Thesis: The United States should allow torture of terrorists so that law enforcement officials can gain valuable information.
   a. International terrorism is increasing, and most of it is aimed at the United States.
   b. Conventional legal punishments fail to deter terrorists.
   c. Although the use of torture is unconstitutional, one terrorist's civil rights are less important than those of the hundreds or thousands his or her actions threaten.
   d. Torture should only be used to prevent future catastrophe, not to punish terrorists for past deeds.

Question each main point to decide the most effective strategy for developing it, and write a paragraph on one of the points. Now write a paragraph using a different strategy. Determine which paragraph is more effective, and explain why.

2. Select one of the two following thesis statements. Never mind whether you agree or not—in fact, choosing one you disagree with would be more challenging.

Thesis 1: When local law enforcement proves inadequate to fight crime, citizens are justified in taking the law into their own hands.

(Narrate a story to establish that the law is often inadequate. Define *justified*. Analyze the effect on society of the present condition. Compare the present condition with a hypothetical state in which citizens *did* take the law into their own hands.)

Thesis 2: It is better to lose a little security to gain freedom than to lose a little freedom to gain security.

(Define *freedom* and *security*. Give examples of each. Divide and classify countries into those that have given up freedom and those that have given up security. Narrate a story about life in each kind of country.)

Write a passage—it could take several paragraphs—advancing your thesis and employing the sequence of strategies indicated in parentheses.

3. Select a past paper that didn't work very well. Examine your thesis carefully, and identify your main points. Revise two of your interior paragraphs using altogether different strategies. If, for instance, you developed a paragraph largely by narration, try comparison and contrast or definition.

4. Identify throughlines in the Nisbet essay and Larry Boyd's response in Chapter 5, Critical Reading.

5. For your next paper, draft a first version in the usual way. Now go through your first draft and look for a paragraph that contains one of the following: narrative, cause and effect, division and classification, extended definition, or assertion and illustrations. Expand your chosen paragraph into three or more paragraphs. The first paragraph should have a very strong controlling statement; the rest need not have strong topic sentences but must follow the lead of the first paragraph. When you have finished, read your new passage over and assess how strong the throughline is. If it needs to be stronger, improve it.

6. The following statements establish possible throughlines:
   a. The years between fifteen and eighteen were the least productive/ poorest/quickest-moving/laziest/most surprising years of my life. (Choose one—or make up another adjective that fits; but be specific.)
   b. Over and over in my life I have learned that it pays/does not pay to be kind to people in need. (Choose one.)
   c. A creative person has the ability to be inventive—that is, to transform his or her original thoughts into a form others can appreciate.

   Write a paragraph for each statement, and then write a series of new paragraphs that follow the statement's lead.

10

BEGINNING, ENDING, TITLING

Of all my verse, like not a single line;
But like my title, for it is not mine.
That title from a better man I stole:
Ah, how much better, had I stol'n the whole!
ROBERT LOUIS STEVENSON (1850–1894)
SCOTTISH NOVELIST AND POET

Three of the most important parts of your paper are your opening paragraph, your closing paragraph, and your title. These are your social points, the ones at which you establish and leave your most significant impressions. Too cautious, too timid, a first paragraph can promise a chore to be endured, like a dutiful visit to a sick relative. But overdone, too assertive, your opening will seem rude, as if you just barged in, shouting, "Here I am!" A poor conclusion can seem equally dreary or impolite, depending on whether you repeat the same conversation upon leaving that you had upon arriving or just run off without saying good-bye. And your title—that first glimpse the reader has of your essay—can discourage or invite.

THE FIRST PARAGRAPH: A BOLD BEGINNING

Some opening paragraphs sound like an ancient truck trying to warm up on a very cold day. Old trucks don't offer a very enticing ride, and neither do essays that start off with a grind or a groan. The reader wants a sense of movement and purpose.

229

An introductory paragraph should aim to do three things:

grab the reader's attention

identify the central issue or subject

create the tone of the essay

The way you start will determine how your reader responds to your essay. It is so crucial that many writers draft the first paragraph only after they have finished the essay and can put all their energy and artistry into it. And the good writers we know tune up their openings over and over again. They don't want the engine to die before the reader even turns the corner into the rest of the essay. If you have trouble getting that first paragraph right, try waiting until you finish the essay before writing it. In any case, you will probably need to rewrite it.

Some openings read as though the writer wants to postpone unveiling his or her thought until the last possible moment. First there is a litany of generalities that we already knew and didn't want to hear again ("Human beings are rational creatures, and yet their behavior is not always explicable." Oh?). And then the apology ("I don't pretend to know everything about human nature"—as though anyone did). Such openings usually indicate lack of confidence. When we aren't sure of something, we delay committing ourselves. We walk our thought around the block a few times. We hide behind generalities, platitudes, and other distractions. We hem and haw. The reader gets suspicious: what am I being asked to buy? do I really want to buy it? Don't waste time: get moving.

The Shape of the Opening Paragraph

The thesis statement can appear in the first sentence or in the last or even in the middle of the opening paragraph. In fact, it does not have to be in the very first paragraph at all (but it is a good idea to state it fairly early). Nor must you begin with a series of generalizations. You could start with something descriptive or narrative and then show how this description or narration gives rise to the thesis. Anything that works goes—if it grabs the reader's attention and leads right into your essay.

One especially effective shape for opening paragraphs is the *funnel*, so named by Sheridan Baker. The wide end of the funnel is the first sentence, a focused generalization that provides the necessary context and the subject. Each succeeding sentence narrows the subject. The last sentence is the thesis statement, the least general statement in the paragraph.

Lewis Thomas provides a clear model of this shape in the opening paragraph of an essay entitled "How We Process Information."

According to the linguistic school currently on top, human beings are all born with a genetic endowment for recognizing and formulating language. This must mean that we possess genes for all kinds of information, with strands of special, peculiarly human DNA for the discernment of meaning in syntax. We must imagine the morphogenesis of deep structures, built into our minds, for coding out, like proteins, the parts of speech. Correct grammar (correct in the logical, not fashionable, sense) is as much a biologic characteristic of our species as feathers on birds.

Here Thomas moves from the general idea of genetic endowment to the concept of DNA to the linguistic notion of "deep structures" to his thesis in the last sentence. The ideas rush through that funnel into the rest of the essay just as water rushes through the narrowed nozzle of a hose.

Not all essays open with a funnel. Thomas begins another of his essays, "Natural Science," by stating its point in the first sentence.

The essential wildness of science as a manifestation of human behavior is not generally perceived. As we extract new things of value from it, we also keep discovering new parts of the activity that seem in need of better control, more efficiency, less unpredictability. We'd like to pay less for it and get our money's worth on some more orderly, businesslike schedule. The Washington planners are trying to be helpful in this, and there are new programs for the centralized organization of science all over the place, especially in the biomedical field.

The rest of the paragraph explains what the first sentence means, and the rest of the essay supports it.

Another possible way to begin an essay is the multiparagraph opener, which unfolds in more leisurely fashion. The first paragraph may provide historical background, an extended definition, or a series of illustrations or facts that are then developed in the second paragraph. The following opening reaches its thesis statement at the beginning of the third paragraph:

About 225 million years ago, at the end of the Permian period, fully half the families of marine organisms died out during the short span of a few million years—a prodigious amount of time by most standards, but merely minutes to a geologist. The victims of this mass extinction included all surviving trilobites, all ancient corals, all but one lineage of ammonites and most bryozoans, brachiopods, and crinoids.

This great dying was the most profound of several mass extinctions that have punctuated the evolution of life during the past 600 million years. The late Cretaceous extinction, some 70 million years ago, takes second place. It destroyed 25 percent of all families, and cleared the earth of its dominant terrestrial animals, the dinosaurs and their kin—thus setting a stage for the dominance of mammals and the eventual evolution of man.

No problem in paleontology has attracted more attention or led to more frustration than the search for causes of these extinctions. (Stephen Jay Gould, *Ever Since Darwin*)

The multiparagraph introduction can be graceful and appealing, as this one is. It slides the reader deep into the essay. Remember, though, that regardless of length or shape, the goal of the introduction is a clear indication of the thesis and an attractive invitation to the reader to join you in exploring it.

The First Sentence

Perhaps the most important single sentence in an essay is the first one. An excellent opening sentence is like the first bite of a superb dinner: it stimulates the taste buds and starts the digestive juices flowing. But if the first taste is badly seasoned or poorly cooked, no one will be eager for the next. Here are some ways to provide a good appetizer.

A REVEALING ANECDOTE, HISTORICAL OR PERSONAL.   An essay by Roland Barthes analyzing the significance of the Eiffel Tower begins,

> Maupassant often lunched at the restaurant in the tower, though he didn't care much for the food: *It's the only place in Paris,* he used to say, *where I don't have to see it.* ("The Eiffel Tower")

The humor of this opening entices the reader.

AN INTERESTING OR ILLUMINATING FACT.   An essay on Arab-Israeli tensions could start, "In only forty years, the Arabs and the Israelis have fought six wars." Anyone who hadn't known that would now surely want to know more.

AN ARRESTING IMAGE.   An essay on breeds of dogs begins, "He had eyes like Junior Mints, a body like a chorizo sausage, a tail that could have pulled wine corks, and, while his slavish retainers grasped the edges of the bed to keep from tumbling to the floor, he sat like a king in the middle of a $500 silk comforter." Building an essay on that would not be difficult.

A PROVOCATIVE OPINION ASSERTED PROVOCATIVELY.   Your position can either be supported or refuted: "American doctors have lost their halos, for very good reasons." Remember, though, it is one thing to be provocative and another to be outrageous. You need to arouse interest without offending.

A SHARP QUOTATION.   A quotation such as Sir Isaac Newton's "Errors are not in the art but in the artificer" could introduce an argument favoring genetic engineering. When selecting a quotation, however, be sure you don't choose one that is overused.

Pitfalls to Avoid

We have made some suggestions for good beginnings, but we have hardly exhausted the subject. Indeed, the possibilities are almost limitless. Having said that, we now want to identify some openers that are to be avoided at almost any cost.

THE OBVIOUS DEFINITION. One paper on Marx's *Communist Manifesto* began, "Society is defined as a voluntary association of persons for common ends, and government, which exists in society, is defined as the organization or agency through which a political unit exercises authority." The writer could have safely assumed that the reader knew terms this basic.

FACTS NOBODY NEEDS TO BE REMINDED OF. A paper on John F. Kennedy's foreign policy need not begin "John F. Kennedy, who served as president of the United States . . ." or "Conduct of foreign policy is the responsibility of all presidents of the United States, and so it was with John F. Kennedy." These are tedious.

PLATITUDES. Too many essays begin with sentiments such as "The processes of life are awe inspiring" or "Despite thousands of years' experience of the horrors of war, we seem no closer to controlling our destructive impulses" or "Poetry can be important to our lives." True statements all, but hardly promises of an exciting essay.

APOLOGIES AND EXCUSES. "Ricardo's economic theories are extremely difficult to explain, but I will do the best I can" does not increase the reader's confidence in the writer. And "This essay will be short, because I began it only five hours before it was due" may seem clever to the writer, but it probably will not amuse the instructor. Some apologies and excuses are honest expressions of insecurity, others are mere manipulations. Spare the reader both.

TIPS FOR THE FIRST PARAGRAPH

- Remember that the goals of a beginning are to get the reader's attention, to identify the central issue, and to create the tone.
- Put a lot of thought into your first paragraph. Make it as inviting as you can.
- Remember that your first sentence is perhaps the most important in your essay.

- Don't dawdle—get started.
- Choose the form that suits your subject and your style. A funnel is a good way to begin, but it is not the only way.
- Avoid obvious definitions, well-known facts, platitudes, apologies, and excuses.

Exercises for the First Paragraph

1. Here are four thesis statements, each of which sets forth a controversial or unpopular position:

   In light of the recent upswing in violent crime, police officers should be allowed to use more force during arrests.

   Insurance companies are to blame for putting doctors out of business with their high malpractice rates.

   American children are growing up largely ignorant of the way the federal government functions.

   Minority children need more scientists and intellectuals and fewer athletes and musicians as role models.

   Choose one statement and compose an opening paragraph for an essay arguing for or against that thesis. Your paragraph can be as long or short as you please, but it must start with a provocative or attention-grabbing sentence that employs one of the strategies outlined in "The First Sentence" and end with the thesis statement.

2. Find a recent essay of yours and examine the opening paragraph. Is it effective? What do you think of the first sentence and the way the paragraph unfolds? Revise your paragraph to improve it.

3. Exchange your revised opening from Exercise 2 for a classmate's. Write a paragraph comparing the effectiveness of the two. Now write a final version of your opening, incorporating the good ideas from both.

THE CONCLUSION: FINISHING IN STYLE

We won't claim that your concluding paragraph is as important as your opening one—if you don't give your readers a good start, they probably won't make it to the end. Nonetheless, it is crucial, for it is your last chance to make a good impression. Make it as effective as you can.

A conclusion has three goals:

to make one last effort to convince the reader

to suggest larger implications than you could reasonably assert before you presented your evidence

to provide a satisfying sense of closure

Ending on the Right Note

When so much is riding on your essay, you do not want to leave the impression of limping or skulking off. You want to appear dynamic and confident, fully engaged and in control. Without appearing smug, you want to be seen—figuratively, of course—brushing the dust off the palms of your hands after a job well done.

To achieve this poise, follow two general rules: never apologize and never brag. If a writer apologizes, the reader is very apt to think the whole journey through the essay has been a waste of time. And when a writer brags that he or she has proved a large notion or accumulated a great deal of information, the reader is apt to be annoyed—and inspired to find holes in the argument and faults with the writing. Be honest and modest: don't claim more than your argument fully justifies. A concluding tone of judicious assurance can finish off your essay in style.

The Larger Implications

If you have done your job in the middle of the essay—developing your argument while staying close to the thesis—by the end you should be ready to push your thinking—and your reader's—a little. After all, what you have said surely has some importance beyond the limits of your thesis. You should now be able to tell your reader how the thesis opens a window on a larger idea.

A student in an art history class was asked to write a paper on painting. She narrowed the topic to her favorite painter, Vincent van Gogh, and then to a favorite painting, *Chair and Pipe*. Her thesis was "The physical quality of van Gogh's brushstroke emphasizes the concrete and material reality of his subject." Through the body of the paper she analyzed the painting. In her last paragraph she wrote that *Chair and Pipe* may have led other painters to employ similar techniques reflecting the density of their subjects. She did not have to prove this observation; she only had to suggest it. Her analysis gave her the right to this larger observation.

In a criminal justice class, a student wrote an essay arguing for automatic jail sentences for anyone driving with a blood alcohol count of over 0.5 percent. In the body of the paper, she carefully presented and analyzed information on both sides of her subject. She discussed the effects of the alcohol count on the nervous system, the experience of countries with stringent laws, the increase of alcohol consumption, and the increase in teenage drinking. She admitted negative implications. In her conclusion, she stated that despite problems, the compulsory jail sentence was worth a try. That assertion would hardly have surprised an attentive reader—it was probably assumed in the writer's thesis. But this writer wanted to go beyond the thesis and make an impression on her reader, and so she enlarged her argument:

> Many Americans seem willing to forbid smoking in public places, to insist that guns be prohibited, and to re-institute a nationwide speed limit of 55 miles per hour. Surely the time is right to go after the deadliest killer of them all—driving under the influence.

By shifting the focus to other kinds of socially dangerous behavior, she provided some thought-provoking analogies and expanded the implications of her paper. And she left a strong impression.

An accomplished conclusion, then, is often more in-depth than the essay. It sets the thesis in a larger context, and that larger context helps to clinch the argument, for then the reader understands the importance of the ideas.

Pitfalls to Avoid

A good conclusion adds to an essay; a bad conclusion detracts from it. Many last paragraphs, unfortunately, seem mechanical, embarrassed, lazy, or frenzied. Here are the major pitfalls you should try to avoid in your endings.

THE WASTE BASKET ENDING. Some writers sweep up all the overflow points they could not fit into the body of an essay and present them in the last paragraph. In an essay on the founding of Israel, a writer concluded: "The Palestinians are Sunni Moslem. The Sunnis are one of the great divisions in Islam, the other being Shiite. The two groups separated over the succession to the leadership of Islam following the death of Mohammed." Those facts might have been interesting if the writer had developed them in the essay, but tacked on in the last paragraph, they only confuse the reader. Don't throw into your conclusion bits and pieces that didn't fit elsewhere.

THE FADE-OUT. Have you noticed how some people can tell a fascinating story but seem to lose heart as they get to the end and let their voices dwindle away? Some writers end essays that way. The following concludes a very good essay on how children learn to use language: "Researchers have so much more to discover in this area that I have to admit that we have only scratched the surface. Whatever we say now will be superseded very soon." Those last sentences seem to say, "Maybe this wasn't worth writing after all. Sorry I took your time." An essay should end on a note of confidence.

THE WILD SURMISE. We have noticed that when students fear that their essays are not important enough, they often write a concluding paragraph that leaps far beyond the evidence to a grandiose pronouncement. The concluding paragraph of an otherwise excellent essay on Nigerian bureaucracy suddenly claimed, "From this we see the utter futility of tying aid to underdeveloped nations to the adoption of Western standards." All because of limited experience in Nigeria? How much better it would have been to conclude with "If the Nigerian experience is typical of the Third World, perhaps we ought to re-evaluate the strings we attach to our foreign aid." Qualified claims are better because they are so much likelier to be acceptable.

THE MIRROR IMAGE. Because the mirror image is perhaps the most common error students make in endings, we saved it for last. The writer repeats the thesis and summarizes the main points, as in this example:

> As I said, professional athletes should be allowed to participate in the Olympics. They would add quality to the games. The hypocrisy now rampant would decrease. The Soviet athletes would no longer enjoy an advantage resulting from having "government jobs." We should act immediately to change the Olympic rules.

This kind of conclusion is dull and mechanical. If you have done your job in the body of the essay, you do not need to repeat the whole argument in the last paragraph. The best conclusions do not carry the thought backward but forward.

The conclusion can be one of the most effective parts of your essay. Let it be an elegant and creative farewell.

TIPS FOR THE CONCLUSION

- Your closing is not an afterthought. Pay as much attention to it as to your opening.
- Keep in mind the three goals of an essay's conclusion: to make one last effort to convince the reader, to suggest larger implications than you could reasonably assert before you presented your evidence, to provide a satisfying sense of closure.
- Try to appear poised and confident in your conclusion; never apologize and never brag.
- Push for larger implications, but don't go outside the reach of your essay.
- Avoid the wastebasket ending, the fade-out, the wild surmise, and the mirror-image closing.

Exercises for the Conclusion

1. Here are the last paragraphs of three professional essays:

   "Like bone to the human body, and the axle to the wheel, and the song to a bird, and air to the wing, thus is liberty the essence of life," José Martí, the Cuban poet and patriot, wrote. "Whatever is done without it, is imperfect." (William Pfaff)

   Still, beyond all this is another laugh entirely, that neither condemns, praises, ridicules, nor conspires, but sees into the essential nature of a slip of the tongue and consequently sympathizes. After all, most human endeavor results in a slip of the something—the best-laid plans gone suddenly haywire by natural blunder; the chair, cake or painting that turns out not exactly as one imagined; the kiss or party that falls flat; the life that is not quite what one had in mind. Nothing is ever as dreamed.
   So we laugh at each other, perfect fools all, flustered by the mistake of our mortality. (Roger Rosenblatt, "Oops! How's That Again?")

   So I will try here to be exact. I wish my father had done more headlong, more elegant inventing. I believe he would respect my wish, be willing to speak with me seriously about it, find some nobility in it. But now he is dead, and he had been dead two weeks when they found him. And in his tiny flat at the edge of the Pacific they found no address book, no batch of letters held with a rubber band, no photograph. Not a thing to suggest that he had ever known another human being. (Geoffrey Wolff, "Memories of My Father")

   Can you tell what each essay was about? What hints do you find? What techniques did each author use to make his ending more effective? What do you think of the last line of each paragraph?

2. Exchange with a partner a recent essay but without its concluding paragraph. Write a conclusion for your partner's essay. Then compare your conclusion and your partner's for each essay. What are the weaknesses and strengths of each closing? Which suits the essay better? Write a paragraph analyzing the differences.

THE TITLE: ISSUING THE INVITATION

The title is probably the last thing you write for an essay, but it is the first thing the reader sees, and it ought to be attractive. No title at all or something like "Assignment 3" or "Second Sociology Paper" is pretty unappealing. Even "Hemingway's *The Sun Also Rises*" or "The Albigensian Heresy" won't arouse a reader's wild enthusiasm. These titles are too broad and shapeless.

You need a title that says, "I know something interesting—come and find out." A title like "Four-Letter Words Can Hurt You" or "Running and Other Vices'' or ''Shakespeare without Tears'' intrigues readers and even softens them up to enjoy the essay. Even ''Authorial Intervention in *The Sun Also Rises*'' and ''The Albigensian Heresy and the Rise of Preaching'' tell something about their essays and provide the reader with an entryway.

A title should be an honest advertisement. Something cute and snappy but irrelevant forces the reader to double back and readjust his or her expectations. When ''Six Months behind Bars'' turns out to refer to a summer spent mixing drinks at a fancy resort, the reader will feel tricked—justifiably. Similarly, a serious essay shouldn't have a frivolous title. If, for example, the subject is geriatrics, a title like ''Everything You Always Wanted to Know about Death—But Were Afraid to Ask'' would offend many people.

A well-chosen title will indicate not only the subject but also the tone of the essay. Think for a moment about what your expectations are for these titles: ''A Dog's Eye View of Man,'' ''Motherhood—Who Needs It?'', ''The Reach of Imagination.'' Which essay would you expect to be the most serious? Which would you expect to be confrontational? Titles can—and in these examples do—represent both the thinking and the approach of the essay.

You can find titles in a variety of places. Sometimes a title will come from within your essay. A nice turn of phrase or a recurrent theme may say it all. Or you might pull a quotation out of the text or the subject you are writing about: ''I beg your pardon—I know exactly what to think'' comes from Jane Austen's *Pride and Prejudice* and could serve as the title for a study of the character who made this statement. General Douglas MacArthur said ''I shall return'' when he was forced to leave the Philippines at the beginning of World War II; that quotation would nicely introduce a paper on the Battle for the Philippines.

Sometimes you can find a good title outside your immediate subject. Hundreds of writers have used the Bible and Shakespeare as sources for titles. Peter Cohen wrote *The Gospel According to the Harvard Business School*; his ironic title tells much about his approach. If you were writing about the difficulty of starting college, you might find a title in the words of the Latin poet Virgil: ''Look with favor upon a bold beginning.'' Finally, you may use a twist on an old saying, like ''Two Birds in the Bush'' for an essay about Stanley and Livingstone, or a phrase from a song, like ''My Country, Taint of Thee'' for an essay on environmental pollution. In short, you can find a title anywhere.

TIPS FOR THE TITLE

- Choose a title that is inviting and appealing.
- In devising a title, think about both the content and tone of your essay.
- You can find a title in your essay, in the work or subject you are discussing, in literature, or even in popular sayings.

Exercises for the Title

1. Match the description of an essay in column A to the corresponding title in list B. Why did you make the match you did?

A	**B**
Suggests that the English people fight famine by dining on Irish babies	1. The Importance of Being Ordinary
Compares the tools and methods of different plastic surgeons	2. Was Paul Revere a Minute-Person?
Details a month in the life of a professional art appraiser	3. A Modest Proposal
Draws up a program of absolutely essential education	4. The Cutting Edge
Argues that we should not change our use of English just to avoid sexism	5. In the Eye of the Beholder
Discusses how the rich and famous try to be just like other people in order to improve their public image	6. Is There Any Knowledge that a Man Must Have?

2. Here is a partner exercise. Write an essay that describes eating, compares people who listen with people who watch, or discusses your personal tastes in humor. Then give it to your partner to title. Do you think the title works? Does it capture the essence of your essay? Why or why not?

3. Devise new titles for the last three essays you have written. Ask a partner to judge whether the new titles or the old are better and to state why. Do the same for three of your partner's essays.

PART FOUR

The Art of
the Writer: Sentences,
Diction, Style

11
THE SENTENCE FROM MANY ANGLES

Backward ran sentences until reeled the mind.
WOLCOTT GIBBS (1902–1958)
AMERICAN WRITER AND HUMORIST

You could not write an essay, you could not write a paragraph, indeed you could not express a thought at all without sentences. You could say a word, and thus denote an object or even identify a concept, but you could not say anything about that thing or concept. A sentence expresses the basic unit of thought. By its construction, it discriminates among ideas and signals what is important. Its very form affects its meaning.

Some writers seem to think sentences exist fully grown somewhere in the mind and will come when called. It isn't that easy. Sentences don't write themselves: we have to do the work. Words are in our heads, but we have to put them together to make a whole thought.

In this chapter we will consider the sentence under two main headings:

Structure: A sentence is something you put together. How you put it together always affects its sense and impact. We will examine various ways of assembling sentences and the effect different structures have.

Quality: Writers of good sentences work for three main qualities. They work for emphasis—they manage the force or intensity of expression to make the sentence memorable or impressive. They work for economy—they pack the most meaning into the fewest words. And they work for variety—they mix up different kinds and lengths of sentences to keep the reader interested.

243

PARTS OF A SENTENCE: THE BASIC THOUGHT

Deep in every complete sentence there always exist a simple subject (S) and verb (V) and frequently a direct object (O) or a complement (C). These elements compose the spine of the sentence.

S	V	O/C
Raccoons	harassed	farmers.
I	like	Ike.
Sugar	is	sweet.
Khrushchev	blinked.	

The subject is the topic of the sentence. *Raccoons* is the topic of the first sentence. The verb indicates an action or state of being. *Like* indicates the action in the second sentence; *is* indicates the state of being in the third. The direct object receives the action. *Ike* receives the action *like.* The complement names, identifies, or describes the subject. *Sweet* describes *sugar.*

Not all sentences contain an object or complement. In *Khrushchev blinked,* he didn't blink anything—he just blinked. Still, the thought and the sentence are complete.

Some sentences contain both an indirect object (IO) and a direct object. The indirect object indicates to whom or for whom the action was done.

S	V	IO	O
The hamburger	cost	us	money.

Spines provide the substructure for thought, and often they are all we need. "I love you," "War is hell," and "You shut your mouth" hardly require embellishment.

MODIFIERS: ENRICHING THE THOUGHT

Usually we want to go beyond the simple statement to ask subtle questions, voice reservations, describe in detail what we see, give complicated commands, explain with precision. The unembellished subject-verb-object/complement will seldom convey a complex meaning.

Here is an unembellished sentence:

The people supported a law.

We can enrich it by adding adjectives, adverbs, phrases, or clauses.

Long before pollution reached international proportions, *the people* of Dortmund, West Germany, *supported a law* making public health a higher priority than any other political consideration.

Although still there, our original sentence is hardly recognizable, for now we have added modifiers that explain, qualify, and amplify the central thought. We know when the people passed the law, where they lived, and what the law said.

Adding Adjectives and Adverbs

We can hang a modifying word on any part of the spine. Suppose our sentence is

Raccoons harassed farmers.

We can make this sentence more pictorial and more exact by adding an adjective to modify the nouns or an adverb to modify the verb.

The marauding raccoons harassed the farmers.
The raccoons gleefully harassed the farmers.
The raccoons harassed the hot-tempered farmers.

We can combine these possibilities and write a fairly lively sentence.

The marauding raccoons gleefully harassed the hot-tempered farmers.

Now we have told our readers more about the raccoons, the harassment, and the farmers.

If we wish, we can add more than one adjective to any noun and more than one adverb to any verb.

Crusty, cantankerous Khrushchev blinked rapidly twice.

(For more on adjectives and adverbs, see Chapter 19.)

Building with Phrases and Clauses

So far we have added fairly simple modifiers. But we can also attach more complicated modifiers—phrases and clauses—to sentence spines.

A *phrase* is a group of words lacking either a subject or a verb. We can hang phrases on any part of the spine.

Blue from the cold, the mountain climbers plunged *into the Jacuzzi.*

To get even for the harsh and petty measures of the Roman officials, the Visigoths rebelled *against Rome.*

We do have to be sure, though, that we hang phrases close to the words they modify. We might confuse the reader if we wrote

The mountain climbers plunged into the Jacuzzi *blue from the cold.*

Is the Jacuzzi blue from the cold?

A *clause* is a group of related words containing both a subject and a verb. Clauses come in two varieties. One variety, called *independent,* can stand as a complete sentence.

> Babe Ruth started his baseball career as a pitcher.

The other variety, called *dependent,* cannot stand alone.

> After Babe Ruth pointed his bat at the center field bleachers

Although this clause contains a subject and a verb, it is not a complete thought, and it needs an independent clause to support it.

> After Babe Ruth pointed his bat at the center field bleachers, he hit a home run.

Dependent clauses, like phrases, can be attached to any part of the spine.

> The conquistador Balboa, *who was the first European to view the Pacific from the Western Hemisphere,* claimed the entire Pacific coast for the Spanish crown.
>
> *While he was preparing an expedition to Peru,* Balboa was accused of treason.

Again like phrases, clauses must be placed close to the part of the spine they modify. We would confuse our reader if, for instance, we wrote

> General Lee presented his sword to General Grant, *which he had carried throughout the Civil War.*

Lee most certainly did not carry Grant throughout the Civil War. (For a further discussion of phrases and clauses, see "Phrases, Clauses, and Sentences" in Chapter 19.)

Modifiers carry information, and where and how they carry it makes all the difference. We must follow the rules of syntax, grammar, and usage. And, of course, we must show restraint and choose our modifiers carefully. Piling on modifier after modifier can make near-gibberish of writing.

> On a cold and rainy January morning, in a fit of pique, and blue from the cold, marauding raccoons who had reconnoitered at dawn gleefully harassed the furious, hot-tempered farmers, which was their way of getting even for harsh and petty measures.

The human mind simply cannot sort out so many ideas and images at once. A few well-chosen modifiers will make the point more clearly and forcefully. A single sharp image may have more impact than a lengthy description. Often a simple noun is better all alone. *Gorilla* hardly needs *hairy* or *scary,* and *howled* hardly needs *wildly.* If, however, the gorilla is bald and simpering, add the modifiers.

TIPS FOR MODIFIERS

- Use carefully chosen modifiers to sharpen or enrich your thought.
- Place modifiers as close as possible to the part of the spine they modify.
- Show restraint: use only as many modifiers as the spine can easily carry and the reader's mind take in.

Exercises for Modifiers

1. Make these sentences livelier by modifying each at three places, using adjectives or adverbs.
   a. Mother wrote a book.
   b. Politics is absurd.
   c. The boss provided us with transportation.
   d. The crane hit the pavement.

2. Modify each of these sentences with both a phrase and a clause. (Make up attributes and events if you need to.)
   a. I study metallurgy.
   b. The hurricane destroyed the house.
   c. Sherman attacked Atlanta.
   d. The Spartans defeated the Athenians.

3. Modify each of these sentences by adding at least one adjective, one adverb, one phrase, and one clause.
   a. Harry Truman succeeded Franklin Roosevelt.
   b. Economics is dismal.
   c. The instructor flunked me.
   d. Sigmund Freud wrote *Interpretation of Dreams*.

   First, let yourself go. Make them as wild as you like. Then revise the sentences to make them acceptable for a school essay. But keep them lively.

COORDINATION AND SUBORDINATION: SHAPING THE THOUGHT

Modifiers are only one way of shaping and directing sentences. Now that we have seen how they work, we can begin to look at the others. In this section, we discuss how to structure the sentence.

The Simple Sentence

The simplest construction is a simple sentence. It consists of a single independent clause.

The Irish elk is a deer.
Leonardo da Vinci invented the bicycle.

The simple sentence can have a compound subject.

In 1940, *Sammy Baugh* and *the Washington Redskins* lost the National Football League championship to the Chicago Bears by a score of 73–0.

It can also have a compound verb.

The Scottish poet Robert Burns *wrote* the words to "Auld Lang Syne" but *did not write* the music.

Both these sentences contain only one independent clause.

The simple sentence can express complicated ideas and contain a good deal of information.

Woodrow Wilson, the twenty-eighth president of the United States, had been a practicing lawyer, a professor of political science, president of Princeton University, and governor of New Jersey.

The simple sentence can also come right out and say what is what. From it the reader can quickly pick up the main idea. (For more on simple sentences, see "Phrases, Clauses, and Sentences" in Chapter 19.)

Young children use simple sentences almost exclusively. Their writing sounds like this:

Dear Mom and Dad,

I am having a lot of fun at camp. We learned how to swim yesterday. Then we went on a hike. We got on top of a mountain. It was high. You could see a long way. I got dizzy. I like Counselor Howard. I don't like the food so much. Give Frisky a big kiss. Say hi to Grandma.

Love,
Patty

What gives such writing its charm—and makes it sound childish—is its way of putting the same emphasis on everything. Each sentence runs in a straight line, from locomotive to caboose. Patty writes with clarity and directness, all right—even Grandma could hardly miss the meaning—but her prose lacks variety and depth. No one, of course, would criticize a nine-year-old for this kind of writing. Readers, however, expect mature writers to be able to use not just the hammer and the saw but all the tools of the trade. And they expect the right tool for the job.

Coordination

Rather than having a string of choppy sentences, an older Patty could combine her simple sentences into compound sentences.

> We learned how to swim yesterday, and then we went on a hike. I like Counselor Howard, but I don't like the food so much.

A *compound sentence* contains at least two independent clauses and no dependent clauses. Patty now expresses her experience more clearly. She shows the relations between ideas. She points out how camp activity is structured and how one event immediately follows another. Finally, to show the range of her experiences, she combines a like and a dislike in one sentence.

This process is called *coordination*. When we coordinate sentences, we are saying that the clauses enjoy the same importance. They are costars and deserve equal billing. (For a further discussion of compound sentences, see ''Phrases, Clauses, and Sentences'' in Chapter 19.)

By placing two independent clauses in the same sentence, we imply that they are so integrally connected that they must perform in the same show. The two independent clauses should reinforce each other; each thought should benefit from being coupled with the other.

> Give me liberty or give me death! (Patrick Henry)
>
> Candy
> Is dandy
> But liquor
> Is quicker.
> > (Ogden Nash)

If the two ideas are not closely related, they should not be in the same sentence. When we hook together disparate ideas, our sentences tend to fly apart.

> Michelangelo painted the Sistine Chapel, and Pope Julius II was a great patron of the arts.

These two clauses have no apparent connection.

Even if both parts of the sentence treat the same subject, they may not mesh.

> Leonardo da Vinci painted *The Last Supper*, and he was a Florentine.

The connection between these two ideas is too casual to justify putting them together, and we can hardly imagine a context in which the ideas would be equally important.

To connect independent clauses, insert between them either a comma with a coordinating conjunction or a semicolon. (Without one of these devices, you would commit the error called a comma splice. See "Comma Splices and Fused Sentences" in Chapter 20.)

Coordinating conjunctions (*and, but, for, nor, or, so, yet*) indicate the relation between the independent clauses. Each carries its own logic. You would not use *and* when one clause contradicts the other. You would not use *yet* when you meant *nor*.

Writers sometimes face the decision of whether to use a conjunction or a semicolon.

> The pollsters predicted a close election, but the smart money predicted a landslide.

> The pollsters predicted a close election; the smart money predicted a landslide.

Often this choice is a matter not of grammar but of intuition. The semicolon signals a closer relation between the two clauses. It rivets the reader's attention on the connection. Even if the comma and conjunction seem more natural to you, try a semicolon occasionally. It will give your clauses a tighter link.

Subordination

A prose consisting only of simple sentences and coordination can tire your reader. Even though you may add interesting modifiers, the basic beat goes on until the reader goes away. When every idea is in an independent clause, the reader can't distinguish between what is more important and what is less.

Remember our tortured sentence about the raccoons and the farmers? Suppose we had presented the information this way:

> It was a cold January morning, and it was rainy too. It was dawn, and the marauding raccoons reconnoitered. They were blue from the cold, but they were piqued. They were determined to get even. The farmers' measures had been harsh; they had been petty. The raccoons harassed the farmers. The farmers were furious; they were a hot-tempered bunch. And, oh yes, the raccoons were gleeful.

This series of independent clauses fails to identify what is important and what is not. Everything comes at the reader willy-nilly. For all its silliness, our original involuted sentence makes better reading. Intelligent readers will make some educated guesses about the priority of each bit of information. But why should they have to do the work? It is the writer's responsibility to make the point clear and to indicate relative importance, to *subordinate* the less important ideas to the more important. As coordination indicates equal significance of ideas, subordination indicates that one idea is more significant than the other.

> Although it was a cold, rainy January morning, the raccoons were determined to get even with the farmers.

From this sentence the reader knows that the weather and time of day are less important than the raccoons' determination.

When we subordinate, we bring the main idea front and center in an independent clause and push less important ideas back into a dependent clause. The main idea should *always* appear in the independent clause. The subordinate ideas depend on and are secondary to that main idea and should be housed in a dependent clause.

> When I finally left the casino, I had lost my last dollar.

The main idea is losing that last dollar and it is expressed in the main clause. Had the main idea been leaving the casino, the writer would have put it in the main clause.

> After I lost my last dollar, I finally left the casino.

The writer could clearly improve the next sentence by subordinating one idea to the other:

> Hunger had finally driven him wild, and Big Foot Sam began to stalk the Milwaukee suburb looking for food.

There is nothing wrong here—except that there is no weighing of the ideas. Is the hunger more or less important than the stalking? And what is the connection between them? The intelligent reader figures out the meaning and silently rewrites.

> Because hunger had finally driven him wild, Big Foot Sam began to stalk the Milwaukee suburb looking for food.

You can have more than one subordinate idea in a sentence, and you can put them in different places, depending on meaning and style.

> Muhammad Ali, *who had won the heavyweight title from Sonny Liston and again from George Foreman,* became the first man to win it three times *when he took it from Leon Spinks.*

To join a dependent clause to the independent clause, use either a subordinating conjunction or a relative pronoun. (One of each appears in the Muhammad Ali sentence.) The subordinating conjunctions you are most apt to read and use are *after, although, as, because, before, if, in order to, since, so that, unless, until, when, whenever, where,* and *while.* Each of these indicates a particular relation between the dependent clause and the independent clause—what caused what, when, where, why, and how.

Although he never learned to juggle, Raoul had a certain unwashed charm about him.

The postman refused to deliver the mail *because* my Great Dane bit him on the rump and tore his britches.

(Caution: some of these words also function as prepositions—*before the vending machine, because of you, since Tuesday.* To identify a clause, look for both a subject and a verb.)

The relative pronouns are *that, which, who, whom,* and *whose.*

The question *that* this essay poses has baffled all the critics *who* have wrestled with it.

Some sentences contain both a subordinating conjunction and a relative pronoun.

Because a small, barred window *that* looked down on the prison yard provided the only light in the cell, he could not read.

As these examples demonstrate, subordination can create flexible, energetic, precise, and subtle sentences. Subordinated sentences can be either *complex*—having one independent clause and one or more subordinate clauses—or *compound-complex*—having at least two independent clauses and one subordinate clause. (For further discussion, see "Phrases, Clauses, and Sentences" in Chapter 19.)

TIPS FOR COORDINATION AND SUBORDINATION

- Remember that too many simple sentences may sound childish.
- When two thoughts are equal and reinforce each other, coordinate them in a single sentence.
- Use subordination to convey the relative importance of thoughts.
- Put main thoughts in independent clauses and subordinate thoughts in dependent clauses.

Exercises for Coordination and Subordination

1. Combine each of the following groups of sentences to make one sentence.
   a. Inflation most drastically affects the lives of people on fixed incomes. These people depend on Social Security. The Social Security laws

provide for increased payment based on the cost of living. We should protect that part of the law.

b. Each year, the swallows come back to Capistrano. They come in the summer. They are small birds. In flight they are graceful. Their plumage is an iridescent black or blue.

c. The obelisk is a monument. It is four sided. Usually it is made of a single piece of stone. It tapers toward the top. In ancient Egypt, obelisks were dedicated to the sun god.

d. The Mississippi is a mighty river. It is sometimes as thick and brown as mud. It curls like a snake in motion. It is one of the world's greatest waterways. Vast cities have been built on its banks.

e. San Marco is a church in Venice. It contains beautiful mosaics of stone, glass, and gold. Its foundations are in watery soil. The air is damp. These factors threaten the permanence of the artworks. They also threaten the stability of the church.

f. The channel catfish will eat almost anything. It is a scavenger. It is a predator. It can find food by sight and also by touch and taste with its fleshy barbels. You can bait your hook with minnows. You can also use frogs and chicken innards. Artificial lures attract the channel catfish. It is omnivorous.

2. Revise the following sentences as directed.
   a. The boss turned her back, and Carl and Tony stuck out their tongues. (Use subordination.)
   b. Margaret Mead was able to throw herself into tribal life because she possessed remarkable gusto. (Make into a simple sentence.)
   c. After he took a fabulous bite out of the Big Apple upon his arrival in New York, he was hooked. (Use coordination.)
   d. There is no other drink as potent as the zombie, and I know that from recent, painful experience. (Use subordination.)

3. In a few sentences, discuss each change you made in the sentences in Exercise 2, stating whether it was an improvement or not, and why.

4. Revise the following to make subordinate sentences.
   a. I played the piano, and Mary sang.
   b. Galileo had artistic ability and might have turned out to be a painter or a musician.
   c. Williams voted for Phillips and so Phillips won the election.
   d. Many old people watch the actions of the young with nostalgia, regret, and sometimes horror, but few young people take an equally strong interest in the old.
   e. A history of philosophy and theology could be written in terms of grudges, wounded pride, and aversions, and it would be far more instructive than the usual treatment.
   f. She came up behind the man, and she looked gaunt in the gray, shapeless garment and the sunbonnet, and she wore stained sneakers.

EMPHASIS: STRENGTHENING THE THOUGHT

Some sentences should have punch; others should not. An essay that came on like gangbusters all the time would soon exhaust and irritate the reader. Reading it would be like listening for hours to a prize fight. You want variety. You want some sentences to start with a punch, some to end with a bang, a few to proceed evenly from start to finish.

Ending with a Bang

All of us want occasionally to make a truly emphatic statement, to cue the trumpets and train the spotlights as the big point arrives. The big moment will very likely occur at the end.

Take the money and run.

Those who make peaceful revolution impossible will make violent revolution inevitable.

Reverse the order of the ideas and they lose that strong emphasis.

Run after you take the money.

Violent revolution will be made inevitable by those who make peaceful revolution impossible.

A sentence generally wants to get somewhere. It wants to gather momentum as it travels.

Beethoven had been deaf for five years when his Ninth Symphony was first performed.

This sentence is grammatically correct but hardly emphatic. Suppose it had been written this way:

When his Ninth Symphony was first performed, Beethoven had been deaf for five years.

Here we have the same words, same ideas, same independent clause, same dependent clause, but the different order provides a greater impact. The notion of the great composer's deafness is not slipped in but slammed home.

In the passages that follow, we discuss four versions of an opening sentence for a paragraph in praise of the lowly hot dog. Each sentence contains the same set of ideas, but the arrangement of those ideas makes each sentence quite distinct.

The most American of all foods is still the hot dog, which is a thought that makes great chefs bristle.

Few readers would realize that the writer of this sentence intended to praise the hot dog. That homely object lies buried in the middle, where the main clause dies a murky death. Highlighted, unfortunately, is a weak, barely breathing *which* clause. This clause reads like an afterthought, or a thought the writer did not know how to include.

> The most American of all foods is still the hot dog, although great chefs bristle at the thought.

This is much better. It still reverses the flow of energy and sends the reader backward looking for the target, but the *although* at least indicates that something contrary, and therefore perhaps interesting, may follow. Now see what happens when the writer moves the *although* clause to the front.

> Although great chefs bristle at the thought, the hot dog is still the most American of all foods.

That hot dog is obviously the point of the sentence—not the chefs, not American foods—and the writer ought to place it in the most prominent spot.

> Although great chefs bristle at the thought, the most American of all foods is still the hot dog.

Now the reader gets the full impact of the idea.

Sometimes you simply cannot place your main idea at the end, however. The sense of the sentence may dictate otherwise.

> Because he was rich, he thought people adored him.
>
> He thought people adored him because he was rich.

These two sentences do not express the same thought. You would probably dislike the fellow in the first version but pity him in the second. Placing the modifying clause near the word it modifies is as important as strong emphasis.

Opening with a Punch

Although the ending is the most emphatic part of a sentence, the beginning is a close second. When you start your sentence with a strong idea, you step right out and say, "Here it is, folks—take it or leave it."

> The cold grave is the fate of humankind.

That sentence packs a wallop from the first word. To reverse it would be to weaken it.

> · The fate of humankind is the cold grave.

Even for less stunning assertions, the opening can make a reader sit up and take notice.

> Be cheerful while you are alive.
>
> Stealing apples can lead to trouble.

Some writers muffle a strong opening idea in a construction that weakens the impact.

> There isn't anyone who can stop him now

is less emphatic than

> No one can stop him now

and

> It was frequently said that lust for applause was his worst fault

is bland compared with

> Lust for applause, it was frequently said, was his worst fault.

In this revision, the writer buried the least interesting idea in the middle.

THE SECOND SPOTLIGHT.   Even when you put your main idea at the end, start off with the second most important idea. Read these two sentences:

> Because every day the city sees the influx of thousands of people, Mexico City is a sprawling mess.
>
> Because thousands of people enter the city every day, Mexico City is a sprawling mess.

Sprawling mess is, of course, the most compelling idea in the sentence and rightly goes at the end. But *thousands of people* is the second most compelling and should have the second spotlight, the beginning. (For further discussion of sentences, see "Phrases, Clauses, and Sentences," in Chapter 19.)

Revising for Emphasis

THE LIMP SENTENCE.   Limpness (not a technical term) in a sentence can have three causes. First, it can come from adding a weak and unnecessary phrase or clause to a sentence.

> Hamlet hated King Claudius, so it seems.
>
> But through all the trouble, he loved his mother, in a way.
>
> He was of several minds, so to speak.

With phrases like these, even the best sentence will sag.

Second, limp sentences may result from using a *passive voice* construction. In these constructions, the subject of the sentence is not the actor but the recipient of the action.

Yesterday all my hair was cut off by John the barber.

The reader must go back to the beginning of this sentence to find the target of the action. In the meantime, the sentence loses both energy and emphasis. Had the writer followed the natural flow of the simple English sentence, this one would have read

Yesterday John the barber cut off all my hair.

(For further discussion of passive voice, see "Be Active" in Chapter 12.)

Third, ending with a preposition can make a sentence limp. Note the difference in emphasis between

Toxic waste dumps are hazards to keep away from

and

Toxic waste dumps are hazards to avoid.

That *from* at the end makes the idea trail off weakly, while *to avoid* provides a firm closing.

You should not twist your sentences into knots just to avoid this construction. To tease pedants, Winston Churchill said that to worry about ending sentences with prepositions was something "up with which I will not put." It is not a crime—it is just not a strong finish.

THE ANTICLIMAX.   Anticlimax will undermine even the most interesting sentence. When you write a sentence of several more or less equal elements, watch your order of presentation. That order can make or break your sentence. The obvious, and easy, way to present a list is chronologically. But not all items occur in sequence, and indeed sometimes strict chronology leads to anticlimax, as in this sentence:

She flew a balloon in France; she hunted lions in Africa; she fought a revolution in Chile; she drove a taxi in Philadelphia.

Philadelphia? a taxi? Fortunately, the revision does greater justice to an exciting career.

In Africa, she hunted lions; in France, she flew a balloon; in Philadelphia, she drove a taxi; and in Chile, she fought a revolution.

This new order is called the *relay race* because, as on most relay teams, the second best leads off and the best runs the last lap. Driving a taxi takes, as it should, a less important position even though it occurred after the other events.

The writer also improved this sentence in another way. In the original, place comes last in each clause and thus receives the emphasis. But what happened is more interesting than where it happened. In revising, the writer put the action at the end of each clause. *She fought a revolution* provides a fitting climax.

Equal Emphasis: Treating Ideas Alike

So far we have seen sentences in which one idea dominates and therefore deserves the most emphasis. Now we turn to sentences in which two or more related or similar ideas deserve equal billing. We create such sentences by means of parallelism and correlatives.

PERFORMING ON THE PARALLEL.   In parallel construction equal or similar ideas are presented in the identical grammatical form.

> I came, I saw, I conquered.

Follow Caesar's lead: put parallel ideas in parallel grammatical form. Parallel construction requires that all like elements be treated in the same manner. They should be expressed in the same grammatical construction, whether clauses or phrases, passive or active voice.

> The farmer takes a wife, the wife takes a child, the child takes a nurse, the nurse . . .

Because of the parallel construction of this traditional song, children have no difficulty understanding the story. Without parallel construction you might get something like this:

> The farmer takes a wife, the child is taken by that wife, and it in its turn has an opportunity to choose its nurse, and then a choice is made by the nurse . . .

In this version, the ideas do not function as an organized team but rather as a motley mob of straggling thoughts.

Maintaining parallelism is particularly helpful in comparing and contrasting two things. Although the following example contains all the elements of a comparison, the writer has presented them in a confusing manner:

> The Sahara was a verdant region in 10,000 B.C., but seven millennia later you would have seen fewer lakes and forests.

Not only is this sentence limp, but also the reader must reorganize elements to figure out exactly what it says. The revision is clear and forceful.

> In 10,000 B.C., the Sahara was a verdant region, but by 3,000 B.C. it had become a desert.

Verdant region and *desert* offer a sharper contrast; using dates for both periods of time makes the point clearer; repetition of the subject-verb construction underscores the comparison.

In constructing a list of complicated thoughts, we ignore parallelism at our peril, as the writer of this sentence discovered:

> The main priorities of Hitler's campaign were encouraging the German people, and fewer debts, the subjugation of France, and he wanted to become the sole power in Europe.

This is a jumble. The reader has to get in there and straighten it out.

> The main priorities of Hitler's campaign were to encourage the German people, to reduce the German debt, to conquer France, and to become the sole power in Europe.

Now the reader will grasp Hitler's goals more easily.

Although in parallelism all parts must have the same construction, they need not all possess the same length or cadence. Here is a parallel sentence in which one element is much fuller than the other:

> For its well-being, Mississippi depends largely on agriculture, but for its well-being, Georgia depends on business, commerce, and manufacturing as well as agriculture.

MAINTAINING YOUR BALANCE. Balance is a stylistic variation on parallelism. In a balanced sentence, the length and rhythm, as well as the grammatical elements, are the same in both parts. We could find no better illustrations of balance than in the orations of Brutus and Mark Antony over the body of Caesar in Shakespeare's *Julius Caesar.*

> Not that I loved Caesar less, but that I loved Rome more. . . . As he was valiant, I honor him; but as he was ambitious, I slew him.

With these balanced cadences, Brutus sways the Roman crowd. In opposition, Antony uses the same technique with even greater effect.

> The evil that men do lives after them,
> The good is oft interred with their bones.

The reader here feels the exquisite tension of perfect balance—that of an elegant gymnast on the high bar.

We cannot write as Shakespeare did, but we can strengthen even our everyday sentences by balancing the ideas. A sentence like

> Although Stephen Douglas triumphed in the debates, the presidency went to Abraham Lincoln

can become

> Stephen Douglas won the debates, but Abraham Lincoln won the presidency.

> He had a passion to discover things and that pushed him onward, but he was held back by a fear of failure

can become

> His passion for discovery pushed him onward, but his fear of failure held him back.

Revised, both these sentences are balanced.

JOINING WITH CORRELATIVES.   When you are working out on the parallel bars or trying to balance on the high beam of a sentence, you can find help by turning to correlative conjunctions: *both . . . and, either . . . or, neither . . . nor, not only . . . but also, whether . . . or.* These pairs firmly tie two thoughts together by showing exactly how they are related.

> Both Joe Louis and Rocky Marciano were great heavyweights.

> Either he would get his way, or he would not play.

> Neither screaming men nor rivers of blood could stop the war.

> Francis Bacon was not only a philosopher but also an essayist and a statesman.

When you use these pairs, you show that the two parts of your thought are equally important and closely related. You can forge a stronger and more emphatic bond with correlatives than with the coordinating conjunctions, such as *and, but,* and so on.

Bonding carefully is both grammatically and stylistically important. When using correlative conjunctions, make sure the grammatical form of the first phrase or clause is repeated in the second. It is incorrect to write

> Either you are part of the solution or part of the problem.

It should be

> Either you are part of the solution or you are part of the problem

or

> You are part of either the solution or the problem.

By using correlatives, you can strengthen grammatically correct but uninspired sentences. You can, for instance, change a rather dull sentence like

> At Abu Simbel, Ramses II built an immense temple in his own honor and he built another one as an honor for Queen Nefertari

to the livelier

> At Abu Simbel, Ramses II built not only an immense temple to honor himself but also one to honor Queen Nefertari.

Caution: The words *both, either,* and *neither* are not always correlative conjunctions; they can also function alone as pronouns or adjectives.

> Because both played well, either side could have won, but neither was overwhelming.

TIPS FOR EMPHASIS

- Remember that the place of greatest emphasis is the end of the sentence. The second most emphatic position is the beginning.
- Avoid limp sentences and anticlimaxes.
- When you express more than one important thought, put them in parallel grammatical form.
- Balance elements in a sentence to emphasize the equality of the thoughts.
- Correlative conjunctions tie thoughts together, but when you use one of the pair, you must use the other. Be sure the thoughts are expressed in the same grammatical form.

Exercises for Emphasis

1. Change the following sentences so that the emphasis comes at the end.
   a. The mayor acts as though she dislikes street vendors more than anybody in the United States.
   b. The airport is where I would like this taxi to take me.
   c. Virtually all agree that we must find a new source of fuel to be able to meet our increasing energy demands in the future.
   d. The paintings of Giorgione are enjoying a period of immense popularity because there is an exhibition at the museum of his works.

2. Rewrite the following sentences so that the emphasis falls at the beginning.
   a. What it is that's important is doing your homework.
   b. A bad way to bring about change is mob rule.
   c. The languages of the Bantu and the Arabs combined to form Swahili.
   d. People are telling the truth when they say he is conventional.

3. Rewrite these sentences to emphasize the most important point.
   a. Born in the fifteenth century, Lucrezia Borgia had her second husband murdered, although she was the daughter of a pope.

    b. Cotton has been spun, woven, and dyed since prehistoric times, including long before Europeans settled in the Western Hemisphere.

    c. Pacifists, celibates, and egalitarians, the Shakers have virtually vanished as a religious group, although they were a relatively popular offshoot of the Quakers in the nineteenth century.

    d. Copper is a useful element because it is a good conductor of heat and is used in alloys such as brass and bronze, in addition.

4. Revise the following sentences to make them parallel, balanced, or both.

    a. Women should earn just as much as the opposite sex, and I think they also ought to be able to feel as good about themselves.

    b. People should save their money so that they can put it in investments of one kind or another, but money earning something would be important too.

    c. Although he thought he was probably extremely prejudiced, behaving in a fair manner was something he knew he was capable of doing.

    d. He was an excellent plumber, and I was surprised to learn that he worked really well doing carpenter work.

ECONOMY: REDUCING THE VERBIAGE

Some people write as though they believe that the more words, the better the writing. Of course, that is not true. We have all read passages in which the writing sags from sheer volume of verbiage. In this section we discuss how to write a trim, economical prose.

Excess Weight

"Under the impression," said Mr. Micawber, "that your peregrinations in this metropolis have not as yet been extensive, and that you might have some difficulty penetrating the arcana of the modern Babylon . . . in short," said Mr. Micawber in a burst of confidence, "that you might lose your way . . ." (Charles Dickens, *David Copperfield*)

Mr. Micawber takes twenty-nine words to say what he could have said in six. He is a glutton for words. In contrast, good writers look for that one word that will do the work of ten. This restraint is much to their credit, for in English the longer and the more repetitious the statement, the weaker.

Here is a sentence from a student paper that is laboring under a great deal of excess weight:

> Carl Sagan opens up an area of interest to me with the content of his essay, which cites explanations of how monkeys can be observed to learn to communicate through the use of language.

Even the most physically fit reader would sweat under that load.

The writer put the sentence on a diet. If the area is *of interest to me,* then it is *interesting,* period. The *content of his essay* is nothing more than *his essay,* so *content,* farewell. *Can be observed to learn* is unnecessary and confusing, because the focus is not on someone's observing, but on the monkeys' learning. *The use of language* is only a long way of saying *language.* So now the writer had

> Carl Sagan opens up an interesting area with his essay, which cites explanations of how monkeys can learn to communicate through language.

From thirty-four words down to twenty-two without losing a thing. With such success, the writer became a little bolder and began to change some verbs and nouns around. *Cites explanations* became *explains.* Then she realized that *opens up an interesting area* could be tucked into *essay.* And she didn't need the uninteresting word *interesting.* She was down to twelve words and a much more vigorous sentence.

> In his essay, Carl Sagan explains how monkeys can learn to communicate.

In the next few pages, we discuss the kinds of surplus that you can easily jettison.

BLAH PHRASES. Sometimes your prose will be invaded by blah phrases, groups of uninteresting words that contribute nothing to your sentence. Whenever you see tiny words in your sentences, beware. *It, that, of, do,* and many more are waiting to weigh down your sentences. They form flocks: *due to the fact that, in the event that, it is also of importance that, when it comes to, in the matter of, has to do with.* Flocks of tiny words can be a bad omen in writing. They burden your reader.

> Due to the fact that the death of the previous captain had to do with a quarrel over a black hen, the effect is that of providing a preview of what Marlow himself will face in the future.

We can eliminate many of these tiny words.

> Because the previous captain died after a quarrel over a black hen, Marlow understands what he will face.

Frequently, we can translate a flock of tiny words into a single one: *in the event that* can become *if, has to do with* can become *concerns,* and *when it comes to* can usually shrink to *when.* As in the example, *due to the fact that* can become the simple *because.*

Blah phrases do not necessarily consist of tiny words; they are often simply long ways of expressing things. Sometimes they conceal perfectly good ideas.

> Lincoln decided that he would go to Ford's Theater to see the play even though he had been somewhat disturbed by thoughts that there might be some kind of danger if he went.

We can often find energetic one- or two-word substitutes for these limp strings.

> Despite his premonitions of danger, Lincoln went to Ford's Theater to see the play.

Twenty blah words at the end of the original have condensed to five crisp words beginning the revision.

In revising, we can often condense overlong modifying clauses or phrases—especially *who* or *which* clauses that end a sentence—into an adjective or shorter phrase with the same meaning and then embed that adjective elsewhere in the sentence. Finding an equivalent will sometimes take some imagination; just as often, though, it is quite easy.

> The emperor, who had been drinking to the point of intoxication, staggered here and there through Rome, until he eventually found a place to sleep in the garbage dump, which all the Romans used

can easily become

> The emperor, drunk and staggering, eventually slept in Rome's garbage dump.

REDUNDANCY. *Redundant* refers to words used when the meaning is clear without them. We culled this from a newspaper:

> We will do all we can to do everything in our power to see that the incumbent does not return to Capitol Hill as senator for another term.

We certainly got the point, but we could have gotten it more quickly and enjoyably if we hadn't had to push our way through all the unnecessary verbiage. After all, *all we can* is *everything in our power,* and if the incumbent returns as senator, that will be *another term,* and surely it will be to *Capitol Hill.*

Repetition is not bad in itself and can sometimes come in handy. We may want to emphasize a point by repeating it, as in "I said no, No, NO!"—but we should be on our guard. Redundancies are useless repetitions; they creep into speech and once there are hard to extricate. How many times have you heard *the general public* instead of *the public, the sta-*

dium's total capacity instead of *the stadium's capacity, personally I think* instead of just *I think,* or *my close personal friend* instead of *my friend?*

Redundancies appear in several guises. Often writers use a modifier for a noun or verb that already contains the modifier's meaning.

Thomas Edison was the original inventor of the electric light bulb.

Inventor means "originator," and the only thing we call a *light bulb* is electric. We should settle for

Thomas Edison invented the light bulb.

Sometimes writers pile on adjectives with the same meaning.

She did not strike him as an open-minded, impartial, or objective judge.

These adjectives mean about the same thing. Any one alone is ample.

She did not strike him as an impartial judge.

Occasionally an idea already implied in one part of a sentence is made explicit elsewhere.

Unlike his friend Cassius, who seems to have made his decision quickly in comparison with Brutus, Brutus has made his decision slowly, as his opening words show.

Because this sentence obviously contrasts the two men, the phrase *in comparison with* is redundant. Nor is it necessary to spell out how both men acted. The writer can imply Cassius's quickness by focusing on Brutus's slowness.

Unlike Cassius, Brutus has made his decision slowly, as his opening words show.

This problem is harder to identify and avoid than simple one-word redundancies; the best prevention is to pay close attention to the meaning of your sentence. Develop your "redundancy detector." Weed out useless repetitions in pursuit of spare, efficient English.

LONG, RUNNING JUMPS AND EXPLETIVE OPENERS. Look for excess at the beginning of the sentence. Some sentences take a long run before leaping into the thought. In the following sentence, so many words run by that the reader would have to watch the replay to remember the subject:

Clearly, activity in the oil industry over the last ten months is indicative of the fact that, far from being on a decided wane, the efforts of OPEC and cartels like it are all the more likely to continue.

The sentence improves with a shorter run.

Oil profits for the last ten months show that, far from waning, the success of OPEC and cartels like it is likely to continue.

The problem of the long running jump is particularly acute in sentences that begin with a subordinate clause or a lengthy phrase.

> Even if it were true that you and your mate enjoy a perfect marriage, it would still be just as true that, if certain sociologists are to be believed, there are 125,000 other possible mates who would suit you just as well.

From the revision, we realize that the sentence contains an interesting idea.

> Even if you and your mate enjoy a perfect marriage, certain sociologists claim that 125,000 other possible mates would suit you just as well.

Many long, running jumps start with *It is* or *There are.* This opening is called the *expletive,* meaning that *It* or *There* acts as the formal (though not the real) subject of the sentence. Sometimes expletive openers are the most appropriate way to start a sentence. They are, for instance, wonderful for pointing out things that simply exist. The first line of Jane Austen's *Pride and Prejudice* is

> It is a truth universally acknowledged, that a single man in possession of a good fortune must be in want of a wife.

And sometimes no other opener can capture just the right mood.

> There is a tavern in the town, in the town. . . .

Frequently, however, the expletive seems to conceal more than it clarifies, as in this sentence regarding intervention in international currency markets:

> There were occasions when there was agreement to intervene and to intervene in a coordinated manner. There was some concerted intervention after January 31 and last week.

Without the expletives, the sentence is much clearer and shorter.

> On occasion the parties agreed to intervene in a coordinated manner. Some concentrated intervention occurred after January 31 and last week.

Sometimes the expletive only condemns the reader to additional words that postpone the moment of truth.

> It is true that many people believe there are some ways in which football has become the national pastime.

The revision is compact, like a running back.

> Many people believe football has become the national pastime.

We can hardly talk without the expletive, for it gives us time to shape our thoughts. But when we write, and therefore have time to revise, we ought to cast away unnecessary verbiage, and that often means the expletive. We are not suggesting that you never use *It is* or *There are*—they have their uses. You just should not overuse them or fall back on them to avoid a little extra effort or thought.

Qualifiers Vague, Timid, or Loud

Three kinds of qualifiers—vague, timid, loud—are often verbal fillers rather than informative elements in a written sentence.

VAGUE QUALIFIERS. Often writers use words such as *very, actually,* and *really* to pump up adjectives. But these vague qualifiers frequently have the opposite effect. The unadorned

That rhinoceros was huge

suggests more hugeness than

That rhinoceros was really very huge.

How big is *very*? How real is *really*? It was huge, period.

By overusing vague qualifiers, we diminish the power of language. The word *terribly* once meant "in a manner to cause fear and dread," as in *The wounded rhino closing in on me roared terribly.* Now we blithely say, *I had a terribly good time at your tea party.* The word *terribly* is, like the rhino, wounded, but it lacks the energy to roar. We can no longer convey in a single word "in a manner to cause fear and dread."

We are not suggesting that you should or could make every sentence absolute (few get close enough to say *The rhino weighed 847 pounds and head to tail measured 9.33 feet*). And we are not saying you should rid yourself of every *very*. If *very* is as close as you can get to what you mean, and the context makes the meaning clear, then you should use the word. But do not lean on vague qualifiers to avoid making careful assessments.

TIMID QUALIFIERS. Cousins to the vague qualifiers are the timid qualifiers. How big is *a bit*? To what degree is *somewhat*? Is *a lot* the same as *a good deal,* or is it more like *much*? How much is *rather*? Like their kin, these words pop up almost unbidden. They may save you the work of being precise, but they can blur your writing. If we say *East German swimmers are rather superior,* what do we mean? Do we mean that they won one more race than the competition, or that they won all the races but by a narrow margin? If we say *Our friend is somewhat of a hypochondriac,* do we suggest one major complaint a week or a dozen minor ones each day?

No writer can do without timid qualifiers; indeed, they keep prose responsible. They are reminders of the imprecision of estimates and the tentativeness of opinions. You should not pretend to a certainty you do not possess. But use these qualifiers only when they convey your thought as precisely as possible.

Loud Qualifiers. Loud qualifiers also add verbiage without much meaning. "Oh wow! That is absolutely the most *fantastic* thing I ever heard! That's just *incredible!*" Perhaps you know people who talk like this. You may even like their enthusiasm. But when they talk this way all the time, complete with exclamation points, italics, flashing lights, and explosions, you probably begin to wonder what they find important.

The problem with constant emphasis, whether in writing or in speech, is that it fails to make distinctions. What did the person find so *fantastic* and *incredible?* Did someone rise from the dead? That is indeed incredible. Did a rich uncle die, bequeathing an island off the coast of Greece? That does sound like a fantasy. If, however, the writer just attended a movie, maybe it was only *good,* or—to be more informative— maybe *the acting was effective* or *the camera work helped convey the mood. Incredible*s and *fantastic*s do not tell what somebody thinks. "How was the movie?" "Fantastic!" "But how was the movie?"

Careful writers avoid artificially emphatic words. They try to convey their enthusiasms without shouting. They want to show their readers exactly what excited them.

Wasteful Constructions

The requirements of the thought should determine the size and construction of a sentence. Overextended, a sentence can appear awkward or even incomprehensible.

> When he was in the village, he saw the timbered houses, which had been built by the colonists, who brought the style from England, and they were now occupied by the aborigines, who had entered the village after the colonists had retreated.

In revising, the writer wisely broke the sentence in two.

> When he was in the village, he saw the timbered houses, built by the colonists in a style brought from England. Ever since the colonists had retreated, the aborigines had occupied the houses.

The passage gains in both clarity and strength. Never do violence to the complexity or subtlety of your thought, but when you can shorten and simplify, do so.

The English language offers numerous ways to compress thoughts without changing meaning. Sometimes you can move elements around and substitute a few words for a long clause.

> Dirty tricks in political campaigns are as old as the American republic, and they will probably be around until its end because they have frequently been effective when politicians have resorted to them.

Compressed, the sentence is easier to read.

> Frequently effective, dirty tricks in political campaigns are as old as the American republic and will probably be around until its end.

The writer combines the two independent clauses into one main clause. *Frequently effective* takes the place of *because they have frequently been effective when politicians have resorted to them.* The writer does not mention *politicians* in the revised sentence because the reader can assume the word from the main clause.

We can also use appositives to condense. *Appositive* refers to a word or group of words placed beside a noun or noun substitute to supplement its meaning. An appositive can take the place of a wordy clause.

> Cairo, which is the largest city on the African continent, has a daytime population estimated at 12 million, which is 2 million more than its estimated nighttime population

can become

> Cairo, Africa's largest city, has a daytime population estimated at 12 million, 2 million more than its estimated nighttime population.

Changing a dependent clause to an adjective phrase can often create a shorter, more energetic sentence.

> Philadelphia, which is called the City of Brotherly Love because it was founded as a Quaker colony, served as the American capital during the Revolution

can become

> Founded as a Quaker colony and called the City of Brotherly Love, Philadelphia served as the American capital during the Revolution.

You may have noticed that many of the changes we recommend in this section get rid of a *which* clause. As a general caution, beware the *which* clause, which is much overused, which is a shame, which is an example. *Which* clauses tend to inefficiency as well as windiness.

We are not suggesting you should excise all clauses that begin with *which*. Here, for instance, is an elegantly turned sentence:

> Punishment, which is inflicted by all civilized societies, is not a virtue but a necessity.

No serious writer could do without the word *which*. But when saving words, check your *which* clauses.

TIPS FOR ECONOMY

- Look for blah phrases and cut them out of your prose.
- Remove, delete, and get rid of redundancies, repetitions, and saying the same thing twice.
- Beware of overusing expletive openers.
- Watch out for vague, timid, or loud but empty qualifiers.
- Remember that the complexity of a sentence should be determined by the complexity of the thought.
- When you can shorten and simplify without distorting meaning, do it.
- Look for the *which* clause when you are searching for excess.

Exercises for Economy

1. Reduce the following sentences to a minimum without losing sense.
   a. In view of the fact that she is a person who is likely to monopolize the conversational talk, men and women alike have experienced a wish to go elsewhere and in fact do go elsewhere when she is speaking.
   b. It is unbelievable for you to say that if a person who smoked marijuana regularly did not fear that he or she might come into conflict with the law in an unpleasant manner and subsequently serve time in a jail, marijuana would very likely be smoked in public places more often than in fact it now is.
   c. When people are a bit too quick to do things, it is a fact that they often end up making an awesome mess of what they are trying to do.
   d. It is a fact that many human beings, including both men and women, who stay up late at night seeking excitement in its very many guises and in all ways driving themselves a bit too much, may find that later in life their chances to live to a ripe old age have been in point of fact fabulously curtailed.

2. Exchange with a partner two paragraphs from an essay you wrote for an earlier assignment. Revise each other's paragraphs for economy. Then revise your own paragraphs. Compare the revisions, and discuss the effectiveness of the changes.

3. Find two- or three-word substitutes for the italicized parts of the following sentences.
   a. My father was *a person who was born and lived in Italy before he came to the United States.*
   b. He *uses a lot of words that repeat each other.*
   c. My mother married *when she was very young and in fact was not even twenty years old.*

> d. Franklin Roosevelt *was the thirty-second president of the United States and was the only president to be reelected three times.*

4. Using appositives, revise these sentences to make them less wordy.
   a. Auburn is a university in the state of Alabama, and it has an agricultural school and an architectural school.
   b. Abraham Lincoln, who was a citizen of Illinois though he was born in Kentucky, was the sixteenth president of the United States.
   c. The Napa Valley is located just north of San Francisco and is famous for its many varieties of wine.

VARIETY: CHANGING THE PACE

There may come a time in your writing when you want to take a chance and try something different, something you haven't tried and don't see very often in your school reading. When that mood strikes, go ahead. Dive in. Here we describe two ways to vary the construction of sentences—inverting the natural order and using fragments.

Inverting the Natural Order

A writer's natural inclination is to move through a sentence from subject to verb to object—along the way, of course, hanging modifiers on the spine. Most of the time, this is how you will construct your sentences. But occasionally you may want to try an unusual construction, such as

A genius he isn't.

By inverting the natural order, you undercut your reader's expectations and quicken his or her interest. Used sparingly, inversion can transform a bland sentence into a sharp one. Compare

We shall always have the poor with us

with

The poor we shall always have with us.

Using Fragments

A group of words set off as a sentence is a fragment if it lacks either a subject or a verb, or if it contains a dependent clause but no independent clause.

Walking fast in order to get home by dusk.

The building designed by Frank Lloyd Wright.

Because I said so.

Although they are grammatical errors—complete sentences must contain both a subject and a verb—fragments sometimes appear in published works; we have used a few in this book. Employed rarely and carefully, a fragment can add a little zing to writing as in this example.

> Had you gotten off the Harbor Freeway and driven into Watts before the 1965 riots, you would have seen the scars of official indifference. For Watts had been forgotten by those responsible for the city. On either side of the freeway you would have seen once-pleasant houses now with broken windows and crumbling walls, once-verdant gardens now junk heaps, a once-prosperous commercial area now half-occupied and wholly dilapidated. You would have seen teenagers—and adults— lounging against liquor stores, with absolutely nothing in the world better to do. What were the elements that turned their quiet lethargy into violent rebellion? *A very hot summer day. Some radio and television stations hungry for news. A handful of frightened police officers. A small event.*

When experienced writers use fragments, they prepare the ground so carefully that the reader understands the ideas very well and can supply the missing words without thinking.

An occasional and deliberately designed fragment can intensify a thought and add complexity to a paragraph. But you must take great care to lay the groundwork and make sure that your meaning is clear and your writing smooth. We have a peculiar rule for writing fragments: don't ever write a fragment unless you know that is what you are doing, and be sure the missing part is clearly and strongly implied. (For more on fragments, see "Phrases, Clauses, and Sentences," in Chapter 19.)

Summing Up the Sentence

Short sentences are fine. They say what they came to say. Then they leave. They are clear. They are direct. They are efficient. They can be punchy. But they can become exhausting. Too many in a row will not do. Your readers will get irritated. They will put down your writing. You will lose them. Try again.

And so the time comes when you wish you had written not sentences with more wit, for your sentences were clever enough; and not even stronger sentences, for those short ones were as strong as an uppercut; but longer sentences, sentences that took their time getting to their appointed end, sentences that stopped every so often en route to the period to consider not only where they had been but also where they were most likely to be going. However, and this is an important point, the simple act of writing longer sentences, as tantalizing as it may be and as much as it seems to promise greater complexity of thought, wider command of all possible aspects of the subject matter, and that adroitness, that panache, that *je ne sais quoi* for which every writer strives, frequently fails to deliver and all too often becomes a way of stretching out the little you have to say over as many words as you can find to stuff into the sentence in an effort to avoid having to come to the end of saying that little. Your readers will get irritated. They will put down your writing. You will lose them. Try again.

Mix up your sentences. Add a little variety to your writing. Try not to have the same shape sentence after sentence. Include all four constructions: simple, compound, complex, compound-complex. Perhaps a fragment. Why not try an occasional question? Don't get stuck in one rhythm like a rutted phonograph record. Have some long sentences, some medium, some as short as a word. Don't try to dazzle your reader with the brilliance and power of every sentence, but make sure your reader occasionally sits up and takes notice.

TIPS FOR VARIETY

- Be a little adventurous: invert the natural order and try an occasional fragment.
- Change your pace by mixing up constructions, sentence length, and placement of emphasis.

Exercise for Variety

Rewrite the following to give it variety.

The young people in our culture seem to be suffering from a lot of anxiety. This anxiety has many causes. The young people fear they will not have jobs. They won't be able to afford to own houses. Children are expensive. If they have them, will they be able to educate them? And of course they worry about nuclear bombs. When they travel, they worry about terrorism and anti-American feeling abroad. Some people tell them they are lucky anyway. It is possible that they are lucky. But maybe they are not so lucky.

Be sure to include one inversion, one fragment, and one question.

12

WORKING WITH WORDS

When we write, we are always choosing words. Most of our words just appear on the page, without our quite knowing where they come from. Crucial moments arise in writing, however, when we consciously rack our brains for exactly the right word. *Diction* is the art of choosing that right word. It is the art of finding words that will present our thought exactly, clearly, and attractively.

Although words are neither good nor bad but only used well or badly, every word counts. We want to repeat that: every word counts, the ones that just appear on the page and the ones you worry over. Note the different meanings in these sentences:

A dog has fleas.

The dog had fleas.

The dog has the fleas.

The dog has ticks.

The cat has fleas.

The dog has the cat.

Every single word, including the verb as it changes and the article *the*, carries specific meaning. In simple sentences like these, we have no problem. We know whether we mean all dogs or only this one, fleas or ticks, and so on, and we write accordingly. As the ideas become more complicated, however, so does the job of choosing the right words to fit them. As we write and revise, we fret over our choices, conscious and unconscious.

Writers have in common with musicians a reliance on their hearing. We have all known people who have such perfect pitch that they can tell what note the doorbell hits when it rings, and we have all known people who sound as though they are moaning for help when they sing "Jingle Bells." Similarly, some people have a talent, a good ear, for words. They instinctively go for the right one at the right time. What they say sounds right, and what they write looks right. Most of us, however, are not so blessed. We have occasional attacks of sickly word choice. A few of us even seem to suffer from chronic tin ear, invariably putting the wrong preposition with a verb or derailing a sentence with the wrong noun.

Like our ear for music, our ear for words can be trained. People who thought they couldn't carry a tune have learned to sing—albeit not in the Metropolitan Opera. And people who thought they could never be happy with pen in hand have learned to write well. This chapter should help you to train your ear and your eye.

Our first piece of advice is this: read and read and read some more. You should read in all directions, but be sure you read good writing. If you are a speed-reader, slow down and listen to the words. Try to feel their shape and size and strength and rhythm. Notice the company they keep. When an excellent stylist uses a phrase that you have never used, say it aloud several times and use it in a sentence. Analyze a superb essay. If the words seem strange or awkward, write them down in a notebook. Try them out.

In this chapter we will discuss working with words to attain precision, vigor, appropriateness, and flair.

WRITING WITH PRECISION: SEEKING THE EXACT WORD

All good prose is precise. Good writers don't settle for a word that is nearly or almost what they mean. They want the exact word. As a soprano would be embarrassed to hit C-sharp when she meant to hit C, so a careful writer avoids words that do not communicate the precise meaning.

Connotation and Denotation

Most words have a number of different meanings, or shades of meaning. Take the word *gross.* It derives from the Latin *grossus,* which meant "thick." It still means thick. But it has also developed many additional meanings. To accountants and economists, it means an overall total, as in *gross national product.* To merchants, it means twelve dozen of anything ordered. To many people, it means anyone big or overweight. To college students, however, it has come to mean something disgusting. If we say, "That person is gross, isn't he?" you might reply, even though he weighs 300 pounds, "On the contrary, he is the nicest person I know." Because the word *gross* has one meaning for you and another for us, we would not be communicating.

Words both *denote*—indicate or point to something in the world— and *connote*—suggest a range of meanings surrounding that something. Denotation is the explicit meaning. Connotation refers to all that is associated with the word, the feelings and references it calls up.

Let's look at the word *government.* According to the primary dictionary definition, *government* means "an organization that exercises authority over a particular political unit." That is its denotation, on which everyone would agree. Its connotations vary, however. When some people think of *government,* they think of exorbitant taxes, corruption, and officials meddling in their private lives. To them the word connotes something bad. But when others think of *government,* they think of law and order, care for the poor, protection and security. To them, *government* connotes something good.

Connotation is composed of the suggestions and feelings that each word carries with it. It is molded by a word's history—is it from Old English, like *half-wit,* or from Latin and Italian via French, like *prestidigitation*? Each word has been shaped by the way people habitually use it. For instance, people have *hangovers,* but roofs have *overhangs.* Even a word's physical properties—such as sound and length—help determine its connotation. Think of *niggle, smug,* and *rump* as opposed to *worry, self-satisfied,* and *derriere.* Because of all these shades of suggestion, English has few if any exact synonyms, that is, words with precisely the same meaning. Brothers and sisters, yes, but no identical twins.

If a word has several near-synonyms, chances are that each, while denoting the same thing, will connote something slightly different. *Police officer* denotes the same thing as *cop, flatfoot,* and—to those who disliked them in the late 1960s—*pig,* but the connotation worsens with each synonym.

Word choice depends on the situation and the writer's purpose. Was the officer who gave you the speeding ticket a *slender police officer* or a *scrawny pig*? The first phrase has a touch of delicacy and respect; the second suggests you think you were framed and want to fight.

Simple choices, like that between *police officer* and *pig,* don't cause much trouble. When the words are more abstract or remote, however, diction becomes a fine art. Welfare recipients receive *handouts, payments,* or *entitlements,* depending on who is talking. We constantly read, hear, and use phrases such as *nuclear freeze, affirmative action,* and *Third World,* and words such as *materialism, socialism,* and *gay.* All are loaded with connotation. Handle with care: be sure both you and your audience know exactly what you mean.

We don't have a formula for choosing the right word every time. Good word choosers develop their skill through years of training. We do, however, have a few suggestions.

1. Handle overloaded words with care. Some words, like those just listed, have acquired such a weight of meaning that no two people would agree on their proper definition; writers who use them without thinking risk confusing and misleading their readers. Still, we can hardly talk about politics without using words such as *democracy, liberty,* or *equality.* Therefore, our next suggestion:

2. Define your terms. If, for instance, your essay is on entitlement programs, don't assume that your reader will correctly interpret the phrase *safety net.* Fairly early in the essay, provide a definition: "By *safety net,* I mean a package of government benefits that would bring the recipient's income to the government-designated poverty level." (See "Definition: Establishing What a Word Means" in Chapter 9 for a discussion of definition and a model of a longer definition.)

3. Use your dictionary. It can help you choose the word with the right connotation.

Using Your Dictionary

The great dictionary maker himself, Samuel Johnson (1709–1784), said, "Dictionaries are like watches; the worst is better than none, and the best cannot be expected to go quite true." While it may not "go quite true," a good dictionary can be a writer's valuable friend, and most writers keep one close at hand.

You may be surprised at all you can find in a dictionary. It will give you preferred pronunciation—sometimes you have a choice, as with *pajamas* and *advertisement.* It will tell you where to divide between syllables—is it *in-nards* or *inn-ards*? It will provide synonyms and antonyms. If it is a fairly good dictionary, it will also trace the derivation of a word, whether it comes from Greek, Latin, Old English, or another language, and what prefix or suffix is appropriate for it—whether, for instance, we *legitimize* or *legitimate.*

The surprise about good dictionaries is that they can inform us about not only denotation but also connotation. The word *tolerate,* for example, has several meanings in most dictionaries: (1) to allow without opposing or prohibiting; (2) to recognize and respect the rights, opinions, and practices of others; (3) to bear or put up with someone or something not especially liked. Follow these denotations a bit and you will arrive at the word's various connotations: indifference, appreciation, mild hostility.

The *Oxford English Dictionary,* known familiarly as the *OED,* is a veritable education in itself. It contains nearly a half million English words and over a million and a half quotations illustrating their use at various times in history. It traces the development of words and their meanings in detail. Not many of us can afford to own this publication, but almost every library has a copy. Browse through the *OED* and learn more about the wonderful world of words.

Another storehouse of words is the thesaurus. It is popular with writers because it contains synonyms (and often antonyms) for words. At this point, we want to flash a giant caution sign. A thesaurus is a good servant but a bad master. What it gives you are all the rough equivalents for your word; what it does not give are differences in connotation. Beware: a near-synonym may have the proper denotation but a wrong connotation.

Some writers are afraid of repeating a word, so they run to the thesaurus for a synonym. Or they fear that their vocabulary doesn't sound intelligent enough, and the next time *policeman* pops up in an essay on crime prevention, it appears as *constable* or *minion of the law.* Imagine a love letter:

> Dear Laura,
>   I have been sitting next to you all day and just can't believe how pretty you are. Your voice is like music, and your eyes are like moonlight. I know that beauty isn't skin-deep, for I saw you laughing at our teacher, which shows good sense. I think we could get on well together. Let me know what you think.
>
>   Love,
>   Name Withheld

Fearing that Laura would find his note unexciting, the writer scurried to his thesaurus. There, of course, he found all sorts of replacements for his plain words. The trouble was, the resulting stew of mismatched words would have sent even the most receptive Laura into paroxysms of laughter.

> Dear Laura,
>   I have been straddling you daily and simply cannot fathom how comely you are. Your vociferation approximates a sonata, and your peepers resemble lunar illumination. I comprehend that pulchritude isn't subcutaneous, for I ogled you sniggering at our pedagogue, which illustrates beneficent cranial capacity. I formulate in my mind that we would have a positive response to each other. Inform me of what you reason about.
>
>   Charity,
>   Name Withheld

This writer is not necessarily stupid—he just doesn't trust his natural, comfortable vocabulary. Luckily for him, his pedant/instructor/educator intercepted the missive/epistle/correspondence and saved him some embarrassment/incommodity/loss of face, for which he was profoundly/deeply/intensely grateful.

If you use a thesaurus, use it along with—not in place of—your dictionary and your own imagination. Use it to remind yourself of what you already know—to draw out a word momentarily forgotten or to help you find a more exact word. Don't use it to inflate your language.

The Idiom

Do we go to town or downtown or uptown? Should we nurse our cold or nurture it or nourish it? When we are under the weather, are we out in the rain or inside the house? When we pass an exam, do we say hello? Few dictionaries and no thesaurus will answer these questions. Nor are there any rules that will predict their answers. When a word is appropriate and in what context is a matter not of decree but of accepted usage—idiom.

Idiom refers to the way native speakers speak a language and good writers write it. Idiom is the customary way people put words together, the peculiar twist that a group gives to its language. Americans look under the *hood* of the car and put their tools in the *trunk,* while the British look under the *bonnet* and put their tools in the *boot.* Southerners say, "I'm fixing to eat dinner," but you would not hear that sentence from a northerner.

For nonnative speakers, idiom is the hardest part of a language to master. It does not follow rules the way grammar does. In answer to the question *Who wants to shampoo the Great Dane?* most of us will cry, *Not me*—bad grammar but good idiom. And *Cecil spent all his hardly earned cash* is good grammar but bad idiom. Nonnative speakers often use words that seem fine to them but are simply not idiomatic: *I have traveled a long space* or *I cannot tell you how much indignation I feel to this proposal.* Both sentences sound wrong, but try to say why. Try to explain why a student can be *late* or *tardy* for school but why a party may begin *late* in the afternoon but not *tardy.* Or why a case of pneumonia, though it is always *bad,* is never *reprehensible,* but a mean act is both.

If you grew up speaking English, its ins and outs are second nature to you. Even so, you may still be uncertain about some idioms. Again, use your dictionary if a phrase you have written does not sound right to you. And keep an ear out—not *on* or *in* or *at*—for the often irrational twists and turns that idiom takes.

The Specific and the General

The difference between the specific and the general is the difference between *Aunt Tabitha* and *woman*, or *bow tie* and *item of clothing*. A specific term refers to the individual item, the thing itself. A general term encompasses all the items of a kind or class.

These are not absolute terms but relative, a matter of degree rather than of opposites. *Bow tie* is not as specific as *purple polka-dot bow tie*, and *woman* is not as general as *living creature* or *thing*.

In the following lists, you can see increasing specificity:

> crime, felony, murder, first-degree murder, the murder of a man in a purple polka-dot bow tie

> food, meal, entrée, chicken Kiev, burned chicken Kiev, the chicken Kiev Aunt Tabitha burned last night

We need general terms to show relationships and concepts, and we need specific terms to appeal to the reader's senses and create exact images.

As our words become more specific, they sharpen and solidify the image in the mind of the reader. The reader can picture the prostrate body of the man in the bow tie, Aunt Tabitha weeping over the charred chicken. The more specific the language, the closer the reader will come to understanding what we mean. And to enjoying what we write.

Sometimes writers use general terms when something specific and pictorial would serve much better:

> The governor sent fire-fighting equipment to the scene of the fire.

A few specifics could make the sentence more visual, more interesting, more informative:

> Governor Cuomo ordered bulldozers, fire trucks, and air transport carriers to the forest fire near Elmira.

A sentence such as

> Emperor Nero of Rome was obese

is not incorrect, but

> Emperor Nero of Rome weighed 360 pounds

is more specific. *Obese* only skitters across the surface of Nero's fatness; the revision gives us the fat emperor pound for pound. A writer would bore us with

> An official said that the United States suffered recently from economic problems

but might get us to read further with

> The United States suffered from record-setting deficits and high interest
> rates in the late 1970s, according to Genevieve duPres of the Treasury
> Department.

Specific terms help our writing come alive for the reader, but we
cannot always be discussing a particular chicken or a particular murder.
We may want to discuss the qualities common to all chickens, or ideas
about felonies in general, not just murder. The more complex the ideas
and relationships we want to discuss, the more necessary are general
terms.

To generalize means to think of a quality apart from a particular context and to construct an idea that will cover the individual items that share
the quality. "Politics is the art of the possible," said Otto von Bismarck,
generalizing from his experience as the first chancellor of Germany and
saying a great deal about politics everywhere. "Believe that your life is
worth living," said the psychologist William James, "and your belief will
help create the fact." The sentence is full of general ideas, such as *believe*,
worth living, fact, ideas we can all understand. We cannot make serious
statements without such words, and it would be absurd to try.

Sometimes, however, we use general words in such a vague way
that our reader cannot possibly know what we mean. Remember our
failed love letter? How likely was it that Laura would know what "we
would have a positive response to each other" meant? A positive response
could be anything from a passionate embrace to a belly laugh. Some writers bandy terms such as *good, beautiful, truth,* justice—and could mean
almost anything.

Good serious writers ground the general in the specific. They explain
difficult general ideas by reference to the specific. The evolutionary biolo-
gist Stephen Jay Gould handles general ideas as a scientist but grounds
them in the concrete. In discussing Freud's idea that to ensure civilization,
human beings must "renounce more and more of our innate selves,"
Gould writes,

> Freud's argument is a particularly forceful variation on a ubiquitous
> theme in speculations about "human nature." What we criticize in our-
> selves, we attribute to our animal past. These are the shackles of our
> apish ancestry—brutality, aggression, selfishness; in short, general nas-
> tiness. What we prize and strive for (with pitifully limited success), we
> consider as a unique overlay, conceived by our rationality and imposed
> upon an unwilling body. Our hopes for a better future lie in reason and
> kindness—the mental transcendence of our biological limitations. "Build
> thee more stately mansions, O my soul." (*Ever Since Darwin*)

Gould makes these complex ideas clear by using specific, familiar language. Having clarified what Freud meant, he can now refer simply to

"Freud's argument." He concludes with a line from a once-popular poem by Oliver Wendell Holmes.

Once you have made your point clear, you will often use a general term to stand for that point. In a discussion of the fire in Elmira, for instance, you would not continue to say "bulldozers, fire trucks, and air transport carriers." You would just say "the equipment." First, however, be sure you bring your ideas out into the concrete world you share with your reader.

TIPS FOR PRECISION

- Know the difference between what a word denotes and what it connotes before you use it.
- Read all the information about a word in the dictionary.
- Resort to a thesaurus with a critical eye and consult it along with, not instead of, your dictionary.
- Be sure to use words in their idiomatic, or commonly accepted, sense.
- Be as concrete and specific as you can.

Exercises for Precision

1. For each of the following pairs of synonyms, write a sentence in which either would fit: *hold/grasp, evening/dusk, throttle/choke, obsequious/humble, humiliate/embarrass, refuse/garbage, teeth/dentures, inebriated/drunk, crazy/insane.* Discuss the connotations and analyze how the sounds of these words do or do not reinforce their meanings.

2. For each of the following phrases, provide at least three synonyms that carry different connotations.
   a. unwillingness to change one's mind
   b. an object that costs less than one expected
   c. not telling the truth
   d. one's parent of the opposite sex
   e. a member of the House of Representatives

3. Go to a large dictionary, preferably the *OED*, and look up the following pairs of words: *empathy/sympathy, enormity/enormousness, notoriety/notoriousness, uninterested/disinterested, ensure/insure.* Write a paragraph comparing the meanings of each pair.

4. Practice using a large dictionary by investigating the derivations of the following words: *engineer, sarcasm, gossip, oxygen, circle, corespondent.*

Write a paragraph about two of them, tracing their meanings from their earliest usage to the present.

5. Make the following sentences more concrete or specific.
   a. The creature took the food into the room.
   b. Attendance at secondary educational institutions has been correlated with participation in athletic endeavors.
   c. The woman took down the garment and concealed it about her person without the store personnel's awareness and then went to the escalator and descended.
   d. When exposure and malnutrition are present, support from various levels of government should be forthcoming.

WRITING WITH VIGOR: MAKING PROSE ENERGETIC

Some writing seems crisp and energetic; other writing seems limp and tired. We have already dealt with some of the causes of limp, tired writing, such as imprecision and verbosity. Here we give direct advice on how to make your writing more vigorous.

Be Active

The verb makes things happen in your sentence. It builds muscle. It generates energy. If your sentence begins to sag, blame the verb. If it zings home its meaning, credit the verb. Nurture your verb as though the life of your sentence depends on it.

ACTIVE AND PASSIVE VOICE. English verbs come in two voices: active and passive.

The fire fighter grabbed the hose.

The hose was grabbed by the fire fighter.

The first sentence is in the active voice. The subject (*the fire fighter*) performs the action (*grabbed*). The second sentence is in the passive voice. The subject of this sentence (*the hose*) receives the action (*was grabbed*). The passive consists of the past participle of a verb (*grabbed*) preceded by some form of the verb *to be* (*was*).

For good reason, good writers prefer the active voice most of the time. It is clearer and more direct, and it packs more punch. Also, it immediately identifies the responsible actor.

> Bill struck Tom.
> Professor Beerbohm spilled coffee on my term paper.

We know exactly and immediately who did what to whom. Passive voice tends to be unemphatic and wordy.

> Tom was struck by Bill.

It is sometimes evasive.

> Coffee was spilled on my term paper.

Thus does Professor Beerbohm escape blame.

Much official writing resorts to the passive voice, frequently erasing all signs of personal responsibility.

> It has been decided that farm subsidies must be decreased.

This sentence makes it sound as though a disembodied law of nature made this fiscal decision rather than the people announcing it. If the writers recast their sentence in the active voice, they would have to admit that

> We have decided to decrease farm subsidies.

Some student writers employ the passive because they think it sounds more important.

> It is agreed by most scholars that the superego was meant by Freud to be portrayed as a force by which the id is prevented from getting what it wants.

Four passive constructions in a single sentence are not so much weighty as wooden. In an effort to remove all evidence of the passive, the student revised the sentence.

> Most scholars agree that Freud meant to portray the superego as a force that prevents the id from getting what it wants.

She reduced thirty words to twenty-two and wrote a much clearer, more direct, more active, more enjoyable, and more informative sentence.

The passive voice is not always bad, however. You should not tie yourself into a pretzel to avoid it. Sometimes it is awkward to state the subject of the sentence. If you just want to say

> Los Angeles is well supplied with water

it would distort your meaning to twist the sentence into the active voice this way:

> Canals, conduits, pipes, and a series of reservoirs supply ample water to Los Angeles.

When an important baseball game is cancelled because of the weather, it is only natural to write

> The game at Fenway Park was called on account of fog and rain

instead of

> Ed Kunkel, Paul Runge, and the rest of the umpiring crew called the game at Fenway Park on account of fog and rain.

When used with finesse and restraint, the passive voice can even add variety to prose.

> The slumbering household was slowly awakened by the twittering of tiny birds.

The problem is misuse. Pseudoscientific and pseudoofficial prose is everywhere, tempting writers into the passive voice. Resist. Write in the active voice whenever you can.

VIGOROUS VERBS.   Many dynamic verbs are vanishing into extinction. And some of the best are converting into nouns, leaving the work of sentences to weak, deflated verbs. In this sentence,

> The police made an investigation into reports of explosions near the Capitol

the writer has turned a fine verb—*to investigate*—into a noun—*investigation*—and the uninteresting verb *to make* has taken over the action. Result: more words, less action. The rewrite,

> The police investigated reports of explosions near the Capitol

saves three words and restores the action.

Some writers apparently abhor the powerful and direct use of good verbs. But how much stronger our prose would be if we changed

I have admiration for	to	I admire
You will show deference to		You will defer to
She is in need		She needs
They gave approval		They approved

Writers are sometimes seduced from the specific by fancy sounding verbs, such as *interact*, *relate*, *impact*, and *deal with*. Unfortunately, in meaning almost anything, verbs like these mean almost nothing.

> I interacted with Alex yesterday.

What did the writer do with Alex? Did she kiss him? stab him? hand him a subpoena? All these would be *interactions*, but no one knows exactly what happened.

Likewise, *impact* as a verb has almost no impact.

Brazil's failure to meet its debt obligations has impacted upon American interest rates.

Was the effect good or was it bad? You can always replace *impact* with a more specific action.

Brazil's failure to meet its debt obligations has driven up American interest rates

Perhaps less blatant but still debilitating is writing that contains an abundance of general-purpose verbs, such as *go, seem, do, make, have,* and *become.* While useful beasts of burden, these verbs cannot carry the specific meanings that vivid prose demands. As much as possible, good writers choose verbs that tell exactly what the action was. This sentence badly needs a good verb:

Ingesting plant fiber has a positive effect on the risk of heart disease.

As readers, we must use our imaginations to find our way through this. Just what does *has a positive effect on* really mean here? Is there a verb out there that will say the same thing? Perhaps *decreases* will do; it is certainly more active than *has* and tells us something more precise about that plant fiber.

Ingesting plant fiber decreases the risk of heart disease.

When you revise your prose, seek verbs with energy.

Not *to Be*.   You may have noticed that forms of *to be* crop up frequently in inactive sentences. This verb links the subject of the sentence to a word or words that describe the subject's condition.

Max is a friendly Doberman pinscher. He really is.

The town with the lowest zip code number in the United States is Agawam, Massachusetts.

I am Gunga Din.

The little verb *to be* is one of the most necessary verbs in English. Many sentences would not be without it. For instance, you couldn't convey a complete thought by saying

I hungry!

The baby disgruntled!

The bathtub overflowing!

With so many forms of *to be* around, however, writers can fall into the habit of using them for almost everything. Verb deflation frequently occurs because we use forms of the verb *to be* followed by a noun followed by a preposition.

> She was understanding of
>
> This episode is an example of

These phrases have lost the services of the vigorous verbs *understood* and *exemplifies*.

> We tend to overwork the verb *to be* in other ways as well.
>
> Demosthenes was a more effective speaker than Cato was.
>
> If it had not been for the unfair taxes the British imposed, there might not have been an American Revolution.

We can turn a static condition into an action by substituting for the verb *to be*.

> Demosthenes spoke more effectively than Cato did.
>
> Without unfair British taxation, the Americans might not have revolted.
>
> Very long and complicated sentences often rely too heavily on forms of the verb *to be*.

> Stein is saying that American governing philosophy is in a situation where it is becoming an area that is under the domination of men who are not really sincere about what is good for the public, men who are attracted only by what is advantageous to them and to the special interests that it is their function to represent.

As this sentence shows, when a writer overuses the verb *to be*, other problems frequently emerge. The revision, short and to the point, eliminates many *to be*s, the passive voice, and verbosity.

> Stein maintains that the men who have dominated American governing philosophy are less interested in the public good than in their own advantage and that of the special interests they represent.

In revising a first draft, try circling each occurrence of *to be* (don't forget to include *is, am, have been,* and other forms), and search for a better word. You won't be able to change every one (nor should you), but try especially hard to reword when you see bunches of circles.

Prefer People

> Imagine being confronted with the following sentence:
>
> Renouncing a former state to obtain real existence is an adjustment requiring understanding of what is seen, comprehending its causes, and coping with it.

Can you figure out who is doing the renouncing, or who must adjust, understand, comprehend, and cope? The sentence is depopulated, yet the writer seems to be writing about human beings.

Now look at the sentence:

> In order to renounce their former state and improve themselves, clients must understand how they perceive the world, why they perceive it that way, and how they can cope with it.

Although a little longer, this sentence is much clearer and more interesting. We know who is doing what.

Why did the writer depopulate that sentence? Perhaps he thought impersonal prose sounded more serious. But aren't you more interested in reading about what people do or have done to them? Wouldn't you rather read *The actor playing Othello made the audience weep* than *The performance of the role of Othello brought tears*? Even a small move toward putting people in a sentence can make a difference. People add strength and vibrancy to your sentences.

Impersonal writing can be both boring and confusing, as is this passage on how tennis players should choose the food they eat:

> Careful selection of foods containing all the proper nutrients is important for maintaining health and adequate energy. Whether food is prepared at home or eaten out, resistance to disease can be increased and energy rate maximized through careful nutritional food selection.

Tennis players, anywhere? Not a person within a mile of those sentences, although people ought to be doing almost everything in them. You have probably spotted some of the ways the writer has kept the passage impersonal: overuse of the passive voice, nouns where there might be verbs, too many *to be*s. It doesn't make you want to rush out and try the diet, does it?

A revision puts the people back where they belong.

> To stay healthy and full of energy, tennis players must select foods that contain all the proper nutrients. Whether they cook their meals at home or eat out, they can better resist disease and maximize their energy by carefully choosing nutritional foods.

We are not claiming that every sentence must contain a person. It would be absurd, perhaps impossible, to try to stick people into sentences such as

> Art is the accomplice of love. (Remy de Gourmont, 1858–1915)

or

> Land is immortal, for it harbors the mysteries of creation. (Anwar Sadat, 1918–1981)

When people are involved, though, good writers put the people in. And they put them in as human beings, not as abstractions or congregations. We wouldn't say *members of the student body* or *members of the elector-ate*. We would say *students* and *voters*. We ought to follow this natural inclination when we write.

We can go a step further and use the good old names for occupations and professions. When we write *teacher* or even *professor*, we picture a human being, perhaps even someone we know, but when we refer to an *educator*, we imagine a faceless bureaucrat. When we write *banker*, again we picture a person, but when we say *financial executive*, we don't even pretend a human being is concealed inside that gray eminence. Indeed, our prose takes on a slightly gray quality itself.

We don't advise you to make everything in your writing sound chatty. As we discuss in Chapter 13, there is a tone appropriate to college writing, and chatty it isn't. But neither is it depopulated. When possible and where appropriate, keep your prose alive with people.

Say It Straight

Even with energetic verbs and people, prose can be flat and uninter-esting. Often, the problem is indirectness. Many of us apparently like to hold off saying what we came to say or try to conceal our thought beneath a variety of indirect constructions. Just as English tends to move straight ahead from subject to verb to object, it also works best when it goes straight to the point. Our moral here is "Say it straight." Readers don't have time to play hide and seek with thoughts. You can help them under-stand your meaning.

We discuss here three bad habits that often block understanding.

DISCLAIMERS. No doubt you have read *opinions to the contrary notwith-standing, it is conceivable* (or *arguable* or *possible*) *that one might say, an opin-ion might be hazarded that,* and phrases such as these. They may seem like security blankets, but they are more like smoke screens. Some of these disclaimers self-destruct if you think about them; our two favorites are *needless to say* and the immediately comic *needless to repeat*.

WEAK-HEARTED NEGATIVES. As George Orwell pointed out in his es-say "Politics and the English Language," overuse of the negative is a form of circumlocution—"talking around" your meaning. Orwell quotes this sentence:

> I am not, indeed, sure whether it is not true to say that the Milton who once seemed not unlike a seventeenth-century Shelley had not become, out of an experience ever more bitter in each year, more alien to the founder of that Jesuit sect which nothing could induce him to tolerate.

Once you untie all the negatives, you have the following (we think):

> Out of an experience more bitter each year, the Milton who once resem-
> bled a seventeenth-century Shelley had come to resemble the founder of
> that Jesuit sect which nothing could induce him to tolerate.

Less outrageous, but more frequent, is the use of the negative to fog
a disagreeable opinion: *They did not honor their debts as they had promised*
instead of *They reneged*, or *She did not play her clarinet very admirably* instead
of *She played her clarinet abominably*. In each case, the first may sound more
polite, but the positive is stronger and clearer.

Think of the statements *The president was not inarticulate*, or *The book
is not uninteresting*. The reader has to cancel out the double negative and
even then cannot be sure what the sentences mean. Was the president
articulate or only a cut above mumbling? Is the book interesting or just
this side of the trash basket?

EUPHEMISMS.   Writers of euphemisms substitute neutral terms or agree-
able words for words with strong or unpleasant associations. They say *salvage engineers* when they mean *junk dealers*, *remains* when they mean
corpse, *fib* when they mean *lie*, and *water closet, comfort station, necessary
room*, or almost anything else when they mean *toilet*.

Euphemisms sometimes spare feelings—to say *I'm sorry your mother
passed on* might be gentler than to say *I'm sorry your mother died*. Too frequently, though, people slip in euphemisms to conceal meaning. Hitler
used the term *rectification of the frontier* when he forced thousands of people
to march miles from their homes; some government bureaus have referred
to murder, execution, or assassination as *termination with extreme prejudice*.
These phrases conceal the awful truth: Hitler uprooted large populations;
people were killed.

You should try to say exactly what you mean in the most honest
manner you can. Try to be graceful rather than crude, of course, but say it
straight.

TIPS FOR VIGOR

- Prefer the active voice to the passive.
- Seek vigorous, fresh verbs, and avoid tired, general ones.
- Don't overuse forms of *to be*.
- Put people in any sentences in which they can fit.
- Avoid disclaimers, weak-hearted negatives, and euphemisms.

Exercises for Vigor

1. Rewrite the following sentences to make them more vigorous.
   a. The decision was announced by the referee, and the loud cheers were emitted by Jack Dempsey's supporters.
   b. Open-heart surgery will be performed on me tomorrow.
   c. Absconding with the family heirlooms was the accusation made against Señor Ortega by Señora Sanchez.
   d. Asia was overrun by Genghis Khan and the hordes of warriors who had been enticed by him to join his army.

2. Replace the weak verbs in these sentences with more energetic ones.
   a. He made a very tasty sauerbraten and then gave a party.
   b. My cousin went through India in eight days and then came home in a big hurry because she had a job to go to.
   c. Admiral Darlan, who had been the head of the French navy during the Second World War, seemed to become a different person when he became minister of defense in the Vichy government.
   d. My decision was to go to the head of the department and to make a strong case for a raise in what I got in my job.

3. Reread an essay you've written recently and circle every use of the verb *to be*. Then revise the whole essay, using *to be* as little as possible.

4. Revise the following sentences to make them more direct.
   a. One is not unwilling to hang-glide although one is not unfamiliar with the difficulties one may encounter.
   b. When in the vicinity of vipers capable of making what might be called a fatal attack, I have a tendency to experience unpleasant emotions and to prepare to exit as quickly as possible, in a manner of speaking.
   c. Once the animal custodian picked up the little dog, it was not unlikely that in a short period of time the underground engineer would be called in to perform, if he has not been intemperate with alcohol lately, though far be it from me to claim to know about his private habits.

WRITING AN APPROPRIATE PROSE: LANGUAGE THAT FITS

All of us want our prose to express our sensitivity, our distinctiveness, and our taste. At the same time, we want what we say to fit both the audience and the subject. Yet we sometimes slip into language that does not express what we mean, let alone who we are. In the pages that follow, we examine five ways to avoid sour notes.

Choosing Slim Words over Fat Words

Remember from Chapter 11 that Mr. Micawber said in twenty-nine words what he could have said in six? With this lovable old duffer, Dickens poked fun at people who invariably choose the impressive polysyllabic word rather than the short, familiar one. Mr. Micawber is not alone. You will find inflated language in legal, bureaucratic, academic, technical, and editorial writing.

Winston Churchill said, "Short words are best and the old words when short are best of all." Practically all great literary stylists agree. Yet some writers think that the more complicated and unusual the language, the more serious the thought. Windiness is not elegance, however, and difficulty is not profundity. It is no more elegant and profound to say *Precipitation appears imminent* than to say *It's going to rain.*

Many of the shorter, plainer words in English come from Old English: they preserve the Anglo-Saxon in our language, growling out practical and durable monosyllables: *house, thief, stone, want, help.* Such words are concrete, familiar, and useful. *I want to get an ice cream cone* is more direct and understandable than *I desire to procure a frozen gelatinous confection; want* and *get* are the functional words you need in this sentence, not the overdressed *desire* and *procure,* and that *gelatinous confection* sounds nauseating.

The thesaurus provides a list of synonyms for *get,* including *procure, secure,* and *acquire.* These words came into English later than *get,* via Latin and French. Like most travelers of this route, they are longer than their Old English near-equivalent and have connotations that *get* does not. The dictionary tells us that *get* is a "very general term and may or may not imply initiative." *Procure,* however, suggests "effort in obtaining something"; *secure* implies downright "difficulty in getting"; *acquire* has it easy by comparison, implying "an addition to what is already possessed." Good writers would neither abandon *get* just to have more letters and syllables nor use *get* when they mean *procure* or *secure.*

Keep in mind this simple rule from George Orwell: "Never use a long word where a short one will do."

This does not mean that you must speak in Tarzanlike monosyllables. Longer is better when that is the clearest way to say something. Here is Orwell writing clearly but not in monosyllables:

> Now, it is clear that the decline of a language must ultimately have political and economic causes: it is not due simply to the bad influence of this or that individual writer. ("Politics and the English Language")

No one would call that sentence pretentious. The "long words" (*language, ultimately, political, economic, influence, individual*) are all familiar ones, and

Orwell obviously used them because they are the ones he needed. No other words mean what those words mean.

If we used only one-syllable words, our essays would be about as subtle as telegrams. Long words often help us to be precise and to convey the right nuance.

> Karl Marx said that rich people keep poor people from being free

is direct, but

> Karl Marx's economic theories depict the efforts of the powerful capital-ist classes to oppress the workers of the world

tells us more, and more exactly. *Capitalist classes,* for example, suggests more than just rich people, and *oppress* implies both action and purpose. The longer sentence is truer to Marx's thought. Orwell would have agreed with this corollary to his little rule: use a long word when it, and only it, is the word you need.

Another rule we think Orwell would have agreed with is When two words bear more or less the same meaning, select the one more familiar and natural to you and your reader. Prefer *limit* to *circumscribe, the rest* to *the remainder,* and *use* to *employ.* Remember that English has a great heri-tage of short, direct, familiar words. They are where the language began. When we need to be clearest in our writing, they are waiting for us. Read-ers tire of long parades of peculiar or pompous words, and they become suspicious of the writer who uses them. Writing can be both simple and intelligent. Use complex words only when they carry just the shade of meaning, just the distinction you want.

Prioritizing Dejargonization

Technical terms emerge in every discipline. They take the place of lengthy descriptions or definitions. In law, we speak of *torts* and *liability* and *double indemnity;* in computer science of *interface, systems, bits,* and *bytes,* and in economics of *balance sheets* and *cartels.* Of course, we must use the terms of the discipline we are discussing.

A problem emerges, however, when technical terms are used unnec-essarily or inappropriately. Then they are *jargon,* a special language often unintelligible to anyone outside the group that devised it. Can you, for instance, figure out this Hollywood jargon?

> The veepees and the exex of the new org were skedded to orb the Eu-ropix in an all-day sesh.

or this psychological babble?

The process of representational guidance has been found to be essentially the same as response learning under conditions where an externally depicted pattern was followed by a person who is then *directed* through a series of instructions to enact novel *response* sequences.

Both these examples are comical, but the second sometimes fools readers because it sounds academic.

Often prose riddled with jargon is depopulated, and the passive voice dominates. Common words, such as *direct*, receive a special twist. The writer piles adjectives one on top of another in the interest of precision. Business writing can come up with some whoppers.

Problem determination procedures indicated that parallel reciprocal mobility was supported by management options.

And we wouldn't want you to think that English studies is lagging behind in the jargon race.

Plot is the structure of action in closed and legible wholes; it thus must *use* metaphor as the trope of its achieved interrelations, and it must *be* metaphoric insofar as it is totalizing.

Thus many writers abandon the common language and common usage in favor of a private language that is bewildering to outsiders and often incomprehensible even to other professionals. Jargon poses a threat to the most basic principle of writing: communication between people.

Whether you write about an engineering project, a painting, or a computer program, you should try to avoid jargon. Always strive to write so that any literate person with an interest in the subject could understand you. Write in standard, vigorous English.

Giving Clichés the Kiss of Death

Clichés are a dime a dozen. Some people use them right off the bat, even though they may have a sneaking suspicion that brave souls would give them the cold shoulder. But make no bones about it, good writers have other fish to fry and could care less. That's the bottom line.

A cliché is a worn-out saying or expression, an expression we have heard so much that it no longer creates an image for us. The first time they appeared, the clichés in the preceding paragraph offered fresh images or fresh views. *The kiss of death*, for instance, was what Alfred E. Smith said when he learned that William Randolph Hearst was supporting Smith's opponent in the election for governor of New York. Smith suggested that Hearst's help was like Judas kissing Jesus and would lead to political death. His opponent lost. At the time, the expression was fresh (fresh enough to go down in Bartlett's *Familiar Quotations*). Since then, however, overuse has exhausted it.

Most clichés start out as efforts to make an idea vivid. A speaker or writer puts a new twist on something to illuminate it. When the twist is pithy, others adopt it—we can imagine Smith's supporters chortling as they repeated *the kiss of death*. Even though the original context fades, the saying may struggle on, mechanically, thoughtlessly, pointlessly. Whenever fresh expression fails, out trots the cliché.

When people string several clichés together, the result can be hilarious: "He is one of those people who stand up and tell it like it is and go against the powers that be whenever they have their turn at bat." "My target is to explore every avenue to relieve the bottleneck in our backlog of orders." The mind reels.

Another form of cliché is the trite expression. *Gone but not forgotten, easier said than done, better late than never, in a very real sense* are a few of the ubiquitous phrases out there enticing us into dreary prose. They may once have carried thought, but now they carry only ennui.

Akin to the trite expression is the automatic pairing of a noun with a particular adjective. In this group we find *solemn oath, heavy burden, foreseeable future, crushing blow*. The list could go on and on.

The attraction of clichés is that they are ready-made. Rather than struggle with a fresh image, we reach for the nearest cliché. Using them may be excusable in speech—we are often in a rush to get our opinion stated. Writing is different. We—and our readers—have time to examine our prose. When we state even the most imaginative and reasonable idea in clichés, it will seem flabby and vague. Precision in thought and energy in expression are what good writing is all about, and that means getting rid of cliches.

The Private Language of Our Crowd

Slang refers to the special and spontaneous language a group develops. Often it can revitalize and rejuvenate the standard language. It keeps English slightly off balance and prevents it from becoming rigid. Like the unmannerly, vital yokel who crashes the tea party, slang brings in energy. Terms such as *zoo on* or *dogging* when we mean *insult*, *dylan* when we mean *bad*, or *fried* when we mean *extreme* can sometimes add vitality to what we say.

Slang is not universal or standard throughout society. People on different blocks in the same neighborhood—not to mention people on different coasts or people in different social or cultural groups—may use words to mean quite different things. *Get wasted* means drink too much, take too many drugs, or be killed, depending on where you are. In the 1960s *up-*

tight meant overly tense to whites and ready to go to blacks. The word *fag* has meant, at various times to various people, a servant, a cigarette, and a homosexual.

Slang is often a signal that a person belongs to a certain group: youth, jazz lovers, the political left, the country club. Creating new words or giving old words new meanings helps form a group's identity. Although some slang expressions filter into everyone's vocabulary, they usually take a long time to do so, and by then the originators have probably gone on to other slang words.

Most slang changes quickly. The slang our grandparents used— *scram, lollapalooza, nix, rats!*—has a pleasantly old-fashioned sound today. Even slang from the 1950s and 1960s has lost its currency: think of *Mary Jane* for *marijuana*, or *groovy* (itself a word resurrected from the 1940s) for *good*. Sometimes it seems that contemporary slang fades before we learn to use it. Occasionally slang achieves a desirable effect in writing.

> With their vote in the municipal runoffs, the residents of Bedford-Stuyvesant have told the all-white city council, "If you can't hang with it, stroll."

College writing generally requires a level of diction offensive to none and understandable to all. You should write *bewildered* rather than *freaked out*, *overwhelmed* instead of *blown away*, and *frustrated* rather than *bummed*—or are our examples already out of date?

Avoiding Sexist Language

We have all heard words that disparage the opposite sex or suggest sexual assault. Sometimes using these words is only the result of carelessness or a wish to appear part of the gang and tough. But often we must assume the speaker intends to express hostility, a need to feel superior, or a desire to inflict pain. Using such words seems to indicate the speaker's personal problems. Whether deliberately assaultive or a result of ignorance, these words have no place at all in writing.

Not all sexist language is overtly cruel and crude, however. Words such as *bird, doll, tomato, hunk,* and *stud* can be affectionately or admiringly intended. Even so, they carry connotations that to some suggest a less than fully human person, a plaything, an object. Innocent though many may find these terms, they often suggest disrespect for the opposite sex and almost always reflect slovenly writing habits. Like the harsher terms, they have no place in expository writing.

Sexist assumptions permeate our language. In the higher ranking professions, the male seems to be the norm and the female the aberrant. Without intending insult, many of us say *the lady veterinarian* or *the female lawyer,* although we would never say *the gentleman veterinarian* or *the male lawyer.* We tend to call the hypothetical doctor *he* and the nurse *she.* Positions of leadership and responsibility in many fields contain masculinity in their denotative words: *chairman, congressman, policeman, fireman.* Yet we know that women can and do hold positions of prestige and responsibility in these fields.

In addition, many grammatical conventions favor men and ignore women. Traditionally, it has been grammatically correct to say *A writer must choose his words carefully* or *To each his own.* Some people think these constructions suggest that the female was an afterthought, to be subsumed under the dominant category "male."

Some of our common expressions seem to support this bias favoring males. The rallying cry of the American Revolution—"All men are created equal"—seems to exclude women. Some people argue that the term *man* encompasses the entire species and that objections to its use are foolish. But others note that during the time of the Revolution the "equal" did not include women, for they were not allowed to vote or serve on juries, and a married woman could not dispose of her own property without the consent of her husband.

These usages reflected the society in which they grew, a society dominated and documented by males. The complaints that females may have had about the laws and the language would not have been well known or recorded. Society has changed drastically, and so has language.

The English language is now, as always, in a state of flux, growing and adjusting to new perceptions. Recognizing that sexism has no place in intelligent prose, sensitive writers are trying to get rid of it. Unfortunately, sexism in language is much easier to criticize than to weed out, but we have five suggestions for writing nonsexist prose.

1. Avoid stereotypes about men and women. Treat both sexes with respect and appreciation, and treat individual people as individuals. Think of all the exceptions there are, for instance, to the stereotypes *insensitive men* and *irrational women.* (For more on this subject see "Opening the Mind" in Chapter 3.)

2. Keep your writing free of gender-determined words, from obscenities to apparently innocent terms like *man and wife* and *coed. Man and wife,* for instance, suggests that women are an attachment; *coeds,* that they are an afterthought.

3. Avoid sexist usage. Find broader, more inclusive terms for words that denote only males. Instead of *policeman,* say *police officer.* Instead of *chairman,* say *chairperson.* If that usage sounds awkward or condescending, say *chair* or *head.* The point, of course, is to avoid the implication that only males hold high positions.

4. Steer clear of what many people consider sexist grammar. When you write about a nonspecific person, an *anyone,* use the plural instead of

the sexist masculine singular pronoun. In place of *A writer should choose his words carefully,* say *Writers should choose their words carefully.* Shifting to the plural means that you avoid the suggestion of sexism without resorting to either the ungrammatical *a writer should choose their* or the questionable *s/he.*

5. Be ever gracious and inclusive: on the rare occasions when you cannot avoid the singular, write the unobtrusive *he or she, him or her, his or hers.*

TIPS FOR APPROPRIATE PROSE

- Prefer short, plain words to long, fancy ones.
- Avoid jargon; strive to write so that any literate person can follow your thought.
- Get rid of clichés.
- Keep slang out of your writing.
- Avoid sexist language.

Exercises for Appropriate Prose

1. Revise these sentences by removing jargon, clichés, and slang.
   a. Incrementally compatible programming will always impact on total management options.
   b. Although the horror movie freaked me out, I thoroughly enjoyed the evening, most particularly when I flashed on the fact that I cannot relate to that other dude because he does not give me ego reinforcement. That's when I decided to be up-front with you, sweetie pie.
   c. What you say may be true, but if I hear that bromide one more time, I will flip.
   d. The Bard of Avon was a great writer and had a mind like a steel trap.

2. For fun, construct two sentences using at least two of the following words in each sentence: *dialectical, functioning, heuristic, conceptualized, metonymy, partial need factor, systematized, reciprocal, time-phase, feedback, logistic, hermetic.* Be sure your sentences *mean* something. If you don't know the words, look them up in the dictionary.

3. Eliminate the sexist bias from the following sentences.
   a. Three students—a man and two girls—were murdered in their composition class because they had misplaced a modifier.
   b. The lawyer's husband lets her travel alone, but a senior partner would have his own reasons for objecting.

> c. The dean presented awards to both John Smith and Ellen Jones. Smith's was, of course, for athletics and Ellen's for art.
> d. When I went to the ladies' room, my escort went to the men's room.

WRITING WITH FLAIR: RISKS THAT PAY OFF

Although much of our book has been prescriptive—do this, don't do that—we want you to be adventurous and courageous in your writing. Take chances, even if you risk failure. At that, you may be shaking your head: why should I take a chance of falling on my face? That question has four answers.

One, nothing communicates what we are and how we think more powerfully and completely than prose. It tells what we value and why. Stodgy prose therefore implies that the writer is stodgy.

Two, good writing leads to good thinking and vice versa. As you strive to interest your reader, you challenge your own thinking. Struggling to find a particular image or an exact phrase may open up a new range of thought.

Three, almost all A papers in the world possess personality and imagination. Aim high. Stretch toward excellence.

Four, writing with flair is more fun.

Although you should never sacrifice sense and integrity, you should actively seek the vivid. Indeed, vivid writing will often add to sense and integrity. The following three passages demonstrate some different ways of employing vivid language.

The first was written by a funny man who obviously enjoys his words.

> There is no question that there is an unseen world. The problem is, how far is it from midtown and how late is it open? Unexplainable events occur constantly. One man will see spirits. Another will hear voices. A third will wake up and find himself running in the Preakness. How many of us have not at one time or another felt an ice-cold hand on the back of our neck while we were home alone? (Not me, thank God, but some have.) What is behind these experiences? Or in front of them, for that matter? Is it true that some men can foresee the future or communicate with ghosts? And after death is it still possible to take showers? (Woody Allen, "Examining Psychic Phenomena")

The humor in this passage is provided by the sudden invasion of the absurd. Allen juxtaposes two different worlds, that of psychic phenomena and that of daily concerns. The incongruity of the two is unexpected and forces the reader to look at ideas anew.

The strength of the second passage comes not from the collision of ideas but from the strings of memorable images or mental pictures used to describe the prose of President Warren Gamaliel Harding.

> . . . He writes the worst English that I have ever encountered. It reminds me of a string of wet sponges; it reminds me of tattered washing on the line; it reminds me of stale bean-soup, of college yells, of dogs barking idiotically through endless nights. It is so bad that a sort of grandeur creeps into it. It drags itself out of the dark abysm (I was about to write abscess!) of pish, and crawls insanely up the topmost pinnacle of posh. It is rumble and bumble. It is flap and doodle. It is balder and dash.
> But I grow lyrical. (H. L. Mencken, "Gamalielese")

This passage is a feast of vivid writing. Mencken is certainly having fun, and providing fun, but he is also expressing his strong opinion about Harding's intelligence.

Neither of these passages is particularly complicated. Both make fairly simple points. But vivid language is not limited to the simple, as you can see in the following passage:

> It seems to me that there is a historical parallel, in white American history, between the treatment of the land and the treatment of women. The frontier, for instance, was notoriously exploitative of both, and I believe largely for the same reasons. Many of the early farmers seem to have worn out farms and wives with equal regardlessness, interested in both mainly for what they would produce, crops and dollars, labor and sons; they clambered upon their fields and upon their wives, struggling for an economic foothold, the having and holding that cannot come until both fields and wives are properly cherished. And today there seems to me a distinct connection between our nomadism (our "social mobility") and the nearly universal disintegration of our marriages and families. (Wendell Berry, "Discipline and Hope")

Berry, a naturalist and poet, brings an intriguing and complex point to life.

As you can see, good writing comes in many shapes, sizes, and colors—and can be the result of different intentions. Sometimes we forget that with a little effort we too can write a prose that has more flair. Perhaps a few precepts can help to translate what we admire into what we write.

Appeals to the Senses

Earlier in this chapter, in the section entitled "Writing with Precision," we said that the best writing is concrete and specific. Not all concrete and specific descriptions, however, are vivid. Take this one:

The child played ball on the sidewalk.

The description is both concrete and specific, but it is not particularly vivid. In revising we wanted to create a picture, a mental image, in the reader's mind.

First we visualized the subject: *boy* is more visual than *child*, but we thought harder about the image and tried to picture physical qualities. Then we turned to what the child was doing. We imagined as vividly as we could.

The frizzy-haired little boy slashed line drives to himself off the brick wall.

We thought the reader could better see the boy when we described his frizzy hair. *Slashed* conveys a specific action: the stroke of the boy's arm. The brick wall completes the picture.

According to an ancient Chinese proverb, one picture is worth more than ten thousand words. But by using words, we can create a picture in the reader's imagination, as James Baldwin does here:

[My father] looked to me, as I grew older, like pictures I had seen of African tribal chieftains: he really should have been naked, with war-paint on and barbaric mementos, standing among spears. (*Notes of a Native Son*)

By creating an exact image, Baldwin clearly illuminates his father's personality.

Unfortunately, dull language is as hard to fight in writing as crabgrass in a lawn. When we get the least bit lazy it springs up. This kind of sentence results:

Many residential structures were destroyed for redevelopment.

It is a sensible sentence and we understand it. But if we wish the reader to share our indignation, we need a more vivid image.

To clear the way for a new glass box, the wreckers sledgehammered the Victorian mansions and reduced them to rubble and dust.

Now the reader hears the wrecking ball, sees the rubble, and can taste the dust. Only the redeveloper hoping to go unnoticed would be happy with that first version.

All things being equal, we would not recommend additional words. But if you want to appeal to your reader's senses, you may need more words. Brevity is not the only virtue of good writing.

Vivid writing is important for two reasons. First, it makes understanding easier and quicker for the reader. In the "Victorian mansions" example, only the image of rubble and dust could quickly tell the real damage. Second, vivid writing pleases readers. We all like to read about the world of sight and sound and smell and taste and touch.

Figurative Language

Most good writing contains figures of speech, that is, words and expressions not used for their literal sense. Writers make figures of speech by describing one idea or object in language that properly belongs to another. If we say

Doubt crucified the president

we borrow feelings and ideas the reader has about actual crucifixion to illuminate the idea of painful doubt. By comparing one thing to another this way, we can reveal a new world for our readers and often ourselves.

The three major forms figurative comparisons take are similes, metaphors, and analogies.

SIMILES. A simile is an explicit comparison of one thing with another: the writer clarifies one idea or thing by claiming it is like another. A simile always includes *like* or *as*. In describing his father, James Baldwin said that people thought him ingrown "like a toenail." This simile conveys the isolated, pained, and disturbing old man. Here are more similes:

During the swing, the golf club bends like a whip.

Seen from a distance, the brightly dressed crowd in the market looked like a basket of summer fruit.

Like a mysterious, fog-enshrouded island approached by explorers, atomic energy fascinated and frightened the scientists.

An apt and nicely shaped simile can not only paint a vivid picture but also illuminate an idea. Shakespeare's work is rife with similes that make pictorial the nonpictorial opinion or abstraction. Near the end of *King Lear*, the Duke of Gloucester expresses his despair at human existence.

As flies to wanton boys, are we to the gods;
They kill us for their sport.

The successful simile, like this one, is brief and to the point. You shouldn't try to keep a comparison rolling just because you can. It can become silly and tedious if carried too far. But you should occasionally enrich your prose with an apt simile.

METAPHORS. A metaphor compares two things without making the comparison explicit: two things, the metaphor suggests, are the same.

A mighty fortress is our God,
A bulwark never failing

wrote Martin Luther.

> Religion . . . is the opium of the people

said Karl Marx.

"The metaphor is probably the most fertile power possessed by man," said the Spanish philosopher José Ortega y Gasset, relying on metaphor to make his point. A good metaphor lets us think and talk about the world in fresh ways by converting vague ideas into images.

Sometimes a longer metaphor can illuminate a complex situation. The following extended metaphor by the historian Barbara Tuchman describes marriage among ruling families of the Middle Ages:

> Marriages were the fabric of international as well as inter-noble relations, the primary source of territory, sovereignty, and alliance, and the major business of medieval diplomacy. The relations of countries and rulers depended not at all on common borders or natural interest but on dynastic connections and fantastic cousinships. . . . At every point of the loom sovereigns were thrusting in their shuttles, carrying the strand of a son or a daughter, and these, whizzing back and forth, wove the artificial fabric that created as many conflicting claims and hostilities as it did bonds. [The leading families of Europe] were all entwined in a crisscrossing network, in the making of which two things were never considered: the sentiments of the parties to the marriage, and the interest of the populations involved. *(A Distant Mirror)*

Because of Tuchman's metaphor, her reader is able to understand how tightly connected the various families were and how important these connections were. By representing an abstraction in concrete terms, she achieves the persuasiveness of illustration. Moreover, her metaphor adds energy to ideas and observations that might otherwise have been dry or tedious. Imagine that passage written in abstract, purely analytical language. The metaphor makes the idea dramatic and visual.

Some people dismiss metaphors and similes as too "literary." They need not be, however. Politicians have frequently used them, as Theodore Roosevelt did when he recommended that the United States

> Speak softly and carry a big stick.

Franklin Roosevelt spoke metaphorically when he said,

> I pledge you, I pledge myself, to a new deal for the American people.

Athletes and sportswriters instinctively use metaphors when nicknaming the greats: Ted Williams is "the Splendid Splinter" and Earvin Johnson is "Magic." Likewise, scientists often find that a simile or metaphor will help explain a difficult concept, as did Loren Eiseley when he titled an essay "The Ghost Continent" and another "The Angry Winter."

You shouldn't force figures of speech—gone wild they will undercut an essay. But make an effort to think of a natural simile or metaphor and then use it. For there are occasions when, despite all the evidence, reasons, or analysis you come up with, your reader is still a step away from understanding your ideas. Then a well-chosen, forceful comparison—simile or metaphor—may clarify and persuade.

ANALOGIES. An analogy is an extended comparison, drawn point by point, between two things or ideas. Its purpose is generally to explain a complicated or remote phenomenon by reference to a more accessible one. The advantage of an analogy comes from its careful elucidation of an idea.

The Bible is full of analogies. The parable of the prodigal son is an example. In it Jesus discusses God's forgiveness of sinners by suggesting it is like a father's treatment of his wayward son. The remote idea of the deity is made clear by reference to the homely idea of the father.

Sigmund Freud said, "Analogies prove nothing, that is quite true, but they can make one feel more at home." Because they do make readers feel more at home, analogies appear everywhere, even in instructions for using a soldering iron.

> Soldering is the joining of metal surfaces by a melted metal or metallic alloy. We can compare this roughly with the gluing of two pieces of wood. Instead of wood, the solderer joins two pieces of metal and instead of glue, he or she uses a melted alloy or metal that, like the glue, hardens and forms a bond.

Analogies can be surprising when used to compare things not obviously similar. In the sixteenth century, a band of thieves waylaid a parson and forced him to make a speech praising all thieves. At the height of his oration, he conferred high praise indeed, drawing an analogy between the thieves and Christ.

> I marvel that men can despise you thieves, since in all points (almost) you are like Christ himself. For Christ had no dwelling place; neither have you. Christ went from town to town; so do you. Christ was laid wait upon in many places, and so are you. Christ at length was captured; so shall you be. He was brought before the judges; so shall you be. He was condemned; and so shall you be. He was killed; so shall you be. He thereupon went to heaven—and that you shall never do.

That little twist at the end goes to show that even the best analogies should not be pushed too far—no two things are alike in all particulars (or they would be the same thing). The thieves must not have noticed, though, for according to the legend, "they went away well pleased." (See Chapter 7, Using Evidence, for more discussion of analogies.)

> ## TIPS FOR FLAIR
>
> - Take some risks with your writing.
> - Write to appeal to your reader's senses; make pictures as vivid as possible.
> - Try for an occasional simile, metaphor, or analogy.

Exercises for Flair

1. Write a vivid sentence to describe a specific experience with each of the five senses.
2. Complete each of the following sentences with a simile.
   a. The bird's raucous song was like
   b. The entire team sprawled on the turf, looking like
   c. He hated tap dancing just as . . . hated
   d. For Napoleon, those winter months in Moscow were like
   e. Dealing with inflation is like
3. Make an apt metaphor based on the following ideas.
   a. A bird and a squirrel quarreling
   b. Pollution in the city during a rainstorm.
   c. An old woman on a park bench on a cold winter day
   d. The state legislature during a heated debate
   e. The Concorde taking off
4. Make an analogy for two of the following sets.
   a. The circulatory system and a college or university
   b. A lion and her cub and a teacher and her student
   c. The solar system and a family
   d. Crime in a society and chicken pox
   Remember that you are using the known to explain the unknown.
5. Revise passages in an essay you wrote for an earlier assignment to include a simile, a metaphor, and an analogy.

13
STYLE

Oh tain't what you do, it's the way that cha do it. . . . Tain't what you say, it's the way that cha say it—That's what gets results.

SY OLIVER (b. 1910) AND
TRUMMY YOUNG (b. 1912)

Style is what the artist does with the raw material of the art, what the writer or the speaker does with the thought to be communicated. Every decision you make while writing—the words you select, the construction of sentences, paragraphing—will contribute to your style. In that sense, this book has been discussing style all along, especially in the sections on sentences and words. In this chapter, however, we want to bring all the foregoing elements together to concentrate on the way that cha say it, the way that *you* present *you*.

THE PERSONAL VOICE:
BEING THERE IN YOUR WRITING

We should not underestimate the importance of style. The way that we say or do something is distinct and makes even the most common thought or gesture our own. We hear a few bars of music and we say, "That's Brahms" or "That's Beethoven." We read a paragraph from a novel, and we probably know it is by Faulkner, Woolf, or Hemingway. We read the inaugural addresses of John Kennedy, Richard Nixon, Jimmy

Carter, and Ronald Reagan, and even though the sentiments expressed are pretty much the same, we know whose speech each is. We know by the style. Style is the indelible signature of personality.

All saying much the same thing, some very important military commanders presented themselves in these statements:

> My first wish is to see this plague of mankind, war, banished from the earth. (George Washington, 1732–1799)

> There is many a boy here today who looks on war as all glory, but, boys, it is all hell. You can bear this warning voice to generations yet to come. I look upon war with horror. (William Tecumseh Sherman, 1820–1891)

> I know war as few other men now living know it, and nothing to me is more revolting. I have long advocated its complete abolition, as its very destructiveness on both friend and foe has rendered it useless as a method of settling international disputes. (Douglas MacArthur, 1880–1964)

> I hate war as only a soldier who has lived it can, only as one who has seen its brutality, its futility, its stupidity. (Dwight D. Eisenhower, 1890–1969)

These quotations all convey the same thought: war is bad. But the styles of the speakers differ, and so do our responses to them.

Read the quotations again. Which commanders attract you and which put you off? Would you like to know any personally? Which ones would you trust? Imagine for a moment that the statements involved complicated, arguable ideas about matters that affect you directly—say, nuclear armaments or registering for military service. Judging purely by the style of these quotations, which commander would you be most apt to believe?

We do not want to push this analysis too far—these quotations are taken out of context and are too short to be a fair representation of the person. Nevertheless, they do illustrate that behind the words we can sense the attitude of the person. Words convey values and feelings as well as thoughts. They express a person's style.

Too frequently, people think style is just so much verbiage to be slathered over thought like a rich coat of paint over wood. It isn't. It isn't filigree and curlicue added to substance. It isn't fancy packaging. It isn't decoration at all. Style is an integral part of the message. It is the voice of the writer in the message. When Sherman said, "but, boys, it is all hell," his words in their very bluntness conveyed his personality as well as his attitude toward both subject and audience.

Look closely at Sherman's statement. The abrupt use of commas, representing pauses in his speech, rivets the attention, and then the word *hell* hammers home the simple message. The use of the word *boys* establishes a friendly, though paternalistic, relationship between Sherman and his audience, all former soldiers. By his choice of words, phrasing, and punctuation, Sherman has perfectly matched the language to his meaning. We hear his voice in his words. That is style. Behind the style we sense the man William Tecumseh Sherman.

Although some lucky few seem born with a distinctive writing style, most of us must work to develop one. Improving our writing style is at least as hard as improving our guitar-playing style or our tennis-playing style or even our having-a-good-time-at-a-party style. And as with these, improvement results from observation, practice, and imitation. Don't be afraid of imitating—most professional writers imitated other writers they admired before developing their own style. And don't be afraid of trying and failing. You will get better if you are willing to write, rewrite, rewrite again, and perhaps rewrite again. (This chapter has been rewritten at least five times.)

We cannot set up absolute standards for style. Some very good styles are simple and direct, some are florid, some are sinuous, some are muscular. The following passages, all excellent, demonstrate how varied good style can be:

> To everything there is a season, and a time to every purpose under heaven.
> A time to be born, and a time to die;
> A time to plant, and a time to pluck up that which is planted;
> A time to kill, and a time to heal;
> A time to break down, and a time to build up;
> A time to weep, and a time to laugh;
> A time to mourn and a time to dance . . .
> (Ecclesiastes 3:1–4, King James Version)

> It is difficult to imagine, with what obstinacy truths which one mind perceives almost by intuition, will be rejected by another; and how many artifices must be practiced, to procure admission for the most evident propositions into understandings frighted by their novelty, or hardened against them by accidental prejudice: it can scarcely be conceived, how frequently in these extemporaneous controversies, the dull will be subtle, and the acute absurd; how often stupidity will elude the force of argument, by involving itself in its own gloom; and mistaken ingenuity will weave artful fallacies, which reason can scarcely find means to disentangle. (Samuel Johnson, *The Adventurer*)

> Man, it is well to remember, is the discoverer but not the inventor of fire. Long before this meddling little Prometheus took to experimenting with flints, then matches, and finally (we hope not too finally) hydrogen bombs, fires had burned on this planet. Volcanoes had belched molten lava, lightning had struck in dry grass, winds had rubbed dead branches against each other until they burst into flame. There are evidences of fire in ancient fossil beds that lie deep below the time of man. (Loren Eiseley, "Man the Firemaker")

Well, evolution *is* a theory. It is also a fact. And facts and theories are different things, not rungs in a hierarchy of increasing certainty. Facts are the world's data. Theories are structures of ideas that explain and interpret facts. Facts do not go away when scientists debate rival theories to explain them. Einstein's theory of gravitation replaced Newton's, but apples did not suspend themselves in mid-air pending the outcome. And human beings evolved from apelike ancestors whether they did so by Darwin's proposed mechanism or by some other, yet to be discovered. (Stephen Jay Gould, "Evolution as Fact and Theory")

In the pages that follow, we refer to these passages. For now, we want to point out that these four very different stylists all treat an interesting subject respectfully and put their stamp upon it.

CHARACTERISTICS OF GOOD STYLE: BEST FOOT FORWARD

Although a good style cannot be defined in a single set of qualities, all good styles share three characteristics: clarity, appropriateness, and interest.

Clarity

First, a good style is clear. When readers have to work too hard to reconstruct our thought, they are apt to be irritated and give up. Whether we ever develop a great style, we can with care, thought, and practice learn to write clearly.

Reread the Gould quotation—can anyone mistake its message? Or even that of Eiseley, though he wrote in a more leisurely and complex style?

Clarity requires that we follow the rules of the English language. When a reader must translate a plural pronoun into a singular one to match up with a verb, or figure out where the commas and periods should go, that reader will miss much of the meaning—and perhaps think you also are befuddled. Mastery of the rules is essential to a clear style. (For more on grammar, see Chapter 19, Basic Grammar.)

So is a rich but natural vocabulary. To write six words instead of the single appropriate word weakens prose. Look at the word *artifices* in the passage from Samuel Johnson. It means "skill or ingenuity; a clever expedient; a sly or artful trick." In one word, Johnson, the great eighteenth-century stylist, brings all these meanings into his sentence. At the same time, if readers must constantly scurry to the dictionary, they may not return to the manuscript. Had Eiseley begun his first sentence with ''The tellurian hairless biped . . .'' we probably would not have arrived at the verb. (See Chapter 12, Working with Words, for more on the subject of diction.)

Proper organization and emphasis contribute to clarity. The parallelism in the passage from Ecclesiastes, for instance, helps to keep the ideas exactly ordered. Without the parallelism, we might read something like

> We are born at a given time and planting takes place every spring— although to be perfectly rational about it, some people die by accident and that can hardly be said to be happening at a special or preordained time. In the fall is when farmers and their helpers get up really early in the morning because it's the harvest. Which brings me to hunting, I think. . . .

Clear writing is the writer's courtesy to the reader.

Appropriateness

A good style must be appropriate to subject, audience, and self. If Sherman had been addressing the U.S. Congress—instead of a reunion of old soldiers who had served under him—he no doubt would have been the same blunt soldier, but he would have couched his message in more sophisticated terms, and he most assuredly would not have called his listeners ''boys.''

Style must be appropriate to the subject. Samuel Johnson wrote about the complex relations of reading, thinking, and writing, and that subject required complex treatment. The writer of Ecclesiastes treated simple, straightforward ideas in a simple, straightforward way.

Audience also makes demands on style. Had Gould been trying to persuade an audience of fundamentalists, he no doubt would have couched his thought in different language. Had he been addressing a scientific audience, he no doubt would have assumed greater knowledge. But his language was appropriate for readers of *Discover* magazine, where his essay appeared.

Finally, style should fit the writer's personality and situation. We have read essays that sounded—or tried to sound—as if some graybeard had written them. It seems to us appropriate for Samuel Johnson to use a neoclassical style—he lived in that age. Gould, however, is young and American, and his prose appropriately sounds young and American. Style should fit like good shoes.

We are not suggesting, though, that you write exactly as you speak. Your writing style should represent you at your considered best.

Interest

No law says that an academic paper, a personal letter, a law brief, or any other writing must be boring. Nobody—not even the world's greatest pedant—wants to read something written in a dull, uninteresting style.

What makes a style interesting? Colorful imagery. The unexpected twist of a phrase, a startling comparison, an illuminating allusion to any other work. The sentences are rhythmic, vigorous, varied. An interesting style avoids the overblown, the quaint, the pretentious. It is down-to-earth and sincere without being ponderous. It has personality without self-preening. It conveys wit, insight, sensitivity. The most interesting style is the most interesting you that you can get on the page.

TONE: THE VOICE FROM DEEP WITHIN

Perhaps the most important ingredient of style is tone, that is, the atmosphere or attitude the words convey. In speech, the way we say something—the tone of our voice—will telegraph our attitude, even if the words are neutral. Our voice indicates whether we are being sincere, bewildered, amused, or any of dozens of other possibilities. To change the tone, we make small changes in pronunciation or pacing. For instance, the sentence *The college newspaper critic said this was the best movie of the year, and so it must be really great* could be sarcastic, pompous, innocent, deadpan, and so on—the difference depending on a subtle adjustment of tone.

Tone in writing is not as unconsciously or automatically achieved as tone in speech. A writer cannot "drip sarcasm" by anything as simple as modulating the voice. In writing, to change "the way that cha say it," you have to change what you say. Choice of words, length of sentence, rhythm, and punctuation all contribute to the atmosphere in which the ideas exist. They help the writer express an attitude toward the subject.

Too much writing today, unfortunately, sounds as though it issued from a vending machine—cold, detached, nonhuman. Three sentences for a quarter. Some students actively seek tonelessness, believing that tone has no business in academia. That notion is mistaken. Tone in writing is a significant part of the message. Reread the first two sentences of the Eiseley passage on page 308 and compare them with this paraphrase:

This planet knew fire before there were human beings.

The paraphrase gets the fact across, but that is all it does. Eiseley's tone illuminates the matter: we human beings are not as great as we think. His words challenge the reader and prepare the way for the argument he will make.

Not all tones are acceptable in college writing or any kind of writing. Some can be downright unattractive. In this section, we will discuss six tones that you should keep out of your papers.

Flippancy

When something is flippant, it indicates a disrespectful levity. Here is the opening of an essay on utilitarian philosophy:

> Suppose Jesus Christ had truly lived and suppose he had fallen in love with some Egyptian girl who jilted him for a pharaoh. Brokenhearted, he had committed suicide before he had spread his word to the people. Now, by committing suicide, more grief would have been caused, and therefore the utilitarian must say that his act was immoral.

This flippancy is inappropriate to both the audience (an instructor) and the subject, serious and to some people sacred. With such a tone, almost no argument, however cogently reasoned, could salvage the paper. Flippancy can be fun to say or write—maybe fun to hear—but almost never fun to read. To be flippant about a subject indicates that we do not take it seriously. Instructors, and bosses, are unlikely to appreciate that approach.

Sarcasm

Sarcasm is a contemptuous remark or taunt, often couched in words opposite to the speaker's real meaning.

> If only the rest of us misguided students were one-quarter as intelligent as my roommate, what a brilliant student body we would be.

In an essay, sarcasm is even less attractive than flippancy. When you think of that word, don't you picture a sneering, superior look on someone's face? We do, perhaps because when we succumb to sarcasm that is the way we feel. A sarcastic tone may create in the reader's mind that image of the writer.

Sentimentality

Sentimentality means forced or shallow feeling, and it is another tone to avoid. It is good to express feeling in our writing, of course, but only honest—not pumped up—feeling. Excessive sentiment in an essay casts doubt on both the thinking and the sincerity of the writer. When people overstate their feelings, their writing is apt to deteriorate. They begin to dredge up clichés and trite sayings to back up an emotion they don't have.

> Tears spring to my eyes when I think of that helpless little kitten—gone but not forgotten these many years.

We doubt those tears—we even doubt the kitten.

Self-righteousness

Akin to sentimentality is the self-righteous, or holier-than-thou, tone. Some writing seems to suggest that the writer has a special claim to virtue. Often this tone is accidental. The following, from an autobiographical essay, was written by a modest but naïve young man:

> The well-being of my mind, body, and spirit is the result of my family life. My parents love and respect life. This love has inspired me to use my gifts to the height of their potential so that I perform at my best throughout my life.

Appreciating one's parents is a virtue, but a recognition that things are not always as they seem and no one is perfect would have added depth to this essay.

Belligerence

The belligerent writer comes right at the reader, chin thrust forward, fists doubled, like the schoolyard bully, threatening to beat up anyone who dares to disagree. We once read a letter to the editor of a college newspaper that began, "I just can't believe how ignorant and stupid some people are regarding nuclear weapons. They just like to protest something in between hits of the old weed." Not many people would want to associate themselves with views expressed that way.

Some ideas are, of course, worth fighting for. It would be absurd not to show feeling about important issues, such as hunger in Africa, missing children in America, or the torture of animals. Indeed, honest indignation can contribute to effective argument.

There is a line, however, between belligerence and acceptable indignation, and that line should be carefully observed. State your opinion with a tone of indignation, but back it up with evidence. Do not bully us into agreement but respect us enough to want to persuade us with argument. The tone of the letter writer, in contrast, offers no evidence of argument but only more bullying: "Take my word for it or else."

Apology

The opposite of belligerence, and equally inappropriate, is the apology, what might be called the po'-li'l-me tone. With this, the writer claims that he or she is modest, diffident, and hardworking and thus deserves special consideration.

> Even after reading T. S. Eliot's "The Hollow Men" five times, I could not figure it out. I know it is a great poem, and I realize I have not received the education necessary to understanding it.

Professors seldom give A for effort, and they never do when they realize they are being manipulated for a grade. They want ideas, not the writer hat in hand. Imagine Samuel Johnson saying "I know I don't know much, but . . ." Like Johnson, confidently say what you think.

THE HIGH INFORMAL STYLE: THE RIGHT BALANCE

For work in college, seek to write in what could be called the *high informal style.* This style is high because it shows respect, for the reader and for the subject. It observes the rules of argument and of etiquette, including correct grammar, syntax, and punctuation. It avoids silliness, breeziness, overfamiliarity, and vulgarity.

Seriousness does not mean "academic writing." As university instructors, we are particularly sensitive to this kind of writing. For centuries, academics have been pilloried and parodied for being precise to the point of pedantry and pomposity. Yet some of the best writing in the country comes from academics. Lewis Thomas, Helen Vendler, and C. Vann Woodward are only three professors who write with elegance, imagination, and personality. Look up some of their writing. They are well worth imitating.

Some writers, unfortunately, imitate the worst kind of academic writing, the kind that really is pedantic. They insert ten-dollar words when nickel ones would be better. They pile clause on clause, modification on modification, until their sentences and paragraphs teeter and collapse. Along the way, they are apt to lose touch with their thought and certainly with themselves. Imagine how baffled the instructor was when she read the following passage:

> If it were in my power to change one aspect of modern living, I would prioritize change in the capitalist ideology that is predominant socially at the present point in time. It is because of this ideology that pursuit of truly valued goals is prevented. Many settle for conditions that create the possibility of generating sufficient income for inordinate materialistic wants. Stifled by the deluding paradigm of materialism, indi-

vidual hopes and dreams are stillborn, poverty is the norm while the wealthy survive, and many people are forced into molds that will reflect a wealthy life-style.

This sort of writing will "amaze the unlearned and make the learned smile," as the eighteenth-century poet Alexander Pope put it. It is not all the writer's fault, however. She was trying, too hard, to write the way she thought she was expected to write. And so she stumbled over awkward combinations of words, the complex ways of saying simple things, the strained effort to sound intelligent.

The high informal style shifts a little toward informality. It gives the impression of natural speech—without, of course, lapsing into error in form or diction.

In the revision, the writer relaxed and began to sound more like herself and less achingly formal and pretentious:

> If I could change one thing in the world, I would change the empha-sis on materialism that I see today. Because of the rush to get rich, many people cannot pursue what they really find valuable in life, like teaching or farming or social work. Instead, many settle for being doctors, law-yers, bankers, not because these careers interest them, but because the salaries will provide material rewards. It is very sad to see the dreams and aspirations of so many people destroyed by the search for money. But perhaps we cannot expect anything else in a world where the poor struggle or perish and the wealthy have much more than enough.

Writing like this preserves the high aspect of style—the need for respect and seriousness—and adds the informal, the personal, the sense that someone is talking. We know full well what this writer believes and cher-ishes. In her examples, she puts her stamp on the thought. An appropriate style is always a personal style. It should include not only your values but also your humor, your tolerance, your quirky way of viewing the world.

Be as fine a stylist as you can be. Don't settle for the first sentence that emerges. Work in an occasional metaphor or analogy. Notice what writers you admire do in their writing and try it on for size. Just as you may experiment with different styles of clothing, experiment with different styles of writing. Challenge yourself. Stretch for a fine style.

TIPS FOR STYLE

- Keep in mind that your style is the you that you present to your reader.
- Think about the qualities and techniques that make a style clear, appropriate, and interesting.

- Read your work critically so that you can evaluate whether your tone is the one you want to convey.
- Avoid flippancy, sarcasm, sentimentality, self-righteousness, belligerence, and apology.
- Seek the high informal style, a mixture of respect, seriousness, and informality.
- To learn how to get yourself across in your style, observe and imitate what good writers do, and practice.

Exercises for Style

1. Here are passages by seven professional writers. How would you characterize the styles?

   a. A word is dead
      When it is said,
      Some say.
      I say it just
      Begins to live
      That day.
         (Emily Dickinson)

   b. Have I not walked without an upward look
      Of caution under stars that very well
      Might not have missed me when they shot and fell?
      It was a risk I had to take—and took.
         (Robert Frost)

   c. We shall now meet my cousin Yuri, a thin, sallow-faced boy with a round cropped head and luminous gray eyes. The son of divorced parents, with no tutor to look after him, a town boy with no country home, he was in many respects different from me. . . . From his earliest boyhood, he was absolutely fearless, but was squeamish and wary of "natural history," could not make himself touch wriggly things, could not endure the amusing emprisoned tickle of a small frog groping about in one's fist like a person, or the discreet, pleasantly cool, rhythmically undulating caress of a caterpillar ascending one's bare shin. (Vladimir Nabokov, *Speak, Memory*)

   d. That year in New Jersey lives in my mind as though it were the year during which, having an unsuspected predilection for it, I first contracted some dread, chronic disease, the unfailing symptom of which is a kind of blind fever, a pounding in the skull and fire in the bowels. Once this disease is contracted, one can never be really carefree again, for the fever, without an instant's warning, can recur at any moment. It can wreck more important things than race relations. There is not a Negro alive who does not have this rage in his blood— one has the choice, merely, of living with it consciously or surrendering to it. As for me, this fever has recurred in me, and does, and will until the day I die. (James Baldwin, *Notes of a Native Son*)

e. The world has heaped contumely on my people, even on the one of us who is President [Jimmy Carter]. But do we try to make people feel guilty for the misunderstanding? No. Do we file antidefamation suits? No. That ain't my people's way. We don't even like to *wear* suits. (Roy Blount, Jr., *Crackers*)

f. Many years ago, as a solitary youth much given to wandering, I set forth on a sullen November day for a long walk that would end among the fallen stones of a forgotten pioneer cemetery on the High Plains. The weather was threatening, and only an unusual restlessness drove me into the endeavor. Snow was on the ground and deepening by the hour. There was a rising wind of blizzard proportions sweeping across the land. (Loren Eiseley, *The Unexpected Universe*)

g. The emphasis on skills was a response to what had been the major weakness of Peace Corps programs in the 1960s. There has always been a debate within the agency about whether its emphasis should be on socioeconomic development or cross-cultural exchange. In theory, one goal is as important as the other. In the 1960s, however, too many projects tended to focus on the second goal of the Peace Corps Act (the people-to-people aspect) and neglected the first goal (the supply of *trained* manpower). (Gerald T. Rice, *Twenty Years of Peace Corps*)

What kind of person do you think each writer is? Analyze the texts to support your opinion.

2. Choose two of the passages in Exercise 1 and write a paragraph about each in which you analyze their sentence structure and diction.

3. Describe the tones of the following passages.
   a. Abortion is a vicious crime and any person who encourages another person to have one is an accomplice in a murder and should be prosecuted to the fullest extent of the law.
   b. Males are so honorable by nature that they would naturally take the high moral position on this issue of abortion because of course it affects them so greatly and they have so much to lose if abortion is recriminalized.
   c. I don't care about the issue—what's one more aborted fetus or one more unwanted baby? People have always had abortions and people have always hated their children. The thing that amuses me is how excited people who are centuries past the childbearing years can get about this. Now that is worth pondering.

4. Revise the three statements in Exercise 3 to remove the offending tones. Write the passages in the high informal style.

5. Write six sentences, using a different unacceptable tone in each. Revise the sentences to make the tones acceptable.

PART FIVE

Putting It

All Together:

College Writing

14

DOING RESEARCH

My library
Was dukedom large enough.
WILLIAM SHAKESPEARE (1564–1616)
THE TEMPEST, 1.2.109–110

Somewhere along the way it is going to happen. A teacher, an employer, or a colleague will ask you to study a topic thoroughly, gather information, and write a paper that communicates your research in an accessible form. A time-honored response is to wait until the last moment, then whirl in a frenzy to the library for two days, thence to the typewriter and correction fluid, pencils, erasers, and coffee, to bash out an overnight wonder. This method has a world of drawbacks. The results are almost always shabby. Worst of all, last-minute researchers waste a real opportunity to do something challenging and significant.

Research gives us an excellent chance to pull together what we have learned in a course and to learn a great deal on our own about an important topic. If researched haphazardly and written carelessly, a research paper can be a tedious, sloppy mess; if treated with care and consideration, it can be a source of pride.

Modern researchers have a powerful arsenal of tools and techniques. The most powerful is still the mind, its interests, its way of seeing things. Research tells you almost as much about yourself as about your topic. That may be why so many people like doing it. Research has its own suspense, its close calls, its mystery trails, its revelations. Enjoy it.

No research project happens all at once. Like any writing project, it emerges out of a process. We will divide that process into ten stages and look at each in this chapter and the next. The stages are:

Choosing a General Subject

Compiling a Working Bibliography

Limiting Your Area of Research

Formulating a Tentative Thesis

Reading and Taking Notes

Restating Your Thesis

Preparing an Outline

Writing a First Draft

Documenting Your Sources

Revising, and Writing the Final Draft

If these stages sound like repetitions of much of our book, all the better: a research paper requires us to combine all our critical and analytical skills with all our writing skills, from drafting and inventing to choosing words.

The order of these stages varies from project to project, but few research papers are written without involving all of them. Some stages repeat themselves; research is a recursive rather than a linear process. Be ready to restate your thesis many times, to return to the library again and again, to go back over steps you thought you had left behind.

CHOOSING A GENERAL SUBJECT

A research paper has to be about something. That seems perfectly obvious, but, strangely enough, some writers neglect this essential requirement. They circle a possible topic page after page, switch to another one, and perhaps somewhere near the end, discover what it was they should have been discussing all along. By then, of course, it is too late. The first step in writing a research paper is to choose the general subject you will study.

Research topics will come to you along different paths. Your instructor may explicitly define the topic or leave it as broad as possible.

Working with an Assigned Topic

When you are given a topic for writing, read the assignment carefully. You will want to stay within its limits. Look closely at the questions or statements your instructor provides. You may find clues in them to direct you. Here, for instance, is a research assignment for an African studies class:

> Examine studies done by Warner, Junker, Adams, and Edwards. Compare their thinking about black group stability on the basis of class, economics, and social structure.

Go straight to the command words, *examine* and *compare*. They lead to both the sources (the various studies) and the subject (*their thinking about black group stability*). The assignment even provides subheadings (*class, economics, and social structure*) that could help you organize your paper.

Here an instructor limits a topic in a different way:

> What in your opinion were the main causes of the Johnson administration's "failure" in Vietnam in 1964–1967? Argue for your opinion on the basis of references to documents, debates in the press, and major scholarly interpretations.

Rather than asking for an analysis of what scholars have written, this instructor wants you to defend an opinion. He has been unusually kind, providing not only the topic and a suitable strategy (cause and effect) but also a possible theme: *"failure."* Those quotation marks are asking you to define the term, perhaps even to disagree with the verdict that the administration's policy *was* a failure. The assignment also specifies a time frame (1964–1967) and three broad kinds of sources. It will be up to you to limit the topic further in your research paper. But again, the way the question is phrased has given some idea of how to begin.

Discovering Your Own Topic

Frequently you will have free rein to do research on any aspect of a course. You will find your own topic. You might discover a topic in the form of a surprise in the course. In the assigned reading for a course on architecture, for instance, you might come upon this sentence:

> Now Jefferson's plan [for Monticello] prefigures that by Frank Lloyd Wright of the Ward Willitts house of 1902.

If you had never thought of Thomas Jefferson as an important architect, that might lead you to consider whether other architects were deeply influenced by him. Your research project would be your opportunity to find out. Or in a psychology class your lecturer may comment in passing that

> Communist governments have heretofore been critical of Freudian forms of therapy.

If you want to know why, you may have a research topic.

Take pains to choose a subject area large enough to offer you interesting research but small enough to allow you to treat it fully. No single paper can cover the whole field of Soviet-American relations or American fiction in the twentieth century. Researching a large, amorphous subject can be like trying to serve Jell-O with your fingers.

Begin thinking about your subject early. Go over your textbooks, notes, and assigned readings. Think about the possibilities. Brainstorm. Free-write. Question yourself and the subject systematically. Write out a few ideas. Let your ideas ripen.

You may have trouble brainstorming if you don't know much about a topic. In that case, off to the library immediately: crack open some encyclopedias and other general reference works on the subject. Get some background. Talk to your instructor. See how the subject looks before trying to narrow it.

When you have found a subject, you will need to start narrowing it to a manageable size. Here are ways of narrowing the two broad subjects we mentioned earlier.

> Soviet-American relations
> > Soviet-American relations and *glasnost*
> > > Soviet-American relations and Russian dissidents
> American fiction in the twentieth century
> > American short fiction in the twentieth century
> > > American short fiction in the 1920s

These topics are still too broad to write on, but they are a proper size for starting a research project.

Christina Gerke, who wrote the paper reproduced at the end of Chapter 15, had complete freedom in her freshman composition class to choose her research topic. She was also taking a course entitled Contemporary American Society, which had made her interested in the changes taking place in America. She knew that this topic was far too broad for a research project, so she began to whittle it down.

> Recent changes in American society
> > Minorities and recent changes in American society
> > > Minorities and the educational system

Now she still had a broad subject, but she had enough direction to make her first sweep of the library.

COMPILING A WORKING BIBLIOGRAPHY

Once you have chosen a general subject, it is time to begin your library work. Notice that this is the groundwork for more extensive research later. You are scouting ahead, getting the lay of the land, so that when the time comes for the real journey to begin, you will know where everything is.

Your main aim during this first sweep, which will take a number of visits to the library, is to compile a working bibliography, or a list of the books, articles, and other sources to be consulted in your research. The working bibliography will help you come up with the list of works cited in your final paper. Many instructors also require that you submit a preliminary bibliography early in the research process, and this stage will help you compile one.

You will find titles of and leads to sources in many of the places we discuss in this section; you will also find them in the bibliographies of the books and articles you consult. Each source will send you to more sources, and so your working bibliography will grow. Make your list using notecards—they are the neatest and easiest way (see a system for note taking in "Taking Notes"). Add to and delete from your working bibliography as you extend your research.

Time Management

You will want to use your research time as efficiently as possible. Here are five hints on how to do so.

1. Start early on all projects. As we suggested in Chapter 1, a good rule of thumb is to start writing about halfway between the time you receive the assignment and the deadline. That means that your research should have been started well before then—certainly before a third of the time has passed. Remember that every step will take half again as long as you think it will. Do not rely on the pressure of an advancing deadline to squeeze a project out of you.

2. Make frequent two- or three-hour visits to the library. This method usually works much better than marathon sessions. First, it gives you more time to ponder what you find. Second, you will remember and understand more in shorter sessions than when you are fatigued, hungry, and under pressure—for instance, frantically researching at three o'clock in the morning during the last week of the term.

3. Since few of us are at tip-top form all day, do your most challenging and creative work at your best time, whether that is early morning or late evening. Search, read, and take notes then; review notes and drafts when you begin to run down.

4. Schedule your research visits for the same time every day, if possible. Like you, your brain likes habits.

5. Find a place free of distraction for your work. If your dorm room is a popular conversation spot, avoid it. If the library is a social center,

check out the books and flee. Take frequent short breaks; get a drink of water or just gaze out the window. But make the breaks short, don't steal time from yourself.

Using Notecards

Here you are, in the best place at the best time, notecards and sources at hand. Yes, notecards. Even at this early juncture, you will want to retain what you read. Do not rely on memory. Take careful notes.

For each source you plan to consult in detail, make a *bibliography card*. This card will contain all the vital information about the source. Put down the author's last and first name, the title, the journal name (for articles), and all publication information (place, publisher, date). To save yourself work later, follow the MLA format for list of works cited (see "Documenting Your Sources" in Chapter 15). Be sure you include the library call number. And in case you need to return to it, write down where you found the source—what list, bibliography, or subject heading. Put the author's last name in capital letters in the upper-left-hand corner of the card. Losing or garbling any bibliographic information could cost you time later—or even the ability to cite a promising source.

Figure 14.1 shows a bibliography card that Christina Gerke made during her research. Note that her entry is exactly as it might appear in a list of works cited.

We will discuss note taking in more detail in "Taking Notes." Here we want to emphasize that you should always make a complete record of every source that you expect to consult in any extensive way.

Figure 14.1   Bibliography Card

BERK

LB   Berk, Ronald, ed.

3060.62   <u>Handbook of Methods for Detecting</u>

H 36   <u>Test Bias</u>.

Baltimore: Johns Hopkins UP 1982.

SUBJECT CATALOG: "Test bias —

congresses"

The Modern Library

Although most research will rely on the written word, college and university libraries house more than stacks of books. Researchers now must know more than how to look up an article or a book title. Computer data bases, record collections, audio- and videotape collections, motion picture catalogs, and interlibrary loan services are among the resources available. Few libraries have all these, but most offer many of them.

If a researcher was studying "The Treatment of Japanese-American Servicemen during the Second World War," the traditional and necessary first approach would be to amass the titles of relevant books and articles. But it is not hard to think of materials that would augment the information in printed sources: newsreels and photographs, audio- and videotapes of interviews with Japanese veterans, even memorabilia in a university collection. This kind of research can aid the traditional kind in creating a fully rounded and persuasive project.

Therefore, *know your library.*

As early as possible in your education, take a tour of your school's main library and learn the locations of any other libraries on or near the campus. If your school offers guided library tours, take one. If your library offers informational pamphlets, read them. Detailed knowledge of a college or university library system would take a research project in itself, but you will find it useful to develop a general idea of what materials are where. You might not have planned to step into the campus geology library, for instance, but you may find it useful if you do a report on the San Francisco earthquake of 1906. Also, learn about other institutions affiliated with yours. Become familiar with your school's information network.

Oh, yes—know the hours the libraries keep. Save yourself disappointment later.

Finally, get to know the librarians. People are often a library's most valuable resource. Librarians have been trained to know their collections and other available resources and to help those who do not know them as well. Reference librarians are paid to answer your questions, so ask them. And circulation librarians can help you locate a book if you cannot find it on the shelf; if it is checked out and you need it badly, they may even be able to call it back for you.

Primary and Secondary Sources

In the library you will find two kinds of materials: primary and secondary sources. You will probably use both, but it is important to distinguish between the two.

Primary sources are the contemporaneous documents relating to a subject: letters, interviews, polls, eyewitness accounts, experiments, speeches, and surveys. To write an essay on the battle of Vicksburg during the Civil War, you could consult *The Official Records of the War of the Rebellion between the Armies of the United States and the Armies of the Confederacy,* which contains primary documents, including military orders. Most instructors want you to examine available primary sources at some stage in your research. You can even create your own primary sources when you conduct interviews or take polls. For a discussion of this topic, see "Being Your Own Source," pages 338–339.

Secondary sources are what other investigators have said about a subject. Douglas Southall Freeman's great tome *Lee's Lieutenants,* a scholar's informed study of the decision makers in Lee's army, is a highly useful secondary source on the battles of the Civil War. (For a discussion of how to evaluate and use the expert evidence that secondary sources represent, see Chapter 7, Using Evidence.)

Most instructors want you to consult whatever primary documents are involved with your topic, but do not ignore the helpful insights in secondary sources.

The Reference Section

The main library will probably be your research center, and its reference section will be an early stop. Here you will find overviews of virtually every subject and guides to getting right to the more detailed information. Start big. Consult general surveys of your topic. Once you get an overview, you will know much better what aspect you want to pursue. Encyclopedias are especially good for background reading; they can provide you with the main terms, controversies, and people in your subject. Even if you do not have a subject yet, you may find one while looking through general reference works. Among the many types of resources available in the reference section, we will describe eight that you will find especially helpful.

GENERAL ENCYCLOPEDIAS. General encyclopedias offer broad overviews of a variety of topics. Under the entry for your subject you can find a capsule survey, including a list of books for further reading. General encyclopedias are *not* adequate in themselves as research sources. They may, however, be helpful first steps. Christina Gerke consulted encyclopedia entries for "Intelligence" and "Education" as a first step in her research. Among the best general encyclopedias are *Collier's Encyclopedia, Encyclopedia Americana, Encyclopaedia Britannica* and *New Encyclopaedia Britannica.*

SPECIALIZED ENCYCLOPEDIAS. Almost all fields have their own encyclopedias. These books can help you with definitions of special terms and recurrent themes within a subject. Gerke, for instance, looked in *The Encyclopedia of Education* for a discussion of educational testing. Here are some other specialized encyclopedias:

> *Encyclopaedia of Religion and Ethics*
> *Encyclopedia of World Art*
> *International Encyclopedia of Film*
> *International Encyclopedia of the Social Sciences*
> *McGraw-Hill Encyclopedia of Science and Technology*
> *Oxford Companion to English Literature*

DICTIONARIES. Dictionaries offer not only spellings, etymologies, and histories of words but also rules of punctuation, indexes of foreign phrases, and lists of famous people and places. Dictionaries become important at many points in research. When Gerke needed a good, solid definition of *intelligence,* she consulted the dictionary, where she discovered that the word refers not to one thing but to many, including understanding, quickness, and wisdom. She realized that measuring intelligence would not be an easy task. The dictionary she consulted is generally viewed as the most comprehensive and scholarly in English, the *Oxford English Dictionary.* Also among the most wide-ranging and thorough is *Webster's Third New International Dictionary of the English Language.* (For more on dictionaries, see the discussion in Chapter 12 called "Using Your Dictionary.")

BIOGRAPHICAL WORKS. Biographical works contain brief, informative entries on prominent people, detailing their lives and achievements. Such directories exist for people living and dead, for particular countries, and for various fields. Some are periodicals, and some are updated every few years. Consult them if you want to know more about the people in your study, or if you wish to follow up on unfamiliar names. Gerke consulted *Who Was Who* to learn more about Alfred Binet, and *Who's Who in America* for more on Arthur Jensen, both influential figures in educational testing. Other valuable biographical works include

> *American Men and Women of Science*
> *Biography and Genealogy Master Index*
> *Biography Index*
> *Chambers's Biographical Dictionary*
> *Current Biography*
> *Dictionary of American Biography*
> *Dictionary of National Biography* (British)

International Who's Who

Notable American Women

Webster's New Biographical Dictionary

GUIDES TO BOOKS.   Guides to books can tell you what is currently being published in your field. Two general guides are *Books in Print*, yearly lists of books by author, title, and subject, and *Book Review Digest*, which offers summaries of book contents and reviews.

ATLASES.   Atlases contain more than maps. They can help you locate unfamiliar place names and also give you extremely useful facts and statistics about topology, population, economics, and forms of government. There are atlases for the whole world, for single countries, for specific regions, for the oceans, and for the heavens. There are atlases for the modern world and for the ancient world. Here is a small sampling: *Historical Atlas of the World, National Atlas of the United States of America,* and the *Times Atlas of the World.*

YEARBOOKS.   Yearbooks summarize the issues, events, and statistics of a given year. Many are connected with encyclopedias. They chronicle a year's major events. A few examples are *American Annual, Britannica Book of the Year,* and *Facts on File Yearbook.*

ALMANACS AND GAZETTEERS.   Almanacs, such as *The World Almanac and Book of Facts,* can be either compendia of broad, general information arranged by the days of the year or annual general reviews of statistics and facts of all kinds. Gazetteers, such as the *Columbia Lippincott Gazetteer of the World,* are geographic dictionaries. Both contain useful information.

   If you cannot find the reference works you need, ask your reference librarian.

Book Files and Catalogs

   If you spend some time doing patient and alert reading in the reference section, you will emerge with a list of authors and titles of books. You may well return to the reference section later as you learn more about your subject. But now you need to know which of these books the library has. The library's book files and catalogs are your next stop.

   If you are not familiar with the following files and catalogs, take time to learn their location and their use. Many libraries now have catalogs in different forms, including card catalogs, bound books, microfilm or microfiche, and computerized "on-line" catalogs. The most familiar form is the card catalog, which lists each book the library owns on a separate card. The cards are arranged alphabetically by author, by title, and by subject heading. Some libraries house these catalogs separately, and some combine them in a central card catalog. Each card provides the call number, by which you can locate a book on the shelves.

In a bibliography on educational testing, Christina Gerke discovered a listing for "Smith, Frank, *Insult to Intelligence.*" Figure 14.2 shows the "main entry" or *author card* she found for that book under *S* for Smith in her library's author-title catalog. The subtitle told her that this was a book worth looking at. The call number in the upper-left-hand corner led Gerke to the right floor of the library, then to the right shelf, then to the right book. The "tracings" near the bottom of the card gave her some additional headings for further research.

The *title card* (see Figure 14.3) is exactly the same as the author card, except that it has the title at the top and is filed alphabetically by the first word of the title, not counting *a, an,* and *the.*

The *subject card* lists the work alphabetically under the subject heading or headings shown on the author and title cards. The subject card for Smith under the heading *Education—Aims and objectives* also appears in Figure 14.3.

Card catalogs also contain *reference cards,* which direct you to other related subject headings via a "See" or a "See also."

Figure 14.2   Main Entry Library Card

Figure 14.3   Title and Subject Library Card

```
                Insult to intelligence.

    LB          Smith, Frank.
    1025.2      Insult to intelligence: the bureaucratic
    .S59        invasion of our classrooms.--New York:
    1986        Arbor, 1986.

                        EDUCATION--AIMS AND OBJECTIVES.

                LB
                1025.2      Smith, Frank.
                .S59        Insult to intelligence: the bureaucratic
                1986        invasion of our classrooms.--New York:
                            Arbor, 1986.
```

Subject headings can be a good lead in your research. If your library uses the Library of Congress classification system, the reference desk will have books called *Library of Congress Subject Headings,* which list all the subject headings most library catalogs use. Consult them to see the range of headings that may apply to your subject. If your library uses the Dewey Decimal classification system, consult the *Dewey Decimal Classification and Relative Index* for a directory of subjects. In either case, once you have the headings, you can examine the catalogs to learn what your library has on the subject. Gerke first searched under the heading *Educational psychology;* a cross-reference sent her to *Educational tests and measurements,* under which she found this list of other possible headings:

Ability—testing

Character tests

Examinations

Grading and marking (students)

High school placement test

Iowa tests of educational development

The subject heading directories cannot tell you which headings will fit your subject and which will not—you must determine that. Since most of us start off as novices in our subject, we must use our imaginations to decide which leads to follow. *Ability—testing* and *High school placement tests* were closer to Gerke's interest; *Character tests* and *Grading and marking (students)* did not seem relevant. She could now return to the card catalog and see what books the library had under the headings she had chosen. More and more, she gravitated to tests and their effect on minorities. The process of going from reference works to catalogs to subject headings, and deciding which titles and subjects to follow and which not, can help narrow a subject.

When using the files and catalogs, be a sleuth. Follow leads. Trace connections between ideas. When you know a few names, check under the authors' listings to see if they have written other books on the subject. Check subject headings under major key words you find in your study—*testing, educational psychology.* And do not forget to complement your search for books with an equally vigorous search for articles in periodicals.

Periodical Catalogs and Guides

The library's periodical catalog lists all the newspapers, newsletters, magazines, journals, and other periodicals the library owns. College writers sometimes avoid periodicals, probably because the process of finding books seems more familiar and less complicated. Locating an article is occasionally more difficult than tracking down a book, but the rewards can be great. Periodicals are rich, varied research sources. Their articles focus on very specific topics. They carry the latest scholarship and debate: you cannot ignore them if you want to know what people are thinking or learning *now.*

You can locate the issues you want in a general or specialized periodical index. Recent issues will be out on the shelves in what is often called the periodical room. Older issues are usually bound and located in a special section of the library. Many libraries are now putting older periodicals on microfilm to save space. Learning to use material stored on microfilm is easy and well worth the effort.

Indexes of periodical sources may be either general—that is, covering a broadly defined area—or specific—that is, covering articles in a narrowly defined area. Some indexes even provide *abstracts,* brief summaries of the contents of articles.

GENERAL PERIODICAL INDEXES. General periodical indexes are invaluable directories to articles. They are organized in different ways, alphabetically or chronologically, but it will only take a moment to figure out the organization. Four extremely helpful general indexes are the *Essay and General Literature Index,* the *Newspaper Index,* the *New York Times Index,* and the *Readers' Guide to Periodical Literature.* Each of these sources contains a guide to its use and an explanation of the abbreviations employed. Find these helps and use them.

The *New York Times Index* is a traditional source for many research

projects on current events or recent history. In the 1975 volume of the
index, Gerke found one of her sources (see Figure 14.4). At first she had
looked under the heading *Scholastic Aptitude Test,* which referred her to the
heading *Colleges and Universities—United States—Grading of Students.* One
article listed there sounded promising. To find it she went to the microfilm
room of the library, got the spool that included the May 4, 1975, issue of
the *New York Times,* located the proper section, and read the article. She
thought the information well worth her search. She also checked under
the same heading in volumes for other years: 1979, 1980, and so forth. As
a rule of thumb, you should check under the same heading starting in
volumes for ten years in the past and work your way to the present.

The *Readers' Guide* is also a good starting point for research. It indexes articles in popular periodicals by year, by quarter, and by month,
and it lists articles by author and by subject. Be careful with it, though—

Figure 14.4 Entry from the New York Times Index

Main subject heading	**COLLEGES and Universities – United States – Finances – Cont** Nathan Kolodney disagrees with Prof Richard Gambino's remarks on Jews in Dec 8 article on high cost of coll educ, lr, D 20,26:5 NY Times survey of NYC's fiscal crisis notes leading social scientists see parallel between that plight and plight of univ; notes costs have spiraled for colls, and tuition often exceeds means of students, while full-time teaching load is 6-8 hours per week in many insts, with 4-month vacations; Yale Univ Prof Douglas Yates cites 'unconscious acceptance of past practice' (M), D 29,50:7
Subheadings and list of other relevant subheadings	●*Foreign Students.* **See** subhead Foreign Study ●*Fraternities and Sororities.* **See also** names Pres Ford on Dec 31 signs bill containing amendment following up regulation on sex discrimination in educ activities issued by HEW; measure exempts from provisions membership practices of tax-exempt social fraternities and sororities (S), Ja 1,36:4 ●*Grading of Students.* **See also** subhead US – Adult Education, Ag 3. Subhead US – Equal Educ, Ja 16. Subhead US – Student Activities, My 18

Author's name Detailed summary	Jackson never graduated from hs; NCAA official Bill Hunt comments on increased violation of acad rules; King illus (M), F 7,22:3; Diane Ravitch article explores history, theory, purpose, value and other aspects of Scholastic Aptitude Test (SAT), which will be given this yr to some 1.5-million hs srs seeking to enter coll; notes supporters of tests view them as reliable indicators for predicting coll performance, while critics contend tests are racially and culturally biased; some educators concede tests may be culturally biased to extent that reading is culturally linked; many colls are now giving weight to other factors, such as depth of preparation and unusual personal qualities, in admitting students; modifications expected in some aspects of tests but prospects for future is that testing, evaluation and assessment on national basis will be a regular and pervasive aspect of educ policy; samples of typical
Date, section of the paper, and page on which the article begins. Note: you must consult the article itself for the title and pagination.	questions from SAT exams; student taking exam illus (L), My 4.VI,p12; Mrs Charles M Apt lr on Diane Ravitch May 4 article on College Entrance Examination Bd holds manner in which exam dates are set militates against public school students; Ravitch replies; illus, Je 8,VI,p54; efforts on some coll campuses to do away with grade inflation, by

Figure 14.5 **Entry from the Readers' Guide to Periodical Literature**

Main subject heading ———————— **Educational tests and measurements**
——————————————— *See also*
Related subject headings ——————— Aptitude tests
Educational Testing Service
Intelligence tests
Scholastic aptitude test

Alternative ways to identify learning-disabled
children. R. A. Berk. Educ Dig 47:51-3 Mr '82
Are U.S. schools on the way up again? [rise in
achievement test scores] U S News World Rep
93:8 O 4 '82
Do aptitude tests encourage laziness? [compari-
son with achievement tests; views of Christopher Jencks and James Crouse] C. T. Cory.
Psychol Today 16:20+ F '82
Go to the head of the class [better public school
performance in reading and math test scores]
D. A. Williams, il Newsweek 100:64-5 O 4 '82

Title of article ——————— Is SAT a dirty word? [study by C. Jencks and
L. Crouse contrasting SATs with achievement
tests] D. A. Williams. il Newsweek 100:68 Jl
19 '82
Brief summary ——————— SAT and other test scores rise for first time in
19 years. Phi Delta Kappan 64:222 N '82
S.A.T.s aren't so smart [achievement tests vs.
SATs] A. Hulbert. New Repub 187:12+ D 20
Author, title of periodical,   '82
volume number, pages, ———— Should we relabel the SAT...or replace it? [ex-
date   cerpt from New directions for testing and
measurement; ed. by William Schrader] C.
Jencks and J. Crouse. bibl f Phi Delta Kappan
63:659-63 Je '82

not all the periodicals it covers are authoritative. Check the title of the
journal and the author's credentials (see "Recognizing Good Sources,"
page 342).

Gerke consulted the *Readers' Guide* for up-to-date entries on standardized testing. In the March 1982–February 1983 volume, for example,
she found a source (see Figure 14.5). First she looked under the heading
Aptitude tests, which referred her to the heading *Educational tests and measurements,* and there she saw an article with a possibly relevant title. Her
next step was to locate where older issues of *New Republic* magazine were
shelved in the library and look for the December 20, 1982, issue.

SPECIALIZED PERIODICAL INDEXES AND BIBLIOGRAPHIES. Specialized periodical indexes and bibliographies list articles and books in particular fields. They are a natural resource as your subject focus narrows and
you need more specific information. After using the general indexes, Gerke
consulted the *Social Sciences Index* and the *Education Index,* both of which
yielded further leads. Almost every field has an index; here are a few:

Applied Science and Technology Index

Art Index

Business Periodicals Index

General Science Index

Humanities Index

MLA International Bibliography

Guide to U.S. Government Publications

ABSTRACTS.   Abstracts list journal articles in specific fields and offer brief article summaries. Reading the summaries does not take the place of reading the articles, but the summaries do tell you whether an article is what you want. *Abstracts in Anthropology, Historical Abstracts, Psychological Abstracts,* and *Science Abstracts* are among the abstracts you may find helpful.

COMPUTERIZED CATALOGS.   Many if not most university and college libraries now have on-line catalogs that are quite user-friendly. Most of us are familiar with the computer terminals stationed throughout the library, those screens that guide even the most computer-illiterate user through the few steps needed to find a book or periodical. If what you seek is on the shelves, the on-line catalog can tell you its location in a couple of keystrokes. Often, you can search for a book by author, title, subject, or key word, and you can also call up lists of books by the same author, or with related titles, or on the same or similar subjects. A few libraries have similar catalogs for periodical articles. If your library has an on-line catalog and you have not already learned how to use it, do so. At many institutions, a student with a computer and modem can gain access to on-line catalogs by phone. Learn what your library has and how to use it.

COMPUTERIZED INDEXES.   Computerized indexes for newspapers and magazines are generally much easier to use than the old bound indexes. At the touch of a key, many will print out a list of useful sources.

DATA BASES.   A data base is a collection of highly specific information— for example, indexes, bibliographies, and bibliographic materials—in a highly specific field. For example, many libraries now own the *Modern Language Association Bibliography,* a data base that lists the research done on major world literary topics, including writers and their works, since 1966. A student doing a research project on, for example, *Romeo and Juliet* might go to the research librarian, who would then use the *MLA Bibliographic Index* to obtain a printout of citations of all the books and articles written on that play in the past twenty years. That list would be huge, and the student wouldn't be able to use all of it—but with it he or she would have begun to compile a working bibliography.

Similar data bases exist for research in nearly every major field of study. Libraries now purchase data bases just as they do books; many libraries have a separate catalog for them. Some libraries charge a fee for using them, while at others you can gain access through your computer and modem. Consult your research librarian for details on your library's holdings and how to use them.

Other Library Resources

We have been discussing the main reference works your library offers. These will doubtless be somewhere on your itinerary, but they do not exhaust the library's resources. Depending on your research, you may have many other places to visit, including the following five.

RECENT ACQUISITIONS LIST. Listings for recently purchased books and periodicals take a while to get into the library's catalogs. Thus, most libraries have separate up-to-date lists of relatively new materials, usually on computer printouts or microfiche. Consult these lists, especially if your topic concerns very recent events.

MICROFILM HOLDINGS. More and more libraries now own microfilm copies of old and rare books, newspapers, and public and private documents. Many, for example, own microfilms of books printed in English before 1640. Usually, the card in the author-title catalog will tell you if a work is on microfilm.

SPECIAL COLLECTIONS. Because some library collections are marked *special,* you may be intimidated. Don't be. The books are there to serve you, and some of them can be quite helpful. For instance, in writing a paper about the history of Boston, you may find that one of your library's special collections includes a privately printed booklet about one of the city's earliest merchant families. Materials in special collections may be listed either in the author-title catalog or in separate catalogs.

GOVERNMENT DOCUMENTS. Many libraries have a special area in which they house government documents, that is, publications by various state, federal, and foreign governments. These documents are not as dry or narrowly focused as they sound. The U.S. government, for example, publishes material on everything from international arms negotiations to how to collect honey from bees. The *Congressional Record* is an unsurpassed primary source for what goes on in the U.S. Congress. The government documents area is definitely worth a detour.

COMPUTER SEARCHES. Many libraries subscribe to local, state, national, and world computer information services. That means that if your library does not have the information you need, the reference librarian may be able to do a "computer search," which can either obtain a printout of the needed material or tell you the nearest place that owns it. Other services can suggest books on the same or a related subject; still others can give you cross-references along with related subject listings. As of this writing, most libraries charge a fee for a computer search. Again, make it your business to know what your library has and how to use it.

Computers have revolutionized the process of making preliminary bibliographic searches. But such searches are *only* preliminary. Nothing takes the place of checking the stacks, paging through promising sources, and scanning recent periodicals.

Being Your Own Source

You need not limit yourself to material you can find in libraries. You can also generate your own primary source information, and some of it can be quite exciting. Here are six examples.

INTERVIEWS.   You can interview people involved with your subject. Ask them about their experiences and what they know. One report on the social organization of a local Quaker congregation included interviews with elders and members.

There is an etiquette to interviewing. First, ask your interviewee if you may use a tape recorder. Taping the interview can save time and allow you to devote more attention to the interview and less to taking notes. When you conduct an interview, do not waste time; have your questions written out in advance. Always offer to let interviewees listen to the tape later, or better yet, read a typed transcript of the interview. These courtesies will allow them to verify what they have said and thus lend more authority to your evidence.

CORRESPONDENCE.   You often can get helpful information by writing to people involved with your topic, such as congressional representatives, your governor or mayor, or people in business, sports, or entertainment. If you write a respectful, serious letter, the results can be surprising. One memorable research project on the Mercury astronauts was based in part on correspondence with John Glenn, Wally Schirra, and Alan Shepard. Be sure to leave ample time for an answer to your letter.

POLLS.   One of our favorite essays included polls measuring audience response to three different performances of Henrik Ibsen's play *Hedda Gabler*. Unfortunately, polls are easy to get wrong. If you do not have experience with them, consult a friend or teacher who does. The better the instrument, the better the data. (For a brief discussion of polling, see Chapter 7, Using Evidence.)

FIELDWORK.   Some researchers can go right out into the field to collect information. For a research paper on Indian burial grounds in the San Francisco Bay area, one student visited an archaeological excavation on the site of a planned subway station. Eventually, he started digging himself.

EXPERIMENTS.   Much writing in the natural and social sciences is based on experiments the writer has conducted. To test extrasensory perception, a student designed a set of cards and asked all the students on his dorm floor to identify what was on the hidden side of each card. He analyzed the responses, and then, disappointed to learn that only chance was operating, he valiantly wrote up the experiment anyway.

OTHER PERSONAL EXPERIENCES.   You can do research on your own experience or background. Did your family name change when your ancestors came to America? You could discuss when and how it changed in a paper on immigration history. Have you ever had to testify in court? Your experience could contribute to a paper on the legal system.

Personal experience has both its own authority and its own limitations. When using it, work especially hard for objectivity and relevance. You should be at least as careful when you are your own source as when you use library research. For a brief discussion of personal experience as evidence, see Chapter 7.

LIMITING YOUR AREA OF RESEARCH

As you learn more and more about your subject, you will begin to see how it divides into parts. This will suggest ways to narrow the subject to exactly what you want to research.

One of the leading killers of research projects is an overly large topic. If you take on too much, you will not be able to shape your material effectively. If you neglect the research necessary to cover the topic, your ideas will lack the background or support they need. Your paper will be as deep as a teacup. You should aim to work on a topic *small enough to cover well but challenging enough to be worth covering.*

After Christina Gerke had scouted the reference books, the card catalog, and the periodical indexes, she saw that her topic, *minorities and the educational system,* was far too broad. She brainstormed a list of attractive aspects of the subject.

> affirmative action in colleges
> busing
> changing populations in city schools
> Supreme Court decisions on minorities in education
> incorporating minority views into history
> the effects of standardized testing

She paused there. While compiling her working bibliography, she had discovered that standardized tests were a hot issue. People argued about what the tests measured, how they were designed, and what effects they had on future careers. There was obviously a good deal more to learn about testing, particularly about its effects on minorities.

By eliminating some possibilities and focusing more intently on others, Gerke narrowed her topic this way:

> Recent changes in American society
>> Minorities and recent changes in American society
>>> Minorities and the educational system
>>>> Standardized tests and their effects on minorities

Cutting subjects down to a workable size is essential. Let's return to our examples from early in the chapter and hone them further.

> Soviet-American relations and Russian dissidents
>> Andrey Sakharov's influence on Soviet-American relations
>>> Sakharov's return from exile and its effect on Soviet-American relations
> American short fiction in the 1920s
>> Women and American short fiction in the 1920s
>>> Women writers of short fiction and the American magazine industry in the 1920s

These topics are now limited to a manageable size for a research project.

As you read more and narrow your subject further, you no doubt will begin to identify controversies to be settled, causes to be traced, patterns to be explained, questions to be answered. While you consider the possibilities, ask yourself a series of questions about your direction and focus.

> Do I like this topic?
> Do I feel in control of it?
> Do I have enough time to do thorough research on it?
> Will I be able to find out enough about it in the sources available to me?
> Will I find adequate support for my ideas?

Is the topic appropriate for the assigned length?

Is it too elementary?

Is it too technical?

Is it worth my while?

Will it interest my audience?

Know the answers to these questions before you write. Early in the project, your instructor may advise you on some of them.

FORMULATING A TENTATIVE THESIS

At this point, a tentative thesis can help you organize your thoughts and direct your research. A tentative thesis in a research project is like a working hypothesis in a scientific experiment. It is the "idea" the research will examine, so it serves as the basis for further investigation.

You may find it helpful to express your topic in the form of a question and your position as an answer. That answer can often be your tentative thesis. This is what Christina Gerke wrote:

QUESTION	In light of the effects of standardized tests on the careers of minority students, should educators continue to use the tests?
ANSWER	We should do away with standardized tests because they perpetuate prejudice against minorities.

Gerke was fully aware that her ideas might change. Her thesis was truly tentative; by the end of the research process, she would very likely discard, change, or modify it.

Stating a narrowed topic as a question will often produce a workable tentative thesis statement, as it could for the Soviet-American relations and twentieth-century American fiction project.

QUESTION	Has the return from exile of Andrey Sakharov affected Soviet-American relations?
ANSWER	Sakharov's return has been ignored by American policymakers because they don't trust Mikhail Gorbachev's *glasnost*.
QUESTION	Was short fiction by women an important factor in the American magazine industry in the 1920s?
ANSWER	Short fiction by women did not greatly influence the economics of the American magazine industry in the 1920s.

At this stage, don't lock yourself into a set proposition. The intensive search you are about to undertake may—probably will—uncover facts and opinions that will make you change your ideas. Further research would show, for instance, that women writers *were* economically important to the American magazine industry in the 1920s. Welcome the opportunity to change your thesis as the material guides you.

We have so far been discussing the tentative thesis with an argumentative edge. Some research assignments, however, only want you to gather information and report it. Your report will still need an organizing thesis to give shape to your research. (For a full discussion of the organizing thesis for a report, see Chapter 16, The Report.)

READING AND TAKING NOTES

Back to the library, tentative thesis in mind.

Here among the stacks, you will now read more intensively, collecting evidence to support, or correct, your tentative thesis. Don't stint on gathering information. Search the stacks. When your research leads you to a book with a particular call number, look also at the books around it on the shelf. Perhaps they too will be promising sources. Page through a few books and evaluate them. Flip through your bibliography cards. Look for other books by the same authors. Follow interesting leads. Chase ideas through periodicals. Collect the details of your subject, the uncommon facts, the competing theories. Whenever possible, trace all references back to their original sources. You probably will not use everything you amass, but the more you know, the more confidence you can have when you sit down to write.

Recognizing Good Sources

A kind of reasonable panic may set in at this point. "I'm going to have 3,000 notecards! It could take weeks just to write everything down. How can I decide which materials are authoritative and which I can leave alone?"

Excellent question. Not all your sources are going to be good ones. Some will be popularizations, summaries, quick-and-easy presentations of topics you need to read about in depth. To sort out the useful from the fallible, test each book or article you find in these five ways.

RELIABILITY OF THE AUTHOR. Ask yourself whether you have seen the author's name in other references. Check his or her background in a biographical or bibliographic index. Consult the *Book Review Digest* for reactions to his or her writings. Ask the reference librarian or your instructor for help.

QUALITY OF THE PERIODICAL OR PUBLISHING HOUSE. Try to get a sense of which periodicals are truly authoritative for your topic. *Time* magazine offers mostly glossy and simplified versions of events. A *Time* account of recent heart transplant techniques would not be nearly as detailed and reliable as one in the *New England Journal of Medicine. Scientific American* is a respected science magazine, but it is hardly as authoritative as the more scholarly *Nature.* For books, assess the publishing house. Is it a university press or one of the well-established trade houses? Have you heard of it before? Have you seen it in other references? Again, ask your reference librarian or your instructor.

CURRENCY OF THE MATERIAL. Check dates of all sources. With most topics, especially current issues, you will want sources as up-to-date as you can find. Suppose your topic is the economy of Pakistan. Pakistani politics and external relations are changing so rapidly, few books more than five years old will be authoritative. Some topics, of course, have standard references that are quite old. Sir James Frazer's *The Golden Bough,* for instance, is still a classic source in anthropology, although it was first published in 1907. But even in a relatively established field, such as Elizabethan drama, most authoritative studies are less than thirty years old. If a source seems out of date, look for newer material.

COMPLETENESS OF THE PRESENTATION. Look for both detail and comprehensiveness. Do not rely wholly on summaries. Prefer Professor Y's original journal article to a brief excerpt from her informal talk to high-school students. For clues to the completeness of a book or article, check the title and subtitles, the length, the table of contents, chapter headings and subheadings, the bibliography, and the index.

SLANT OR BIAS. Some sources have a bias arising from politics, nationality, the methods of research used, or the sponsors of the study. Books or articles out of the conservative Hoover Institution or the Heritage Foundation may have a different slant from those out of the liberal Brookings Institution or Common Cause. We are not suggesting that you should ignore works from these organizations. That would be foolish, for they can be useful and scholarly. But whatever you consult, be alert to bias. Read prefatory chapters carefully: authors sometimes bring their affiliations and their prejudices to light at the beginning of a work. Notice the tone: does it seem judicious? Look also for a balance between opinion and substantiation. Is opinion clearly and consistently distinguished from fact? If so, the source may be a responsible one; if not, you should have your doubts.

Taking Notes

Never sit down with any source unless you are prepared to take notes. Taking notes on what you read serves two purposes: it helps you store information for easy recall, and it helps you organize your essay. You will reap these benefits only if you gather and arrange your notes carefully. Review Chapter 5, Critical Reading, and apply the principles there to any source on which you take notes. As always, read critically.

We all have our own ways of taking notes, and no system in this or any other book can guarantee brilliant results. The following suggestions, however, have worked well for many people.

Take notes on notecards. Although some people use sheets of paper when they take notes, we think notecards are a more efficient way to store information. They are flexible: you can move them around in a pack as you wish, and, as you will see, you can group them to help you shape your essay. Unlike bibliography cards, which contain factual information about the works consulted, notecards remind you of the *content* of sources.

Whenever you find something interesting or significant—a quotation, an idea, a piece of information, a reference, a picture, a statistic, a graph—make a note of it on a notecard. Develop notecards on all the books and articles you consult in any depth.

Use one card for each major point. Avoid covering cards with too many notes; otherwise you will not be able to file them efficiently. It is much better to make a separate notecard for each point. In the upper-left corner, write the author's name. In the upper-right corner, write the topic of the note in a key word or short phrase. Never forget to write down the *exact* page numbers on which the noted material appears: you may well need to find your way back to important information, you may well need page numbers for documentation later. In the notecard in Figure 14.6, Christina Gerke used the key phrase *minority performance.*

File each notecard under the key word or phrase. As you accrue notes, you will be compiling stacks of cards on the various aspects of your subject. They will all be together when you need them. Under each key word or phrase, alphabetize your notecards by the author's last name. If the author is anonymous, use the first word of the title of the source. This will be helpful later when you want quick access to specific points; you can go directly to the exact spot in the stack.

Keep your cards grouped together with rubber bands. You may want to use different colors or sizes of cards to keep notecards separate from bibliography cards. Three-by-five-inch cards will be adequate for bibliog-

Figure 14.6 Key Phrase Notecard

Berk   Minority Performance

183-184: minority students give answers
          that are right for them but
          show up wrong on tests

raphy cards, but use four-by-six-inch cards for notes, because they have more room. Edit your notes frequently—that is, delete old or useless sources often.

There is no rule for how many notecards are enough, though you can usually tell when your research is skimpy. An old high-school rule of thumb says, with some reason, that forty is a lower limit for a ten-page paper. It is not unusual, however, to get into the hundreds. Do not be afraid of a rich supply.

What kinds of notes should you take? You have three choices, and you should probably use them all:

> *quotation*—a precise, word-for-word rendering of the author's original statement
>
> *paraphrase*—a rendering that follows the order and emphasis of the author's original statement but puts it in your own words
>
> *summary*—a concise, condensed presentation of the essentials of the author's original statement.

QUOTATION.   Sometimes an author will make a point with such eloquence or authority that you will want to write down the exact words. Don't misquote. Carefully spell and punctuate exactly as the author did. Note the page numbers; put quotation marks around the material. If you decide you do not need the entire quotation, indicate where you have omitted any words (see "Integrating Quotations into Your Text"). After you complete the transcription, check your card against the text. This may seem slow, but it will save you grief later.

Sometimes you will quote a passage because of its particular aptness or authoritativeness. In an article by George F. Madaus, Gerke found a passage that expressed fears similar to her own about standardized tests.

> The more one knows about the technology of testing, the more one realizes the potential for harm when a test score is used as the sole or primary criterion on which to make an important decision affecting an individual's future.

She had already made a bibliography card for Madaus, so now she made a notecard on which she quoted this passage exactly (see Figure 14.7).

At other times you may wish to quote a passage because of the way in which it is phrased, for the language as well as the content. While reading Andrew J. Strenio's *The Testing Trap,* Gerke found a passage that she knew immediately was worth writing down word for word. Strenio was arguing that many people have the right skills for a job yet would do poorly on a standardized test on such skills.

> Can't you just see Richard Petty asking an applicant for one of his racing crews to take a standardized test on internal combustion engines? Or Red Auerbach telling Larry Bird to quit the Celtics until he scores well on a standardized test about passing lanes in basketball?

Right away she made a bibliography card and a notecard with the quotation on it.

If the material you are quoting is lengthy, you may wish to photocopy it—especially if you can't take the source out of the library, as with noncirculating journals, reference books, and special collections materials.

Figure 14.7   Quoted Passage Notecard

> Madaus   "Effects of Tests"
>
> "The more one knows about the technology of testing, the more one realizes the potential for harm when a test score is used as the sole or primary criterion on which to make an important decision affecting an individual's future."
>
> (93)

Photocopying can save you hours of copying by hand. Make sure to record all the information you'll need to document the source you're copying. Record this information both on a bibliography card and at the top of the first page of the photocopied material.

Photocopying has three important limitations. First, the cost of photocopying can add up. Second, copyright laws govern the amount of material you may photocopy and the purpose for which you may use it. The library staff should know the laws and be able to advise you. Third, photocopying only lets you take the material with you—it is no substitute for thinking and taking careful notes.

Quote only when the elegance, forcefulness, or authority of the author's original words is absolutely essential. When *what* the author says is more important than *how* the author says it, you may wish to paraphrase or summarize.

PARAPHRASE.   Use paraphrase whenever

> an idea or passage seems important but the exact wording is not essential
>
> a good idea is couched in difficult language.

Paraphrase is a useful way to make an author's ideas accessible to a reader. Paraphrasing information is also useful to you in two ways. First, it helps you get a handle on the material and preserve your understanding. Second, because the paraphrase is already in your own words, you can easily work it into your first draft. It represents much of the analysis and context that your final paper will offer.

A good paraphrase must be faithful to the content and order of the original while being expressed in completely different language. Therefore, when paraphrasing, follow the author's thought closely but recast it in your own words; your version will be about as long as the original. But it will probably take longer to write a paraphrase than it will to quote the original because paraphrase includes analysis and translation.

In her research, Gerke read a particular passage that struck her as important.

> The systematic testing of school children that began in Britain in the early years of the present century was closely linked with an influential eugenics movement, primarily motivated by a fear of uncontrolled fertility and inherited intellectual inadequacy in the poorer classes. The preferred solutions to what in those days was seen as a potential threat to the race were usually birth control and sterilization. (Frank Smith, *Insult to Intelligence: The Bureaucratic Invasion of Our Classrooms*)

Gerke liked the point but did not feel that the language merited direct quotation. So she wrote her own version (see Figure 14.8). To see the

Figure 14.8   Paraphrased Passage Notecard for Smith Passage

Smith   Insult

Testing began in Britain early in the twentieth
century because of a eugenics movement that
was founded on the idea that the poorer
classes were inferior and that the growth
of these classes threatened the purity of the
upper classes. The spread of such
inferiority could be checked by birth
control and sterilization.   (132–133)

difference between quoting and paraphrasing, look at Figure 14.9, which shows how the Madaus material in Figure 14.7 might have been recorded if Gerke had decided to paraphrase instead of quote.

Do not let the author's language sneak into your paraphrase. If, however, you are struck by a phrase of the author's, jot it down at the bottom of the card but enclose the phrase in quotation marks. Include exact page references for all paraphrases.

Figure 14.9   Paraphrased Passage Notecard for Madaus Passage

Madaus   "Effects of Tests"

Test scores have the potential to hurt
students when educators use the
scores as the only or the most
important basis for making decisions
that can influence the students'
futures.   (93)

SUMMARY. If you don't think you will need the author's exact words or an extensive paraphrase, summarize your findings. Summary fits meaning into a smaller space; it is the art of distilling the essential. You might condense a whole paragraph into a few words, a whole page or section into one or two sentences. Good summaries are accurate (they faithfully represent the main points), comprehensive (they don't miss any main points), and independent (they do not rely on the original at all for order, emphasis, or wording). They concentrate exclusively on meaning.

The author of the original must define terms and provide illustrations, prove or explain ideas; however, the summary captures only the main ideas in as few words as possible. This may require combining snippets of ideas from different parts of a passage. It most certainly will require ignoring interesting details. Carefully edit out the following:

illustrations

quotations

lengthy explanations

definitions

elegant phrasings

speculation on side issues

digressions

repetitions

hemmings and hawings

Here is an example of a writer summarizing a passage.

lengthy
xplanation

illustration

~~One difference between war and football~~, ~~though, is that~~ there is little or no protest against football. ~~Perhaps the most extraordinary thing about the game is~~ that the systematic infliction of injuries excites in people not concern, ~~as would be the case if they were sustained at, say, a rock festival~~, but a collective rejoicing and euphoria. ~~Players and fans alike revel in the spectacle of a combatant felled into semiunconsciousness, "blindsided," "clotheslined," or "decapitated." I can remember, in fact, being chided by a coach in pro ball for not "getting my hat" injuriously into a player who was already lying helpless on the ground. (On another occasion, after the Stampeders had~~

another
lengthy
illustration

~~traded the celebrated Joe Kapp to BC, we were play-~~
~~ing the Lions in Vancouver and Kapp was forced on~~
~~one play to run the ball. He was coming "down the~~
~~chute," his bad knee wobbling uncertainly, so I sim-~~
~~ply dropped on him like a blanket. After I returned~~
~~to the bench I was reproved for not exploiting the~~
~~opportunity to unhinge his bad knee.)~~ (John Mc-
Murtry, "Kill 'Em! Crush 'Em! Eat 'Em Raw!")

SUMMARY

Football players are encouraged to inflict as
much injury as possible, and no one complains.

McMurtry's original is intelligent, humorous, and horrifying, but in this
case the main idea counted most, and a sentence was enough.

For one method of writing a summary, see ''The Précis'' in Chapter
16. Figure 14.10 shows how the notecard might look had Gerke summarized the Madaus passage in Figure 14.7. Be sure to indicate on your
notecard exactly where you found the summarized material: you may decide to go back to get the precise language, and in any case you want your
reader to know where you found the information.

We discuss plagiarism in more detail under ''Documenting Your

Figure 14.10   Summary Notecard

Madaus   "Effects of Tests"

The use of test scores to determine
students' futures is potentially
harmful.
                                        (93)

Sources" in Chapter 15. Here we want to point out that good notes can protect you from that worst of academic problems. Record all information accurately. Put quotation marks around *all* quoted material. Identify whatever you paraphrase or summarize. If while taking notes you get your own idea on the same subject, write your idea on the same notecard, but put it in brackets or write it with a different colored pen. Don't intermingle your thoughts and the original. That would create trouble.

Using the Computer

This section is for those of you with word processors. We know we cannot cover everything computers do; these lovely machines can be very useful tools for research. Although they will be most important when you start writing, they can come into play at almost every stage of research.

STORING NOTES. Computers are excellent places to keep your notes. Some programs can alphabetize for you, and some can find your note in a split second when you give them a key word. They can also store important passages and your reactions to them. If you get more ideas later, you can always insert them. You can also highlight key words, phrases, or passages that you may want to use later. And typing, unlike handwriting, is rarely illegible. Smearing and destruction by fingers and food are hazards foreign to the well-maintained word processor. Of course, computers can't replace cards in all respects—especially if your instructor requires that notecards be handed in with the completed paper. Still, if you write your papers on a word processor, storing your notes on it could save you a great deal of work.

Don't forget the three cardinal rules of word processing:

1. Save your work often, every fifteen to twenty minutes. This is an extremely useful superstition.
2. Make backup copies of your work on a separate disk.
3. Never forget to follow rules 1 and 2.

DOCUMENTATION. You can also build your list of works cited on the computer. Programs such as Nota Bene can build one for you as you go. If your program does not have such a feature, do it yourself. Each time you use a source extensively, make a complete entry for it in a file named, let us say, LIST. Put the entry at the correct alphabetical position. By the time you have finished your research, you should have a fairly complete bibliography. Paring it down to your actual list of works cited is as easy as a delete command. Print out a draft of your list of works cited to check for completeness and accuracy—most researchers forget to enter one or two sources. Then you can add your list of works cited to the end of the file that contains your paper.

Some word-processing programs, such as Word and WordPerfect, can also make footnotes and endnotes automatically. Know what features your program has for handling notes and references.

RESTATING YOUR THESIS

Now you are back from the stacks with plenty of notes and a much better understanding of your topic. You should be able to tell at this point whether your tentative thesis needs modifying. The temptation will be strong to ignore contrary or qualifying evidence and start writing immediately. Beware: do not defend a thesis that should be changed. Instead, interrogate it in the light of your research.

Do you still believe it?

Does your research amply support it?

Should you modify it in any way?

In the light of her research, Christina Gerke had begun to question her tentative thesis, which had been

We should do away with standardized tests because they perpetuate prejudice against minorities.

This statement now seemed to her too extreme. Her research did not fully support it. After her reading she thought that some tests had value and that the bias in them was often accidental. During her research she had asked herself more probing questions, such as *Why* are the tests harmful to minorities? And from her reading she had developed an answer: they are harmful because a low score on a test can determine much of a person's future. Her revised thesis shows how research had refined her ideas.

Standardized tests often shape the course of people's lives, not to mention their self-image and their society's image of them. Since there is still so much controversy about standardized tests, employers and institutions should place less emphasis on test performance as a criterion for admissions and hiring and more on aptitude and personal characteristics.

Gerke had gone from an ill-defined general feeling to a refined and arguable thesis, one that mattered to her and would guide a rich essay.

Examine your thesis, write it out, and be sure it is clear. If you are in doubt, state it to someone else. The response should tell you a great deal. Be sure it is worth arguing. Be sure you have time and space to do it justice. Take time to reconsider the thesis at least once during each day of work.

PREPARING AN OUTLINE

You and your project are still together after all these trials. Now you have a thesis and a mass of research to mold into some shape. A first step toward that goal is to make an outline. This will help you in three ways.

It will put your argument or exposition down on paper for the first time.

It will force you to organize and develop your material.

It will carry you a long way toward your completed essay.

Think of your outline as an opportunity to combine each of your ideas with relevant evidence or background and to place each idea in its proper relation to your other points.

To devise an effective outline, you should have completed your research and have your notecards stacked in order, your authorities and accurate quotations at your elbow. Now is the time to think carefully about your approach to the subject.

First, go through all your notecards. Note which topics have grown largest. Make a scratch list of the main points that emerge. Try arranging your notes into piles according to these important topics. Look for a natural form for your discussion. If the organization "wants" to go in a certain direction, follow it and see how it works. Think about where you might employ different strategies: description, process analysis, cause and effect, comparison and contrast, definition (see Chapter 9, Strategies for Developing Your Thoughts). Determine what will be the crucial parts of your paper. Write out a few trial outlines.

Christina Gerke decided to begin her paper with general background on standardized tests, move to an overview of the controversy, and then present her thesis. Later, she could treat the debate in more detail and present one test—the Scholastic Aptitude Test—as a case study. Her outline, which appears just before her paper in the next chapter (see pp. 394–397), reflects these decisions.

For an assignment as large as a research paper we recommend that you devise a formal outline—that is, an outline that presents the shape and direction of your paper as exactly as possible. Choose either a phrase outline that identifies in short phrases the topics your paper will cover, or a sentence outline that makes a statement in a complete sentence about each topic. (See Chapter 2, Putting Words on Paper, for a full discussion of outlining.) Many instructors require that students submit an outline at some stage of research, so be sure you know what is expected of you.

Once you have made your outline, go back to your notecards. Working by the topic key words and phrases, organize your cards according to the outline. If a note pertains to your conclusion, it belongs on the bottom of the pile; if it pertains to your introduction, it belongs near the top. Once you have your notes in order, reading through them ought to be like surveying a compressed version of your paper. Do not worry about having too much material. As writing proceeds, you can decide which pieces of support you need most. It is far easier to cut excess material than it is to search for new sources at the last moment.

The research project's most important elements—organization, argument, evidence—should all be there when you finish a good outline. Even now, much about your outline may be provisional. Problems may stick out. You may see that one part needs more work or that one of your main points is out of place. Many writers find it painful to sit down, bash out the shape of the argument, and arrange all the evidence without writing the paper at the same time. But correcting problems in an outline is more efficient than trying to fix a finished product. A little work ahead of time will make things easier later.

WRITING A FIRST DRAFT

Once you have an outline and notecard order that seem to work, you are ready to begin writing your first draft. With something as complex as a research paper, you won't get everything right—ideas, references, commas—the first time. The whole point of the first draft is to be flexible. You may find, for example, that your outline, so painstakingly thought out, doesn't work in all parts. Some of your most cherished ideas may go up in smoke. Some may require more research. You may even need a different thesis, a whole new approach. Take all such discoveries with good humor: the purpose of a first draft is to help you figure out what you want and need to say. Nothing characterizes research more than global revisions at every stage.

Two issues will be especially important to you at this stage: using your evidence and integrating different sources.

Using Your Evidence

In an argumentative project, your ideas make your paper go; they make it new and worth reading. But assertion of opinion—no matter how brilliantly phrased or original—is not enough. You must show how you arrived at your ideas, or why they are justified. That is why you did all that research. When you provide appropriate evidence, you allow your reader to make an educated decision about the validity of your argument.

Let your reader review all the evidence. Don't suppress information contrary to your thesis. Presenting the opposition and responding to it can only strengthen your argument. (For a discussion of how to construct a complete argument, see Chapter 6, Writing to Persuade.)

In the section on note taking, we discussed the differences among quoting, paraphrasing, and summarizing. Here we discuss when and how to incorporate these techniques into a paper.

QUOTATION.   When should we include quotations in essays? Here is what a great language expert says:

> A writer expresses himself in words that have been used before because they give his meaning better than he can give it himself, or because they are beautiful or witty, or because he expects them to touch a chord of association in his reader, or because he wishes to show that he is learned and well read. Quotations due to the last motive are invariably ill-advised. (H. W. Fowler, *A Dictionary of Modern English Usage*)

Almost all research contains quoted material because it is such good evidence. For example, quotations can help you amplify or clarify a point, as this one does:

```
Baseball players have an unusual approach to lan-
guage, as in Yogi Berra's famous line, "The game
isn't over till it's over" (Bartlett 903).
```

In the examples given here, the parenthetical reference after the quotation follows the Modern Language Association's system for documenting sources. Other systems of documentation are discussed in the first appendix.

Or quotations can prove a specific point or attach weight to a theory or opinion, as this one does:

```
As the complexities of nuclear policy grow, it be-
comes more and more difficult to decide which infor-
mation is good and which is propaganda.  As one stu-
dent of international politics wrote, "Reality in
the nuclear age tends to become what people whose
voices carry say it is" (Newhouse 41).
```

If you are using a short quotation, you can include it in the text, enclosed in quotation marks.

```
Perhaps it would be best for everyone to follow Wil-
liam Least Heat Moon's advice and "Beware thoughts
that come in the night" (3).
```

When you have quotations of more than four lines, however, make them easier to read by setting them off from the text, indented ten spaces from the left margin, double-spaced, and without quotation marks, as Christina Gerke does in this passage:

> Sometimes it is difficult to ascertain exactly what qualities the tests actually measure. Scientists do not yet agree on a single definition of the word <u>intelligence</u>, for example, and as the meaning of the word changes, so do the tests that try to measure it ("Brave New World"). Furthermore, a test item designed to measure one ability may actually test different abilities in different people. This accidental shifting can occur in something as simple as a spelling test, as John R. Bormuth explains:
>> Asking for the spelling of a given word may require a student who was previously drilled on the word merely to recite from rote memory a string of letters but require a student who was not taught this word to analyze it into syllables and phonemes and then to apply his phonics knowledge to the task. (23)
> Consequently, a test item aimed at a specific ability (phonics knowledge) tested something quite different (ability to memorize).

Note that Gerke does not sprinkle her work with unexplained quotations; she shows the reader the reason for her reference. She makes clear how the quotation supports her opinion.

INTEGRATING QUOTATIONS INTO YOUR TEXT. When you are using a writer's words, you must be careful to fit those words into your own writing. Here are four suggestions on how to integrate quotations gracefully into your own text.

1. *Give the source's full name when you first refer to that source.* No acknowledgment is clearer than the kind you make in the text itself. In-

clude the person's credentials if possible. Gerke did just that in a passage from her research paper.

> For example, Harvard University's Arthur Jensen,
> noted and controversial critic of standardized
> tests, claims that the overall difference between
> whites and blacks is 15 points, and the gap between
> rich and poor is 12 points (44).

Jensen is surely a big name in the field. Mentioning his name and credentials added authority to her evidence.

2. When possible, give some background to your quotations. Transition from your text to quoted material and back will be easier if you suggest the topic of the coming quotation.

> Against those who charged that women had not proven
> themselves especially virtuous, Mary Wollstonecraft
> Shelley wrote, "It is vain to expect virtue from
> women until they are in some degree independent of
> men."

3. Fit quotations into the grammatical structure of your sentence. A quotation that doesn't fit is as awkward as if you had made the error yourself. Note the difference between the following examples:

ORIGINAL PASSAGE

Black women are called, in the folklore that so aptly identifies one's status in society, "the *mule* of the world," because we have been handed the burdens that everyone else—*everyone* else—refused to carry. [Alice Walker, "In Search of Our Mothers' Gardens," *The Norton Anthology of Literature by Women,* ed. Sandra M. Gilbert and Susan Gubar. New York: Norton, 1985: 2378]

AWKWARD QUOTATION

> Today, according to Alice Walker, the black woman
> "are called, in the folklore that so aptly identi-
> fies one's status in society, 'the mule of the
> world'" (2378).

In this instance the writer's subject (*woman*) does not agree with Walker's verb (*are*). Such problems are usually easy to correct. Here are four ways to fit your sources' words in with your own.

a. Change your sentence structure to fit the quotation.

```
Alice Walker's view of the plight of the black woman
is clear: "Black women are called, in the folklore
that so aptly identifies one's status in society,
'the mule of the world'" (2378).
```

b. Use only a part of the quotation.

```
Today, according to Alice Walker, the black woman is
called "'the mule of the world'" (2378).
```

c. Change or add material in the quotation by using brackets. Brackets tell the reader that you are adding words of your own to clarify the quotation or smooth the transition between it and your own prose.

```
According to Alice Walker, the black woman has been
taken for granted "because [she has] been handed the
burdens that everyone else--everyone else--refused
to carry" (2378).
```

d. Delete words from the quotation by using ellipses. (See "Ellipses" in Chapter 21.)

```
        Alice Walker explains that "black women are
called . . . 'the mule of the world'" (2378).
```

Use brackets and ellipses sparingly. If you change too much, the quotation will no longer be a quotation.

```
Alice Walker claims that "black [people, especially
American black women] have been . . . 'the mule of
the world [which is really the same thing as being a
woman anyway]'" (2378).
```

4. *Identify and introduce quotations, smoothly; use a variety of methods.* There are plenty of acceptable and elegant ways to work a quotation into a sentence. Here are four ways you should master.

INTRODUCTION AND COLON

```
Alice Walker identifies one main reason black women
have been denigrated in folklore: "we have been
```

```
handed the burdens that everyone else--everyone
else--refused to carry" (2378).
```

INTRODUCTORY PHRASE

```
According to Alice Walker, black women have "been
handed the burdens that everyone else--everyone
else--refused to carry" (2378).
```

Other introductory phrases include "In Alice Walker's view," "For Alice Walker," and so forth.

SUBORDINATION USING *THAT*

```
In the face of racism and antifeminism, Walker de-
clares that "black women have been called . . . 'the
mule of the world'" (2378).
```

The word *that* subordinates the rest of the sentence. The same thing goes for quotations as well. When using *that* as a way into a quotation, you may lowercase the first letter of the quoted material whether or not that material begins a complete sentence.

INTERRUPTED QUOTATION

```
"We have been handed the burdens," declares Walker,
"that everyone else--everyone else--refused to
carry" (2378).
```

Here is a very experienced book reviewer using quotation confidently and with great variety. He is quoting from the American poet Wallace Stevens's journal entries about Stevens's hometown of Reading, Pennsylvania. Note how smoothly the writer has interwoven his own commentary with Stevens's original.

> Coming home from Harvard for Christmas of 1898, he wrote in his journal, "The city was smoky and noisy but the country depths were prodigiously still. . . . Coming home I saw the sun go down behind a veil of grime." The journal entries balloon when he is back in Berks: "Country sights both purge and fill up your fancy," he notes, and says, having described a raindrop slipping from leaf to leaf of a clematis vine, that "it was certainly a monstrous pleasure to be able to be specific about such a thing." Paragraphs are devoted to local botany and atmospheric effects; he ends one entry "Salut au Monde!" and another "The splendor is almost too great: things seem a little overdressed, a little overdone."

(John Updike, "The Heaven of an Old Home," review of *Souvenirs and Prophecies*)

PARAPHRASE.   If a paper contains excessive quotation, a reader will suspect that the writer has not fully digested the material, has few ideas of his or her own, or is showing off. Your instructor wants to know if you have understood the information and what you can do with it. A quotation may indicate that the information has been swallowed whole. A paraphrase means you've chewed the information.

You may need to help your reader understand difficult material. You have no doubt read much more of the author's work than your reader has, at least recently, and you have grown accustomed to the way the author presents ideas. Furthermore, you are more familiar with the context in which the material appears. Since you can't possibly reproduce the entire text, you need to break out the ideas and put them in language that doesn't require that context.

A paraphrase must be acknowledged—even though the words are yours, the ideas still belong to the author. To start a paraphrase by identifying the source provides a context and is a courtesy to the reader. No one wants to have to go back and reread in the light of a late-arriving source. If Gerke had used the paraphrase in Figure 14.9, she might have begun with, "As Madaus points out" or "According to Madaus." Or she might have begun the paraphrase but then seized an early opportunity to identify the source.

```
Test scores have the "potential" for hurting stu-
dents, so says George F. Madaus.  He believes
that . . .
```

Notice the quotation marks around "potential": any important word or phrase used in the original must be identified. To signal the end of the paraphrase, immediately cite the exact reference in a note.

SUMMARY.   Much of a research paper will be summary. In fact, such an essay could be viewed as an interpretation of a compendium of summaries sprinkled with quotation and paraphrase. You probably won't use quotations or paraphrases nearly so much as summaries. In some ways, summarizing ideas is more fraught with peril than quoting because it *seems* so easy that we become careless. We need to be as accurate in summary as in quotation. We don't want either to include false data or to create false impressions.

The nicest writing, of course, will have a feeling of seamlessness, the summary, the paraphrase, the quotation flowing into the text.

Integrating Different Sources

As you write, you may be pulling information from books, articles, and other sources much separated in time and different in style and point of view. One of the most delicate tasks in writing your first draft is that of weaving these various sources into your argument. Here are three tips on this process.

1. Make sure your sources exactly support your claim.
One student paper had the following passage:

Many researchers are in favor of teachers retiring
when they reach age sixty-five. According to the
National Bureau of Statistics, there are no teachers
over eighty-five now active in the United States
(123).

Interesting fact, but it does not really fit the claim. Putting the two together will confuse the reader. Resist the temptation to plug in a reference because it is "close" to your own thought. Close gets no cigar.

2. When you use more than one reference to back up a point, compare the references closely to make sure they truly agree.
In her first draft, Christina Gerke wrote this passage:

Another challenge points to the difficulty of ascertaining exactly what qualities the various standardized tests actually measure. Scientists do not yet
agree on a single definition of the word intelligence, for example, and, as the meaning of the word
changes, so do the tests that try to measure it
("Brave New World"). H. J. Eysenck, a prominent expert in the field of human intelligence, suggests
that since we lack a better definition, intelligence
is what is measured in IQ tests (78). It is also
possible that a test item designed to measure one
ability will in reality test different abilities in
different people.

Her first reference was indeed appropriate, but her second did not really agree with it. The paragraph treats the problem of "ascertaining exactly what qualities" the tests measure. Eysenck's quotation threatens to derail the paragraph into a discussion of how *intelligence* is defined. In the end Gerke decided to drop it, much as she wanted this expert to appear in her paper.

Some writers put in references out of desperation or the desire to appear informed. But you should never use a reference you don't need. Every reference should push your point forward, not merely add to what you have already established. Your instructor will be able to determine the quality of your research without padding.

3. Be sensitive to the way passages are worded, to the context from which you have taken material, and to the background and point of view of the author. If you weave together uneasy companions, the result will be a strange paragraph, one that may confuse the reader because its pieces of evidence do not follow directly from one another.

The following three suggestions should help you pick and choose among your sources:

Prefer the concrete—facts, statistics—to the general.

Choose firsthand accounts over second- and thirdhand ones.

Prefer recent sources to older ones.

As you add body and detail to the skeleton of your outline in your first draft, you may very well find—no surprises here—that you need to make further modifications. Enjoy your first draft, but treat it as the first version of what will eventually be a solid, polished piece of writing.

TIPS FOR DOING RESEARCH

- Choose a general subject that is both interesting and specific enough to cover adequately in your research paper.
- Know your library.
- Make a working bibliography as a basis for later research.
- Make your bibliography cards carefully to save yourself work later.
- After initial research has helped you narrow your topic, formulate a tentative thesis. Be ready to change your tentative thesis at any time.
- Read sources critically. Evaluate sources according to the reliability of the author, the quality of the periodical or publishing house, the currency of the material, the completeness of the presentation, and slant or bias.
- Take careful notes.

- Quote directly if a passage is unusually striking in aptness, authoritativeness, or phrasing.
- Paraphrase when the content of a passage is more important than the wording, or when an important idea is couched in difficult language.
- Summarize passages in which only the main points are essential.
- Restate your tentative thesis often.
- Prepare a formal outline for any extended research project.
- Use your evidence critically. Remember the criteria for good evidence and the rules of argument.
- Integrate quoted material smoothly with your own writing. Use a variety of methods to introduce quotations.

Exercises for Doing Research

1. The following is a treasure hunt. Find the answers to these questions by consulting the appropriate source in your library. When you have located each answer, report on how you found it and in what source. State what sent you to that source in the first place?

   What country produced the largest amount of chromium in 1968?
   What did movie critics say about *The Jazz Singer* when it first appeared?
   How did people do the Big Apple?
   How and when was Tanzania formed?
   Where did the word *swastika* come from?
   Who was the last man Don Larsen faced in his perfect game in the World Series, and how did Larsen get him out?
   Who was the second person to walk on the moon?
   What was a rumble seat?
   What was the latest in women's fashions in 1932?
   Why do some Americans say "Gosh!" and "Gee Whiz!"? When did these expressions originate?
   Which country has the oldest continuously operating form of government?
   What was the worst zeppelin crash in Europe's history?
   Name all the members of the present cabinet and report on what they did before becoming cabinet members.
   Who were the members of the Miles Davis Quintet, and why were they important?
   Does either Neptune or Uranus have any moons?
   Who were the leading man, leading lady, producer, and director of the film *You Gotta Stay Happy*? What was the plot?
   Name four cannibal tribes.

2. Look up one of the following names and give a short account of the person's life. Where did you find the information, and why did you go there?

Sigrid Undset
Napoleon Lajoie
Alessandro di Mariano Filipepi
H. Rap Brown
Yevgeny Yevtushenko
Le Corbusier

Walter Gropius
John Dewey
Bessie Smith
Harun al-Rashid
Bahaullah
William Wheeler

3. Find and present an example (through a recording, photocopy, still photograph, plot summary, short excerpt, or other means) of five of the
following. Discuss the creators and what makes the works distinctive.
Finally, discuss how you found your information. What sources did you
use?

a song by John Dowland
a painting by Jan van Eyck
a building by Frank Lloyd Wright
a photograph by Edward Steichen
a movie starring Ingrid Bergman
a newspaper article by Damon Runyon
an essay by Jessica Mitford
a discovery by Louis Pasteur

a statue by Constantin Brancusi
a mural by José Orozco
an invention by Thomas Edison
a theory by John Maynard Keynes
a discovery by L. S. B. Leakey
an essay by Julian Bond
a poem by Elizabeth Bishop
a study by Mary Douglas

4. Imagine that you are doing a research paper on the presidency of John
F. Kennedy. What would you take notes on in this passage? What
would you quote, paraphrase, or summarize? Why?

Kennedy was called an intellectual very seldom before 1960 and very often
thereafter—a phenomenon which deserves explanation.

One cannot be sure what an intellectual is; but let us define it as a person
whose primary habitat is the realm of ideas. In this sense, exceedingly few political leaders are authentic intellectuals, because the primary habitat of the political
leader is the world of power. Yet the world of power itself has intellectual and
anti-intellectual sides. Some political leaders find exhilaration in ideas and in the
company of those whose trade it is to deal with them. Others are rendered uneasy
by ideas and uncomfortable by intellectuals.

Kennedy belonged supremely to the first class. He was a man of action
who could pass easily over to the realm of ideas and confront intellectuals with
perfect confidence in his capacity to hold his own. His mind was not prophetic,
impassioned, mystical, ontological, utopian or ideological. It was less exuberant
than Theodore Roosevelt's, less scholarly than [Woodrow] Wilson's, less adventurous than Franklin Roosevelt's. But it had its own salient qualities—it was objective, practical, ironic, skeptical, unfettered and insatiable.

It was marked first of all, as he had noted to Jacqueline, by inexhaustible
curiosity. Kennedy always wanted to know how things worked. Vague answers
never contented him. This curiosity was fed by conversation but even more by
reading. His childhood consolation had become an adult compulsion. He was
now a fanatical reader, 1200 words a minute, not only at the normal times and
places but at meals, in the bathtub, sometimes even when walking. Dressing in
the morning, he would prop open a book on his bureau and read while he put
on his shirt and tied his necktie. He read mostly history and biography. . . . His
supposed addiction to James Bond was partly a publicity gag, like Franklin Roosevelt's supposed affection for "Home on the Range." Kennedy seldom read for
distraction. He did not want to waste a single second. (Arthur M. Schlesinger, Jr.,
A Thousand Days)

5. Summarize one of the following passages. After writing your summary, discuss what you left out, what you left in, and why. What problems did you encounter putting the passage into your own words? How does your summary compare with the original in terms of clarity and comprehensiveness?

> We have now surveyed, in such a cursory manner as time permits, the commonest types of psychic intervention in Homer. We may sum up the result by saying that all departures from normal human behavior whose causes are not immediately perceived, whether by the subjects' own consciousness or by the observations of others, are ascribed to a supernatural agency, just as is any departure from the normal behavior of the weather or the normal behavior of a bowstring. This finding will not surprise the nonclassical anthropologist: he will at once produce copious parallels from Borneo or Central Africa. But it is surely odd to find this belief, this sense of constant daily dependence on the supernatural, firmly embedded in poems supposedly so "irreligious" as the *Iliad* and the *Odyssey*. And we may also ask ourselves why a people so civilized, clear-headed, and rational as the Ionians did not eliminate from their national epics these links with Borneo and the primitive past, just as they eliminated fear of the dead, fear of pollution, and other primitive terrors which must originally have played a part in the saga. I doubt if the early literature of any other European people—even my own superstitious countrymen, the Irish—postulates supernatural interference in human behavior with such frequency over so wide a field. (E. R. Dodds, *The Greeks and the Irrational*)

> Are viruses very simple forms of life? Can they give us clues to the nature of a precellular living system of which no fossil is likely to remain? As information increases on the nature of viruses and, in particular, of their relationships with host cells, this interpretation of viral origins seems less and less likely. Viruses are able to reproduce and to make their protein coats only because they are capable of commandeering the enzymes and other metabolic machinery of the host cell. Without this machinery, they are as inert as any other macromolecule, lifeless by many criteria. It seems more likely that viruses are cellular fragments that have set up a partially independent existence. (Helena Curtis, *Biology*)

6. You and a partner separately write a paraphrase of the following passage. If you come upon portions that are difficult or vague, work on the difficulty together. When you are finished, compare paraphrases. How well does each capture the content of the original? Which is more faithful to the author's original order? What problems did you encounter trying to stay away from the author's original words?

> [A brief look at history] may suggest the mutual interdependence of the scientific revolution and the industrial revolution. Upon the one hand, modern industry *is* so much applied science. No amount of desire to make money, or to enjoy new commodities, no amount of mere practical energy and enterprise, would have effected the economic transformation of the last few centuries and generations. Improvements in mathematical, physical, chemical and biological science were prerequisites. Businessmen through engineers of different sorts, have laid hold of the new insights gained by scientific men into the hidden energies of nature, and have turned them to account. The modern mine, factory, railway, steamship, telegraph, all of the appliances and equipment of production, and transportation, express scientific knowledge. (John Dewey, "Some Historical Factors in Philosophical Reconstruction")

7. Read each of the following quotations, and then fit it into the types of introductions and sentence structures given.

> To be an existentialist, one must be able to feel oneself—one must know one's desires, one's rages, one's anguish, one must be aware of the character of one's frustrations and know what would satisfy it. (Norman Mailer, "The White Negro")

   a. The existentialist, according to Norman Mailer, must
   b. Mailer called on the existentialist to know four things:
   c. When speaking of the existentialist, Mailer said that
   d. The existentialist should not only know his or her "frustration"; for Mailer, one should also
   e. "[part of quotation]," said Norman Mailer, "[another part of quotation]"
   f. Norman Mailer declared,

> And we do not quite say that the new is more valuable because it fits in; but its fitting in is a test of its value—a test, it is true, which can only be slowly and cautiously applied, for we are none of us infallible judges of conformity. (T. S. Eliot, "Tradition and the Individual Talent")

   a. Eliot did not claim that [part of quotation], but instead he claimed that [other part of quotation]
   b. The reason that we must be cautious in judging the new, says Eliot, is that
   c. Eliot called the test of conformity [use ellipses to omit words from the quotation]
   d. No one can ever be completely confident of his or her taste in the new because he or she is only a [use brackets to work quotation into sentence]
   e. Eliot believes that the best test of something new is its

15

WRITING RESEARCH

And time yet for a hundred indecisions,
And for a hundred visions and revisions

T. S. ELIOT (1888–1965)
AMERICAN POET AND CRITIC

The process of preparing a research paper for handing in not only involves the writing but also involves precise documentation of your sources, revision, and careful presentation of the final manuscript.

DOCUMENTING YOUR SOURCES

Documentation is an essential part of presenting evidence. You must identify the source of every quotation, fact, statistic, graph, or opinion about your subject that you include in your research paper. You must tell your reader exactly where you got every bit of information that you use. Further, you must list for your reader every source you have cited in your paper. In short, you must thoroughly document your research.

You must do this for three reasons:

Documentation provides a guide for any reader who wants to study your subject.

It indicates the extent of your research.

It gives credit where credit is due.

If writers document their sources sloppily or not at all, they disappoint curious readers and undermine confidence in the quality of the research. Worse, they run the risk of plagiarism.

Plagiarism

Plagiarism is the use without due acknowledgment of the thoughts, writing, scholarship, or inventions of another. In college and university writing, as in most other walks of life, people put a great value of knowing what is yours and what belongs to someone else. Therefore, plagiarism is a serious moral issue.

Plagiarism is often the result of carelessness or ignorance: sometimes a student does not fully understand the importance of the issue or does not know the right way to acknowledge sources. The remedy is to learn. Sometimes, however, people in full awareness submit as their own the ideas or work of someone else. Compare this passage from a book on fifteenth-century art with the way a writer used it in a paper on the same subject:

SOURCE

The diminishing role of gold in paintings is part of a general movement in western Europe at this time towards a kind of selective inhibition about display, and this shows itself in many other kinds of behaviour too. It was just as conspicuous in the client's clothes, for instance, which were abandoning gilt fabrics and gaudy hues for the restrained black of Burgundy. This was a fashion with elusive moral overtones. (Michael Baxandall, *Painting and Experience in Fifteenth Century Italy*)

USE

At this time, western Europe was moving toward inhibition of display, which shows up in the diminishing role of gold in paintings as well as in many other kinds of behavior, including the abandoning of gilt fabrics and gaudy hues in clothing. This fashion had moral overtones, though elusive.

In this case the writer has obviously used material belonging to another without crediting the source. He or she has used the same words and phrases, in only slightly altered form. This is plagiarism.

Even if you do not quote any of the words of a source, borrowing ideas can also be plagiarism. Compare this passage from an original source with its use in a paper called "The Psychology of Children's Play":

SOURCE

Just as for its growth an organ needs nourishment in proportion to its functioning, so each mental activity, from the most elementary to the highest, needs for its development to be fed from without by a continuous flow, which [in the case of children's play] is purely functional, not material. (Jean Piaget, *Play, Dreams, and Imitation in Childhood*)

USE

```
Children play as part of the normal process of grow-
ing and developing.  Like any bodily organ, the mind
needs constant nourishment and exercise as it grows.
When children play, they exercise and nourish the
mind and assist it in its growth.
```

These ideas may be in the writer's own language, but he or she has borrowed them from the source without acknowledgment. If the writer did this knowingly and deliberately concealed the source, it is a kind of theft.

Here is the general rule for avoiding plagiarism and providing appropriate documentation: give enough information so that a reader can examine the sources you have used.

Now, here are seven guidelines for applying the general rule.

1. When you incorporate into your paper sentences, paragraphs, or apt phrases from the work of another, you must use quotation marks around the borrowed words—or indent passages longer than four lines—and you must identify the source. In the case of Baxandall's material about fifteenth-century painting, the writer should have credited the source and put borrowed phrases inside quotation marks, like this:

```
According to Michael Baxandall, people in fifteenth-
century western Europe were tending toward an "inhib-
ition about display," which manifests itself in "the
diminishing role of gold in paintings" as well as in
other cultural practices, including "abandoning gilt
fabrics and gaudy hues" in clothing.  As Baxandall
says, "This was a fashion with elusive moral over-
tones" (14).
```

2. When you rely on another person's ideas or train of thought but change the actual words used or the order of the ideas—that is, when you paraphrase—you still must acknowledge your source. To avoid plagiarism, the writer who borrowed from Piaget should have written this:

```
Jean Piaget claims that children play as part of the
normal process of growing and developing.  Like any
bodily organ, the mind needs constant nourishment
and exercise as it grows.  He goes on to say that
```

> when children play, they exercise and nourish the
> mind and assist it in its growth (87).

Notice that Piaget is named in the text, not merely in a note. The material was Piaget's own, and he should receive clear and obvious credit. An opinion or an original interpretation of the facts—whether quoted, paraphrased, or summarized—should be part of the text; otherwise, it might appear that the writer doing the quoting is claiming the opinion.

3. When the material you use is widely known and generally available—that is, not an interpretation—you can acknowledge the source simply in a parenthetical reference rather than in the text. Christina Gerke acknowledges the sources of some facts in this way:

> The French psychologist Alfred Binet originally for-
> mulated his Binet scale of intelligence in 1905 to
> place advanced and handicapped children in special
> schools (Wardrop 8; Jensen 141–43).

4. When your ideas or opinions have been influenced in a general way by material you have read or lectures you have heard, you must also acknowledge your debt. In a paper on modern linguistics, a writer indicated the source of a borrowed idea in this fashion:

> Paradoxically, linguists can no longer confine them-
> selves to language to understand how language works.
> They must now take into account the time, the place,
> the speaker, the listener, and the actual situation
> of each single utterance. Mikhail Bakhtin's analy-
> sis of these sociolinguistic elements is exception-
> ally insightful (383).

5. When you rely on factual material gathered by another person, you must state this as well.

> My discussion of Samoan marriage ceremonies will
> draw heavily on Margaret Mead's <u>Letters from the
> Field</u>.

6. When you have benefited from another person's way of organizing material that is widely known, you must still acknowledge.

```
When researching the movies of Preston Sturges, I
found Simonson's History of American Film extremely
helpful.
```

7. Finally, when you employ another writer's method of analyzing material, you must give credit where it is due.

```
If we agree with David Riesman's view of American
society in The Lonely Crowd, we can see that . . .
```

There are practical exceptions to the general rule, however. Some things are just common knowledge and it would be nearly impossible to acknowledge them. For instance, you need not identify a source for facts that almost everyone knows or could easily learn and that no one needs to prove.

Columbus sailed to America in 1492.

The chemical symbol of water is H_2O.

How could we ever remember where we learned those things? Nor do you need to provide a source for an idea expressed by many people.

Hamlet is one of Shakespeare's greatest tragedies.

Hostility has existed between Israel and the Arab nations since Israel became a nation.

Err on the side of overacknowledgment, however. Be generous and open in giving credit for any source of help.

There are three common practices that also qualify as plagiarism. Avoid them in all the work you do.

1. *Never submit another student's paper as your own.* This practice is obviously unethical. Worse, it can actually harm both you and the other student. If you wish to use the ideas of a classmate or other student, do so and acknowledge the source. But submit work only you yourself have written.

2. *Never submit a paper that you have obtained from a "paper mill" or paper-writing service.* All instructors expect that the work you turn in is your own. Submitting a professionally written paper is simply putting up a false pretense. "Paper mills" cater to the worst aspects of people: their laziness, their eagerness to take the easy way out. Turning in a professionally written paper makes a mockery of the entire reason we teach and learn. Besides, most of the "paper mill" papers we have read have been awful. Have nothing to do with such papers: Do not use them, do not quote them, do not read them.

3. *Never turn in the same paper to more than one class.* This practice is simply plagiarizing yourself. Instructors expect original work. Do not turn in a paper you have written for any other class. Avoid using sections of such works as the basis for other papers. If you find yourself writing on a topic you have treated before, consider writing on something else unless you have something new to say. Ask your instructor for permission.

Every discipline has its own way of documenting sources. Many humanities researchers use the Modern Language Association (MLA) system; social scientists often use the system advocated by the American Psychological Association (APA); the natural sciences use a number system. Indeed, methods of documentation will vary somewhat from course to course. Some instructors will require footnotes; others, endnotes. We will cover the MLA system of parenthetical references in this chapter. You can read about this system in more detail in Joseph Gibaldi and Walter S. Achtert, *MLA Handbook for Writers of Research Papers,* 3rd ed. (New York: MLA, 1988), widely considered by English instructors as the arbiter on such matters. The MLA standard format for notes and bibliography and the author/year or APA style appear in the first appendix, Other Systems of Documentation.

The MLA Parenthetical References and List of Works Cited Format

The preferred MLA format uses parenthetical references that generally give the author's name and the page number after the quoted material. If readers want to know more, they can refer to a list of works cited at the back of the paper. In most cases this system allows you to acknowledge your sources immediately and in a relatively unobtrusive manner. We'll look first at how to present the list of works cited and then discuss how to handle references to these works in the text.

LIST OF WORKS CITED. Type your list of works cited on a separate sheet at the end of your paper. This list will include *only books you actually cite in your paper, not all the books you consulted in your research.* Center the words *Works Cited* one inch from the top of the page and two lines above your first entry. Double-space all entries; arrange them alphabetically by author's last name or, when there is no author, by title.

In each entry give the author's or authors' names (last name first), the title of the book or article, and then the necessary publication information: city, publisher, and year of publication for books; name of periodical, volume number and/or date, and page numbers for articles. For each entry, indent all lines after the first one five spaces. Skip two spaces after each period. Whenever italics are called for (as with book titles, for instance), you should underline. Finally, continue to number your pages all the way through the list. See Christina Gerke's list of works cited at the end of her paper for a model (pp. 413–415).

Sample Entries

In the following pages you will find examples of the kinds of references you will be most likely to use. Some preliminary notes to keep in mind:

    a. Omit titles (Ph.D., M.D., and so forth) from an author's name.
    b. Omit words such as *Company, Publishing,* and *Inc.* from a publisher's name.
    c. The words *University Press* are abbreviated UP, without any periods, even if they appear apart: Johns Hopkins UP, U of Pittsburgh P.
    d. Always list the city in which the book was published—but list the state only if the city is obscure, has a common name, or is likely to be confused with another city with the same name: Oxford, Mississippi; Athens, Georgia.
    e. Drop the word *The* from all periodical titles: *Los Angeles Times,* not *The Los Angeles Times.*

BOOKS BY ONE AUTHOR. Give the author's name, last name first, the title underlined, and the city, publisher, and year of publication.

    Field, Syd. <u>Screenplay</u>. New York: Dell, 1982.

Note the periods after the author's name, the title, and the year. If there is a subtitle on the title page, follow the title with a colon and capitalize the first letter of the subtitle.

    Smith, Frank. <u>Insult to Intelligence: The Bureau-
        cratic Invasion of Our Classrooms</u>. New York:
        Arbor, 1986.

ARTICLES IN PERIODICALS. Start with the author's name, if you know it. Put the title of the article in quotation marks. Follow the title with the underlined title of the periodical. If the periodical uses *continuous pagination* throughout the annual volume (for example, if the first issue ends on page 413, the second issue picks up at page 414), simply follow the title with the volume number, the year of publication in parentheses, a colon, and then the page numbers.

```
Barnet, Sylvan.  "Some Limitations on a Christian
     Approach to Shakespeare."  English Literary
     History 22 (1955): 81-92.
```

Some periodicals have *noncontinuous pagination*—that is, every issue begins with page 1. In that case, give the volume number, a period, and (without a space after the period), the issue number, then proceed as just described.

```
Klein, Asher.  "Secrets of Writing."  Interior Re-
     view 51.6 (1959): 25-38.
```

ARTICLES IN MONTHLY OR BIMONTHLY PERIODICALS. If the periodical identifies its issues with the names of months, you need not give the volume and issue number. Instead, give the names of the months and the year, abbreviating all months except May, June, and July. If an issue is identified by two months, put a hyphen between their abbreviated names.

```
Lawren, Bill.  "Why Do Birds Live in Colonies?"  Na-
     tional Wildlife Apr.-May 1988: 53-59.
```

ARTICLES IN DAILY OR WEEKLY PERIODICALS. For periodicals that come out daily or weekly—including most newspapers and magazines—you need not give the volume number. Instead, give the exact date of publication, a colon, and then the page numbers followed by a period.

```
Pfaff, William.  "Reflections: Remembering."  New
     Yorker 7 Dec. 1987: 140-50.
```

Notice that the date appears as day, month, and year with no commas. Give all page numbers on which the article appears. If the article is not on consecutive pages, put a + after the first page number to indicate continuation on a later page.

```
Goleman, Daniel.  "New Insights into Freud from Let-
     ters to a Friend."  New York Times Magazine 17
     Mar. 1985: 31+.
```

(Remember that , though you would use the + in the list of works cited, you would use the exact page number in any citation in your text.)

If the newspaper numbers its pages with numbers and letters (11B, B-10, and so forth), show the page numbers exactly as they appear on the page. For an example, see page 380.

MULTIPLE WORKS BY THE SAME AUTHOR. When you have two or more entries for the same author, don't repeat the name, but type three hyphens and a period and complete the reference. List the author's works alphabetically by title.

> Derrida, Jacques. "La Double Séance." La Dissémi-
> nation. By Derrida. Paris: Seuil, 1972. 199–317.
> - - -. Of Grammatology. Baltimore: Johns Hopkins
> UP, 1976.

Notice that the first entry is an essay and the second a book, both by Derrida.

WORKS BY MORE THAN ONE AUTHOR. When you are citing a work by two or more authors, list the authors' names in the order in which they appear on the title page; this may or may not be alphabetical. Reverse only the first author's name, and type the rest out normally, separating names with commas.

> Gibaldi, Joseph, and Walter S. Achtert. MLA Hand-
> book for Writers of Research Papers. 3rd ed.
> New York: Modern Language Association, 1988.

If there are more than three authors, give only the first name that appears on the title page and follow it with *et al.*, a Latin abbreviation that means "and others." Do not underline *et al.* For the following work, the names on the title page were Elizabeth Waldeman, Allyson S. Grossman, Howard Hayghe, and Beverly Johnson:

> Waldeman, Elizabeth, et al. "Working Mothers in the
> 1970's: A Look at the Statistics." Monthly La-
> bor Review Oct. 1979: 39–45.

ANONYMOUS WORKS. Sometimes the author of a work is not identified. For a book:

> Swimmers for Life. Huntington Beach: Nereid, 1984.

For an article:

> "The Bogus Order of Merit." New Republic 2 Apr.
> 1977: 6.

WORKS WITH TRANSLATORS, EDITORS, OR COMPILERS. For translated works, begin with the original author's name and the title of the work, followed by the label *Trans.* and the name of the translator.

> Chekhov, Anton.   <u>Three Sisters</u>.   Trans. Lanford Wil-
>   son.   New York: Dramatists Play Service, 1984.

Some works have no author but have been assembled by an editor or compiler. Begin citations for such works with the title, followed by the label *Ed.* or *Comp.*, whichever is applicable, and the editor's or compiler's name.

> <u>Tribal Music of Africa and America</u>.   Comp. Donald
>   Rooney.   Atlanta: Feldspar, 1921.

WORKS IN ANTHOLOGIES OR COLLECTIONS. For college papers you may often use works in anthologies or collections. For such sources, give the name of the author of the anthologized work, the work's title, and then the title of the anthology or collection. Then give the name of the editor or compiler, preceding that name with *Ed.* or *Comp.* (Even if there is more than one such person, as in the following example, use *Ed.* or *Comp.*) After the place, publisher, and date, give the page numbers on which the work appears. (Don't count page numbers of introductions or notes.) Here are several such entries:

ESSAY

> Hansberry, Lorraine.   "In Defense of the Equality of
>   Men."   <u>The Norton Anthology of Literature by</u>
>   <u>Women</u>.   Ed. Sandra M. Gilbert and Susan Gubar.
>   New York: Norton, 1985.   2058—67.

If the anthology has more than one volume, specify the number of the volume you used after the editor's name, and put the total number of volumes of the work at the end of the citation. Then precede the page numbers with the number of the volume you used and a colon. The poem in the following citation was on pages 1739—41 of volume 2 of the anthology.

POEM

> Plath, Sylvia.   "Lady Lazarus."   <u>Anthology of Ameri-</u>
>   <u>can Literature</u>.   Ed. George McMichael. Vol. 2.
>   New York: Macmillan, 1974.   1739—41. 2 vols.

If the anthology has more than three editors, give the first editor's name a comma, and then "et al." meaning "and others."

PLAY

Jonson, Ben. Volpone, or The Fox. The Norton Anthology of English Literature. Ed. M. H.
   Abrams et al. 5th ed. Vol. 1. New York: Norton, 1986. 1114–208. 2 vols.

The edition number of an anthology is very important because anthologies change greatly from edition to edition. Place the edition number after the name of the editor or editors. Use abbreviated ordinal numbers (*1st, 2nd, 3rd,* and so forth) and the abbreviation *ed.* for "edition." The following short story was found on pages 906–10 of the second edition of the anthology.

SHORT STORY

Paley, Grace. "A Conversation with My Father." The
   Story and Its Writer: An Introduction to Short
   Fiction. Ed. Ann Charters. 2nd ed. New York:
   Bedford–St. Martin's, 1987. 906–10.

Underline the titles of longer works (novels, epic poems, and plays) even when they are part of an anthology, as with the epic poem *Paradise Lost* in the following example:

Milton, John. Paradise Lost. John Milton: Complete
   Poems and Major Prose. Ed. Merrit Y. Hughes.
   Seattle: Odyssey, 1957. 206–469.

MULTIVOLUME WORKS. If you have used all of the volumes of a multivolume work, put the number of volumes after the title, using the abbreviation *vols.*

Scherrol, Lydia. Russian Writers, 1766–1985. 3
   vols. Washington: Novy Mir Press, 1985.

EDITIONS. An *edition* is a work by one person specially prepared for publication by another person. This second person, called the *editor,* is responsible for the text, the notes, and any other explanatory or accompanying material. To cite an edition, give the original author's name, the title, then the abbreviation *Ed.* and the name of the editor.

Defoe, Daniel. <u>Robinson Crusoe</u>. Ed. Michael Shinagel.
New York: Norton, 1975.

BOOKS THAT ARE PART OF A SERIES. If the title page tells you that the book you are citing is part of a series, follow the book's title with the title of the series, neither underlined nor in quotation marks, and the book's number in that series.

Oquendo, Ignacio. <u>Spraygun Politics</u>. Southwestern
Writers Ser. 4. Los Angeles: Olmec, 1984.

SACRED WORKS. The convention of underlining does not apply to sacred texts, such as the Bible or its books. For books in the Bible, be sure to specify whether they are in the Old Testament (also abbreviated *OT*), New Testament (also abbreviated *NT*), or Apocrypha. Omit "The Book of"; give simply the name or title associated with the book. Give full publication data for sacred texts, especially editors, edition, and page numbers, if you are citing individual books, chapters, or sections.

Bible. Old Testament. Job. <u>New American Standard
Bible</u>. Chicago: Moody, 1972. 647–92.

ENCYCLOPEDIAS AND OTHER REFERENCE WORKS. Include articles in dictionaries, encyclopedias, and other reference works in your list if you used them in your paper. If the article is signed, enter it under the author's name; if not, alphabetize it by its title. After either one, cite the title of the reference work. If the work arranges its entries alphabetically, omit the volume and page number. If the work is well known, you need cite only the date of the edition.
For a dictionary:

"Cytodifferentiation." <u>Webster's Ninth New Collegiate Dictionary</u>. 1984 ed.

For an encyclopedia:

Ulrich, Homer. "Music: Western Music." <u>Encyclope-
dia Americana</u>. 1985 ed.

PREFACES, INTRODUCTIONS, FOREWORDS, AND AFTERWORDS. We do not suggest that students often cite these parts of a book, but when you learn a fact or idea in a preface or an afterword, you must give credit if you use it in a paper. Start the citation with the name of the author and the title of the part being cited—*Preface, Afterword,* and so forth—neither underlined nor in quotation marks. Follow with the title of the entire work. If the author of the part being cited is also the author of the complete work, follow the title of the work with *By* and the author's last name only. Follow the usual publication data with the page numbers of the part being cited (for prefaces, introductions, and forewords, these will often appear as lowercase roman numerals).

> Roszak, Theodore. Preface. The Making of a Counter
> Culture. By Roszak. New York: Doubleday,
> 1969. xi–xiv.

If the author of the part being cited is different from the author of the main work, follow the preceding form, except that after *By* give the full name of the author of the main work.

> Mudrick, Marvin. Afterword. Persuasion. By Jane
> Austen. New York: New American Library, 1964.
> 241–54.

WORKS BY CORPORATE OR INSTITUTIONAL AUTHORS. Many publications have no individual author but are of group or corporate origin. In such a case, enter the name of the originating body as the author's name.

> National Congress of Independent Beekeepers. The
> Backyard Apiary. Taos: Natl. Cong. of Indepen-
> dent Beekeepers, 1984.

If a corporate or institutional name also appears as publisher, abbreviate it the second time.

GOVERNMENT DOCUMENTS. A special group of works by corporate authors are documents put out by the U.S. government. These are especially tricky entries. If the individual author is not known (usually the case), treat the government agency as author. State the name of the government first—that is, the state or country of origin—and then the name of the agency. You may use common abbreviations such as *Dept.* and *Cong.* if the context makes their meaning clear. Then give title, place, publisher, and date as for other book entries.

> United States. Dept. of Health and Human Services.
> Eating to Lower Your Cholesterol. Bethesda,
> MD: Natl. Insts. of Health, 1984.

Make your citation as specific as possible. If a source is published by an agency within an agency, mention all the agencies in descending order of hierarchy.

> United States. Dept. of Health and Human Services.
>   Public Health Service. Centers for Disease
>   Control. <u>Understanding AIDS</u>. Rockville, MD:
>   HHS, 1988.

Again, if the same agency is both author and publisher, abbreviate the name of the agency the second time it is mentioned.

PAMPHLETS. Treat a pamphlet the same way you would treat a book. Give the author, if known; otherwise, begin your entry with the title, underlined.

> Boden, Talbot. <u>Identifying Desert Rocks</u>. San Fran-
>   cisco: Hiker's Aids, 1980.
> <u>Is Your House Burglar-Proof?</u> Washington, DC: Crime-
>   watch, 1956.

EDITORIALS. Cite editorials by giving the author's name, the title of the editorial in quotation marks, and then the label *Editorial,* neither underlined nor in quotation marks. Then give the information as usual for periodicals.

> Timpane, John. "Old Age Is Taking a Turn for the
>   Lengthier." Editorial. <u>San Jose Mercury News</u>
>   14 Feb. 1988: 1P+.

(Note that the page number is 1P, as it appeared in the newspaper.) Some editorials have neither authors nor titles. Then your task is simple.

> Editorial. <u>Bergen Tribune</u> 30 May 1983: 12.

LETTERS TO THE EDITOR. For letters to the editor, begin with the author's name and the label *Letter,* neither underlined nor in quotation marks. Then give publication data and page number. If the letter is in reply to another letter, follow the author's name with the label *Reply to letter of* . . . , then give the name of the author of the initial letter.

> McGrath, Dan. Letter. <u>New York Times</u> 15 May 1988:
>   28E.

> Ghoti, Frank. Reply to letter of Dan McGrath. <u>New York Times</u> 22 May 1988: 17D.

A PUBLISHED INTERVIEW. If you are citing a published interview, start with the name of the person interviewed. Follow with the title of the interview, if any, in quotation marks, or underlined if the interview takes up the whole work. If there is no title, simply write *Interview,* without underlining or quotation marks. If you know the name of the interviewer, place it after the title, preceded by *By.* Then continue the entry as usual.

> Updike, John. Interview. By John Timpane. <u>West</u> 1 May 1988: 4.

A PERSONAL INTERVIEW. If you are citing an interview you have done, give the name of the person interviewed, a label stating the kind of interview (*Personal interview, Telephone interview, Interview by questionnaire*), and the date, using the order day, month, year. If you did a personal interview with Margaret Thatcher on June 7, 1988, the citation would read this way:

> Thatcher, Margaret. Personal interview. 7 June 1988.

A telephone interview with Earvin Johnson on January 24, 1987, would be cited this way:

> Johnson, Earvin. Telephone interview. 24 Jan. 1987.

For some advice on how to conduct personal interviews, see "Interviews" in Chapter 14.

MATERIAL FROM A COMPUTER SERVICE. Computer services, such as DIALOG or Mead, can now give you printouts of abstracts, articles, and other information in many fields. Treat material from computer services as you would any other material. Give the complete original reference (you'll find it on the printout), and add the name of the computer service and the service's identifying numbers for the material cited.

> Smith, Gerry. "The Race for Superconductors." <u>Business Forum</u> May 1987: 27+. DIALOG file 441, item 089473.

MATERIAL FROM AN INFORMATION SERVICE. Again, treat material from an information service, such as the Educational Resources Informa-

tion Center (ERIC), as you would any other material, but add the name
and identifying numbers of the information service at the end.

>   Ogilve, Tanya. Innovations in Teaching the Hearing-
>
>   Impaired. Madison, WI: Special Education,
>
>   1986. ERIC ED 050 675.

FILMS. Citations for films usually begin with the film's title, underlined, followed by the director's name (preceded by the label *Dir.*), the
name of the distributor, and the year. Separate distributor and year with
a comma.

>   It Happened One Night. Dir. Frank Capra. Metro-
>
>   Goldwyn-Mayer, 1934.

If you wish to emphasize the contribution of a particular person, you can
begin with that person's name and his or her contribution.

>   Ford, Harrison, actor. Witness. Dir. Peter Weir.
>
>   Paramount, 1986.

RADIO OR TELEVISION PROGRAMS. Cite radio or television programs
by giving the title of the broadcast (underlined), the name of the network
(if known), the call letters and city of the local station (separated by a
comma), and the date of the broadcast.

>   Day of the Barricades. National Public Radio.
>
>   WNYC, New York. 13 May 1988.

If you are citing a particular episode of a series, give the name of the
episode in quotation marks, the author's name (preceded by the label
Writ.), if known, then the series title (underlined), followed by network
(if known), call letters, city, and date.

>   "The Razor's Nudge." Writ. Walter Hedley. Technol-
>
>   ogy Today. KFWB, Los Angeles. 22 Sept. 1981.

In general, give information that is as detailed as possible, emphasizing the
person whose contribution you are citing. The following entry cites the
work of the writer of a particular episode of a television program and
includes the names of the director and producer.

```
Braddock, Ada, writ.  "The Rainforests: Going Fast?"
    Dir. Frank Koski.  Prod. Charles Upham.  Our
    World.  PBS.  WGBH, Boston.  3 July 1977.
```

RECORDINGS. If you are citing a commercially available recording, you should usually begin your citation with the name of the *person* whose contribution you wish to cite, whether it be the writer or composer of the work, the artists involved, a conductor, or a producer. You will *always* include the title of the work, the artist or artists involved, the manufacturer of the recording, the catalog number (exactly as it appears on the cover of the record), and the year of issue, if known. (If the year is not known, write *n.d.* for "no date.") Follow the manufacturer and catalog number with commas.

```
Berlioz, Hector.  Symphonie fantastique, op. 14.
    Cond. Leonard Bernstein.  New York Philhar-
    monic.  Columbia, MS 7278, n.d.
```

If the recording is a collection or anthology and you wish to cite a single work, enclose the title in quotation marks if the work is short, underline it if the work is long, and do neither if the work is identified only by form, number, or key.

```
Lennon, John, and Paul McCartney.  "Come Together."
    Abbey Road.  The Beatles.  Capitol, MFSL 1-023,
    1969.
Takahama, Miyoshi.  Concerto for Flute in A, op. 77.
    New Works for Flute.  Amerasian Flute Chorus.
    Calliope, GDS 642, 1988.
```

Using References in Your Text

To follow the MLA format, document sources in your text by inserting a short acknowledgment in parentheses. Usually, the author's last name and a page number are enough. We are basing this section on the *MLA Handbook,* especially on pages 155–202 of that book, so a reference is in order (Gibaldi and Achtert 155–202).

We just gave it. Notice that there is no comma between the authors' last names and the page number. Close the parentheses before a period or comma. If you are crediting a longer, indented quotation, skip two spaces after the concluding punctuation mark and give the reference. Christina Gerke does this in this passage from her paper:

Educator George F. Madaus writes,

> The more one knows about the technology
> of testing, the more one realizes the
> potential for harm when a test score is
> used as the sole or primary criterion on
> which to make an important decision
> affecting an individual's future. (93)

Because she mentions Madaus in the text before the quotation, Gerke needs to give only the page number in parentheses. Again, note that the reference comes outside the terminal punctuation and on the same line. If her readers want to know more, they can refer to her list of works cited; there they would find

> Madaus, George F. "NIE Clarification Hearing: The
> Negative Team's Case." Phi Delta Kappan Oct.
> 1981: 92–94.

Whenever Gerke refers to Madaus, she simply uses the brief parenthetical reference and the appropriate page number.

Place such references at natural pauses in your sentences—usually at the end of the sentence, or the end of the phrase or clause that contains the cited material—and as close to the material as possible.

If the names of the authors of your sources already appear in your text, you need only give the page number in your reference. Here is another example from Gerke's paper.

> Robert L. Green and Robert J. Griffore write, "The
> negative aspects of testing procedures are espe-
> cially apparent with respect to racial minorities"
> (25).

We recommend that you mention the names of important sources *often.* Your readers can find the names of the authors in the text, and complete information is always waiting for them in your list of works cited.

Other systems of documentation have used Latin words and abbreviations, such as *loc. cit. (loco citato,* "in the place [previously] cited"), *op. cit. (opere citato,* "in the work [previously] cited"), and *ibid. (ibidem,* or "in the same place"). Because parenthetical references always cite the page number, even if it is the same as that in a previous citation, this MLA system does not use these abbreviations.

Common Kinds of Parenthetical References

WORKS BY ONE AUTHOR.   As mentioned, include the author's name and page number. The following example is straightforward.

> Play, after all, is the way the growing mind gets nourishment (Piaget 87).

WORKS BY MORE THAN ONE AUTHOR.   For sources with two or three authors, give the last name of each in the same order as on the title page of the book.

> Platypuses are bizarre holdovers from ancient animal forms (Stein and Ahmad 223).

For sources with more than three authors, give the first author's name as it appears on the title page, then write *et al.* and give the page number. Thus, for the work with four authors that we cited on page 375, the text citation would be

> As of March 1978 one of every five families with children under the age of eighteen was maintained by a parent who was separated, divorced, widowed, or never married (Waldeman et al. 45).

Notice we kept only Waldeman. If you use a single name as a reference to a multiauthored source, use it also in your list of works cited.

ANONYMOUS WORKS.   If the work lists no author, simply give a short title—usually the first main word of the title—in the reference. If your source is a book, underline the word or words from the title.

> Today's lifeguards not only must know how to swim but must be able to differentiate among many differ- ent kinds of suntan lotion (<u>Swimmers</u> 56).

If your anonymous source is an article, put the title in quotation marks.

> In short, a diet of cotton candy is detrimental to the health of most rodents ("Effect of Cotton Candy" 6).

MULTIPLE WORKS BY THE SAME AUTHOR. If you refer to more than one work by the same author, simply give the author's name, a short title of the work referred to, and page number.

> Meaning is often lost in transit (Derrida, "Séance" 203). Our final destination is often displaced in the search for something else (Derrida, Grammatology 99).

The first reference is to an essay and the second to a book, both by Jacques Derrida. For clarity we separate the author's name from the title of the work with a comma.

MULTIPLE WORKS IN A SINGLE REFERENCE. If you want to support a point by referring to more than one work, separate the references by a semicolon within the parentheses.

> Like the hippies of the 1960s, the yuppies of the 1980s are largely a creation of the press ("Bogus Order"; Nesbitt 6–18).

If you need to refer to three or more sources (a rare event for most college writers), use a footnote or endnote in the text of your paper.

> American teenagers now reach puberty at an average age of 11.5 years, much earlier than at any time in this century.[1]

The corresponding note would look like this:

> [1]Delahay 42; Crossbeck 178; Montemayor 788.

Place these notes on a sheet of paper *before* your list of works cited. Such notes can also be used for explanation and cross-referencing, but use them sparingly. See the two sample endnotes in Christina Gerke's paper, page 412.

MULTIVOLUME WORKS. For a text reference to a multivolume work, show the volume number with an arabic numeral followed by a colon and the page number.

> Though the two never met, Tolstoy admired Dostoyevski (Scherrol 2: 77).

WORKS BY CORPORATE AUTHORS. Some publications have a corporate author whose name is quite long. You may put that name in parentheses, but it is better to cite the title of the work and the name of the originating body in your text, followed by the page number in parentheses.

> In its newsletter, The Backyard Apiary, the National
> Congress of Independent Beekeepers reported a slight
> rise in the number of neighbors who sued members
> over bee stings (44).

LITERARY REFERENCES. Most college papers on literature treat a single work. In this case, establish the author and title of the work you are discussing early and then simply give page, chapter, act, or line numbers in your references. If you are writing about more than one work, give the author's last name and page number in your references as we just described, unless you mention the author or title in your text. In your list of works cited, give a complete entry for the edition you use of each work.

1. Novels. Put the page first, then the chapter (abbreviated *ch.*), in case your reader has an edition with different page numbers.

> When Jo in Charles Dickens's Bleak House is asked
> where his parents are, he replies, "I never know'd
> nothink about 'em" (372; ch. 25).

2. Plays. Cite quotations from plays not by page number but by the division of the play—act, scene, line—in which the quotation appears. Give these divisions in arabic numerals. If you mention the name of the play in the text, you may omit it in the reference.

> In Hamlet, the protagonist's most intense insight
> occurs when he accepts his fate: "If it be now, 'tis
> not to come; if it be not to come, it will be now"
> (5.2.76–77).

Some instructors may prefer roman numerals for acts and scenes; for example, the preceding reference would then be (V.ii.76–77). Follow your instructor's preference.

3. Poems. For a poem, give line numbers cited in parentheses. Use the word *line* or *lines* in your first citations; once you have established that the numbers will indicate lines, use the numbers by themselves.

> In John Donne's "The Good—Morrow," the speaker muses
> to the loved one, "I wonder, by my troth, what thou,
> and I/Did, till we lov'd?" (lines 1—2). Later, the
> poet says that any idea he had of beauty before
> meeting his love was only "a dream of thee" (7).

If you quote two or three lines of poetry, use slashes to separate them in the text. If you quote more than three lines, begin the quotation on a new line, indented ten spaces from the left margin. Break the lines exactly as they appear in the original.

If there are divisions (cantos, books, parts) in the poem you are quoting, give the division number before the line numbers.

> When he sees what he has done, Milton's Adam gives
> one of the most moving laments in Paradise Lost:
> "The more I see/Pleasures about me, so much more I
> feel/Torment within me" (9.119—21).

ENTIRE WORKS.   The best way to cite an entire work is to do so in your text.

> The furthest development of the Russian novel is
> still represented by Tolstoy's War and Peace.

Give a complete entry in your list of works cited for any entire works you cite.

INDIRECT SOURCES.   As we mentioned in "Primary and Secondary Sources" in Chapter 14, you should prefer firsthand sources to all others. Sometimes, however, you may only be able to find an indirect source, such as someone quoting someone else. If you quote or paraphrase material quoted in another source, put the abbreviation *qtd. in* (for "quoted in") before the indirect reference you cite in parentheses.

> Even a compulsive worker like Harry Truman was heard
> to mutter, "Even I need a day off once in a while"
> (qtd. in Giuseppe 55).

Then cite the indirect source in your list of works cited.

> Giuseppe, Raphael.   Type A Personalities in
>   American History.   Seattle: Workplace, 1981.

REVISING AND WRITING THE FINAL DRAFT

Putting your research paper into final form will call on everything you have learned about writing: style, grammar, and punctuation; paragraphing, persuasion, and documentation; claim, evidence, and warrant. We hope you will refer to this book often in the course of rewriting. Be sure you reread the section "Revising: Getting the Writing Right" in Chapter 2.

Before typing the final draft, read your paper twice, first for content and then again for mechanical correctness. Contrary to popular belief, you cannot read for both content and correctness at once. While hunting down an errant comma, you may miss a faulty warrant. One time-honored method of checking spelling is to start with the last word and read word by word backwards.

Try reading aloud too.

After you finish revising, your paper will go to your reader. Don't unleash a disheveled paper on the world. Turning in even the most closely reasoned and well-supported paper with incorrect spelling and poor grammar is like going out on a special date with dirty fingernails and greasy hair. If your instructor has given explicit directions regarding title page, binding, footnotes, and the like, follow them. If not, here are twelve guidelines for good form.

1. Use 8½-by-11-inch white paper—not too flimsy or easily smeared. Rule out onionskin and certain kinds of erasable papers. If you use computer paper, remove the perforated sides and separate the pages.

2. Type. Be sure the type is clear, dark, and black. Avoid blue, green, and red ribbons, pretty as they are; and do not use italic types. If you use a computer printer, make sure the ribbon is new, especially if the printer is dot matrix. Do not use strange or unusual fonts for the typeface. Also, make sure the "justify" feature of your word-processing program is turned off. It is standard for college papers to have a ragged right edge (that is, lines of unequal length). If "justify" is on, there will be ugly, confusing gaps in your text.

3. An inch below the top of the first page, even with the left-hand margin, type your name, your instructor's name, your course title and number, and the date on separate lines, double-spacing between each.

4. Double-space again and type your title in the center of the line. Do not underline the title or put it in quotation marks. Double-space between the title and your first line of text. Figure 15.1 shows the standard format for the first page of a research paper.

Cover sheets are not required for most research papers. We do, however, suggest that you use a cover sheet if you have included an outline for your paper. (That is what Christina Gerke did.) On a cover sheet, cen-

Figure 15.1   First Page of a Research Paper

Page number ½ inch
below top of page.   1

Name 1 inch below
top.

|

Subsequent lines
double-spaced.

|

Title centered, neither
underlined nor quoted.
First line indents 5
spaces.

1-inch side margins.

1-inch bottom margin.

Christina Gerke

Professor Resnick

English 102

2 May, 1988

     The Standardized Testing Controversy

     Standardized tests have become an Ameri-
can way of life. They now help determine who
will be accepted to college; which students
must take remedial classes and which must
take advanced classes; who will make the best
soldiers, civil servants, lawyers, state em-
ployees--even who may drive a car. According
to James L. Wardrop, more than 200 million
such tests are administered in the United
States each year (16). It may come as a surprise, then, to learn that something so common is the subject of a national controversy.

     Educators, psychologists, and experts in
test design stand on both sides of the debate. Advocates argue that standardized
testing is still the best available method of
assessing a person's abilities. They claim
that existing tests are "not biased against
minority groups" (Herbert) and are "valid
predictors" of a person's future success
(Eckland 12). In short, they see the tests
as services to the community.

     Opponents believe that the tests may do

ter your title about a third of the way down the page. Do not underline it or put it in quotation marks. An inch below the title, type *By* followed by your name. An inch below your name, type your instructor's name, the name and number of the course, and the date, each on a separate, centered line. On the first page of text, center the title (again, neither underlined nor in quotation marks) two inches from the top of the page. Begin the text two lines below the title. See Christina Gerke's paper (pp. 393–397) for the proper form for papers with cover sheets and outlines.

5. Number all your pages in the upper-right-hand corners, one-half inch below the top of the page and an inch from the right-hand edge. Since papers tend to fly apart, it is also a good idea to give your last name with the page number—for example, "Gerke 6"—from page 2 on.

6. Double-space your text. That includes long quotations, endnotes (if any), and list of works cited.

7. Leave margins of at least an inch at the bottom, top, and sides of each page.

8. Leave two spaces after any period or other end-of-sentence punctuation.

9. Make sure your references, endnotes (if any), and list of works cited follow the proper form. If you use endnotes, type them on a separate page, numbered as part of the paper. Center the heading *Notes* one inch from the top of the page. Double-space the notes. Indent the first line of each note five spaces from the left margin. The number of the note (corresponding to the raised number in the text) is raised a half-space above the note. For the proper format, see Christina Gerke's endnotes on page 412.

The list of works cited begins on a separate page following the text and endnotes (if any). The page is numbered as part of the text, and the heading *Works Cited* is centered one inch from the top of the page. Entries are double-spaced throughout, with the first line of each entry even with the left margin and subsequent lines indented five spaces. Authors are listed alphabetically, with the first author's name inverted and additional authors' names (if any) in normal order. Anonymous works are alphabetized by the first important word of the title (not *a, an,* or *the*). See Christina Gerke's list of works cited on pages 413–415.

10. Use correction fluid if necessary, but retype a heavily corrected page or passage rather than submit anything sloppy or unreadable.

11. Fasten the pages together with a paper clip or a staple of adequate strength. Plastic binders and stiff cardboard can be a nuisance to your reader.

12. Keep all written work away from food and drinks, especially coffee, to which papers seem to have a magnetic attraction. Make a copy of your paper for safekeeping.

CASE STUDY: A SAMPLE RESEARCH PAPER

Here is a formal outline of Christina Gerke's research paper, followed by the paper itself. Notice that she uses the MLA parenthetical reference and list of works cited system of documentation.

Gerke includes a
formal outline with
her paper, so she uses
a separate title page.

The Standardized Testing Controversy

By Christina Gerke

Professor Resnick

English 102

May 2, 1988

The outline is placed between the title page and the text. Gerke centers the title of the paper one inch from the top of the page. She double-spaces and types her thesis. This is a formal, sentence outline.

Each major point of the outline corresponds to a part of the thesis. Each subdivision relates directly to the main division under which it appears.

The Standardized Testing Controversy

Thesis: Since there is still so much contro-
        versy about standardized tests, em-
        ployers and institutions should place
        less emphasis on test performance as
        a criterion for admissions and hiring
        and more on aptitude and personal
        characteristics.

I. Standardized tests are a fact of life
   in the United States, but their design
   and effects are a matter of continuing
   controversy.
   A. They determine who graduates from
      high school, who attends the best
      colleges, who gets the best jobs,
      even who drives a car.
   B. Educators and experts disagree about
      their usefulness.
      1. Advocates say they are the best
         available instrument for assess-
         ing a person's abilities.
      2. Opponents charge that because the
         tests are biased, they may do
         more harm than good.
   C. This paper argues that employers and
      institutions should continue to use
      the tests, but they should de-empha-
      size them.
II. The controversy stems from the tests'
    social origin and social impact.

ii

A. The tests have replaced older prejudicial ways of choosing candidates
   for college admission and employment.
B. Advocates praise the tests on two
   grounds.
   1. The tests have predictive value.
   2. They are reputedly fair.
C. Opponents, however, point out bias
   in tests.
   1. Minorities score lower.
   2. Use of standardized English auto-
      matically discriminates against
      those for whom English is a sec-
      ond language and those who use
      dialects.
   3. Most tests emphasize reading and
      vocabulary, both of which are
      culturally linked.
   4. Test items can be "differentially
      attractive."
III. Because of further inherent problems in
    test design itself, critics doubt the
    ability of standardized tests to pre-
    dict future performance, and they ques-
    tion the tests' value in assessing
    knowledge.
    A. Tests ignore personality factors
       that could influence a person's per-
       formance.

Outline pages are numbered with lower case roman numerals about a half-inch from the top of the page, in the upper-right-hand corner, beginning with *ii* (the first page is counted but not numbered). The pages of the text are numbered with arabic numerals, beginning with the first page.

    B. Candidates may be quite qualified for a position and still may perform poorly on tests.

    C. It is sometimes difficult to ascertain exactly what the tests measure.

       1. Intelligence is not clearly defined.

       2. Tests may measure different abilities in different people.

IV. The Scholastic Aptitude Test (SAT) is a case study in the history and controversy surrounding standardized tests.

    A. The SAT is the largest, most widespread standardized test.

    B. Students' performance on the SAT may have more to do with which high school they attend than with their intelligence.

    C. Minorities and the less affluent perform less well on the SAT.

V. Standardized tests may actually reinforce the subordinate position of minority groups.

    A. Low scores mean a limited future.

    B. Despite efforts to eliminate accidental bias, even minimum competency tests (MCTs) still maintain hierarchies that restrict candidates' future chances.

VI. Still, standardized tests are useful within limits.

iv

    A. In general, standardized tests can measure performance, predict future success, and indicate aptitude for various things.

    B. SATs can predict students' college success to some extent.

    C. It is useful, for better or for worse, to learn how to survive in a white, middle-class world.

Neither the introduction nor the conclusion is named as a separate part of the outline. Instead, Gerke includes sentences that describe the content of these sections.

VII. We should not, however, rely on tests so much.

    A. They are overused, and they have too much power to determine candidates' futures.

    B. Some schools are already downplaying the tests in favor of other standards.

VIII. I propose that we adopt an "opportunity quotient" test.

    A. Such a test would compare a person's opportunity with his or her achievements.

    B. An "opportunity quotient" test would present a fairer and more comprehensive picture of a student.

1

The Standardized Testing Controversy

Standardized tests have become an American way of life. They now help determine who
will be accepted to college; which students
must take remedial classes and which may take
advanced classes; who will make the best soldiers, civil servants, lawyers, state employees––even who may drive a car. According to
James L. Wardrop, more than 200 million such
tests are administered in the United States
each year (16). It may come as a surprise,
then, to learn that something so common is
the subject of a national controversy.

Educators, psychologists, and experts in
test design stand on both sides of the debate. Advocates argue that standardized
testing is still the best available method of
assessing a person's abilities. They claim
that existing tests are "not biased against
minority groups" (Herbert) and are "valid
predictors" of a person's future success
(Eckland 12). In short, they see the tests
as services to the community.

Opponents believe that the tests may do
more harm than good. In their eyes, the
tests fail to recognize the cultural diversity of our society. Constructed according
to the styles and standards of the white,
middle–class, male community, the tests, opponents say, are biased against minorities
and less affluent whites. Robert L. Green

Four-paragraph
introduction: one on
general background,
one for each side of
the controversy, and
one stating the thesis.

Since Wardrop is
mentioned in the text,
only the page number
appears in the
parenthetical
reference.

Effective transition
from "national
controversy" in para. 1
to "the debate" in
para. 2.

Gerke smoothly
combines material
from two sources with
her own writing. The
reference to the
Herbert article has no
page number since the
article is one page
long.

Gerke 2

and Robert J. Griffore write, "The negative
aspects of testing procedures are especially
apparent with respect to racial minorities"
(25). By failing to recognize cultural diversity, they argue, test makers permanently
handicap large numbers of people whose poor
performances land them where they do not be-
long--in "slow" classes with restricted cur-
ricula and even more restricted opportunities.

In her thesis
paragraph, Gerke
distinguishes her
position from both
sides of the debate.
Her thesis promises a
direction, raises some
questions to be
answered (*Why* should
tests be de-
emphasized?), and
commits the paper to
an argument.

My discussion will look at both sides of
this issue in more detail but will not agree
completely with either side. Standardized
tests are useful, but they are also very powerful: test scores can affect the course of
people's lives, not to mention their self-image and their society's image of them. Since
there is still so much controversy about
standardized tests, employers and institutions should place less emphasis on test performance as a criterion for admissions and
hiring and more on aptitude and personal
characteristics.

In these paragraphs,
Gerke gives readers
background
information. This
section of the paper
corresponds to II.A. in
the outline.

In the past employers and institutions
based their selections on factors such as a
candidate's social class and family background. College admissions boards, especially those for private institutions,
weighed these values more heavily than proven
ability. Diane Ravitch points out that as
late as the 1940s, admissions boards tended

Gerke 3

to select students from a small number of
well-known public and private institutions
(55). This practice, obviously unfair to deserving candidates from disadvantaged back-
grounds, maintained the homogeneous nature of
the colleges.

Standardized tests arose out of the
prejudicial atmosphere of the early twentieth
century. Testing began in Britain in the
early twentieth century because of a eugenics
movement that was founded on the idea that
the poorer classes were inferior and that the
growth of these classes threatened the purity
of the upper classes. The spread of such inferiority could be checked by birth control
and sterilization (Smith 132-33). At the
same time, however, there was a move toward
standardization, partly to correct such institutionalized prejudices. The French psychologist Alfred Binet originally formulated
his Binet scale of intelligence in 1905 to
place advanced and handicapped children in
special schools (Wardrop 8; Jensen 141-43).
Binet's test began the long history of standardized placement examinations.

In the eighty years since, standardized
tests have often drawn praise as the most
democratic possible means of social selection
because they aim only to "predict performance
in school and on the job" (Herbert). Bruce K.
Eckland, professor of sociology at the Uni-

Note how two
different sources are
cited in a single
parenthetical
reference.

Gerke establishes the
authority of her source
by giving his
credentials in her
introduction to the
indented quotation.

Gerke 4

versity of North Carolina, gives the standard
defense:

Long quotation
indents ten spaces
from left margin.
Ellipses indicate that
something is omitted
from the original.
Since Eckland is
already mentioned,
only the page number
appears in the
reference.

> There is no factor that has a
> stronger, more consistent effect in
> the college attainment process in-
> dependent of race, social class,
> sex, or any other observed charac-
> teristic . . . than individual
> ability as measured by standardized
> tests. (12)

Here and elsewhere,
Gerke analyzes and
evaluates her sources.
This appeal to reason
shows that she has
thought about
Holden's position and
has a response.

Advocates often seem to suggest that this
ability to predict exonerates tests from
charges of bias. One defender writes that
the tests "can predict equally well for members of minority groups as for nonwhites"
(Holden), as if this accuracy can somehow
sidestep the question of whether or not the
prediction is self-fulfilling.

Yet the charge of test bias against minority groups has become the central issue in
the debate. One consistent trend has proved
most embarrassing to those who favor standardized tests: in general, minorities score
lower on standardized tests than do middle-
class whites. For example, Harvard University's Arthur Jensen, noted and controversial
critic of standardized tests, claims that the
overall difference between whites and blacks
is 15 points, and the gap between rich and
poor is 12 points (44).

If such figures provide powerful evi-

Gerke 5

By suggesting that the next piece of evidence will be more convincing than the first, Gerke makes an effective transition.

dence of bias, problems in the design of the tests are even more telling. One obvious example is the use of standard English in most tests. Peter Farb says that students for whom English is a second language, or those who speak a dialect such as black or Appalachian English, may have a handicap before they even sit down to take the test (162–63).

In Gerke's first draft, the Farb information came later in the paper. In her revision she grouped it earlier with similar evidence.

Further, many tests emphasize reading and vocabulary ability, which studies have shown to be culturally linked (Ravitch 54)—that is, a student from a background where reading is either unavailable or not encouraged will come to a standardized test at a great disadvantage. And some questions may similarly contain quite accidental bias. Consider this test question:

Collie is to dog as trout is to ____.
The correct answer, of course, is <u>fish</u>, but if a student came from a background where people never used the word <u>trout</u>—or, more likely, used a slang or dialect equivalent instead—he or she would miss the question, not through lack of ability but, as Wardrop claims, through being different (53).

Here Gerke closely paraphrases a passage from Wardrop. She carefully documents her source

This paragraph contains a claim and a lengthy quotation for evidence. It then concludes with a strong warrant.

In the parlance of the experts, certain test items may have characteristics that "are differentially attractive" to different population subgroups. As Janice Dowd Scheuneman, vice president of the Eastern Educational Research Association, states,

Gerke 6

Unexpected differences in item performance can occur as the result of
. . . urban-rural distinctions,
climatic differences, economic advantage or disadvantage . . . cultural characteristics or values
. . . Spanish language heritage
. . . black English dialects, and
the interpersonal style and communication modes of different ethnic
cultures. (185)

This means that a person's background shapes
his or her perception of the world.

A test constructed by a white, middle-
class male will necessarily reflect many of
his norms and value assumptions. Obviously,
these may differ markedly from those of a
lower-class Hispanic woman, who may be penal-
ized for selecting answers that are true for
her. Her selection of different answers,
however, does not necessarily indicate that
she lacks ability or intelligence. Scheuneman gives the example of one test of auditory
discrimination in which children were asked
to select a picture of the object which began
with the same sound as a word given by the
teacher. In one item,

Gerke uses brackets to
insert material into the
quotation for clarity.

the key word was "heart," and the
correct choice was [the picture of
a] "hand." The first option, however, was a [picture of a] large,

Gerke 7

> fancy car . . . called a "hog" in
> black dialect . . . this option, in
> fact, had drawn a disproportion-
> ately large number of black chil-
> dren. (183–84)

Thus, although the answer was technically incorrect, the children demonstrated that they
actually had the skill being tested. Such
built-in inequities may not happen in most
test items, but they do happen often enough
to support the conclusion that standardized
tests, while "highly perfected" (Ravitch 13),
may not be humanly sensitive.

By referring to *bias* (the umbrella term for the first set of criticisms against the tests), Gerke makes a smooth transition to the next set.

Bias is not the only point of conten-
tion. The great selling features of standardized tests––their ability to predict future performance and their value in assessing
knowledge––are now also under attack. In a
report of the Committee on Ability Testing of
the Assembly of Behavioral and Social Sciences, Alexandra K. Wigdor, study director of
the committee, cites the

Gerke adds italics to emphasize a passage not originally stressed in the source. Her phrase *italics mine* in brackets immediately following the material indicates that this is her addition.

> limited predictive powers of the
> tests . . . the constraints on as-
> sessment <u>introduced by the very</u>
> <u>process of standardization</u> [italics
> mine], the traditional concentra-
> tion of the tests on a limited
> range of cognitive skills . . . and
> the inability of the tests to as-
> sess adequately other important

Gerke 8

characteristics such as motivation, creativity, or perseverance. (6–7)

Problems arise, then, whenever we try to measure people by a single yardstick. Standardization prevents tests from taking into account intangible differences among people, differences in personality factors, such as Wigdor's "motivation, creativity, or perseverance," that might be valuable or crucial to a person's success. Most tests cannot address aspects of character because test takers are often confined to multiple choice answers ("Jensen's Rebuttal"). Yet any truly predictive test must measure such qualities, since what people lack in strictly intellectual or cognitive abilities they can sometimes offset with other abilities or with hard work and dedication. The tests may therefore have the serious shortcoming of ignoring significant predictors of future performance.

Further, not all talented people are talented test takers. Many people acquire skills informally or by habit and are not skilled at recapitulating their knowledge in a test environment. An extremely skilled gardener could flunk a state examination, for example, because he or she is semiliterate or poor at mathematics. Such people can perform deceptively poorly on a standardized test that is designed only to produce a number.

Gerke 9

Critic Andrew J. Strenio says that not accepting a talented individual because of a
low test score is like "Red Auerbach telling
Larry Bird to quit the Celtics until he
scores well on a standardized test about
passing lanes in basketball" (167).

Here is a claim.

No warrant is
necessary for this, the
first piece of evidence.

Sometimes it is difficult to ascertain
exactly what qualities the tests actually
measure. Scientists do not yet agree on a
single definition of the word intelligence,
for example, and as the meaning of the word
changes, so do the tests that try to measure
it ("Brave New World"). Furthermore, a test
item designed to measure one ability may actually test different abilities in different
people. This accidental shifting can occur
in something as simple as a spelling test, as
John R. Bormuth explains:

Here is a second piece
of evidence. The
quotation that follows
makes the evidence
more specific.

> Asking for the spelling of a given
> word may require a student who was
> previously drilled on the word
> merely to recite from rote memory a
> string of letters but require a
> student who was not taught this
> word to analyze it into syllables
> and phonemes and then to apply his
> phonics knowledge to the task. (23)

The warrant explains
how the evidence
works with the claim.
In fact, Gerke makes
the warrant very
detailed: it takes two
sentences.

Consequently, a test item aimed at a specific
ability (phonics knowledge) tested something
quite different (ability to memorize). This
shifting happened because of the different

Gerke 10

experiences of the students being tested,
something that no test may ever fully take
into account. If designers cannot limit what
their questions test, their tests may not
really identify specific abilities and test
for them accurately and fairly.

The Scholastic
Aptitude Test (SAT) is
used as a case study of
standardized tests.

Gerke follows an
important term with
its abbreviation in
parentheses. In later
references she uses just
the abbreviation.

The title of the book is
used when there is no
author. If the title is
very long, a brief form
can be used.

Inequities occur on the largest scale in
the largest, most standardized test of all.
The Scholastic Aptitude Tests (SATs) evaluate
high-school applicants to colleges and universities. Taking SATs has become a senior-
year ritual for more than a million students
every year (On Further Examination 1), and,
despite the disagreements over their value,
SAT scores are still very important parts of
any college application. SATs aim to measure
the student's innate capacity. However, SAT
results may have more to do with one's school
than with intelligence. In an article in New
Republic magazine, Ann Hulbert says that "the
SAT is in fact yet another exam that reflects
the quality of the schools students happen to
attend, rather than a transcendent test that
measures some ambiguous 'aptitude' they possess" (12). Certain schools gear the senior
and sometimes the junior year to preparing
students for the SATs; others run mock exams
or hold classes on how to use the multiple
choice format to help eliminate inaccurate
answers. Thus, the SAT may handicap people
who have intelligence and potential but

Gerke 11

Gerke uses the word *further* to make a smooth transition.

have not attended schools with these programs.

Further, the familiar gaps in average score exist between rich and poor and between racial groups on the SAT as on other tests. Students from families with income under $6,000 per year average about 100 points lower on the verbal and the mathematics parts of the test than those from families with incomes over $18,000 per year. According to the College Entrance Examination Board, blacks average 100 points below the overall average on the verbal part and 115 points below on the mathematics (On Further Examination 15).

This paragraph summarizes the article "Jensen's Rebuttal" since only the main sense of the article was needed.

The great danger of the SATs and other standardized tests is that they may reinforce social hierarchies by the simple fact that a low test score is a social disadvantage. Because of their low test scores, minority children have often been labeled slow or retarded and placed in special schools or, worse yet, have received no further education. Studies show that such children grow up thinking they are stupid and suffer further hardship, since with no education they can expect fewer prospects in society ("Jensen's Rebuttal").

The raised number refers readers to a content note at the end of the paper.

Even minimum competency tests (MCTs), which were designed to reveal basic skill deficiencies so that they could be rectified (Popham 91), may contribute to the problem.[1] The aim behind these tests was to eliminate the gap between racial and economic groups,

Gerke 12

but the tests may reinforce class differenti-
ation and hold back deserving students.

Once the system classifies people according to test results, it tends to perpetuate and accentuate the differences among
them. Although students are no longer rated
"slow" or "fast" learners, Andrew R. Trusz
and Sandra L. Parks-Trusz discovered that a
specific number are classified as "pigeons,"
"hawks," or "eagles" according to their MCT
scores (17). While "eagles" learn the entire
curriculum on which later examinations will
test them, "pigeons" are given only a part of
it, which causes them to fall further and
further behind. The rest of the story is familiar. "Pigeons" could fail to earn a high-
school diploma and thus be cut off from further opportunities at school and at work.
The handicap of social labeling could ensue:
"remediation evokes labelling . . . attaching
a negative label to an individual's actions
causes the individual to develop a negative
self-image. The result is a self-fulfilling
prophecy of failure" (17). Though they are a
result rather than a cause of social assumptions, standardized tests begin this circular
pattern.[2]

Despite these problems in design and social sensitivity, standardized tests have
many uses. They can, in general, effectively
measure performance. To some extent they can

Gerke concedes that tests are valuable in certain ways. This concession will strengthen her thesis when she reasserts it in the next paragraph.

predict how well you or I will do in our future lives; within limits, they can also indicate our aptitudes for various things. For
example, Scientific American reports that SAT
scores are good predictors of how well high-
school seniors will do in their first year in
college ("Scores" 88). Test design has become a science to itself, and, as it develops, its products will improve. And even if
the critics of SATs and MCTs are right, the
political issue of bias by itself is not
enough to justify doing away with testing.
The world of work and school is, whether we
like it or not, still white and middle class,
and, until this changes, everyone needs to
learn how to live and succeed in that world.

Gerke does not just string sources together; she uses her critical faculties and imagination to create a real argument.

The thesis is reasserted at the end, strengthened by the judicious qualifications in the previous paragraph.

We should not, however, rely on standardized tests to the extent we do now. We
should not use them to pigeonhole people, nor
should we allow them to influence our opinions of them. Even such a proponent as Arthur Jensen admits that the tests are overused ("Jensen's Rebuttal"). Educator George
F. Madaus writes,

> The more one knows about the tech-
> nology of testing, the more one
> realizes the potential for harm when
> a test score is used as the sole or
> primary criterion on which to make
> an important decision affecting an
> individual's future. (93)

Gerke 14

Tests may be able to suggest what this or that person's future might be like, but it would be wrong to let them determine that future.

In a neat argumentative move, Gerke notes that other institutions and people think the way she does. This point again strengthens her thesis.

Some colleges and universities have already begun to downplay applicants' test scores in favor of "progressive validity indices" that balance SAT scores with high-school grades, class rank, and the quality of the high-school program (Ravitch 55). Perhaps this practice will start a trend. Perhaps parents, teachers, and administrators—who know students as people—will concentrate on getting as comprehensive a picture of each student as they can and passing that picture on.

The conclusion steps out of the argument, now finished, and makes a proposal, well in keeping with the tone and direction of the paper. This ending is a creative way to finish the paper.

Ironically, perhaps what we need is another test—one for OQ, or "opportunity quotient." This would compare the amount of opportunity in a person's background with that person's achievements. The motivated but disadvantaged student could score well over 100, while the advantaged but only mildly active student might score below. If this sounds whimsical, it may only be because many of us are not used to thinking in minority ways. An OQ test could reveal people whose drive balances their handicaps in other areas. When they try for that job or that place at Harvard, the Naval Academy, or the foreign service, they should have a dossier that shows them not just as a point along a scale but as a person with potential.

The paper ends with a strong closing sentence that appeals to sympathy and humor.

Gerke 15

Notes

Note 1 gives additional information about the MCTs. Gerke originally included this material in the text, but she changed it to a content note so she could focus on her own argument.

[1]Popham believes that MCTs will "restore meaning to a highschool diploma" (91), but opponents like Anderson and Pipho believe that "testing minimal competencies primarily affects low achieving students. . . . It can discourage those who are average or below" (212).

Endnotes can also refer readers to additional sources of information, as in note 2.

[2]See Jaeger for more information about the relationship between standardized tests and student failure.

Gerke 16

Works Cited

Article with two authors.

Anderson, B., and C. Pipho. "State-mandated Testing and the Fate of Local Control." Phi Delta Kappan Nov. 1984: 209-12.

Book with two editors.

Austin, Gilbert R., and Herbert Gardner, eds. The Rise and Fall of National Test Scores. New York: Academic, 1982.

Berk, Ronald, ed. Handbook of Methods for Detecting Test Bias. Baltimore: Johns Hopkins UP, 1982.

Name of publisher is shortened.

Bormuth, John R. On the Theory of Achievement Test Items. Chicago: U of Chicago P, 1970.

Anonymous article, alphabetized by title.

"Brave New World of Intelligence Testing." Psychology Today Sept. 1979: 13.

Eckland's piece is a chapter in Austin and Gardner. Chapter title, in quotation marks, is followed by book authors' names and chapter page numbers. Book is cited in full earlier.

Eckland, Bruce K. "College Entrance Examination Trends." Austin and Gardner 9-34.

Farb, Peter. Word Play. New York: Knopf, 1973.

Green, Robert L., and Robert J. Griffore. "Standardized Testings and Minority Students." Education Digest Feb. 1981: 25-28.

Herbert, W. "Ability Testing Absolved of Racial Bias." Science News 6 Feb. 1982: 84.

Holden, Constance. "NAS Backs Cautious Use of Ability Tests." Science 19 Feb. 1982: 950.

First page number followed by + indicates article is not paged continuously.

Hulbert, Ann. "S.A.T.s Aren't So Smart." New Republic 20 Dec. 1982: 12+.

Gerke 17

Jaeger, Richard M. "The Final Hurdle: Mini-
    mum Competency Achievement Testing."
    Austin and Gardner 223—46.

Jensen, Arthur. Bias in Mental Testing. New
    York: Free, 1980.

"Jensen's Rebuttal." Newsweek 14 Jan. 1980:
    59.

Madaus, George F. "NIE Clarification Hear-
    ing: The Negative Team's Case." Phi
    Delta Kappan Oct. 1981: 92—94.

On Further Examination. New York: College
    Entrance Examination Board, 1977.

Popham, W. James. "The Case for Minimum Com-
    petency Testing." Phi Delta Kappan Oct.
    1981: 89—91.

Ravitch, Diane. "The College Boards." New
    York Times. 4 May 1975, sec. 6: 12+.

Scheuneman, Janice Dowd. "A Posteriori Anal-
    ysis of Biased Items." Berk 180—98.

"Scores." Scientific American Sept. 1978:
    88+.

Smith, Frank. Insult to Intelligence: The
    Bureaucratic Invasion of Our Classrooms.
    New York: Arbor, 1986.

Strenio, Andrew. The Testing Trap. New
    York: Rawson, 1981.

Trusz, Andrew R., and Sandra L. Parks—Trusz.
    "The Social Consequences of Competency
    Testing." Education Digest Apr. 1982:
    15—18.

This anonymous book is alphabetized by the title.

Gerke 18

Wardrop, James L. Standardized Testing in
    the Schools: Uses and Roles. Monterey:
    Brooks, 1976.

Wigdor, Alexandra K. "Ability Testing: Uses,
    Consequences, and Controversies." Edu-
    cational Measurement: Issues and Prac-
    tice 1 (1982): 6–7.

Article in a journal
that paginates
continuously
throughout the year.

TIPS FOR WRITING RESEARCH

- Avoid plagiarism. Be generous in giving explicit acknowledgment to the sources of any ideas that you use in your writing. Give enough information so that the reader can examine the sources you have used.
- Learn and use the MLA parenthetical references and list of works cited format; it is a practical, unobtrusive system for acknowledging sources.
- Careful revision is especially important in a research paper.
- Prepare your manuscript carefully for submission; never turn in anything that is sloppy or illegible.

Exercises for Writing Research

1. Go to the library (and other places!) and find an example of each of the following entries. Type out the entry exactly as it would appear in a list of works cited.
   a. a book with more than one author
   b. an article in a bimonthly periodical
   c. a poem in the second edition of an anthology
   d. a book of the Koran
   e. an edition of *King Lear*
   f. a book in a series
   g. a foreword
   h. a newspaper editorial
   i. a film
   j. a record
   k. a television program

2. Do you know the correct format for the preparation of the research paper? Try answering the following true or false questions. Use this book as a reference.
   a. Endnotes and list of works cited pages are not numbered.
   b. First pages of text are numbered.
   c. There is a comma between the author's name and the page number in a parenthetical reference.
   d. Outlines are numbered in arabic numerals.
   e. Abbreviations are no longer used for entries in lists of works cited.
   f. The list of works cited includes all sources you have consulted.
   g. Your name should appear with the page number on every page beginning with page 2.
   h. It is all right to use computer printouts for research papers.
   i. You can use any kind of paper for your final manuscript.

     j. You may never use correction fluid.

     k. Binders and plastic folders are a good idea.

     l. You never need to use endnotes anymore.

     m. If you cite the author's name before giving a quotation from that author, you need to give the author's name again in the parenthetical reference.

     n. When you indent a long quotation, you should place the parenthetical reference inside the terminal punctuation, just as you do in the text.

3. Write a research paper using at least three book sources and at least two periodical sources. Follow all the rules in this chapter for citation of sources and preparation of the manuscript.

16

THE REPORT: WRITING IN ALL DISCIPLINES

I come not, friends, to steal away your hearts.

I am no orator, as Brutus is;

But (as you know me all) a plain, blunt man

MARC ANTONY IN *JULIUS CAESAR* (3.2.216–218)
WILLIAM SHAKESPEARE (1564–1616)

During your college career, and probably afterward as well, you frequently will be called on to write a report—that is, a brief, reliable summary of a large body of information. Your history instructor might say,

> Write a four-page report on Fernand Braudel's *The Mediterranean and the Mediterranean World in the Age of Philip II.*

Thirteen hundred pages of a book in a few pages of report! Your work is cut out for you. You want to give the reader a good idea of what is really in Braudel's book, but you must be brief. Your emphasis will be on analyzing, summarizing, organizing, and conveying information. You would perform pretty much the same tasks for chemistry lab reports and for reports on new products for your boss.

The report differs from the argumentative essay in that it presents material as objectively as possible, without focusing primarily on expressing an opinion. It differs from the research paper in not requiring wide-ranging, original research. Rather, it tries to represent the knowledge and research of others. In the society of writings, the report is plain and blunt.

Good writing, of course, matters in the report. How we say something determines whether or not our readers understand us and enjoy our writing. But a report is only as good as it is clear, reliable, accessible, and sufficient. Although wit, metaphor, and imagery can help, they cannot substitute for these basic qualities.

As with other writing tasks, we go through a process when we write a report. We can divide this process into seven steps:

determining your scope

getting a handle on the subject

reviewing

devising an organizational thesis

outlining

writing

revising

Because we have spent this entire book discussing writing and revising, we will concentrate here on the other five steps.

DETERMINING YOUR SCOPE

In report writing, determining the scope usually doesn't take very long. Your art instructor assigns a five-page paper on the career of the Russian painter Wassily Kandinsky, or your biochemistry instructor says, "Report on what's been written on the side effects of prednisone." Or your boss says, "We need a report on the performance of middle managers in the Marketing Division yesterday."

Scope, then, depends on purpose. Direct and simple as the stated purpose so often is, you still need to analyze it. Most teachers and most bosses leave some, maybe the largest part, of the assignment unspecified. What is the report supposed to accomplish? How wide a scope should you give it? Does that biochemistry instructor really want a summary of *all* the literature? All the journals? periodicals? drug company blurbs? Does the boss want to know exactly which middle managers are pulling their weight or how Marketing as a whole is doing?

The problem is what to include and how detailed and precise you should be. Aristotle writes that audience, occasion, and purpose will tell you how long and how detailed to make your presentation. To see how these three factors function, read the following chart:

AUDIENCE	OCCASION	PURPOSE
Rocket scientists	Twentieth Annual International Conference of Rocket Scientists for Arms Control	To give a background briefing on the growth of nuclear armaments in the Third World

Your art class	Daily meeting	To introduce for discussion the work of Georgia O'Keeffe
Corporate directors and senior officers	Board meeting	To provide the basis for acquiring your main competitor for $150 million

In each case, audience, occasion, and purpose will help determine the length and detail of the report. Whenever you write, after all, you make certain assumptions about what your audience does and does not already know. If your readers are well informed, you may not need to dally with introductions and elementary issues; instead, you can begin at a sophisticated, detailed level. But if your readers know very little or have differing levels of expertise, those introductions and elementary issues may well be in order.

In the first example, the report need not be very long: the interested and educated audience probably needs only to be reminded of the situation; the occasion is not to discuss the Third World except as a symptom of a larger problem, and the words *background briefing* suggest that the large picture, rather than detail, is in order. In the second example, the report should provide an overview broad enough for an uninformed audience—your art class—to take in but with enough detail to give them a basis for discussion. In the third example, well, you had better be very careful and very thorough: the future of the company depends on the accuracy of your report, and so does *your* future. The directors will no doubt require a high level of detail before making such a momentous decision.

As a final word on length and level of detail, we want to share the best advice we ever heard uttered, by a tough advertising manager to his young employee about to write his first report: "Do a little more than they expect—but not a whole lot more."

GETTING A HANDLE ON THE SUBJECT

Once you know your audience, occasion, and purpose, you can begin to pull together the information for your report. Start off by scouting the topic. If you rush right in, you could get lost in the thickets. You need to know how far afield you should go. If you are reporting on a single book, read that book, and then check in some bibliographic dictionaries for information about the author (see "The Reference Section" in Chapter 14). Find out what reviewers and critics have said. If you are reporting on a fairly limited subject, such as the life and works of Georgia O'Keeffe, perhaps two or three books will suffice. For some subjects, however, such as nuclear armaments in the Third World, you may need to go to the library and look into many books and periodicals. (For a discussion of research processes, see Chapter 14, Doing Research.)

Whatever your project—be it a book report, a lab report, a progress report, or an accident report—take copious notes. You probably will not be able (or willing) to do your work twice—so do it once thoroughly. Note more, not less, than you think you need—you can toss what you don't need, but it is painful to find what you lack. And take careful notes. Write down authors' names, titles, publishers, dates, and page numbers for your sources. (For a discussion of quotation and paraphrase, see "Taking Notes" and "Using Your Evidence" in Chapter 14.)

We vastly prefer notecards to notebooks, and we like to note very little on each card. Why? Because these cards with sparse notations are so flexible. When you've completed your analysis, you can arrange the cards in all kinds of ways. You can make an outline with them (see "Getting from Thesis to Outline" on page 432), and you can even arrange them according to how you intend to write your paper.

But first comes analysis of the subject. In the pages that follow, we suggest five ways to analyze information.

The Précis

When instructors ask you to report on a book or passage, they are probably asking for a précis, that is, a concise summary or condensation. The point of such an assignment is to ensure that you have read the material and understand it. (If instructors also want an evaluation, they say so, and that usually will come in a paragraph or two after the précis.) In the working world, mastering the précis may help you condense material for someone who hasn't the time to read it in toto.

Here are the ten steps for writing a précis:

1. Map the text before starting to read. (See "An Overview: Mapping the Text" in Chapter 5.)

2. After mapping, write out what you think the author's main point is. Doing this will help you to recognize and evaluate the main ideas.

3. Go back to the first paragraph and begin reading. Carefully. If it occurs to you that you did not identify the main point, restate it. You need that point to keep your reading on track.

4. Write a brief summary, on a notecard or separate sheet of paper, for each major idea. If the reading is short, summarize each paragraph in a note. For longer works, try to combine ideas even when they are spread over several paragraphs.

5. Make a page reference for each summary. You'll need this later.

6. Briefly note particularly significant or interesting supporting ideas so you can return to them. When the main ideas are very complex or unclear, be sure to note the supporting details that will clarify them.

7. Avoid direct quotation. Only when you translate the ideas into your own words can you be sure you understand them—and when you write your report, your instructor will want your words in order to be sure you understand the reading.

8. Retain the author's order, emphasis, and tone. By order, we mean the general arrangement of major points. You may well need to combine snippets of ideas from different parts of the piece—but adhere to the general arrangement. Similarly for emphasis. If a twenty-page essay on dog breeding devotes fifteen pages to training and only five to grooming, observe that general three-to-one ratio of discussion in your paraphrase. And it is essential to preserve the author's tone. If you don't, you will misrepresent the author and mislead your reader. Imagine a paraphrase that was serious when the author was only fooling—or vice versa. In either case, the writer and reader would miss the point together. Remember—your reader depends on your summaries to convey what is actually in the work.

9. Avoid interpretations and evaluations. Keep your opinions to yourself. This is harder than it sounds. It is not merely a matter of not stating agreement or disagreement. Opinions may slip into the tone in which you couch your summaries. Be careful. An intrusion of your opinion not only will confuse you when it comes to writing but will also confuse the reader later.

10. Once you complete the reading, check your summary notes against the text and identify the contours of the argument.

The Pentad

The critic Kenneth Burke devised a set of five questions that offer a way of analyzing any piece of expository prose—newspaper, magazine, book, history text, primary document. These questions, called the pentad, are fairly obvious, but asking them systematically can help you understand a text and thus begin a report.

Suppose you were asked to report on a rather lengthy article entitled "Bourgeois Self-interest and Human Rights." Here is how you might use the pentad to analyze it.

1. *What does it say?* Summarize or paraphrase the article to get its main point. ("American concern for human rights proceeds from the bourgeois-capitalist misconception of the importance of individualism.")

2. *Who wrote it?* Check the bias, special interest, and expertise of the author, and his or her biography if possible. ("Anatoli Goncharov of the Washington Bureau of the Soviet news agency Tass. He has been in the United States for four years and has maintained a steady anti-Americanism.")

3. *In what source was it published?* Check the source's general reputation. Is it considered objective and reliable? ("Published in *New Worlds a-Coming: Marxist Journal of Opinion,* a strongly pro-Soviet journal, unlikely to offer a balanced opinion but a good reflection of Soviet thought.")

4. *When and where was it published?* Look at the source in regard to historical and geographic background, as well as its intended audience. ("Published in Auckland, New Zealand, in 1986, during a period of animosity between New Zealand and the United States over nuclear weapons on U.S. ships stopping at New Zealand ports. Subscribers are leftist New Zealanders.")

5. *What is its purpose?* Think about the immediate purpose as well as the ultimate and even ulterior purpose, if any. ("By suggesting that the U.S. emphasis on human rights is self-serving and hypocritical, the author intends to undercut the United States among New Zealanders and perhaps to influence New Zealand opinion about nuclear-armed U.S. ships. But in the light of *glasnost* and the opening of Communist societies, the article could reflect an internal issue in leftist circles.") Read it again.

The Journalistic Method

Sometimes you may be reporting on events rather than on reading. If so, the journalistic method, mentioned in Chapter 1, provides a list of headings under which you can take notes or analyze your material into its most important elements. This method, used by beginning reporters, asks six questions: who? what? when? where? how? and why? By answering these questions, you gain control of the subject.

Suppose you were asked to report on the election of Richard Nixon to the presidency in 1968. Try asking the six questions:

Who? Richard M. Nixon, former congressman, senator, vice president; previously defeated for the presidency

What? won a contentious U.S. presidential election

When? in 1968, during the height of the Vietnam War and the attendant protests

Where? in all parts of the nation, though his victory margin was slim

How? most experts agree Nixon won because most voters thought he could end the war and bring back stability to society

Why? because the nation saw itself in the throes of upheaval and uncertainty and feared that opponent Hubert Humphrey would continue outgoing president Lyndon Johnson's policies

This analysis provides a structure for a report, complete with all the details, the numbers, the narratives, the explanations.

For events that do not involve people—volcanic eruptions, for instance—use the "headless" method: drop the Who? and answer the other five questions.

Format for Analyzing Raw Data

Scientists and social scientists often present their experiments and collections of data according to a format—that is, a generally accepted arrangement of the various aspects of the study. (Who "accepts" this arrangement? The community of other scientists. Again, audience is important.) Such a format can help you to get a handle on a large amount of raw data. Perhaps the most useful, and common, is this one:

problem or purpose
review of the literature
method
data
discussion

PROBLEM OR PURPOSE. In the "Problem" section, you set forth the problem you studied: What happens when I add this chemical to that and turn up the heat? What are the religious habits of the people of Abilene, Kansas? You will perhaps want to indicate the relevance of the problem to a larger field and how you differentiate it from similar problems. You might find it helpful to narrate or describe how you arrived at the problem and to define various terms. (In some formats, this section is called "Purpose," but that is not much different; your purpose is usually to address the problem.)

REVIEW OF THE LITERATURE. In collecting your own raw data or performing experiments, you will sometimes be required to review important studies of the subject. (Ask your instructor whether a review of the literature will be required.) Reviews of the literature accomplish three things: they establish that the problem really is a problem, they let the reader know what research has been done in the field, and they establish that you are informed enough to undertake the study. The literature you review should be recent, authoritative, and well known in the field. Don't list all the studies, but concentrate on those that have most significance for your discussion.

METHOD.   Your most important sections will be "Method" and "Data," because in them you will describe how you gathered the material and what you found out. Under "Method," you narrate how you went about your study, what steps you followed in what order. In lab reports, you describe how you designed your experiment; in a field study in the social sciences, you describe the interviews, polls, and quantitative techniques you used to amass your information. As a rule of thumb, this description should be detailed enough for someone else to follow exactly in your footsteps and presumably to arrive at the same conclusions.

DATA.   The data section is all-important. In it you gather the information your study has produced. Don't interpret: report. Here is where you would tell that you changed lead into gold in the lab—or blew up six retorts and got tar in your test tube. Here is where you would present the statistics you amassed on church attendance in Abilene. Write your data section as objectively and clearly as possible. Only then will you know—and your ultimate reader believe—that your study has been successfully conducted.

DISCUSSION.   In the discussion section, you make sense of the data. You go beyond the sheer facts of the study to discuss their meaning and their importance. Here you might explain why you think you blew up the lab just as the lead was turning into gold, or why the people of Abilene are such big churchgoers. If in the process of doing this analysis, you discovered other lines of inquiry, this would be the place to mention them.

Here is an outline of a psychiatric study of depressed patients.

Problem: Some depressed people are merely depressed. But others have "psychotic depression"—that is, they not only are depressed but have delusions or hallucinations. We wondered if such people were more or less likely to commit suicide than were people with simple depression.

Review of the Literature: [Reviews eight other studies—"by Guze and Robins, by Pokorny, by Weissman . . . "—that have defined and treated the problem.]

Method: We looked back over the files of all depressed patients who had committed suicide over 25 years at the Psychiatric Institute in New York. We classified them into a "depressed suicide group" and a "control group" of depressed patients who had not committed suicide. We further classed each group into those that had psychotic features and those that did not.

Data: Here is what our survey found:

	Psychotic Features	Nonpsychotic
Suicide group	10	4
Control group	9	19

Out of 14 suicides, 10 patients had psychotic features and 4 did not. In our control group of 28 patients, however, only about a third had psychotic features. We thus figured the odds ratio:

$$\text{Odds ratio} = \frac{10 \times 19}{4 \times 9} = 5.3 \text{ relative risk}$$

Discussion: A depressed patient with psychotic features is 5.3 times more likely to commit suicide than a depressed patient without such features. Patients with psychotic depression should thus be treated quickly and effectively, and they need to be watched more carefully if they are institutionalized. "Once hospitalized, the patients still require special suicide precautions and must be regarded with a high degree of caution, even when they appear recovered." (Based on S. P. Roose et al., "Depression, Delusions, and Suicide")

Division and Classification

In addition to helping you develop your thoughts (see Chapter 9), division and classification can help you get a handle on a large topic. (Indeed, any of the strategies can be helpful.) Some subjects are so large that to get a handle on them at all we need to break them down into smaller units. How impossible it would be for biologists to think about "living creatures" without breaking down the subject into the categories of kingdom, phylum, class, order, family, genus, and species! These categories help us sort out the myriad individuals according to similarities and differences.

The trick is to discover the most helpful way to break down a big subject. Suppose your history instructor asked you to report on the geography of Africa. What an enormous subject! Right off, you would divide the subject to make it more manageable: north, south, east, west, central. You would then gather data about each of these areas.

But as you gathered data you probably would begin to see more significant and revealing divisions. That Mali is in the west is not nearly so important as that much of it is desert. You might decide on a different division, one based on climate or terrain: the Sahara, the Sahel, the Congo region, the plains, and so on. Once you have divided up this enormous subject in a rational way, you will begin to see which parts of it you can report on.

Or suppose you were taking a course in nutrition. The first division of foods is fairly obvious: fats, proteins, and carbohydrates. But you wouldn't understand very much about nutrition if all you could do was throw a foodstuff into one of these categories. Not all proteins are the same, not all fats are alike, not all carbohydrates possess identical nutritional value. Time to divide again.

Fats:
saturated   monounsaturated   polyunsaturated

Carbohydrates:
sugars   starches

Proteins:
simple   fibrous   conjugated

Under each heading you would begin to place the appropriate foodstuffs. Dividing and classifying is a handy way to organize vast amounts of information.

COGITATING AND REVIEWING

Go over your notes early and often. We have had the experience of so intently jotting down notes that not one piece of information blowing by actually stuck to our brain. We might not have even been able to state the subject. But when we went over those notes, it all made sense. Once you have a pretty good handle on the subject, carefully review all your notes, card by card. After each review, sit back and cogitate.

Ask yourself these questions about the material:

What is the most significant aspect of the subject?

What are four or five other significant aspects?

What connections have I noted?

Can I find similarities with another topic?

Can I find recurring themes?

Is there a natural way to organize the information?

This is where the organizational thesis comes in.

DEVISING AN ORGANIZATIONAL THESIS

In "The Thesis" in Chapter 2, we pointed out the differences between the argumentative thesis and the organizational thesis. The argumentative thesis sets out the opinion or evaluation or view that the essay will attempt to prove. The organizational thesis does not focus primarily on an argument but rather establishes the writer's approach to the body of information. It says, "I have surveyed this material, and this is how we will travel over it." Your organizational thesis is your plan for the trip. It tells both you and your reader where you intend to go and what you intend to do along the way.

In the following pages, we discuss seven possible forms the organizational thesis can take. Most reports will have a thesis that takes one of these forms.

Establishing Chronological Order

In writing about history or explaining how something happens, we quite naturally narrate events in the order in which they occur or occurred. An organizational thesis establishing chronological order lets the reader know the way we will organize this report, as this famous anthropologist does:

> The life of the day begins at dawn, or if the moon has shown until daylight, the shouts of the young men may be heard before dawn from the hillside. Uneasy in the night, populous with ghosts, they shout lustily to one another as they hasten with their work. As the dawn begins to fall among the soft brown roofs . . . (Margaret Mead, *Coming of Age in Samoa*)

Now we know that Mead will follow Samoan life through a typical day, from dawn to sunset.

Indicating Main Divisions

This is one of the simplest kinds of organizational thesis. It merely tells the reader how the subject will be divided and what the order will be.

> I will describe the society into which Virginia Woolf was born, offer an account of her life, and conclude with an annotated bibliography of major critical studies of her work.

This thesis statement plainly and bluntly informs the reader into what segments the material is divided and when to expect each segment.

Suggesting Recurrent Themes

As you study a topic, you will notice themes that arise again and again. Your stack of notes will be larger under certain headings than under others. Those large stacks indicate a recurring theme in your subject. Such themes can help you organize your thoughts. And when you encapsulate the recurrent themes in your organizational thesis, you tell your reader what is important.

After studying disputes over gun control laws, a student found that these themes kept popping up:

> the constitutional right to bear arms
>
> the necessity for owning guns in some parts of the country
>
> how easy it is for anyone, including criminals, to buy guns
>
> the relation between the crime rate and ownership of guns

He devised this organizational thesis for his report:

> The two sides line up over the issue of individual rights and needs as against society's need.

Indicating the Means of Discussion

Often the most helpful bit of information is *how* the discussion will be conducted. A thesis that indicates this provides the context within which the reader can evaluate the material. In the following, a musicologist explains how he will conduct a discussion of music in Africa:

> In this chapter we will examine some of the general characteristics of African music, and we will draw heavily on the work of a few scholars who have made an effort to condense their broad experience into brief summaries. To illustrate these characteristics I will rely mainly on my own greater familiarity with Dagomba and Ewe drumming . . . (John Miller Chernoff, *African Rhythm and African Sensibility*)

Description of the subject, the sources, the kinds of examples, and the way they connect helps to orient the reader to the discussion that follows.

Defining the Subject

A definition often can point out the arrangement of an essay. In the following, the authors define their terms in order to tell us what they will and will not discuss:

> No cheeses have such loyal supporters and such vociferous critics as the very strong cheeses such as Limburger, Liederkranz, Livarot and a half-dozen others, which have in common an aroma as unequivocal as a thunderclap. People who like them extol as virtues the very qualities that others deplore. Looking at Liederkranz that is *à point*, an enthusiast will see below its russet mantle the creamy, smooth cheese within—a

cheese with something of the flavor of a Camembert or Brie intensified
many times over. To him the flavor is robust, the aroma awe-inspiring.
But to his opposite number, that aroma, in the words of Oscar Burdett,
can "cling and penetrate with the tenacity of cigar smoke. Perhaps for
this reason," he adds, "the puritan nose twitches in indignation." (Vi-
vienne Marquis and Patricia Haskell, *The Cheese Book*)

The authors are not going to discuss cottage cheese or bologna, and they
are going to tell us about those smelly cheeses.

Establishing the "Angle"

Webster's Ninth New Collegiate Dictionary defines the word *angle* both
as "the precise viewpoint from which something is observed" and as "a
special approach, point of attack, or technique for accomplishing an objective." Just as in journalism, in many reports it is essential to establish your
angle—where you stand, what your special approach or attack will be—
before you begin to tell your story. In the following paragraph, an author
rejects several possible angles in favor of the one he will use in his book
on South Africa:

> It wasn't the problem of the color bar that gripped me—"the color
> bore," an English journalist once wrote—or even the great mystery of
> how it would turn out in the end. Least of all was I preoccupied by
> South Africa's supposed strategic significance for the West. It was the
> place itself, its actual workings, its here and now. (Joseph Lelyveld, *Move
> Your Shadow*)

"The place itself," then, is Lelyveld's angle, where he chooses to stand.
That is enough to organize his view of South Africa and give us an authoritative, detailed look.

Setting Up a Comparison

Sometimes you may be asked to compare and contrast two objects,
two theories, two events, two proposals. Other times you may see that
you can more brightly illuminate one subject by comparing it with a similar subject. In either case you need to set out for your reader what you
will compare as well as suggest the attributes that will go into the comparison.

As we discussed in Chapter 9, Strategies for Developing Your
Thoughts, a comparison can be either item by item—that is, a complete
presentation of one side before going on to the other—or attribute by attribute—that is, a thorough comparison of the two sides under one head-

ing before comparing them under the next. Which method you will follow should be clear in the organizational thesis.

In an essay on the simultaneous invention of the telephone by Alexander Graham Bell and the obscure Elisha Gray, David Hounshell concludes his brief introduction with this clear statement of his organizational thesis:

> In the history of the telephone, the world of the professional and the world of the amateur appear at almost every turn, as will be made clear by a brief exploration of the two worlds, first Gray's and then Bell's. ("Two Paths to the Telephone")

Thus, Hounshell establishes what he will do—narrate the story of the two inventions—and how he will do it—complete one before going on to the other.

If you intend to compare attribute by attribute, that too should be clear from your organizational thesis.

> The Soviet and American electoral systems might even seem superficially similar, except for the issues of who may vote, how one votes, whether the ballot is secret, and whether the choice is among a representative range of candidates.

Although she could hardly keep a straight face, the writer had clearly established an attribute-by-attribute organization.

The organizational thesis tells both you and the reader how the report will be organized. It provides the frame on which you can hang all the material you have gathered.

Here are some suggestions for choosing the right organizational thesis.

1. Make it interesting and accessible. No matter how dull you think the subject, how automatic the assignment, rise to the occasion and catch the reader's interest. Avoid overly technical language, slang, facetiousness. Make the thesis readable so that the reader can get into the report and the harder, more complex, issues with you.

2. Avoid overcomplicating your thesis. What the reader needs is a map, not a directory of gasoline stations and cafés along the way. If, for instance, the authors of the cheese book had included the name and locale of every strong cheese, along with some distinctions between strong cheeses and overripe cheeses, the reader would likely be confused. The authors take care of all that later in the report, where it belongs.

3. Be sure your thesis suggests all the major points of the paper. It need not state them by name but should suggest the range of the exploration.

Like the argumentative thesis, the organizational thesis should authoritatively sum up the entire scope of the discussion.

GETTING FROM THESIS TO OUTLINE

Once you have your organizational thesis clearly in mind, the next step is to outline your report (see "Developing, Organizing, Drafting" in Chapter 2). And where is all your evidence? Where are the major and minor points? In your notes, of course. Go through them, and identify the major ideas. Be relaxed about it: don't aim for a specific number, but if an idea seems important, hold on to it.

Now stack behind each of these major ideas any related smaller ideas. If, for instance, you were writing on the architectural theories of Frank Lloyd Wright, you might have a major card dealing with Wright's idea of "the natural house." Under this card, you might file cards with entries on building materials and cards with entries on building sites. Under each of these you might file cards detailing smaller ideas, for instance, "glass" or "Wright's hostility to suburbs."

Go through your entire packet, and try to place every card. If something absolutely will not fit anywhere, don't throw it out—you may need it—but put it in a "Miscellaneous" stack. If that stack begins to climb too high, check your organizational thesis to be sure you really have selected the right road over this material—your road, after all, ought to pass by most of the major attractions. If your thesis doesn't allow for that, you probably need a new one. Don't be afraid of devising another thesis.

Once you have placed all your cards, take a fresh look at the major ideas. Are they all equally important? Are they mutually exclusive, or does one overlap another? Are there any obvious gaps between the ideas, or do they seem to cover the subject? Do you need more information about any of them? If everything is in order, try making an outline. With a strong outline and well-organized notes, your writing will be little more than filling in.

PARTING SHOTS

We want to close this chapter with three pieces of advice.

1. Your report, like any essay, should have a beginning, a middle, and an end. At the beginning provide the necessary background, and define terms the reader needs at the outset. Then, of course, state your organizational thesis to tell the reader what is coming. Reports often become disorganized in the middle, so concentrate on those paragraphs. Follow your outline; include what it includes in the same order. If you find yourself discussing ideas not in your outline, go back and see if you can fit

them into the outline. If you can't, either drop the ideas or change the outline. At the end of reports, it is permissible—often required—to summarize your most important points. Even so, good conclusions give a sense of closure, of "wrapping up." Don't miss this chance to give your reader one last good grip on the subject. Never trail off in a whirl of loose ends.

2. Package your information; don't dump it. Each paragraph should be organized around a single main idea, all sentences should relate to that main idea, and the connections between ideas should be smooth and clear. Some report writers, unfortunately, treat paragraphs as little "information dumps." They simply unload a handful of information in each one, and it doesn't matter whether any is related or organized.

> Not all brain hemorrhages are fatal, although the brain tissue may be damaged. The rate of survival depends on age, concomitant health status of the patient, and other pre-existing factors. There may be some paralysis or loss of sensory capabilities. Hemorrhages are often caused by atherosclerosis. Along with cerebral infarctions, cerebral hemorrhages are a prime cause of stroke. A burst blood vessel floods an area of the brain. Cerebral infarctions are often caused by atherosclerosis too.

All important bits of information, but when dumped out in a jumble like this, not much use to the reader. In the revision, the writer packaged the information. In one paragraph he combined the information on causation and pathology of hemorrhage, and in a second he discussed recovery.

> Cerebral hemorrhage is the bursting of a blood vessel that serves the brain. Like infarctions, hemorrhages are often caused by atherosclerosis, in which deposits inside the blood vessels constrict the passageway for blood. When this happens, the arteries may become hardened, lose their resilience, and become vulnerable to blockage or breakage. Along with cerebral infarctions, cerebral hemorrhages are a prime cause of stroke.
>
> Not all brain hemorrhages are fatal, although brain tissue damage is usually sustained. The rate of survival depends on age, concomitant health status, and other pre-existing factors. But even in patients who survive and apparently recover well, there may be some paralysis or loss of sensory capabilities.

Much better. You don't have to be a neurosurgeon to follow the discussion. (Actually, most neurosurgeons would find the original just as jumbled as we did.) Watch out for information dumps; they are especially common after the midpoint of an essay, when the writer, close to deadline, is working down to the end of the note pile.

3. Plan to revise. With a strong outline and well-organized note-cards, you are well prepared to write, but even so you will find it difficult to get every idea firmly nailed in place. In your effort to get in all the

information, you may find yourself writing, "Oh, yes, I forgot to say on page 3 that . . ." Reread your report most carefully from the midpoint on to scout out information dumps, loose ends, and gaping holes in the development. Remember, a report is only as good as it is clear, reliable, accessible, and sufficient.

TIPS FOR THE REPORT

- Let audience, occasion, and purpose determine the scope of your study.
- Take careful and detailed notes.
- To get a handle on the subject, consider using the précis, the pentad, the journalistic method, the ready-made format for analyzing raw data, or division and classification.
- At some point in your study, just sit down, review your notes, and cogitate.
- Formulate an effective organizational thesis that will tell your reader, and you, how you plan to cover the material.
- Based on your thesis, prepare an outline, and organize your notes around it.
- Make sure your report has a beginning, a middle, and an end.
- Don't just dump information, package it.
- Revise a report just as you would any other writing.

Exercises for the Report

1. Here is a series of topics. Choose one and follow the process for writing a report outlined in this chapter. With the help of your classmates and instructor, determine your scope. Then review your subject, devise your organizational thesis, write, and revise.

   the trial of Socrates
   the Crédit Mobilier scandal, 1867–1872
   the Supreme Court's *Roe* v. *Wade* decision, 1973
   the Ethiopian famine, 1981–82
   how geese know it's time to fly south for the winter
   the career of photographer Margaret Bourke-White
   what supply-side economics is
   the Sumerian epic *Gilgamesh*
   the murder trial of Fatty Arbuckle
   why superconductivity is important
   the career of American poet Robert Lowell

the career of English anthropologist L. S. B. Leakey
the construction of the Golden Gate Bridge
the gypsy moth

2. Discuss how audience, occasion, and purpose would dictate scope and depth in the following reports:

   a report on the career of Arnold Schwarzenegger to be delivered orally for your "Physical Training" class

   a report on a new technique of laser surgery of the eye for a convention of the American Ophthalmological Society

   an end-of-term report on the Palestine Liberation Organization for your class "Mideast History, 1970–1985"

   a report on your car crash last week for your insurance company

   a report on the Super Bowl for the front page of tomorrow's *New York Times*

   a report on the toxic effects of a new drug for a committee of the Food and Drug Administration that is considering that drug for public use

   a report to the mayor on the moral profile of a policeman being considered for the open position of chief of police

   a report on the recent extraction of your wisdom teeth, for your mother, who hasn't seen you in four months

3. Read one of the following essays and write a précis of it. Discuss the special problems you encountered in writing your précis. What did you leave out? What did you include? Why?

   Walter Lippmann, "The Indispensable Opposition"
   Karl Marx, "The Communist Manifesto"
   Woody Allen, "My Speech to the Graduates"
   Brigid Brophy, "The Rights of Animals"
   Richard Nixon, "The 'Checkers' Speech"
   James Rachels, "Active and Passive Euthanasia"
   Joan Didion, "Bureaucrats"
   Alison Lurie, "Male and Female"

4. What methods of analysis—including the précis, the pentad, the journalistic method, the format for analyzing raw data, or division and classification—would work best with the following topics? Explain.

   the patterns of college attendance by minority students
   The Autobiography of Alice B. Toklas by Gertrude Stein
   the changing place of protists in biological schemes of classification
   the space shuttle disaster of 1986
   starlings, grackles, and crows
   methods of irrigating and fertilizing desert regions
   the eruption of Mt. St. Helens
   an experiment in which cats were trained to walk tightropes

5. Read each of the following organizational theses and discuss what it tells the reader and what kind of report you expect based just on reading the thesis.

   A close look at what does actually take place may explain in large measure the undertaker's intractable reticence concerning a procedure that has become his major *raison d'être.* (Jessica Mitford, *The American Way of Death*)

Here, after all, were two forms of nature in collision: the elements and human nature. Last Wednesday, the elements, indifferent as ever, brought down Flight 90. And on that same afternoon, human nature—groping and flailing in mysteries of its own—rose to the occasion. (Roger Rosenblatt, "The Man in the Water")

A definition that should really define [beauty] must be nothing less than the exposition of the origin, place, and elements of beauty as an object of human existence. (George Santayana, "The Nature of Beauty")

Many now agree that the sexual revolution of the 1960s worked a profound change on our society's family values and personal relationships. Certainly, the seeds of upheaval were present before that critical decade. But a major change that occurred in the mid-sixties was an explicit rejection of the common values about sexual and family relationships that most Americans in the past had held up as an ideal. (George Gallup, Jr., and William Proctor, *Forecast 2000*)

17

READING, INTERPRETING, AND WRITING ABOUT LITERATURE

There are three points of view from which a writer can be considered: he may be considered as a storyteller, as a teacher, and as an enchanter.

VLADIMIR NABOKOV (1899–1977)
STORYTELLER, TEACHER, ENCHANTER

Many of the most intense and moving moments in our lives have come thanks to literature. It has clarified our thinking and feeling, and changed us in ways we cannot put into words. We have been entertained, taught, and enchanted by it.

The challenges of literature are bracing. Responding to poems, plays, novels, and stories calls for both sensitivity and clarity. It demands an open mind as well as close attention. Yet far from "taking the fun out of literature," accepting its challenges increases both our understanding and our enjoyment.

In the pages that follow, we treat the study of literature as a three-part process of reading, interpreting, and writing.

READING LITERATURE

Reading literature is different from reading a textbook, editorial, or essay. If you tried to use the eight questions in Chapter 5, Critical Reading, on Albert Camus's *The Plague*, T. S. Eliot's *The Waste Land,* or Anton Chekhov's *Three Sisters,* you would not have much success. Literature does not follow the rules of argument. Rather, it presents the world as the writer views it. And it presents this world in a language that is important for itself as well as for what it conveys. To get at the world of the writer and the beauty of its language, the eight questions offer little help.

So—how should you read a poem, a play, a novel, or a short story?

First of all, you should respect the world the work describes. Literature is always a product of a particular time and a particular place. Good readers try to view a work within its own context. Of course, no reader can wholly escape being culture bound; our customs and codes of behavior are too firmly planted. But good readers try to control the bias of their own class and era. They recognize that though values may be eternal, their expression is finite and various. Social relationships may be different. Definitions of acceptable behavior may have changed.

Plan to read any work of literature more than once. If you read an expository or argumentative essay carefully, you may well get its whole meaning with one pass—few would read an editorial twice. But literature will not yield its fullness of meaning in one reading. On the first reading, simply read. Don't try to be critical. Give yourself up to the work. Let it possess you.

When reading a poem, read aloud, slowly. Let the rhythms of the poem control the tempo and cadence of your reading. Listen to the music of the poem. Get a friend to read it with you. Never confine a poem to your head. Perform it and listen to the performance. As you read, think about the words themselves, their denotations and their connotations and how they join with the music to create the total effect.

When reading longer works, set aside at least one, preferably two, hours for uninterrupted periods of reading. Dive in and stay in until you get the feel of the work. Whenever you pick it up, give yourself time to settle in. If you only read piecemeal, five pages at a time, you may end up with a piecemeal view of the work.

Keep your mind open during the first reading. Don't try to make the story or poem mean what you expect; let it show you its own meaning. Literature is often startling, outraging, and bewildering. It may ridicule or deny your most cherished beliefs. Do not reject it: learn from it.

On this first reading, don't take notes. They are apt to break your connection with the work by introducing the critical element. If something strikes you, pencil a little check in the margin or circle a phrase (except if it's a library book). Later you can return to these spots to make full notes.

Warning: no one can skim a piece of literature and expect to get much out of it. You may learn some facts, but you cannot comprehend the quality of the work. Nor can you get much when you rely on the assessments or interpretations of others. There are notes, summaries, and shortcuts on the market today that promise a quick way through novels, plays, and poems. They, too, give facts, but the one thing these shortcuts can never give you is the work itself. There simply is no substitute for a sensitive reading of the text. Don't cheat yourself.

When you have finished this first reading, meditate on what you have read. Think about the ideas, the events, the language. Write a short paraphrase, like these, of the main concern of the work—or your main response to it.

> This poem is about the anguish of unrequited love and how its not being returned makes the loved one more attractive.

> There are a lot of marriages in this novel, but not all are happy because the people are silly or too selfish to adjust.

Thorough readers have been performing such exercises for centuries: they help firm one's hold on the material.

Now reread the work. This time, annotate the text. Write notes on notecards or in a separate notebook. If you scribble all over your book, your notes will stay unorganized, and you may not be able to find them again.

If the work is long, summarize each chapter. If it is short, paraphrase the whole thing. When you come across one of your checks or circled passages, analyze what struck you the first time. Don't hesitate to go back and forth, to compare different sections. Pause at important junctures. If the characters are confusing, make a list of them. If the language strikes you as unusual, describe its qualities. Take special note of whatever you find arresting. Make exact page references.

General Topics in Literature

What do we look for when we read literature? Literature is so rich that no discussion could possibly cover it. In this section, however, we deal with three important elements common to all literature: theme, symbolism, and language. (Later we will discuss special topics in fiction and poetry.)

THEME. A literary work often expresses the values of the writer and his or her conceptions of the human condition. But these values and conceptions are rarely simple and obvious. A work of literature cannot be reduced to a simple moral. Nor can it be treated as though it were a philosophical or sociological treatise. Usually, though, the reader is left with a sense of the point or meaning of a work. This is what we call the theme.

This theme is expressed throughout the work, as either a recurrent idea or a general preoccupation. Examples of a theme might be frustrated desire in Emily Brontë's *Wuthering Heights,* obsession in Herman Melville's *Moby-Dick,* the alienation of modern life in T. S. Eliot's *The Waste Land.* As you read, you can note what changes the theme undergoes and what significance it has either in the world of the work or in your world.

SYMBOLISM.   A symbol is a sign standing for something else. The thirteen stripes in the American flag symbolize the original colonies, and the fifty stars symbolize the fifty states. In literature, a symbol is an image that stands for more than its physical properties indicate. When Hamlet holds up Yorick's skull, that skull stands not just for the remains of a human being but also for death, the certainty that it will come to everyone, including Hamlet.

How can you tell when an image is a symbol? Repetition is one great clue. In *Moby-Dick,* the whale and its whiteness are everywhere and on everyone's mind; they are more than a physical reality. Sometimes the environment of a work will indicate which images you should see as symbolic. When Hamlet holds up Yorick's skull, for instance, he is standing beside a grave and debating death with a grave digger. Hamlet knows his own death is near. You would have to try hard to miss the symbolic function of Yorick's skull in these surroundings. Often shared experiences can lead you to symbols. When you see a human skull, you can hardly avoid thinking of death. When T. S. Eliot, in "The Love Song of J. Alfred Prufrock," writes

Do I dare to eat a peach?

you recognize that it is hardly a brave act to eat a peach, and so you may conclude that eating a peach is symbolic: Eliot is telling you that even innocent acts can be threatening in our time.

LANGUAGE.   Another common focus of our reading literature is various aspects of language, such as tone and imagery. *Tone* is the atmosphere an author creates by the way he or she uses language. It often indicates an attitude toward the subject or toward the audience. When we seek to determine the tone of a work, we are trying to understand the actual voice in which it should be read—serious, sarcastic, playful, or whatever. Edgar Allan Poe begins "The Fall of the House of Usher" with this:

> During the whole of a dull, dark, and soundless day in the autumn of the year, when the clouds hung oppressively low in the heavens, I had been passing alone, on horseback, through a singularly dreary tract of country.

His choice of words, with all those dull *d* sounds, and the slow, ponderous cadence create an atmosphere heavy with threat. Solemn and ominous, the tone shapes our responses.

One very common tone in literature is *irony.* Irony expresses a disparity between opposites: appearance and reality; the ideal and the real; the literal and the implied; what we mean and what we say. Think of the many times you use irony in your daily talk. If someone rams your car, you might say, "That's just great." No one standing by would misunderstand the tone. Or you might resort to understatement, saying, "Seems like you left a scratch in the side of my car'' when the whole door has caved in.

You will find all kinds of irony in literature. The Eliot line about eating a peach is ironic because there is a disparity between the apparent innocence of the act and the fear the speaker expresses. Irony often lends itself to humorous effects. Grace Paley opens her story ''The Loudest Voice'' this way:

> There is a certain place where dumb-waiters boom, doors slam, dishes crash; every window is a mother's mouth bidding the street shut up, go skate somewhere else, come home. My voice is the loudest.

The irony of the tone is carried through in the plot: Jewish children play leading parts in a school Christmas play.

Sometimes a reader knows something the characters don't know and therefore understands the deeper significance of words and deeds. This situation is called *dramatic irony*. Perhaps the most famous example of this knowing occurs in Sophocles' *Oedipus the King*. The audience knows that Oedipus, by a terrible series of mischances, has slain his father and married his mother. Unaware of these facts, Oedipus wants to discover the truth, and he cries, ''I shall not cease until I bring the truth to light.'' The audience's prior knowledge of what his search will reveal makes his endeavors appear ironic.

Imagery is another important aspect of literary language. Writers seek to stimulate mental images in the minds of readers. Identifying and appreciating such imagery is one of the great pleasures of reading literature. The word *imagery* can refer to pictures, but it is most commonly used to denote the sum of sensual language in a work—the figures of speech and vivid individual images.

Despite its name, an image is not necessarily visual. Several senses are involved in this stanza from Robert Browning's ''Meeting at Night'':

> Then a mile of warm sea-scented beach;
> Three fields to cross till a farm appears;
> A tap at the pane, the quick sharp scratch
> And blue spurt of a lighted match,
> And a voice less loud, through its joys and fears,
> Than the two hearts beating each to each!

The words that make the passage vivid are images, from simple nouns such as *beach* and *farm* to insistently concrete phrases such as *the quick sharp scratch/And blue spurt of a lighted match.*

Literature achieves many of its effects through unexpected and startling figures of speech, such as *similes* and *metaphors*. A *simile* is an explicit comparison of two things, usually using *like* or *as*. Archibald MacLeish's poem ''Ars Poetica,'' which we discuss in ''Special Topics in Poetry,'' is a series of similes.

> A poem should be palpable and mute
> As a globed fruit. . . .
>
> A poem should be wordless
> As the flight of birds.

Similes occur in fiction also, as you will see when you read Isaac Babel's "My First Goose" in "Special Topics in Fiction." In describing the commander, Babel writes that

> His long legs were like girls sheathed to the neck in shining riding boots.

Rather than making an explicit comparison, *metaphor* draws an identity between two things. Toward the end of "Ars Poetica," MacLeish describes the experience of grief in metaphoric terms.

> For all the history of grief
> An empty doorway and a maple leaf.

We find metaphors in fiction too, including this one in "My First Goose" of a man unable to concentrate on what he reads:

> the beloved lines came toward me along a thorny path and could not reach me.

Metaphor's power comes from its unspokenness; it draws us into the possible likenesses between things we had previously assumed were unalike.

We have more to say about similes and metaphors in "Figurative Language" in Chapter 12.

Special Topics in Fiction

In addition to theme, symbolism, and language, each kind of literature has its own concerns and terms to be mastered. To prepare for our discussion of the four major elements of fiction—plot, character, setting, and point of view—please read Isaac Babel's "My First Goose." Don't forget to give yourself to it on the first reading and then go back to make notes.

My First Goose
Isaac Babel

Savitsky, Commander of the VI Division, rose when he saw me, and I   1
wondered at the beauty of his giant's body. He rose, the purple of his
riding breeches and the crimson of his little tilted cap and the decorations stuck on his chest cleaving the hut as a standard cleaves the sky.
A smell of scent and the sickly sweet freshness of soap emanated from

him. His long legs were like girls sheathed to the neck in shining riding boots.

He smiled at me, struck his riding whip on the table, and drew toward him an order that the Chief of Staff had just finished dictating. It was an order for Ivan Chesnokov to advance on Chugunov-Dobryvodka with the regiment entrusted to him, to make contact with the enemy and destroy the same. 2

"For which destruction," the Commander began to write, smearing the whole sheet, "I make this same Chesnokov entirely responsible, up to and including the supreme penalty, and will if necessary strike him down on the spot; which you, Chesnokov, who have been working with me at the front for some months now, cannot doubt." 3

The Commander signed the order with a flourish, tossed it to his orderlies and turned upon me gray eyes that danced with merriment. 4

I handed him a paper with my appointment to the Staff of the Division. 5

"Put it down in the Order of the Day," said the Commander. "Put him down for every satisfaction save the front one. Can you read and write?" 6

"Yes, I can read and write," I replied, envying the flower and iron of that youthfulness. "I graduated in law from St. Petersburg University." 7

"Oh, are you one of those grinds?" he laughed. "Specs on your nose, too! What a nasty little object! They've sent you along without making any enquiries; and this is a hot place for specs. Think you'll get on with us?" 8

"I'll get on all right," I answered, and went off to the village with the quartermaster to find a billet for the night. 9

The quartermaster carried my trunk on his shoulder. Before us stretched the village street. The dying sun, round and yellow as a pumpkin, was giving up its roseate ghost to the skies. 10

We went up to a hut painted over with garlands. The quartermaster stopped, and said suddenly, with a guilty smile: 11

"Nuisance with specs. Can't do anything to stop it, either. Not a life for the brainy type here. But you go and mess up a lady, and a good lady too, and you'll have the boys patting you on the back." 12

He hesitated, my little trunk on his shoulder; then he came quite close to me, only to dart away again despairingly and run to the nearest yard. Cossacks were sitting there, shaving one another. 13

"Here, you soldiers," said the quartermaster, setting my little trunk down on the ground. "Comrade Savitsky's orders are that you're to take this chap in your billets, so no nonsense about it, because the chap's been through a lot in the learning line." 14

The quartermaster, purple in the face, left us without looking back. I raised my hand to my cap and saluted the Cossacks. A lad with long straight flaxen hair and the handsome face of the Ryazan Cossacks went over to my little trunk and tossed it out at the gate. Then he turned his back on me and with remarkable skill emitted a series of shameful noises. 15

"To your guns—number double-zero!" an older Cossack shouted at him, and burst out laughing. "Running fire!"   16

His guileless art exhausted, the lad made off. Then, crawling over the ground, I began to gather together the manuscript and tattered garments that had fallen out of the trunk. I gathered them up and carried them to the other end of the yard. Near the hut, on a brick stove, stood a cauldron in which pork was cooking. The steam that rose from it was like the far-off smoke of home in the village, and it mingled hunger with desperate loneliness in my head. Then I covered my little broken trunk with hay, turning it into a pillow, and lay down on the ground to read in *Pravda* Lenin's speech at the Second Congress of the Comintern. The sun fell upon me from behind the toothed hillocks, the Cossacks trod on my feet, the lad made fun of me untiringly, the beloved lines came toward me along a thorny path and could not reach me. Then I put aside the paper and went out to the landlady, who was spinning on the porch.   17

"Landlady," I said, "I've got to eat."   18

The old woman raised to me the diffused whites of her purblind eyes and lowered them again.   19

"Comrade," she said, after a pause, "what with all this going on, I want to go and hang myself."   20

"Christ!" I muttered, and pushed the old woman in the chest with my fist. "You don't suppose I'm going to go into explanations with you, do you?"   21

And turning around I saw somebody's sword lying within reach. A severe-looking goose was waddling about the yard, inoffensively preening its feathers. I overtook it and pressed it to the ground. Its head cracked beneath my boot, cracked and emptied itself. The white neck lay stretched out in the dung, the wings twitched.   22

"Christ!" I said, digging into the goose with my sword. "Go and cook it for me, landlady."   23

Her blind eyes and glasses glistening, the old woman picked up the slaughtered bird, wrapped it in her apron, and started to bear it off toward the kitchen.   24

"Comrade," she said to me, after a while, "I want to go and hang myself." And she closed the door behind her.   25

The Cossacks in the yard were already sitting around their cauldron. They sat motionless, stiff as heathen priests at a sacrifice, and had not looked at the goose.   26

"The lad's all right," one of them said, winking and scooping up the cabbage soup with his spoon.   27

The Cossacks commenced their supper with all the elegance and restraint of peasants who respect one another. And I wiped the sword with sand, went out at the gate, and came in again, depressed. Already the moon hung above the yard like a cheap earring.   28

"Hey, you," suddenly said Surovkov, an older Cossack. "Sit down and feed with us till your goose is done."   29

He produced a spare spoon from his boot and handed it to me. We supped up the cabbage soup they had made and ate the pork.   30

"What's in the newspaper?" asked the flaxen-haired lad, making 31
room for me.

"Lenin writes in the paper," I said, pulling out *Pravda*. "Lenin writes 32
that there's a shortage of everything."

And loudly, like a triumphant man hard of hearing, I read Lenin's 33
speech out to the Cossacks.

Evening wrapped around me the quickening moisture of its twilight 34
sheets; evening laid a mother's hand upon my burning forehead. I
read on and rejoiced, spying out exultingly the secret curve of Lenin's
straight line.

"Truth tickles everyone's nostrils," said Surovkov, when I had come 35
to the end. "The question is, how's it to be pulled from the heap. But
he goes and strikes at it straight off like a hen pecking at a grain!"

This remark about Lenin was made by Surovkov, platoon commander 36
of the Staff Squadron; after which we lay down to sleep in the hayloft.
We slept, all six of us, beneath a wooden roof that let in the stars, warming
one another, our legs intermingled. I dreamed: and in my dreams
saw women. But my heart, stained with bloodshed, grated and brimmed
over.

PLOT. We call the structure and order of events in a work of fiction plot.
A plot is not just a simple chronology of events, however; it focuses on
causation and what forces bring the events about.

We could summarize the plot of "My First Goose" this way:

> A young soldier joins a division of rough Cossacks. As an intellectual,
> he does not fit in. He is ignored or ridiculed. To prove himself and earn
> a place among the soldiers, he bullies an old woman and kills her goose
> for his dinner. He then is accepted. But this incident has taught him a
> bitter lesson about himself.

This is a fairly typical construction, beginning with a situation and characters,
introducing a complication, and then proceeding to a resolution.
But plots do not always move in such a straight line. They may contain
flashbacks to the past, foreshadowings or hints of future events, interruptions,
or events seen from several viewpoints.

To get a firm grasp on a story, look at the plot first, especially the beginning.
Locate the turning points. Master the chain of causation. Summarize
the work. Though it cannot be an essay, a plot summary can be a first step
toward understanding the story.

CHARACTER. Character is a portrait in words of a person imagined by
the writer. This portrait may include physical characteristics, background,
and personality. Anything that explains why a person speaks, feels, or behaves
as he or she does is part of characterization.

Sometimes the narrator will *tell* us something directly, as in this passage from "My First Goose":

> The steam that rose from it [the cooking pot] was like the far-off smoke of home in the village, and it mingled hunger with desperate loneliness in my head.

At other times the narrator will *show* a character in action, through deeds, dialogue, or interaction with other characters.

> "Oh, are you one of those grinds?" [the commander] laughed. "Specs on your nose, too! What a nasty little object!"

We are in no doubt about the commander's opinion of the narrator or, by extension, about his opinion of learning and intellectuals.

Although much of our understanding comes from what a character says and does, we also learn about character from associated symbols: the specs, the newspaper, the trunk, even the goose. And we learn about character from the way language is used. The narrator's tone, for instance, changes from the admiring description of the commander to this depressing sentence:

> Already the moon hung above the yard like a cheap earring.

Literature is full of fascinating characters, and it is quite natural to be interested in them. But their personalities are not so much the point as what they cause to happen and what their actions and reactions tell us. Don't think of them as "real people." They are elements with an important role to play in a piece of fiction. In "My First Goose," for instance, the narrator and the Cossacks work through the age-old struggle of the intellectual and the warrior.

SETTING.   All the events in fiction happen within a time, a place, and specific social circumstances. We call this context the setting. Like all the elements in a story, setting helps determine meaning. The meaning of "My First Goose" is dependent on its setting: a Russian village during the chaotic 1920s, when the Communists were fighting to gain full control of the country. But you need not know the history to discern the unsettled state of life in the story. The landlady twice says she wants to go and hang herself. The narrator reads a speech by Lenin about shortages. In the foreground are the tensions of a violent, confusing time—a time in which a sensitive person brutally kills a goose.

Because setting is important, be sure that you take it into account during your reading and that you take accurate notes on it.

POINT OF VIEW.   Stories have a storyteller, a narrator, who tells us what happens and sometimes even interprets an event. Since these storytellers are our only source of information, knowing their point of view is important. Point of view refers to the angle from which the story is told, the place from which the reader is allowed to see events. Is the storyteller a participant or only a reporter? Are we allowed to know what one person thinks, or many, or none? Are we close to the action or far from it?

Although there are other possibilities, point of view is generally either first person or third person. In *first person,* we see events through the eyes of a single character. This *I* may be the major character or only a witness or observer. In "My First Goose," he is the major character, that is, the one on whom the events register and to whom they matter most. In other works, such as F. Scott Fitzgerald's *The Great Gatsby,* an *I* describes what happens to someone else.

In *third-person* point of view, the storyteller is in no way a participant, although sometimes he or she will interrupt a story to make a judgment. Some third-person storytellers, called *omniscient narrators,* know everything and can move from past to present and from the mind of one character to the mind of another. Other third-person storytellers are *limited narrators,* confined to one character's consciousness. This is not necessarily a loss: though we know only one mind, we know it intensely and immediately. Occasionally, the storyteller is a *direct observer,* reporting only what can be seen or heard. This point of view creates a story resembling drama in that there is no interpretation of events or attempt to probe a character's mind. The reader, watching and listening, is like a fly on the wall.

Always note the point of view in a work and pay attention to how it colors your feelings about what happens. Just for fun, try imagining "My First Goose" told by an omniscient narrator who can go into the minds of the Cossacks and the old lady. Do you think that would have made a better story?

Later in this chapter we will use "My First Goose" as an example of how to prepare to write a literary essay.

Special Topics in Poetry

Poems sometimes tell stories that contain characters, plots, and points of view. And poems are as rich in theme as they are in symbolism, imagery, metaphor, and unusual uses of language. Careful readers notice these aspects when reading poems. They also attend to poetry's special domain: the intense world of musicality. In the pages that follow, we discuss this world expressed in rhythm, music, and rhyme.

Before going on, please read aloud, reread, and take notes on this poem by Archibald MacLeish.

Ars Poetica

A poem should be palpable and mute
As a globed fruit,

Dumb
As old medallions to the thumb,

Silent as the sleeve-worn stone   5
Of casement ledges where the moss has grown—

A poem should be wordless
As the flight of birds.

A poem should be motionless in time
As the moon climbs,   10

Leaving, as the moon releases
Twig by twig the night-entangled trees,

Leaving, as the moon behind the winter leaves,
Memory by memory the mind—

A poem should be motionless in time   15
As the moon climbs.

A poem should be equal to:
Not true.

For all the history of grief
An empty doorway and a maple leaf.   20

For love
The leaning grasses and two lights above the sea—

A poem should not mean
But be.

RHYTHM.   Rhythm in a poem is created by alternating strong and weak stresses on syllables in a line. When you read a line of poetry aloud, you can always feel the rhythm.

A poem should be palpable and mute
As a globed fruit

The stresses force you to attend to certain words and phrases. When you read the lines just quoted, you will hardly be able to ignore the words *mute* and *globed.*

Often a poem will repeat a rhythmic pattern. The word *meter* refers to this measured repetition. MacLeish's line

A poem should be palpable and mute

contains a regular alternation of stressed and unstressed syllables, beginning with an unstressed syllable.

Critics often identify unstressed syllables with a ⌣ and stressed syllables with a '. If we used these marks on MacLeish's line, it might look like this:

Ă póĕm shóuld bĕ pálpăblé aňd múte

We call this a *metered* line. Each kind of metrical pattern has its own name, depending on the number and arrangement of stresses. (Handbooks on poetry will provide you with detailed information about these patterns.)

Rhythm does more than make reading delightful. It can tell you which words and ideas a poet intends to emphasize. Putting the stress on the word *globed,* for example, emphasizes the fruit's physicality and thus reinforces the point.

"Ars Poetica" plays many games with rhythm and meter. Read these two lines aloud:

Dumb
As old medallions to the thumb

That solitary, surprising word *Dumb* has a curious sense of finality to it, in part because it hitches the rhythm up short. MacLeish plays off the short one-syllable line against the next longer and more regular line and then comes down hard on *thumb.*

Now read this pair of lines aloud:

Leaving, as the moon behind the winter leaves,
Memory by memory the mind—

You may feel an almost hypnotic rhythm, regular and gradual. And perhaps that will remind you, as it has many readers, of the way the moon climbs in the sky.

Although all poetry has rhythm, not all poetry has meter. Since the mid-1800s, poets have increasingly turned to what is called *free verse,* poetry that does not repeat any rhythmic pattern. Even when reading free verse, however, you should listen for the rhythms that reinforce the meaning. Two lines from a poem by Walt Whitman show the importance of rhythm in free verse; read them aloud.

Out of the cradle endlessly rocking,
Out of the mocking-bird's throat, the musical shuttle.

In these lines you can hear the rhythms of the rocking cradle and of the mockingbird's song. Words alone would not have made them real; words and rhythm together do.

Music. The general term *music* covers the way a poem sounds. In the line

Twig by twig the night-entangled trees,

you can hear the *t* sound repeated. Such repetition of consonant sounds is called *alliteration*. Again, the purpose is more than sound: the poet uses alliteration to point to objects or feelings in the lines. The repeated *t* sound calls up the physical reality of the twigs and trees.

The repetition of vowel sounds is called *assonance*. In these lines, MacLeish repeats the sound of a long *e:*

> The leaning grasses and two lights above the sea—
>
> A poem should not mean
> But be.

These long *e*'s create a feeling of continuity between the physical world and the poem, which is MacLeish's point. Assonance can also slow the pace of a line. Notice how this line moves:

> Leaving, as the moon behind the winter leaves.

Because of all the long vowel sounds, the line is as slow as the moon itself. The brilliant combination of sounds drives the image home. Read the following lines aloud again slowly, shaping your lips around each word, dwelling on the sounds:

> A poem should be palpable and mute
> As a globed fruit.

The combinations of sound can make you feel as though you were holding the globed fruit in your hand, weight, smoothness, and all.

RHYME. When two words terminate in the same sound, they rhyme: *mute/fruit, dumb/thumb, stone/grown*. Most rhymes in poetry happen at the ends of lines and are called *end rhyme,* as here:

> For all the history of grief
> An empty doorway and a maple leaf.

But frequently poems contain *interior rhyme,* as in these lines written by Gerard Manley Hopkins:

> I caught this morning morning's minion, king-
>   dom of daylight's dauphin, dapple-dawn-drawn Falcon, in his riding.

Sometimes sounds are not exactly alike, but are approximate. These are called *slant rhymes.*

> A poem should be wordless
> As the flight of birds.
>
> A poem should be motionless in time
> As the moon climbs.

Like rhythm and music, rhyme directs us to what is important in a poem—the connection, for example, between *grief* and *leaf* and between *wordless* and *flight of birds*.

INTERPRETING LITERATURE

Once you have thoroughly read a work, interpreting it will come naturally. To interpret a work of literature, you say what you think it means, how it achieves that meaning, what values it expresses, what effect it has on the reader, and how it creates that effect. You look at the world the writer presents and at the artistry of the presentation. The aim is both to understand the work and to appreciate the achievement.

Responsible Interpretation

An odd rumor is going around about interpreting literature, namely that all opinions are equally valid: "You can see whatever you want to see in it. You can say just about anything." There is some truth in that—but not much. The range of possible interpretations is indeed large, but it is not infinite. Flights of fancy may be fun, but they usually contribute little to understanding the work.

When MacLeish writes

Dumb
As old medallions to the thumb,

Silent as the sleeve-worn stone
Of casement ledges where the moss has grown—

you could perhaps claim that the medallions are portraits of knights from old castles and that the poem is about the decline of the British Empire. Or when he writes

Leaving, as the moon releases
Twig by twig the night-entangled trees,

you might say he is comparing the poet and the poem to a mother and her child. But such unlikely interpretations are useless. They have strayed too far from the text.

Some readers seem to believe that literature, particularly poetry, contains some hidden meaning, and that interpretation is the deciphering of a riddle. It is true that the significance of a great work is seldom found on the surface. We have to think about it. But literature is not a riddle, and interpretation has little in common with doing crossword puzzles.

One important way in which interpretation is different from doing crossword puzzles is that the puzzles have correct answers, to be published next Sunday. There are facts about literature too. *"Hamlet* was written before 1961" is a statement of fact. About meaning in literature, however, there are no absolutely right answers—nor any that are completely wrong. Few writers provide a key to fix a work's meaning forever. Even when a writer does say what a work is about, that is only one interpretation. There will be others, probably just as illuminating. (This may sound like a paradox, but it is true. Virtually all writers acknowledge that there is much more to their work than they have consciously put there.)

Our job as interpreters is not to invent the fanciest answers we can or to discover a secret, but to articulate the meaning of a work.

When interpreting literature, keep two principles in mind.

First, the interpretation must fit the facts. A sound interpretation will not be contradicted by any element or event in the work. In interpreting the lines about the medallion in MacLeish's poem, you can't assert that the poem is about the British Empire when all the evidence points to its being about poems.

Second, the interpretation must be comprehensive. It should account for much of the work and should not neglect any important parts of it. Again, in interpreting MacLeish's poem, you would hardly neglect the facts of rhyme, music, and rhythm. Nor would you ignore the fact that MacLeish illuminates what poetry should do by reference to many physical objects.

Bases for Interpretation

The question is, On what shall we base our readings? There are three possible bases for interpretation: impressionism, factual analysis, and informed speculation.

IMPRESSIONISM.   Some interpretations are all impression. They stray so far from the text that they run off into the land of unbridled feeling. Rather than interpreting, impressionistic readers only treat the emotions they have about a text. Instructors are glad to see students who appreciate what they read. They are not glad, however, to receive personal effusions that sound like *True Confessions.* Here is one:

> Hamlet is as brave as a lonely alpine skier. He thrills to the risks he runs. He's an adventurer, afraid of nothing, willing to take a chance; he's a flyer. He loves speed. He loves to go over the moguls as fast as he can. But then a blinding snowstorm comes up. He can't make out the trees.

Speed? Moguls? Snowstorm? The problem is obvious: the writer never speaks of Shakespeare's play. He is not articulating meanings within the work: he is conveying pictures that flashed through his mind. There may be some good ideas in here—Hamlet does seem to like risk—but they are so submerged in a rush of feeling that the reader can't figure them out.

FACTUAL ANALYSIS. Good interpreters start with the facts of the text and stay close to them. Their readings are plausible because their insights are grounded in the text. Interpreters of MacLeish's poem, for instance, might begin with the fact that the poet refers to physical objects to illuminate what poetry should do. And in elucidating, they would stay close to that idea and use the text to prove it: "He uses fruit, medallions, trees . . ."

The most conservative interpreters stick exclusively to the text. They analyze *only* the facts of the work. In interpreting MacLeish's poem, for instance, a cautious interpreter might discuss the rhyme scheme, the rhythm or assonance, or the repetition of images.

In an essay on *Othello,* a conservative interpreter began this way:

> Iago is the most important character in *Othello,* as we can tell by an examination of the number of lines he speaks and the amount of stage action given to him.

To support her thesis, she went on to present a statistical analysis of the play's lines and action.

The possibilities for this kind of interpretation are large. Facts exist in plots and characters: what actually happens and what causes it; the names, ages, social standings, traits, and number of characters, and how these influence the plot. We can interpret aspects of the setting: whether it is rural or urban, domestic or foreign; whether the time is the present or the past. We can also base interesting interpretations on the physical makeup of the work: number of pages and lines; features of rhythm, meter, sounds, rhyme; use of verbs, nouns, adjectives.

INFORMED SPECULATION. Often interpretation goes beyond the facts to what would be called informed speculation. It is informed because it starts with the facts of the text; it is speculation because it goes beyond the facts to the possibilities they imply. Informed speculation ventures opinions on the meanings behind the words.

Do not worry if you feel insecure about this approach to interpretation. Everyone, no matter how experienced, feels some uncertainty, some risk. It is obviously safer to discuss a rhyme scheme or the use of alliteration than it is to speculate on what the rhyme and alliteration are telling us. When we speculate, we run the risk of being wrong—but we gain the power of offering fresh insights into a work. In any case, informed speculation about a work is a very fine way to know literature.

Levels of Speculation

When we speculate, we build arguments, not on hard evidence but on connotations. Read the following two lines from "Ars Poetica":

> A poem should be motionless in time
> As the moon climbs.

At the most concrete level, there are sounds: long *o* sounds and *i* sounds that take time to say. These are lines no reader can rush. An alert interpreter wrote,

> The long sounds in these two lines slow the lines down and direct us to the long, slow climbing of the moon, a climbing that is so gradual that it indeed appears motionless.

That is a lovely reading. It has speculated on the level of *the physical facts about the poem.* But there are other levels of speculation.

A second level involves speculation about *the literal meaning of the lines.* Take the poet absolutely literally.

> A poem should be motionless in time
> As the moon climbs.

Now, what does that mean? An alert speculator might write,

> But that is a contradiction. To climb is to move in time. The moon is never really motionless; it only seems that way because its passage is so gradual.

And this might naturally lead us to a third level, in which we speculate about *implications:*

> Perhaps MacLeish knows all along that a poem must move in time. Even reading it takes time, after all. Why does he make this apparent contradiction? For one thing, it seems to imply that there is something in the way the moon moves that defies our ordinary sense of motion. Try as we might, we can't see it move, even though we know it does. Perhaps MacLeish wants the poem to defy our ordinary sense of motion too—always to have something that we can't quite grasp, that eludes our demand for clear-cut certainty. And, of course, he, like many poets, probably wants the poem to seem as permanent, changeless, and inevitable as the natural world.

We are not talking about sounds or about words now but about implications. On the second level we asked, What do these lines mean? and on this one we asked, What is the significance of saying something like that? Note that we have not strayed very far at all from the poem. Those two lines are standing by waiting for us to reread them in the light of this new speculation. (We can press even further: Should a poet *want* a poem to be as permanent, changeless, and inevitable as the natural world?)

We might discuss a work's ideas *as* ideas, or build our argument on appeals to shared experiences—as we did with our description of the moon climbing. We could analyze our impressions (Why *does* the moon seem to stand still?) or evaluate the author's methods. And always we must identify those places in the text that give rise to our response.

With this kind of interpretation, our intelligence intersects with the text and brings forth fresh meaning.

WRITING ABOUT LITERATURE

When we turn our understanding and enjoyment of literature into writing, we stake out a claim on the work. In accounting for our thoughts and reactions, we take possession of the work. It becomes more deeply and securely ours. Writing about literature, then, is an opportunity to experience more profoundly the art of the storyteller, the teacher, and the enchanter.

Before setting out on your writing, revisit the text and your notes. Return to arresting moments, high points, themes that attracted you. Meditate a moment. Listen to your inclinations, what likes, dislikes, confusions, or enthusiasms have stayed with you.

You may want to consult outside works. Biographical works can tell you more about the author. Isaac Babel's life, for instance, closely paralleled that of the narrator in "My First Goose." Facts about his life may clarify parts of the story or suggest ideas about it. Historical works will provide information about the setting and social environment of a work. If you want to know more about Lenin, the Cossacks, or the state of Russian society in the early 1920s, you can consult encyclopedias or histories of Russia. Your main source, of course, remains the text.

The best-kept secret about papers on literature is that they are argumentative. When you write about a poem, a play, a novel, a short story, or any other literary work, you argue for your interpretation, using the text as your major evidence.

Now the search is on for a thesis you can argue—an idea that will direct your paper and interest your reader, yet be limited enough to treat within the assigned page limit. Your thesis will present an aspect of your interpretation. To arrive at this thesis, use your favorite form of invention—free writing, clustering, or whatever. (See "Invention: Generating Ideas" in Chapter 1 and "Subject and Thesis: Saying Something" in Chapter 2.)

Once you have decided on your thesis, return to the text and your notes for evidence. Determine major supporting points, and group your evidence from the text under them. During this developing stage, rather than copying out all the quotations, you might want to use page numbers or abbreviations. Just be sure you can go back to the exact quotation you want.

Writing about "My First Goose"

In the pages that follow, we describe the process of preparing to write a six-page essay on "My First Goose."

We can hardly tackle a story like this without being analytical. Without breaking it down into its component parts, we will not be able to say anything significant about it. ("It was great." "It was boring." "It was fun to read.") We can arrive at a worthwhile interpretation only by examining the story under literary topics such as the ones we have been discussing.

As we read, we keep in mind plot, character, setting, point of view, theme, symbolism, and language. Some of these topics will attract us more than others. Suppose, for example, that we are particularly drawn to the central figure in the story, the lonely, idealistic young man who kills the goose. We decide to begin with this character.

We do not want to force a thesis, so we return to the story and read it yet again. We want our presentiments to coalesce. When writing about literature, we must go through the same steps over and over, from making notes to reading to thinking to reading to making notes. Nothing appears in exactly the same light twice, for we see the action—the commander's laughter, the slaughter of the goose—differently each time. That is what makes literature so great: it is inexhaustible.

We note the protagonist's characteristics: his admiration for Savitsky, his intellectuality, his "desperate loneliness." We see how he responds to the Cossacks and to the landlady. We observe as the narrator scrambles to gather up his things from his broken trunk, pushes the landlady, and kills the goose. After a few readings, we will have listed many more events and characteristics.

We certainly want to avoid the trap of writing a mere "character study." Having made a list of characteristics, some writers would simply plow through the items, devoting a paragraph to each until the bottom of the list announced the end of the paper. That kind of paper would be mechanical to write and boring to read. Instead, we must account for the character's place in events, and how he illuminates human experience.

Now we confront a second trap: plot summary. From character, we naturally move to thinking about the plot. But the instructor has read the story and need not be told the plot again. Lengthy plot summaries are a waste of everyone's time. What we and the instructor want is critical judgment.

We find ourselves reading the killing scene again, and we ask why the narrator kills the goose. True, he is hungry, but there is more than that. To get at it, perhaps we freewrite about the scene.

> The way the narrator crushes the goose with his boot and digs into it with his sword is too vicious to really have anything to do with that goose. This fellow seemed sensitive, not like the other soldiers, but then this. He becomes just like them, as though he has given in to the brutality he sees around him.

Through reading and analyzing we move closer to a thesis. We now go back to the story to refine what we mean by "the brutality he sees around him." We find all sorts of brutality, though most of it is implied: the commander's insolent power, the jokes about the spectacles, the quartermaster's remarks about soldiers and women, the flaxen-haired lad's insulting behavior, the landlady's despair. We think about the setting of the tale. Brutality seems to be behind almost every action. Why? Perhaps because the story is set in a time of upheaval.

With each reading, we learn new things and put them more firmly together. Eventually, we can say something significant about the story based on our analysis.

> In "My First Goose," the killing of the goose signifies the surrender of the young narrator to the brutality of an uncertain time, a brutality that directs the actions of all the characters and permeates the story.

Our early leads changed, and with them changed the direction of our ideas. Our analysis of the character led to the plot and on to a reexamination of the killing scene, which ultimately led to our thesis. This thesis promises that we will show how brutality directs the characters and how the narrator capitulates to this fact of life.

To show this, we must create classifications under which to put evidence. We recognize that examples of brutality occur at every point in the story and on every social level. Commander Savitsky enforces his authority by belittling the narrator. The Cossacks enforce their exclusivity by insults and intimidation. The protagonist bullies the landlady. Examples of the uncertainty of the times are also plentiful: the troubles hinted at in Lenin's speech; Surovkov's remark that truth is to be "pulled from the heap"; the tensions among the characters. We list these examples and prepare to use them in our argument.

Similarly, our reading has prepared us to discuss the story's ending. The narrator is thrilled to be accepted and exultantly reads Lenin's speech. Later, his exultation falls flat. As in many good stories, the last line here is particularly telling: "But my heart, stained with bloodshed, grated and brimmed over." Now when we make an assertion, we can reach into our notes and pull out an example from the text to support it.

Writing about any work of literature usually follows a pattern much like this: reading, forming a preliminary interest, rereading, solidifying an idea, perhaps rereading again, formulating a thesis, collecting and classifying examples, arranging classified material beneath the thesis. Now we can proceed fully equipped to the challenge of making our thinking clear on paper.

Some Do's and Don'ts

Let the structure of your argument take priority over the structure of the text. Too many papers start with line 1 or Chapter 1 and plow through straight to the ending. If you simply follow the text, your argument will have no shape or direction. Organize your argument first, and then arrange your notes and evidence to fit that organization.

Use the language of the text as your evidence. Nothing persuades quite so quickly and thoroughly as the text itself. Sometimes you may need to summarize or paraphrase a section for convenience or clarity, but when you can use the author's own words, do so.

Tie each piece of evidence in to your discussion. Warrants are essential in all papers on literature. Some writers pile on quotations without showing how they apply to the argument, as here:

> "Ars Poetica" tries to be the things it portrays. In the first two lines, "A poem should be palpable and mute/As a globed fruit," there are many *p* and *b* sounds.

Not so fast. What is the connection between the claim and the evidence? Until the writer shows *why* those sounds prove the claim, she will not carry her point.

> "Ars Poetica" tries to be the things it portrays. One of the ways it does this is with sound. In the first two lines, "A poem should be palpable and mute/As a globed fruit," there are many *p* and *b* sounds. These sounds force the reader to work the mouth and give the impression of real weight and texture.

This is the form the warrant takes in literary papers—the demonstration that the evidence fits the claim.

Do not praise the text or the author, no matter how great they are. One of the rewards of studying literature is the constant discovery of brilliant insights and technical mastery. But, then, everybody already knows that Honoré de Balzac, Thomas Mann, and Virginia Woolf are "great." Concentrate, rather, on showing how they achieve their great effects.

Write in the present tense. By convention, one writes as though the events of the poem, play, novel, or story are taking place in the present.

> When the old lady says, "I want to go and hang myself," the narrator responds by pushing her in the chest.

Give your *interpretation, not that of professional critics.* Most instructors want to know what *you* make of the text. Books of criticism can help to illuminate a difficult text, but use them with great care. Do your own reading and build your own opinions. Exceptions to this rule are the book report and the research paper. But for interpretive essays on literature, *do not let experts do the thinking or writing for you.* Ask your instructor for suggestions on how to use the experts. And always acknowledge all sources that contributed to your essay.

TIPS FOR READING, INTERPRETING, AND WRITING ABOUT LITERATURE

- Give yourself to the reading the first time through, and make your notes on the second reading.
- Remember that theme, symbolism, and language are concerns in nearly all literary works.
- When reading fiction, think about plot, character, setting, and point of view.
- Read poems aloud, and, as you do, think about rhythm, music, and rhyme.
- Make sure your interpretation fits the facts and does not neglect major aspects.
- Try to go beyond factual analysis to an informed speculation about the meanings in the work.
- Identify what interests you most, and use that as a basis for your analysis.
- Develop an essay on literature as you would other argumentative essays, with a thesis, evidence, and warrants.
- Avoid mere character studies and plot summaries.
- Let the structure of your argument take priority over the structure of the text.
- Do not praise the author.
- Write in present tense.
- Remember that your instructor wants your critical judgment of the work.
- Stay close to the text: the best evidence is the author's own words.

Exercises for Reading, Interpreting, and Writing about Literature

1. Read the following sonnet by William Shakespeare and write an essay in which you first describe the situation presented and then argue for what you believe to be the central anxiety in the speaker's mind. What

is the origin of the anxiety? Has the speaker taken any steps at the end of the poem to address his problem? Back up your argument with detailed references to the poem's language, rhythms, and any other technical or thematic material you believe supports your thesis.

Sonnet 138

When my love swears that she is made of truth,
I do believe her, though I know she lies;
That she might think me some untutored youth,
Unlearnèd in the world's false subtleties.
Thus vainly thinking that she thinks me young,
Although she knows my days are past the best,
Simply I credit her false-speaking tongue;
On both sides there is simple truth suppress'd.
But wherefore says she not she is unjust?
And wherefore say not I that I am old?
O, love's best habit is in seeming trust,
And age in love loves not to have years told.
Therefore I lie with her, and she with me,
And in our faults by lies we flattered be.

2. Analyze the language and symbolism of the sonnet in Exercise 1. Are there metaphors, similes, vivid images? Which words are symbols, and for what ideas?

3. Discuss what would not constitute plausible interpretations of Sonnet 138. Try to speculate as far from the text as you can. At what point does your interpretation become impressionistic?

4. Take the last two lives from the sonnet in Exercise 1 and try writing a paragraph in which you speculate on the three levels—the physical facts, the literal meaning, and the implication. If you feel brave, press one step further, to the implication of the implication. Exchange your paragraph with a partner's and compare.

5. Choose one of the following short stories and identify its central symbol. What makes this symbol significant? What relation does it have to the story's main theme?

   Delmore Schwartz, "In Dreams Begin Responsibilities"
   John Steinbeck, "Flight"
   Nathaniel Hawthorne, "Young Goodman Brown"
   Flannery O'Connor, "A Good Man Is Hard to Find"
   Ernest Hemingway, "The Snows of Kilimanjaro"

6. Analyze the use of point of view in the story you selected in Exercise 4. Write a paragraph describing the advantages or disadvantages of that point of view. Now write another paragraph analyzing the effect a change in point of view would have had.

7. Choose another one of the stories listed in Exercise 4, and write a three- or four-page essay about it. At the end, append a description of where you started your analysis and what route you followed to arrive at your thesis.

18

THE IN-CLASS ESSAY EXAMINATION

Examinations are formidable even to the best
prepared, for the greatest fool may ask more
than the wisest man can answer.

CHARLES CALEB COLTON (1780–1832)
ENGLISH WRITER

When your instructors require an essay examination in a course, they generally have two purposes in mind. First, they want to know how much you have learned about the materials and concepts of the course and how well you can use them. Their second purpose is more educational than evaluative: they want you to synthesize your knowledge and thus to understand it better and possess it more securely. Using knowledge is a superb way of making it yours. An essay exam, then, can be a great learning experience.

Essay exams take many formats. They can last from one to four hours. They can be open or closed book. They can consist of several short questions or a single long one. They have in common a premium on time. You must organize information quickly and respond clearly and concisely to the questions posed. Ease in writing in-class essays depends largely on your knowledge of the material and on your physical and mental state at the time of the test. We hope the advice in the pages that follow will help you to get the most out of yourself.

STUDYING FOR THE EXAM

When studying your notes, look for broad themes and patterns. Differentiate major ideas from supporting points. Analyze how the major points are related, and how the evidence supports them. Notice changes and developments.

461

You may find it helpful to consolidate class notes and reading notes by transcribing them in an orderly way. The act of writing down the information is an excellent reviewing technique. In addition, when you group the information, you improve not only your grasp but also your memory.

A good method for consolidation is to put the basic themes of the course across the top of a sheet of paper as column headings and to list the major divisions of the subject down the left-hand margin. In a Western civilization course, for example, you might put major concerns—justice, religion, ethics—across the top and put various philosophers—pre-Socratics, Plato, Aristotle, Cicero, and so on—down the side. Under each topic, you would write out the ideas of each philosophical approach. You could then easily compare the major ideas of the course.

As you study and organize your notes, think about what areas of the subject the instructor favored. Try to anticipate test questions. In the Western civilization course, for instance, you might anticipate a question like this one:

Compare Plato's idea of justice with that of Cicero

or

In what ways is Augustine's idea of freedom a purely Christian concept and in what ways is it a continuation of the Greco-Roman idea of freedom?

Questions, even ones you invent, can help you structure your studying. You may find it both reassuring and informative to share this process with a friend in the class who might have different ideas about the subject.

As you identify probable areas the test will cover, think of major issues and supporting ideas. If, for instance, you think the instructor is particularly keen on the idea of justice, look closely at your reconstructed notes on that subject and know what you think about it. If a major theme remains vague to you, reread the textbook or the original material. Try to arrive at the exam with ideas that tie the course together.

Avoid anxiety as much as possible. Think about the examination not as just a test but also as a learning opportunity. When you can view the exam as intrinsically worthwhile rather than as an ordeal, you will reduce the concern you feel about it. While studying, try to maintain your usual habits of eating and sleeping. Staying up late, missing meals, or ingesting large amounts of coffee or other stimulants can upset both your memory and your thinking patterns. Cramming may push information you already know out of your mind. Try to take the pressure off. Before the exam, get a good night's sleep. Eat a full breakfast—your brain needs fuel just as your body does.

Immediately before the test, read over your summary notes. Don't try to cram in facts: just remind yourself of patterns and themes. At this point, do not rehearse questions with others. It is too late for that to serve any purpose, and if someone brings up a subject you have not anticipated, it will no doubt increase your anxiety.

Arrive for the exam on time and fully equipped with pens or pencils and scratch paper. Bring a watch with you. Keeping track of time is essential, and you cannot count on a clock or instructor to do it for you. If you have a free choice of seats, sit away from distraction—doors open to the corridor, windows that look out on busy thoroughfares, even other students who might want to socialize.

Relax. If you feel nervous, try one of these methods for relaxing: either breathe in until your lungs are full, add another quick breath, breathe out slowly, and repeat the process several times, or consciously relax each and every muscle of your body, beginning with your little toes. (The first time you try this, you may laugh, which is relaxing in itself.) Clear your mind.

TAKING THE EXAM

Well prepared, confident, and relaxed, you will be ready, perhaps eager, to show what you know when the instructor says "Go."

When you receive the question sheet, read the instructions and all the questions slowly and thoroughly. Take the time to understand what is expected. Listen to all verbal directions. If you have any problems of interpretation, ask the instructor right away. Know when the test starts and when it will end. Synchronize your watch.

Organizing Your Time

Know exactly how much credit you will receive for each answer, and allot your time accordingly.

Start with the question you feel most ready to answer. Not only is this encouraging and even soothing but also it taps right in on your best ideas. As you write about something you feel fairly confident of, ideas about other questions may occur to you. Be sure to keep your scratch paper handy so that you can jot down these ideas.

Noting Significant Words in the Question

Pay close attention to all command words, key words and phrases, and texts mentioned in each question. These tell you what to do and often how to do it.

COMMAND WORDS.   Command words tell you exactly what the instructor wants you to do: *compare, define, demonstrate, evaluate, isolate, trace,* and so on. These are the action verbs in the question. You might, for instance, receive this instruction in a sociology class:

> Define *individualism* in America and trace the development of this concept.

This question asks something specific of you: to *define* individualism (identify the meaning of the term) and to *trace* its development (show its origin, its history, and its present application). Remember that you must perform both tasks. Doing just one will answer only half of the question. It does not ask you to compare American individualism with something else or to evaluate it. Be sure you know and follow the exact command.

Some command words—*discuss, explain, explore, describe*—are more general; they put you on your own. In answering a question that uses one of them, you will have to figure out whether to define, compare, evaluate, and so on. In an American history class, you might be asked to respond to this kind of open-ended question:

> John Adams estimated that one-third of the colonists were loyal to the British Crown during the American Revolution. Discuss the treatment of these loyalists during and after the Revolution.

Don't just start free-associating about the loyalists. Even when the instructor does not tell you exactly what to do, you still must construct a reasoned, organized answer. Figure out your own commands. Here, you might identify who the loyalists were according to economic class, occupation, and geographic location. Then you might trace their history and their fate. Finally, you might analyze their motives and the motives of those who, in punishing them, confiscated their property.

KEY WORDS AND PHRASES.   With or without clear commands, a question may contain a key word or phrase that can help you organize your answer. This question certainly does:

> What was the origin of the Monroe Doctrine? Examine three occasions before 1900 on which this doctrine was invoked.

The key words and phrases are, of course, *origin, Monroe Doctrine,* and *before 1900.* They strongly suggest a course for a response: define the doctrine, summarize its origin, then turn to the period in question, and select the three occasions. With each occasion, you might say why the doctrine was invoked and what the result was. You might conclude with an evaluation of the doctrine's effectiveness as an instrument of foreign policy in the nineteenth century.

If the key words in a question need definition, define them early and go right to a discussion of why they are significant. Then you can use that definition and evaluation as a basis for your entire answer.

REFERENCES TO TEXTS. If the question mentions an author or a text, note them and prepare to treat them specifically in your essay. The instructor is providing you with a focus. Here is a question for a linguistics class that provides a sharp focus:

> Continental linguists criticize Noam Chomsky's theories of language on the ground that they are based on the behavioristic tradition of J. B. Watson and B. F. Skinner. With reference to Chomsky's *Language and Mind* and to Skinner's *Beyond Freedom and Dignity*, evaluate this criticism.

In answering, you would look first at the command word, *evaluate*. That word calls for a balanced response, neither enthusiastic agreement with nor dismissal of the criticism. You should express your own opinion, but the command asks you to be alert to both sides. Next, you would turn to the key words, *criticism* and *behavioristic tradition*. You would probably define *behaviorism*. Then you would pick up on the authors and texts mentioned. You would describe Chomsky's theories and relate them specifically to those of Watson and Skinner. You would include pertinent analyses of *Language and Mind* and *Beyond Freedom and Dignity*.

Fully understanding the question and identifying the important words in it can carry you a long way toward a persuasive answer.

Shaping Your Answer

The first moments of your exam are important. Once you understand what the question asks, start thinking. It is sheer folly to begin writing your answer the moment the gun goes off. Some good test takers use up to a quarter of the exam time to organize their thoughts before they write their answer. They then have a good idea of what to write and can be cool and collected when they begin.

Remember: an essay examination asks you to write an essay, and an essay has a thesis. Your instructor does not want a mess of unsorted facts or a list of vague feelings. Though the conditions of an exam are somewhat different from those of the usual essay, you can apply much of what you have learned in *Writing Worth Reading*.

Take the first few minutes to formulate your thesis. Use that scratch paper. Employ any of the invention devices. Brainstorm. Free-write. Write down your thesis.

Spend the next few minutes organizing. Make a scratch list of everything pertaining to the question. Don't waste time trying to retrieve something you can't remember. Either it will surface or it won't, and it is more likely to if you don't force it.

Turn your scratch list into an outline. Sort out the major ideas. Be ruthless: by combining, condensing, or discarding, reduce your list of major points to three or four. These will be the prominent subheadings under your thesis. Put these points in proper order. If the question lends itself to chronological treatment, as does the one regarding the Monroe Doctrine, use that organizing principle. Otherwise, arrange your answer either according to the order of the relay race, with the second strongest point first and the strongest last, or in ascending order to climax. What you want, of course, is to end on a strong note. (See "Coherence" in Chapter 8 for a discussion of ordering points.)

Flesh out your points. Virtually all graders prefer specific essays to general ones, the concrete to the abstract. The more specific your answers, the better. As you go over your scratch list, identify the support for all your major points. This is a good time to make sure you have included the major points and the evidence for them.

Writing Your Answer

Write legibly. Illegible handwriting is worse than useless; it is a positive irritant. Use conventional mechanics. Write an economical, plain, direct prose.

If you are using a blue book, skip lines and write on only one side of each page. That way, if you want to add something later you can put it in the empty line or on the blank side of the opposite page with an arrow showing where it fits. The grader will not mind incorporating the new material if its place is clearly designated. In any case, double-spaced writing on one side of the page generally makes reading easier.

Write a brief introduction that contains the general area you will cover in your answer, as well as your thesis. Put your thesis in the last sentence of the introduction and underline it. Don't restate the question. That not only wastes time but also can irritate the grader. A strong thesis will tie your discussion firmly to the question.

Now you are ready to move into your answer. Check the remaining time. Plan so you have ample time to spend on the important points. You don't want to be gasping for breath as you leave a question.

Make paragraph breaks at important pauses. Write emphatically. Do not be afraid to underline your major point in each paragraph. Construct each paragraph with claim, evidence, and warrant in mind. Your claim will be the major point of the paragraph, perhaps stated as a topic sentence. Support each point with evidence: example, quotation, paraphrase, statistic, or what have you. Be sure you have at least one piece of evidence, and preferably more, for each point. We have never heard an instructor complain of too much evidence in an exam. And clearly tie the evidence to the claim with a short discussion, or warrant.

Write confidently. If a new idea about the subject strikes you, write it. Great revelations can come in the pressure cooker of the essay exam. But don't be diverted from your overall structure. You simply do not have time for digressions or stray points. Discipline is important. Keep the question clearly in mind. If you are to compare and contrast A and B, do not spend 90 percent of your time on A, and do not throw in C.

Leave yourself a few minutes for a conclusion. Ending in style will help any essay. Reiterate what you have said, but try to wrap up the essay with an observation that indicates the importance of what you have written. Your conclusion need not be long, but it ought to have a feeling of finality. Here is the conclusion to an essay analyzing George Washington's warning against getting involved with "foreign entanglements":

> The new United States was still wary from its war with England, and its first president understandably insisted that the country make its own way. But countries cannot exist in a vacuum, and, as the rest of U.S. history has shown, no country can keep out of foreign entanglements for long.

If you can, close each essay answer with a good authoritative last line. (See "The Conclusion: Finishing in Style" in Chapter 10 for more on closing lines.)

If you run into trouble during the writing, don't panic. To get those juices flowing again, try free writing on scratch paper.

Adding, Reviewing, Polishing

Leave time to review the whole exam. Use the blank sides of your blue book pages for new ideas or clarifications. Don't forget those arrows to indicate insertions: the grader won't want to reconstruct the order of your ideas. If you run out of space on the nearest blank page, go to the end of the book.

When reviewing, read your work critically, as though you were the grader. Try to catch inconsistencies, incoherent sentences, unfulfilled promises in your essay. Check your grammar and syntax. But don't make your paper look as if armies of pens and pencils had been in combat over it. Make sure your essay is presentable; then hand it in.

CASE STUDY: AN IN-CLASS EXAMINATION

The following answer was written by Jeri Shikuma in response to the question

> Drawing on readings and lectures, discuss (1) whether (and in what sense) you think Americans are individualistic, and (2) the possible

causes and *consequences* of that individualism in America's religious origins, stratification patterns, and forms of political power.

Notice how she responds to the command words. In the first paragraph she sets up her thesis and the major topics she will pursue. After the brief introduction she gets right into her argument. Each following paragraph takes up a topic. She carefully develops evidence and always ties it to the claim. She has a strong conclusion. Notice how she bolsters her judgments by reference to sources.

> Individualism has characterized America since its beginnings with the idea of the rugged individualist. This individualism has grown and influenced America's stratification patterns as well as its forms of political power.

> Americans are individualistic in the sense that they place a great deal of importance on being unique and offering something special. This is manifested in art as well as commerce. Many great American novels portray a hero who must stand alone, outside society, to fight for justice. One such is Herman Melville's *Billy Budd.* Captain Vere accepts the responsibility as well as the loneliness of his command as he sends Billy to his death. Individualism, according to Blumberg, is even manifested in America's architecture. Isolated apartments and one-occupant flats emphasize the individual alone. Even the stress on the nuclear family—mother, father, children—is in opposition to the wider society.

> This individualism was probably founded at the very beginning of the nation with the arrival of the Protestants. According to Weber, the Protestants were deeply ingrained with the sense of the individual alone in the world, and they placed a high importance on individual acts. Calvin's idea of God's being so transcendent that he never interferes with one's life led the Calvinists to believe that they were alone on earth, with no one to turn to for help. Furthermore, because their afterlife was predestined for either salvation or damnation—though they did not know for which—the Doctrine of Proof, in which their proof of salvation showed in their actions, made individual actions very important. Thus, the Protestants, and particularly the Calvinists, perpetuated an ethics of rational, systematic self-evaluation, which grew into a general idea of individualism.

> This individualism has permeated every aspect of society. In politics, it manifested itself in pluralistic theories advocating particularistic interests as essential for the health of democracy. To theorists, the pursuit of personal, particular interests in the political arena keeps society from being split down the middle and thus prevents class conflict and, in the long run, tyranny. Mobilization around special interests also prevents deep ideologies from forming and promotes compromise.

> Furthermore, individualism has affected stratification patterns. People are inherently different, and, in society like that in America in which these differences are exploited, stratification is inevitable unless the society directly tries to prevent it through redistributive means. Indeed, as

Black said, the idea of individualism in the sense of inherent differences is essential for the justification and legitimation of inequality. Upper-class people can say they have privileges and advantages because they are inherently more capable. The idea simultaneously placates the lower classes by making them feel that they are on the bottom not because of any unfair system but because of human nature. It also lets them feel that they may rise in society if they really try and make the most of their unique talents.

Thus, individualism has been a very prominent force in shaping American society. And though people seem to be caught up in issues of society as a whole, such as unemployment and the arms race, individualism is still important. As Tocqueville recognized in the early nineteenth century, individualism is a deeply ingrained characteristic of American life.

SHORT ANSWERS

Short-answer essay questions require a different strategy from that used in long essays. Scan the identification section of the test. Note the number of questions and the credit you will receive for each one.

Spend the most time on questions that have the highest number of points. You can afford to botch or omit a five-point question, but not a thirty-five-point one.

Work on questions you know first; save harder ones for later. Generally, people write more easily and quickly on questions about which they feel confident, and much more slowly when they are uncertain.

Write short answers as crisply and specifically as you can. Some instructors want the *shortest* answer possible, and some will stipulate that complete sentences are not necessary. Again, make sure you know what your instructor expects. In any event, vague or general answers lose points. Recall what was said in class about the question at hand. What points did the instructor repeat? What important distinctions or details will he or she probably want to see? Here are two short essay examination answers to a question worth ten points. The first answer, brief and very general, received four points, and the second, more specific one received the full ten.

QUESTION	Identify the term *oxymoron*.
ANSWER 1	Oxymoron is a figure of speech used in poetry where two words contradict.
ANSWER 2	Oxymoron is a poetic figure of speech in which two terms seem to contradict. *Seems* is the important word, because although the two words

may contradict, together they make a paradox. An example is *loving hate.* The two words seem to contradict, except that there are so many times when love involves feelings close to hatred that the oxymoron makes sense.

TIPS FOR THE IN-CLASS ESSAY EXAMINATION

- Make summary notes of lectures and reading.
- Anticipate the questions or at least the probable areas to be covered.
- Get a good night's sleep, and eat a full breakfast before the test.
- Avoid anxiety by breathing deeply and steadily or consciously relaxing each muscle.
- Pay attention to command words, key words and phrases, and texts mentioned in the test question.
- Before beginning, formulate a thesis and organize your answer.
- Write legibly and use conventional grammar, syntax, and mechanics.
- Construct paragraphs with claim, evidence, and warrant in mind.
- Save time for writing a conclusion and adding, reviewing, and polishing.
- Make short answers direct, emphatic, and as specific as possible.

Exercises for the In-Class Essay Examination

1. Read these hypothetical essay examination questions. Focus on the command words, key words and phrases, the texts mentioned, the way the questions are put, and any other clues to possible organization. What is each question asking for? How would you organize an answer to it?
   a. Ten days before the San Joaquín revolt of 1886, the duke of Calabria said, ''The people will never revolt. They depend too much on us.'' To what extent did the people of San Joaquín depend on the nobility? Trace the causes of revolt, with reference to Smith's *Urban Armies of Italy.*

   b. Discuss the major differences between a hunter-gatherer society and an early agrarian society.
   c. In recent years the Federal Reserve Board has attempted to control the supply of money in our economy. Compare what a monetarist would say about such efforts with what a supply-sider would say.
   d. Design a program that uses positive reinforcement to help you cure yourself of some undesirable habit. Refer to the steps given in Gibson and Baker.
   e. Would the Athenian citizens have considered the American form of government a democracy? Why or why not?
   f. What was the role of John Foster Dulles in the formation of America's international policy after World War II? Back up your discussion with examples from Raub and Williams.
   g. Read the following passage. Keeping in mind all we have read and learned about American stylists, say whether the passage was written by Faulkner, Fitzgerald, or James. What aspects of the style led you to make this identification?

   But for the moment she was so happy, so lifted up by the belief that her troubles at last were over, that she forgot to be ashamed of her meagre answers. It seemed to her now that she could marry him without the remnant of a scruple, or a single tremor save those that belonged to joy.

2. Your instructor will design an essay examination based on a selection the class will have read in preparation. Before actually taking the exam, the class will discuss how to respond to the question, what clues might help organize the answer, and what the instructor is looking for. The instructor will not confirm or deny anything: the class must reach a consensus before writing.

PART SIX

The Nuts and Bolts: A Handbook of Grammar, Punctuation, Mechanics, and Usage

19

BASIC GRAMMAR

*Grammar, which knows how to control
even kings.*
MOLIÈRE (1622–1673)
FRENCH DRAMATIST

Grammar deals with the forms and structures of words and with their conventional arrangements in phrases, clauses, and sentences. In this chapter we discuss key grammatical terms.

THE PARTS OF SPEECH AND THEIR FUNCTIONS

Nouns

A **noun** is the name of a person, place, thing, condition, or idea, everything from Mrs. Smith to catfish, from honesty to Albania. **Proper nouns** name a particular person, place, or thing: *Caesar, Utah, Coca-Cola.* **Common nouns** name general categories: *politician, state, soft drink.* **Collective nouns** name a number of individuals considered as a single entity: *congregation, covey, jury.* **Concrete nouns** refer to tangible things: *iron, telephone, fingernails.* **Abstract nouns** refer to conditions, states, and ideas: *health, consciousness, technology.*

Pronouns

A **pronoun** is any word that stands for a noun or noun substitute (a word or phrase functioning as a noun). In the passage *Maud shot the sheriff. She shot him with a .44, she* stands for Maud and *him* stands for sheriff. Words such as *I, each, him, that,* and *which* are all pronouns.

Every pronoun must have an *antecedent*—a specific noun or noun substitute to which it refers. The pronoun must agree in person, number, and gender with its antecedent. In *Maud bought her gun at a pawnshop when she went to town,* both *her* and *she* agree with the antecedent *Maud.*

Pronouns come in many varieties and perform many functions.

Personal pronouns refer to a specific person or thing. Examples of personal pronouns are *I, you, him, hers, it, we, theirs.* (See "A Special Word about Pronoun Case" on page 477 for more on personal pronouns.)

Relative pronouns are *who, whom, whose, that,* and *which.* These pronouns introduce a subordinate clause and relate it to a noun or noun substitute in the main clause.

Sam, who had never ridden a Brahma bull before, won the rodeo that took place in Amarillo.

Who introduces the subordinate clause *had never ridden a Brahma bull before,* and *that* introduces the subordinate clause *took place in Amarillo.*

When the antecedent of the relative pronoun is an animate object, use *who, whom,* and *whose. Sam,* an animate object, is the antecedent of the *who* clause. Use *which* or *that* when the antecedent is an inanimate object. *Rodeo,* an inanimate object, is the antecedent of the *that* clause. (See the Glossary under *"that, which"* for a discussion of when to use *that* and when to use *which.*)

Intensive and **reflexive pronouns** are *myself, yourself, himself, herself, itself, oneself, ourselves, yourselves, themselves.* An intensive pronoun emphasizes a noun or noun substitute.

I *myself* witnessed the dastardly crime.

It stands beside the noun because it is part of the noun. A reflexive pronoun indicates that a subject is acting upon itself.

Judas hanged *himself.*

The pronoun follows the verb because it is the direct object.

Demonstrative pronouns are *this, that, these,* and *those.* These pronouns point at the noun and make the reference unmistakable.

Those plants are poisonous; *these* are edible.

Indefinite pronouns include *all, any, anyone, each, either, everyone, few, most, nobody, none, no one, some, somebody,* and *someone.* These pronouns refer to people or things generally rather than specifically.

Nobody loves me, *everybody* hates me, I'm going out in the garden and eat worms.

Reciprocal pronouns are *each other, each other's, one another,* and *one another's.* They express a mutual relationship. Use *each other* when referring to two people, *one another* for more than two.

Although we are told we should love *one another,* those two hated *each other.*

Interrogative pronouns are *what, which, who, whom,* and *whose.* These pronouns introduce questions.

To *whom* shall I tell my story?

A Special Word about Pronoun Case.   The form a personal pronoun or a relative pronoun takes will depend on **case,** that is, on the pronoun's function in the sentence. The case shows the pronoun's relation to neighboring words. English observes three cases:

subjective—when the pronoun is the subject of the verb: She *shot the sheriff.*

objective—when the pronoun is the direct or indirect object of the verb: *Maud shot* him *and then gave the gun to* me.

possessive—when the pronoun shows either ownership or association: *It was* my *gun, unfortunately.*

Here are the cases for all personal and relative pronouns:

SUBJECTIVE	OBJECTIVE	POSSESSIVE
I	me	my, mine
you	you	your, yours
he, she, it	him, her, it	his, her, hers, its
we	us	our, ours
you	you	your, yours
they	them	their, theirs
who, that, which	whom, that, which	whose, of which

Most of us use the correct form unconsciously most of the time, but in the following paragraphs we discuss some particularly tricky usages.

1. The verb *to be* can be tricky. We may naturally say

Was it him?

But for the high informal writing style, use the subjective case.

Was it *he*?
It wasn't *I.*

2. *Who* and *whom* can cause trouble. If the relative pronoun is the subject of the verb in the subordinate clause, then the pronoun should be in the subjective case.

Do you know *who* ate all the pickles?

Who is the subject of the verb *ate*.
If the relative pronoun is the direct or indirect object of the verb in the subordinate clause, then the pronoun should be in the objective case.

Do you know from *whom* they were stolen?

If the relative pronoun shows possession or association, use *whose* when the antecedent is an animate object.

It was Old Dog Tray *whose* smell permeated the car.

If the antecedent is inanimate, use *of which* for the possessive.

The fire, *of which* the source was old rags, raged through the night.

3. Be careful with compound subjects. Be sure that all parts are in the correct case.

He must not let ill will grow between *him* and *me*.
Professor Krantz and *I* disagreed about my grade.
The judge gave the lawyer, the defendant, and *me* a lecture.

To test whether the compound subject is correct, read the sentence as if the problematic pronoun were the only subject.

Me disagreed about my grade.
The judge gave I a lecture.

4. When using a pronoun to modify a gerund (that is, a verb or verb phrase functioning as a noun), use the possessive case.

His acting made me laugh.
He adores *my* having fun.

Nouns modifying gerunds also take the possessive case, as in

Martin Luther objected to the *clergy's* selling priestly offices.

5. Making a comparison using the word *than* followed by a pronoun can be confusing. The case depends on whether the pronoun is the object of the preposition *than* or the subject of an unspoken but understood verb. To test this, fill in the silent words.

He loved her more than [he loved] *me*.
He loved her more than *I* [loved her].

6. Writers are sometimes confused by a pronoun acting as an appositive—that is, a noun or noun substitute placed right beside another noun or noun substitute to provide additional identification.

We Americans have an "omnipotence complex."

The appositive takes the same case as the word it stands beside. *Americans* is the subject of the sentence, and therefore the pronoun must be in the subjective case.

This "omnipotence complex" has injured *us* Americans.

Now *Americans* is the direct object of the verb *injured,* and the pronoun takes the objective case. To test for correctness, read the sentence with the appositive pronoun only.

This "omnipotence complex has injured we."

Exercises for Pronouns

1. For each of the following sentences, choose the correct word in the parentheses.
   a. We looked forward to (them, their) coming home at Christmas.
   b. Men generally misunderstand (we, us) women.
   c. (We, Us) men are largely misunderstood by women.
   d. We (ourself, ourselves) are happy at the election's outcome.
   e. All the basketball players got in (each other's, one another's) way.
   f. The most valuable player award went to the entire team, including (I, me, myself).
   g. Just between you and (I, me, myself), she has bad breath.

2. Correct the following sentences for pronoun errors, if any.
   a. The woman never regretted hiring we students.
   b. The strike whose cause was low wages ended peacefully.
   c. My sister who lives in England wrote a letter to Mother, Father, and I.
   d. Here is a painting about which much should be said.
   e. Me and Eddie both participated in the track meet, but he pole-vaulting was funnier than me trying to high-jump.
   f. The man that tried to hang-glide last Saturday is doing nicely in the hospital, but the doctor that attended him is worried. So are his wife and me.
   g. I know three movie stars who Goldwyn discovered in drugstores.

Verbs

Verbs express actions, processes, or states of being.

He *ran* outside when the object *appeared* in the sky, but she *was* horrified.

Verbs are the energy at the center of all sentences.

KINDS OF VERBS. We classify verbs according to whether they take a direct object or a complement or help other verbs to perform.
Transitive verbs take a direct object.

The lion *ate* the wildebeest.

Intransitive verbs describe activities and states without an object.

Queen Victoria *sneezed* and the empire *trembled.*

Linking verbs act as equal signs between nouns and their complements, that is, words that complete the meaning of the sentence.

William *is* a clown, but he *appears* miserable.

To be is the most frequently used linking verb; other common ones are *appear, become, feel, look,* and *seem.*
Auxiliary verbs, also called helping verbs, join with the infinitive, past participle, or present participle of a verb to form a verb phrase.

The new phone book *has* arrived.

The verbs *to be* and *to have* are the most common auxiliaries. (*To be* also functions as a linking verb.) Other auxiliaries are *can, could, do, may, might, must, need, ought, should, would.*

VERB FORMS. The principal parts of the verb are the *infinitive,* the *past tense,* and the *past participle.* Changes in verb form rely on these basic parts. To form the past tense and the past participle of regular verbs, add *-d* or *-ed* to the infinitive.

INFINITIVE	PAST TENSE	PAST PARTICIPLE
help	helped	helped
traverse	traversed	traversed

Sometimes the present participle is considered a principal part of the verb. It is formed by adding *-ing* to the infinitive (*helping, traversing*).

Many English verbs are irregular, and ways of forming their past tenses and past participles vary greatly. Sometimes an internal vowel changes, sometimes a consonant ending, sometimes both. Occasionally, the past or past participle will have two acceptable forms. Here we list the most common irregular verbs. If a verb you want to use is not on the list, consult your dictionary.

INFINITIVE	PAST TENSE	PAST PARTICIPLE
arise	arose	arisen
awake	awoke, awaked	*awaked, awoken

INFINITIVE	PAST TENSE	PAST PARTICIPLE
bear	bore	borne
begin	began	begun
bite	bit	bitten
blow	blew	blown
break	broke	broken
burst	burst	burst
choose	chose	chosen
come	came	come
draw	drew	drawn
drink	drank	drunk
drive	drove	driven
eat	ate	eaten
fall	fell	fallen
fly	flew	flown
forbid	forbad, forbade	forbidden
forsake	forsook	forsaken
freeze	froze	frozen
get	got	gotten, got
give	gave	given
go	went	gone
grow	grew	grown
hang	hung, hanged	hung, hanged
know	knew	known
lay	laid	laid
lie	lay	lain
lose	lost	lost
prove	proved	proved, proven
ring	rang	rung
rise	rose	risen
see	saw	seen
set	set	set
sing	sang	sung
sit	sat	sat
slay	slew	slain
speak	spoke	spoken
spring	sprang, sprung	sprung
steal	stole	stolen
strive	strove, strived	striven, strived
swear	swore	sworn
swim	swam	swum
take	took	taken
teach	taught	taught
tread	trod	trodden, trod
write	wrote	written

For all verbs, to form the present participle add *-ing* to the infinitive.

TENSE. Tense refers to time. All verbs change according to when the action occurs, how it is related to another action, and whether it is continuous.

The **simple tenses** are present, past, and future. *Present tense* indicates current action.

> She *sings* well.

Past tense indicates completed action.

> She *sang* that song last night.

Future tense indicates action that will be completed later.

> She *will sing* it again tomorrow.

To form the future tense, combine the infinitive of the verb with the future tense of *to be.*

The **perfect tenses** indicate an action that was or will be completed after another action. *Present perfect* indicates past action continuing up to the present.

> She *has sung* that song every night.

Past perfect indicates action completed before another past activity.

> She *had sung* it nearly fifteen hundred times before her big break came.

Future perfect indicates action expected to be completed later.

> By July 4, she *will have sung* that song to a million people.

The perfect tenses are formed by combining the past participle of the verb with the present, past, or future tense of *to have.*

The **progressive tenses** indicate ongoing action.

> She *was singing*, she *has been singing*, she *will be singing*, she *is singing* her life away.

These tenses can indicate ongoing actions past, present, or future. They are formed by combining the present participle of the verb with the appropriate form—present, past, future—of *to be.*

Be consistent with your tenses. Sudden and incorrect shifts can confuse and irritate the reader.

> **INCONSISTENT**   After Robespierre initiated the Reign of Terror, he controls the revolution and has Danton guillotined.

Because *initiated* is in the past tense, the other verbs should also be in the past tense.

REVISED After Robespierre *initiated* the Reign of Terror, he *controlled* the revolution and *had* Danton guillotined.

VOICE. English has two **voices,** active and passive. In **active voice,** the subject of the sentence performs the action.

The diva *sang* an aria from *Aida*.

In **passive voice,** the subject of the sentence receives the action.

Even the stagehands *were moved*.

See "Be Active" in Chapter 12 for more on active and passive voice.

MOOD. The **mood** of the verb tells us whether the speaker views the action or state expressed in the sentence as fact, question, command, or likelihood. English has four moods. The **indicative mood** makes an assertion.

She *will win* the race.

The **interrogative mood** asks a question.

Did she *win* the race?

The **imperative mood** issues a command.

Win that race!

The **subjunctive mood** has several functions. It can express a wish—

I wish I *were* running,

a statement contrary to fact—

If I *were* you, I *would run* faster,

a remote possibility—

I *might get* in shape someday,

and a command—

I *demand* that your laughter *be* stopped.

This form is slowly dying out in English, but careful stylists still use it.

Exercises for Verbs

1. Write two sentences using a transitive verb, two using an intransitive verb, two using a linking verb, and two using an auxiliary verb.

2. Provide the appropriate form of the verb for each sentence in this paragraph.

> Before the snows have melted, my neighbor (to plant) his garden. He (to work) in his garden every day. He always (to have) tulips and daffodils by April. By the middle of May, the tulips (to begin) to droop. One year, however, they (to bloom) still in June. When he (to work) during the hot summer months, I am often afraid he (to suffer) heat stroke. I think he (to like) flowers.

3. Using a single verb (such as *to race* but not that one), write sentences for all the different moods.

4. For the following sentences, determine the tense and voice of the verbs.
   a. Viewers of this program were dazzled by his performance.
   b. The quotation came from the *New York Times*.
   c. Studying the acquisition of language is instructive.
   d. You will be happy with his speech.
   e. Playing serves several functions in children.
   f. Coffee has sometimes been thought a cause of headache.
   g. Medicine is not yet considered a science.
   h. In April, she will have served as mayor for ten years.
   i. A surprising conclusion was drawn from the evidence.
   j. You will need a derrick to remove your car.

Adjectives

Adjectives are words that modify nouns or noun substitutes.

It was a *brilliant* idea to build a *gravel* road.

They answer the question What kind of person, place, or thing is this? They also tell us how many people, places, and things there are.

Innumerable bumblebees chased the *four* children.

They sometimes follow a linking verb and modify the verb's subject.

The night was *bright*, and the horse looked *blue* in the moonlight.

The articles—*a, an,* and *the*—are also adjectives. *The* is the **definite article** and is used to refer to a definite, known thing.

The book was torn by *the* baby.

A and *an* are **indefinite articles** and are used to refer to nonspecific things. *A* precedes nouns that begin with consonants, and *an* precedes nouns that begin with vowels.

To some people *a* rat is less repulsive than *an* eel.

One exception occurs before nouns that begin with a long *u* sound; these take *a* as their article.

Although you may think it *an* underhanded trick, it is *a* universal practice.

To some Americans, the phrase *an historical event* sounds and looks right. If it sounds natural to you, use it. Generally, however, Americans do not use *an* before *h*.

Comparative and *superlative* refer to the degree to which a person, place, or thing possesses an attribute. When a person, place, or thing possesses an attribute more than another does, the adjective is in the *comparative* form.

My daddy is *stronger* than your daddy.

When a person, place, or thing possesses all of an attribute or possesses it in greater degree than does any other in a group of three or more, the adjective is in the superlative form.

My daddy is the *strongest* daddy in the world.

Most adjectives simply add *-er* for the comparative and *-est* for the superlative. Some, however, change form with degree (*good, better, best*). And some adjectives of two or more syllables require *more* or *most* to indicate their comparative or superlative form.

Chocolate is *more delicious* than strawberry; it is the *most delicious* flavor.

When in doubt, check your dictionary.

Adverbs

Adverbs modify verbs, adjectives, and other adverbs. They indicate how, when, where, why, how often, and in what manner. Most adverbs end in *-ly* (*swiftly, intelligently*), but some do not (*very, beyond*).

Like adjectives, adverbs may be compared, but unlike most adjectives, they require the terms *more* and *most* to signal their comparative and superlative forms.

She ran *more swiftly* than I did; in fact she ran *most swiftly* of anybody.

Exercise for Adjectives and Adverbs

Choose a passage of fifty words and underline all the adjectives and all the adverbs. Provide the comparative and superlative forms for all the words you have underlined.

Conjunctions

Conjunctions join words, phrases, and clauses. **Coordinating conjunctions** join equal ideas.

Bill and Phil hated the movie, *but* they liked the popcorn.

You can remember the coordinating conjunctions by remembering *fanboys—for, and, nor, but, or, yet, so.*

Subordinating conjunctions join a dependent clause to an independent clause.

If you hurry, you will catch the train.

Some common subordinating conjunctions are *although, because, if, since, unless, whenever, whereas.*

Correlative conjunctions are pairs of conjunctions that help balance the sentence and relate different parts of it to each other.

Either you leave *or* I leave.

The correlative conjunctions are *both/and, either/or, neither/nor,* and *not only/but also.* The same grammatical construction must follow both elements of the pair.

Caligula *not only* destroyed the pride of the Romans *but also* wasted Rome's resources.

Conjunctive adverbs provide a logical link between two independent clauses.

You misbehaved, and, *therefore,* you will have no supper.

We guarantee nothing; *however,* we hope to please.

Some common conjunctive adverbs are *however, moreover, nevertheless, therefore, thus,* and phrases such as *on the contrary.* Set them off with punctuation. Other punctuation is exactly as if the conjunctive adverb were not there.

Exercises for Conjunctions

1. Write seven sentences, using a different coordinating conjunction in each.
2. Write five sentences, using a different subordinating conjunction in each.
3. Write four sentences, using a different pair of correlative conjunctions in each.
4. Write four sentences, using a different conjunctive adverb in each.

Prepositions

A **preposition** ties a noun or noun substitute to another word in the sentence. In

The baseball rolled into the sewer,

the preposition *into* ties the sewer to the baseball. Constructing a complete list of prepositions would be nearly impossible—and certainly unneccessary. They range all the way from the common ones, such as *in, to,* and *with,* to rarer compound prepositions, such as *inasmuch as* and *on behalf of.* A preposition and its object form a **prepositional phrase**. Such phrases function in several ways. They can serve as adjectives to modify nouns.

John Maynard Keynes conceived a passion *for the ballerina with the long, beautiful legs.*

They can serve as adverbs.

On VJ Day, Americans danced *in the streets.*

They can also serve as nouns.

In the streets was the place to be that day.

Prepositions can combine with verbs to create multiword verbs.

She can't *put up with* a man who won't *give up on* a car that always *falls apart.*

Unfortunately, prepositional phrases tend to pile up in a sentence, as in E. B. White's famous burlesque:

What did you bring the book I can't stand to be read to out of up for?

When prepositions pile up, rewrite the sentence.

Exercises for Prepositions

1. Write three sentences in which the prepositional phrases function as adjectives, three in which they function as adverbs, and three in which they function as nouns.
2. Write five sentences which have more than one prepositional phrase.

Interjections

Interjections express feelings, not thoughts. Words such as *gosh, hey, oh, ouch, pshaw, say,* and *well* are interjections. They never constitute sentences on their own and appear only rarely in high informal writing.

PHRASES, CLAUSES, AND SENTENCES

Phrases

A **phrase** is a group of related words that lacks either a subject or a verb or both. It modifies another word in the sentence or modifies the sentence as a whole.

> *Standing in the sunlight,* the man *in the red sweater* squinted *at the photographer.*

A **prepositional phrase** begins with a preposition and can act as an adjective, adverb, or noun. See the section "Prepositions."

A **verb phrase** is a verb expressed in more than one word.

> By this time tomorrow, Los Angeles *will have traveled* in a 27,000-mile circle.

See the section "Verbs."

A **verbal phrase** is a form of the verb used not as a verb but as another part of speech. An **infinitive phrase** is a verbal phrase that contains the infinitive, its object, and any modifiers. In *To err is human,* the infinitive *to err* serves as the subject of the sentence, a noun or noun substitute. The infinitive phrase can also serve as an adjective or adverb:

> The Yankees are almost always the team *to beat.* (adjective)
>
> Drew juggled three chain saws *to show his talent.* (adverb)

A **participial phrase** includes a participle, its object, and any modifiers. It functions as an adjective.

> Police were on the lookout for a man *driving a 1951 Hornet.*

A **gerund phrase** is the present participle used as a noun. It functions as either the subject or the object of a verb.

> *Rising early* is healthy, but how I hate *getting up.*

An **absolute phrase** modifies a whole clause or sentence, not just a single word.

> *Weather permitting,* we'll boat over the rapids tomorrow.

It contains a participle and a noun or pronoun. Usually, we drop the participle if the verb is *to be.* In the following example, putting *Being* before *Weary and hungry* is not necessary.

> *Weary and hungry,* the field hockey team trudged homeward.

An **appositive phrase** is placed next to another word or phrase to provide pertinent elaboration of it.

Clarence, brother of Richard III, was drowned in a barrel of malmsey.

Brother of Richard III is an appositive, providing apt information about Clarence. Using appositives can help you maintain a lean, vigorous prose. We have more to say about them in ''Economy: Reducing the Verbiage'' in Chapter 11.

Clauses

A **clause** is a group of words that contains a subject and a verb. Clauses can be independent or dependent. When they are **independent**, they can stand alone.

Volcanoes rumble before spewing.

When clauses are **dependent**, they cannot stand alone.

Whenever volcanoes rumble

The dependent clause requires an independent clause to complete its meaning.

Whenever volcanoes rumble, the villagers begin to fret.

A dependent clause (also called a *subordinate clause*) begins with a subordinating conjunction (such as *although, if, whenever*) and can function as an adjective, adverb, or noun.

The witch doctors, *whose geological training was slight,* said they had nothing to fear. (adjective)

The villagers knew better *when the lava began to flow.* (adverb)

Whether they should flee was the pressing decision. (noun)

Sentences

A **sentence** is a complete thought. It contains a subject and a verb. It indicates what happened to the subject or what the subject caused to happen. For a detailed discussion, see Chapter 11, The Sentence from Many Angles.

Sentences come in four constructions. A **simple sentence** contains one independent (or main) clause and no other clauses. It may, however, have a compound subject.

Lewis and Clark explored the Northwest Passage.

It may have more than one verb.

They tried and tried but could not find their way.

As long as it has only one independent clause, it is a simple sentence.

A **compound sentence** contains at least two independent clauses but no dependent clauses. The independent clauses can be joined either by a comma and a conjunction or by a semicolon.

You take the high road, and I'll take the low road.

Diplomacy without defense is folly; defense without diplomacy is madness.

A **complex sentence** contains only one independent clause and at least one dependent clause.

When John Adams was president, his wife hung the family wash in the East Room of the White House. (dependent-independent)

On the other hand, George Washington, who preceded Adams in the presidency, never occupied the White House. (independent interrupted by dependent)

A **compound-complex sentence** contains two or more independent clauses and at least one dependent clause.

Men over age thirty-five should have a medical checkup regularly even if they are feeling fine, and they should begin to cut down on the sugar, salt, and cholesterol in their diet. (independent-dependent-independent)

In addition, sentences can be distinguished according to when the main idea is completed and where the emphasis falls. A sentence is called *loose* or *cumulative* when the main idea is introduced at or near the beginning and then modified by less important elements. The information piles up along the way in a rather casual and unemphatic fashion.

Bats are obliged to make sounds almost ceaselessly, to sense, by sonar, all the objects in their surroundings. (Lewis Thomas, *The Lives of a Cell*)

This kind of sentence is very natural to speech, when we usually start with a subject and amplify it as thoughts occur to us.

A sentence is called *periodic* when the main idea is not completed until the end. Along the way, less important elements—modifiers, subordinate clauses, and the like—are presented, but the emphasis comes at the conclusion.

No matter how many areas of the world the British colonized, the jewel in the crown was always India.

Most good writers combine these two forms, using the periodic to
particularly important point.

Exercises for Phrases, Clauses, and Sentences

1. Identify the various kinds of phrases in the following passage.

   Like ill-trained shamans, rock singers manipulated the energies they could
   scarcely keep in tow. This was closely akin to their self-destructive streak; they
   loved putting their heads in the lion's mouth, and several were dead before the
   sixties ended. Janis Joplin was particularly naked in her vulnerability to the audience, in her visible need of them. (Morris Dickstein, *The Gates of Eden*)

2. Write a sentence containing one of each kind of phrase.

3. Ify the various kinds of constructions in the following passage and determine which sentences are loose and which are periodic.

   Anyone who has observed a dog doing his neighborhood rounds and leaving
   his personal mark on each convenient post will have already guessed how the
   wolves marked out *their* property. Once a week, more or less, the clan made the
   rounds of the family lands and freshened up the boundary markers. . . . This
   careful attention to property rights was perhaps made necessary by the presence
   of two other wolf families whose lands abutted on ours, although I never discovered any evidence of bickering or disagreements between the owners of the various adjoining estates. I suspect, therefore, that it was more of a ritual activity.
   (Farley Mowat, *Never Cry Wolf*)

4. Change the following passages as directed.
   a. Into a simple sentence: Thomas Marshall, who was vice president
      under Woodrow Wilson, said, "What this country needs is a good
      five-cent cigar."
   b. Into one complex sentence: Chinese chefs serve food in bite-size
      pieces. Bite-size pieces cook faster. That saves fuel.
   c. Into a compound sentence: Money is the root of all evil. Few people
      bury it or burn it.
   d. Into a compound-complex sentence: My Uncle said he had a terrific
      television show to watch, and he insisted on turning to another sta-
      tion, and then he sat in his big green easy chair; he was snoring in
      five minutes.

5. Construct two loose sentences and two periodic sentences.

20

PROBLEMS IN SENTENCES

since feeling is first
who pays attention
to the syntax of things
will never wholly kiss you
E. E. CUMMINGS (1894–1962)
AMERICAN POET

SUBJECT-VERB AGREEMENT

The verb of a sentence must agree in number and person with the subject.

The scarlet macaw lives in the jungles of South America.

The singular noun *macaw* takes the singular verb *lives*.

Macaws have long tails and large hooked beaks.

The plural noun *macaws* takes the plural verb *have*.

Subject-verb agreement can become complicated. Here are some difficult constructions and the rules that govern them.

1. Intervening words. Subject and verb must agree even when other words come between them.

The sight of red and blue macaws thrills the spectator.

Sight is the subject, and *thrills*, the verb, must agree with it, even though *macaws*, a plural noun, is next to the verb. An *intervening clause* with a plural verb can be quite confusing.

The sight of red and blue macaws, which are the largest of all the parrots, thrills the spectator.

Sight is still the subject, and *thrills* agrees with it.

Phrases beginning with prepositions *(along with, as well as, in addition to, like)* are never part of the subject and cannot affect the verb.

> President Johnson, as well as Presidents Truman and Kennedy, was once a senator.

What applies to Johnson also applies to the other two, but Johnson alone is the subject, so the verb is singular.

2. Collective nouns. Words like *committee, family, group, jury*, and *team*, take a singular verb when you want to emphasize the group as a whole.

> The jury has decided.
>
> The family agrees about religion.

These collective nouns take a plural verb when you want to emphasize separate entities.

> The jury are in there arguing about the verdict.
>
> The family disagree, however, about sex and politics.

Apply the same rule and reasoning to *majority of, mass of, number of*, and other references to quantity or size. They take the singular to emphasize the totality and the plural to emphasize the separate entities.

> The number of mistakes is sometimes disheartening.
>
> But the majority of people make them.

3. Compound subjects. When a compound subject connected by *and* is viewed as separate entities, the verb should be plural.

> Harpo and Groucho are my favorites of the Marx Brothers.

When the compound subject is viewed as a unit, the verb should be singular.

> Peanut butter and banana is my favorite snack.

When a compound subject is joined by *nor* or *or*, the closer subject determines the verb.

> Either the Brownie Scouts or Ms. Peabody was lying about the rampaging bear.
>
> Either Ms. Peabody or the Brownie Scouts were lying about the rampaging bear.

When this rule leads to an awkward construction, rewrite the sentence.

> **AWKWARD**   Either Clara or I am the worst tennis player on the team.

REVISED   Either Clara is the worst tennis player on the
                                 team or I am.

4. Numbers. Numbers that act as a unit take a singular verb.

Ninety-five cents is too much to pay for a soft drink.

Numbers viewed as individual items take a plural verb.

Ninety-five dogs in the kennel were barking.

5. Singular words in plural form. Some words ending in *-s* that refer to a single item or idea take a singular verb.

Mumps is usually a childhood disease.

But some take a plural verb.

Scissors are hard to sharpen.

Idiom controls the form. Consult your dictionary.
Some words ending in *-ics* will be singular in one context but plural in another.

Statistics is a branch of mathematics.
Statistics are not always reliable.

In the first example, *statistics* is singular because it refers to a body of knowledge viewed as a unit. In the second, it is plural because it refers to items viewed separately.

6. Noun substitutes. When the subject of a sentence is a phrase or clause used as a noun substitute, the verb is always singular.

Smuggling parrots has become a lucrative business.
Why the smugglers persist is hardly puzzling.

Smuggling parrots is the subject of the first sentence, and *Why the smugglers persist* is the subject of the second. Both require singular verbs. When, however, two or more noun substitutes are the subject, the verb is plural.

Smuggling parrots and selling them are violations of the law.

7. Linking verbs. A linking verb (*appear, be, feel, look, seem, smell,* and so on) agrees with its subject, not with the noun or pronoun that is the subject's complement.

Pink cockatoos are an Australian native.

Pink cockatoos is the subject; *Australian native* is the complement.
In sentences that begin with *There* or *Here* followed by a linking verb, the verb agrees with the real subject following the verb.

There is a tavern in the town.

There are many customers.

8. Relative pronouns. The singular or plural status of the relative pronouns *that, which, who, whom,* **and** *whose* **is determined by their antecedent, the noun to which they refer.**

I love dogs that have a sense of humor.

The antecedent of *that* is *dogs,* and so the verb is plural.

I love a dog that has a sense of humor.

Now the antecedent is *dog,* so the verb is singular.

A problem may arise when the word *one* appears in the sentence.

Thomas Mann was one of the German intellectuals who were willing to stand up to Hitler.

Who refers to *German intellectuals* and takes a plural verb.

Mann was not the only one of the German intellectuals who was willing to stand up to Hitler.

Who now refers to *one,* a singular pronoun, and takes a singular verb.

9. Indefinite pronouns. Indefinite pronouns, such as *any, each, either, everybody, someone,* **and so on, generally take a singular verb.**

Everyone loves fudge.

A few indefinite pronouns (*all, any, few, none, some*) can take either a singular or a plural verb, depending on whether they refer to individual items or the group as a whole.

Some fudge has nuts.

Some people make themselves sick gorging on it.

Careful stylists generally prefer the singular when using *none,* and always use the singular when using *no one.*

None was more gluttonous than William, who ate two pounds.

No one was surprised when he got so sick.

Exercises for Subject-Verb Agreement

1. In the following sentences choose the correct word in the parentheses to make the subject and verb agree.
   a. The list of books (stays, stay) on my table.
   b. The committee (reviews, review) applications at night.

    c. Neither the coach nor the players rewarded (himself, themselves) for the victory.

    d. The collections of antique silver (shows, show) taste.

    e. Either the guards or the warden (was, were) responsible for the trouble.

    f. When measles (is, are) epidemic, I keep my children at home.

    g. The ethics of all who have vaccine (is, are) under scrutiny.

    h. She was one of those brainy people who also (loves, love) sports.

    i. The couple living next to the Bishops (drinks, drink) too much.

    j. Each one of the dogs that belonged to Jennie Vickers (has, have) fleas.

2. Correct any mistakes in subject-verb agreement in the following sentences.

    a. His collection of spiffy sports cars were impressive.

    b. The family is fighting viciously over the will.

    c. No one in all the display rooms were surprised at the brilliance of the artists.

    d. He is one of the salesmen who, having sold over a million dollars in policies, are going to Hawaii.

    e. Everybody clapped and were happy.

    f. Neither his clothes nor the car were paid for.

    g. The sound of the dogs, who barked all night, have driven her to distraction.

    h. Tommy, along with all his friends, are going to the circus.

    i. A favorite creature of mine are koala bears.

    j. How the accountants manage on April 15 are puzzling, but preparing income taxes is a laudable occupation.

PRONOUN-ANTECEDENT AGREEMENT

As we said earlier, a pronoun must agree in person, number, and gender with its antecedent, that is, the noun or noun substitute to which it refers.

Dachshunds require special care because of their long backs.

The pronoun *their* matches in person and number its antecedent, *dachshunds*.

Our male dachshund requires special care because of his back.

The pronoun *his* matches in person, number, and gender its antecedent, *our male dachshund*.

Occasionally, a pronoun will precede its antecedent in a sentence.

While performing his tricks, the elephant fell on his nose.

Here we discuss four potentially confusing constructions.

1. Antecedents joined by *and* usually take a plural pronoun.

As Fido and Rover ate, they snarled at each other.

2. Antecedents joined by *nor* or *or* take singular pronouns when both parts of the antecedent are singular.

Either the flanker or the tight end missed his assignment.

When one of the nouns is plural, the closer noun determines the pronoun.

Neither the coach nor the players admit their mistake.

To avoid an awkward construction, put the plural noun closer to the verb.

AWKWARD	Neither the Brownies nor Ms. Peabody was able to find her way home.
REVISED	Neither Ms. Peabody nor the Brownies were able to find their way home.

3. A pronoun referring to a collective noun (such as *audience, committee*) should be singular when the emphasis is on the group as a whole.

The committee has its proposal ready.

The pronoun should be plural when the emphasis is on individual entities within the group.

The audience are slowly taking their seats.

4. Indefinite pronouns (*everyone, none, some*) are usually treated as singular and take singular pronouns.

No one eats her lunch before noon at Miss Blaine's School.
Each of the boys appears in his uniform on Fridays.

Sometimes, however, an indefinite pronoun suggests more than one and should be treated as a plural.

Some of the teachers eat their lunch alone.

When treating the indefinite pronoun as a singular, writers have traditionally used the generic *he, him, his.*

Everyone has his faults.

Many, however, have come to consider this usage sexist. To avoid the problem, recast your sentence.

All have their faults.

(For a general discussion of sexist language, see "Avoiding Sexist Language" in Chapter 12.)

Exercises for Pronoun-Antecedent Agreement

1. In the following sentences, choose the appropriate pronoun in the parentheses.
   a. Neither Brecht nor Beckett typed (his, their, theirselves) manuscripts.
   b. The awards committee split (its, their) award between Conklin and Dumanian, and the chair asked each winner to express (her, their) appreciation.
   c. The family quarreled with one another because of (its, their) religion.
   d. Some of the members voiced (its, his, their) personal convictions.
   e. Either the manager or his assistants missed (his, their) chance to correct the error.

2. Correct any mistakes in pronoun-antecedent agreement in the following sentences.
   a. To sail in the America's Cup, every member of the crew must do their job.
   b. The family sat down to their Thanksgiving dinner.
   c. Neither the Contras nor Ortega likes the proposal.
   d. All the meat was ground up and the sausages put in its cases.
   e. Charles and the Parkers driving home in his car really took their sweet time.
   f. Each member of the committee wanted to put forward their individual proposals.
   g. Either the secretary of state or the secretary of defense failed to assume their responsibility.

PRONOUN REFERENCE

A pronoun should refer specifically and unmistakably to one and only one antecedent.

Lincoln would have had a difficult time in his second term because his cabinet had turned against him.

All the pronouns in this sentence clearly refer to Lincoln. Unclear antecedents can cause the reader to misread the sentence. The following rules will help you avoid this kind of misreading.

1. When you use more than one noun or noun substitute to which the pronoun could refer, double check to make sure the reference is unmistakable.

UNCLEAR   After Schmeling fought Louis, he was never the same.

The pronoun *he* could refer to either boxer.

CLEAR   After he fought Louis, Schmeling was never the same.

Now the pronoun can refer only to Schmeling. The writer revised the sentence so that the second noun is not mentioned until after the pronoun reference is established.

2. When a group of words intervenes between the antecedent and the pronoun, the reference may be unclear.

UNCLEAR   The jury was served doughnuts in the lunchroom that tasted stale.

The lunchroom, we assume, is not what tasted stale. Reframing the sentence so that the pronoun is beside its antecedent clears up the problem.

CLEAR   In the lunchroom, the jury was served doughnuts that tasted stale.

UNCLEAR   The lawless and intuitive character of modern art is a familiar theme that Professor Longstreth delights in criticizing.

Does Professor Longstreth delight in criticizing the theme, or in criticizing the lawless and intuitive character of modern art?

CLEAR   The lawless and intuitive character of modern art that Professor Longstreth delights in criticizing is a familiar theme.

Now the pronoun stands beside the subject that is its antecedent. It could not be thought to refer to *theme*. If the writer had intended the clause to modify *theme,* he or she might have put it this way:

CLEAR   The lawless and intuitive character of modern art is a familiar theme, a theme that Professor Longstreth delights in criticizing.

Repeating the noun *theme* makes the statement unambiguous. Don't be afraid of repeating a word in the interest of clarity.

3. A pronoun should refer to the subject of the previous clause, as this one does:

New models had arrived at the showrooms, and they were all different colors.

We know that the models, not the showrooms, were different colors. When the pronoun refers not to the subject but to some other part of the clause, however, we may be confused.

UNCLEAR   If your children refuse to eat their vegetables, slice them up and hide them in a savory beef pie.

What, we may well ask, is to be sliced up? Does the pronoun refer to the subject of the clause, *children,* or to the last noun in it, *vegetables*?

> CLEAR   Slice up the vegetables and hide them in a sa-
>   vory beef pie if your children refuse to eat them.

The writer has saved the children from a horrible fate.

4. Avoid confusion with demonstrative pronouns, such as *this,* *that, these,* and *those,* particularly when they begin a sentence.

> UNCLEAR   Otto nibbled at the frosting and finally took a
>   little slice of the wedding cake and began to eat
>   it. This so angered the bride that she dumped
>   the whole cake on his head.

What angered the bride? the nibbling? taking a slice? eating it?

> CLEAR   Otto nibbled at the frosting and finally took a
>   little slice of the wedding cake and began to eat
>   it. Seeing him eating it so angered the bride that
>   she dumped the whole cake on his head.

When using a demonstrative pronoun, be sure its reference is clear.

5. Avoid problems in vagueness with the ubiquitous *it.*

> UNCLEAR   The sheepdog sniffed the Chihuahua, and then
>   it went to sleep on its side.

Which dog went to sleep? And did it go to sleep on its own side or on the other dog's side?

> CLEAR   The sheepdog went to sleep on its side after sniff-
>   ing the Chihuahua.

6. Do not use a pronoun with an unstated antecedent.

> UNCLEAR   At the New York Stock Exchange, they buy or
>   sell securities listed on that exchange only.

Who is *they*? There is no antecedent.

> CLEAR   At the New York Stock Exchange, traders buy
>   or sell securities listed on that exchange only.

Antecedents implied in adjectives, adverbs, or possessives can also be confusing.

> UNCLEAR   She laughed raucously, and that unnerved him.

Raucously is an adverb and cannot function as an antecedent.

> CLEAR   Her raucous laughter unnerved him.

| UNCLEAR | Tommy Manville was a much-married million-aire. It was usually to starlets and dancers. |

Much-married is an adjective and cannot serve as an antecedent for *it.*

| CLEAR | Tommy Manville was a much-married million-aire. Usually he married starlets and dancers. |

In almost all problems of reference, the reader can figure out the meaning, but the writer should make it clear.

Exercise for Pronoun Reference

Rewrite the following sentences to correct any problems in pronoun reference and to clarify the meaning you think the sentence has.

a. After Clarence overdosed on hot fudge while Rudolph ate peanut butter, he never trusted him again.

b. We all ordered chicken at the North Beach restaurant that had a tasty red sauce over it.

c. I have never seen a mother totally reject her daughter, no matter how angry and even humiliated she was.

d. I have never seen a mother totally reject her daughter, no matter how dissolute and degenerate she was.

e. If you compare the morals of people today with those of the most devout and enlightened people of the Middle Ages, you will see that they fall short.

f. When the players persist in breaking all the rules, change them.

g. The students in the dormitories made such messes on the floors of the dining rooms that Mrs. Hassenfuss had the staff hose them down and sweep them out.

h. In the women's dressing room, they often leave wet towels on the floor, and I have to nag at them.

i. Liz Taylor has lost thousands of pounds. It can't be either healthy or fun.

j. Getting into medical school isn't easy. They have to do well in college and on their MCATs.

COMMA SPLICES AND FUSED SENTENCES

Independent clauses of a compound sentence are joined either by a conjunction and a comma or by a semicolon.

Brutus was careful, but Cassius was cunning.

Jack Sprat could eat no fat; his wife could eat no lean.

When two independent clauses are joined by a comma alone, the error is called a *comma splice.*

> **COMMA SPLICE**   I sauntered happily down Connecticut Avenue, it reminded me of my old neighborhood.

Expecting a dependent clause or a phrase to follow a comma alone, the reader may misread. To correct the problem, the writer could add a conjunction or replace the comma with a semicolon.

> **REVISED**   I sauntered happily down Connecticut Avenue, for it reminded me of my old neighborhood.

When two independent clauses are joined by no internal punctuation at all, the error is called a *fused* or *run-on sentence.*

> **FUSED**   Sudan is the largest country in Africa its land mass is larger than California's.

Absence of punctuation forces the reader to rethink the sentence to figure out the meaning. A comma and a conjunction or a semicolon will do the trick.

> **REVISED**   Sudan is the largest country in Africa; its land mass is larger than California's.

The comma splice and the fused sentence can also be corrected by making two sentences.

> **REVISED**   I sauntered happily down Connecticut Avenue. It reminded me of my old neighborhood.

Exercise for Comma Splices and Fused Sentences

Correct the errors in the following sentences.
  a. Walt Whitman's *Leaves of Grass* was poorly received its reception subjected Whitman to embarrassment.
  b. When he was a senator, Nixon's votes on domestic affairs were conservative, his votes on foreign affairs were more liberal.
  c. People call Salinas, California, the lettuce capital of the world also many artichokes are grown in the area.
  d. Jefferson and Adams wrote the Declaration of Independence, they died on the same day.
  e. Comma splices and fused sentences are a problem, they catch us unawares.
  f. These articles and essays provide an education, it is a humane and even entertaining one.

g. The water for the Genoan fountains came from aqueducts, the water also powered the mills nearby.

h. The grain in Sri Lanka is broadcast over cleared fields they are fertilized with ashes.

i. Long ago, salt was used as money in parts of Africa, rain could be a disaster.

j. Population increases come in spurts there was a prolonged rise in the late Middle Ages.

SENTENCE FRAGMENTS

From time to time we are all guilty of careless writing. We have a thought, and, before it is completed, another intervenes and knocks the first off the track. The result can be the error called a *sentence fragment*. A sentence fragment lacks either a subject or a verb, or contains a dependent clause but no independent clause.

The building designed by Frank Lloyd Wright

Walked fast in order to get home by dusk

Because I said so

Not complete sentences, these are not complete thoughts. What is being said about the building? Who was walking home, and what about it? Because you said so, what? The thought is fragmented, left hanging in mid-air.

Sometimes you can catch fragments by reading aloud. A sentence lacking either a subject or a verb will sound flat and toneless. A sentence that is only a moorless dependent clause will sound unfinished.

For a discussion of the proper use of a fragment, refer to "Using Fragments" in Chapter 11.

Exercises for Sentence Fragments

1. Identify the fragments in the following brief passages.
   a. The Seine was seldom used for anything but commerce. Although some sightseers on Sundays going to Saint-Cloud.
   b. Less consumption of beef but more of fish and chicken. Many people have become vegetarians.
   c. He was exhausted and his feet hurt. His shoulders and calves as well, having run so very far. Sitting down felt good. Then getting up and running on.

> d. When she opened the letter she found a check for one hundred dollars from her aunt. Thinking that it was quite a lot of money for a birthday present when she turned sixteen. She laughed.
> e. These times that try men's souls. Said Thomas Paine.
> f. East German money had a picture of happy schoolchildren on one side. A picture of Goethe on the other side.
> g. Tell me why stars shine. Composed of fire, like the sun?
> h. This essay is by far the most important I have written. Because it runs counter to prevailing opinion.
> i. Plato says the youth of Athens taught games and songs and dancing to the very gods themselves. Apollo, Athena. Plato wasn't too interested in literary studies. Poetry largely for the sake of the music.
> j. I have learned much in school. If, indeed, because people have forced me to study subjects in which I had no natural interest.

2. Rewrite this passage so that there are no sentence fragments.

> Beyond the maze of alleys was an indoor market. Women guarded the tables. Loaded with fruits, vegetables, and melons. They chatted and nursed babies. Their social life. The mounds of produce came from the big local plantations. A false but incredibly vivid illusion that all was abundance in that poor country.

MODIFIERS:
MISPLACED, SQUINTING, AND DANGLING

When we don't make it clear which word a modifier is related to, we run the risk of confusing our readers. The three types of unclear modifiers are misplaced, squinting, and dangling.

1. Misplaced modifiers. A modifier is misplaced if it seems to apply to the wrong word in the sentence.

> MISPLACED   Gooey, sticky, and sweet, my friend Celeste put the finishing touches on the Baked Alaska.

At first glance, we have to assume the writer is calling Celeste "gooey, sticky, and sweet." What a friend! But perhaps he meant the Baked Alaska.

> REVISED   My friend Celeste put the finishing touches on the gooey, sticky, and sweet Baked Alaska.

Sometimes we have to snicker at the effect of a misplaced modifier.

> MISPLACED   Coming around the corner, the Empire State Building stood before the newly arrived immigrants, then the tallest in the world.

REVISED	The Empire State Building, then the tallest in the world, stood before the newly arrived immigrants coming around the corner.

In the revision, the modifiers are placed close to the items they modify, and the meaning is clearer, though not so amusing.

Sometime even long clauses are misplaced.

MISPLACED	People should not toy with knives and forks who are eating their supper.
REVISED	People who are eating their supper should not toy with knives and forks.

2. Squinting modifiers. Some modifiers straddle a sentence and seem to "squint" in both directions. The reader cannot know which part of the sentence such a modifier belongs to.

SQUINTING	That he cleaned up the car thoroughly pleased her.

Did he thoroughly clean up the car, or was she thoroughly pleased?

REVISED	That he thoroughly cleaned up the car pleased her.
	That he cleaned up the car pleased her thoroughly.

Some adverbs (*just, merely, only, simply,* and so on) often seem to float blithely through a sentence, whimsically dropping between any two words they fancy. *Only* is particularly capricious. Think of all the places it could fall in this sentence.

I have eyes for you.

Be sure to place these adverbs firmly and unambiguously.

I have eyes for only you.

Sometimes a long phrase or clause will squint badly.

SQUINTING	The coach said while the game was in progress he would make no substitutions.

Did the coach make the statement before or during the game?

REVISED	The coach said he would make no substitutions while the game was in progress.
	While the game was in progress, the coach said he would make no substitutions.

3. Dangling modifiers. If a sentence simply lacks the word the modifier is supposed to modify, that modifier is dangling.

> **DANGLING**   Before riding the horses, all pets should be tethered.

Reading a sign like that, we do a slight double take: the *pets* will be riding the horses? Then we rewrite the sentence.

> **REVISED**   Before riding the horses, riders should tether all pets.

Most of the time, the dangling modifier occurs because the writer has not brought the modified term forward from the previous sentence.

> **DANGLING**   We went to the Smiths' last night. The evening passed pleasantly, eating candy and playing music.

Eating candy and playing music dangles because the writer has left *we* in the previous sentence.

> **REVISED**   We went to the Smiths' last night. We passed the evening pleasantly, eating candy and playing music.

Exercise for Modifiers

Rewrite the following sentences to make clear which words the modifiers modify.
 a. While telling a joke to friends, a boa constrictor coiled menacingly over Conroy's head.
 b. Rationing food and experiencing nightly air raids, the war was extremely difficult for the British.
 c. Some say the German people had themselves only to blame.
 d. Listening to the glorious voice of Leontyne Price, the opera *Aida* was a marvelous occasion.
 e. Second-guessing the coach's strategy, a football game can be a Monday morning social encounter.
 f. More than a millennium and a half before Evelyn Waugh wrote *Brideshead Revisited,* amid the pagan influence of late antiquity, Augustine defined the very theology on which Waugh based his beliefs.
 g. Eerily similar to my own experience, my friend returned to her car to find an old lady sitting in the front seat.
 h. Whatever happens, I only want the best for you, not your other boyfriend.
 i. Sugarcane appeared as a common food during the sixteenth century only of the rich.
 j. The instructor said during the exam no one should look at either notes or the textbook.

PARALLEL CONSTRUCTION

1. When thoughts are parallel, express them in the same grammatical construction.

> To be Italian is to be fortunate.

By so doing, you not only indicate the connection between the thoughts but also create a more vigorous prose. When, in contrast, you present similar or equally important ideas in grammatically different forms, you make reading more difficult and less interesting. Compare these two sentences:

> **NONPARALLEL** France's foreign policy irritates the British because of its arrogance and it is chauvinistic.
>
> **REVISED** France's foreign policy irritates the British because of its arrogance and its chauvinism.

Ideas in parallel form are more easily grasped. Be particularly careful in constructing a series of equal parts. Whatever form you use for the first part, repeat for each subsequent part.

> **NONPARALLEL** Use epoxy to fix broken dishes, for patching cracked glass, if your favorite knickknack is broken, and as a sealant for almost any broken surface.

In this example each item has a different grammatical construction—and the result is a mess.

> **REVISED** Use epoxy to fix broken dishes, to patch cracked glass, to repair a favorite knickknack, and to seal almost any broken surface.

Sometimes in keeping a list parallel, you will need to repeat a word to maintain clarity.

> **UNCLEAR** We chased the fox through the woods, the hills, the creek, and a dozen trees.

At first we thought the chase was through the hills, through the creek, and through a dozen trees.

> **REVISED** We chased the fox through the woods, over the hills, over the creek, and up a dozen trees.

Writers can commit more grievous errors than repetition—confusion for one.

2. When you use a coordinating conjunction, be sure you have the same grammatical construction on both sides.

NONPARALLEL   The woman hated all kinds of music but who
                               loved painting.

In this construction *who loved painting,* a dependent clause, is in a different
grammatical form from *The woman hated all kinds of music,* an independent
clause.

REVISED   The woman hated all kinds of music but loved
                               painting.

**3. When you use correlative conjunctions (*both/and, either/or, nei-
ther/nor,* or *not only/but also*), use the same form following each
member of the pair.**

NONPARALLEL   Either he is a genius or a fraud.

In this example, *either* is followed by an independent clause, but *or* is followed only by a noun. Both should be followed by the same grammatical
form.

REVISED   Either he is a genius or he is a fraud.

                               He is either a genius or a fraud.

Exercise for Parallel Construction

Rewrite these sentences to make the thoughts parallel.
  a. For years, Ryan had three things on his mind: watching out for his
     brother's temper tantrums, what his friends thought of him, and he
     wanted to break away from his overprotective mother.
  b. Many consider Titian the greatest Venetian painter, but some think-
     ing Tintoretto achieved equal greatness.
  c. Either the instructor knows his subject or should be fired.
  d. Not only was Jimmy Carter a farmer but an engineer.
  e. The mechanic told Mrs. Filoli that the spark plugs ought to be re-
     placed, she needed a new fan belt, and relining the brakes for the car
     to run well.
  f. You will either pay your rent or you will have to move.
  g. Some historians believe the major reason the British colonized Aus-
     tralia was to head France away from India, but sending criminals to
     get rid of them according to other historians.
  h. She had many plans: to travel to China, getting married and having
     a family, and she had a legal career in mind.

i. The rich were quite aware of fashion in the sixteenth century: women not only wore short stilts to protect themselves from the muddy streets, which fashion had first appeared in Venice, the mantilla from Spain, and they also wore many jewels as well as ruffs of fine lace.

j. To linger over dinner having a fine glass of wine at hand is what can make a person glad to be alive.

21

PUNCTUATION

*No steel can pierce the human heart so
chillingly as a period at the right moment.*
ISAAC BABEL **(1894–1941)**
RUSSIAN WRITER

When you use periods, commas, semicolons, and other punctuation, you are instructing your reader on how to read your work. Punctuation, therefore, isn't an afterthought or window dressing; it is your practical partner in the effort to be clear. Careful punctuation gets your message across; careless punctuation hinders communication.

ENDINGS

Periods

Periods mark off the endings of sentences. They tell your reader, "This is the end of a complete thought." They also signal abbreviations: *Gov., St. Augustine, Ibid., reg. U.S. Pat. Off.* (See "Abbreviations" in Chapter 22.) And they mark off letters and numbers in outlines and figures: *A. Endings.*

Exclamation Points and Question Marks

The exclamation point tells your reader that your sentence is emphatic; the question mark, that it is a question.

> I see a ghost! Or is it my kid brother in a sheet?

In formal prose, use exclamation marks stingily. They are all right in quotations.

> When Shelley writes "Oh world! Oh life! Oh time!" he tells us . . .

They are also proper in the rare situation that calls for dialogue.

> Newspapers are like a neurotic friend ever at your elbow who cries, at every event whether large or small, "What a decision! What a cataclysm! This is unprecedented!"

But let your own sentences be emphatic without bullhorns.
Never double end punctuation. You would not, for example, write

> Who wrote *What Price Glory??*

One question mark is ample.

COMMAS

You will use commas more than any other punctuation mark. They tell your reader how to read your sentences. Commas have many uses. Here are the eleven you will encounter most often.

1. Before coordinating conjunctions. Use a comma before a conjunction that connects two independent clauses, that is, before the *and, but, for,* and so on in a compound sentence.

> He liked sports, but he never exercised.

2. In a series. Use a comma between all elements in a series of three or more nouns, verbs, or phrases.

> The pen, the pencil, and the typewriter all failed her.
> She whistled, tap-danced, and yodeled better than her mother.
> Playing jacks, eating candy, and chatting with friends occupied her days.

3. Between coordinate adjectives. Coordinate adjectives are adjectives you can arrange in any order without changing the meaning.

> Here we are at the lush, moist, comforting oasis.

Not all adjectives in a series are coordinate, however. The adjective next to the noun sometimes combines with the noun to form a unit, and the other adjectives modify the whole unit.

> Early fliers hated the long, weary dawn patrols.

Dawn and *patrols* cannot be separated; *long* and *weary* modify *dawn patrols*. To check whether you are dealing with coordinate adjectives, see if an *and* can logically be placed between the last two adjectives, as in the following:

> Here we are at the lush and moist and comforting oasis.
>
> Early fliers hated the long and weary and dawn patrols.

4. After introductory material. Use a comma to set off an initial long phrase or dependent clause from the main part of the sentence.

> Because of the coldest frost in thirty years, half of Florida's orange crop was lost.
>
> After I had swum across the Amazon River, I dried my hair.

The comma tells the reader to pause and not to run the thoughts together. You can, however, omit the comma after a very short introductory phrase.

> After swimming the Amazon I dried my hair.

When in doubt, use your ear, and put the comma at the pause.

5. In quotation. Use a comma to separate a direct quotation from its attribution, whether the attribution is at the end, at the beginning, or in the middle.

> "We are not amused," said the queen.
> The king asked, "Who is not amused?"
> "Who," asked the court jester, "wants to know?"

6. For nonessential information. Use commas to tell the reader whether information is or is not essential to the meaning of the sentence.

Use a comma to set off words, phrases, or clauses that provide nonessential information (also called *nonrestrictive elements*).

> Harry's wife, Deirdre, was named den mother of the year.

Because Harry has only one wife, the name *Deirdre* is not essential to understanding the sentence and so is set off by commas.

Do not use commas to set off words, phrases, or clauses that provide essential information (also called *restrictive elements*).

> As a result, Harry's son Russell became an Eagle Scout.

Because Harry has two sons, the name *Russell* is essential to the meaning of the sentence and therefore should not be set off by commas.

In the following sentence, the commas make a great deal of difference:

> All the test pilots, who drink too much, will be grounded without pay.
>
> All the test pilots who drink too much will be grounded without pay.

When *who drink too much* is set off by commas, the sentence means that (1) all tests pilots drink too much, and (2) all will be grounded without pay. When *who drink too much* is not set off by commas, the sentence means that (1) at least some test pilots do not drink too much, and (2) only those who do will be grounded.

7. With parenthetical and interruptive elements. All sorts of expressions and words pop into the middle of a sentence but have no real connection to it. Mark them off with commas.

ASIDES	The emu lives, if you want to call it that, in Australia.
INTERJECTIONS AND EMPHATIC ELEMENTS	The emu, that flightless bird, runs rapidly. Well, no, it is not soothing to look at because its neck is, after all, four feet long.
CONJUNCTIVE ADVERBS	Moreover, it is almost extinct. Its cousin the ostrich, however, is protected for its feathers.
NOUNS OF DIRECT ADDRESS	What do you think of Mr. Steinbrenner, Mr. Winfield?

For other ways to set off parenthetical and interruptive elements, see "Parentheses and Dashes."

8. Between titles and names. Use commas to separate names from titles that follow, such as *Jr., M.D., Ph.D., Inc.,* and *Ltd.*

Harry Horvath, Jr., and his wife, Deirdre Failin Horvath, M.D., are joint owners of Horvath Chinchilla Farms, Inc.

9. After place names. Use commas after both city and state.

Every year Aunt Hepzibah leaves her boardinghouse in Bent Twig, Wyoming, to visit Harry.

10. For day and year. Use commas to set off the year. Do not use commas to set off only the month and year.

On December 7, 1941, the Royal Japanese Air Force bombed Pearl Harbor, and the war ended in August 1945.

11. In long, complicated sentences. Use commas to prevent misreading. When a long, twisty sentence threatens to leave your reader behind, you can sometimes break it into readable hunks with a considerate comma.

In my opinion, aerobic exercise helps develop thick, muscular calves, and minds that are well rested and alert.

Because of its structure, this sentence would not automatically get a second comma. As you can see, however, without that comma, we would have thick, muscular minds, as well as calves that are well rested and alert. But be careful to avoid using commas ungrammatically or indiscriminately.

Exercise for Commas

Add commas at the appropriate places in the following sentences and then state the governing rule for each comma you add.

   a. The intelligence that a man has and most other animals lack at least according to experts lies in the power of language.

   b. Freedom of speech guaranteed by our Constitution is important for without it we would not learn of new not necessarily popular or conventional ideas.

   c. In my long association with books and libraries I have made many friends across the centuries.

   d. Being a tall lithe handsome redheaded talented tennis player she was greeted enthusiastically by hopeful ambitious tournament managers who believed she could draw audiences for their tennis tournament.

   e. Tea which came into Europe from China with the Portuguese did not catch on at once because of its exotic flavor.

   f. I was born on July 30 1972 in the little town of Oneonta Alabama making my parents Andy and Mary Braudel very happy.

PARENTHESES AND DASHES

Two other ways to mark off parenthetical elements are parentheses and dashes. Each has its own function.

Parentheses

Parentheses are more emphatic than pairs of commas because they decisively block off the material between them.

Years from now (and not too many years at that) the sexual revolution will seem as corrupt as the double standard that preceded it.

Parentheses are a cue to the reader to lower the voice, so to speak. Don't overuse parentheses; no one likes a constant whisperer. Enclose material within them that may be interesting but is really a digression.

Present at Yalta were Joseph Stalin, Franklin D. Roosevelt (who would be dead within two months), and Winston Churchill.

Many people are uncertain about how to punctuate when parentheses are present. Here are four guidelines.

1. When the parentheses are within a sentence, punctuate the sentence exactly as if the parentheses were not there.

> Debate used to rage about whether the dog or the cat is smarter (not an unimportant topic for some of us); opinion now leans in favor of Fido.

Be sure not to put the sentence's punctuation inside the closing parentheses.

INCORRECT	Sixteen ounces is the equivalent of 454 grams (a ratio of 28.37 to 1.)
CORRECT	Sixteen ounces is the equivalent of 454 grams (a ratio of 28.37 to 1).

2. When a complete sentence stands by itself in parentheses— that is, when it is not inside another sentence—the period falls within the parentheses.

> Saying the dog is smarter than the cat does not devalue the latter in the eyes of cat fans. (It is doubtful whether anything could.)

In an occasional bizarre case a complete and parenthesized sentence can fall within another sentence. In such a case, omit both the initial capital letter and terminal punctuation for the parenthetical sentence.

> Beekeeping is hazardous (you always risk being stung) but rewarding.

3. Use parentheses when appropriate to enclose acronyms, dates, or numbers.

> Walter Reuther founded the United Auto Workers (UAW).
>
> Derek Walcott's *The Fortunate Traveller* (1981) received excellent reviews.
>
> He comes from Cleveland, Tennessee (pop. 26,415), not Cleveland, Ohio (pop. 573,822).

4. If you like the way they look, use parentheses to set off numbers in a numbered list.

> (1) Name
> (2) Address
> (3) Occupation

Dashes

Even more emphatic than parentheses are dashes. They indicate not whispers but shouts.

Although William Howard Taft was obese—a dinner guest once inquired whether he was expecting—he lived to be seventy-three years old.

Framed by dashes, this joke emerges loud and clear.

1. Use the dash—sparingly—to indicate interruptions, informal breaks in construction, or special emphasis.

My best friend—my dog Kent, I mean—has left me forever.

Muhammad Ali—then known as Cassius Clay—won an Olympic Gold Medal in 1960.

2. In typing, form the dash with two hyphens. Don't leave a space on either side, and do not use any commas, colons, semicolons, or parentheses adjacent to a dash—the dash is the only punctuation needed. When you use a dash before the final element in a sentence, close with the usual period.

Caesar loved Cleopatra—but not as much as she thought.

Like the other components of writing, these emphatic markers become meaningless if you overuse them. Save them for special occasions.

Exercise for Parentheses and Dashes

Place either parentheses or dashes at appropriate places in the following sentences. Explain briefly why you chose the material you did to set off and why you chose either parentheses or dashes.

  a. Cinema has its own traditions and techniques similar to those of the novel but its history is of course much shorter and more dramatic in the rate of change.
  b. Rolf Hochhuth's play has been the occasion for disagreement indeed for riots because it shows not merely suggests that Pius XII did not oppose the Nazis very vigorously.
  c. Most of us wear masks most of the time and our lives are blighted.
  d. At this date April 20, 1988, the National League West leader is Los Angeles won 9 and lost 4 and the National League East leader is Pittsburgh won 9 and lost 3.
  e. After the twelfth century when fireplaces were first built into the wall cooking was done on the hearth with the family huddled close by.

SEMICOLONS

A semicolon announces a pause in the thought in a sentence. In the strength of pause it is exactly halfway between a period and a comma, and to indicate it a period sits on top of a comma. You can use this pause in two ways.

1. Between independent clauses. Use a semicolon to indicate a close connection between independent clauses.

> The pollsters predicted a close election; the smart money knew otherwise.

Used this way, the semicolon tightly holds together two or more complete thoughts. It indicates strong likeness or balance.

> He loved biology; he hated English; he was indifferent to languages.

The semicolon is also effective in suggesting a clash or contrast.

> He endured her for her money; she worshiped him for his soul.

You must have independent clauses on both sides of the semicolon in these constructions.

2. When you have a series of items that have internal punctuation, use the semicolon to separate the items clearly. This use of the semicolon is less common but no less useful. Here too the semicolon connects equal elements.

> At the party we saw Sam, the electrician; Tim, the magician; Bill Jones; Wanda Everts, the land, sea, and air endurance champion of England, China, and Wales; and Everts's dog, Spence.

Without semicolons, this sentence would be hopelessly confusing.

By all means learn to use semicolons; they will add subtlety and grace to your style. Do not overuse them, however, or their power to balance and connect will evaporate.

COLONS

The colon is the vaudeville punctuation mark. Its task is to introduce with a certain fanfare. It says, Here it is folks! Here are the most common uses of the colon.

1. To introduce a series or a list.

> Kate visited three cities in Ohio: Akron, Columbus, and Toledo.

2. To introduce a short quotation.

> Eisenhower said it more than once: "I shall go to Korea."

3. To introduce, and thus emphasize, a single element.

> This element may be as short as a single word.

> When he asked to borrow money, I knew what to say: No.

The element introduced may be a phrase.

> There in the doorway stood something I never dreamed I'd see: my grandfather in a gorilla suit.

The element introduced may be another independent clause.

> Jealousy serves only one purpose for humanity: it alienates people from those they most dearly love.

Many careful stylists do not capitalize after a colon used in this way, except for proper names: what follows the colon is not a new thought but an extension of the existing one.

The colon has formal uses, too.

4. To introduce a long quotation set off from the text. (See "Integrating Quotations into Your Text" in Chapter 14 for a discussion of how to present long quotations.)

5. To introduce the body of a letter after the salutation in formal correspondence.

> Dear Senator Kassebaum:

6. To separate the title and the subtitle of a book.

> *Madness and Civilization: A History of Insanity in the Age of Reason*

7. To separate city and publisher in lists of works cited.

> New York: Knopf

8. To separate chapter and verse in biblical citations.

> Jeremiah 21:3

Note that there is no space after the colon.

9. To separate hour and minutes in reporting time.

> It is 9:43 a.m. as I write this.

There is no space after the colon in this use either.

Exercise for Semicolons and Colons

Place semicolons and colons in the following sentences, and explain your decisions for each.

a. The rain had stopped the sun was out the picnic was on.
b. On Christmas morning I received the present I had always longed for the *Encyclopaedia of Religion and Ethics.*
c. Americans were thrilled by General McAuliffe's defiant response to the demand for surrender at the Battle of the Bulge "Nuts!"

d. The early twentieth century produced a spate of fine writers who were expatriates Thomas Mann a German who lived his last years in Switzerland James Joyce an Irishman who lived in Trieste, Paris, and Zurich and Ernest Hemingway an American who spent much of his adult life in France.

e. I have four favorite things pistachio ice cream cowboy movies playing golf and my gerbil Patsy.

f. This production of *A Midsummer Night's Dream* has a most unusual aspect the same person plays Puck and Oberon.

g. Sanity permeates the literature of the eighteenth century insanity permeates the literature of the twentieth.

h. The whole thing was a mess Tim loved Sue Sue loved Craig Craig loved Carol Carol loved Tim.

APOSTROPHES

Apostrophes serve two important functions: to form possessives and to mark contractions.

1. To form the possessive of nouns and indefinite pronouns. Apostrophes used in this manner signify ownership or association.

To make a singular noun or indefinite pronoun possessive, add an apostrophe followed by an *-s*.

Lincoln's beard

the cat's meow

Amos's bee sting

the business's employees

everybody's favorite

To make a plural noun not ending in *-s* possessive, add an apostrophe followed by an *-s*.

the children's squeals

the Men's Glee Club

To make a plural noun ending in *-s* possessive, add only an apostrophe.

the Mohicans' war cry

the girls' crazy hats

the Richards' dinner party

To make a noun composed of several words possessive, add the *-'s* only to the last word.

my brother-in-law's haircut

To show possession by more than one individual, add an apostrophe followed by an *-s* only to the name of the last individual if the possession is joint.

Harpo and Groucho's brother was named Zeppo. [The brother belongs to both.]

To show possession by more than one individual, add an apostrophe followed by an *-s* to each individual's name if possession is separate.

Harpo's and Groucho's careers were brilliant. [Each has his separate career.]

Avoid awkward possessives by using *of* or other prepositional constructions.

AWKWARD	After the collision, the Williamses' Acura was ruined.
REVISED	After the collision, the Acura owned by the Williamses was ruined.

2. To show contractions. Used in this manner, the apostrophe shows where you drop letters to contract two words into one. Words frequently *elided*, as this is called, are *can, do, does, have, is, not, will*.

If I can't find my algebra book, I'll flunk.

For the most part, contractions are still limited to informal prose and dialogue. Careful stylists keep them to a minimum. High informal prose should not sound chatty or breezy.

BREEZY	Japan couldn't've conquered the whole of Asia because it didn't have the resources.
REVISED	Japan could not have conquered the whole of Asia because it did not have the resources.

You should, however, use contractions when the full form would sound awkward.

AWKWARD	Is this not the same as claiming that Japan would have been defeated even without the United States?
REVISED	Isn't this the same as claiming that Japan would have been defeated even without the United States?

Tiny confusions and mistaken identities plague contractions. The contraction *it's* is often mistaken for the possessive pronoun *its*. There is no apostrophe in the possessive. In the contraction, the apostrophe marks the spot where the *i* in *is* is missing.

INCORRECT	Corsica is French, but its often rebellious.
CORRECT	Corisca is French, but it's often rebellious.
INCORRECT	It's main exports are olive oil, wine, and citrus fruits.
CORRECT	Its main exports are olive oil, wine, and citrus fruits.

Much the same confusion occurs in using *your* and *you're,* and *their* and *they're.* In both cases the first is a possessive form of a pronoun (*you* and *they*), and the second is a contraction of two words (*you are* and *they are*). Perhaps three correct sentences will make the differences clear.

Our beagle always knows when it's time for its dinner.

Your taxi will arrive in five minutes if you're lucky.

They're trying to find their lottery tickets.

You should avoid cutesy apostrophes in your writing. *Steak 'n' eggs* is *steak and eggs, a little bit o' soul* is *a little bit of soul.* Even *rock 'n' roll* suffers little when written *rock and roll. Three o'clock,* however, is standard; most of us do not know that it is a contraction for *three of the clock.*

Do not use an apostrophe before the *s* to form the plural of abbreviations, capital letters, words used as words, or specific decades unless the *s* alone would be confusing.

His high Cs are sharp, but his low Fs are delicious.

It will take sixteen IBMs to compete with one of our EECs.

In some ways, the 1890s were similar to the 1920s.

If, however, the *-s* alone might be confusing, precede it with an apostrophe.

He had difficulty pronouncing S's, A's, and I's.

Here are the do's and don'ts of windsurfing.

Exercises for Apostrophes

1. Place an apostrophe where appropriate in the following sentences, and be prepared to explain what you have done.
   a. I didnt believe Id flunk because its not that hard a course.
   b. The boys game wasnt over until Billy Billings ball bounced over the players heads. Its bounce was at least ten feet and now its gone for good.
   c. The editor-in-chiefs hat sits on the back of his head, and when Im angry its tempting to knock it off.

   d. The company lost its suit in court because its case was so weak.
   e. Its anybodys guess whether the Joneses summer house withstood the
      tornado, but my brothers-in-laws place was completely demolished.
2. Correct any mistakes in placing apostrophes in the following passages,
   and add any apostrophes that are needed.
   a. My friend James father hunts quail and hes taking James' with him
      this weekend. There staying at you're uncles. Im of two minds about
      there plans but they're going anyway.
   b. Fortunately no one was home when the Hopkinses' houseboat blew
      up the other night because it's safety valve melted. I called the Hop-
      kins's but their staying at Mrs. Hopkins' sister-in-law's. They're new
      houseboat won't be ready until June. By then itll be nice weather.
   c. I read in Montaignes essay's that sin "dwells in us as in it's own
      home." He says it's a rare person who conducts life well and they're
      few men admired by there households. Id like to know you're opin-
      ion. Mine is that Montaigne's a bit cynical.

PUNCTUATION OF QUOTATIONS

In this section we discuss when to use quotation marks and how to
punctuate with, in, and around them.

Quotation marks have many uses; we'll focus on three.

1. Use quotation marks when you quote the words of others.

Nixon said, "I am not a crook."

In this example, a comma follows the attribution. Sometimes writers use
the word *that* to introduce the quotation.

Nixon said that he was "not a crook."

Refer to "Integrating Quotations into Your Text" in Chapter 14 for
ways to introduce and use quotations in your writing.

2. Use quotation marks to indicate titles of short works.

POEMS	T. S. Eliot's "Ash Wednesday" is my favorite poem.
STORIES	Eudora Welty wrote "Why I Live at the P.O."
CHAPTERS	Chapter 22 is entitled "German Folklore."
ESSAYS AND ARTICLES	I read Montaigne's "Of Idleness."
SHORT MUSICAL COMPOSITIONS	The band played "Send in the Clowns."
EPISODES IN TELEVISION SERIES	I saw Bruce Willis in "A Tale of Two Cities."

Titles of other kinds of works require italics. See "Italics" in Chapter 22.

3. Use quotation marks around a slang word to show that the use is not standard.

> After all the dancing, everybody at the party was "beat."

Sometimes writers use quotation marks to indicate irony or distaste.

> He was one of the "beautiful people."

If you use such a word a second time in the work, don't use quotation marks: continued use of the word indicates that you have adopted the initial usage and are treating it as standard in this context. The point is, you can't have it both ways: you can't use a word and also dissociate yourself from the usage by enclosing it in quotation marks.

Punctuation marks seem to congregate around quotations. Five standard practices will ease the guesswork involved in how to use them.

1. For a quotation within a quotation, use single quotation marks.

> Harry said to Deirdre, "When I said, 'Life would be easier if I were not married,' I was only speaking figuratively."

2. In American writing, periods and commas always come inside quotation marks, whether they are part of the quotation or not.

> When we speak of "the next wave," we mean the same thing our grandparents meant when they said "the latest thing."

3. Colons and semicolons fall outside quotation marks.

> I mean three things when I say "junk food": hamburgers, potato chips, and Twinkies.

4. Place a question mark or an exclamation point inside the quotation marks if it is part of the quotation. Place it outside if it is not part of the quotation.

> Betty Rollin wrote "Motherhood: Who Needs It?"
> But who wrote "Three Kinds of Thinking"?

5. When quoting a complete sentence, capitalize the first word.

> We can sympathize with King Lear when he cries, "How dost, my boy? Art cold?"

Do not capitalize if you introduce a short complete sentence with *that* or a similar construction.

> When Mark Twain tells us that "training is everything," we should believe him.

Do not capitalize the first word if you are quoting a fragment.

> By "different but equal," women's rights advocates still mean "equal."

Finally, when the attribution comes in the middle of a quoted sentence, do not capitalize after the interruption.

> "The only animal ever to be recorded as having been killed by a meteor," Professor Frohling said, "was an Egyptian dog."

ELLIPSES

Ellipses—that is, spaced periods in the body of a quotation—indicate that material has been omitted. They should never be used to change a meaning, but they can help to shorten a long passage that contains material not directly relevant to your purpose.

Here is a passage in which Charles Darwin extols the lowly worm:

> Archaeologists ought to be grateful to worms, as they protect and preserve for an indefinitely long period every object not liable to decay, which is dropped on the surface of the land, by burying it beneath their castings. Thus, also, many elegant and curious tessellated pavements and other ancient remains have been preserved; though no doubt the worms have in these cases been largely aided by earth washed and blown from the adjoining land, especially when cultivated. The old tessellated pavements have, however, often suffered by having subsided unequally from being unequally undermined by the worms. Even old massive walls may be undermined and subside; and no building is in this respect safe, unless the foundations lie six or seven feet beneath the surface, at a depth at which worms cannot work. It is probable that many monoliths and some old walls have fallen down from having been undermined by worms. (Charles Darwin, *The Formation of Vegetable Mould, Through the Action of Worms, with Observations on Their Habits*)

By placing ellipses where text has been deleted, you can quote just a part of this passage and still convey its point.

> In extolling lowly worms, Darwin says that "they protect and preserve . . . every object not liable to decay . . . by burying it beneath their castings," thus preserving ancient remains. Darwin points out the negative side to this activity, however: "Even old massive walls. . . . have fallen down from having been undermined by worms."

1. If the deleted material comes in the middle of the sentence, use three spaced periods.

> Darwin says, "They protect and preserve . . . every object not liable to decay."

2. If the deleted material includes the end of a sentence, use four spaced periods.

"Even old massive walls. . . . have fallen down."

3. Never use ellipses in place of a colon to introduce or set off material.

INCORRECT   After miles of wandering, they stood before it . . . the sea.

4. And finally, never use ellipses to fade in or out of a sentence.

INCORRECT   Sunsets are beautiful . . .

OTHER PUNCTUATION

Two relatively rare punctuation marks are brackets and virgules.

Brackets

1. Whenever you have to change a quotation to fit your context, enclose your words in brackets to indicate the changes.

ORIGINAL   Darwin says that "a weight of more than ten tons of dry earth annually passes through their bodies. . . ."

REVISED   Darwin says that "a weight of more than ten tons of dry earth annually passes through their [the worms'] bodies."

Warning: Overuse of this form will annoy your readers.

Virgules

1. The virgule, commonly called the *slash,* is used to show that several possibilities are equally appropriate.

King James was a gypsy/god/king.

2. It is also used to show line breaks in poetry when the lines are not indented but are continuous in the text.

When T. S. Eliot writes, "set down/This set down/This," the sense of dislocation is breathtaking.

Exercises for Punctuation

1. Punctuate the following sentences according to proper form.
   a. Heideggers work is difficult I had to read every paragraph several times.
   b. Who was that person shouting help help help outside the police department at six oclock this morning
   c. Her presence her regal walk I mean communicated to us all a sense of confidence poise and financial well-being
   d. Even when I am showered clothed and fed I still have trouble facing up to the mornings most frightening task shaving
   e. Somewhere in a run-down garret in the Spanish-speaking part of Ecuador the most gung ho yodeling choir in the world is practicing for tomorrow nights world championships
   f. All I said to the teacher Bill said was Why are you flunking me you old crow
   g. If you have no money welcome to the club if you do have some lend me five dollars until tomorrow
   h. Monique found three curious items in her grandmothers hope chest a white silk dress still wrapped in the tissue in which it was bought a pair of dancing slippers seemingly made of glass and a jeweled tiara covered with hundreds of fake amethysts
   i. We cant guarantee that you will still be riding your new motorcycle in ten years but we can offer you an insurance policy at very low cost
   j. Oh gosh this is great
   k. Mr. Greaves an old man who has been teaching here for thirty years refers to his rich students as Porsche philosophers
   l. The black-footed albatross also known as the gooney bird can fly well but has terrible trouble with takeoffs and landings
   m. The career of Upton Sinclair shows that success in one field literature does not necessarily lead to success in another politics
   n. He reached into the aquarium and you won't believe this swallowed both goldfish whole
   o. Sometimes I go crazy with all the NFLs NBAs and USHLs don't you
   p. Long before he had told her he would marry someone else

2. Restore the proper punctuation to the following paragraph. Read the paragraph aloud as a first step.

   To this day we cannot understand how a great civilized nation or at least a considerable part of it could in the twentieth century succumb to its fascination with a ridiculous complex-ridden petit-bourgeois man could fall for his pseudo-scientific theories and in their name exterminate nations conquer continents and commit unbelievable cruelties Positivistic science Marxism included offers a variety of scientific explanations for this mysterious phenomenon but instead of eliminating the mystery they tend to deepen it For the cold "objective" reason that speaks to us from these explanations only underlines the disproportion between itself a power that claims to be the decisive one in this civilization and the mass insanity that has nothing in common with any form of rationality (Vaclav Havel, "Thriller")

22

MECHANICS

*Always do right. This will gratify some people
and astonish the rest.*
MARK TWAIN (1835–1910)
AMERICAN WRITER

With punctuation we mark and divide sentences; with mechanics we treat things such as abbreviations, capitalization, italics, numbers, and hyphens. Mechanics are conventions—general and often unspoken agreements about basic procedures—that all writers observe. Your reader will expect you to follow these conventions and may be confused if you deviate from them or are inconsistent. All careful writers learn the proper mechanics to keep their writing clear and correct.

ABBREVIATIONS

Some abbreviations, which we have grouped in three categories, are standard.

1. Abbreviate many titles and terms—such as *Dr., Mr., Mrs., Ms., M.D., Ph.D., A.D., B.C., a.m. p.m., Hon., Msgr., Rev., St., Jr.,* **and** *Sr.*
2. Abbreviate institutional names as appropriate, and note that most are now written *without* **periods:** *AFL-CIO, EEC, EPA, GNP, IBM, NAACP, TWA.*

If your reader may not know what the abbreviation stands for, write the name out the first time you use it, and follow it with the abbreviation in parentheses.

The journalist's assignment was to cover the Environmental Protection Agency (EPA).

Now you could use EPA throughout the rest of the essay. (By contrast, IBM is so universally known as *IBM* that many people would not recognize *International Business Machines.*)

Keep abbreviations to a minimum. Clumps of letters and periods make your writing read like a ticker tape. If your audience uses these abbreviations as part of its language, use them. Careful stylists, however, never use *TV* for *television.*

3. Abbreviate figures and some items in footnotes: *ed., fig., ft., p., sec.* American practice is tending away from abbreviations in footnotes and figures, although *ed.* for "editor" and *p.* and *pp.* for "page" and "pages" are still common. (See "Documenting Your Sources" in Chapter 15 for explicit information on documentation.)

Generally speaking, don't abbreviate days, months (except in lists of works cited), cities, states (except in addressing envelopes), business designations (such as *company, incorporated,* and *limited*), units of measure (such as *ounce, pound, liter, meter, inch, foot, pint, gallon*), or Latin words and phrases (such as *versus* and *et cetera*).

CAPITALIZATION

Every sentence should, of course, begin with a capital letter. This indicates that you are starting a new thought. The capital has additional uses. We have summarized the uses and misuses in three rules.

1. Capitalize the first letter of each word in the following categories.

PROPER NAMES	Michael Jackson
SPECIFIC PLACES	Mongolia
WORKS OF ART AND ENTERTAINMENT:	
BOOKS	*Gone with the Wind*
MOVIES	*Star Wars*
PLAYS	*Hedda Gabler*
PAINTINGS AND SCULPTURES	*The Last Supper, The Thinker*
TELEVISION SHOWS	*L.A. Law*
RADIO SHOWS	*All Things Considered*
NOTABLE OBJECTS AND GROUPS:	
SHIPS	*Queen Elizabeth II*

PLANES	*The Spirit of St. Louis*
FAMOUS STRUCTURES	Golden Gate Bridge
ORGANIZATIONS	United Auto Workers
INSTITUTIONS	Lehigh University
RELIGIONS	Roman Catholic
ETHNIC OR NATIONAL GROUPS	Ute Indians
LANGUAGES	French, Swahili
MARKS ON THE CALENDAR:	
DAYS	Wednesday
MONTHS	April
HOLIDAYS	Passover
HISTORICAL ITEMS:	
ERAS	Middle Ages
DOCUMENTS	Magna Carta
EVENTS	Civil War
SACRED BEINGS AND TERMS:	
DEITIES	God, Allah
SACRED PERSONS	Buddha
SACRED SCRIPTURES	the Koran

Capitalize titles when they precede proper names.

> Senator Howell Heflin came from Alabama.

Do not capitalize titles that stand alone or titles that come after the proper name.

> Howell Heflin was the senator from Alabama.
> Being a senator is hard work.

An exception to this rule is titles of very high and special rank.

> William Rehnquist is the Chief Justice of the United States.

2. Do not capitalize the first letter of words in these categories.

SEASONS	winter
GENERAL GROUPS	the middle class
ABSTRACTIONS	love, art, nature

3. Be aware that some words appear both capitalized and uncapitalized, depending on their use.

Capitalize names of regions.

> New Orleans is the gem of the South.

But do not capitalize directions.

Go west, young man.

Capitalize names of college courses and departments.

I think Anthropology 119 is the best course offered by the Department of Anthropology.

Do not capitalize the names of general subjects.

I love anthropology, but I don't like mathematics.

ITALICS

1. To indicate italics on a typewriter, underline the material. Use italics for titles of

BOOKS	*War and Peace*
PERIODICALS	*Scientific American*
NEWSPAPERS	*San Jose Mercury News*
MOVIES	*Moonstruck*
PLAYS	*Much Ado about Nothing*
TELEVISION PROGRAMS	*Dallas*
LONG MUSICAL COMPOSITIONS	*Resurrection Symphony*
FOREIGN WORDS OR PHRASES	*sine qua non*

2. Use italics to indicate that you are using a word as a word.

When he says *language,* it sounds like music.

Avoid underlining as a way of emphasizing. Writers who are fond of exclamation points also like italics, for with *them* they can *emphasize* every word they think is *crucial.* Let words stand without artificial emphasis. Give your sentences their own punch, and the reader will see the emphasis *without* being *pushed* by shouting, insistent *italics.*

NUMBERS

1. Use figures (2, 98, 92837) for addresses, dates, page numbers, divisions of books, scores. For other usages in nonscientific writing, use figures only for numbers of more than two words.

He was twenty-nine.

My grandfather died at 112.

2. Either spell out all the numbers in a sentence, *three of the six,* **or use figures for all,** *3 of the 6.* **Don't mix the forms.**

3. Spell out any number that begins a sentence.

One hundred and twelve years is a long time to be alive.

HYPHENS

The hyphen is used either to join words or to separate syllables.

1. To join words. Use hyphens to join multiword adjectives that precede the word they modify and multiword nouns.

Harry was a devil-may-care philosopher-poet who claimed he had many out-of-town speaking engagements.

When multiword adjectives follow the noun they modify, however, do not hyphenate them.

Yet he claimed he had many speaking engagements out of town.

There is no hard-and-fast rule governing when to hyphenate compound words. Check the dictionary. If it does not have the entry you seek, write the words without a hyphen.

2. To separate syllables. Use hyphens to show where words have been divided at the end of a line.

Houdini was not only an escape artist but a pres-
tidigitator.

If you type carefully, you should not need to divide words often. (Most word-processing programs have a "word-wrap" function that automatically takes care of word division.) Never divide one-syllable words, and only divide longer words at a syllable break. Check words in your dictionary to determine where these breaks occur. When you must divide a word, the last thing on the line should be the hyphen.

Harry retired to Pocatello for a long vaca-
tion because he had just completed a book.

Avoid breaking a word in a way that leaves only one or two letters on either side.

If you do, the letter will look quite a-
lone, and furthermore it will look silly.

3. Use hyphens to attach certain prefixes to certain root words. The prefixes *ex-*, *self-*, and *all-* are attached by hyphens to the roots.

> Her all-encompassing dislike for her ex-husband is self-evident.

If the root word is capitalized, attach the prefix to it with a hyphen.

> She could not decide whether she was a Pre-Socratic or a postmodernist.

When two prefixes apply to the same word, use a hyphen and a space after the first prefix and attach the second prefix to the word.

> She studied both micro- and macroeconomics.

More often than not, prefixes are joined to their root without benefit of a hyphen. When in doubt, use your dictionary.

4. Use a hyphen to join words that form certain compound nouns.

> daughter-in-law
>
> editor-in-chief
>
> reporter-at-large

Some compound nouns are not joined by hyphens, for instance, *vice president*. Keep your dictionary handy.

5. Use hyphens to indicate fractions and compound numbers.

> three-fourths
>
> twenty-nine

Exercises for Mechanics

1. Edit the following sentences for proper form for abbreviation, capitalization, italics, and numbers.
   a. in the winter of 65, people in the midwest were far colder than people in the atlantic states because of a wintry arctic blast
   b. albert appeared on claudia's doorstep last thursday night, smelling of cologne and lisping sotto voce, "Come with me to the casbah—or at least to cinema five. they're showing tracy and hepburn in woman of the year."
   c. in the epic poem gilgamesh, written down around 2000 bc, a sumerian king, gilgamesh of erech, prays to his patron goddess ishtar, and travels to the land of the dead in search of his friend enkidu.
   d. yesterday I read melville's whaling novel, moby-dick, hemingway's short story with the lean and revealing dialogue, hills like white elephants, and the new popular mechanics.

    e. when senator gass asked tommy what he wanted to be when he grew up, tommy said he wanted to be a senator just like him and serve in congress.

    f. jack meridge, lld, phd, was first a lawyer for the afl-cio, but then he hooked up with the nfl and the cia, which eventually led to a job with rev harold haines, a leader of the naacp.

    g. is twelve midnight am or pm?

    h. 30,000 buffalo took an average of 5 months to migrate from their winter pastures in new mexico to their summer pastures in montana.

    i. at the salt in geneva the ambassador from the united states and the ambassador from the ussr discussed the abm program and the deployment of medium-range icbms and ss-x-25's.

2. Restore proper mechanics to the following passage.

on tonight's episode of houston, dr van slyke discovers fifi's plan to sell his ocean liner, the willie mays, to throckmorton gotrocks, jr, the sixty seven year old former tree surgeon and stunt pilot, in exchange for an autographed copy of his poem, how green the face, six prize st bernard dogs, and 22 us savings bonds. meanwhile, senator rex smith has telephoned his brother roy, governor of the state, to see if he can get free tickets for the exclusive performance of gershwin's porgy and bess, being given by the houston light opera company at the civic center opera house. tonight's episode is based on the short story the big swap by lily upmeier, phd, and is soon to be made into a feature length motion picture, to be entitled grope for gold.

SPELLING

English spelling is irregular. Its rules are far from certain and far from complete. Our first and most important tip: use your dictionary. Everything is in there: how to spell a word, how to divide between syllables, and how to join suffixes of all descriptions.

Your dictionary may list two and occasionally three spellings for the same word. Most of the time, the first spelling given is "preferred," and we recommend you use it. When in doubt, however, choose the spelling that is simpler, modern, and American. Write *encyclopedia* instead of *encyclopaedia*, *theater* instead of *theatre*, and *color* instead of *colour*. Always be consistent. Stick to your choice throughout your writing.

The two most common trouble spots in English spelling are suffixes and homonyms (words that sound alike). Although your dictionary has more information, the following rules will give you some help.

SUFFIXES

Here we set out some guidelines for adding suffixes to words.

Forming Plurals

The plural of most nouns is formed by adding -*s*. There are, however, special cases and exceptions.

1. Nouns ending in -*s*. Form the plural by adding -*es*.

James   Jameses   business   businesses

2. Nouns ending in -*ch*. Form the plural by adding -*es*.

match   matches   lunch   lunches

3. Nouns ending in -*y*. When a word ends in -*y* preceded by a vowel, add -*s*.

boy   boys

When the -*y* is preceded by a consonant, change the -*y* to -*i* and add -*es*.

trophy   trophies

4. Nouns ending in -*o*. When the -*o* is preceded by a vowel, add -*s*.

studio   studios

When the -*o* is preceded by a consonant, add -*es*.

potato   potatoes

5. Nouns ending in -*f* or -*fe*. Some words ending in -*f* or -*fe* take an -*s*.

fife   fifes   chief   chiefs

Some change -*f* to -*ves*.

elf   elves   knife   knives

There are plenty of exceptions to these rules. Check that dictionary.

Doubling the Final Consonant

Is it *traveller* or *traveler*? *Compelled* or *compeled*? Questions like these can sometimes make a writer's head spin. Three factors determine whether you double a word's final consonant before adding an ending:

1. the number of syllables
2. what letters precede the final consonant
3. which syllable is accented

Here are the combinations.

1. Double the consonant when a word of one syllable has a single vowel before the final consonant.

    flip flipped   trap trapped

2. Double the consonant when a multisyllable word has a single vowel before the final consonant and is accented on the last syllable.

    compel compelling   occur occurrence
    forget forgetting

3. Don't double when a one-syllable word has two vowels before the final consonant.

    peel peeled   sear searing

4. Don't double when the word ends in two consonants.

    risk risked   grasp grasping

5. Don't double when the accent shifts away from the last syllable once the ending is added.

    infer inferential   confer conference

6. American writers increasingly prefer the single consonant. Therefore, when you encounter words that could go either way, don't double.

    focus focused   travel traveling

Adding Other Suffixes

1. Adding *-able, -ible, -alogy, -ology, -ance, -ence, -ant, -ent*. No hard-and-fast rules can tell you whether it is *dependant* or *dependent*. If you have not memorized the spellings, use your dictionary.
2. Words ending in *-cede, -ceed, -sede*. This one is fairly easy. *Supersede* is the only word to end in *-sede*. And only three words end in *-ceed: exceed, proceed,* and *succeed*. For the rest, use *-cede: precede, recede*.
3. Words ending in *-y*. To add a suffix to words ending in *-y* preceded by a consonant, change the *-y* to *-i* except when the suffix begins with *-i*.

    happy happiness   merry merrily

When the suffix begins with *-i*, the *-y* stays put.

    carry carrying

HOMONYMS

Some spelling problems occur because two words are homonyms—that is, they are pronounced similarly or the same way but have different meanings and are spelled differently. Here are some common ones.

accent/ascent/assent	ewe/you
accept/except	incredible/incredulous
affect/effect	loose/lose
brake/break	passed/past
capital/capitol	principal/principle
choose/chose	read/reed
cite/sight/site	right/rite/write
conscience/conscious	stationary/stationery
credible/creditable	straight/strait
desert/dessert	than/then
dew/do	to/too/two
eminent/immanent/imminent	weather/whether

We discuss many of these words in Chapter 24, Glossary of Usage.

SPELLING GUIDELINES

The following three spelling guidelines usually work, but hang on to your dictionary.

1. "*I* before *e* except after *c*, or when sounded like *ay*, as in *neighbor* and *weigh*."

thief	friend	pier

after *c*:

ceiling	conceive	conceited

sounds like *ay*:

inveigh	skein	sleigh

There are, of course, exceptions, such as *foreigner, height,* and *weird.* Keep your dictionary warmed up.

2. For words ending in *-e*, retain the *-e* before suffixes that begin with consonants.

battle battlement	shape shapely
hope hopeful	cute cuteness

Drop the *-e* before suffixes beginning with vowels.

believe   believable   scrape   scraping
contrive   contrivance   sanguine   sanguinary

Where confusion could arise with another word, keep the *-e.*

dye   dyeing (instead of dying)

3. For words that end in *-ce* or *-ge*, keep the *-e* to retain their last consonant's soft sound.

change   changeable   notice   noticeable

Exercises for Spelling

1. Add the suffixes indicated to the words that follow them. Check your choice of spelling in the dictionary.
   a. Suffix: -able, -ible
      Words: access, commend, defense, excuse, force, response
   b. Suffix: -ing
      Words: change, commit, pat, prefer, rally, slope
2. Correct all spelling errors in the following paragraph. Use your dictionary whenever you are unsure.

   Last night I made the acquaintance of that imminent playright Carol Dermott. This remarkable woman has kept her eye on the changable tastes of her audience for more than twelve years and has never disapointed her fans. She is embarassed by all the adulation and says that it is all exagerrated. Whether she choses to write a tradgedy or an outragous farce, Dermott has shown her independance. Her first play, *Not for Nothing*, portrays a fisherman who sails alone across the Artic Circle. Her prizewinning drama *Lew's Loss* portrays the lonliness of a cemetary gaurd who falls in love with a waitress at a restarant. But it was not until her eigth play, *Unecessarily Yours*, that her rythmic writing, her wierd but mischevious sence of humour, and her briliant satire of modern beaureaucracy recieved the attention they deserved from the American playgoing audiance.

24

GLOSSARY OF USAGE

"When I use a word," Humpty Dumpty said in a rather scornful tone, "it means just what I choose it to mean—neither more nor less."

"The question is," said Alice, "whether you can make words mean so many different things."

"The question is," said Humpty Dumpty, "which is to be master—that's all."

LEWIS CARROLL (1832–1898)
ENGLISH WRITER

No one could hope to untangle all the snarls in American usage. In this section, however, we offer advice on how to avoid the common errors. We treat troublesome words that sound alike but have different meanings, words that are frequently used incorrectly, quandaries you may often find yourself in when choosing a word. When we have also discussed the problem in the text, we indicate a reference.

a, an   Use *a* before words beginning with a consonant sound and *an* before words beginning with a vowel sound. Check "Adjectives" in Chapter 19 for a further discussion.

accent marks   Accent marks are part of the word and must be used where they are called for, as in *cliché*. Consult your dictionary.

accept, except   *Accept* means "to receive" or "to agree to": *Hirohito finally accepted defeat. Except* as a verb means "to leave out" or "to make exception of" and as a preposition means "excluding": *The ravages of war do not except children, the aged, or the feeble. Everyone got out alive except the cat.*

adverse, averse   *Adverse* is an adjective meaning "hostile" or "unfavorable": *The adverse effects of alcohol include headache and nausea. Averse is an adjective meaning "reluctant" or "in opposition": Repeated hangovers soon made him averse to drinking alcohol.*

advice, advise   *Advice* is a noun meaning "counsel": *Bill went to his broker for advice on the stock market. Advise is a verb meaning "to give counsel": But Bill's broker was unable to advise him.*

affect, effect   *Affect* as a verb means "to influence" or "to pretend to have": *The oil slick did not seriously affect the beach. Professor Honnicutt affected a Boston accent. Effect as a verb means "to bring about" or "to cause to happen" and as a noun means "result": Diplomats are trying to effect a peace in Lebanon. The injections had no effect.*

aggravate, irritate   These words are not synonyms. *Aggravate* means "to make worse": *Running in the sprints, Lewis aggravated his hamstring injury. Irritate means "to make impatient or angry": My little sister irritates me.*

agree to, agree with   We agree *to* a proposal. We agree *with* a person.

all, all of   When modifying a common noun, use only *all: All the world's a stage. When modifying a proper noun or a pronoun, use all of: When all of his teeth were pulled, all of Hollywood cried.*

all ready, already   *All ready* is an adjective meaning "prepared": *We're all ready to dance. Already is an adverb meaning "prior in time": Sven had already cooked dinner by the time we arrived.*

all right, alright   Use *all right; alright* is a misspelling.

allusion, illusion   *Allusion* means "reference to," as in *The "rail-splitter" was an allusion to Lincoln. Illusion means "deception" or "mistaken idea," as in He is under the illusion that he is Napoleon.*

almost, most   See *most, almost*.

along with   Phrases introduced by *along with* are parenthetical and do not change the number of the verb: *The mayor, along with the comptroller and the city council, runs a tight ship. See rule 1 under "Subject-Verb Agreement" in Chapter 20.*

although, though   Used as conjunctions, *although* and *though* are synonyms. Careful stylists, however, prefer *although* in formal writing: *Although he studied for years, Klaus never passed the bar exam. Though also works as an adverb: He tried, though.*

altogether, all together   *Altogether* means "entirely": *Einstein was altogether unprepared for the fame his discoveries brought him. All together means "as a group": Our family stood all together in the dining room for this snapshot.*

ambiguous, ambivalent   *Ambiguous* means "capable of more than one meaning or interpretation," or, more generally, "unclear or confusing": *His statement was ambiguous, and I wasn't sure what he meant. Ambivalent* means "feeling two ways (usually conflicting) about something": *I was ambivalent about the movie and so stayed home.*

among, between   See *between, among.*

amoral, immoral   *Amoral* means "without concern for moral standards": *Don Juan was amoral and so felt no guilt about his seductions.* *Immoral* means "in violation of moral standards": *Cruelty to animals is immoral no matter the situation.*

amount, number   *Amount* refers to the bulk or quantity of something viewed as a whole: *I have had an adequate amount of back talk from you.* *Number* refers to something viewed as separate units: *You have made a number of undeserved criticisms.*

and etc.   *Et cetera* means "and other things." To place it after *and* means "and and other things," an obvious redundancy.

and/or   Avoid this awkward construction. Decide whether you mean "and" or "or." If your sentence contains a third option, add *or both,* as in *We could not decide whether to go to India or China or both.*

ante-, anti-   The prefix *ante-* means "before": *Arlington is an antebellum mansion near Washington. Anti-* means "against": *If poisoned, find an antidote.*

anxious, eager   *Anxious* means "worried, uneasy, brooding": *Most students were anxious about the organic chemistry midterm. Eager* means "full of enthusiasm": *Few were eager to take the midterm.* Be careful not to use one when you mean the other.

anybody, any body, anyone, any one   *Anybody* and *anyone* are single-word synonyms meaning "any person at all": *Anybody (or anyone) can be a star these days.* The phrase *any body* refers to any item of a particular group of bodies: *You students of surgery may dissect any body you find.* The phrase *any one* means "any single one of a particular group": *Can I choose any one of the cadavers, Professor?*

anymore, any more   *Anymore* (less commonly written as *any more*) is an adverb meaning "any longer" and is used in negative situations: *Annie doesn't live here anymore.* Avoid using it in positive constructions to mean "now" or "these days": *Vegetables are certainly expensive now* (not *anymore*). *Any more* usually refers to an addition: *I've had enough sass and don't want any more.*

anyplace, anywhere   Careful stylists prefer *anywhere.*

anyways, anywheres   Avoid these colloquial variations of *anyway* and *anywhere.*

apt, likely, liable   *Apt* means "having a tendency to": *I am apt to be forgetful. Likely* means "probable to happen": *I am likely to forget lunch dates. Liable* means "legally responsible": *If I don't repair that missing stair,*

I'll be liable for damages. Writers sometimes incorrectly use *liable* when they mean *likely* in situations that have negative consequences: *I'm likely* (not *liable*) *to slip on icy sidewalks* is correct.

as *As* can be a preposition, an adverb, or a conjunction. As a preposition, it means "in the role of": *As a cook, he would make a good tennis player.* As an adverb, it means "equally": *She would be just as miserable in Katmandu.* As a conjunction, it introduces an adverbial clause: *He smirked as he ate the goldfish.*

Poor *as* is much overused and abused. It is not a synonym for *because.* Prefer *Billy did not attend school yesterday because* (not *as*) *he had a cold.* It is not a substitute for *that.* Prefer *I don't know that* (not *as*) *I care who wins.* It is not a substitute for *to be.* Prefer *The president appointed her to be* (not *as*) *head of the SEC.* (*To be* is usually so strongly implied it may be omitted.)

as, like *As* and *like* are not interchangeable. *Like* as a preposition can be followed only by a noun or a noun substitute: *Do you think I look like Michael Jackson? Like* should not introduce a clause. Use *as*: *Do unto others as* (not *like*) *you would have others do unto you.*

assure, ensure, insure *Assure* usually means "to give confidence": *He assured her that her stuffed goose was delicious. Ensure* means "to make certain": *Tying Black Bart with a lasso ensured his detention. Insure* means "to get insurance for": *Lloyd's of London refused to insure the trombonist's lip.*

awful, awfully *Awful* is an adjective: *The awful dragon breathed fire. Awfully* is an adverb: *The dragon snorted awfully.* Neither should be used in formal writing to mean "very" or "extremely."

awhile, a while *Awhile* (one word) is an adverb: *Let's rest here awhile. Awhile* cannot be the object of a preposition. *A while* is a noun phrase and can be the object of a preposition: *I will get moving again in a while.*

bad, badly *Bad* is an adjective that modifies nouns or noun substitutes; *badly* is an adverb. The problem arises with linking verbs, such as *feel, appear,* or *look,* that take the complement *bad*: *After eating the pound of chocolate, Hans felt bad* (not *badly*) *enough to call the doctor.*

being as, being that Avoid these colloquialisms. Use *because* or *since*: *Because* (not *Being as*) *I was ill, I could not attend your recital.*

beside, besides *Beside* means "by the side of" or "next to": *The Secret Service agents stood beside the president. Besides* means either "except" or "in addition to": *Besides her, no one volunteered. Three other students besides her received A's.*

between, among Use *between* for two things, *among* for three or more, or when the number is unstated: *Between you and me, I think this party stinks. He was first among equals.*

biweekly, bimonthly, semimonthly, semiannually As a prefix indicating time, *bi-* means happening every two periods of time. *Semi-* means happening twice in one period. *We meet biweekly, or every two weeks. We meet bimonthly, or every two months. We meet semimonthly, or twice each month. We meet semiannually, or twice a year.*

bring, take Someone *brings* something toward you and *takes* it away from you: *Bring me some antacid, and take away this awful soup.*

bunch Careful writers avoid using this word to mean "many."

burst, bust *Burst* is a verb meaning "to come apart forcefully." Its principal parts are *burst, burst,* and *burst*: *What will you do if I burst the balloon? I burst the balloon yesterday. I had burst another balloon a week before. Bursted* is incorrect. *Bust* and *busted* are slang.

but hardly, but scarcely, but however, but yet *But* is superfluous in these expressions. *Hardly, scarcely, however,* and *yet* already carry negative implications.

calloused, callow These words are near-opposites. Calloused means thick or hardened; callow means young and inexperienced.

can, may *Can* indicates capability, as in *I can bench-press 300 pounds on a good day. May* indicates permission, as in *May I please have the salt?* or possibility, as in *I may need salt on my steak.*

can barely, can hardly, can't barely, can't hardly Both *barely* and *hardly* carry negative implications: *I can barely swim and so can hardly save you. Can't barely* and *can't hardly* are double negatives and should be avoided.

cannot, can not *Can not* is not the preferred form; use *cannot.*

can't help but Careful stylists avoid using this colloquial phrase. Prefer *can't help* without *but* or *can't but* without *help*: *I can't help loving you, I can't but be pleased at that.*

censor, censure *Censor* means "to scrutinize works for unacceptable material": *Some totalitarian countries censor private mail. Censure* means "to scold or criticize": *The Senate censured Joe McCarthy for his conduct.*

center around, center on *Center on* means "to focus or concentrate on": *The FBI hunt centered on the town of Rome, New York. Center around* is illogical. Substitute *revolve around: The quest for freedom revolves around human dignity.*

cite, sight, site *Cite* is a verb meaning "refer to": *To prove that the world is round, I need only cite that famous explorer Columbus. Sight* is a noun meaning "a view": *I'm sure Columbus found America to be a beautiful sight. Site* is a noun meaning "place" or "location": *Was Rhode Island the site of his landing?*

climactic, climatic   *Climactic* refers to a peak or high point: *Bogart's farewell to Bergman is the climactic love scene in* Casablanca. *Climatic* refers to weather: *His voice changed according to climatic conditions.*

compared to, compared with   *Compared to* suggests a similarity between two things not usually thought of together: *My boyfriend compared me to Jessica Lange. Compare with* suggests an analysis of differences and similarities: *His essay compared Roosevelt's presidency with Lincoln's under the headings of wartime leadership, intellectual ability, and personal integrity.* As an intransitive verb, *compare* always takes *with,* as in *Today's presidents just don't compare with yesterday's greats.*

complement, compliment   As a verb, *complement* means "to complete" or "to match," as in *The green sweater complements his green eyes.* As a noun, *complement* means "a word or phrase that completes an idea": *"Sweet" is often the complement of "sugar."* As a verb, *compliment* means "to praise": *The mayor complimented the fire department's quick work.* As a noun, it means "a bit of praise": *"You've lost a ton of weight" doesn't sound like much of a compliment to me.*

compose, comprise   To *compose* means "to form the parts into a whole": *I composed a poem in praise of toothpaste.* The whole *comprises* or *consists of* the parts, as in *The Congress comprises (consists of) the Senate and the House of Representatives.* Careful stylists, therefore, would write *Twelve teams compose the National League;* and *The National League comprises twelve teams.*

comrade, camaraderie   *Comrade* refers to a close companion or friend; *camaraderie* refers to the warm feeling between comrades. Note the different spellings.

conscience, conscientious, conscious, consciousness   *Conscience* is a noun referring to our sense of right and wrong: *My conscience hurt because I ate the whole cake by myself. Conscientious* is an adjective meaning "scrupulous, careful": *He was conscientious about homework and did it every night. Conscious* is an adjective meaning "aware of self and surroundings": *He was conscious of the lipstick smear on his cheek. Consciousness* is a noun referring to the state of being aware: *After the blow on her head, she lost consciousness.*

continual, continuous   *Continual* means "happening repeatedly": *His job as jackhammer operator gave him a continual headache. Continuous* means "uninterrupted or unbroken": *The Apennines form a continuous ridge of mountains.*

could of, should of, would of   Avoid all of these. They are incorrect ear-spellings for *could have, should have,* and *would have.*

council, counsel   *Council* refers to an administrative or legislative body, and *councilor* to a member of that body. *Counsel* refers to advice or to a legal adviser, and *counselor* refers to anyone who advises. *Counsel* can also be a verb, as in *Gandhi counseled his followers to resist without violence.*

couple of   In formal English, don't use this phrase to mean "several" but only to mean "two that are connected, a pair": *A couple of horses pulled the cart.*

credible, creditable, credulous   *Credible* means "giving sufficient reason to be believed": *After a vigorous cross-examination, the jury found her a credible witness. Creditable* means "worthy of praise or esteem": *Mattingly did a creditable job at first base. Credulous* means "ready to believe on slight evidence": *He was so credulous I convinced him I'd been to the moon.*

criterion, criteria   *Criterion* is the singular. *Criteria* is the plural. *Stamina is the main criterion for good running. Stamina and will are the main criteria for good running.*

datum, data   *Datum* is the singular form and *data* is the plural. *The data shows a 15 percent decrease* should be *The data show a 15 percent decrease.*

different from, different than   Many people say, and some write, *different than,* but careful stylists prefer *different from: Being a teenager is different from being an adult.*

differ from, differ with   *Differ from* means "to show unlikeness": *California bagels differ from Boston bagels in color and price. Differ with* means "to disagree with": *Oppenheimer differed with Teller over the hydrogen bomb.*

discreet, discrete   *Discreet* means "prudent" or "able to be silent": *He was so discreet about his poker losses that his wife never found out. Discrete* means "separate" or "distinct": *Each country has its own discrete culture.*

disinterested, uninterested   *Disinterested* does not mean "to have no interest" but "to have nothing personal at stake and thus to be impartial": *The dispute between Japanese and Soviet fishermen has been handed over to a disinterested Swiss arbitrator. Uninterested* means "apathetic," or "uncaring": *Deirdre took Harry for a fishing trip, but he was obviously uninterested.*

doesn't, don't   *Doesn't* is the contraction of *does not,* and *don't* is the contraction of *do not.* Be sure you don't use *don't* when you mean *doesn't: He doesn't* (not *don't*) *feel well today.*

due to, because   Avoid using *due to* as a synonym for "because": *Because of* (not *due to*) *rain, the game was called.* Save *due to* for bill paying.

due to the fact that   This long running jump means "because." Use *because.*

each, every   *Each* means "one of a group": *Each carton of milk undergoes careful inspection. Every* refers to all members of a group: *Every writer wishes for fame.* Both take a singular verb.

effect   See *affect, effect.*

e.g., i.e.   These are abbreviations from Latin: *e.g.* stands for *exempli gratia,* which means "for the sake of example"; *i.e.* stands for *id est,* which means "that is." These Latin abbreviations are fading from use in formal writing. Stick to the English equivalents.

either, neither   Both of these words can function as an adjective, a pronoun, or part of a correlative conjunction. As an adjective, *either* means "one or the other": *Guard dogs stand on either side of the gate.* As an adjective *neither* means "not one or the other": *Neither dog has on a muzzle.* As pronouns, *either* and *neither* take singular verbs: *Either is enough to scare off burglars. Neither makes the postman cheerful.* As a correlative conjunction, *either* is followed by *or* and *neither* by *nor.* For further discussion, see "Conjunctions" in Chapter 19 and "Parallel Construction" in Chapter 20.

elicit, illicit   *Elicit* is a verb that means "to pull forth" or "to evoke": *Ted Williams's homer in his last time at bat elicited a huge roar from the crowd. Illicit* is an adjective that means "not allowed": *Ormsby was arrested for possession of illicit drugs.*

eminent, imminent, immanent   *Eminent* means "respected, high ranking, outstanding": *Ben Franklin was the most eminent statesman of his day. Imminent* means "impending": *An imminent storm darkened the horizon. Immanent,* a rare term of philosophy, usually means "inherent" or "resting within": *Romantic philosophers thought divinity was immanent in nature.*

enthuse   Careful stylists avoid using this colloquial term in formal prose. Prefer *enthusiastic*: *New York City was very enthusiastic about baseball in 1955.*

etc.   See *and etc.*

everybody, every body, everyone, every one   *Everybody* and *everyone* are indefinite pronouns referring to all members of a group. Both take singular verbs: *When everybody plays well, everyone cheers loudly. Every body* is a phrase in which the noun *body* is modified by the adjective *every*: *You will find a heart in every body of a mammal.* In *every one,* the pronoun *one* is modified by the adjective *every*: *Every one has lungs as well.*

everyday, every day   *Everyday* is an adjective: *At five each morning, she rose to do her everyday chores.* The phrase *every day* acts as an adverb: *I see him every day.*

everywheres   Avoid this colloquial version of *everywhere.*

except   See *accept, except.*

explicit, implicit   *Explicit* means "stated outright": *I made an explicit offer to buy his car. Implicit* means "unstated but suggested": *Implicit in my offer was that he throw in the whitewall tires and a gallon of gasoline.*

farther, further   Use *farther* to express physical distance: *Is it farther to his house or to yours?* Use *further* to express abstract distance: *Newton probed further into the nature of the universe than any thinker before him.*

few, fewer, less, lesser   *Few* and *fewer* refer to countable items: *We have few friends, and with that attitude, we'll have fewer. Less* and *lesser* refer to a whole not divisible into individual countable units: *I have less money than you, but you are the lesser talent.*

first, firstly   *Firstly, secondly,* and *thirdly* have pretty much faded from use. Prefer *first, second,* and *third*: <u>First</u>, *the economy is weak.* <u>Second</u>, *our foreign policy is in disarray.* <u>Third</u>, *the soda machine doesn't work.*

flaunt, flout   *Flaunt* means "to make an ostentatious display": *The Smiths <u>flaunted</u> their new car in front of the neighbors. Flout* means "to treat disrespectfully" or "to scorn": *The banker <u>flouted</u> convention by coming to the bank in jeans and sneakers.*

former, latter   These words can help avoid repetition. Use them only when you are referring to two things: *Mr. Hobson and his dog are so alike that I sometimes mistake the <u>former</u> for the <u>latter</u>.*

get, got, gotten   *Got* is the past tense of *get*: *Millions of Americans <u>got</u> their income tax forms in the mail yesterday.* The past participle of *get* is either *got* or *gotten,* hence the confusion. Either is acceptable English: *Have you <u>got</u> a tennis racket? I have <u>gotten</u> to bed late every night this week.*

 Americans use *gotten* more often, especially to signal a progression: *The moral standards of the United States <u>have gotten</u> steadily worse.* We also use *got* in informal English as an intense form of *must*: *You have <u>got</u> to help us.* Our advice: don't overuse *get* in formal writing. Although it is a necessary verb, it can be an easy way out of the search for good verbs.

good, well   *Good* is a noun: *I stand for the true, the <u>good</u>, and the beautiful. Good* is also an adjective: *Wouldn't we all love to be <u>good</u> writers? Well* is an adverb: *She plays the bassoon <u>well</u>.* The problem arises, as with *bad* and *badly,* with linking verbs, such as *feel* or *sound,* which take *good* as a complement. *Whenever she ran ten miles, she felt <u>good</u>* (not *well*). In this sentence *good* modifies the subject *she,* not the verb.

good and   Avoid this colloquial equivalent of *entirely* or *very*: *You should be <u>very</u>* (not *good and*) *mad.*

had ought   Avoid this colloquial equivalent of *ought*. Prefer *You <u>ought</u>* (not *had ought*) *to study.*

hanged, hung   As past participles, the word *hanged* is used with people, and the word *hung* with objects: *In the old West, outlaws were <u>hanged</u>. Pictures are <u>hung</u> all over my house.*

hardly   See *can barely, can hardly, can't barely, can't hardly.*

have, of   Do not use the preposition *of* when you mean the verb *have*: *She shouldn't <u>have</u>* (not *of*) *done what she did.*

hopefully   *Hopefully* is an adverb meaning "in a hopeful manner" and modifies the verb, as in *The sick man waited <u>hopefully</u> for the doctor.* This means "As he waited, he was hopeful." The term is frequently misused: *Hopefully, we should arrive at the summit by two.* This means that when the climbers get to the top, they will be full of hope. The speaker meant *I <u>hope</u> we arrive at the summit by two.* Be careful: this misuse is a pet peeve of many people.

house, home A *house* is an edifice; a *home* is an emotional entity in which you live: *A house is where the kitchen is. A home is where the heart is.*

however This word means "in spite of" or "no matter": *We do not have the exact style you ordered; we do, however, have a similar one.* When used as a conjunctive adverb this way, *however* should be set off by punctuation. Never use this word in a clause beginning with *but*: that would be redundant. Careful stylists do not begin sentences with *however*.

human, human being *Human* is an adjective: *Her dog had a human smile.* Although *human* is acceptable as a noun, careful stylists prefer *human being*: *Her dog was almost like a human being.*

i.e. See *e.g., i.e.*

if, whether In speech, we often say *I'll find out if he's home or not.* A better word here is *whether*: *I'll find out whether he is home or not. Whether* indicates a choice or alternative. *If* indicates a contingency: *If he doesn't shut up, I'll scream.*

imminent, immanent See *eminent, imminent, immanent.*

impact Avoid using this word as a verb. Prefer a more specific word: *Years of war depleted* (not *impacted on*) *the treasury of Venice.*

imply, infer *Imply* means "to suggest" or "to indicate," as in *By shaking her head, she implied disapproval. Infer* means "to conclude" or "to understand," as in *I inferred from her nodding that she agreed.*

individual, person, party, people *Individual* emphasizes singularity or separateness: *Our government must protect the individual. Person* emphasizes the actual self or personality: *A person could develop a cough. Party* means a group of people assembled for a purpose. *Our party arrived fifteen minutes late. People* refers to a nation, congregation, class, or company: *Of the people, by the people, and for the people. People* is also used to refer to human beings in general: *People do the darnedest things.*

infer, imply See *imply, infer.*

ingenious, ingenuous *Ingenious* means "especially inventive" or "clever": *With an ingenious contrivance, King Frederick had the kitchen raised into his bedroom. Ingenuous* means "childlike" or "innocent": *When my daughter said I looked a hundred, I forgave her because of her ingenuous smile.*

irrespective, regardless, irregardless *Irrespective* and *regardless* are synonymous and mean "whether taken into account or not," as in *We are all equal irrespective of sex, color, or creed. I am leaving regardless of her opinion. Irregardless* is incorrect.

is when, is where Avoid these awkward constructions. Revise *A double elimination tournament is when teams losing twice are eliminated.* Prefer *In a double elimination tournament, teams losing twice are eliminated.*

it's, its   Because their appearance is so similar, these two words are often confused with each other. *It's* is always a contraction of *it is*: *It's lovely weather if you're a duck. Its* is a possessive pronoun: *My duck is looking for its bowl.* See "Apostrophes" in Chapter 21.

-ize verbs   Many verbs that end in *-ize* are essential, such as *organize* and *civilize.* Try, however, to avoid made-up *-ize* verbs that take the place of better verbs. Prefer *moisten* to *moisturize, finish* or *complete* to *finalize,* and *use* to *utilize.*

kind, kinds   *Kind* is singular and takes a singular modifier and verb, as in *This kind of novel bores me. Kinds* is plural and takes a plural modifier and verb, as in *these kinds of novels bore me. These kinds of cars* is incorrect. Some abstract words, however, such as *irony, beauty,* and *love,* come in different forms and can be used with the plural *kinds,* as in *There are many kinds of love.*

kind of, sort of   In formal writing, avoid using *kind of* and *sort of* to mean "to a degree" or "less than completely." If you cannot indicate the exact degree, prefer *somewhat* and *rather*: *Murray's poems are rather* (not *sort of*) *elusive. Kind* is never followed by *a. He is kind a tough* is incorrect.

lay, lie   *Lay* is a transitive verb and thus takes a direct object. Its principal parts are *lay, laid,* and *laid*: *That comedian will lay an egg tonight, just as he laid one last week, and just as he has laid one every night for the past five years. Lie* is an intransitive verb and thus does not take an object. Its principal parts are *lie, lay,* and *lain*: *I will lie on the beach today; I lay there yesterday, and I feel as though I have lain there all my life.*

lead, led   The verb *lead* becomes *led* in the past tense: *You lead me down the mountain today. I led you up yesterday.*

leave, let   *Leave* means "to depart"; *let* means "to allow." They are interchangeable only when both meanings apply, as in *Let* (or *Leave*) *me alone.*

lend, loan   Careful stylists use *loan* only as a noun, as in *The interest on the loan is 12 percent.* The verb is *to lend,* as in *Will you lend me a dime?*

less   See *few, fewer, less, lesser.*

liable   See *apt, likely, liable.*

like, as   See *as, like.*

loose, lose   *Loose* means "unbound" or "free from restraint": *Electricians traced the blackout to a loose wire. Lose* means "to become unable to find": *Don't lose your train ticket.*

lots, lots of, a lot of, a lot   These are all colloquial equivalents of *much, many,* or *a great deal.* Avoid them in your college writing: *Many* (not *a lot of*) *steamships sailed from Le Havre.*

majority Use this word to refer to more than half of a group of countable items: *the majority of voters stayed home*. Use words such as *most* when the subject cannot be divided into countable items: *Most of the sky is clear*.

may, can See *can, may*.

may be, maybe The phrase *may be* is the subjunctive of *is*: *The aliens may be laughing at us right now*. *Maybe* is an adverb meaning "perhaps": *Maybe they think our taste in clothes is strange*.

medium, media *Medium* is the singular form: *Television is the fastest growing news medium in the world*. *Media* is plural: *Newspapers and network news are the two most important news media*.

moral, morale *Moral* is an adjective meaning "conforming to a standard of rightness or goodness": *Helping poor nations is a moral thing to do*. *Morale* is a noun meaning "mental or emotional condition": *After the Battle of the Bulge, Allied morale was high*.

most, almost *Most* is an adjective meaning "the greater part": *Most people like finding hidden money*. *Almost* is an adverb meaning "close but not quite": *We are almost home*. They are not interchangeable. *I see him most every day* is incorrect.

myself This is a reflexive or intensive pronoun. As a reflexive, it is used when the actor also receives the action: *I hurt myself jogging*. As an intensive, it emphasizes a point: *I guess I myself will have to do it*. It is not a synonym for *I* or *me*. See "Pronouns" in Chapter 19.

nauseous, nauseating, nauseated *Nauseous* and *nauseating* mean the same thing; that is, "causing nausea": *That wig is nauseating. I can't stand any more of his nauseous quips*. *Nauseated* means "feeling nausea": *She is a little nauseated after riding the Ferris wheel*. The sentence *That hotdog made me nauseous* means you were causing others to feel nausea.

none *None* is almost always singular, as in *Of four candidates, none was female*. Treat *none* as a plural, however, when you wish to consider the members of the group as separate entities: *Of all the varieties of life on earth, none are hardier or more resourceful than the insects*.

nowheres Avoid this colloquial equivalent of *nowhere*.

number, amount See *amount, number*.

off, off of *Off* is sufficient, as in *Get off my bunion*. Adding *of* is unnecessary.

OK, O.K., okay Avoid these in your college writing.

on, upon These words are synonyms. To many people, *upon* sounds pretentious.

on account of, because *On account of* should be reserved for partial payment of a debt. Use the shorter and more direct *because*.

one, you   *One* is the third-person impersonal pronoun: <u>*One*</u> *never knows where* <u>*one*</u> *stands these days.* *You,* the second-person pronoun, is often used in its place. <u>*You*</u> *never know where* <u>*you*</u> *stand these days.* Neither is perfect. *One* has the drawback of being associated with pretentious speakers; *you* has the drawback of being a little too chatty for formal prose. Careful stylists still prefer *one,* although they use it sparingly. Sometimes it is simply better to say *I* when referring to your own experience. Don't use *you* unless you are directly addressing the reader.

only   To avoid confusion, place *only* in front of the word you intend it to modify: *Why did you buy* <u>*only*</u> *two bananas?* See "Modifiers: Misplaced, Squinting, and Dangling" in Chapter 20.

pair   Use a singular verb when you are considering the pair as a unit: *A pair of wild horses* <u>*is*</u> *hard to control.* Use a plural verb when you wish to indicate that the two elements of the pair are separate: *Our new* <u>*pair*</u> *of puppies* <u>*are*</u> *getting along well with each other.*

per   This Latin word means "for each." Prefer the English equivalent: *My Oldsmobile gets fifteen miles* <u>*to a*</u> *(not* per*) gallon. I sent the letter* <u>*by*</u> *(not* per*) Express Mail.*

percent, per cent, percentage   *Percent,* now used more commonly than *per cent,* must follow a numeral: *The bond paid 9* <u>*percent*</u>*. Percentage* means "part" or "portion." Do not use it by itself to mean "a small part or portion." It requires an adjective to give it meaning: *A high* <u>*percentage*</u> *of injuries in football are to the knee.*

person   See *individual, person, party, people.*

phenomenon, phenomena, phenomenal   *Phenomenon* is a noun meaning "an observable fact or event": *A hurricane is a frightening* <u>*phenomenon*</u>*. Phenomena* is the plural: *Hurricanes are frightening* <u>*phenomena*</u>*. Phenomenal* is an adjective meaning "extraordinary": *Her skill in doing calculus was* <u>*phenomenal*</u>*.*

plenty of   Careful stylists avoid using *plenty of* to mean a large number or amount: *Philip Johnson has designed* <u>*a great many*</u> *(not* plenty of*) fine buildings.*

plus   Use *plus* only when adding numbers. Careful stylists never use it in place of *in addition to* or *and.*

precede, proceed   *Precede* means "to go before": *Women and children* <u>*precede*</u> *the men into the lifeboats. Proceed* means "to continue on": <u>*Proceed*</u> *directly to the boarding gate.*

presently   Use this word to mean "in a little while": *I'll return* <u>*presently*</u>*.* Do not use it to mean "now."

pretty   Avoid this colloquialism in formal writing. *Mr. Elton is* <u>*rather*</u> *(not* pretty*) drunk.*

principal, principle   *Principal* as a noun means "chief officer," as in *The principal sent Ralph home from school for keeping a frog in his book bag.* As an adjective, it means "foremost" or "most important." *Our principal objective is to defend the ridge until dawn. Principle* (note the spelling difference) is a noun that means "rule" or "truth": *The first principle of long-distance running is relaxation in the midst of arduous physical exercise.*

quote, quotation   *Quote* is a verb, not a noun: *Newspapers often quote rock stars out of context. Quotation* is the noun: *Reporters scramble to get good quotations* (not *quotes*).

real, really   *Real* is an adjective: *A real crocodile lay on the bank. Really* is the adverb: *It was sleeting really* (not *real*) *hard.*

reason is because, reason is that   *Reason is because* is a redundancy, although it is often seen: *The reason Hamlet waits so long to kill Claudius is because there is so much uncertainty in the court of Denmark* is incorrect. Use *reason is that: The reason Hamlet waits so long to kill Claudius is that there is so much uncertainty in the court of Denmark.*

regarding, in regard to, with regard to, as regards   All these words are synonyms for *concerning.* Avoid using *in regards to,* a cross between *in regard to* and *as regards.*

sensual, sensuous   *Sensual* means "preoccupied with bodily pleasures": *The voluptuous Polynesian women in Gauguin's paintings look sensual. Sensuous* means "appealing to the senses": *I love the sensuous colors in Gauguin's paintings.*

shall, should, will, would   *Shall* was once the correct future tense auxiliary for the first person (*I shall be home shortly),* but in American usage it is now reserved for emphasis (*I shall return*) or a request for an opinion or consent (*Shall we see each other again tomorrow night?*) For most purposes, *will* functions as the future-tense auxiliary for all persons. *Should* was once the past tense of *shall* but now indicates obligation: *He should occasionally volunteer to do the dishes. Would* was once the past tense of *will* but now indicates the conditional: *If she played softer music, I would attend her parties.*

should   See *shall, should, will, would.*

should of, should have   See *could of, should of, would of.* All of these expressions are incorrect.

sit, set   *Sit* is intransitive—that is, it takes no object: *Ever since I bruised my coccyx, I have found it difficult to sit. Set* is transitive—that is, it takes an object: *We set the piano in your kitchen.*

situation   This word is much overused and often unnecessary. Whenever possible, use a concrete word to indicate what the *situation* is: *Congress has done nothing to combat the worsening deficit* (not *worsening situation*). When the word is unnecessary, avoid it: *They found themselves in danger* (not *in a dangerous situation*) *high on the rock face.*

so This word can be an adverb, an adjective, or a conjunction. As an adverb, it usually means "in order to" or "to the degree": *She kept the door open so that she could hear the baby.* As an adjective, it is a vague intensifier. Careful stylists prefer *very* or *intensely: Michael Jackson is very* (not *so*) *good looking.* As a conjunction, it indicates result: *The river is still cold, so the fish are still jumping.* Careful stylists avoid starting sentences with *so.*

somebody, some body, someone, some one Both *somebody* and *someone* are indefinite pronouns meaning "an unspecified person": *Won't somebody* (or *someone*) *answer the phone? Some body* is a phrase meaning an unspecified body: *Some body of government ought to examine this problem. Some one* is a phrase that means "an unspecified one": *Some one of the guests committed the murder.*

someplace, somewhere These two words mean "an unspecified place." Careful stylists prefer *somewhere.*

sometime, some time, sometimes *Sometime* is an adverb that means "at an unspecified time": *Come up and see me sometime. Some time* is a phrase that means "an unspecified length of time": *I haven't seen jai alai for some time. Sometimes* is an adverb that means "occasionally": *Cockroaches appeared sometimes one place, sometimes another.*

somewheres Avoid using this colloquialism in your writing.

sort of See *kind of, sort of.*

split infinitives An *infinitive* consists of *to* and the main form of the verb, such as *to deny.* To *split* an infinitive means to place an adverb or a phrase between the *to* and the verb (*to categorically deny*). When a writer places a long phrase between the *to* and the verb, the split infinitive can make comprehension difficult: *I want to categorically and without fear of contradiction from anyone deny all charges.* Careful stylists are known to strenuously object to any split infinitive.

stationary, stationery *Stationary* is an adjective meaning "not moving or moved": *Scientists in antiquity once thought the earth stationary and the universe revolving. Stationery* is what we write letters on.

suppose to, supposed to Use *supposed to* in your writing to indicate what is expected to happen: *The total eclipse is supposed to* (not *suppose to*) *begin tomorrow.*

sure, surely, certainly Avoid using *sure* to mean "surely" or "certainly." *Sure* is an adjective that means "confident": *The scoutmaster was sure we were near the camp. Surely* is an adverb that means "without doubt": *Though cantankerous, Grandpa surely loved his family. Certainly* is even more assured: *He was certainly good at getting people to agree with him.*

take, bring See *bring, take.*

than, then Note the difference in spelling between these two words. *Than* introduces a comparison: *My father is stronger than your father.* When using *than* with a pronoun, be sure the pronoun is in the right case. One method of making sure is to fill in all the words: *He liked her better than* [*he liked*] *me. He liked her better than I* [*liked her*]. See rule 5 under "A Special Word about Pronoun Case" in Chapter 19.

that, which   Use *that* to introduce clauses containing essential information: *The red hat that I lost yesterday was found.* I have other red hats; this sentence refers to the one I lost yesterday. Use *which* to introduce clauses containing nonessential information: *The red hat, which I lost yesterday, has been found.* I have only one red hat and therefore it is not essential to identify the hat further. The words *restrictive* and *nonrestrictive* are frequently used to make this distinction. See rule 6 under "Commas" in Chapter 21, for more on essential and nonessential information.

their, there, they're   *Their* is the third-person plural possessive: *The models put on their eyelashes. There* is an adverb of place: *I saw the baboon over there in the parking lot. There* can also introduce an expletive: *There wasn't a police officer to be found. They're* is a contraction of *they are: They're not eager to accost big animals.* (See "Apostrophes" in Chapter 21 for a discussion of correct usage.)

theirselves   Avoid this colloquialism.

this, these, those   These demonstrative adjectives must agree in number with the noun they modify: *This kind of day is my favorite. These sorts of dresses are always expensive. Those silk scarves cost a fortune.*

this here, these here, that there, them there   Avoid these colloquial expressions.

through, thru   Use *through* in your writing. *Thru* is informal.

till, until, 'til   *Till* is acceptable, but *until* is preferable. *'Til* is incorrect.

to, too, two   *To* is a preposition: *I propose a toast to all the night watchmen of the world. Too* is an adverb meaning "also" or "more than enough": *He was too conceited to notice that everyone was smirking. Two* is a number: *One plus one equals two.*

toward, towards   Careful stylists prefer *toward.*

try and, try to   *Try to* is preferable: *Scuba divers should never try to* (not *try and*) *swim alone.*

unique   *Unique* does not admit of degree or comparison: a thing cannot be more or less or very unique, only unique. At all events, *unique* is much overused these days. It means "only one of a kind," "singular." Reserve it for things you have never seen the like of before.

upon, on   See *on, upon.*

use, utilize, utilization   *Utilize* is an overused *-ize* verb. Prefer *use: We must use* (not *utilize*) *every means at our disposal.* Similarly, prefer the noun *use* to *utilization*: *China condemned any <u>use</u>* (not *utilization*) *of biochemical warfare.*

use to, used to   Past tense is the preferable form when you mean "did habitually": *I <u>used to</u>* (not *use to*) *scream at horror movies.*

viable   The adjective *viable* means "capable of living or growing": *Anaerobic microbes are not <u>viable</u> in oxygenated environments.* Avoid using it to indicate that something will work: *Hydroelectric energy is a <u>practicable</u>* (not *viable*) *alternative to nuclear power.*

way, ways   Avoid using *a ways* to mean "a great distance." Prefer *a way*: *Africa has a <u>way</u>* (not *a ways*) *to go before it can compete with industrialized nations.*

well, good   See *good, well.*

where, where at, where to   In some regions of America it is quite common to hear *Where are you going to?* and *Where is the shoe at?* In writing, however, never use *to* or *at* after *where*. *<u>Where</u> are you going?* is sufficient.

whether   See *if, whether.*

which, that   See *that, which.*

would   See *shall, should, will, would.*

you're, your   *Your* is a possessive pronoun: *<u>Your</u> heart is in the right place.* Do not confuse it with *you're*, a contraction of *you are*: *<u>You're</u> coming to the show tonight, aren't you?* See "Apostrophes" in Chapter 21.

APPENDIXES

Other Systems of Documentation

Style Manuals and Handbooks in Various Disciplines

OTHER SYSTEMS
OF DOCUMENTATION

THE MLA NOTES AND BIBLIOGRAPHY SYSTEM

If, like us, you were brought up with notes and bibliographies, you may be in an elegiac mood now that a different system has been adopted. But do not be sad. Many college writers and instructors still ask for notes and bibliographies in their papers. Practicality therefore dictates that you review footnotes, endnotes, and bibliography. Instead of citations in the text, in this system you use raised numerals to direct your reader to references located either at the bottom of the page or on a separate page at the end of your paper.

Notes

To indicate a reference, put an arabic numeral half a space up after the final punctuation of your sentence. Number your notes consecutively throughout the paper. If you prefer (or if your instructor requires) endnotes, list them on a separate sheet of paper just before the bibliography. If you use footnotes, be sure to leave enough space at the bottom of the page on which your reference occurs. Skip four lines after the last line of text; indent five spaces; type in the appropriate number and information.

Here are the note forms you will most often need.

BOOKS BY ONE AUTHOR.

> [1]David M. Potter, <u>The South and the Sectional Conflict</u> (Baton Rouge: Louisiana State UP, 1968) 12.

BOOKS BY MORE THAN ONE AUTHOR. Give the first and last name of each author in the same order as on the title page of the book, and then proceed with the entry.

> [2]Alexei Abramowitz, Clarrisa Veer, and Thomas Kaplan, <u>Cartels</u> (New York: International Library, 1977) 22.

For books with more than three authors, give the first author's name, followed by *et al.* or *and others*, and proceed.

> [3]Florence Sagforth et al., <u>Canyon Years</u> (Santa Fe: Illusions, 1982) 112.

ARTICLES IN JOURNALS.

> [4]Clair Schulz, "The Seat of Our Affections," <u>Verbatim</u> 4 (1977): 3.

ARTICLES IN OTHER PERIODICALS. For daily, weekly, or monthly periodicals (most newspapers and magazines), follow this form. Our model is from a newspaper, so it uses the newspaper's page number form.

> [5]Anthony Lewis, "White Man's Lawyer," <u>New York Times</u> 6 June 1985: A27.

REPEATED REFERENCES TO A SOURCE. If you have already referred to a source, do not repeat all the information in subsequent citations. Give the usual full information the first time.

> [6]Oliver Sacks, <u>The Man Who Mistook His Wife for a Hat and Other Clinical Tales</u> (New York: Harper, 1985) 95.

Thereafter, simply give the author's name and page number.

[7]`Sacks 19.`

If there are two works by the same author, give the author's name, a short title of the work, and the page number.

[8]`Sacks, `Man` 36.`
[9]`Sacks, `A Leg to Stand On` 45.`

Frequently, especially in book reports and papers on literature, you will refer to only one source in your paper. In this case, fully cite your source the first time; for each subsequent reference, however, you need not use a footnote or endnote. Just put the page number in parentheses *in the text*, followed by a period.

`The author goes on to say, "Here eight thousand mem-`
`bers of the Oglala subtribe of the Sioux, or Dakota,`
`live on land allotted to them by the government"`
`(115).`

BOOKS WITH TRANSLATORS.

[10]`Jean Genet, `Our Lady of the Flowers`, trans.`
`Bernard Frechtman (New York: Grove, 1963) 130.`

BOOKS WITH EDITORS. Some works by major authors have been edited by someone else. In such cases, put the original author's name, followed by the title, a comma, the label *ed.*, the name of the editor, and proceed as usual.

[11]`Margaret Mead, `Letters from the Field`, ed.`
`R. N. Anshen (New York: Harper, 1977) 58.`

Sometimes collections or compilations have no author but have been assembled by an editor. Put the editor's name first, followed by *ed.*, then proceed.

[12]`Feldon Quinn, ed., `Hollywood Writes: The`
`Collected Graffiti of the Stars` (Anaheim: Katella,`
`1977) 39.`

When an author's work has been edited by one or several editors, give the author, the title of the work, then the names of the editor or editors, and proceed.

¹³Harry Stack Sullivan, <u>The Interpersonal Theory</u>
<u>of Psychiatry</u>, ed. Helen Swick Perry and Mary Ladd
Gawel (New York: Norton, 1953) 156.

ANONYMOUS WORKS. For authorless works—pamphlets, newspaper articles, and so on—start with the title.

¹⁴"The Bogus Order of Merit," <u>New Republic</u> 2
Apr. 1977: 6.
¹⁵"The Effect of Cotton Candy on the Intestinal
Fortitude of the Field Mouse," U.S. News and Infor-
mation Service, n.d.: 8.

The abbreviation *n.d.* means "no date provided." The abbreviation *n.p.* would mean "no place of publication" or "no publisher provided."

Many instructors prefer slightly different forms for documentation. Make sure you know what your instructor expects.

Bibliography

The form for the bibliography is the same as that for the list of works cited, except that the word *Bibliography* replaces *Works Cited* above the first entry.

THE AMERICAN PSYCHOLOGICAL ASSOCIATION STYLE

The American Psychological Association or APA style, most common in the social sciences, uses parenthetical text references. Instead of author and page number, however, the basic reference contains the author's last name and the year of publication. Page numbers are not always given because of the frequent necessity of referring to an article or a study as a whole. If you give a page number, precede it with *p*.

Psychoanalysts have generally treated our pleasura-
ble response to works of art as another example of
the release of tension (Freud, 1956, p. 133).

Notice that in the APA system a comma goes between the author and the year. If the author's name appears in your text, you need only give the year and page number in parentheses.

> Freud, like many psychoanalysts before and after
> him, treated our pleasurable response to works of
> art as another example of the release of tension
> (1956, p. 133).

A list of references at the end of the paper contains complete information about each source.

Sample Text References

Here are the most common forms of reference within the text in APA style.

BOOKS BY MORE THAN ONE AUTHOR. Show all the authors' last names the first time a reference to a multiauthor book occurs; then use the first author's last name and *et al.* for subsequent references. For the first reference:

> Babies start smiling, laughing, and trying to con-
> verse at around three months (Miller, Haskell, &
> Golder, 1970).

Later in the text:

> Babies show a preference for bright, striking colors
> and well-defined patterns (Miller et al., 1970).

ANONYMOUS WORKS. Use a short title and the year for anonymous works.

> Cardiopulmonary resuscitation training is absolutely
> essential for the modern lifeguard (<u>Swimmers</u>, 1984).

MULTIPLE WORKS BY THE SAME AUTHOR. When you cite two or more works by the same author, use the author's last name and the year.

```
Psychoanalysis can be related to language (Edelson,
1972) and to the way in which dreams are generated
in the sleeping mind (Edelson, 1975).
```

If an author has published more than one source in the same year, arrange the sources alphabetically by title and assign each one a lowercase letter after the date (1979a, 1979b, 1979c, and so on); use these letters in your references.

Reference List

The reference list is preceded by the word *References* centered at the top of the page. Alphabetize entries by the author's last name, or by the first major word of the title if there is no author. Citations in the APA style differ from the MLA form in four major ways.

1. The APA puts the year immediately after the author's name.
2. The APA does not capitalize after the first word of a title—except proper names and the first word after a colon.
3. Where the MLA uses quotation marks—for titles of articles, chapters, or essays—the APA uses nothing.
4. The APA system uses only initials for authors' first and middle names and uses an ampersand (&) instead of the word *and*.

BOOKS BY ONE AUTHOR.

```
Freud, S. (1956). Delusion and dream. Boston: Beacon
      Press.
```

BOOKS BY TWO AUTHORS.

```
Phelps, E., & Drummer, T. (1985). Whale migration
      patterns and weather changes. Miami: Ourania.
```

BOOKS BY THREE OR MORE AUTHORS.

```
Miller, F. L., Haskell, J. K., & Golder, S. (1970).
      The growth of perception in the human infant.
      Edinburgh: Lanugo.
```

BOOKS BY CORPORATE AUTHORS.

```
National Association for Research into Parasitic
      Diseases. (1981). Schistosomiasis in the third
      world. New York: Harvey.
```

ANONYMOUS BOOKS.

> Swimmers for life. (1984). Huntington Beach: Nereid
> Press.

BOOKS WITH EDITORS.

> Mead, M. (1977). Letters from the field, 1925–1975.
> (R. N. Anshen, Ed.). New York: Harper & Row.

ARTICLES. In journals that paginate continuously throughout the year, use this form.

> Barnet, S. (1955). Some limitations on a Christian
> approach to Shakespeare. English Literary His-
> tory, 22, 81–92.

In periodicals that paginate each issue separately, follow this style.

> Gordon, G. (1985, May). Micro futures. Profiles, 2,
> 24–30.

In newspapers, follow this style.

> Lewis, A. (1985, November 8). White man's lawyer.
> New York Times, p. A27.

STYLE MANUALS AND HANDBOOKS IN VARIOUS DISCIPLINES

The following is a brief list of suggested style manuals and handbooks in a variety of disciplines. Whatever major you choose, purchase the relevant style manuals and handbooks, learn the style, and follow it.

Agronomy

American Society of Agronomy. *Handbook and Style Manual for ASA, CSSA* [Crop Science Society of America] *and SSSA* [Soil Science Society of America] *Publications.* Madison, WI: American Society of Agronomy, 1984.

Biology

Council of Biology Editors. *CBE Style Manual: A Guide for Authors, Editors, and Publishers in the Biological Sciences.* Rev. 5th ed. Bethesda, MD: Council of Biology Editors, 1983.

McMillan, Victoria E. *Writing Papers in the Biological Sciences.* New York: St. Martin's Press, Bedford Books, 1988.

Business

Brusaw, Charles T., Gerald Alred, and Walter Oliu. *The Business Writer's Handbook.* 3rd ed. New York: St. Martin's Press, 1987.

Lesikar, Raymond V. *Report Writing for Business.* 7th ed. Homewood, IL: Richard D. Irwin, 1986.

Markel, Michael H. *Business Writing Essentials.* New York: St. Martin's Press, 1988.

Smith, Charles B. *A Guide to Business Research: Developing, Conducting, and Writing Research Projects.* Chicago: Nelson-Hall, 1981.

Chemistry

Dodd, Janet S., ed. *The ACS Style Guide: A Manual for Authors and Editors.* Washington, DC: American Chemical Society, 1986.

Handbook for AOAC Members. 5th ed. Arlington, VA: Association of Official Analytical Chemists, 1982 [includes a section on submitting articles to the AOAC *Journal*].

Earth Science/Geology

Cochran, Wendell, Peter Fenner, and Mary Hills, eds. *Geowriting: A Guide to Writing, Editing, and Printing in Earth Science.* 4th ed. Alexandria, VA: American Geological Institute, 1984.

Economics

See also "Business."

McCloskey, Donald N. *The Writing of Economics.* New York: Macmillan, 1987.

Officer, Lawrence H., et al. *So You Have to Write an Economics Term Paper.* East Lansing, MI: Michigan State University Press, 1981.

Education

Arnold, Darlene B., and Kenneth O. Doyle, Jr. *Education-Psychology Journals: A Scholar's Guide.* Metuchen, NJ: Scarecrow Press, 1975.

Beedon, Laurel, and Joseph Heinmiller. *Writing for Education Journals.* Bloomington, IN: Phi Delta Kappa Educational Foundation, 1979.

Katz, Sidney B., Jerome T. Kapes, and Percy A. Zirkel. *Resources for Writing for Publication in Education.* New York: Teachers College Press, Columbia University, 1980.

Engineering

See also "Technical Writing."

McGraw-Hill Chemical Engineering Editors. *Effective Communication for Engineers.* New York: McGraw-Hill, 1975.

Michaelson, Herbert B. *How to Write and Publish Engineering Papers and Reports.* 2nd ed. Philadelphia: Institute for Scientific Information, 1986.

Geography

Haring, L. Lloyd, and John F. Lounsbury. *Introduction to Scientific Geographic Research.* 3rd ed. Dubuque, IA: Wm. C. Brown, 1982 (includes a section on writing geographic research reports).

History

McCoy, Florence N. *Research and Writing in History: A Practical Handbook for Students.* Berkeley: University of California Press, 1974.

Stoffle, Carla, and Simon Karter. *Materials and Methods for History Research.* New York: Neal-Schuman, 1979

Law

Columbia Law Review, et al. *A Uniform System of Citation.* 14th ed. Cambridge, MA: Harvard Law Review, 1986.

Mersky, Roy M., et al., eds. *Author's Guide to Journals in Law, Criminal Justice and Criminology.* New York: Haworth Press, 1979.

Linguistics

Linguistic Society of America. "LSA Style Sheet." Published annually in the December issue of the *LSA Bulletin.*

Literature

Achtert, Walter S., and Joseph Gibaldi. *The MLA Style Manual.* New York: Modern Language Association of America, 1985.

Gibaldi, Joseph, and Walter S. Achtert. *MLA Handbook for Writers of Research Papers.* 3rd ed. New York: Modern Language Association of America, 1988.

Mathematics

American Mathematical Society. *A Manual for Authors of Mathematical Papers.* Providence, RI: American Mathematical Society, 1980 (reprint of 1973 ed.).

Swanson, Ellen. *Mathematics into Type: Copy Editing and Proofreading of Mathematics for Editorial Assistants and Authors.* Rev. ed. Providence, RI: American Mathematical Society, 1982.

Medicine

Fishbein, Morris. *Medical Writing: The Technic and the Art.* 4th ed. Springfield, IL: Charles C. Thomas, 1978.

Huth, Edward J. *How to Write and Publish Papers in the Medical Sciences.* Philadelphia: Institute for Scientific Information, 1982.

Manual for Authors and Editors: Editorial Style and Manuscript Preparation. William R. Barclay et al., eds. Los Altos, CA: Appleton & Lange, 1981.

Modern Languages

See "Literature."

Music

Helm, Eugene, and Albert T. Luper. *Words and Music: Form and Procedure in Theses, Dissertations, Research Papers, Book Reports, Programs, and Theses in Composition.* Valley Forge, PA: European-American Music, 1982.

Irvine, Demar B. *Writing about Music: A Style Book for Reports and Theses.* Rev. ed. Seattle: University of Washington Press, 1968.

Nonprint Sources

Fleisher, Eugene B. *A Style Manual for Citing Microform and Nonprint Media.* Chicago: American Library Association, 1978.

Nursing

Dowdney, Donna L., and Donna R. Sheridan. *How to Write and Publish Articles in Nursing.* New York: Springer Publishing, 1986.

Warner, Steven D., and Kathryn D. Schweer. *Author's Guide to Journals in Nursing and Related Fields.* New York: Haworth Press, 1982.

Physical Therapy

American Physical Therapy Association Staff. *Style Manual: Physical Therapy.* Alexandria, VA: American Physical Therapy Association, 1985.

Physics

American Institute of Physics. *Style Manual.* 3rd ed. New York: American Institute of Physics, 1978.

Political Science

Stoffle, Carla J., Simon Karter, and Samuel Pernacciaro. *Materials and Methods for Political Science Research.* New York: Neal-Schuman, 1979.

Psychology

American Psychological Association. *Publication Manual of the American Psychological Association.* 3rd ed. Washington, DC: APA, 1983. For a summary of APA style documentation, see the first appendix.

Arnold, Darlene B., and Kenneth O. Doyle, Jr. *Education-Psychology Journals: A Scholar's Guide,* Metuchen, NJ: Scarecrow Press, 1975.

Hollis, Joseph W., and Patsy A. Donn, eds. *Psychological Report Writing: Theory and Practice.* Muncie, IN: Accelerated Development, 1979.

Sternberg, Robert J. *Writing the Psychology Paper.* Hauppauge, NY: Barron, 1977.

Religion

Sayre, John L. *A Manual of Forms for Research Papers and D. Min.* [Doctor of Ministry] *Field Project Reports.* 2nd ed. Enid, OK: Seminary Press, 1986.

Science, General

See also "Technical Writing."

American National Standards for the Preparation of Scientific Papers for Written or Oral Presentation. New York: ANSI, 1979.

Barrass, Robert. *Scientists Must Write: A Guide to Better Writing for Scientists, Engineers and Students.* New York: Methuen, 1978.

Council of Biology Editors, Committee on Graduate Training in Scientific Writing. *Scientific Writing for Graduate Students: A Manual on the Teaching of Scientific Writing.* F. Peter Woodford, ed. 5th ed. Bethesda, MD: Council of Biology Editors, 1981 (reprint of 1968 ed.).

Day, Robert A. *How to Write and Publish a Scientific Paper.* 2nd ed. Philadelphia: Institute for Scientific Information, 1983.

Social Science, General

Mullins, Carolyn J. *A Guide to Writing and Publishing in the Social and Behavioral Sciences.* Melbourne, FL: R. E. Krieger, 1983 (reprint of 1977 ed.).

Social Work

Markle, Allan, and Roger C. Rinn, eds. *Author's Guide to Journals in Psychology, Psychiatry and Social Work.* New York: Haworth Press, 1977.

National Association of Social Workers. *Information for Authors about NASW Publications.* Silver Spring, MD: NASW, 1985.

Sociology

Gruber, James, and Judith Pryor. Materials and Methods for Sociology Research. New York: Neal-Schuman, 1980.

Richlin-Klonsky, Judith, et al. *A Guide to Writing Sociology Papers.* New York: St. Martin's Press, 1986.

Sussman, Marvin B. *Author's Guide to Journals in Sociology and Related Fields.* New York: Haworth Press, 1978.

Technical Writing

Bell, Paula. *High Tech Writing: How to Write for the Electronics Industry.* New York: John Wiley, 1985.

Bly, Robert W., and Gary Blake. *Technical Writing: Structure, Standards and Style.* New York: McGraw-Hill, 1982.

Markel, Michael H. *Technical Writing: Situations and Strategies.* 2nd ed. New York: St. Martin's Press, 1988.

Sides, Charles H. *How to Write Papers and Reports about Computer Technology.* Philadelphia: Institute for Scientific Information, 1984.

General Guides

Allen, George R. *The Graduate Students' Guide to Theses and Dissertations: A Practical Manual for Writing and Research.* San Francisco: Jossey-Bass, 1973.

Chicago Guide to Preparing Electronic Manuscripts for Authors and Publishers. Chicago: University of Chicago Press, 1987.

(Acknowledgments continued from page iv)

Archibald MacLeish, "Ars Poetica." From *New and Collected Poems 1917–1975* by Archibald MacLeish. Copyright © 1985 by The Estate of Archibald MacLeish. Reprinted by permission of Houghton Mifflin Company.

Ogden Nash, "Reflections on Ice-Breaking." From *Verses from 1929 On* by Ogden Nash. Copyright 1930 by Ogden Nash. By permission of Little, Brown and Company.

The New York Times Index. © 1975 by The New York Times Company. Reprinted by permission.

Robert Nisbet, "Victimology." Reprinted by permission of the publishers from *Prejudices: A Philosophical Dictionary* by Robert Nisbet, Cambridge: Harvard University Press, Copyright © 1982 by Robert Nisbet.

Readers' Guide to Periodical Literature. March 1982–February 1983, from entries under "Educational tests and measurements." Copyright © 1982, 1983 by The H. W. Wilson Company. Reproduced by permission of the publisher.

Arthur M. Schlesinger, Jr. From *A Thousand Days* by Arthur M. Schlesinger, Jr. Copyright © 1965 by Arthur M. Schlesinger, Jr. Reprinted by permission of Houghton Mifflin Company.

INDEX

A Convenient Guide to the Handbook of Grammar, Punctuation, Mechanics, and Usage